CASES IN MARKETING MANAGEMENT

McGRAW-HILL SERIES IN MARKETING

CASES IN MARKETING MANAGEMENT

Joseph P. Guiltinan
University of Notre Dame

Gordon W. Paul
University of Central Florida

McGRAW-HILL, INC.

New York   St. Louis   San Francisco   Auckland   Bogotá
Caracas   Hamburg   Lisbon   London   Madrid   Mexico   Milan   Montreal   New Delhi
Paris   San Juan   São Paulo   Singapore   Sydney   Tokyo   Toronto

CASES IN MARKETING MANAGEMENT

2 3 4 5 6 7 8 9 0 HAL HAL 9 0 9 8 7 6 5 4 3 2

ISBN 0-07-048947-5

This book was set in Optima by Publication Services.
The editors were Bonnie K. Binkert, Mimi Melek, and Bernadette Boylan;
the production supervisor was Richard A. Ausburn.
The cover was designed by Joan Greenfield.
Arcata Graphics/Halliday was printer and binder.

To Our Families

Sharon, Joanna, Jennifer, and
Shannon Guiltinan

Gloria, Christopher, and Bradley Paul

CONTENTS

PREFACE

M anagers of both profit-oriented and not-for-profit organizations must make daily decisions in an environment that could best be characterized as one of constant change. Changing technology, multinational competition, and shifting economic and political forces are but a few of the many factors marketing managers must contend with when making those decisions. Because marketing is a very involved and complex activity, organizations need to develop processes for coordinating the various decisions and activities to ensure a common purpose and direction. Case studies can serve as the means by which students can better understand the complexity of the marketing system and the decisions required by those managers responsible for formulating marketing strategies and programs. The purpose of this book is to provide both undergraduate and graduate students of marketing with the opportunity to apply their knowledge of marketing concepts and tools to a variety of real marketing problems.

The twenty-eight cases in this book have been carefully selected to illustrate a variety of marketing problems and situations. We have chosen cases that cover both consumer and industrial products as well as services. To reflect the growth of and continued emphasis on multinational competition, we have included ten international cases as well as two Canadian cases. In keeping with the focus of the book, these international cases address a variety of situations confronting managers in consumer and industrial product organizations as well as services.

Each case presents a number of issues, and even though the marketing decision may primarily be concerned with one element such as advertising or pricing, the cases have been selected because they reflect the way marketing issues and problems present themselves. As a result, the majority of cases are fairly lengthy and complex, and most of the information relevant to the problem is included.

The cases are organized around the marketing planning process. Part 1 includes cases that illustrate the role and activities associated with marketing in an organization. Part 2 includes a number of cases that illustrate the decisions necessary in conducting a situation analysis for marketing planning. Included are cases that illustrate market analysis, segmentation and positioning, as well as product profitability and productivity related to alternative marketing decisions. The cases in Part 3 have been chosen to provide illustrations of the marketing strategies and programs necessary for implementing the marketing strategy. Part 4 of the book includes cases that illustrate decisions associated with evaluation and control of the marketing strategies and programs because of the variety of issues presented and the information included.

Some cases could appropriately fit in more than one section. We have found that this organization of the cases achieves two things. First, students readily grasp the process by which marketing planning takes place; and second, they are forced to determine for themselves the major problem confronting the decision-maker. Too often, cases are organized under fairly restrictive topical headings such as price, promotion, or distribution; and student analysis and subsequent recommendations can be conditioned by the case's placement in the book.

We are most appreciative of all the case writers as well as organizations that granted permission to use their cases. We are especially indebted to Ms. Silvia Farmanfarma and the International Institute for Management Development (IMD), Lausanne, Switzerland, for her help and cooperation in securing permissions for IMD cases. Diane E. Mitchell, European Institute of Business Administration (INSEAD), Fontainebleau, France, was also most helpful with case permissions. We would like to especially thank Reinhard Angelmar and Christian Pinson of INSEAD and Jean-Pierre Jeannet of Babson College for their generous contribution of cases and notes. In addition, Professors Jacques Horovitz, Terry Deutscher, Dominique Turpin, Paul Strebel, and Robert F. Young of IMD made cases and notes available which were integral to the collection.

It is our hope that the cases in this book will provide marketing management students with a valuable learning experience. It has been our experience that by being able to confront actual problems faced by marketing managers, students quickly see, through in-depth analysis, the excitement as well as the challenges of marketing.

Joseph P. Guiltinan
Gordon W. Paul

INTRODUCTION

I. NOTES ON THE CASE METHOD

Most students have had a great deal of exposure to problem solving during their academic careers. Much of the educational process in disciplines such as economics, statistics, or engineering is geared toward specifying a problem, selecting an appropriate technique, and applying the technique to obtain a specific solution.

If this is your first experience with case studies, the first thing you should know is that a case is *not* a problem. There is no unique solution to a case. Rather there may be multiple recommendations that could be supported. Alternatively, there may not be any course of action that will yield a result that is satisfactory to the decision maker because, in the real world of management, many businesses or projects fail.

Additionally, as in the real world, you (the decision maker) will have to make decisions in the absence of perfect information. The data or intelligence available will usually be incomplete and may not be totally reliable, and yet decisions must still be made because time (or funds) prohibit further data collection.

Essentially, a case is a simulated decision-making situation that is abstracted from an actual, complex situation once faced by managers in the real world. A case presents the situation as the managers saw it, using the data, opinions, and points of view available at the time in which the case took place. The purpose of the case method is to enhance your ability to make complex decisions and to effectively communicate the rationale for a decision. Additionally, when cases are discussed in a classroom setting, you should develop your critical thinking skills by assessing the opinions of other students and analyzing their reasoning.

Today's business environment is becoming increasingly complex and dynamic. In this kind of environment, managers must be able to make the kinds of decisions that require more than a mastery of data analysis techniques. Additionally, such decisions will increasingly be made with the participation of multiple managers, each of which may have different interpretations or perspectives. Thus the ability to critically evaluate and communicate opinions will become increasingly important in the modern business organization.

Doing a Case Analysis

To prepare a case for class it is useful to divide your effort into four sequential phases as shown in Table 1.

TABLE 1   PHASES OF A CASE ANALYSIS

Phase 1: Obtain an overview

- What kind of business is this?
- What decisions must be made?
- Who will make them?
- Why is the decision important?
- What are the potential consequences?

Phase 2: Situation analysis

- Categorize case facts
- Analyze case data
- Distinguish symptoms from problems
- Establish a list of problems

Phase 3: Identify and assess alternatives

- Identify alternative courses of action
- Consider positive and negative aspects of each alternative
- Assess risks associated with each alternative

Phase 4: Recommendation

- Select a course of action
- Clarify key assumptions
- Present action plan

In phase one, you should read the case through in order to get an overview of the situation. Find out the kind of firm involved and the basic types of decisions to be made (as well as who will make them). Finally, in this phase, you should try to assess (in general terms) "what's at stake?" Specifically try to get a sense for why this decision is important, what the consequences are of a good decision, of inaction (if feasible), of a bad decision. By answering these questions you should be able to better define the problem and to establish the key objectives that will be used to evaluate the success of an action in subsequent phases.

In phase two, a more detailed reading and some note taking are appropriate. Here your goal is to categorize the case information to analyze the situation using the outline in Table 2. (We'll discuss the outline below.) By doing this you will have a list of key facts and opinions. Additionally, you should be sure at this point to

---

TABLE 2   COMPONENTS OF A SITUATION ANALYSIS FOR A CASE*

---

1. Corporate-level situation analysis

- Corporate mission and objectives
- Resources and competencies
- Environmental problems and opportunities:
  - Demographic
  - Social-cultural
  - Economic
  - Technological
  - Legal and regulatory
  - Competition
- Portfolio analysis

2. Product-level situation analysis

- Market analysis
  - Describe the product market structure
  - Find out who buys
  - Assess why buyers buy
  - Determine how buyers make choices
  - Determine bases for market segmentation
  - Identify potential target markets
- Competitive analysis
  - Identify direct competitors
  - Assess likelihood of new competitors
  - Determine stage in product life cycle
  - Assess pioneer advantages
  - Assess intensity of competition
  - Determine competitors' advantages and disadvantages
- Market measurement
  - Estimate market potential
  - Determine relative potential of each geographic area
  - Track industry sales trends
  - Assess company or brand trends in sales and market share
  - Make forecasts
- Profitability and productivity analysis
  - Determine the cost structure
  - Identify cost-volume-profit relationships
  - Perform break-even and target profit analyses
  - Make projections of sales or market share impact of marketing expenditures

3. Summary

- Assess performance (identification of symptoms)
- Define problems and opportunities

---

*Developed from Joseph Guiltinan and Gordon Paul, *Marketing Management: Strategies and Programs*, Fourth Edition (New York: McGraw-Hill, 1990), Chapters 2–6.

perform any data analyses that appear relevant. Specifically, you may wish to perform some of the financial analyses discussed in the next section of this book. Or you may want to look for such things as trends in sales, the comparative advertising budgets of different competitors, or key demographic characteristics of customers. Finally, you will want to distinguish *symptoms* from *problems*. Symptoms are the consequences (such as declining market share) that a problem can cause. The key task at this point is to identify the most likely problems based on the case facts and on your knowledge of marketing theory.

In the third phase, your task is to define and evaluate alternative courses of action. It is imperative that you not jump to the first recommendation that comes to mind. Rather you should first attempt to identify a range of alternative actions. The more complex the case, the more important this will be. Indeed a key advantage of participative decision making (such as project teams, committees, or groups of students) is that a wider range of alternatives can usually be generated. Having generated these ideas you then need to consider the positive and negative attributes of each alternative. This involves more than just a simple listing of pros and cons. You should also identify "fatal flaws"—negative consequences that are so severe as to make a given alternative not feasible. Also, it is useful to try to assess the degree of risk associated with each option and compare these to the risk that particular firm should be prepared to take given its objectives.

Finally, in phase four, you must prepare a recommended course of action with your reasoning for your decision. Your recommendation should be accompanied (to the extent feasible) by an action plan which would identify:

- The budgetary support needed for this recommendation to succeed
- The time frame within which actions will be taken
- The performance benchmarks to be used to assess whether the recommended course of action is working

Finally, in communicating your recommendation, it is important to make clear the key assumptions you have made and the reasons for such assumptions. For example, if you recommend a price cut and assume competitors will not follow suit, you should be prepared to defend your reasoning.

Performing the Situation Analysis

In a situation analysis, you attempt to categorize the case data in a way that will help you assess the firm's performance difficulties (symptoms), identify the problems causing these difficulties, or identify opportunities for still better performance. Table 2 provides a useful outline for doing this. Note that there are two levels at which a situation analysis can be conducted. At the corporate level, you should determine the overall company goals, the strengths and weaknesses in the company's resources or skills, and the problems and opportunities posed by a changing environment. These forces can influence corporate strategy decisions such as whether to enter new markets or stick with existing businesses. These forces may also influence the relative attractiveness of the company's various product lines. This may cause the firm to reassess the allocation of resources to various products or to reexamine expectations regarding growth and profits from various products.

At the level of an individual product (or a line of closely related products), the situation assessment should establish the nature of market demand, the competitive dynamics, the size of current and potential growth opportunities, and the financial implications of current and contemplated marketing budgets. The next section of this book provides a detailed discussion of the financial aspects of marketing.

II. FINANCIAL ANALYSIS FOR MARKETING DECISIONS

It is important to recognize that marketing influences both the level of sales volume and the level

TABLE 3   AMERICAN LEATHER PRODUCTS: PROFIT
           AND LOSS STATEMENT
           (In Thousands)

Sales		$10,000
Less cost of goods sold		6,800
Gross profit		$ 3,200
Operating expenses		
Advertising	$480	
Sales promotion	400	
Sales salaries and travel	160	
Transportation	420	
Sales commissions, discounts	200	
Research and development	120	
General and administrative expenses	300	
Total operating expenses		$ 2,080
Net operating profit before taxes		$ 1,120

of profitability that a firm will experience. Actions such as changing a price, increasing an advertising budget, or packaging a product in a different container can not only influence demand but also influence the level and structure of a firm's costs. Consequently, marketing managers must be aware of the kinds of costs associated with marketing activities and with the factors influencing the profitability of the product being marketed.

As most managers know, the income (profit and loss) statement is generally inadequate for analyzing product profitability. Consider, for example, the profit and loss statement for American Leather Products in Table 3.

This table is useful for giving an overview of the company's overall financial position. But if American Leather Products is a multiproduct firm, it tells us nothing regarding the profitability of the various products. Additionally, it provides few clues to how profitability would be influenced by changes in marketing costs. In order to examine those issues we need to first examine the various types of costs that a firm might incur.

Variable versus Fixed Costs

Variable costs are costs that vary with sales volume. Sales commissions, material, labor, and packaging are typically variable costs because they go up proportionately with sales. That is, each of these costs is incurred every time a product is produced and sold.

Nearly all other costs are *fixed*; that is, they remain essentially the same regardless of volume levels—at least as long as increases in the size of a production facility or in administrative and clerical staff are not required. Although some of these costs can be changed by management (such as advertising budgets and sales-force salaries), they do not vary automatically as sales change. For a manufacturer, the cost of goods sold (in the income statement) usually includes both fixed and variable elements. That is, each unit sold is assigned a share of the fixed costs to be added to its variable cost. For a retailer or wholesaler that only resells products made by other firms, the cost of goods sold is only a variable cost because it simply reflects the purchase price of items being resold.

By separating fixed costs from variable costs (as we have done in Table 4), the portion of cost that is sensitive to volume is identified. Out of every $1000 in sales, $560 is spent on the variable costs. The remaining $440 is the amount that is contributed to cover all fixed costs and profit after variable costs have been subtracted.

With costs separated in this way, managers can calculate a very useful measure: the *percentage-variable-contribution margin* (PVCM). This measure indicates the percentage of each additional sales dollar that will be available to help the firm cover its fixed costs and increase profits. The percentage-variable-contribution margin can be calculated in either of two ways:

$$PVCM = \frac{\text{unit price} - \text{unit variable cost}}{\text{unit price}}$$

or

$$PVCM = \frac{\text{variable contribution margin}}{\text{dollar sales}}$$

In the case of American Leather then,

$$PVCM = \frac{\$440}{\$1000} = 44\%$$

TABLE 4   AMERICAN LEATHER PRODUCTS: CONTRIBUTION MARGIN STATEMENT
(In Thousands)

Sales		$10,000
Variable costs		
Variable cost of goods sold (labor, materials, packaging)	$5,400	
Variable selling costs (commissions, discounts)	200	
Total variable cost for manufacturer		$ 5,600
Variable contribution margin		4,400
Fixed costs		
Advertising	$ 480	
Sales promotion	400	
Sales salaries and travel	160	
Transportation	420	
Research and development	120	
General and administrative costs	300	
Fixed cost of production	1,400	
Total fixed cost		$ 3,280
Net operating profit before taxes		$ 1,120

In order to fully appreciate the usefulness of this measure to a marketing manager, it is necessary to understand the distinction between direct fixed costs and indirect fixed costs.

Types of Fixed Costs

When fixed costs are incurred in a multiproduct firm, they are incurred either on behalf of the business as a whole or on behalf of one or more specific products. For example, organizations may design advertisements to communicate a message about a particular product or product line, or they may use *institutional* advertising which presents a message about the company as a whole and may not even mention the specific products or services sold. Costs such as product-specific advertising that are incurred on behalf of a specific product or service are known as *direct fixed* costs. Costs such as institutional advertising that are incurred to support the total business are *indirect fixed* costs.

In practice, firms recognize that there are really two categories of indirect cost: traceable and nontraceable. *Traceable* costs are indirect costs that can be allocated to various products on some nonarbitrary basis. For example, if a common sales force is used to sell two or more products, the total selling cost is usually allocated between the two products on the basis of some factor such as the percentage of selling time devoted to each one.

The purpose of distinguishing the various types of fixed costs is to provide a basis for evaluating the contributions made by different products or services to the overall profitability of the firm. Thus, firms assign direct and traceable indirect costs to products in order to gauge the costs of supporting each product. But nontraceable indirect costs are not assigned.

Table 5 illustrates how the profitability of individual products and services can be measured once management has separated the fixed costs. The bottom line for the individual products and services is no longer net operating profit but *total contribution*. The total contribution is the amount that an individual product or service "contributes" to the coverage of nontraceable indirect costs and to profit.

By examining Table 5 we can see that briefcases generate the larger total contribution of the two products even though the dollar volume of travel bag sales is larger. One reason for this is that briefcases incur a smaller level of direct

TABLE 5 AMERICAN LEATHER PRODUCTS: CONTRIBUTION BY PRODUCT
(In Thousands)

	Company total	Travel bags	Briefcases
Sales	$10,000	$ 6,000	$ 4,000
Total variable cost of production and selling	5,600	3,600	2,000
Variable contribution margin	$ 4,400	$ 2,400	$ 2,000
Direct, traceable fixed costs:			
Advertising	$ 480	$ 320	$ 160
Sales promotion	400	320	80
Sales force	160	80	80
Transportation	420	220	200
Production	1400	720	680
Total	$ 2,860	$ 1,660	$ 1,200
Total contribution	$ 1,540	$ 740	$ 800
Indirect, nontraceable fixed costs:			
General and administrative overhead	$300		
Research and development	120		
Total	$420		
Net operating profit before taxes	$1,120		

and traceable costs. The data suggest that travel bags require more advertising than briefcases and more sales promotion expense, perhaps reflecting greater competition in the travel bag market.

The second factor influencing the relative profitability of the products and services is the percentage-variable-contribution margin. Table 6 summarizes the PVCM calculations for the two products. On a percentage basis, briefcases are more profitable than travel bags. For each additional $1,000 in sales of briefcase sales, the company will retain $500 after variable costs are subtracted. For travel bags $400 would be retained if sales rose by $1,000.

By identifying the fixed and variable components of cost and by distinguishing between direct and indirect costs, managers will be able to examine some of the profitability implications of pricing and marketing expenditure de-

TABLE 6 AMERICAN LEATHER PRODUCTS: VARIABLE CONTRIBUTION MARGINS

	Travel bags	Briefcases
Units sold	40,000	40,000
Manufacturer selling price	$150	$100
Manufacturer variable cost per unit	$ 90	$ 50
Variable contribution margin per unit	$150 − $90 = $60	$100 − $50 = $50
Percentages variable contribution margin	$\frac{$150 - $90}{$150} = 40\%$	$\frac{$100 - $50}{$100} = 50\%$

cisions. Specifically, by understanding the profitability structure of a product, managers can identify *cost-volume-profit relationships* and can perform break-even and target profit analyses.

Cost-Volume-Profit Relationships

In many organizations, a large portion of the total operating costs is essentially fixed. In these situations, managers will generally pursue policies which take advantage of economies of scale. These economies will exist when a large change in volume leads to a significant change in the average cost of a product.

Consider, for example, Table 7. As sales volume doubles (from 40,000 to 80,000 units) total costs increase by a smaller percentage amount because a high proportion of total costs are fixed. Consequently, the average cost per unit is reduced from $80 to $65.

The existence of strong cost-volume-profit relationships means that managers should be more willing to increase marketing expenses or cut prices, if these actions will lead to significant increases in volume. Returning to Table 7, we can see that at a price of $80 per unit, the firm will just cover its average costs at a volume of 40,000 units. If, however, sales could be doubled by lowering prices, the firm could price the product as low as $66 per unit and still make a profit.

Break-Even and Target Profit Analyses

Once a manager has obtained a knowledge of the cost-volume-profit relationships for a product, the budgetary implications of making changes in prices or marketing expenditures can be readily determined. Specifically, target profit analysis can be used to determine the required sales impact of a change in the marketing budget. Break-even analysis is a special case of target profit analysis which permits a manager to identify the level of sales required to achieve a zero (break-even) profit.

Specifically, target profit analysis involves calculating the level of sales required to achieve the minimum acceptable target contribution for a given budget. This calculation requires three pieces of profitability information:

- The percentage-variable-contribution margin (or the variable contribution margin per unit) based on the expected prices and variable costs
- The total direct and traceable fixed costs to be incurred (including any expected changes in the marketing budget)
- The minimum target contribution that will be acceptable to top management

Given this information, the *required level of sales* can be calculated using the following formulas.

$$\text{Total dollar sales required} = \frac{(\text{target total contribution}) + (\text{total direct or traceable fixed costs})}{\text{PVCM}}$$

or

$$\text{Total unit sales required} = \frac{(\text{target total contribution}) + (\text{total direct or traceable fixed costs})}{\text{PVCM per unit}}$$

TABLE 7 AMERICAN LEATHER PRODUCTS: ECONOMIES OF SCALE FOR BRIEFCASES

	Annual sales volume	
	40,000 units	80,000 units
Unit variable cost	$ 50	$ 50
Multiplied by volume	40,000	80,000
Total variable cost	$2,000,000	$4,000,000
Total direct fixed cost	$1,200,000	$1,200,000
Plus total variable cost	2,000,000	4,000,000
Total direct cost	$3,200,000	$5,200,000
Divided by volume	40,000	80,000
Average unit cost	$ 80	$ 65

For a simple break-even analysis, target total contribution would be $0.

To see how this process works, assume that American Leather Products is considering a $200,000 increase in the advertising budget. Implementing this increase would result in increasing the total direct costs to $1,400,000 (from the $1,200,000 shown in Table 5). If management is willing to accept the current level of total contribution to indirect cost and profit of $800,000 (see Table 5), then

$$\text{Total dollar sales required} = \frac{\$800,000 + \$1,400,000}{0.5}$$
$$= \$4,400,000$$

$$\text{Total unit sales required} = \frac{\$800,000 + \$1,400,000}{\$50}$$
$$= 44,000 \text{ units}$$

For break-even,

$$\text{Total dollar sales required} = \frac{\$0 + \$1,400,000}{0.5}$$
$$= \$2,800,000$$

$$\text{Total unit sales required} = \frac{\$0 + \$1,400,000}{\$50}$$
$$= 28,000 \text{ units}$$

Note that if any changes in the target total contribution are made or if prices, variable costs, or other direct or traceable fixed costs are also changed, then the total sales required will change.

"What If" Analyses

With the widespread availability of financial spreadsheet programs today, managers are likely to use sensitivity analysis (also known as "what if" analysis) in examining the financial implications of a budget change. Spreadsheet programs enable managers to quickly assess a wide range of possible profitability consequences that might result when the sales impact of a change in marketing effort is uncertain.

Consider, for example, Table 8 which portrays a small number of the many possible levels of industry sales and market share and their financial consequences that Americans might face as a result of making the $200,000 additional investment in advertising. The challenge for management at American Leather Products is to determine which scenario is most apt to occur.

Distributor Margins

To a large extent, a firm's profitability is influenced by the margins it pays to wholesale or re-

TABLE 8   AMERICAN LEATHER PRODUCTS: RESULTS OF SENSITIVITY ANALYSIS
(In Thousands)

	Current year	Possible scenarios for next year			
		1	2	3	4
Industry unit sales	2,000	2,200	2,200	2,000	2,000
X American market share	2%	2.5%	2%	2.5%	1.5%
American unit sales	40	55	44	50	30
X price	$ 100	$ 100	$ 100	$ 100	$ 100
Sales	$4,000	$5,500	$4,400	$5,000	$3,000
X PVCM	0.5	0.5	0.5	0.5	0.5
Variable contribution margin	$2,000	$2,750	$2,200	$2,500	$1,500
Direct, traceable fixed costs	1400	1400	1400	1400	1400
Total contribution to indirect costs and profit	$ 600	$ 1350	$ 800	$ 1100	$ 100

tail firms for stocking and distributing its products. In many cases, distributors charge a fixed percentage margin for their activities, while in other cases, the margin is negotiable. In either case, it is important to be clear about the calculation of the margin.

Basically the *dollar margin* is the absolute difference between selling price and unit cost. A retailer who pays $4 for an item and sells it for $6 has a $2 margin.

The *percentage margin* can be calculated in two ways: as a percentage of cost or (more typically) as a percentage of selling price. For our hypothetical retailer:

$$\text{Percentage margin on selling price} = \frac{\$2}{\$6} = 33\frac{1}{3}\%$$

$$\text{Percentage margin on cost} = \frac{\$2}{\$4} = 50\%$$

In some cases, multiple levels of distribution are involved, requiring multiple margin calculations. For example, if our hypothetical retailer purchased the item for $4 from a wholesaler who purchased the item for $3 from a manufacturer, the margins and prices would be as follows:

Retail selling price	$6
Less retail margin	−2 (33⅓% of
Wholesale selling price	$4 retail price)
Less wholesale margin	−1 (25% of
	wholesale
	price)
Manufacturer's selling price	$3

Manufacturers must take the distributor's margin expectations into account in developing the marketing budget. For instance, assume that American Leather Products used retail and wholesale distributors who charged margins such as those just cited. If the firm wanted a retail price of $150 for one of its leather briefcases, it would have to have the following price and margin structure:

Retail selling price	$150
−Retailer margin ($150 × 33⅓%)	−50
Wholesale selling price	100
−Wholesaler margin ($100 × 25%)	−25
Manufacturer selling price	$ 75

MANAGERIAL PERSPECTIVES ON MARKETING

M arketing has become recognized as a basic motivating force in most organizations. The evolution of both business firms and nonprofit organizations from being product-oriented, to sales-oriented, to market-oriented has been widely reported. Firms practicing the marketing concept strive to satisfy customers' needs and wants while, at the same time, achieving their organizational objectives. To provide customer satisfaction requires a thorough understanding of customer needs, wants, and behavior. In addition, it is necessary that marketing decisions are coordinated and integrated with the other functional areas of an organization. The best way to achieve organizational goals and ensure long-term survival is by focusing on customer needs and integrating all the organization's activities including production, finance, accounting, and personnel on satisfying those needs.

Planning is a means for an organization to control its future. A plan is essentially a statement of what the organization hopes to achieve, how they will achieve it, and when it will be achieved. Marketing planning is the systematic process for developing and coordinating marketing decisions.

Marketing management has been defined as "the analysis, planning, implementation, and control of programs designed to bring about desired exchanges with target markets for the purpose of achieving organizational objectives. It relies heavily on designing the organization's offering in terms of the target market's needs and desires and on using effective pricing, communication, and distribution to inform, motivate and service the market."[1] However, even in a market-oriented organization, it is not a simple matter to implement the marketing concept. Organizations are faced with many alternative markets and customers as well as a variety of alternative policies and programs for meeting customer needs. Organizations cannot pursue *all* possible buyers, and *all* possible marketing actions cannot be taken because human and financial resources are limited. The cases in this section illustrate the role and complexities of marketing decision making in two service organizations.

[1] Philip Kotter, *Marketing Management: Analysis, Planning and Control,* 5th ed. (Englewood Cliffs, N.J.: Prentice-Hall, 1984), p. 14.

CASE 1

ROGERS, NAGEL, LANGHART (RNL PC) ARCHITECTS AND PLANNERS

It was August 1984. John B. Rogers, one of the founders and a principal stockholder in RNL, had just completed the University of Colorado's Executive M.B.A. program. Throughout the program John had tried to relate the concepts and principles covered in his courses to the problems of managing a large architectural practice. In particular, he was concerned about the marketing efforts of his firm. As he put it, "Marketing is still a new, and sometimes distasteful, word to most architects. Nevertheless, the firms that sur-

vive and prosper in the future are going to be those which learn how to market as effectively as they design. At RNL we are still struggling with what it means to be a marketing organization, but we feel it's a critical question that must be answered if we're going to meet our projections of roughly doubling by 1989 and we're giving it lots of attention."

RNL

With 1984 sales (design fees) of approximately $3,300,000, RNL was one of the largest local architectural firms in Denver and the Rocky Mountain region. The firm evolved from the individual practices of John B. Rogers, Jerome K. Nagel and Victor D. Langhart. All started their architectural careers in Denver in the 1950s. The partnership

This case was prepared by H. Michael Hayes, Professor of Marketing and Strategic Management, University of Colorado at Denver, as the basis for class discussion rather than to illustrate either effective or ineffective handling of an administrative situation. Copyright ©1985 by H. Michael Hayes (Rev. 7/23/90)

13

of Rogers, Nagel, Langhart was formed from the three individual proprietorships in 1966 and became a professional corporation in 1970.

In 1984 the firm provided professional design services to commercial, corporate, and governmental clients, not only in Denver but throughout Colorado and, increasingly, throughout the western United States. In addition to basic architectural design services, three subsidiaries had recently been formed:

• Interplan, which provides pre-architectural services—programming, planning, budgeting, scheduling, and cost projections—utilized in corporate budgeting and governmental bond issues
• Denver Enterprises, formed to hold equity interests in selected projects designed by RNL and to take risks by furnishing design services

early in a project and by participating in the capital requirements of a project
• Space Management Systems, Inc. (SMS), which provides larger corporations with the necessary services (heavily computer system supported) to facilitate control of their facilities with respect to space, furnishings, equipment and the cost of change

In 1984 the firm had 72 employees. John Rogers served as the Chairman and Vic Langhart served as President. Nagel had retired in 1976. (See Exhibit 1 for an organization chart.) Development of broad-based management had been a priority since 1975. The firm had seven vice presidents. Two of these vice presidents, Phil Goedert and Rich von Luhrte, served on the Board of Directors, together with Rogers and Langhart.

EXHIBIT 1   ORGANIZATION

Note: RNL does not have a formal organization chart, as such. The following was developed by the case writer to portray the general nature of work assignments and reporting relationships in the firm. As a general rule, project managers report either to John Rogers or to Vic Langhart. Most administrative staff functions report to Vic Langhart. At the operational level, Interplan and SMS projects are handled similarly to RNL projects.

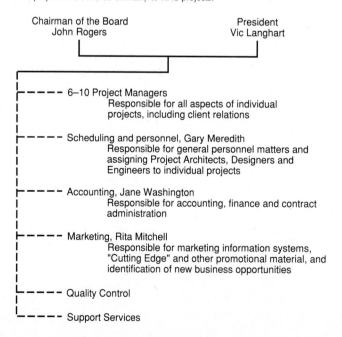

Growth was financed through retained earnings. In addition, a plan to provide for more employee ownership, principally through profit sharing (ESOP in 1984), was initiated in 1973. Rogers and Langhart held 56% of RNL stock, and 66% was held by the four board members. The Colorado National Bank Profit Sharing Trust held 12% in its name. The remaining 22% was controlled by 23 other employees, either personally or through their individual profit sharing accounts. It was a goal of the firm to eventually vest stock ownership throughout the firm, in the interest of longevity and continuity.

The firm's principal assets were its human resources. Rogers and Langhart, however, had significant ownership in a limited partnership which owned a 20,000-square-foot building in a prestigious location in downtown Denver. In 1984 RNL occupied 15,000 square feet. Use of the remaining 5000 square feet could accommodate up to 30% growth in personnel. Through utilization of automation and computers, RNL felt it could double its 1984 volume of work without acquiring additional space.

ARCHITECTURAL SERVICES

Architecture: the profession of designing buildings, open areas, communities and other artificial constructions and environments, usually with some regard to aesthetic effect. The professional services of an architect often include design or selection of furnishings and decorations, supervision of construction work and the examination, restoration, or remodeling of existing buildings. (*Random House Dictionary*)

Demand for architectural services was closely tied to population growth and to the level of construction activity. The population in the Denver metropolitan area grew from 929,000 in 1960 to 1,620,000 in 1980, and it is estimated to grow to 1,958,000 by 1990. Denver's annual population change of 3.4% in the decade 1970–1980 ranked tenth for major American cities (Dallas and Phoenix ranked one and two). The projected population growth for the Denver metropolitan area from 1978 to 1983 ranked third in the nation, and Colorado was predicted to be one of the ten fastest growing states during the 1980s.

Commercial construction permits grew from 340 in 1970, with an estimated value of $70,818,000, to 1235 in 1980, with an estimated value of $400,294,000. This growth was not steady, however. Year-to-year changes in dollar value of commercial construction varied from 0.2% to 91.6%, and the number of permits dropped from a high of 2245 in 1978 to 1235 in 1980. Similar patterns of growth and variation characterized industrial construction.

Translating construction growth into estimates of demand for architectural services was difficult. One rule of thumb held that each additional person added to the population base required 1000 square feet of homes, schools, churches, offices, hospitals, manufacturing facilities, retail and shopping facilities and transportation facilities. In the Denver Metro area alone this could mean 338,000,000 square feet. At $50 average per square foot, total construction expenditure over the decade could reach $16,900,000,000, involving as much as $845,000,000 in design fees during the 1980s.

The past and projected growth in demand for architectural services was accompanied by a significant growth in the number of architects in Colorado. From 1979 to 1982, the number of state registrations of individual architects grew from 1400 to 3381, an increase of 141.5%. Over 100 architectural firms competed actively in the Denver market. (Over 500 architects are listed in the yellow pages of the Denver Metro Area phone directory.) In recent years a number of national firms (e.g., Skidmore, Owens and Merrill) opened offices in Denver. Other major firms came to Colorado to do one job and then return to their home offices (e.g., Yamasaki for the Colorado National Bank Office Tower and TAC for Mansville World Headquarters). Of the 26 major firms working on 38 selected jobs in Denver in 1983, 16, or 61.5%, were Denver based. Of the other ten, which had headquarter offices elsewhere, all but two had offices in Denver.

Major categories of customers for architectural services include:

Industrial
Commercial
   Owner
   Developer
Government
   Federal
   State
   Municipal
Residential (Note: RNL did not compete in this market.)

Within these categories, however, not all architectural work was available to independent firms and not all architectural work on a project was awarded to one architect. A recent Denver survey, for example, indicated that of 49 commercial jobs under construction with a known architect, 11 were handled by an "inside" architect. Of the remaining 38 jobs, 20 included shell and space design whereas 18 involved space design only. In the 18 space designs only 50% were actually done by architects.

The rapid growth in the construction market in Denver came to an abrupt halt in February 1982. Triggered by the broad realization that the oil boom was over, or at least had slowed significantly, project after project was put on hold. Construction of office space literally came to a halt. Of particular concern to RNL, which had just completed negotiations for a $1,000,000 contract with Exxon, was the Exxon announcement of the closure of its Colorado Oil Shale activities at Parachute, Colorado.

It was against the backdrop of these changes that RNL felt the pressing need to review its marketing activities.

MARKETING OF ARCHITECTURAL SERVICES

The basis of competing for architectural work had changed dramatically over the past several decades. As John Rogers recalled:

At the beginning of my practice in 1956, you could establish an office, put a sign on your door, print calling cards and have a "news" announcement with your picture in the *Daily Journal* that you had established a new practice of architecture. Beyond that, it was appropriate to suggest to friends and acquaintances that I was in business now and I hoped that they might recommend me to someone they knew. The Code of Ethics of the American Institute of Architects, like many other professions at the time, prohibited any kind of aggressive marketing or sales effort as practiced in recent times.

In fact, after convincing one School Board member (an artist) in Jefferson County that design was important, and then being awarded a commission to design an elementary school, which led to another and another, it was not surprising to read in the *Daily Journal* that the School Board had met the previous evening and had elected me to design a new junior high school, one that I hadn't even known about. I called and said, "Thank you." Marketing expense was zero with the exception of an occasional lunch or courtesy call here and there.

Today, the situation is vastly different. We have to compete for most jobs, against both local firms and, increasingly, large national firms. Clients are becoming more sophisticated regarding the purchase of architectural services (see Exhibit 2 for a brief description of buyer behavior). Promotion, of some kind, and concepts such as segmentation have become a way of life.

During the 1960s, development of an architectural practice was a slow process, characterized by heavy reliance on word of mouth regarding professional experience and expertise. Overt communication about an architect's qualifications was limited to brochures. Personal acquaintances played a significant role in the development of new clients. Personal relations between principals and clients were an important part of continuing and new relations. This method of practice development tended to favor local firms, whose reputation could be checked out on a personal basis, and small firms, whose principals could provide personal management and design of client projects.

EXHIBIT 2   BUYER BEHAVIOR

Purchase of architectural services is both complex and varied. Subject to many qualifications, however, there seems to be a number of steps that most buying situations have in common.

- Development of a list of potential architects
- Identification of those architects from whom proposals will be solicited for a specific job (usually called the "short list")
    - Invitations to submit proposals
    - Evaluation of proposals and screening of final candidates
    - Selection of a finalist, based on proposal evaluation or
    - Invitations to finalists to make oral presentations to an evaluation group

From a marketing standpoint, the focus of interest is the process of getting on the short list and the process by which the final selection is made.

THE SHORT LIST

Prospective clients find out about architects in a variety of ways. Those who are frequent users of architectural services will generally keep a file of architects, sometimes classified as to type or practice. Additions to the file can come from mailed brochures, personal calls, advertisements, press releases or, in fact, almost any form of communication. When a specific requirement develops, the file is reviewed for apparent fit. With many variations, a short list is developed and proposals are solicited.

Those who use architects infrequently tend to rely on various buiness or social networks to develop what is in essence their short list. In either case, a previously used architect is almost always on the short list, provided the past experience was satisfactory.

As the largest single customer for architectural services, agencies of the federal government follow a well-defined series of steps, including advertisement in the *Commerce Business Daily* and mail solicitation of local firms.

THE SELECTION PROCESS

The selection process is significantly influenced by the nature and scope of the work and its importance to the firm. Architect selection on major buildings is usually made at the highest level in the organization: by a principal or the president in a private organization or by various forms of boards in not-for-profit organizations such as churches. In some instances the principal, president or board are actively involved in all phases of the process. In others the management of the process is delegated to others who develop recommendations to the decision makers. On smaller jobs, and those of an ongoing nature (e.g., space management), the decision is usually at lower levels and may involve a plant engineer or facilities manager of some kind.

Regardless of the level at which the selection process is made, there seem to be two well-defined patterns to the process. The first, and predominant one, evaluates the firms on the short list, taking into principal consideration non-price factors such as reputation, performance on previous jobs and current work load. Based on this evaluation one firm is selected and a final agreement is then negotiated as to the scope of the work, the nature of the working relationship, the project team and the specific details concerning price. The second, and of limited but growing use, attempts to specify the requirements so completely that a firm price can accompany the proposal. In some instances the price and the proposal are submitted separately. Evaluation of the proposals includes a dollar differential, and these dollar differentials are applied to the price quotation to determine the low evaluated bidder.

Regardless of the process, there appear to be three main criteria on which firms are evaluated:

- The ability of the firm to perform the particular assignment. For standard work this assessment is relatively easy and relies on the nature of past work, size of the organization, current backlogs and so forth. For more creative work the assessment becomes more difficult. Much importance is put on past work, but the proposal starts to take on additional importance. Sketches, drawings and sometimes extensive models may be requested with the proposal. In some instances there may actually be a design competition. Much of this evaluation is, perforce, of a subjective nature.

• The comfort level with the project team that will be assigned to do the work. For any but the most standard work there is recognition that there will be constant interaction between representatives of the client's organization and members of the architectural firm. Almost without exception, therefore, some kind of evaluation is made of the project team, or at least its leaders, in terms of the client's comfort level with the personalities involved.

• Finally, there is the matter of cost. While direct price competition is not a factor in most transactions, the cost of architectural services is always a concern. This has two components. First, there is concern with the total cost of the project, over which the architect has great con-

trol. Second, there is growing concern with the size of the architect's fee, per se.

At least some assessment of the reputation of the architect with respect to controlling project costs is made in determining the short list. Once final selection is made there is likely to be much discussion and negotiation as to the method of calculating the fee. The traditional method of simply charging a percentage of the construction price seems to be on the wane. Increasingly, clients for architectural services are attempting to establish a fixed fee for a well-defined project. The nature of architectural work, however, is such that changes are a fact of life and that many projects cannot be sufficiently defined in the initial stages to allow precise estimation of the design costs. Some basis for modifying a basic fee must, therefore, be established. Typically this is on some kind of direct cost basis plus an overhead adder. Direct costs for various classes of staff and overhead rates obviously become matters for negotiation. In the case of the federal government the right is reserved to audit an architect's books to determine the appropriateness of charges for changes.

As Denver grew, the market changed. The advantage of being a successful local architect and knowing the local business community diminished. Newcomers to Denver tended to rely on relationships with architects in other cities. For local architects there wasn't time to rely on traditional communication networks to establish relationships with these newcomers. The size of projects grew, requiring growth in the size of architectural staffs. Personal attention to every client by principals was no longer possible.

Concomitantly, there was a growing change in the attitude toward the marketing of professional services. New entrants in the fields of medicine and law, as well as architecture, were becoming impatient with the slowness of traditional methods of practice development. A Supreme Court

decision significantly reduced the restrictions that state bar associations could impose on lawyers with respect to their pricing and advertising practices. In a similar vein, the American Institute of Architects signed a consent decree with the Justice Department which prohibited the organization from publishing fee schedules for architectural services.

Perhaps of most significance for architects, however, was the start of the so-called proposal age. Investigations in Maryland and Kansas, and other states, had revealed improper involvement of architects and engineers with state officials. Financial kickbacks were proved on many state projects. Formal proposals, it was felt, would eliminate or reduce the likelihood of contract awards made on the basis of cronyism or kickbacks. Starting in the government sector, the requirement for proposals spread rapidly to all major clients. In 1984, for example, even a small church could receive as many as 20 detailed proposals on a modest-sized assignment.

MARKETING AT RNL

In 1984, RNL was engaged in a number of marketing activities. In addition to proposal preparation, major activities included:

• Professional involvement in the business community by principals, which provides contacts with potential clients. This included memberships in a wide variety of organizations such as the Downtown Denver Board, Chamber of Commerce, Denver Art Museum, etc.

• Participation in and appearances at conferences, both professional and business oriented.

• Daily review of the *Commerce Business Daily* (a federal publication of all construction projects) along with other news services that indicate developing projects.

• Maintenance of past client contacts. (RNL found this difficult but assigned the activity to its project managers.)

• Development of relationships with potential clients, usually by giving a tour through the office plus lunch.

• VIP gourmet catered lunches for six invited guests, held once a month in the office. These involved a tour of the office and lively conversation, with some attempt at subsequent follow-up.

• Participation in appropriate local, regional or national exhibits of architectural projects.

• Occasional publicity for a project or for a client.

• The *Cutting Edge*[1]

• An assortment of brochures and information on finished projects.

• Special arrangements with architectural firms in other locations to provide the basis for a variety of desirable joint ventures.

RNL participated in a number of market segments which it identified as follows, together with its view of the required approach (see table below).

Net fee income and allocation of marketing expenses by major segments are given in the table on page 20. The general feeling at RNL was that there is a lapse of 6 to 18 months between the marketing effort itself and tangible results such as fee income.

---

[1] The *Cutting Edge* is an RNL publication designed to inform clients and prospects about new developments in architecture and planning and about significant RNL accomplishments (see Exhibit 3 for a typical issue).

Segment	Approach
Government	
City and county governments	Personal selling, political involvement
School districts	Personal selling (professional educational knowledge required)
State government	Political involvement, written responses to RFPs (Requests for Proposals, from clients), personal selling
Federal government	Personal selling, very detailed RFP response, no price competition in the proposal stage
Private sector	Personal selling, social acquaintances, referrals, *Cutting Edge*, preliminary studies, price competition
Semi-private sector (includes utilities)	Personal selling, *Cutting Edge*, referrals, continuing relationships, some price competition

EXHIBIT 3   THE CUTTING EDGE

PLANNING FOR PARKING

The recent boom in downtown Denver office building has resulted in tremendous increases in population density in Denver's core, bringing corresponding increases in the number of vehicles and their related problems as well.

Auto storage, or parking, is one of the major resulting problems. Most building zoning requires parking sufficient to serve the building's needs. Even building sites not requiring parking are now providing parking space to remain competitive in the marketplace.

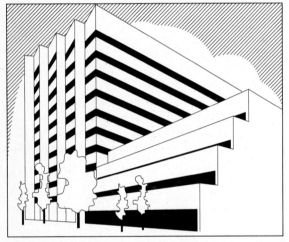

RNL's design for this above-grade parking structure at 1700 Grant aided in facilitating lease of the office building.

Parking solutions can range from a simple asphalt lot to a large multi-floor parking structure: the decision is based on many factors including site access, required number of spaces, land costs, budget and user convenience.

For many suburban sites, where land costs are sufficiently low to allow on-grade parking, design entails mainly the problems of circulation and landscaping. Circulation includes issues of easy site access and optimal use of the site. Landscaping, including landforming, can visually screen automobiles and break up ugly seas of asphalt common to poorly designed development.

At the opposite end of the parking spectrum are downtown sites where high land costs necessitate careful integration of parking into the building concept. This is often accomplished by building parking underground, below the main structure. Parking design, in this case, becomes a problem of integrating the circulation and the structure of the building above. While building underground eliminates the need for acceptable outer appearance, the costs of excavation, mechanical ventilation, fire sprinklering and waterproofing make this one of the most expensive parking solutions.

Between on-grade parking and the underground structure is the above-grade detached or semi-detached parking structure. This solution is very common in areas of moderate land cost where convenience is the overriding factor.

Site conditions do much to generate the design of an above-grade parking structure, but where possible the following features should ideally be included:

1 Parking is in double loaded corridors, i.e., cars park on both sides of the circulation corridor to provide the most efficient ratio of parking to circulation

2 Parking is at 90 degrees to circulation corridors rather than at angles, once again the most efficient use of space.

3 Access to different garage levels is provided by ramping the parking floors, efficiently combining vertical circulation and parking.

4 A precast prestressed concrete structure (this structure economically provides long spans needed to eliminate columns which would interfere with parking circulation and the fireproof concrete members have low maintenance surface that can be left exposed).

5 Classification as an "open parking garage" under the building code, meaning that the structure has openings in the walls of the buildings providing natural ventilation and eliminating the need for expensive mechanical ventilation of exhaust fumes.

6 A building exterior in a precast concrete finish, allowing the designer to combine structure and exterior skin into one low-cost environment.

RNL recently completed work on the $20,000,000 1700 Grant Office Building for Wickliff & Company. The inclusion of a 415-car parking garage in the 1700 Grant project provided one of the amenities necessary for successful leasing in a very depressed leasing market.

	1982		1983		1984 (est.)		1985 (est.)	
	Net fee	Marktg. exp.	Net fee	Marktg. exp.	Net fee	Marktg. exp.	Net fee	Marktg. exp.
Government	$ 800*	$104	$1,220	$101	$1,012	$150	$1,200	$140
Private	1,376	162	1,261	140	1,200	195	1,616	220
Semi-private	88	11	118	24	100	25	140	30
Interiors	828	40	670	30	918	100	1235	110
Urban design	95	20	31	10	170	30	220	40
Total	$3,187	$337	$3,300	$305	$3,400	$500	$4,411	$540

* ($000)

Salient aspects of budgeted marketing expense for 1985, by segment, were:

• Government. Heavy emphasis on increased trips to Omaha (a key Corps of Engineers location), Washington and other out-of-state, as well as in-state, locations plus considerable emphasis on participation in municipal conferences.

• Private. Personal contact at local, state and regional level with corporations, banks, developers and contractors plus local promotion through Chamber of Commerce, clubs, V.I.P. lunches, *Cutting Edge*, promotion materials and initiation of an advertising and public relations effort.

• Semi-private. Increased level of personal contact and promotional effort.

• Interiors. Major allocation of salary and expenses of a new full-time marketing person to improve direct sales locally plus other promotional support.

• Urban design. Some early success indicates that land developers and urban renewal authorities are the most likely clients. Planned marketing expense is primarily for personal contact.

Additional marketing efforts being given serious consideration included:

• A more structured marketing organization with more specific assignments

• Increased visibility for the firm through general media and trade journals, paid or other (e.g., public relations)

• Appearances on special programs and offering special seminars

• Use of more sophisticated selling tools such as videotapes and automated slide presentations

• Increased training in client relations/selling for project managers and other staff

• Hiring a professionally trained marketing manager

• Determining how the national firms market (i.e., copy the competition)

• Expansion of debriefing conferences with successful and unsuccessful clients

• Use of a focus group to develop effective sales points for RNL

• Training a marketing M.B.A. in architecture versus an architect in marketing

RNL CLIENTS

RNL described its clients as:

1 Having a long history of growing expectations with respect to detail, completeness, counseling and cost control

2 Mandating the minimization of construction problems, including changes, overruns and delays

3 Having an increased concern for peer approval at the completion of a project

4 Having an increased desire to understand and be a part of the design process

Extensive interviews of clients by independent market researchers showed very favorable impressions about RNL. Terms used to describe the firm included:

- Best and largest architectural service in Denver
- Innovative yet practical
- Designs large projects for "Who's Who in Denver"
- Long-term resident of the business community
- Lots of expertise
- Designs artistic yet functional buildings

RNL's use of computer-aided design systems was seen as a definite competitive edge. Others mentioned RNL's extra services, such as interior systems, as a plus, although only 35% of those interviewed were aware that RNL offered this service. In general, most clients felt that RNL had a competitive edge with regard to timeliness, productivity and cost consciousness.

Two major ways that new clients heard about RNL were identified. One was the contact RNL made on its own initiative when it heard of a possible project. The other was through personal references. All those interviewed felt that advertising played a minor role, and in fact, several indicated they had questions about an architectural firm that advertises.

Clients who selected RNL identified the following as playing a role in their decision:

- Tours of RNL's facilities
- Monthly receipt of the *Cutting Edge*
- Low-key selling style
- RNL's ability to focus on their needs
- Thoroughness in researching customer needs and overall proposal preparation and presentation
- RNL's overall reputation in the community
- Belief that RNL would produce good, solid (not flashy) results

Clients who did not select RNL identified the following reasons for their decision:

- RNL had less experience and specialization in their particular industry.
- They decided to stay with the architectural firm used previously.
- They decided to go with a firm that has more national status.
- Other presentations had more "pizazz."

Overall, clients' perceptions of RNL were very positive. There was less than complete understanding of the scope of RNL services, but their current approach to clients received good marks.

MARKETING ISSUES AT RNL: SOME VIEWS OF MIDDLE MANAGEMENT

Richard von Luhrte joined RNL in 1979, following extensive experience with other firms in Chicago and Denver. In 1984 he led the firm's urban design effort on major projects, served as a Project Manager and participated actively in marketing. He came to RNL because the firm "fits my image." He preferred larger firms that have extensive and complementary skills. He commented on marketing as follows:

> RNL has a lot going for it. We have a higher overhead rate, but with most clients you can sell our competence and turn this into an advantage. I think RNL is perceived as a quality firm, but customers are also concerned that we will gold-plate a job. I'd like to be able to go gold-plate or inexpensive as the circumstances dictate. But it's hard to convince a customer that we can do this.

> For many of our clients continuity is important, and we need to convey that there will be continuity beyond the founders. RNL has done well as a provider of "all things for all people," and our diversification helps us ride through periods of economic downturn. On the other hand we lose some jobs because we're not specialized. For instance, we haven't done well in the downtown developer market. We're starting to do more, but if we had targeted the shopping center business, we could have had seven or eight jobs by now. One way to operate would be to jump on a trend and ride it until the downturn and then move into something else.

There's always the conflict between specialization and fun. We try to stay diversified, but we ought to be anticipating the next boom. At the same time, there's always the problem of overhead. In this business you can't carry very much, particularly in slow times.

I like the marketing part of the work, but there's a limit on how much of it I can, or should, do. Plus, I think it's important to try to match our people with our clients in terms of age and interests, which means we need to have lots of people involved in the marketing effort.

Oral presentations are an important part of marketing, and we make a lot of them. You have to make them interesting, and there has to be a sense of trying for the "close." On the other hand, I think that the presentation is not what wins the job, although a poor presentation can lose it for you. It's important that the presentation conveys a sense of enthusiasm and that we really want the job.

As Comptroller, Jane Washington was involved extensively in the firm's discussions about its marketing efforts. As she described the situation:

There is little question in my mind that the people at the top are committed to developing a marketing orientation at RNL. But our objectives still aren't clear. For instance, we still haven't decided what would be a good mix of architecture, interiors and planning. Interiors is a stepchild to some. On the other hand it is a very profitable part of our business. But it's not easy to develop a nice neat set of objectives for a firm like this. Two years ago we had a seminar to develop a mission statement, but we still don't have one. This isn't a criticism. Rather, it's an indication of the difficulty of getting agreement on objectives in a firm of creative professionals.

One problem is that our approach to marketing has been reactive rather than proactive. Our biggest marketing expenditure is proposal preparation, and we have tended to respond to RFPs as they come in, without screening them for fit with targeted segments. From a budget standpoint we have not really allocated marketing dollars to particular people or segments, except in a pro forma kind of way. As a result, no one person is responsible for what is a very large total expenditure.

Another problem is that we don't have precise information about our marketing expenditures or the profitability of individual jobs. It would be impractical to track expenditures on the 500 to 1000 proposals we make a year, but we could set up a system that tracks marketing expenditures in, say, 10 segments. This would at least let individuals see what kind of money we're spending for marketing, and where. We also could change from the present system which basically measures performance in terms of variation from dollar budget to one that reports on the profitability of individual jobs. I've done some studies on the profitability of our major product lines, but those don't tie to any one individual's performance.

Rita Mitchell, who had an M.S. in Library Science and Information Systems, joined RNL in 1981. Originally her assignment focused on organizing marketing records and various marketing information resources. In her new role as New Business Development Coordinator she had a broader set of responsibilities. According to Rita:

We definitely need some policies about marketing, and these ought to spell out a marketing process. In my present job I think I can help the board synthesize market information and so help to develop a marketing plan.

I do a lot of market research based on secondary data. For instance, we have access to Dialog and a number of other on-line databases, using our PC. Based on this research, and our own in-house competence, I think I can do some good market anticipation. The problem is what to do with this kind of information. If we move too fast, based on signals about a new market, there is obviously the risk of being wrong. On the other hand, if we wait until the signals are unmistakably clear, they will be clear to everyone else and we will lose the opportunity to establish a preeminent position.

With respect to individual RFPs, our decision on which job to quote is still highly subjective. We try to estimate our chances of getting the job, and we talk about its fit with our other work, but we don't have much hard data or policy to guide us. We don't, for instance, have a good sense of other RFPs that are in the pipeline and how the mix of the jobs we're quoting and the resulting work fits with our present work in progress. The Marketing Committee (consisting of John Rogers, Vic Langhart, Phil Goedert, Rich von Luhrte, Dick Shiffer, Rita Mitchell and, occasionally, Bob Johnson) brings lots of experience and personal knowledge to bear on this, but it's not a precise process.

We have a number of sources of information about new construction projects: the *Commerce Business Daily* (a federal government publication), the *Daily Journal* (which reports on local government construction), the Western Press Clipping Bureau, Colorado trade journals and so forth. Monitoring these is a major activity, and then we have the problem of deciding which projects fit RNL.

Bob Johnson, a Project Manager and member of the Marketing Committee, commented:

The way the system works now we have four board members and 12 project managers, most of whom can pursue new business. They bring these opportunities before the Marketing Committee, but it doesn't really have the clout to say no. As a result, people can really go off on their own. I'd like to see the committee flex its muscles a little more on what jobs we go after. But there's a problem with committing to just a few market segments.

Right now we're involved in something like 30 segments. If we're wrong on one, it's not a big deal. But if we were committed to just a few, then a mistake could have really serious consequences.

For many of us, however, the major problem is managing the transfer of ownership and control to a broader set of individuals. Currently the prospective owners don't really have a forum for what they'd like the company to be. My personal preference would be to go after corporate headquarters, high-tech firms, speculative office buildings and high-quality interiors. But there probably isn't agreement on this.

MARKETING ISSUES:
THE VIEWS OF THE FOUNDERS

Vic Langhart started his practice of architecture in 1954 and had taught design in the Architecture Department of the University of Colorado.

He was instrumental in developing new services at RNL, including Interplan and SMS, Inc., and was heavily involved in training the next level of management. In 1984 he supervised day-to-day operations and also served as President of Interplan and SMS, Inc. Looking to the future, Vic observed:

Our toughest issue is dealing with the rate of change in the profession today. It's probably fair to say there are too many architects today. But this is a profession of highly idealistic people, many of whom feel their contribution to a better world is more important than dollars of income and so will stay in the field at "starvation wages." We wrestle with the question of "profession or business?" but competition is now a fact of life for us. The oil boom of the 1970s in Denver triggered an inrush of national firms. Many have stayed on, and we now have a situation where one of the largest national firms is competing for a small job in Durango. We're also starting to see more direct price competition. Digital Equipment recently prequalified eight firms, selected five to submit proposals that demonstrated understanding of the assignment and asked for a separate envelope containing the price.

Our tradition at RNL has been one of quality. I think we're the "Mercedes" of the business, and in the long haul an RNL customer will be better off economically. A lot of things contribute to this—our Interplan concept, for instance—but the key differentiation factor is our on-site-planning approach.

In 1966–1968 we were almost 100% in education. Then I heard that they were closing some maternity wards, and we decided to diversify. Today we have a good list of products, ranging from commercial buildings to labs and vehicle maintenance facilities. In most areas the only people who can beat us are the superspecialists, and even then there's a question. Our diversification has kept our minds free to come up with creative approaches. At Beaver Creek, for example, I think we came up with a better approach to condominium design than the specialists. Plus, we can call in special expertise, if it's necessary.

Over the past several years we've had a number of offers to merge into national, or other, firms. We decided, however, to become employee owned. Our basic notion was that RNL should be an organization that provides its employees a long-time career opportunity. This is not easy in an industry that is characterized by high turnover. Less than 10% of architectural firms have figured out how to do it. But we're now at 35% employee ownership.

I'm personally enthusiastic about Interplan. It has tremendous potential to impact our customers. In Seattle, for instance, a bank came to us for a simple expansion. Our Interplan approach, however, led to a totally different set of concepts.

We've had some discussion about expansion. Colorado Springs is a possibility, for instance. But there would be problems of keeping RNL concepts and our culture. We work hard to develop and disseminate an RNL culture. For example, we have lots of meetings, although John and I sometimes disagree about how much time should be spent in meetings. A third of our business comes from interiors, and there is as much difference between interior designers and architects as there is between architects and mechanical engineers.

In somewhat similar vein, John Rogers commented:

In the 1960s RNL was primarily in the business of designing schools. We were really experts in that market. But then the boom in school construction came to an end, and we moved into other areas. First into banks and commercial buildings. We got started with Mountain Bell, an important relationship for us that continues today. We did assignments for mining companies and laboratories. In the late 1960s no one knew how to use computers to manage office space problems, and we moved in that direction, which led to the formation of Interplan. We moved into local and state design work. One of our showcase assignments is the Colorado State Judicial/Heritage Center.

In the 1980s we started to move into federal and military work, and this now represents a significant portion of our business. We have done some developer work, but this is a tough market. It has a strong "bottom line orientation," and developers want sharp focus and expertise.

As we grow larger, we find it difficult to maintain a close client relationship. The client wants to know who will work on the assignment, but some of our staff members are not good at the people side of the business.

Currently we're still doing lots of "one of a kind" work. Our assignment for the expansion of the Rocky Mountain News building, our design of a condominium lodge at Beaver Creek, our design of a developer building at the Denver Tech Center are all in this category. A common theme, however, is our "on-site" design process. This is a process by which we make sure that the client is involved in the design from the start and that we are really tuned in to his requirements. I see this as one of our real competitive advantages. But I'm still concerned that we may be trying to spread ourselves too thin. Plus, there's no question that there is an increased tendency to specialization, "shopping center architects," for example.

We need to become better marketers, but we have to make sure that we don't lose sight of what has made us the leading architectural firm in Denver—service and client orientation.

SOFTWARE ARCHITECTS (A)

Harvey Mayerowicz, the president and founder of Software Architects, was in the process of reviewing the business strategy for 1982–1983. Software Architects (SA) was a data processing consulting firm which provided customized computer programming services and technical seminars on various topics to companies in the Chicago area. A small entrepreneurial enterprise, SA had enjoyed modest growth and profitable performance in the two-and-a-half years since its founding. Harvey's concern was to develop a clear understanding of the factors which had contributed to SA's past success, and to position the company for continued success in an industry that was experiencing rapid growth, increasing competition, and technological change.

Financial support for this case was provided in part by the Strategic Management and Marketing Management Programs of the Graduate School of Business, Stanford University. This case was prepared by Professor Tom Kosnik. Reprinted with permission of Stanford University Graduate School of Business © 1983 by The Board of Trustees of The Leland Stanford Junior University.

COMPANY BACKGROUND

Software Architects was founded by six individuals in late 1979. Harvey Mayerowicz was the president, elected by his colleagues on the board of directors. The other five directors were Gloria Petersen, Gene Petrie, Edward Wroble, Bruce Parrello, and Fritz Wolf. All of the directors were experienced systems programmers, who performed technical consulting tasks in addition to their duties of managing the company.

Decision making at SA was a consensual process, with each of the six directors contributing ideas and opinions at the meetings held every one or two weeks. An idea which was of interest to a particular director was often explored outside of the meetings so that he or she was able to make recommendations and advocate a particular position to the others.

Responsibility for business functions was shared among the directors in the following way. Harvey and Gloria were responsible for marketing and new client development. Bruce, who had developed the automated accounting systems used by SA, was concerned with the financial side of the business. Fritz, Gene, and Ed focused their attentions on the conduct of consulting projects themselves, including technical work, supervision of SA employees, and managing the delicate relationships with SA clients.

In addition to the six founders/directors of SA, there were five other technical consultants who performed project work. Harvey anticipated that these employees might be groomed to take on additional responsibilities in marketing or project management as SA grew. They were encouraged to take initiative and to accelerate the timetable for their development, in an effort to provide challenge and stimulation on the job.

Financial Performance

The directors all took pride in the fact that SA had been profitable since the time the firm was established. Income statements for the 1980 and 1981 fiscal years indicated that retained earnings for 1981 had almost tripled the 1980 figure. The results for the first six months of the 1982 fiscal year (July through December of 1981) showed revenues of over $400,000 and before-tax income of over $140,000.

The accountants who reviewed SA's financial reports had given Harvey a set of financial performance ratios for firms in the computer programming and software services industry. The results of high-, average-, and low-performing companies are provided in Exhibit 1. It appeared to Harvey that SA was doing reasonably well, especially in view of the fact that it was a new venture in a fairly competitive marketplace.

Services Offered

SA provided services to clients in three main areas:

1 *Systems programming:* The design and programming of systems software to augment that provided by the hardware manufacturer. Examples included programs for measuring systems efficiency, compilers, utilities, and report generators.

2 *Application programming:* The design and programming of software to perform specific applications for the client, such as accounting, inventory management, and planning systems.

3 *Technical education:* The development and presentation of training seminars for employees in client organizations on a variety of technical subjects in which SA had special expertise.

EXHIBIT 1   KEY FINANCIAL RATIOS FOR FIRMS IN THE COMPUTER PROGRAMMING AND SOFTWARE SERVICE INDUSTRY COMPARED WITH SOFTWARE ARCHITECTS' RESULTS

Financial performance measures	Industry performance in 1981			Software Architects results for 1981
	High performers	Average performers	Low performers	
% Profit before tax/sales	N/A	8.4%	N/A	13.6%
% Profit before tax/net worth	73.5%	45.2%	20.8%	59.3%
% Profit before tax/assets	22.1%	14.2%	5.7%	19.7%
Sales/receivables	7.7	5.7	3.8	2.6
Sales/assets	3.0	2.2	1.5	1.9
Debt/worth	1.1	2.0	3.6	2.0
Current ratio	1.8	1.4	1.0	1.6

Source: Robert Morris Associates (1981) and Software Architects' internal records.

Additional descriptions of systems and application software are provided in Appendix A.

SA had also done a project on a microcomputer network in the last year. It was possible that there might be other opportunities for SA related to microcomputers in the future, but it was not clear what form those opportunities might take.

SA's costs and revenues for the services it provided were largely based on the time spent by SA consultants to complete design and programming tasks on each project. The custom development of software was usually broken down into several phases. Although the tasks performed in each phase varied depending upon the methodology that was being used, most of SA's projects consisted of:

1 *General design:* In which the overall framework for the new system was developed and the needs of the users which were to be satisfied by the system were identified.

2 *Detailed design:* During which the general guidelines from the previous phase were elaborated to provide a clear, explicit blueprint for subsequent programming.

3 *Implementation:* During which programs were written, tested individually and as an overall system, and the final system was introduced into a "live" environment for use in day-to-day operations.

SA spent more time than many of its competitors in the detailed design phase. However, they were convinced that extra effort there allowed even greater time savings during implementation. In essence, their detailed planning allowed a smoother, faster execution and much less time in testing and debugging programs.

Keys to Success

In discussions with other members of the board, Harvey and Gloria expressed their feelings that in a consulting relationship, technical competence was a necessary but not sufficient condition for success. There were other essential ingredients as

well. Harvey believed that a programming consultant had to have three qualities to satisfy most clients and earn an invitation for follow-on work. The individual had to be honest, competent, and personable. Gloria felt that the most important characteristic was the ability of the consultant to be empathetic with the client, understanding and listening to the client's business and personal concerns.

Their continuing discussions had yielded a list of factors which they believed were important to a prospective client in deciding whether or not to accept a proposal from a particular software consulting firm:

1 *Availability:* The ability of the consultant to meet staffing levels, start dates, and completion dates required by the client.

2 *Cost:* Measured in terms of both an hourly billing rate and an estimate of overall project costs.

3 *Honesty:* The willingness of the consultant to admit that he or she either does not know the answer or had made a mistake; in addition, the unwillingness of the consultant to make promises in a proposal that the firm may not be able to keep, e.g., the promise to meet a deadline desired by the client.

4 *Professionalism:* The consultant's respect for the client's work environment rules, punctuality, neatness, and personal appearance.

5 *Quality of past work:* As evidenced by either the recommendations of other satisfied clients or the quality of sample programming documentation, articles, technical papers, etc., provided by the consultant for review by the client. The quality of the analysis supporting the proposal was also important.

6 *Rapport:* A combination of what Harvey had identified as the personable quality and Gloria had called empathy. The sense of shared understanding, values, and personal friendship between the client and the consultant.

7 *Technical fit:* The match between the consultant's areas of competence and the client's needs for specialized expertise. It was possible for a highly technical individual to be undesirable to a client if the expertise was out of date or was not relevant in the client's problem situation.

Harvey and Gloria wondered whether their clients saw the keys to success in software consulting the same way that they did. They were also curious about how potential clients perceived SA in each of the areas above. In what respects was SA's position strong relative to its competitors? What were the major areas needing improvement? Were there other considerations in the decision to hire a firm like SA that the two of them had overlooked?

It seemed that getting answers to the questions above was crucial to understanding what SA had done right in the first two years. It was also critical to keeping SA well-positioned for the future.

SOFTWARE ARCHITECTS' EXTERNAL ENVIRONMENT

Prospective Clients

As suppliers of customized programming services and technical education, SA had a wide variety of potential clients. However, the realities of the marketplace and the values of the SA principals both served to focus attention on a reasonably small group of companies.

The cost of custom programming was prohibitive for many organizations. SA believed that the size of the data processing budget was related to the annual revenues of a company, and its main targets were therefore the largest industrial firms. Because SA had only one office and the professional staff preferred not to travel out of town, Harvey generally restricted his clients to those in the Chicago metropolitan area. SA did not attempt to specialize in a particular application area (such as general ledger systems) or industry group (such as banking or forest products). However, it did try to concentrate on its areas of primary technical expertise. As a result, potential clients were screened based upon the hardware and systems software that they had in their data processing centers. SA preferred to work with

IBM hardware and software, and rarely competed for projects in other hardware and software environments.

SA's potential clients, then, included large businesses in the Chicago area with IBM computer equipment. Most of the 19 clients for which they had worked in the first two years had all three of these characteristics. There were almost 50 prospective clients which met the three criteria and showed high potential for future SA work. Market research had identified approximately 50 other firms which were large enough and were based in Chicago. It was not yet determined what hardware and software was in place in each of the second group of companies.

The Chicago area was not a center of high-technology manufacturing like the areas outside Boston, Massachusetts, and San Jose's Silicon Valley. As a result, few of SA's potential clients made computer-related products. Most used computers for their internal administrative, accounting, inventory, and planning systems. The data processing departments varied in size from a few to several hundred people. Nearly every organization suffered from a shortage of skilled programming personnel. In fact, the shortage of people and technical skills was what provided the principal raison d'être for the hundreds of systems consulting firms which operated in the Chicago area.

The data processing departments of most organizations had at least three separate groups. One was responsible for systems programming, and maintained the technical environment in which the other two groups worked. The technical skills required to work as a systems programmer were greater than those of other data processing personnel. The second group was responsible for application development. This group designed and tested programs for accounting, planning, or other functions which had been requested by non-technical users in the organization. The third group was responsible for operations. They "ran" the hardware and software in order to process information and produce reports desired by management for planning and control purposes. Computer operators were typically the least technically skilled of the three groups.

The decision to acquire consulting services from a firm like SA was sometimes made by the manager in charge of the systems programming group. At other times, the person in charge of the entire data processing operation was the final decision maker. Occasionally, and especially when a manager from another part of the potential client company had requested that an application system be developed to meet his or her needs, non-technical management were involved in the process. If the contract was for a large dollar amount (greater than $50,000), or was for a project of critical importance to the organization, senior management approval was usually required.

No matter who was involved in the process of choosing the consultant, SA's "client" was almost always a member of management in the data processing organization. This individual was often under a great deal of stress to develop a new system under tight budget and deadline constraints. If the project timetable "slipped" or there were cost overruns, the manager's job could be in jeopardy. With billing rates between $30 and $120 an hour for outside programming support, a small error in estimating the scope of the project resulted in a large increase in cost.

The stories of projects that had been placed in the hands of data processing consultants and had subsequently gone awry were many. There were also frequent accounts of outsiders who had installed a system and left when the initial contract had expired. When the client later found "bugs" during the day-to-day operations of the system, there was often no one in-house who knew enough about the system to make the necessary repairs. The consultants were seldom available for assistance. The programmers were immersed in other projects with new clients. Frequently, the people who had actually worked on the system had moved on to other employers. Turnover among software programming houses was notoriously high.

Thus, the potential clients of SA shared two major concerns about the use of consultants: the fear of project delays and budget overruns in the short run, and the worry about being left "high and dry" when the project was over. Many companies had policies against the use of outsiders for system development. Unfortunately, that rarely offered protection from the two key risks. Inability to meet deadlines was at least as much a problem for internal programmers as it was for firms like SA. So was turnover. The competition for technical people was fierce enough that programmers were often lured away by other employers.

Harvey believed that if SA were able to demonstrate its technical competence and its ability to meet deadlines to a client, the chances for follow-on business were good. Firms who could deliver on promises made at the time of the initial proposal were rare. Repeat business also served to reduce the client's second area of risk. If the SA programmer were working on another project in the same firm, he or she would be accessible to answer questions or provide a "quick fix" if problems arose.

The problem for Harvey was how subtly to address what he thought were the two areas of concern for most clients. He was unsure of how SA might demonstrate its competence and its willingness to provide continuity in a way that sounded like an honest promise, rather than a sales pitch.

The clients for SA's technical seminars were sometimes the same individuals as for the programming services. At other times, people in the organization's professional training and development staff got involved. Although the risk of a poorly conceived and executed seminar did not appear to be as great as those for a computer system, the two groups shared something in common. They had to commit money and their reputations in advance to an outside supplier of a product which did not yet exist. This often made the criteria for selection difficult to articulate. The decision was rarely clear-cut. Usually, the client had to rely on "gut feel" and hope for the best.

Competitors

Harvey and his colleagues were not certain who their closest competitors were in the systems and applications programming area. One study (see Appendix A) had estimated that there were thousands of firms providing custom design and programming services in the United States. Of these, there were only about 2,000 competitors nationwide who generated more than $250,000 each in annual revenues. There was no market research data available on the firms in the Chicago area. Harvey had found over 200 names of data processing consultants in the Chicago yellow pages. However, neither SA nor several of the firms against which they had bid on past projects were listed in the yellow pages. He was not sure how many firms were actually providing a similar type of service to the same target clients.

Harvey and Gloria had developed a list of potential competitors which included those against whom SA had prepared bids for work in the past, as well as those about whom SA had heard from clients and other contacts. Exhibit 2 contains information about billing rates of SA's major competitors on past projects.

SA's known competitors included several very large national firms, such as Arthur Andersen and McAuto. There were also a number of smaller companies. It was unclear what the best strategy might be for SA's positioning relative to this wide variety of opponents. How did potential clients perceive SA relative to a company with the re-sources and reputation of Arthur Andersen? Were there needs that SA might fill better than a larger, better-established firm? Where were the client's sensitive spots in dealing with an entrepreneurial company that Harvey had to address? Further, did SA appear to be special in the eyes of the client, or was it one of a myriad of small, nondescript "body shops" that abounded in the marketplace?

Learning where SA was from the client's point of view was an important first step. Creating an image for the firm as a high-quality, high-priced source of services was the next item on the agenda.

Industry Facilitators

Although software consultants typically marketed their services by direct sales calls on potential clients, there were other institutions in the marketplace which could aid in the spread of reputation and the generation of leads for new business. Harvey considered at least three types of "industry facilitators":

1 *Hardware vendors:* Who often provided purchasers of equipment with the names of several software consulting firms if there was a need for help in setting up new applications

2 *User groups:* Who met to discuss new ideas and common problems with hardware or software that they all had at their respective sites

3 *University MIS professors:* Who provided consulting firms with programmers, and who also

EXHIBIT 2   ESTIMATED HOURLY BILLING RATES OF SOFTWARE ARCHITECTS' COMPETITORS

Competitor name	Estimated hourly rates for			
	Programmer/ analyst	System designers	Project leaders	Partners/ Principals
Arthur Andersen	$38–$40*	$45–$55	$50–$85	$100–$150
Consumer Systems	$27–$31	N/A	$38	N/A
Farlow Associates	$25–$28	N/A	N/A	N/A
Giles Associates	$24–$32	$26–$36	$35 and up	N/A
McAuto	$46–$58	$66–$83	$109–$136	$127–$159

* For every five programmer/analysts, Arthur Andersen provided an experienced consultant as supervisor at no charge to the client.

referred technical consulting business that they could not handle because of time commitments to software houses that they considered "top notch."

It seemed that SA should have a coherent strategy for their dealings with each of these industry groups. Harvey also wondered whether there were other "facilitators" that he might have overlooked.

Growth and Technological Change

Appendix A provides growth rates for different segments of the software industry. Professional services for custom software development showed a 20% annual growth forecast for the 1981–1986 period. Harvey had no data for the growth in demand for software services in the Chicago area.

Technological change was an important and troublesome issue for SA's future planning. The manufacturers of hardware and systems software improved their products and developed new technologies at a breakneck pace. As a result, technical expertise became obsolete almost as fast as the products did. There was always a lag in the decline in demand for services, because clients who already owned older hardware did not discard it as rapidly as the technology changed.

Harvey had developed a list of the technological changes which offered the greatest risk of obsolescence (and opportunity for new business) for SA:

1 Changes in systems software technology
2 Development of application generators
3 Proliferation of microcomputers

There were two impending changes in systems software technology that threatened SA: (1) IBM's promise of operating systems that eliminated the need for systems programmers and (2) new database management software. SA's special expertise was in systems programming for IBM mainframe computers. That firm had recently announced a new operating system called the SSX

system, which it claimed made it unnecessary to hire systems programmers. The software was supposed to allow a non-technical user to start and operate the system without programming commands in Job Control Language (JCL). Harvey was a bit skeptical about IBM's claims but felt that in the future, systems software might become more "user friendly." In fact, some of the minicomputer manufacturers had made great strides in that area.

SA's experience with database management systems was with a pair of competing technologies known as hierarchical and network architectures. Most of the database packages that had been sold in the last ten years had been one of those varieties. While extremely powerful, these systems were known for their technical complexity, and database design and programming skills were in short supply. SA had a wealth of experience in several of these products, including IBM's flagship IMS, Cullinane's IDMS, and Software AG's ADABAS.

There had been a great deal of interest in the trade press in a new, simpler technology called relational database management systems. There were two or three new products that were actually on the market, and IBM had been working for several years to develop a relational DBMS of its own. If and when the new software came into widespread use, the threats to SA were twofold. First, it was a technology in which they did not have expertise to differentiate them from competitors. Second, the systems were supposed to be much simpler and "user friendly," reducing the need for specialized systems programming experience.

The shortage of skilled programmers and rising salary costs for technical personnel had provided the incentive to reduce the labor intensity of systems development. Many suppliers had developed application software packages which a client could buy "off the shelf" and use with little or no additional programming. A more radical solution to the problem was the concept of a product known as an application generator. This was an off-the-shelf package that a non-technical person could use to translate English-like commands into machine-readable code. In essence, the idea of the application generator was to eliminate the "middleman" between the non-technical user and the machine. If such a product were perfected, the need for application programmers would all but disappear.

Thus far, no one had succeeded in developing the concept of the application generator to its full potential. Nevertheless, products which vastly improved programmer productivity had been introduced. For example, Cullinane Corporation had recently advertised a package which it claimed reduced the time required for programming by 90%.

Most of SA's past experience had been with large IBM mainframes. IBM's share of the data processing industry's total revenues was almost 40% in 1980. Its nearest competitor, NCR, had 5% share of market in 1980. The large installed base of IBM mainframes made it the obvious choice of hardware in which to develop specialized expertise.

However, there were considerable differences in the growth trends for different segments of the hardware industry, as shown in Exhibit 3. In particular, sales of microcomputers had grown 85% from 1979 to 1980. Many industry observers believed that microcomputer sales might grow at a faster rate in the 1981–1986 period, as new suppliers entered the marketplace, the technology improved, and the selling price per unit declined.

The massive influx of microcomputers was both a threat and an opportunity for SA. If users moved away from dependence on large mainframes and centralized data processing departments to meet their needs, SA's traditional clients might be faced with less work, lower data processing budgets, and less power in the decision to bring in consultants. On the other hand, many of the users of microcomputers were non-technical people who preferred not to write their own programs. SA might be able to develop application software for micros and sell it to a large number of users.

Harvey was confident that SA had the technical skill to develop such software. In fact, SA had a TRS-80 microcomputer, and Bruce Parrello had written programs to do the company's project accounting, accounts payable and receivable, and general ledger in his spare time. However, SA

EXHIBIT 3   SELECTED DATA PROCESSING INDUSTRY GROWTH RATES, 1979–80

TABLE I   TOP 10 DP REVENUES
           (In $ Millions)

		1980	1979	% growth rate
1	IBM	21,367	18,338	16.5
2	NCR	2,840	2,528	12.3
3	Control Data	2,791	2,273	22.8
4	DEC	2,743	2,032	35.0
5	Sperry	2,552	2,270	12.4
6	Burroughs	2,478	2,442	1.5
7	Honeywell	1,634	1,453	12.5
8	Hewlett-Packard	1,577	1,147	37.5
9	Xerox	770	570	35.1
10	Memorex	686	658	4.3
	Total Top 10	39,438	33,710	17.0
	Total	55,626	46,220	20.4
	Top 10 as a percent of total	70.9%	72.9%	

TABLE III   TOP 20 REVENUE GROWTH RATE
(In $ Millions)

		Total dp % growth rate	U.S. dp % growth rate	Foreign dp % growth rate	1980 Dp rev.	1980 Earnings
1	Sanders Assoc.	206.5	91.5	NM	145.0	49
2	Apple	175.1	163.4	224.7	165.2	47
3	Philips Information Sys.	100.0	100.0	NM	50.0	96
4	Tandem	93.9	58.7	179.4	128.8	53
5	Intergraph	91.3	80.1	153.7	56.5	90
6	Dysan	86.1	79.9	127.7	62.9	85
7	Computervision	85.5	72.7	108.3	191.1	41
8	Paradyne	83.2	74.0	108.9	75.9	77
9	Prime	75.0	59.9	95.8	257.6	27
10	Teletype	72.4	62.1	NM	250.0	29
11	CPT	68.9	44.7	157.7	76.4	76
12	Wang Labs	66.1	68.8	61.5	681.8	11
13	Lanier	64.1	60.6	129.7	128.0	54
14	Triad Systems	61.0	61.0	NM	60.2	87
15	Anacomp	60.1	60.1	60.0	57.0	89
16	Commodore International	54.1	−13.2	105.2	98.7	66
17	Applicon	51.4	35.2	136.6	68.5	82
18	Auto-trol Technology	51.3	58.5	27.1	50.8	97
19	AM International	49.0	49.0	49.0	98.8	65
20	Printronix	48.8	37.7	93.0	48.9	99

NM = Not Meaningful

TABLE IX   DP REVENUES BY PRODUCT SEGMENT
(In $ Millions)

	1980 $	1980 %	1979 $	1979 %	% Growth rate
Systems					
Mainframes	15,148	27.2	13,312	29.0	13.8
Minicomputers	8,840	15.9	6,916	15.0	27.8
Microcomputers	769	1.4	416	0.9	84.9
Word processing	881	1.6	538	1.2	63.8
Total systems	25,638	46.1	21,182	46.1	21.0
Oam peripherals	3,968	7.1	3,128	6.8	26.9
End user peripherals	6,910	12.4	5,943	12.9	16.3
Data communications	1,141	2.1	927	2.0	23.1
Software products	1,738	3.1	1,347	2.9	29.0
Maintenance	8,588	16.0	7,372	16.0	20.6
Service	6,432	11.6	5,329	11.6	20.7
All other	911	1.6	772	1.7	18.0
Total	55,626	100.0	46,000	100.0	20.9

Source: Wright, P., "The Datamation 100," Datamation, June 1981.

had no idea how to market microcomputer software once it was developed. They had deferred discussion on diversification into that area until they learned more about the marketing channels for microcomputer software.

SA directors knew that the company could not expect to be writing systems and applications programs for IBM mainframes in 20 years. But how fast would the technology change? What could SA do in 1982 to anticipate these changes and to build a viable niche in the future data processing arena? With limited time and financial resources, he wondered where he should place his bets in the next two years. The alternatives were almost too numerous to list, much less scrutinize in detail. And it seemed imperative that SA move quickly to establish its position for the future.

SOFTWARE ARCHITECTS' BUSINESS OBJECTIVES

The business objectives which Harvey and the board established for Software Architects were:

1 Preserve the quality of life of the SA employees and directors.

2 Recruit additional consultants to support the growth in revenues and earnings without sacrificing SA's requirements for technical competence and the potential ability to deal effectively with clients and others in the firm.

3 Maintain exceptional quality of SA work product.

4 Differentiate SA from competitors by demonstrating a perceptibly higher quality of work to existing and potential clients.

5 Charge a premium price based on the value of higher-quality work to the client.

6 Increase annual billings to $700,000 in 1982 and $1.2 million in 1983.

7 Achieve a target percentage of before-tax income to total billings of 30% in both 1982 and 1983.

8 Explore new products and services for SA to introduce in order to meet its targets for growth and profitability, and to position the firm favorably in a rapidly changing technological environment.

The projected billings by category of service and staffing levels for SA are included in Exhibit 4. SA performance for the first five months of the 1982 fiscal year made the targets for billings and income seem reasonable. Year-to-date billings were $411,000, with before-tax income of over $147,000. This performance had been achieved with minimal requirement for overtime work.

EXHIBIT 4   PROJECTED BILLINGS, INCOME BEFORE TAX[1] AND STAFFING LEVELS FOR SOFTWARE ARCHITECTS

		Period ending	
Billings by line of business	June 1981 (actual)	June 1982 (projected)	June 1983 (projected)
Systems software	$203	$245	$ 240
Custom application software	75	335	600
Education/training programs	60	105	360
Microcomputer systems	5	15	0
Total billings	$343	$700	$1,200
Income before tax	$ 47	$210	$ 360
Staffing levels			
Number of software architect consultants	7	15	25
Number of support staff	0	1	2
Number of subcontractors	½	1 ½	2 ½

[1]Billings and income are in thousands of dollars.

SOFTWARE ARCHITECTS' BUSINESS STRATEGY

A strategy was under development to address each of SA's eight business objectives. While not yet completed and approved by the board of directors, most of the elements of the plan had fallen into place.

Quality of Life

The six founders of SA had all worked previously for other employers. They had left those organizations because they were dissatisfied with the stress, red tape, and sluggishness they had encountered. Each of them wanted to learn more in the technical area. They also shared the desire to develop their interests outside of their careers, and wanted to avoid the frenetic pace of tight deadlines and 60-hour workweeks that were the rule in many software consulting firms. Therefore, the quality of life for SA personnel was of tremendous concern to Harvey, Gloria, and the other directors. They had adopted the following policies to demonstrate their commitment in this area:

1 The billable hours targeted for each employee were 1,680 a year, considerably lower than targets in other firms. This helped to prevent excessive overtime on projects.

2 Each employee was allowed 12 days of vacation, 12 days of sick leave, two weeks for training/development, and 10 holidays a year.

3 To prevent the stress of out-of-town travel, SA limited its marketing activities to the Chicago area. The directors had occasionally turned down lucrative contracts that required prolonged travel to other locations.

Recruiting and Staff Development

Harvey, with his board's approval, devised a strategy for preserving quality of service to customers that was closely tied to his staffing plans. Every professional at SA was a graduate of a rigorous program in Computer Science at Northern Illinois University. The school had achieved a prominent reputation in the Midwest for producing graduates of unquestioned technical competence who also had an appreciation for the needs for practical data processing solutions to business problems. Harvey planned to recruit Northern Illinois University students on campus, as well as graduates who had been in industry for a year or two. He also provided funds for continuing development of the technical and interpersonal skills of current SA employees. They were encouraged to take seminars in state-of-the-art technical subjects, as well as those which might refine their skills in marketing, managing subordinates, and interacting with clients.

SA had planned to add several members to the staff in late 1981. They had not yet been brought on board. Several people who had been made offers accepted jobs elsewhere. One indicated that he did not feel technically qualified to "measure up" to the current SA staff. Although there was some concern that SA might be too selective in its recruiting criteria, the directors were convinced that maintaining high standards of technical competence was critical to the preservation of the quality of the work on which SA's reputation was based.

Quality of Service

It appeared that the major causes of failure in systems development projects were the imposition of unrealistic deadlines, the use of programmers without relevant experience, lack of adequate planning in the design phases, and poor documentation in the implementation phase. Harvey and Gloria felt that their strategy for quality of service addressed each of those problems.

SA refused to commit to completion dates when submitting proposals for new business. They insisted on being able to work on the problem a few days or weeks in order to gain information to make realistic estimates of the elapsed time required to finish the job. This prevented the premature establishment of a timetable that was doomed to failure.

Many of SA's competitors staffed projects with one or two seasoned programmers and a large number of "green troops." SA used smaller project teams and experienced programmers almost exclusively. When a new person joined the firm, he or she was put on a project with several SA veterans to learn the ropes and ensure that the quality of the new programmer's work was consistent with the rest of the firm's.

SA spent more time and energy doing detailed design than many of its competitors. Planning and the preparation of detailed specifications reduced the risk of problems and delays during implementation. SA also documented their programs more extensively than did most other firms. Although this was somewhat time-consuming during the first writing of the program, it made it much easier to test the program later on. Also, modifications were simpler once the program was installed. There was less dependence on a particular programmer, because good documentation was easily decipherable by someone who had not written the original code.

SA's directors agreed that all of these things made the company's work product better than that of most of their rivals. But they were not sure whether their clients perceived a difference in quality. Nor were they confident that such subtle gradations in quality of service could be effectively communicated to a prospect who was unfamiliar with SA.

Differentiation from Competitors

The strategy for differentiating SA from its competitors was still under review. The firm was considering a policy of guaranteeing their custom software work for a period after contract expiration. This practice was rare in the software industry, where the costs of time spent on "free" warranty work rather than billable projects were high and extremely visible. Harvey was not sure how effective a warranty might be in convincing potential clients that SA provided a quality advantage. It was not clear how to assess the potential benefits of new business versus the costs of honoring the warranty if the client encountered a problem.

Harvey and Gloria, in making their sales pitch, stressed the fact that SA programmers were all Northern Illinois University graduates in the be-

lief that the school's reputation for data processing instruction might help to distinguish SA from other firms. But they needed to establish other unique advantages for SA which could be communicated to prospective clients. Harvey was trying to generate creative ideas for doing this.

Pricing Strategy

Harvey was not sure whether SA's billing rates were set at a "premium price." This was mainly due to uncertainty over the pricing strategies of competitors. It was difficult to obtain good estimates of what each firm charged for its services, since there were no industry guidelines for billing rates. Moreover, rates quoted by consultants in response to general inquiries were generally higher than those submitted during competitive bidding. Price-cutting in order to win new business occurred frequently. The amount of the reductions varied and was impossible to predict.

It was evident that the rates customers would accept varied, depending upon the service performed. System software development skills were in short supply in the industry, and SA had no trouble charging $50 an hour for such projects. SA hourly rates for application software development, which was less complex and less specialized, ranged from $33 to $37. Database design and application programming in special environments commanded rates between $34 and $44. The development of technical seminars brought $50 to $65 an hour, while giving the seminars to clients often paid $75 to $100 per instructor hour. However, clients typically wanted a more experienced individual to prepare the technical training than for programming tasks; thus the higher billing rates were offset by higher salaries and opportunity costs for SA. (Case 13, Software Architects (B), contains estimates of SA billing rates and project size and duration for typical projects in each area.)

Marketing Strategy to Achieve Target Growth and Profits

It appeared to Harvey that the keys to meeting the goals for growth in revenues, profit, and staffing levels were effective recruiting and marketing programs. The recruiting strategy has already been discussed. The marketing strategy consisted of several elements:

1 Concentrate on the largest private sector enterprises in the Chicago area.

2 Where possible, use the growing network of key decision makers familiar with SA to obtain referrals to new prospective clients.

3 Where referrals are not possible, initiate "cold calls" on key technical managers in target organizations to expose them to SA and discuss current and future needs for services provided by the firm.

4 Concentrate on organizations using IBM hardware and system software, because of the specialized expertise of SA consultants in those systems.

5 Wherever possible, adopt the premium quality and price approach. In competitive bidding situations, if the potential for repeat business is high, reduce the hourly rate to not less than $33 an hour for the first contract. Increase the hourly rate for follow-on work, once the client has seen the high quality of SA consultants' performance.

6 Stress the links between SA and Northern Illinois University in order to develop the image of SA as a source of updated technical talent and high-quality work.

Development of New Products and Services

While the first seven objectives (see p. 27) were addressed by the strategy Harvey had developed, he was uncertain about the best approach to meet the objective of exploring new products and services. There was no shortage of ideas from within the firm about potential areas of new business. Some of the suggestions included:

1 Development of application software for microcomputers, including a project accounting and general ledger system for a company in a service business like SA's.

2 Development of software to collect information on telephone calls made in a company using Bell equipment. The information would subsequently be used to produce accounting and resource usage reports for management.

3 Development of systems software packages for users of IBM computers in many organizations.

4 Preparation and presentation of courses on programming using techniques that SA had perfected.

5 Joint presentation of technical seminars in cooperation with several of the faculty members from Northern Illinois University.

6 Establishment of an institute in which nontechnical personnel provided by SA's clients would be given an accelerated course in programming. Harvey estimated that a bright liberal arts major could be transformed into a crack application programmer in four to six months.

These were but a few of SA's potential alternatives. What was missing was a method by which to review these and other alternatives from the strategic perspective. How might one assess the potential of alternative projects to contribute to SA's growth and profitability? How might one discern whether one project or another provided a better hedge against the risk of technological obsolescence? Developing a strategy and a system for the last objective appeared to be the most difficult task of all.

CONCLUSION

As Harvey reviewed the elements of the strategy he had assembled, he had three major concerns:

1 Was the strategy realistic, given SA's resources and the realities of the external environment?

2 Were the elements of the strategy internally consistent?

3 How might the short-term strategy be modified to better equip SA to deal with its long-term prospects?

The issues were important enough that he wanted an outside opinion. He decided to bring in a consultant that Gene Petrie had recommended to help him think them through.

DATAGUIDE REPORT ON THE FUTURE OF THE SOFTWARE INDUSTRY

Software

Warren N. Sargent, Jr. and Paul Colen
Palo Alto Management Group

The software industry is booming! By 1986 it will be a $38 billion industry. Market growth will average 30% per year for the next five years. Today companies spend over $10 billion on external software expenditures.

This may seem an extraordinary growth from other market-size estimates of $3.5 billion today and $10 billion at mid-decade. However, it is important to realize that most estimates ignore the two largest segments of the software marketplace: professional services and turnkey software, each of which is as lucrative as the combined market for applications and systems software packages, as explained below.

Software is provided to users in two ways: standard off-the-shelf packages and customized products. In addition, software may be packaged with computer hardware and called a turnkey system. The software industry can be graphically depicted as shown in Figure 1.

Turnkey systems can use either standard off-the-shelf software products or can be customized for a client (professional services). It is estimated that between 50% and 60% of all turnkey systems use off-the-shelf software products while the other 40% to 50% use software created specially for the client through a professional services arrangement.

Turnkey systems are generally perceived to be a relatively recent product innovation, although the concept is at least 15 years old. Historically, software vendors sold software products and/or professional services, but rarely involved computer hardware in the sale. Today, computer manufacturers offer quantity discounts to turnkey system vendors, who can then add software and sell the system to a user, theoretically generating profit from the software as well as the hardware

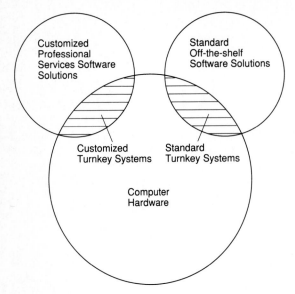

FIGURE 1 SOFTWARE INDUSTRY COMPOSITION IN 1981

(marked up to the list price for the user). More will be said about this theoretical relationship later.

Software can be separated into two categories. Systems software enables the computer/communications system to perform basic operations. Applications software provides solutions to specific user requirements. It is the application software that is most visible to the user, while the systems software supports the functions called for by the application. Figure 2 depicts a computer system showing the main functions of systems and applications software.

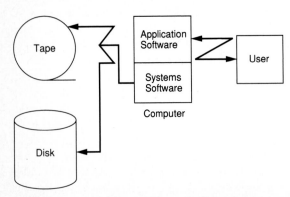

FIGURE 2 COMPUTER SYSTEM ARCHITECTURE

Each of the four elements of the software industry will grow rapidly (see Figure 3). Turnkey systems user expenditures will grow the fastest: 35% per year for the next five years. The practice of computer manufacturers charging separately for systems software products will continue to increase over the next five years and will therefore drive the growth forecast for these products to over 30% per year.

The rate of growth in user expenditures for application software products, 25% per year, is deceptive. Turnkey systems use application software products in at least 50% of the cases, and turnkey systems user expenditures are growing at 35% per year. Therefore, the true growth for all uses of application software (products and turnkey systems) exceeds 30% per year. Professional services user expenditures, excluding turnkey systems, will grow at 20% per year for the next five years. However, the true growth rate for all types of professional services (including turnkey systems) will be 25% per year.

SYSTEMS SOFTWARE

Systems software, which enables the computer communications system to perform basic func-

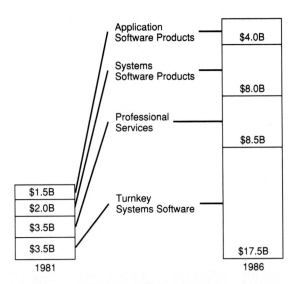

FIGURE 3 USER EXTERNAL SOFTWARE EXPENDITURES

tions, is classified by three types—system operation, system utilization, and system implementation.

System operation products manage computer communication system resources during program execution. Examples of such products are operating systems, database management systems, and telecommunication monitors.

System utilization products help manage the computer system operation more efficiently. Performance measurement systems, job accounting systems, and system utilities are examples.

System implementation products prepare applications for execution by assisting application design, programming, testing, and related functions. Examples of such products are assemblers, compilers, software design productivity aids, report writers, and program library systems.

There are probably 4,000 or more systems software products, marketed by nearly 1,000 vendors today. It is extremely difficult to count vendors and products because of the changing nature of the industry. Some vendors announce a new product and subsequently drop it because they can't generate sales, or they decide to sell the product and licensing rights for the product to another vendor. Vendors change the name of some products to create a new image even though the product is not actually new. There has been an explosion of new products for personal and small computers. Since many of the vendors of these systems software products are still operating regionally, it is difficult to identify their market presence.

At one time over 80% of user expenditures for systems software products were for IBM and IBM-compatible large computers. That percent is decreasing as users of small computers become more sophisticated and realize the value of the systems software products available in the marketplace.

The industry trends of increased use of telecommunications and automation in the office have a positive impact on the market for systems software products. Systems software is the "glue" that joins the computer hardware and application software together. Changing functionality in the computer hardware creates a need for new systems software. Enterprising organizations have recognized this need and have been responding with new and improved products.

Computer manufacturers have historically fostered this industry by their attitude toward independent software vendors, in that they have not "locked out" the independent vendor's software from operating on the manufacturer's computer. Manufacturers have tacitly encouraged independents to develop user-friendly systems that facilitate computer use: the easier computers are to use, the more will be sold.

The future of the systems software market is unclear in the late 1980s and beyond. On the one hand, the computer manufacturer must consider its users and cannot lock out independent systems software products. On the other hand, computer manufacturers could develop similar product capabilities to the independent vendors' products. The investment required to do this is probably prohibitive. The computer manufacturer is left in a precarious position: i.e., how can it maintain control over its customers?

One solution to this dilemma is to combine the systems software and the computer hardware (firmware) together in future computer generations. As users buy these new computers, they will not have a need or perhaps the ability to add additional systems software products to their computers. Will this happen? Intel has stated that software (including applications) will be combined with the hardware in the 1980s. It is unlikely that all systems or application software will be combined with hardware in this decade, but it appears clear that a substantial part of the systems software *could* be combined with the computer hardware in the next 10 years.

APPLICATION SOFTWARE

Application software products perform specific application functions for end-user organizations. These products solve specific user problems.

Application software products can be divided into two types: cross-industry products and industry-specialized products. Cross-industry products perform applications common to many industries, such as payroll, general ledger, fixed asset accounting, accounts receivable, or inventory management. Industry-specialized products perform applications specific to industries such as banking, medical, or insurance. Examples of industry-specialized applications are demand deposit accounting (banking), shop scheduling (manufacturing), and policy administration (insurance).

Users of application software products are people involved in day-to-day company business. Thus, typical users of an accounts receivable product include clerical personnel who perform data entry, credit managers who use CRT terminals for online inquiry, and the vice-president of finance who uses summary reports. All of the functions described are performed by the application software product. Generally, the people involved with computer operations are not the users of application software products. Computer operations personnel typically use systems software products. However, both groups of people help evaluate application software products for company use.

Nearly 10,000 applications software products are marketed by approximately 2,000 vendors. These numbers grow daily due to the tremendous growth in use of small computers. No vendor, including computer manufacturers, has captured more than 10% of this market. At one time the majority of application software products was written for IBM and IBM-compatible mainframes, but this is no longer true today. Over one-half of the application software products and vendors now serve the personal and small computer used by many user markets.

Application software product vendors have penetrated the banking, insurance, and discrete manufacturing sectors with industry-specialized application products to the extent that nearly 60% of user expenditures for application software products occur in these three industries. Discrete manufacturing application software expenditures is the fastest growing section due largely to the need for distributed applications for plant operations in diverse locations. However, other industries such as retail, process manufacturing, and transportation will also experience rapid growth in user expenditures for application software products, as these industries have not yet been heavily penetrated by product solutions.

PROFESSIONAL SERVICES

Professional services are used for the design and programming services performed for users who require software tailored to their specifications. In some cases, users want software capabilities that are not available in standard products. In other cases, the user wants very specific functions performed according to set procedures that rule out product solutions. Most professional services are for application software although some systems software is written for mainframes or unique distributed processing projects.

There are thousands of professional services vendors. Every independent consultant who designs software or programs on a custom basis provides professional services. However, probably 2,000 vendors each generate more than $250,000 revenue in professional services per year. The amount of client contact required means these vendors generally serve geographical markets. There are only several hundred firms that offer professional services in more than one geographical area.

The use of professional services is increasing primarily due to the backlog of programming work in data processing departments, the shortage of software designers and programmers, and the lack of specific skills in data processing departments needed to develop certain applications. The backlog of application development in most data processing departments is 24 months and growing. The only way to reduce this backlog without hiring permanent employees (assuming that they could be found) is to use outside professional services. The shortage of software designers and programmers tends to raise the compensation level for people with these key skills. In order to attract and retain these people, professional services firms offer higher salaries and more diverse project experience. This creates a greater personnel shortage in other types of firms, reinforcing the need for outside professional services.

Professional services firms have developed technical skills to handle new applications in distributed processing, telecommunications, database systems, and office automation. Most companies don't have the diversity of needs to have developed these skills in-house. Now that these skills are required, it may be more economical to obtain them from a professional services vendor.

Many professional services vendors have begun offering turnkey systems to their clients. Although it is too early to measure the success of most of these offerings, the professional services firm is extremely well positioned to offer unique turnkey systems because of its established base of technical expertise.

TURNKEY SYSTEMS

Turnkey systems solve an application problem for a user. The key features are that the computer hardware and software are sold at the same time, and that the problem addressed is an application (as opposed to systems software). Application software not sold at the same time as the computer hardware is considered a product (or professional service) and would be included in the application software product (or professional service) category. User expenditure data shown in Figure 3 includes only the software portion of the turnkey system sale. The computer hardware, training, supplies, and computer hardware maintenance components are independent of and not included in Figure 3.

There are approximately 5,000 turnkey system vendors. Some turnkey system vendors also sell software products and/or professional services. The largest turnkey system suppliers today provide systems for computer-aided design and manufacturing (CAD/CAM). Approximately 15% to 20% of all turnkey system user expenditures today are for CAD/CAM. The smallest turnkey system suppliers typically serve the general business accounting environment. The supplier sells payroll, accounts receivable, accounts payable, and general ledger software along with the computer hardware. Most of these suppliers are marginally profitable due to intense competition in this market.

The key to successful turnkey systems is offering specialized systems to a narrow audience. Industry-specialized turnkey systems have been successfully sold and serviced and are easily sold by custom referrals. Vendors who have specialized systems have less competition, can command higher prices, and have higher profits. Vendors that offer generalized systems have intense competition (from computer processing services firms and computer manufacturers, as well as other turnkey system suppliers) and generally have to discount list prices of hardware. Thus, it is a myth that the generalized turnkey system vendor will make profit on *both* the computer hardware and software.

The future for independent turnkey system vendors should involve the packaging of small computers with highly specialized software. The more unique the system, and consequently the smaller the market niche, the better for the vendor. The successful vendor will become the leader in serving these market niches and hence move down the experience curve and ultimately raise the barriers of entry to the competition.

Computer manufacturers will concentrate on offering generalized solutions that will appeal to many buyers. However, these solutions will not have the specialization needed to serve small market niches.

DRIVING FORCES

The past five years have shown a dramatic increase in user demand for software. Substantially improved computer hardware cost-performance has lowered the threshold and opened new application areas. A new generation of management is (by education and training) increasingly more aware of the types of applications that can be addressed with computer software. Increased scarcity of software designers and programmers, coupled with the impact of inflation on personnel costs, has forced managers to explore alternatives to in-house software development.

Computer manufacturers have devoted most of their resources to development and marketing of computer hardware and systems software, leaving voids to be filled, particularly in application software. Computer manufacturers such as Atari and IBM are encouraging software developers to write software for the manufacturer's hardware. Government regulation in such industries as banking and insurance, and in such functional areas as human resources and taxes, has had a substantial impact on demand for external software. The net result has been the entry of many small companies, with a corresponding proliferation of software.

New forces are coming into play that will add to the factors influencing the software marketplace in the next five years. Computer manufacturers such as Honeywell and Burroughs and other large companies such as Xerox and Exxon are entering the marketplace. The accompanying buying process (better coordinated, more sophisticated, demanding improved support service) will force greater competition among vendors of software solutions. Advances in technology in areas such as database, microprocessors, image processing, telecommunication networks, and distributed processing will fur-

nish new opportunities for new software solutions. Future success will require vendors to excel in software development, sales, marketing, and in customer maintenance and support. Computer manufacturers and selected large companies, together with large independent computer software solution firms, will aggressively acquire smaller vendors, resulting in a market consolidation in which a relatively small number of firms will dominate the profitable market sectors.

WARREN N. SARGENT, JR., a principal of the Palo Alto Management Group, has 17 years' experience in the computer services industry. He has held management and technical positions in both user and computer services vendor organizations. He has a B.S. in Mechanical Engineering, an M.S. in Mechanical Engineering, and an M.B.A. from the University of Connecticut. He is a Ph.D. candidate in International Marketing and Finance at the University of Texas.

PAUL COLEN, a principal of the Palo Alto Management Group, has more than 25 years' experience. He was President of Advanced Management Systems and was also founder of the Corporation for Information Systems Research and Development. He has held a number of technical and management positions with Burroughs and Honeywell. He has a B.S. from Northwestern University and an M.S. in Business Economics from Claremont Graduate School.

PART TWO

SITUATION ANALYSIS

Marketing activities start with a clear understanding of the organization's mission and objectives. This provides the direction to marketing management by specifying the industry and the role of the organization in that industry as well as a precise statement of what the organization is trying to accomplish. Successful marketing of a good or service depends first of all on having sound understanding of the market. In addition, marketing success depends on how many resources are applied in developing the market offer and how effectively these resources are used. Middle-management marketing decisions need to be consistent with the broad decisions that top management makes with regard to the long-term purposes and direction of the organization.

The marketing manager must analyze and monitor the position of the firm in terms of its present and future situation. In order to develop a logical, planned approach to selecting the appropriate marketing strategies and programs necessary to achieve the product objective(s), managers must understand the specific problems and opportunities confronting a product or product line. A variety of forces affect the marketplace, and the marketing manager must be cognizant of those forces and their impact on the market.

By performing a situation analysis, managers should be able to identify the problems and opportunities that will guide them in selecting appropriate marketing strategies and programs. Of particular importance is the process of market analysis. Identifying and understanding how buyers (and potential buyers) are likely to respond to different marketing actions and identifying possible target markets are crucial tasks in the marketing planning process. In addition, managers must assess the current and potential competitive situation in the market since the extent of the market opportunity also depends on competition. The sources of competition must be identified as well as the relative strengths and weaknesses of competition attempting to serve the same market.

One of the most important decisions a marketing manager will make is that of selecting a target market. This requires not only a thorough understanding of the environment and buyer characteristics but also a comprehensive and objective assessment of the organization's strengths and limitations. With such an understanding, the marketing manager can begin to formulate the appropriate marketing strategies and programs for the desired market. The cases in the following section focus upon issues that have, as their central problem, an appreciation and understanding of external market opportunities and the internal capabilities of the illustrated organizations.

CLUB MED SALES INC. (A)

It was still raining in New York on May 31, 1983, when Serge Trigano, Chairman and CEO (Chief Executive Officer) of Club Med Sales Inc. (C.M.I.), returned to his office. He sat and went over in his mind the events of the meeting he had just attended. When the bookings for summer 1983 of C.M.I. had gone 3% below those of the previous summer, a meeting with C.M.I.'s advertising agency had been called to examine the situation.

The advertising agency's answer to the dip in sales was to send a discount coupon for September vacations to people who had been to Club Med in the recent past. Club Med's immediate reaction had been, "Was a discount suitable for the Club Med customer?" It became clear during the meeting that no specific definition of a Club Med customer existed. No formal market research had yet been done on the American consumer. Did

Club Med need to do this research? If so, what kind should be done, and where? What could be done in the short term to help boost sales? Were there other more important issues that should be addressed?

BACKGROUND

History

From its inception as a non-profit venture in 1950, Club Méditerranée, C.M.I.'s parent, was a unique enterprise. Shelter for vacationers was furnished in a way never before seen in France. Gilbert Trigano, part-owner of a family tent-making business, rented the required tents to Club Med with no down payment.

In 1954, Gilbert Trigano formally joined Club Méditerranée and turned it into a profit-making business. The original concept of the straw hut village was born. It was meant to create a Polynesian "back to nature" atmosphere. The huts were bare of any luxury, and the showers were communal. Outdoor activities were the main focus of daily life. From this type of village came the image that Club Méditerranée has represented to this day—sun, sea and sport.

This case was prepared by Research Associate Juli Dixon under the direction of Professors Jacques Horovitz and Terry Deutscher as a basis for class discussion rather than to illustrate either effective or ineffective handling of an administrative situation. Copyright ©1987 by IMEDE, Lausanne, Switzerland. IMD International, resulting from the merger between IMEDE, Lausanne, and IMI, Geneva, acquires and retains all rights. Reproduced by permission.

Club Méditerranée expanded quickly, often adding one or two resorts per year. In 1956, the first ski resort opened in Switzerland. Club Méditerranée moved into what would become known as the American zone in 1968. However, Europe continued to be its main target. By 1982, Club Med was represented in 24 countries by 98 villages (one-fifth were ski resorts), 58 residences and 6 resort hotels. Financially, Club Méditerranée was very profitable (see Exhibit 1). Another indication of Club Méditerranée's success was that it had become a household word in France, where it was known simply as "le Club."

The Club Med Concept

The Club Med concept was unique. Any package vacation that Club Méditerranée offered had the same basics: a prepaid, fixed-price holiday including airfare, meals (with unlimited wine and beer), sports, sports instruction and other activities such as a discothèque, arts and crafts, classical concerts and cabaret shows at night. Sports were varied and included pastimes such as archery, snorkeling, deep-sea diving, horseback riding and yoga, as well as standard favorites like swimming, tennis, sailing, golf and many others. Vacationers could choose either to take part or not in these activities. The villages also contained other facilities such as a shop, car rental and an excursions office, which were all within walking distance. Club Med was famous for selecting the best available beach area in every country where it had summer villages.

A no-hassle, relaxed atmosphere was created, since Club Méditerranée arranged meals and leisure time. Each village staff member (called Gentil Organisateur, or GO) had responsibilities in an area such as applied arts, sports, excursions, food, bar or receptions. There were about 80 to 100 of these organizers per village. They would move to a different village every six months. The GOs were encouraged to mix with the vacationers (called GMs for Gentils Membres) and performed the various roles of hosts, friends, teachers and entertainers rather than staff.

Another aspect of the Club Med concept was the absence of the real world in the form of

EXHIBIT 1   FINANCIAL STATEMENTS: CLUB MÉDITERRANÉE S.A.
(000's of French Francs)

	1980–81 US $1 = FFr 5.67	1981–82 US $1 = FFr 7.25
Gross income	3,180,523	3,953,812
Gross margins	1,994,388	2,486,948
	(62.7%)	(62.9%)
Earnings	142,128	174,331
Consolidated EPS	43.99	50.46
Hotel days spent in zone (winter and summer) (000's)		
North America	1,279	1,464
All other zones	5,635	5,693
Average bed occupancy rate total	71.51%	71.27%
Average bed occupancy rate		
Europe/Africa	76.66%	75.76%
South America	50.44%	44.33%
North and Central America	59.24%	61.93%
Asia, South Pacific, Indian Ocean	65.18%	68.21%

Source: Club Méditerranée Annual Report 1982–83.

clocks, phones, radios, money, tips and rigid dress code; people could dress casually or more formally as they wished. Extra drinks were purchased using prepaid bead necklaces.

Club Méditerranée had ensured that it was fundamentally different from other packaged tours. First, the homogeneity of the villages provided a predictable fantasy within a Club Méditerranée world anywhere, so that Club Méditerranée was not really selling a destination like other tour groups. Secondly, the way of life in the village, with its lack of money and formality, broke down the established barriers of class and wealth among vacationers.

Furthermore, Club Méditerranée had overcome the seasonality problem by opening some resorts all year round, and by providing both winter and summer vacation locations. Also, Club Méditerranée had been operating for a long time and had built up much goodwill; 70% of their European vacationers had been to Club Méditerranée before.

International Business Week (Sept. 27, 1982) called Club Méditerranée "the innovative French vacation specialist." The company earned this reputation by refusing to sit back and let its proven formula work. It was continually adjusting and adding to its offerings. Its success was so great that it received the compliment of having the "capacity to anticipate the needs of (its) clients" (*International Business Week*, Aug. 3, 1981).

The Gentil Membre

Broadly speaking, a whole range of holiday makers were represented among the Club Med customers. However, there was a larger representation of office workers, executives, and professional people. Club Méditerranée had not yet examined its customer base in detail.

THE AMERICAN MARKET AND CLUB MED SALES INC.

The Economic Climate

According to the *Economist*, (Oct. 1982), despite the worsening recession, the number of tourists had increased (see Exhibit 2). One point that favored Club Med in the travel industry was that packaged tours generally remained popular; however, people were starting to take cheaper or shorter holidays or stay closer to home.

Deregulation in the U.S. airline industry in 1979 had contributed to substantial changes in the packaged tour business. The ensuing price war had slashed travelers' costs, uncovering a new mass market for cheap air travel. The

EXHIBIT 2   DESTINATIONS OF U.S. TRAVELERS ABROAD, 1980 to 1982[a]

	1980 ('000)	1981 ('000)	1982 ('000)
Canada[b]	11,171	11,374	10,974
Mexico[c]	3,442	3,432	3,580
Europe and Mediterranean	3,934	3,931	4,144
Caribbean and Central America	2,624	2,453	2,637
South America	594	567	529
Other areas	1,011	1,089	1,200
Total	22,421	22,846	23,064

Source: U.S. Department of Commerce, Bureau of Economic Analysis.
Notes: [a] Includes business travel; excludes cruises, travel by military personnel and other government employees stationed abroad.
[b] Visitors staying one or more nights in Canada.
[c] Visitors staying one or more nights in Mexico.

number of travel agents had increased from 7000 in 1970 to over 22,000 in 1983. Travel agents demanded higher commissions when group selling became a large part of their business. With the subsequent increase in commissions, it became even more attractive to set up an agency. As in Europe, travel agents were the primary channel for sales in the travel business.

Club Med felt that it occupied a unique position in the market and had no directly com-

Club Méditerranée in North America

In the mid-1970s, Club Méditerranée started to target the North American market specifically. In 1980, Club Méditerranée was restructured so that marketing and operations were more closely linked. North and South America made up the American zone, which had its own profit responsibilities. By 1983, North Americans represented 15% of the Gentils Membres worldwide, but less than one half of 1% of the North American popu-

	Club Med (one-week vacation)	Competitor (one-week vacation)
Before decrease	$799*	$505**
After decrease	$799	$399

* Includes airfare of $400, shelter, all meals, all sports and other activities.
** Includes airfare, hotel and breakfast.

parable competitors. However, its closest competition did come from other packaged tour operators.

As a result of deregulation, some prices for airline tickets had recently dropped by 30%. Club Med had not yet incorporated these decreases into their prices. The following table gives an example of the price structure, comparing a trip with Club Med from Los Angeles to Puerto Vallarta, Mexico, with a competitive package sold by an airline.

It was estimated that some 4.5 million residents of the United States had gone on packaged tours in 1982, including about 1.5 million who had taken cruises. Many others took vacations to "sun destinations" without using packaged tours. For example, it was projected that in 1983 about 1.5 million people from the U.S. mainland would go to Puerto Rico, a destination that was within the same geographical area as five Club Med villages. Another 2.5 million were expected to go to the Caribbean islands, and 500,000 to Bermuda. Exhibit 2 gives a breakdown by destination of U.S. travelers abroad during 1980–82.

lation were Club Med clients. Total sales in North America were almost $140 million in 1981–82, representing some 120,000 Gentils Membres.

In 1980, Serge Trigano took charge of the American zone. He made the improvement of Club Med's image in the North American market his first priority as there was a feeling in the organization that an image of sexual permissiveness was deterring many Americans from patronizing the Club. Club Méditerranée felt that the North American market represented a sound base for growth.

By the beginning of 1983, Serge Trigano felt that he was well on the way to achieving the goals he had set. Revenues had grown by 6% over the previous year. Profits had exceeded his expectations, and he also felt that good progress had been made toward improving Club Med's image. A new campaign—the Antidote for Civilization—had set Club Med apart from other travel advertisers. Club Med spent several million dollars a year on this image-oriented consumer advertising, emphasizing the uniqueness of the concept. The campaign had generated considerable favorable public relations for the organization, and it had been nominated for a prestigious CLIO award in the advertising industry.

CLUB MED SALES INC.: STRATEGY

Organization

The organization in the American zone was such that Serge Trigano, as CEO, had about 25 people reporting to him directly (i.e., public relations, transportation, operations, advertising agency co-ordinator, finance, sales promotion, etc.). In the sales promotion area, there were 7 regional sales managers (about 35 years old) who supervised 14 district sales managers. (In contrast, one single airline had 40 sales representatives for the New York market alone.)

Marketing

All the regional and district sales managers were former GOs. They were to make sales calls to the travel agents, give them brochures and talk to them about the Club Med concept. No formal system had been set up regarding which agents to visit at what time. As a result, each representative performed his job differently. Each one also operated independently in developing creative ideas to boost sales. Some representatives had consumer shows where people could hear about the Club Med concept. Others participated in professional travel shows or ran cooperative advertising with their own copy. This arrangement was consistent with the company culture, which allowed the person running a Club Med village to be his own master in designing enjoyable vacation programs.

Regional representatives were earning over $50,000 a year with an additional bonus up to 25%, while district representatives earned a straight $25,000 a year. These figures did not include expenses, which were approximately $500,000 for all representatives, including travel.

Serge Trigano was the final decision maker for sales promotion and advertising. The total marketing budget for 1983 is presented in Table 3-1.

TABLE 3-1   TOTAL MARKETING BUDGET (1983)

Advertising (5.7% of sales)	$8 million*
"Push"**	2 mn
Brochures	2 mn
Reservation Center (Toll-free 1-800 number)	4 mn
Travel agents' commission (10% of sales)	12 mn
Miscellaneous	1 mn
	$29 million

* Advertising in 1980 had been $2.5 million.
** Sales managers' salaries and expenses, trade-advertising, travel agents, familiarization trips, promotional material directed at travel agents.

Club Med used the words "tactical" and "image" to distinguish between its two types of advertising. Image advertising intended to build up in people's minds a long-term concept of Club Med and what it represented. Television, magazines and sometimes billboards were considered the most effective media for this type of advertising. Tactical advertising, on the other hand, was a call for action in the short term which would generate revenue the following week. Club Med used radio and newspapers for this type of sales-oriented advertisement. One-third of the advertising budget was currently allocated to tactical advertising. (See Exhibit 3 for an example of a tactical advertisement.)

Eighty-six percent of C.M.I.'s sales came through travel agents. Club Med had a reservation center in Phoenix with 100 reservation employees who serviced the public as well as the bookings from agents. (In contrast, only 35% of Club Med sales were indirect in the French market.)

American travel agents received a 10% commission from Club Med, the usual rate given for business (such as airplane tickets). Competitors, however, frequently raised commissions with special promotions. For example, if a travel

EXHIBIT 3

CLUB MED PRESENTS THE SUMMER CLUBS.

Club Med serves up intensive Tennis for players at all levels. There'll be 2 1/2 -hour daily lessons, ball machines, closed-circuit video and training films. Paradise Island, Bahamas May1 to Oct 31 From $790 to $885 (depending on date) for one week including air fare from New York.*

Professional artists and proformers at our fine Arts and Music Festival will exhibit their talents and help you develop yours in special classes and workshops. Magic Hatti. Hatti July 1 to July 31. Special 10-day package only $980 including air fare from New York* Week-long packages also available.

Aerobics, jogging, running, yoga, gymnastics and more are the components of our special Fitness Month vacations. They'll prove to you that shaping up really can be fun. Caravelle, Guadeloupe, to Oct 31 From $900 to $940 (depending on date) for one week including air fare from New York.*

This years International Bridge Festival bids to be the best ever. Enjoy the camaraderie of players from around the world. In team and mixed-doubles competitions. Punta Cana Dominican Republic. Sept. 4 to Sept. 11 Only $880 for one week including air fare from New York.*

Learn how to harness the wind and the sea during our Windsurfing Weeks. Intensive teaching will help you master the techniques of the masters. And you'll find yourself competing in our grand regattas. Magic Haiti, Haiti June 5 to June19 Only $790 for one week, including air fare from New York.*

Our French Immersion vacations feature daily audiovisual language labs. French film classics and tables where only French is spoken at mealtimes. So you'll learn a new language almost effortlessy Caravelle, Guadeloupe, July 1 to Aug 31. Special 11-day package only $1135 including air fare from New York.* Week long packages also available.

DAYS ARE LONGER. ACTIVITIES ARE BROADER. PRICES ARE LOWER. AND GOOD-BYES ARE HARDER.

There is a vacation that is far removed from the petty annoyances of ordinary vacations.

A week full of sports like tennis, waterskiing and sailing. And gourmet meals. And glittering entertainment. At a special vacation village designed only for your amusement. On an exclusive beach tapped by cool tropical waters.

It is Club Med.

At Club Med villages all year round you can enjoy this unique vacation for one very reasonable all-inclusive price.

But in the summer theres even more to enjoy a range of sports and unusual activities that will make your vacation more of a celebration than ever before. At lower prices than in the wintertime.

Our Summer Club special events are described in greater detail above. But whats almost indescribable is the feeling of relaxation and harmony you will discover at Club Med this summer.

You see, we've done everything possible to make sure that at Club Med the living is easy. So only the leaving for home is not.

CLUB MED
The antidote for civilization.
Call your travel agent or 1-800-528-3100

agent's volume exceeded a certain level, the commission would be increased, or if a travel agent sold packages during certain periods, he earned more. Sometimes a direct cash bonus was offered for selling certain packages. Large travel agent organizations that did a sizable volume of business for a competitor often got a higher base commission. The net effect of these programs was that travel agents could sometimes earn 15% commissions and, on rare occasions, even as much as 20%. Club Med did not have such offers.

THE CURRENT SITUATION

The Advertising Agency Meeting of May 31, 1983

The climate of the meeting was tense since Serge Trigano was not pleased that bookings had dropped to 3% below the sales of the previous summer, after a growth averaging 5 to 6% (before inflation) in recent years. The advertising agency had reserved a conference room in the Hotel Meridien in New York and had asked its own CEO to make an elaborate presentation (booklet, overhead, and past TV spots shown on video as well as current summer newspaper advertising). The agency was anxious to appease Serge, who they sensed was very concerned. Jean Rambaud was also attending the meeting along with ten representatives from the agency. Jean had been invited to the meeting to be briefed on C.M.I.'s advertising strategy since he had recently agreed to become assistant to the Chairman and CEO of Club Med Sales, with major responsibilities in sales and marketing.

One of the main ideas presented by the advertising agency was to send recent Club Med members a gift certificate for a $100 discount on a September holiday. Otherwise, despite the dip, the agency proposed to continue the same newspaper advertising campaign that had started in April.

When asked for his opinion about the discount idea, Jean said:

> The advertisements you just showed me on video, used mostly in the winter, appear to be targeted at

an upscale customer. If Club Med is attracting that kind of person, how will they react to a discount on the same holiday they paid full price for last year? I'd worry that they might wonder just who will start coming to Club Med. We might lose this upscale customer and attract another kind. Is that what we want?

Furthermore, Serge felt that the present newspaper advertising campaign was not aggressive enough and would not attract sales in the short term. Also, September was the end of the season, and Serge questioned waiting so long before attempting to remedy such an immediate problem.

The agency indicated that it felt Club Med was overreacting and that business would pick up. "Don't worry, our plan will work," the agency replied. It also suggested that bookings would increase if the agency sweetened the sales opportunities for the travel agents.

The Club Med people tested this assumption:

> You seem sure that the Club Med customer will rush to the villages because of a $100 discount. But who is the Club Med customer?

Taken aback, the agency admitted that, without any recent formal market research, it could not accurately describe the Club Med customer. This answer strengthened Jean's resolve to examine the discount suggestion more closely. He remarked that it would be a good idea to do some market research. The agency agreed.

After the meeting, Serge and Jean talked over the potential for market research. Serge encouraged Jean to develop a research proposal, and also to offer other suggestions which would address the problem. Both agreed that, in the short run, it was important to stay within the current $29 million marketing budget (see Table 3-1).

Jean returned to his hotel and thought through the situation. There were several important questions. What should Club Med do in the short term to improve its bookings? Was a market research study necessary, and if so, what kind and where? What did they need to know, and what would they do with the results when they got them? Jean was aware that C.M.I. had not done formal market research before and that, for results to be used effectively, the project would have to be carefully implemented in the organization.

Preliminary inquiries by Jean the next day provided a list of the different types of research and their associated costs (see Exhibit 4).

EXHIBIT 4   COMPARATIVE DIRECT COSTS PER COMPLETED INTERVIEW*

Data collection method	Approximate cost
1. Mail survey (costs depend on return rate, incentives, and follow-up procedure)	$5–$10
2. Telephone interviews	
(a) 7-minute interview with head of household in metropolitan area	$8–$10
(b) 15-minute interview with small segment of national population from central station	$15–$25
3. Personal interviews	
(a) 10-minute personal interview in middle-class suburban area (2 callbacks and 10% validation)	$20–$30
(b) 40- to 60-minute interview of national probability sample (3 callbacks and 10% validation)	$40–$50
(c) Executive (VIP) interviews (1–2 hours)	$150
(d) One focus group of 15 people (includes analysis and a report on the session)	$3000–$4000

* Including travel and telephone charges, interviewer compensation, training, and direct supervision expenses.

CLUB MED SALES INC. (B)

Club Méditerranée offered packaged vacations all over the world. It had been concentrating on the American market in recent years because it considered North America to be a growth market. When, in the spring of 1983, bookings for summer vacations in the American zone had dipped to 3% below sales of the previous summer, an urgent meeting with Club Med Sales Inc.'s advertising agency had been called by Serge Trigano, the CEO of the American zone. Jean Rambaud, a previous associate of M. Trigano, had attended the meeting because he was going to join the company in July 1983 to do a six-month project on the work methods of the sales organization.

At this meeting, the advertising agency suggested offering a discount to customers in order to increase sales. However, there was some doubt as to whether or not a discount was suitable for the type of customer that frequented Club Méditerranée. When the agency was unable to

adequately describe the Club Med customer, it was agreed that market research was needed. Jean Rambaud was to take the lead by identifying Club Med's needs, designing the research and implementing the results.

Background information on Club Med Sales Inc. is available in Club Med Sales Inc. (A).

AFTER THE MEETING

Club Med did not follow the agency's suggestion to introduce the discount idea. It did, however, immediately drop prices in the California market, where Club Med air travel prices were 30% higher than those of competing package tours. Also, the advertising was changed to state all the activities, meals, etc., included in Club Med's price that were not available in other tours (see Exhibit 1). These advertisements demonstrated that Club Med provided good value for the money in a market where airline deregulations were enabling many cheap packages to be offered.

Data from Club Med's own computer revealed that 12,000 of the 22,000 travel agents in the United States had sold at least one Club Med trip in the past year. Fifty percent of Club Med's sales were generated in 2000 of these agencies, but half of these top sellers were different from year to year.

RESEARCH

Five studies were done to help Club Med learn more about its customers and its market.

1 The first study gave a demographic profile of the Club Med members (see Exhibit 2).
2 The second study compared the profile of Club Med members with a cluster of 40 groups representing all U.S. residents. This information, available from a data bank called PRIZM, helped determine what "types" of people were interested in Club Med and where they came from. After the major "types" were identified, detailed data from the Simmons Market Research Bureau (on media habits, activities, interests and opinions of a panel of 20,000 people) were correlated with the "types" in order to distinguish likely tastes of Club Med members. (See Exhibits 3a, 3b, 3c.)
3 In the next stage, a detailed two-phase study of the consumer market was conducted for Club Med.

   (a) Phase One, called Focus Groups (see Exhibit 4), consisted of an in-depth discussion with small groups of Club Med members and non-members to elicit hypotheses for a thorough survey of members and prospective members.
   (b) Phase Two, called the Quantitative Study (see Exhibit 5), was a survey which:
      (i) Helped understand members' and prospects' opinion of Club Med (see Exhibit 6)
      (ii) Helped draw a picture of Club Med members and prospects (see Exhibit 7)
      (iii) Identified members' and prospects' expectations of vacations (see Exhibits 8 and 9)
      (iv) Helped Club Med understand the impression their members were communicating (see Exhibit 10)

   (v) Helped understand members' booking behavior (see Exhibit 11)
   (vi) Helped Club Med understand the prospective customer's cost perception of a Club Med vacation (see Exhibits 12 and 13)
   (vii) Demonstrated Key Prospects' interest in particular vacation activities and services (see Exhibit 14)

Most of the findings presented in these exhibits represent the responses of Key Prospects and Key Members. (To be designated as "Key," a person must have answered that he would probably or definitely consider a Club Med vacation in the near future, either as a repeat purchase or as an initial trial.) A summary of how "Other Members" responded to the survey is also given (see Exhibit 15). The 11 exhibits (exhibits 5 to 15) are a condensation of more than 400 pages of research results.
4 The fourth study looked at U.S. travel agents to determine their attitude toward Club Med so that Club Med could improve its working relationship with the agents (see Exhibit 16).
5 The last study, the Destination Study, determined the number of inhabitants from selected cities who traveled to particular geographical locations (see Exhibit 17).

After the data were collected, Club Med had another set of decisions to make. Did the company's current strategy fit with the findings? If not, what changes should be made in positioning, communications, product, pricing and distribution? C.M.I. had to decide who should be its customer and how to persuade this potential customer to patronize Club Med's villages.

READER'S GUIDE TO EXHIBITS

   Exhibit 1: Tactical Advertising, 1983
   Study One: Demographic Profile Study (Exhibit 2)
   Study Two: The Prizm Study (Exhibits 3a, 3b, 3c)

Study Three: A Study of the Consumer Market
(i) Exhibit 4: Focus Groups
(ii) Exhibits 5 to 14: Quantitative Study
Exhibit 5: Description of the Quantitative Study
Exhibit 6: Panel A—Likelihood to Consider a Club Med Vacation in the Next Year or So Panel B—Overall Opinion of Club Med
Exhibit 7: Demographic Profile of Key Prospects vs. Key Members
Exhibit 8: Difference between Key Prospects and Key Members for Vacation Attitudes and Lifestyles That Are Important to Key Prospects
Exhibit 9: Vacation Benefits: Importance and Rating of Club Med

Exhibit 10: Impressions of Club Med Members Held by Key Members and Key Prospects
Exhibit 11: Booking Behavior for Last Club Med Visit
Exhibit 12: Perception of Comparative Cost of a Club Med Vacation
Exhibit 13: Perceptions of Things Included in Cost
Exhibit 14: Vacation Activities and Services of High Interest to Key Prospects
Exhibit 15: Summary of Data on Other Club Med Members
Study Four: The Travel Agent Study (Exhibit 16)
Study Five: The Destination Study (Exhibit 17)

EXHIBIT 1

DEMOGRAPHIC PROFILE STUDY
(July 1983)

Cost: $7000 US

Purpose: To determine major characteristics of Club Med customers.

Sample: 1000 people who booked Club Med vacations in summer of 1982 (506 calls)
               or in the winter 1982–83 (494 calls) in a North American village.

Methodology: Telephone interviews

Data: Forty percent of the Gentils Members interviewed had been to Club Med
               more than once

Age	Winter vacations	Summer vacations
35+	60%	44%
25–30	32%	50%
less than 25	8%	6%

Marital status	%
Married	51
Single	36
Separated	1
Divorced	11
Widowed	1

Education	%
Graduate School	38
College Graduate	40
Some College	13
High School or less	9

Community of residence	%
City	43
Suburb	49
Rural	7

Number in party	%
One	25
Two	52
Three or more	24

Household Income	%
Less than $30,000	16
$30,000 – 39,999	20
$40,000 – 49,999	14
$50,000 – 59,999	12
$60,000 – 79,000	16
greater than $80,000	22

Sources of information about Club Med vacation	%*
Friends/Associates	62
Travel Agent	25
Advertising – TV	7
– Magazine	4
– News	7
Brochure	6
Direct from Club Med	1

*sum to more than 100 because multiple answers were allowed

Occupation

93% Employed —— 85% White Collar —— 35% Managerial
5% Blue Collar 33% Professional
2% Service 17% Other (clerical, etc.)

7% Unemployed

EXHIBIT 2   DEMOGRAPHIC PROFILE STUDY (July 1983)

EXHIBIT 3a   THE PRIZM STUDY (Fall 1983)

PRIZM is a data base produced by an organization named Claritas and used for postal code marketing. The use of PRIZM is based on the hypothesis that the same kind of people tend to live in the same postal codes (called zip codes in the United States).

Cost: $3700.

Purpose: The study was to help determine "group types" of people most likely to be interested in Club Med. The company planned to use the information for direct response purposes (mailing lists of people fitting the appropriate profile could be purchased), to determine the choice of message and the way in which the message would be written for the Club Med consumer, and to help choose appropriate media.

Sample: In the PRIZM data base, the census data from 36,000 zip codes were clustered into 44 homogeneous neighborhood groups based on education, income, mobility, ethnicity, housing stock, degree of urbanization, age, family composition, etc. Club Med compared the zip codes of its customers with the clusters obtained from the PRIZM data base to identify what kind of people went to Club Med.

Data: *Index of concentration*: See Exhibit 3b, Club Med PRIZM Analysis.

Definition of index of concentration: The index of concentration is calculated by dividing the *percentage of Club Med members* whose addresses (i.e., zip codes) would place them in a given PRIZM cluster by the *percentage of population* in the PRIZM cluster and multiplying by 100.

Take, for example, Urban Gold Coast, the first cluster listed in Exhibit 3b. The zip codes of 5.41% of Club Med members fall in this cluster, but the membership of the cluster itself is only 0.31% of the U.S. population.

Then, the index of concentration

= 5.41 divided by 0.31 times 100
= 1745

Therefore, the percentage of Club Med members from Urban Gold Coast is 17.45 times higher than the percentage of Urban Gold Coast people in the United States.

EXHIBIT 3b   CLUB MED PRIZM ANALYSIS: TOTAL MEMBERS

Cluster	Index of concentration[1]
Urban Gold Coast[2]	1745
Blue Blood Estates[3]	637
Bohemian Mix[4]	556
Money and Brains[5]	437
Furs and Station Wagons[6]	291
Two More Rungs	279
Young Influentials	269
Pools and Patios	214
Sun-Belt Singles	186
Blue to White	150
Young Suburbia	135
Old Melting Pot	134
God's Country	114
Blue-Collar Catholics	80
Blue-Chip Blues	74

[1] Only the 15 highest clusters on the index of concentration are shown in this exhibit. They collectively represent 39.64% of the U.S. population, and 81.18% of U.S. Club Med members.

[2] Of all 44 PRIZM clusters, the Urban Gold Coast cluster has the highest concentration of income, is the most densely populated, and has the highest percentage of young adults, singles, professionals, renters, childless householders, and residents of New York City.

[3] The Blue Blood Estates cluster has the most affluent people and the most well traveled. Also included are a large number of young adults living with their parents.

[4] The Bohemian Mix cluster can be described as "high-rise singles."

[5] The Money and Brains cluster has heavy consumers of adult luxuries in apparel, restaurants and travel.

[6] The Furs and Station Wagons cluster consists of well- educated and mobile professionals.

EXHIBIT 3c

Market Potential Index
Definition:
This part of the study ranked various cities according to the prevalence of PRIZM clusters with a high proportion of Club Med members (relative to 100).

Washington	241	Miami	151
New York	207	Chicago	149
San Francisco	195	Los Angeles/Palm Springs	147

Activity and Media Analysis
In this analysis, data from the Simmons Market Research Bureau were used. This information has been collected in the United States every year from a panel of 20,000 people who were asked detailed questions about their media habits (television, radio, magazines and newspapers) and lifestyles. When these data were combined with the PRIZM data, it was possible to determine the tastes of the clusters full of Club Med members. An index measuring how frequently each cluster did an activity was correlated with the index of concentration. This correlation was done for income, education, marital status, sports tastes, tastes in reading and media preferences.

Results: It was determined that the total membership was upscale in income and education, more likely to be single, more likely not to have children, more likely to travel a lot, likely to be sports-oriented (racquetball, jogging, sailing, tennis), and own an American Express Green Card. As far as media were concerned, newspapers and magazines were better cluster fits than TV or radio. Tennis viewers were the only TV watchers with a similar profile to members. Radio did have *some* high correlations: Classical 0.867, All-News 0.822, and Talk Shows 0.802 (in contrast, Country Music −0.681).

Magazines and newspapers	
New York Times Magazine	0.889*
New Yorker	0.856
New York Times (daily edition)	0.782
Gentlemen's Quarterly	0.777
Time	0.764
Wall Street Journal	0.737
Harper's Bazaar	0.733

* This number is the correlation coefficient between a measure of clusters' readership of the *New York Times Magazine* and the index of concentration for each cluster. Each of the following correlation coefficients is created in the same way.

EXHIBIT 4   A STUDY OF THE CONSUMER MARKET FOCUS GROUPS (Summer 1983)

Cost:	$15,000.
Purpose:	To develop hypotheses to be tested in the quantitative research to follow. C.M.I. wanted to be sure that it did not miss any important questions and that the questions were asked in the consumer's language.
Sample:	Four groups of 15 people each: two groups from New York and two from San Francisco; two male groups, two female groups; 60% members, 40% non-members.
Methodology:	C.M.I. subcontracted this research to another firm, which made up a list of questions relating to the subject of vacations in general. Questions such as "Where did you go on your vacation?" "What did you get out of your vacation?" and "Why did you choose this vacation?" were asked. Each group met in a room for two hours, led by the head of the research group (a trained psychologist) and watched by Jean Rambaud (and sometimes Serge Trigano and regional sales managers) from behind a one-way glass partition. Club Med could identify its members since their name tags were different from those of non-members. The group did not know Club Med was sponsoring the research. After the focus groups were finished, the psychologist did a content analysis on the sessions. This last part helped to build the questions (as it highlighted important themes such as attitudes toward vacations and expectations from vacations), and it also helped to build the scales for the questions (on a scale of one to ten, like/dislike, etc.).
Results:	Club Med made a list of questions or hypotheses which it could use for quantitative research. Each question and element was something that had been mentioned in the focus groups. The quantitative study would test from a larger group whether these hypotheses were true.
	Example: In the focus group, one person might say, "When I'm on vacation, I like to take tours through museums." To test if people really do like museum tours on vacation, Club Med asked (in the section on Interest in Activities and Services) whether people wanted this service offered.
	During the focus groups, respondents were asked, "Where did you go on vacation?" It was interesting to note that people gave an actual destination (e.g., Hawaii) *unless* it was a Club Med vacation. In the latter case, they simply answered "Club Med."

EXHIBIT 5   A STUDY OF THE CONSUMER MARKET DESCRIPTION OF THE QUANTITATIVE STUDY
(Sept. 21 to Oct. 3, 1983)

Cost: $50,000.

Purpose:

1. To serve as the foundation for a new consumer marketing approach by providing information on past Club Med vacationers (prospective repeat customers) and prospective new Club Med members
2. To identify Key Prospects and where they could best be found
3. To position Club Med
4. To develop Club Med's communication strategy by determining what should be communicated and how it should be communicated (e.g., in what tone and manner)
5. To identify how the distribution strategy could be refined (e.g., how to make the best use of travel agents)
6. To determine what the optimal pricing policy should be
7. To determine if and how the Club Med "product" should be modified

Sample: Six markets in three regions (see table below).

| | Sample Sizes | | |
Region	Club Med member sample	Prospect sample	Total
North	167	130	297
Southeast	123	93	216
West	170	129	299
Total	460	352	812

1. Members: Random sample of U.S. residents who visited in the past year.
2. Prospects: A 1 was added to the last digit of Club Med members' phone numbers to create a parallel universe of non-members in the same neighborhoods.

Definition of a Prospect

The person had to be between 25 and 49 years old. If he were married, he had to earn at least $35,000 a year; if he were single, he had to earn at least $25,000 a year. Furthermore, the person must have taken a vacation at least one week long within the past year (or intend to take one within the next year) that had prepaid accommodation and was either on a cruise ship or required plane transportation.

Methodology: A 40-minute phone interview was then followed by immediate mailing of a survey. Though refusal rates among both members and prospects were low, it took many calls to generate the prospect sample; only 7% of those called qualified as a prospect.

EXHIBIT 6   QUANTITATIVE STUDY
PANEL A   LIKELIHOOD TO CONSIDER A CLUB MED VACATION IN NEXT YEAR OR SO

Question 10 (phone): Thinking about the next year or so, how likely are you to consider a vacation at Club Med—definitely, probably, probably not, or definitely not?

	Members %			Prospects %	
Definitely will not	8			20	
Probably will not	18			35	
Probably will	40			39	
		Key			Key
		Members			Prospects
Definitely will	34			6	

Key Members and Key Prospects are defined as those people falling in the bottom two sections.

PANEL B   OVERALL OPINION OF CLUB MED AMONG KEY MEMBERS/PROSPECTS VS. OTHERS

Question 7 (phone): Thinking of everything you know about Club Med, what is your overall opinion of Club Med as a place at which to have a wonderful vacation—poor, fair, good, very good, or excellent?

	Members		Prospects	
	Key %	Others %	Key %	Others %
Fair, poor	1	27	7	27
Good	7	27	31	41
Very good	37	32	49	29
Excellent	55	14	13	3

EXHIBIT 7   QUANTITATIVE STUDY: DEMOGRAPHIC PROFILE KEY PROSPECTS VS. KEY MEMBERS

	Key Prospects	Key Members	Compared with Key Prospects, Key Members are
	%	%	%
Education			
Some college or less	42	24	−18*
College graduate	41	40	− 1
Post graduate	17	36	+19*
Income			
Under $30,000	8	23	+15*
$30,000 to $39,999	23	19	− 4
$40,000 to $59,999	40	29	−11*
$60,000 or more	29	29	0
Occupation			
Professional/semi-prof.	24	35	+11*
Proprietor/manager	32	31	− 1
Clerical/sales	21	19	− 2
Full-time homemaker	7	2	− 5
Sex			
Male	45	60	+15*
Female	55	40	−15*
Age			
Under 30 years	28	24	− 4
30 to 34	26	25	− 1
35 to 39	19	22	+ 3
40 and over	27	29	+ 2
Average	35	36	+ 1
Marital status			
Married/couples	55	43	−12*
Singles	32	36	+ 4
Ex-married	13	21	+ 8
Have children at home	36	23	−13*
Under 12 years	23	17	− 6

* Indicate a difference of at least 10 percentage points. These differences were also maintained on every item when all members were compared with all prospects.

EXHIBIT 8   QUANTITATIVE STUDY: DIFFERENCES BETWEEN KEY PROSPECTS AND KEY MEMBERS ON VACATION ATTITUDES AND LIFESTYLES THAT ARE IMPORTANT TO KEY PROSPECTS

Key Prospects rate these items[1] to be of:	Compared with Key Prospects, Key Members rate the importance of the item to be:		
	Higher	Similar[5]	Lower
Very high importance[2]			
I make my own decisions		X	
Vacation is an escape from everyday life		X	
My goal in life is to experience as many things as I can			X
Vacation is a reward for hard work			X
I have fun doing things with others		X	
High importance[3]			
I like to live to the fullest			X
I like to be pampered on vacation			X
I prefer a beach vacation	X		
I like doing things my way			X
I am anti singles bars and vacations			X
I do my own thing despite others		X	
I want peace and quiet on vacation		X	
Moderate importance[4]			
There is no worry re vacation cost		X	
I feel free since I won't see people again			X
I am anti going/doing things by myself		X	
I enjoy planning my vacation			X
I don't like being surrounded by people who talk to each other in a foreign language		X	

[1] Question asked: I would like to know how you feel generally about vacations. I am going to read you a list of phrases. Could you rate on a scale of 1 to 10 (with 1 being the lowest) how much this phrase describes you and how you feel about vacations?

[2] At least 50% of Key Prospects chose 9 or 10 on the 10-point importance scale.

[3] From 30 to 49.9% chose 9 or 10 on the importance scale.

[4] From 10 to 29.9% chose 9 or 10 on the importance scale.

[5] Key Members and Key Prospects are categorized "similar" if their importance scores (% choosing 9 or 10 on the 10-point importance scale) are within 10 percentage points of each other.

EXHIBIT 9   QUANTITATIVE STUDY   VACATION BENEFITS IMPORTANCE AND RATING OF CLUB MED

Benefits	Importance ratings[1]		Rating of Club Med[4]	
	Key Prospects[2]	Key Members vs. Key Prospects[3]	Key Prospects[2]	Key Members vs. Key Prospects[3]
Everything works right	Very High[2]	– [3]	Moderate[2]	Similar[3]
Can do what/when you want	Very High	Similar	High	+
Allows you to relax	Very High	Similar	High	+
Good value for money	Very High	Similar	High	+
No hassles/problems	Very High	Similar	High	Similar
Beautiful location	Very High	Similar	Very High	Similar
Good, interesting food	Very High	–	High	Similar
Activities you like	High	Similar	High	+
Well-managed	High	Similar	Moderate	+
Can be spontaneous	High	Similar	Moderate	Similar
Easy to arrange	High	–	High	+
Lots of fun	High	Similar	High	+
Lot or little contact	High	Similar	Moderate	+
See variety of places	High	–	Moderate	–
Status, $ unimportant	High	–	Low	+
Explore local area	Moderate	Similar	Moderate	+
Very exciting	Moderate	Similar	Moderate	Similar
Good place for couples	Moderate	–	High	Similar
No extra $ payment for singles	Moderate	Similar	High	+
Can arrange last minute	Moderate	Similar	Moderate	Similar
No worry about your looks	Moderate	Similar	Low	Similar
Dance and drink till late	Moderate	Similar	High	+
People not wild	Moderate	–	Low	Similar
Have vacation romance	Moderate	–	High	Similar
Lots of sports to do	Low	Similar	High	+
Good place to go alone	Low	+	High	+
All paid in advance	Low	Similar	High	+
All in walking distance	Low	Similar	Moderate	+
Learn, improve skills	Low	Similar	Moderate	+

[1] Question asked: I would like to know how you feel about certain benefits derived from a vacation. I am going to read you a list of phrases. Could you rate on a scale of 1 to 10 (with 1 being the lowest) how important these benefits are to you?

[2] Judgment categories for Key Prospects were determined as follows for both importance of benefits and ratings of Club Med:

Importance Category (or Club Med rating category)	% of Key Prospects rating a benefit (or Club Med) at 9 or 10 on a 10-point importance scale
Very high	At least 65%
High	50 to 64.9%
Moderate	39 to 49.9%
Low	Less than 30%

[3] Key Members and Key Prospects are categorized as "similar" if their scores (% choosing 9 or 10 on the 10-point scale) are within 10 percentage points of each other. A "+" means that Key Members ratings were more than 10 percentage points higher; a "−" means that they were more than 10 points lower.

[4] Question asked: I would like to know how well you think Club Med delivers certain vacation benefits. I will read you a list of benefits. Could you rate on a scale of 1 to 10 (with 1 being the lowest) how good you think Club Med is at delivering these benefits.

EXHIBIT 10   QUANTITATIVE STUDY: IMPRESSIONS OF CLUB MED MEMBERS[1]
(% Rating "Describes Most People")

Most people are:	Agreement by Key Prospects[2]	Compared with Key Prospects, Key Members tend to agree		
		More	Similar[3]	Less
In their 30s	Strong			X
Active	Moderate	X		
Americans	Moderate			X
Self-confident	Moderate		X	
Successful	Moderate		X	
Professionals	Moderate		X	
Swinging singles	Moderate			X
Intelligent	Moderate	X		
Interesting	Disagree	X		
Good-looking women	Disagree		X	
Good-looking men	Disagree		X	
Sports experts	Disagree		X	
Just interested in sex	Disagree		X	
Immature women	Disagree		X	
Immature men	Disagree		X	
Couples	Disagree			X
Secretaries	Disagree			X
Rich	Disagree			X

[1] Question asked: I would like to have your impression of the people who vacation at Club Med. Please indicate which of the following items describe most people who vacation at Club Med. Multiple answers are permitted.

[2] Agreement categories were determined as follows:

Agreement category	% of Key Prospects agreeing
Strong	At least 65%
Moderate	35 to 64.9%
Disagree	Less than 34.9%

[3] "Similar" means that the percentage of Key Members who agreed with the statement was within 10% of the percentage of Key Prospects who agreed.

EXHIBIT 11   QUANTITATIVE STUDY: BOOKING BEHAVIOR FOR LAST CLUB MED VISIT

Booked Through	Key Members
	%
Club Med	16
Travel agent	82
Reasons Club Med not used*	
Unaware could use, didn't know how/where	26
More convenient	21
Needed advice, had complex arrangements	13
Habit	11
Know, trust agent	7
No advantage	2
Don't know why not	17

* Multiple answers were permitted.

EXHIBIT 12   QUANTITATIVE STUDY: PERCEPTION OF COMPARATIVE COST OF A CLUB MÉDITERRANÉE VACATION

Compared with other places, the cost at Club Med is:	Key Prospects %	Compared with Key Prospects, Key Members are
Very low	2	0
Fairly low	0	+ 9
Moderate	57	+ 6
Fairly high	39	−14
Very high	2	− 1

Four percent of Key Prospects thought a Club Med trip was more expensive than it really was.

EXHIBIT 13   QUANTITATIVE STUDY: PERCEPTIONS OF THINGS INCLUDED IN COST[1]

The things the basic cost covers	Key Prospects[2]	Compared with Key Prospects, Key Members perceptions are		
		Higher	Similar[3]	Lower
+ Nighttime entertainment	Very high	X		
+ Sports instruction	Very high	X		
+ Most sports equipment	Very high	X		
+ Wine at meals	High	X		
+ Ski lifts	High	X		
+ Books and games	High	X		
Sightseeing tours	High	X		
+ Air transportation	Moderate	X		
Tips	Moderate			X
Drinks at bar	Low			X
+ Items included in the basic cost				

[1] Seven items are not listed. Key Prospects and Key Members agree that meals+, exercise classes+, maid service, and ground transportation+ are included in the basic cost, while a high percentage of each group believe that food between meals is not included.

[2] Percentages of Key Prospects believing that the cost covers the item fall into the following categories:

Very high	At least 80%
High	70 to 79.9%
Moderate	30 to 69.9%
Low	Less than 30%

[3] Key Prospects and Key Members are categorized as "similar" if their perceptions are within 10 percentage points of each other.

EXHIBIT 14   QUANTITATIVE STUDY: ACTIVITIES AND SERVICES OF HIGH INTEREST TO KEY PROSPECTS

Key for own room
Variety of dinner menu
Food/beverages all hours
Flexible mealtime hours
Private rooms for singles
Choice of restaurant
Phone in room

These 7 items were selected from a list of 64 activities (ranging from jazz concerts to 24-hour room service to supervision for children). These 7 items presented above were the only ones for which more than 70% of Key Prospects reported that they were "Very Interested." None of the 7 were currently offered at the majority of Club Med villages. Key Members were much less interested (by 15 to 60 percentage points) in these activities.

EXHIBIT 15   SUMMARY OF DATA ON OTHER* CLUB MEMBERS

Other Club Members have fairly low future visit intentions. They do not think that they belong at Club Med and also do not think that status and money are unimportant at Club Med.

They are disaffected with Club Med. Their alienation is not related to whether they are first-time visitors or repeaters, to whether they visit in-season or out of season, or to the degree of Club Med knowledge. Their alienation *is* highly related to:

1. The vacation attitudes and benefits sought, in that they have more interest in doing things on their own and have more interest in seeing and doing new things

2. The fact that they are less receptive to the essence of Club Med since they have less interest in fun, sociability, activities, and internationality, and are less willing to give up privacy and services

3. Their experience at the Club in that many benefits they consider important to a vacation are not delivered by Club Med to their satisfaction (for example, independence, smooth operations, spontaneity, activities they like), and they did not feel that they belonged at the Club

4. Their expectations not being met

---

* To be defined as "Other" Club Member (as opposed to "Key"), a member had to have said that he probably or definitely would not consider a Club Med vacation in the near future.

EXHIBIT 16   THE TRAVEL AGENT STUDY (Summer 1983)

Cost:	$1000 (plus travel and administrative expenses) (Performed by a student full-time for a summer project. He received no salary.)
Purpose:	To discover how travel agents felt about Club Med and how to improve Club Med's working relationship with them
Sample:	- Some large and some small travel agencies in terms of Club Med sales - Geographically diverse—six cities: New York, Houston, Atlanta, Los Angeles, Philadelphia, Chicago - Three groups emerged:

(a) Those with an increase in sales over the last year
(b) Those with a decrease in sales over the last year
(c) Those with no sales in 1983 but some in 1982

Methodology: First, ten personal interviews were conducted with travel agents in New York to develop the questionnaire. Then, 170 personal interviews were held with travel agents in the six cities.

Findings:

1. Reported number of people recommended to Club Med by the travel agent in the past 6 months

17%—none	18%—20 to 40
21%—1 to 10 people	35%—more than 40
9%—11 to 19	

2. Eighty-five percent of the agencies found the Club Med product easy to sell.
3. The Club Med concept of an all-inclusive vacation was ranked best by 84% of the agencies when compared with the firms the agencies ranked as their top three competitors.
4. The Club Med brochure was considered superior to that of the competition by 90% of the travel agents.
5. There is still much misperception about the Club Med's activities: especially in the midwest area, it is considered as a singles place with a wild reputation.
6. There is a lack of familiarity with the Club Med concept: some think there is too much structure and regimentation.
7. Sixty-five percent of the travel agents have never visited a Club Med village.
8. Travel agents did not feel that there was a need to increase the number of reservation employees.

EXHIBIT 17   THE DESTINATION STUDY (November 1983)

Cost:	Minimal out-of-pocket costs, aside from Club Med and advertising agency staff time.
Purpose:	The study helps determine geographically where certain cities' inhabitants went when they traveled abroad and how many went from each city. In this way, Club Med could follow the path of least resistance. For example, if New Yorkers tended to go to Mexico on vacation, there was no point in wasting resources promoting the packages for Tahiti vacations to them.
Sample:	Club Med received data on arrivals and departures from 20 cities to destinations similar to Club Med village locations. This data helped determine which prime markets to focus on in the short term, which packages to sell in certain cities, and which cities were potential future markets.

Source: Civil Aeronautics Board of the United States.

THE MISTRAL SKISAILER (A)

On March 15, 1987, David Varilek went to seek advice from several faculty members at IMEDE, the international business school in Lausanne, Switzerland. A week earlier, the marketing director of Mistral Windsurfing AG, the world's leading company in sailboarding equipment, had informed David that sales were disappointing for the Skisailer, a new product that David had invented four years earlier. Despite these initial setbacks, David Varilek felt that a negative conclusion was premature. In his opinion, the Skisailer still had a viable commercial potential.

THE SKISAILER CONCEPT

Skisailer was based on a concept that combined alpine skiing and sailboarding in a new sport: skisailing. As a Swiss native, David Varilek was almost "born on skis." However, he had always been frustrated by not being able to ski on the

This case was prepared by Assistant Professor Dominique Turpin as a basis for class discussion rather than to illustrate either effective or ineffective handling of an administrative situation. Copyright ©1988 by IMEDE, Lausanne, Switzerland. IMD International, resulting from the merger between IMEDE, Lausanne, and IMI, Geneva, acquires and retains all rights. Reproduced by permission.

flat snow surface that surrounded his home in the winter season.

In 1983, in his own garage, David Varilek invented a connection bar which could be fixed onto regular skis while still allowing them to be directed with great flexibility. A surf-sailing rig could then be installed on the connection bar, and with enough wind, flat snow surfaces could become great fun for skiing. The idea was subsequently patented under Swiss law. A major feature of the invention was that the Skisailer's unique design also allowed windskiers to use regular alpine skis and almost any type of usual sailboard rig, an innovation that limited the user's budget requirements. The connection bar and the surfsail were easy to install. Lateral clamps used for attaching the connection bar to the skis did not damage them in any way except for a small groove on the side of the ski. Only 5 cm of the ski's length was held rigid, and the rest retained normal flexibility. Safety had also been an important consideration when developing the Skisailer, and three self-releasing safety mechanisms had been included on the product.

Instead of being powered by gravity, as in normal skiing, moderate wind in the sail served as the Skisailer's motor. Skisailer could be used on either smooth slopes or flat surfaces. The ideal surface for skisailing was on the kind of hard-packed snow usually found on groomed ski slopes, but the Skisailer could also be used on ice where it could achieve considerable speed (up to 100km/h). Skisailing in deep snow or slightly uphill required stronger wind. For use at high speeds, wearing a safety helmet was recommended.

According to David Varilek, skisailing was as much fun as sailboarding even though it had to be done in cold weather. David claimed that "for identical sensations, skisailing was easier to learn and handle than sailboarding." For many beginners, it was not easy to stay balanced on a sailboard, and it was frustrating to fall off into the water repeatedly and try to get up on the board again. Many people gave up sailboarding because of these difficulties. With the Skisailer, such frustrations were minimized. According to David, "You can get on and get off the Skisailer easily, and you are always on your feet. Another great thing with the Skisailer is that you can take advantage of the terrain to perform the same kind of loopings as on sea waves. The Skisailer is a great vehicle for discovering variety in the surroundings."

MISTRAL WINDSURFING AG

Mistral Windsurfing AG, was a company affiliated with the ADIA Group. ADIA, a $1 billion conglomerate with headquarters in Lausanne, Switzerland, had its activities centered around ADIA Interim, a company providing interim personnel to companies in Switzerland and around the world. With offices in Austria, Belgium, Canada, Denmark, France, Great Britain, Holland, Ireland, the United States, and West Germany, ADIA Interim was second in revenue only to Manpower, the international leader.

At the end of 1980, ADIA had bought out Mistral as part of a diversification strategy for the group. The acquisition of the sailboard company was seen as an opportunity to acquire a com-

pany in a rapidly growing industry. Consistency in marketing and product policy over the past 10 years had made Mistral a leader in the worldwide sailboarding industry. This constant success was grounded in technological competence, permanent innovation, the highest quality standards, a selective international distributorship policy and solid financial backing. Thus, in a fiercely competitive market, characterized by the rise and fall of brands and manufacturers, Mistral was occupying a place apart. To Martin Pestalozzi, the President of ADIA, the Skisailer represented a good opportunity to extend Mistral's product line, especially since Mistral management was concerned about the future of the sailboarding market.

MISTRAL AND THE SAILBOARDING MARKET

The fathers of the modern sailboard were two Californians, Hoyle Schweitzer and James Drake, who had developed the Windsurfer brand. They had applied for and received a patent in 1970 for their device, which combined a surfboard and sailboat.

In the early 1970s, Schweitzer bought out Drake and developed his firm, Windsurfing International, from a living-room operation into a multi-million-dollar corporation with branches in six countries. As a result of controversy over the Windsurfer patent, sales in the United States and Canadian markets were inhibited, and Windsurfing International was able to hold a virtual monopoly until 1979, when a number of other firms entered the sailboard market.

Meanwhile, competition in the European marketplace was many years ahead of North America. First introduced to the European market by Ten Cate, a Dutch textiles firm, sailboarding had an unprecedented growth, particularly in France and Germany. Even as the industry matured, it maintained growth in terms of dollar volume, if not in units.

Sailboarding's rapid growth over the past six years had thrust this new industry into the limelight. During these few seasons, interest in the sport had grown from a small pool of participants to being among the top (Olympic) participation sports on an international basis. The worldwide population of sailboarders in 1986 was approximately 2 to 3 million people. (In comparison, the worldwide ski population was estimated at approximately 30 million.)

Established in 1976 in Bassersdorf near Zurich (Switzerland), Mistral rapidly won an international reputation among sailboarders. Its success was enhanced by two major factors. First, right from the start, Mistral had signed up Robby Naish, a young Californian who easily managed to win all the major distinctions and titles in this sport. Using Mistral equipment, Robby Naish had become the 1977 World Champion at age 12, and he had been dominating this sport ever since. In 1986, he won the world title for the 10th time in a row. Mistral's other successful early strategy had been to provide several hundred sailboards free to such leisure businesses as Club Méditerranée.

Over the years, part of Mistral's strategy had been to build sales and market share on Robby Naish's success. Mistral also enjoyed a competitive advantage over other sailboard manufacturers by concentrating on the upper range of the market. Worldwide, Mistral's equipment was considered the best.

Robby Naish's name and the high quality and reliability of Mistral's products had helped build an extensive network of distributors in 30 countries around the world. The company had its own organizational structure in the American market, where it enjoyed about one-third of its global sales. Mistral was also directly represented in a number of European countries such as France, Germany, and the Benelux. For the rest of the world, Mistral used exclusive agents who were responsible for selling Mistral products in specific geographical regions.

RECENT DEVELOPMENTS IN THE U.S. SAILBOARDING MARKET

During the 1986 season, the number of board suppliers to the American market declined drasti-cally for two reasons: the patent and home-based failures. The drop in unit sales in the United States from 73,000 to 62,000 reflected two problems. The 1985 market share leaders Bic (with sales of 14,000 units) and Tiga (with sales of 2,300 units), as well as several smaller concerns, did not obtain licenses and therefore could not sell in the United States.

Furthermore, Akutec, the European firm which marketed the successful HiFly brand, went bankrupt as did Wayler in Holland, Surf Partner in Sweden, as well as Sodim, Star Surf, and Skipper in France. Added to these problems were F2's takeover (and bankruptcy of its German marketing subsidiary) and the Crit factory fire.

With fewer suppliers, retailers' options became more limited, and the pressure to sell was reduced. Since mid-1982, F2 had been refinanced, HiFly brand bought by Rotex, Wayler re-opened by Ozo, and Surf Partner reformed out of bankruptcy.

RECENT DEVELOPMENTS IN THE EUROPEAN SAILBOARDING MARKET

There had never been a sport in Europe—snow skiing included—which had grown so dramatically in such a short time period. The proliferation of boards in Europe had come about because of the expense of gasoline (for running power boats), limited water accessibility, the desire for a fast and exciting sport, profitability of boards and the European's willingness to be instructed, which had consistently added new sailers to the pool of potential customers.

The two leading markets in Europe were in France and in Germany, but other major markets existed in Italy, Holland and Switzerland.

According to the French research group EN-ERGY, sales rose from less than 600 units in France in 1974 to more than 70,000 units in 1980. For the 1983 season, which was regarded as "poor" by most French companies, 108,000 units were sold, a drop from 115,000 in 1982. However, a study completed in 1984 by the "Groupement Industrie de Planche à Voile," an association of French manufacturers, found the decrease less than previously estimated. In 1983, industry specialists estimated that the German sailboard market accounted for sales of around 100,000 units.

The 1984 season in Europe showed a decline in sales, as markets aged and weather conditions put a damper on summer activities. Estimates placed the decline at 25 to 30%, with France and West Germany as the biggest losers. Sales in 1985 and 1986 showed a continued slight decline in most countries, with a leveling off in others. Sales in Italy in 1985 were around 35,000 units; between 45,000 and 70,000 units were sold in Holland for 1985–1986 (depending on the source of information) and 12,000 to 15,000 units in Switzerland (where the population was relatively smaller). These declines were due not only to weather and economic conditions but to an increasing emphasis on shorter boards and higher technology sails as well.

In 1986, the French market led as the number one country in European sales. That market continued to be dominated by Bic and Tiga, which accounted for 45,000 of the country's 65,000 units. Mistral was the top imported brand and number three overall with 5,000 units. In Germany, the market fell to just below 60,000 boards sold, led by Klepper with over 12,000 units in sales. Despite its failure as a company, HiFly boards were number two in Germany with sales of 10,000 units, followed by Fanatic and Mistral. The 10-year-old European market had reached a level of maturity where new unit sales were slowing down. However, the market continued to be strong despite a reduced number of suppliers.

THE SKISAILER AND MISTRAL'S DIVERSIFICATION POLICY

Windsurfing AG Mistral had contacted David Varilek at the beginning of 1984 after ADIA management learned about the Skisailer from a four-page article in a major Swiss magazine. David Varilek was particularly interested in establishing a relationship with Mistral as the company was the world leader in sailboarding.

The Skisailer seemed to offer an appropriate product line diversification for Mistral. It also looked superior to various similar products that were appearing on the market. The Skisailer not only was an extension of Mistral's product line but also fit in with the new line of winter sportswear and other ski-related products that Mistral's new management was planning to develop. Moreover, Mistral had full support from ADIA to launch the project.

In spring 1984, a contract for developing, manufacturing, and distributing the Skisailer was formally signed between David Varilek and Mistral. For the duration of the agreement, all Skisailer patent and trademark rights would be transferred to Mistral, but David would serve as technical adviser to Mistral and would receive 2% royalties on its sales. It was also agreed that David would demonstrate the Skisailer in windski competitions and exhibitions where Mistral was participating. Should total sales not reach 5,000 units by the end of 1986, either party could terminate the agreement, with trademarks and patents reverting to David Varilek. Mistral could cancel David's termination rights in 1987 and 1988 for a fixed royalty of $22,000 per year. Mistral could also counter any competitive offer made to David, a so-called first right of refusal.

LAUNCHING THE SKISAILER

During the summer of 1984, two prototypes were developed for presentation in November 1984 at ISPO, the largest annual European sports exhibition, held every year in Munich. Between May and November 1984, Mistral engineers developed several innovations that were added to the Skisailer. For example, the board and the support blocks were strengthened to resist shocks and low temperatures. The connection bar was also modified to accommodate only Mistral windsurf sailing rigs. (These mast feet could be used with most surfsail and mast types.)

In Munich at ISPO, the Skisailer was widely acclaimed as a truly innovative product which would certainly win public enthusiasm.

However, at this early stage of development, the product still lacked promotional support. No pamphlet, video, or pictures had been developed to present the product and educate potential users. David thought that the pictures used to introduce the product to Mistral's distributors were not attractive enough to trigger a buying process. Nevertheless, some distributors liked the product and placed immediate orders.

Starting in December 1984, 50 Skisailers were manufactured by Mistral and sold mainly in Canada and Scandinavia at a retail price of $360. However, these Skisailers broke down rapidly, as some plastic and/or rubber parts tended to break under cold temperatures.

THE COMPETITION

In the early 1980s, a number of products similar to the Skisailer had been introduced around the world. About 20 different models had appeared in various publications during the last five years. However, only three or four companies were reported to have succeeded in developing a viable product.

Among competitive models that were already on the market in 1985, most windski products had been invented by sailboarders who had adapted the sailboard concept to ski conditions. However, nobody except David had thought to do just the reverse, namely adapt skis to the sailboard concept. As a result, most competitive models were more difficult to maneuver. Few could be turned swiftly to the right or the left, and all lacked the great flexibility or the speed of the Skisailer. Finally, most of these new products had been launched by inventors turned entrepreneurs, eager to commercialize their own products by themselves. As a result, most lacked the experience, the financial support, and the distribution network that Mistral had to offer. Some characteristics of Skisailer's three closest competitors were as follows:

Icesurfer

Developed by Ingo Merz, a German entrepreneur with 30 employees, the Icesurfer was a fairly sophisticated windski product, capable of reaching high speeds (up to 160 km/h). Using a board with three ice skates, the product had one major drawback: it could be used only on an icy surface. The Icesurfer was sold mainly in Germany and Scandinavia at a retail price of around $700 (not including the price of the sailing rig).

Winterboard

Winterboard, a light sailing boat with skis, had been invented in Finland. It could be used on both ice and snow, and its performance was impressive. David Varilek rated the Winterboard as the best performing windski after the Skisailer. In terms of sales, Winterboard had been the most successful windski product. Over the last five years, 4,000 units had been sold, mainly in Scandinavia and the United States in regular sports shops. Winterboard was being sold at a retail price of $395 excluding the sailing rig. The skis were already integrated with the board and did not need to be purchased as an extra. However, their quality was considered rather poor.

Windskier

According to David Varilek, Windskier could also be a serious competitor for the Skisailer. The company Windskier, based in Newport Beach, California, seemed to be extremely well managed and to be spending a lot of money to promote its product worldwide. In 1985, Windskier had established a subsidiary in Monaco to distribute the Windskier in Europe. However, the product did not perform well, lacking some flexibility in maneuvering. But David Varilek estimated that the Windskier could certainly be rapidly improved as the company was heavily supported financially. Windskier was also the most expensive competitive model. The board itself retailed at $730, and this cost did not include the skis or the sailing rig.

American-Made Ski Sailer

On a trip to the United States, David Varilek had discovered another snow-sailing product also called the Ski Sailer. The Ski Sailer had been invented by a young Californian, Carl Meinberg, who eventually became David's close friend. The American Ski Sailer also used a small board mounted on skis and was similar to the product developed by David Varilek (see Exhibit 1). On his own, Carl Meinberg had sold about 50 Ski Sailers at $220 each. During the winter season, Carl Meinberg would tour a number of ski resorts, demonstrating the Ski Sailer, and then spend the rest of the year selling his product.

Australian-Made Ski Sailer

A third Ski Sailer also existed. Developed by Richard O'Neill in Australia, this device was initially distributed in the United States by Australian Surf and Sail in Laguna Beach, California, and sold for $90, a much cheaper price than Mistral's Skisailer.

This product was essentially a simple bar with a mastfoot on it which could be attached to normal ski boots (see Exhibit 2) and used with either conventional skis or roller skates. The Ski Sailer had an equalizing slide and joint mechanism, and so maneuvers such as parallel turns, jump turns, and snowplowing were possible. Any sailboard rig could be fitted to the Ski Sailer's mast post. The manufacturer of the Ski Sailer said that jibbing could be easily performed by a full boom rotation, and tacking accomplished by either a duck tack under the boom or by jibbing around and coming back upwind.

David gathered most of the data on competitors by himself. Sporting events were the best opportunity for David and Mistral to learn more about the competition. Because the sport was so new, little information concerning this industry was available. Actually, nobody, including Mistral, had a clear idea of the potential market size for windski equipment. Because the concept was so appealing, most companies thought that pushing the product would be the optimum way to understand the market and observe the public's reaction.

DISTRIBUTION AND PROMOTION OF THE SKISAILER

In Europe, the Skisailer was distributed in large and medium-sized cities through Mistral franchise shops and other sports shops, focusing attention on cities near ski resorts (i.e., less than a 100-minute drive). For example, in Lausanne (Switzerland) with 130,000 inhabitants—250,000 including its outskirts—there were about 30 ski stores and 3 sailboard shops. Of the three stores selling the Skisailer, two specialized in ski equipment and the third one sold only sailboard equipment.

In the winter of 1984–1985, David Varilek participated in various sporting events and demonstrations in Switzerland, Western Europe, and Scandinavia, mostly sponsored by the skisailing equipment manufacturers. The International Federation of Windskiing had also recently been established by a number of Winterboard fans. Although Winterboard and Windskier had a similar concept, the Skisailer's competitors claimed there were some differences, which were then used to disqualify David. As a result, David felt that he had been unfairly stripped of the 1985 and 1986 World Windski Championship titles.

SITUATION IN APRIL 1987

Since the beginning of 1985, David Varilek had been disappointed by what he perceived as Mistral's low marketing effort. David felt that Mistral was not spending the resources needed to promote the product. Although five people were directly involved in the project, no one at Mistral was exclusively responsible for the Skisailer. Working priorities for Mistral's staff were concentrated on the sailboard business rather than the Skisailer.

EXHIBIT 1

SNOWSAILING

A Blast in the Face of Winter

BY CHACO MOHLER

Carving through a field of whitecapped peaks, flying into the sky for a mule kick, brace for speed with legs taking the jolts like shock absorbers. What sport are we talking about here? Boardsailing? Snow skiing? Both.

The similarities in control, speed and freedom of skiing and boardsailing has not been ignored by athletes in mountain towns across America, where spring sees a rapid switch from ski racks to board racks. It was inevitable that some ingenious lover of both sports would mate the frictionlessness of snow with the power of the wind in an exhilarating new hybrid: "snowsailing."

"I was cross-country skiing in a big storm", says Carl Meinberg of Wind Performance Products, "when I opened my jacket and the wind blew me right across the snow. A friend had a sailboard rig; it wasn't to long until I had it on skis."

First practiced on frozen stretches of Scandinavia, snowsailing's been reinvented "Stateside" by entrepreneurs like Meinberg, owner of one of six companies now marketing equipment here. Each of these contraptions is slightly different, but they fall into two main categories: boards on runners, or devices which attach a universal joint directly to skis or boots. The "Windskier," tested with the help of Anne Gardner Nelson and Karen Calvert, is a small board mounted on skis, which allows the sailor to stand across the direction of travel, as on a sailboard. Meinberg's "Ski

Sailor" has the universal connected to a plate which bolts onto four rubber power joints on the front of the skis. Facing forward in his or her ski boots, the snowsailor twists sideways to lean out on a close reach. But for experienced skiers, the Ski Sailor gives incredible control, high speeds, and even, yes *massive air!*

"I've jumped 30-foot cornices," says Meinberg, "and gotten upside down off big snow ripples." Meinberg has also been clocked at 48 mph on his Ski Sailor, and routinely puts in 100-mile days across the snow-covered meadows near his home at Mammoth, California.

For Meinberg and a few of his friends, snowsailing has become the perfect transition, both in terms of conditioning and skills, between skiing and boardsailing seasons.

"We ski the mountain on spring mornings," he says, "and when the wind comes up in the afternoon, we pop on the Ski Sailors and go snowsailing. In the late spring, we snowsail in the morning on the firm snow and then drop down to the lake in the afternoon for boardsailing."

Meinberg has used snowsailing to teach his friends the basics of boardsailing. Water starting (or in this case, snow starting) and duck jibes can be learned easier on skis, for instance. And you swallow less water.

But this is more than a transition sport or teaching aid. Says Meinberg: "When there's fresh snow and the mountain's socked in and the wind's ripping through the meadow and you know there'll only be a few

chairlifts open, it's time to go snowsailing." With enough breeze, the rigs will push right through fresh powder, the snow flying up over the sail's foil (high-clew sails come in handy). But hard pack and corn snow are ideal for the control and speed of the rig. Strong winds can blow you right up steep hills. Then the snowsailor turns around, luffs the sail, and skis down. Incredibly high angles to windward are also possible because skis set on edge don't slip sideways like a sailboard.

And you can really cover some distance on these things, like the 30-mile broadreaches that Meinberg's crew screams through at Mammoth. They also sail to hot springs in the area, sometimes towing a couple of grateful cross-country skiers with them.

And then, there's air. The wind forms natural waves of snow between trees and rocks in the backcountry, sometimes peeling over the perfect glassy, frozen point waves. Choose your spot on this snow swell and your skis are soon pointing heavenward. Landing, however, is not quite as soft as in Mother Ocean; it's easy letdown. No safer, but perhaps easier to control, flights for distance off small mounds. A snowsailor can reach such wild speeds that it doesn't take much of a ramp to get airborne.

If you're a boardsailor *and* a skier, you already own two-thirds of the equipment you need for snowsailing. When the wind's blowing people off the mountain in a winter storm, you'll be out carving up a frozen version of Hookipa. When spring rolls around for the real boardsailing season, your arms will already be in shape without having to hang from booms in the living-room all winter. And then there's the other big plus of snowsailing: like boardsailing, the lifts of this sport don't require a ticket!

Chaco Mohler WIND SURF'S Tahoe correspondent, likes his water hot and cold and frozen and every which way nowadays.

Source: *Windsurf Magazine.*

EXHIBIT 2

SKISAILING

New Dimensions From the Land of Oz

BY RICK O'NEIL

Who'd have thought of it? But it's true: this amazing land downunder has snowfields as well, and when the cooler ocean currents start tingling the sunny shores of Oz, the Snowy Mountains are the place to head for.

The Australian snowfields are concentrated in two main areas in the southeastern corner of the continent, within easy access of most of the population. New South Wales skiers from Sydney reach the snow in about six hours, past Canberra and on the resorts of Thredbo, Perisher Valley and Charlotte Pass. These villages surround the Australian alpine area, which extends above the treeline of "Snow Gums" to the highest peak of Mt. Kosciusko at 7,314 feet. Melbourne skiers have about a three hour drive to the Victorian resorts of Mt. Buffalo, Mt. Hotham or Falls Creek, near the snow covered tableland of the Bogong High Plains.

The snowfields are sparsely populated, but they're home to many native animals, including wombats, wallabies and a few stray foxes. It is not unusual to see these guys chewing casually on a few eucalyptus morsels, or just sunbaking, watching the skiers go by.

The Australian snowfield regions encompass an area rivaling that of the Swiss Alps; there's ample room for alpine and nordic skiing and for the wintertime boardsailer, ample plains and mountain areas for windskiing.

Windskiing, or skisailing, in Australia is a natural. Since the popularization of the freestanding rig, windskiing has developed in two different directions. Performance sailors are using high-aspect-ratio rigs off their wavejumpers for speed and skill events, as was witnessed at the last windskiing regatta

in August. Alternatively, a more relaxing pastime is cross-country touring, which has literally taken on new dimensions. Ski tourers are now skisail tourers, using lightweight, foldaway masts and rigs to travel long distances, with the wind doing most of the work.

Boardsailing gear no longer has to be stored away for half the year—the same sail and rig can be used to tour on snow or ice in the wintertime. What is more, a "Ski Sailer" adaptor system attaches to the sailor in conventional alpine or nordic skis simply by strapping around the ski boots. No modifications to skis or rigs are required. With this sort of versatility and the low cost of the adaptors, families that boardsail in summer and ski-tour in winter can now combine the two what a great way to beat all those other guys trudging to make camp by dark!

It is possible to windski uphill, especially if snow conditions are good and the wind is from a favorable direction (i.e. not from the direction you want to travel—even a boat can't sail directly into the wind). In flat or gently undulating country, winds are relatively clear (compared to the mountain country), and if trees are not blocking the wind, rides comparable to those on a sailboard are possible.

Traversing large mountains under windpower is not only a lift to the body, but a lift to the spirit as well. Naturally, you're going to meet mountains that defy any angle of attack—either too steep or the winds aren't right—and it's at these times that releasable heels, mountaineering bindings and a set of "skins" come in handy.

The lock-down, releasable heel mountaineering bindings, with a strong steel-edged ski, allows the full power of the wind and the rig to be utilized. The ski has to handle side forces on it's edges caused by the side component of the wind in the sail, depending on how hard the sailor wants to pull, he controls the edge forces on the skis. These forces are not, however, any higher than normal alpine skiing, and the Ski Sailor adaptor, by attaching to the boots, carries the forces directly to the user—the wind forces are not carried through the thin and fragile top layers of the ski. These side-wind forces interacting with the body gravity forces of the sailor result in a vertical load at the ski center (i.e. under the ski boots) so that the overall system of sail and rig, sailor and skis can take the full advantage of the ski design, and balance perfectly at the ski and sail center.

Also, by attaching the adaptor to his boots, the skier is attached to his skis by the usual binding method; with the mast mounted on a slide-release fitting, quick and safe separation from the skis and rig is assured.

Unmodified downhill skis are ideal for high-performance ski sailing, and handle all snows and even ice (because weight shifting is easy). With mountaineering skis and a set of "skins", the impossible mountains become possible. By unclipping the heel release and fitting the skins, you can *climb* that mountain.

A conventional ski sailing rig can be packed up and carried on the back, but to make it really easy (especially in cold weather), the three-piece masts and light weight booms that are becoming available allow all the gear to fold into a neat, compact backpack for skiing back down through the trees.

For the more easygoing sailor, light weight nordic skis are well suited for sailing the snow, though for up-wind sailing, a steel-edged ski is recommended. However, when not sailing hard up on the wind, edge loads on skis with their good gliding ability, are a very comfortable way to travel. But remember, skiers on starboard tact have the right of way, and yes, you won't need a lift ticket, though you'd appreciate an occasional lift.

Source: *Windsurf Magazine*, December, 1984.

David believed that some strong promotional material should be developed to expedite the Skisailer's success. Although Mistral had invested $18,000 over a two-year period to develop the Skisailer, little money had been spent on publicity. In 1986, the 20-page Mistral Windsurf Catalogue made only a brief reference to the Skisailer in the upper corner of one page. In a meeting with Mistral's management, David told the marketing manager that the company should hire a professional to produce a good video film and take some quality pictures suitable for calendars, posters, and other promotional tools that would enhance awareness and sell the product. The cost of making a good video was estimated at $35,000, which the marketing manager felt was too high.

In March 1986, David decided to arrange for shooting a video on his own. Together with a photographer, David flew to Mammoth Lake in California to make the film and then spent the whole summer editing it. He also hired a mu-

sician to compose some background music. In September 1986, the video was refused at first, but it was later accepted after some minor modifications. Mistral also agreed to reimburse David Varilek the $10,000 that the video had cost him.

In October 1986, Mistral decided to manufacture 2,000 Skisailers to be sold at a retail price of $410, excluding the sail rig (average retail price about $590) and the skis (average retail price $415). Margins for the distributors and the retailers were estimated at $74 and $110, respectively.

On March 20, 1987, Mistral had sold only 708 units, a small fraction of what the company had targeted. Following these disappointing results, Mistral management decided to reconsider the Skisailer project. David Varilek knew there was a high possibility that "his" Skisailer would be dropped. Therefore, he decided to consult the IMEDE faculty, who had been involved in the early days of introducing his invention to ADIA and Mistral.

CASE 6

THE MISTRAL SKISAILER (B)

In April 1987, David Varilek presented the Skisailer promotion film to the M.B.A. participants and several faculty members at IMEDE, along with the information given in the (A) case. An analysis of the situation provided several suggestions for ways to market the product more professionally.

Further discussions with ADIA top management resulted in setting up an M.B.A. project to assess the viability of the Mistral Skisailer given the situation in October 1987. Based on the outcome, a strategy and implementation plan for either product re-introduction or inventory liquidation would then be developed. The (B) case summarizes additional information which was available in October 1987.

This case was prepared by Assistant Professor Dominique Turpin as a basis for class discussion rather than to illustrate either effective or ineffective handling of an administrative situation. Copyright ©1988 by IMEDE, Lausanne, Switzerland. IMD International, resulting from the merger between IMEDE, Lausanne, and IMI, Geneva, acquires and retains all rights. Reproduced by permission.

MISTRAL'S SKISAILER INVENTORIES AND HISTORICAL COSTS IN OCTOBER 1987

A visit to Mistral in Basserdorf, near Zurich (Switzerland), and various interviews with distributors of Mistral products determined that Mistral's total investment in the Skisailer had been as follows:

Development costs	
Engineering & tooling	$214,000
Other costs	74,000
	288,000
Inventory: assembled & spares	
At central warehouse	180,000
At distributors	68,000
	248,000
Total investment	$536,000

The following shows the distribution, sales, and inventory levels estimated by the distributors interviewed, which left Mistral with a high investment without return.

Country	To distributors	To retailers	To end users
U.S./Canada**	233	98	45*
Germany	250	50*	10*
Switzerland	42	30*	1
France**	56	40*	20*
Benelux**	60	0	0
Others	67	12*	4*
Total shipped	708	230*	80*

* Estimate.
** Owned by Mistral.

POTENTIAL MARKET

The consulting team found that 300,000 sail-boards and 5 million pairs of alpine skis had been sold worldwide in the past year. The team also identified a number of filters which had restricted the estimated realizable market for the Skisailer to a fraction of the potential market.

Filter 1: Customer Type

The innovator: 15–25 years old, sportive but without much money

The early adopter: 25 years old and above, sportive, image conscious and relatively wealthy

Another dimension (beginners, advanced, and experts) was also influencing buying behavior across the different segments (see Exhibit 1).

Filter 2: Location

Users of the Skisailer reported that skisailing required flat, ice- or snow-covered land which was also easily accessible.

Filter 3: Climate

Climate was an important restricting factor for skisailing. The Skisailer required suitable snow or ice, regular and frequent wind (>20km/h), and

EXHIBIT 1   END USERS' PROFILE OF THE SKISAILER

	Beginner	Advanced	Expert
Main experiences	+Interest created by deep powder/freestyle action	+"Entry"-board is not sufficient any more	+Faces different conditions: needs special boards for different purposes
	+Starts on slopes—with difficulties	+Surfs on slopes as well as off piste	+Uses the boards in extremes
Benefit sought	+Easy learning and handling	+Design and quality for the freak +Additional appearance and brand image for the show-off yuppy	+Design, quality, appearance
Price sensitivity	+High for the freak, who is short of money +Medium for the yuppy	+Medium for the freak, who somehow gets the money +Low for the yuppy	+Low

EXHIBIT 2   DATA ON WIND IN LOCATIONS IN OR NEAR THE ALPS

Total eight-hour periods in the years indicated, with average wind strength as shown on Beauford scale:

		0	1km/h	2	6–11	4	20–28
		1	1–5	3	12–19	5	29–38

Davos — Winter 1901–1980

Wind	Total	N	NE	E	SE	S	SW	W	NW
0	13457	577	5463	1840	1764	1336	2073	251	153
1	2282	35	1005	442	172	70	480	59	19
2	468	3	315	47	11	5	74	10	3
3	36	0	31	2	1	0	2	0	0
4	1	0	1	0	0	0	0	0	0
5	0	0	0	0	0	0	0	0	0

Lausanne — Winter 1931–1980

Wind	Total	N	NE	E	SE	S	SW	W	NW
0	2007	158	305	441	291	242	191	200	179
1	4527	260	1177	753	306	328	710	660	333
2	1344	25	629	40	11	1	185	405	48
3	222	1	106	0	0	1	40	71	3
4	21	0	12	0	0	0	2	7	0
5	3	0	3	0	0	0	0	0	0

Leysin — Winter 1931–1980

Wind	Total	N	NE	E	SE	S	SW	W	NW
0	5307	126	1058	21	30	26	1240	1762	1043
1	693	25	110	7	2	5	122	368	54
2	123	5	21	0	0	1	21	66	9
3	32	0	5	1	0	0	7	19	0
4	4	0	0	0	0	0	3	1	0

"mild" weather. (See Exhibit 2 for wind conditions in a selected number of locations in the Alps.)

Filter 4: Competing Products

Four competitive products were identified, but all lacked brand image, wide distribution, and product sophistication.

COMPETITIVE SKISAILING PRODUCTS

In Autumn 1987, the consulting team was able to gather some additional information on competitive skisailing products.

Australian-Made Ski Sailer

In Australia, a series of events had been sponsored by Sony (the Japanese electronics manu-

Product	Price	Sales quantity	Sales area
Winterboard	$395	4,000 Est.	Finland, U.S.
ArticSail	$285	3,000 Est.	Canada, U.S.
Ski Sailer (U.S.)	$220	300 Est.	U.S.
Ski Sailer (Australia)	$ 90	3,500 Est.	Australia, U.S.
Skisailer (Mistral)	$360	80 Est.	U.S., Canada, E.C.

facturer). An inventor symposium, with approximately 200 participants, had been organized for the Ski Sailer. Sony had invested about $2,000 in these promotions.

The U.S. distributor for this product reported sales of about 3,000 units (30% through ski shops, 70% surf shops) at a retail price of $90 each. He admitted that he lost interest in the product when he realized that only customers who were tough and resistant to the cold enjoyed sailing in the wintertime. This meant a much smaller customer base than for his usual surfing and leisure/sportswear products. One user of the Ski Sailer mentioned that sometimes the release mechanism had not worked properly, causing him to have a bad fall.

ArticSail Board

This product was essentially a W-shaped surfboard for use on snow, ice, or water. It was distributed by Plastiques L.P.A. Ltd. in Mansonville, Quebec, approximately 50 miles from the U.S.-Canadian border.

The Series 1000 board was 2.44 meters long and weighed 11 kilos. It was delivered with a towing eye, aluminum edges, rear filler plates and skegs, and adjustable footstraps. The 1000 model was designed for use on snow.

For ice conditions, the Series 2000 model was equipped with four pivoting skates incorporated into the structure of the board. The four pivoting skates were easy to install for icy conditions and could be removed for snow use.

The ArticSail was especially designed for snow and ice, but it could also be used on water. For summer operation, the rear filler plates would be replaced by tow ailerons, which were supplied with the board. Adjustable footstraps included with the board also had to be repositioned for use on water.

The product was made of special plastic, usable at both normal, above freezing, *and* very low temperatures; the ArticSail needed time to normalize with existing temperatures before full operation. The company warned users to watch

for objects which could damage the underside of the sled.

"We think it's a beautiful sport to do in the winter," said Pierre F. Arcouette, president of the company. The company reported total sales of approximately 3,000 (600 estimated for the 1987–88 winter), mostly sold in Canada at $285 each (including 38% retail shop margin). Promotion expenses were about 15% on Canadian and U.S. sales, mainly spent on a two-man team demonstrating at skisailing resorts.

Winterboard

The Winterboard, invented by Mr. Saami Tuurna from Finland, was a small surfboard with two built-in skis for snowsailing (see Mistral case A). In October 1987, Winterboard was running a business in the New England states in the United States. According to the president of the company, Mr. Robert Brotherus, Saami was the inventor, but he was the one who knew more about building a business.

To date, total sales had been approximately 4,000 units at a retail price of $395 each (winter 86–87). This price, which was expected to rise to $450 for the next season, included a normal 40% margin for the retailer. Sales through surf shops had been much more successful than those through ski shops, which had a different type of customer.

Mr. Brotherus had discovered that prices, margins, promotion, etc., were relatively unimportant. Key to the success was organizing *events*. People wanted sportive social gatherings on weekends in the winter. When they had to go out snowsailing in the cold by themselves, they quickly lost interest.

As in sailboarding, there were two types of consumer: the "image" customer, who bought the product, used it a few times, and then left it standing in the garage; and the "sportive" customer, who actively attended snowsailing events on winter weekends. There were about 200 active snowsailers in Finland and about 1,000 active snowsailers in the United States (see

Exhibit 3). Sales had doubled every year, and Robert hoped that 1987–88 would be a breakthrough season with sales of about 1,000 and enough momentum to get other people to organize events.

As president of the International Skisailing Association, Robert had been involved in organizing World Cup races in the United States (56 participants from six nations), in Munich (30 participants), and in Finland (100 participants). The event organizer in Sweden had stopped his activities, and as a result, local interest in the sport had dropped dramatically.

Although Robert did not like the unnatural position for handling the sail with the Mistral Skisailer, he had created a separate category for it, hoping to broaden the customer base for snow-sailing. As president of the Association, he was concerned about the sport's reputation and about safety when using alternative devices such as the Australian Ski Sailer.

Robert hoped that competitors (Mistral with its good image) would also engage in organizing events to stimulate snowsailing as a new sport.

Other Snow and Ice Sailing Products

The Windskier (see Mistral case A) had not reached sales levels that were high enough to justify the company's heavy marketing expenditures. Therefore, it had stopped activities and offered its inventories to Winterboard. Many other products, which had been described in a special

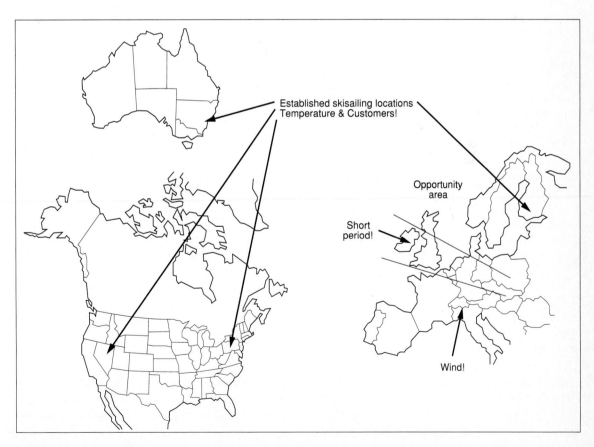

EXHIBIT 3

report on sailboards in 1984, were no longer being made or were still at the prototype testing or early market development phase in October 1987.

RECENT DEVELOPMENTS IN THE WORLD SKIING MARKET

As skisailers use not only a surfsail but also alpine skis, the project team obtained information on the ski market as well. This market was much more established and mature than the sailboarding market. (The 1985–86 season sales of alpine and cross country skis are given in Exhibit 4.)

The total world alpine skiing population was estimated at 30 million people in 1987.

Competition in the ski market was heavy, and production capacity exceeded demand by an estimated 25 to 30% in 1987. Prices for skis were under pressure, and so retail shops used good low-priced skis to get customers into the shop. Profits were mostly made on sales of accessories, skiwear, etc.

In distribution, specialty shops were losing market share to the large distribution chains. Production was concentrated, with seven manufacturers controlling 80% of the business. The falling

dollar tended to put the large European producers such as Fischer and Kneissel at a disadvantage in the U.S. market.

Marketing skis depended heavily on having success in world championships and the image associated with the winning skis. There was a good infrastructure in skiing designed to optimize the whole marketing spectrum from creating awareness, to interest, to rental and trial, and finally to buying the latest ski models and associated products. Around 1983, customers in the United States appeared to be losing interest in skiing to some extent, but these signs had not been observed in Europe and Japan, where the sport remained popular at a stable level.

SNOWBOARDS

The snowboard was a product which was rapidly increasing in popularity amongst younger customers. This was essentially a large ski with two ski bindings positioned in a similar way as the footstraps on a sailboard.

The board had been in existence in the United States for many years, being marketed by Burton, the largest supplier. The Burton board could be used in deep snow the way a sailboard was used on water.

Recently, the product had been introduced into Europe by two main suppliers, Burton and Sims. The product had been technically improved, allowing it to be used on icy ski slopes as well as in deep snow.

It was estimated that about 40,000 boards were sold worldwide, with Burton accounting for 50% of this amount. Sales volumes had doubled every year, starting at a low level and then eventually reaching the estimated 40,000 in the 1986–1987 season.

Many manufacturers of winter products had taken advantage of the opportunity and started producing their own versions of the snowboard. The product was very popular in the European distribution channels, and expectations for growth were high. Whether the snowboard was

EXHIBIT 4   WORLD MARKET OF ALPINE AND CROSS COUNTRY SKIING DURING THE 1985–86 SEASON

Alpine ski sales	Pairs sold/year
Austria, Switzerland, Germany	1,450,000
Rest of Europe	1,550,000
U.S. and Canada	1,600,000
Japan	1,100,000
Other countries	300,000

Cross country ski sales	
Austria, Switzerland, Germany	700,000
Scandinavia	800,000
Rest of Europe	400,000
U.S. and Canada	750,000
Other countries	150,000

only a fad was still not known, but the peak in sales had certainly not yet been reached.

END USERS' OPINONS OF THE SKISAILER

The following comments from end users on advantages, disadvantages, and price offer some explanation for the Skisailer's low level of sales.

Advantages of the Product

"Sure, skisurfing in winter is great; it's a lot of fun."

"You can do quick maneuvers, nice turns, beautiful power turns, and fast changes of the grips. It (the Skisailer) gives a good opportunity to train for windsurfing as you have to drive the way you surf—with the pressure on the inner ski."

"I did not have any problem with turns."

"It is not too difficult to learn if you have some feeling for sailing."

"It simulates surfing in your backyard."

"It is the right device if you want to do something on Sunday afternoon (with no time to drive somewhere in your car)."

"Fun, different, new, good."

"It is the only thing with a mountain touch that you can use on the plain."

"It turns. That makes it much more fun than the other products on the market. You can do jives, curve jives, jumps.... It is close to sailing a shore boat.... It is a lot of fun."

"If the conditions are ideal, it's a lot of fun."

Disadvantages of the Product

"The feet get twisted; sailing on the wind requires exceptional twisting of the legs and knees."

"Both of the white caps at the end of the bar sprung, and it was virtually impossible to get spare parts."

"Difficult in heavy snow."

"Difficult to find the perfect conditions."

"You use it three or four times a season. For this, the price is too high."

"It is uncomfortable to use. You have to loosen up your boots, otherwise the rim of the shoe cuts into your twisted leg."

"If the snow is too deep, you cannot use it. What you want is *foehn*."

"For an alternative, the price is too high."

"My problem is that there is hardly any wind in winter."

"In the beginning, I was getting stiff in the unnatural position and my knees hurt, but later I got more relaxed... and with trapeze you have a lot of fun."

"In the high winter, it is too cold to use it; spring is ideal."

RETAILERS' OPINIONS OF THE MISTRAL SKISAILER

Advantages of the Product

"You could sell a lot of them in the first year, but I do not see it as the absolute 'barnstormer.'"

"It is a first year novelty."

"It is a lot of fun in the snow... and for people with a lot of money. It is a new gimmick."

"It combines two favorite sports... skiing and windsurfing."

"It is better than all self-built products... You have full movability."

"Easy to use. It is an original idea."

"You can use your ski, it is flexible and easy to store."

"Very thoroughly constructed, very stable."

Disadvantages of the Product

"Unhappy product. Usable only under specific environmental conditions."

"It is only a fad."

"You just don't drive with your ski to a lake and try it on the ice."

"Maybe it sells better in a winter shop."

"Your position on the skis is abnormal; the snowboard is a better alternative."

"We do not think that it will be *the* fast turning product."

"Impossible to sell; nobody tried it."

"In my environment, there is no space to do it, no lakes, no fields. Maybe we could use artificial lakes."

Retailers' Comments on Price

"For a backyard product, the price is too high. Even Mistral's good image doesn't help. Maybe this will change if the product is better known."

"Customers watched the video with enthusiasm, but when they learned the price, enthusiasm was nil. We are offering our last piece now at a discount of 40%."

"If you ski *and* windsurf, your hobbies cost you a lot of money. Often the early user is the sportive freak with low income. How will you convince him about the product?"

"We got only one piece. It was too risky and too expensive to rent it out. We needed it for promotion and advertising."

"As a result of promotion with Bild and the NDR (local German TV station), some people asked for the product. But the price was definitely too high. . . . Otherwise more people would have asked."

"The missing mastfoot increases the price of the product even more . . . or do they want to sell only to owners of Mistral rigs?"

"For an accessory—too expensive!"

DISTRIBUTORS' COMMENTS ON THE MISTRAL SKISAILER IN VARIOUS COUNTRIES

Distributor for Sweden

"We first learned about the Skisailer at ISPO in Munich and ordered some Skisailers."

"From Mistral we got some folders and the video. If you see it on the video, you want to use the Skisailer right away."

"We did not support the retailers very much because we felt that the Skisailer's marketing was not done professionally from the beginning. For instance, Skisailer deliveries were late."

"The product would have potential if the price were lowered and the promotion were done professionally all the way through."

Distributor in Finland

"We bought the Skisailer, which is good for use in our winter climate, after Mistral contacted us in 1985."

"The product is expensive and not really functional. Our distributors and customers want a surfboard or ski that can be used as a surfboard."

"Promotion was not good enough at all, only a few folders and a video which were not free of charge. When there were product breakdowns, spare parts were not available."

"A Finnish competitor now has captured the market with a product that looks like a surfboard with two skis fitted into it. We have the right places for skisailing here!"

Distributor in the Benelux

"We used all our contacts and spent approximately $7,500 in mid-1987 to promote this product on television."

"The retail price of $345 is too high for a product to be used only a few weekends in the winter."

"The snowboard, especially made for surfing on ski slopes, is much more fashionable."

"Surf and ski shops make higher margins on clothing and accessories that are sold in larger quantities."

"You don't create a product first and then look for the market. This is the wrong way around. The Skisailer is more a product for Scandinavia and similar regions in America or Canada."

Distributor in France

"We know the product and its inventor from the early days and found the demonstration film to be convincing. Therefore we organized ski resort demonstrations in the French Alps at snow-dog racing events where there are many spectators. We also pushed about 40 Skisailers in several retail shops."

"After the first sales, we discovered that lack of wind is a problem in the ski resorts. You really need at least a moderate wind of

Beauford 3 (12 to 19 km/h) and a moderate to strong wind of Beauford 4+ for going uphill or skisailing in deep snow. Also, the retail price of $360 (ex-factory $160, wholesale $250) is quite high for a product that you cannot use very often."

"For this product, finding suitable locations where you can have a training session with wind and snow is necessary."

"We estimate that the retailers have sold about half their inventory, but we do not want to get more involved and have the rest sent back to us. Retailers are looking for customer demand and this is lacking."

Distributor in Canada

"I cannot see further sales of the Skisailer without more product support. At low temperatures the rubber joints failed, but when we asked for replacements, there was no reply from Mistral. In the end we had to strip other Skisailers to get the spare parts."

"We have good skisailing conditions (in South Ontario and Quebec) and a group of interested enthusiasts here. The product has been proposed to thousands of people! The folder and video are very good."

"On a trade show in Toronto, the product was well received except for the price, which is a problem."

MISTRAL BENELUX'S PROMOTION OF THE SKISAILER

There was a positive initial response to the Skisailer idea from Mistral's distributor for the Netherlands, Belgium, and Luxembourg. Sixty Skisailers and some pamphlets were shipped to Mistral in Wierden in the Netherlands shortly after ISPO '85.

Through good personal contacts, it was arranged that a free Skisailer be offered to a key journalist for a story on the product in the largest Dutch newspaper, *De Telegraaf*.

In mid-1987, a 10-minute TV spot in a program on inventors was organized in cooperation with a popular TV company called "Veronica" at a total cost to Mistral Benelux of approximately $7,500. Most of this money was spent on a trip to the Alps to shoot pictures of the Skisailer in action. On arriving in various resorts in Austria and Switzerland, there was no wind. Luckily, a place with the snow *and wind* conditions needed to shoot the scene successfully was finally found in Italy. The team had to go to the Alps because there was not sufficient snow or ice in the Benelux early that winter.*

Ten Skisailers were provided to Mr. Nederpelt, a 50-year-old skisailing enthusiast who had many contacts in the ice and snow sailing community for organizing demonstrations.

In addition, the Skisailer was shown at the two main trade shows and published in the usual trade journals. In Mistral's experience, these trade shows and publications were usually an adequate way to create demand for new products. The only steps not taken to promote the Skisailer were direct mailing and direct sales to retail shops and rental facilities.

The results of all these efforts by Mistral were disappointing: no sales to retailers whatsoever and a write-off of Skisailer inventories in the Benelux.

RECENT DEVELOPMENTS AT MISTRAL HEADQUARTERS

The turnover in Mistral's management had been high. In October 1987, few of the initial managers, who had tended to come up through the ranks of windsurfing enthusiasts, were still at Mistral. Meanwhile competition in the sailboarding market was severe, and Mistral was also involved in legal actions with its competitors on patent rights.

---

*Snow and ice usually lasted only a few weeks in the Benelux (between late December and mid-February), with light to moderate N or E winds from the European–Scandinavian continent. Western sea winds usually kept winter temperatures above freezing. Under freezing conditions, millions of people in the Netherlands would use the canals and lakes for skating.

In September 1987, the marketing manager and former president of Mistral, who had been involved with the Skisailer's introduction, left the company. The new president, Alex Schuster, had become co-manager of Mistral in April 1987. The successful marketing of Mistral products in North America since 1982 under his management had made him well qualified for his new position. In addition to being responsible for sportswear, he had also assumed control of the hard goods operation in September 1987.

Prior to joining Mistral, he had founded Head Sportswear in the United States. Later, under AMF ownership of Head, he had become Deputy Group Executive for companies like Head Ski, Head Tennis, and Ben Hogan Golf. The complexity of Mistral's structure would be substantially simplified through organizational changes: the physical relocation of the administrative functions and the warehousing from Switzerland to Germany.

These reorganizations were undertaken in close cooperation with ADIA and Mistral "to assure Mistral's dominance in the sailboard market and to set the stage for future business development."

The low sales levels for the Skisailer were clearly only one of a wide spectrum of problems faced by Mistral's management in the autumn of 1987. In October 1987, three days before the M.B.A. project team presented the results of the product viability study to ADIA management, stock prices had collapsed in the world stock market on "black Monday." As a result, the value of the stocks of Mistral/ADIA in their own companies dropped significantly.

FOOD LION, INC.

In 1957 three former Winn-Dixie employees opened their first supermarket in Salisbury, North Carolina, under the name Food Town. Cofounders Ralph Ketner, Brown Ketner, and Wilson Smith all had considerable retail experience in the grocery industry; however, Food Town struggled in its early years. Various marketing gimmicks were implemented (the company gave away trading stamps and even free automobiles), but the stores failed to win the loyalty of customers. In fact, Ralph Ketner had to close 9 of the 16 stores during the first 10 years of operation. He blamed much of this failure on the underpricing techniques of Winn-Dixie. By 1966, only seven Food Town stores remained.

In response to the problem, Ketner decided to slash prices on all items sold in the stores. He realized that a drastic increase in volume would be necessary to make this approach work and keep the company afloat. The company theme of LFPINC or "Lowest Food Prices in North Carolina" became popular as both customers and sales increased greatly. Sales rose 54 percent to $8.9 million, and profits rose 165 percent to $95,000 in the first year under the new pricing strategy.[1]

In 1970 the company went public. Etablissements Delhaize Freres et Cie, a Belgium grocery chain, purchased 47.6 percent of the stock in 1974. Today, Delhaize controls 50.6 percent of the voting stock and has 5 of the 10 seats on the board of directors.[2] The company changed its name to Food Lion in 1983 to avoid confusion with another similarly named chain. Also, the company began implementing its expansion program.

Today, Food Lion operates in eight states, from Delaware to Florida, and is considered to be one of the fastest growing retail grocers in the country. (See Exhibit 1.) Food Lion President and CEO Tom E. Smith explains, "Our goal is to bring extra low grocery prices to as many people in the Southeast as possible."[3]

Food Lion has 27,000 employees, and continues to operate conventional size stores (21,000 to 29,000 square feet) and to offer discount prices. The company remains committed to expansion throughout the Southeast and has avoided moving into the sales of general merchandise in its stores. A food consultant's comments highlight the company's success in the aforementioned areas. He states that Food Lion is "probably the best example of commitment to a format and

Prepared by Janet L. Caswell under the direction of Professor Neil H. Snyder, both of the University of Virginia. ©1988 by Neil H. Snyder.
[1] Richard Anderson, "That Roar You Hear Is Food Lion," *Business Week*, August 24, 1987, p. 66.

[2] Ibid.
[3] *1987 Food Lion, Inc. Annual Report*, p. 1.

EXHIBIT 1   STORE DISTRIBUTION

Location	Stores	Percent of total
North Carolina	233	49.1%
Virginia	112	23.5
South Carolina	74	15.6
Tennessee	29	6.1
Georgia	19	4.0
Florida	6	1.3
Delaware	1	0.2
Maryland	1	0.2
Total	475	100.0%

Source: Standard & Poor's Stock Report, p. 3905.

operating style in the industry today. And although it is a conventional store operator, it also stands as an excellent practitioner of niche marketing. The stores aren't fancy, but beat everyone on price, and the company doesn't make many mistakes."[4]

Ralph Ketner

Since cofounding Food Lion, Ralph Ketner has continued to be a force behind its success. In 1968 it was his idea to adopt the strategy of discount pricing and his LFPINC theme which promoted the company. He acted as chief executive officer until 1986, when he passed the reins to President Tom Smith. Despite giving up his CEO title, Ketner still exerts considerable influence over the operation of Food Lion. He remains chairman of the board of directors, and plans to retain this position until 1991. In addition, Delhaize signed an agreement in 1974 to vote with Ketner for 10 years. This agreement was later extended and was in effect until 1989.[5]

[4]Richard DeSanta, "Formats: Growing Apart, Coming Together," Progressive Grocer, January 1987, p. 37.
[5]"Ketner Gives Up Food Lion Reins," Supermarket News, January 6, 1986, p. 18.

Tom E. Smith

President and CEO Tom E. Smith is very much responsible for Food Lion's growth and success. This is largely attributed to his involvement with the company since his youth. At age 17, Smith began as a bag boy at Food Lion's first store. He attended night school at Catawba College and graduated in 1964 with a degree in business administration. He spent the next six years working for Del Monte, when he was hired as Food Lion's sole buyer. Smith developed the successful strategy of stocking fewer brands and sizes than his competitors. He also took advantage of wholesaler specials by purchasing large volumes at discount prices. He was named vice president for distribution in 1974, and later became executive vice president in 1977. His continued success in these areas led to his promotion to president in 1981, at the age of 39. In 1986 he was named CEO.

Smith views himself as a planner who carefully molds the company's growth while keeping a close eye on the operations. This style has enabled him to react to and resolve any problems quickly and effectively. He has been a primary reason for Food Lion's constant commitment to its overall strategy of discount pricing and cost reduction. Smith has also become well-known through his participation in over 50 percent of the Food Lion commercials. This media exposure has brought him recognition not only in the Southeast but as far away as San Francisco and even Scotland.[6] These commercials portray Smith as a hard-working and very trustworthy manager.

FOOD LION'S ATTITUDE TOWARD SOCIAL RESPONSIBILITY

Food Lion is recognized as a corporate neighbor, and it takes pride in performing charitable acts. In 1986 the company received the Martin Luther King, Jr., Award in recognition of its hu-

[6]Anderson, "That Roar You Hear Is Food Lion," p. 65.

EXHIBIT 2   PERCENTAGE OF U.S. RETAIL SALES BY TYPE OF ESTABLISHMENT

Type of establishment	1983	1984	1985	1986	1987*
Food stores	22.0%	21.1%	20.6%	20.4%	20.3%
Eating and drinking	9.9	9.6	9.7	10.0	10.1
Drug and proprietary	3.5	3.4	3.4	3.4	3.6
General merchandise	11.1	11.0	10.9	10.7	11.0
Furniture and appliance	4.6	4.8	5.0	5.4	5.5
Auto dealers	19.8	21.6	22.6	22.9	22.2
Hardware and lumber	4.4	4.7	4.8	5.2	4.7
Clothing	5.3	5.3	5.4	5.5	5.8
Gas stations	8.5	7.8	7.3	6.1	5.7
All others	10.9	10.7	10.4	10.4	11.2

* First six months.
Source: Bureau of the Census (Revised) 1987.

manitarian efforts. Food Lion received the award for its role in donating trucks to aid southeastern farmers during a prolonged drought; the trucks enabled the farmers to transport hay from Indiana. Also, the company was cited for providing equal opportunity employment and establishing express lanes for handicapped customers.[7]

THE SUPERMARKET INDUSTRY

Several trends in the supermarket industry were of concern to many retail grocers. During 1987 there was a decline in the percentage of disposable income spent for food at home. After discounting inflation, real sales did not increase from 1986. As Exhibit 2 shows, food-at-home spending accounted for more retail sales than any other category in 1983. However, slow growth has caused a reduction in this percentage, leaving food stores in second place behind auto dealers. The percentage of retail sales for eating and drinking establishments during this same period has trended upward.

The grocery industry is also experiencing competition from other types of stores. Discount de-

partment and drug stores are starting to sell more packaged foods. Many fast-food restaurants continue to sell a larger variety of prepared foods for takeout. Sales from specialty shops, which concentrate on one particular type of food, have increased as well. Wholesale clubs have also been of concern to retail grocers. These clubs have been effective at luring many customers away from conventional supermarkets. Those supermarkets stressing discount prices have been hurt most by the emergence of the wholesale clubs.

In response to the trends, most grocery chains are stressing the idea of one-stop shopping. New store formats and product offerings are abundant. These ideas are an attempt to obtain a product mix that stresses higher margin items and services, as well as create an atmosphere causing consumers to view the supermarket as more than a place to buy groceries. Items such as flowers, greeting cards, videocassettes, and pharmacy items are appearing more frequently in many supermarkets. There has also been a greater emphasis on stocking perishables.

However, the biggest trend in the industry is the shift to bigger stores. Several experts believe that increased size is necessary to provide the variety that many consumers desire. One chain president expressed this sentiment: "Customer

[7] *1986 Food Lion, Inc. Annual Report,* p. 4.

EXHIBIT 3   CHAIN EXECUTIVES' OPINIONS ON PROSPECTS FOR NEW FORMATS

	Percent		
	Excellent	Good	Fair/Poor
Superstores	56%	36%	8%
Combination	38	53	9
Convenience stores	26	39	35
Super warehouse	22	39	39
Hypermarkets	10	33	57
Specialty	8	37	55
Wholesale clubs	6	30	62
Conventional	4	35	59
Warehouse stores	1	17	79

Source: Progressive Grocer, April 1988.

satisfaction starts with the store design: one-stop shopping, complete service departments, and integrating a drugstore and pharmacy into the store."[8] Much of the one-stop shopping trend is a result of increases in the numbers of working women, dual-income families, single parents, and singles living alone. Time and convenience are two characteristics that consumers fitting into these groups often desire.

The one-stop shopping concept has resulted in several new store formats. Combination stores offer consumers a variety of nonfood items. These stores can be as large as 35,000 square feet, and 25 percent of the space is devoted to nonfood and pharmacy items. Superstores are similar to the combination stores in that they offer a wide selection of general merchandise items. These stores are all greater than 40,000 square feet, and are thought to be the strongest format for the near future. Exhibit 3 shows chain executives' views on the prospects for the various formats that exist today.

The newest and largest of the formats is the hypermarket. Currently, 55 of these stores exist in the United States. The typical hypermarket ranges in size from 125,000 to 330,000 square feet and requires $25 to $50 million in sales per year just to break even.[9] Normally, 40 percent of the floor space in hypermarkets is devoted to grocery items and the remaining 60 percent is used for general merchandise. Freeway access, population density, and visibility are all key variables contributing to a hypermarket's success. A majority of the stores are run by companies which are not U.S. food retailers. For example, Wal-Mart has opened several stores under the Hypermarket USA name. Also, Bruno's, a retail grocery chain, is teaming up with K mart to build a store in Atlanta.[10]

Because of the trend to expand store size, the number of stores declined for the first time in years. However, the larger store sizes resulted in an increase in actual square footage. Many small units have been closed due to the openings of larger stores. In many market areas, there continue to be too many stores and too few customers to support them. This is going to be an even bigger concern given the advent of the combination stores and hypermarkets, since they tend to attract customers from a wider area than the conventional stores.

[8]"Retail Operations: The New Basics," *Progressive Grocer*, September 1987, p. 56.

[9]David Rogers, "Hypermarkets Need Something Special to Succeed," *Supermarket Business*, May 1988, p. 26.
[10]Ibid.

EXHIBIT 4   STORE ATTRIBUTES DESIRED BY CONSUMERS

Rank	Characteristic
1	Cleanliness
2	All prices labeled
3	Low prices
4	Good produce department
5	Accurate, pleasant clerks
6	Freshness date marked on products
7	Good meat department
8	Shelves kept well stocked
9	Short wait for checkout
10	Convenient store location

Source: *Progressive Grocer*, April 1988.

Although the majority of retailers believe that the bigger stores are necessary to be successful in the future, there is a large group that believes the industry is going overboard in its attempt to provide one-stop shopping. Chain executive Carole Bitter believes that the emphasis on size is unfounded. "There has been an ego problem in the industry that has led to overbuilding and has driven up store sizes and has increased the number of formats."[11] Proponents of conventionals claim that the larger stores are too impersonal to be attractive to everyone. They also believe that many consumers desire the conventional type of store, and that this format will continue to be successful. Although many consumers claim that they want more service departments, studies have shown that the shoppers are not willing to pay enough for such departments to make them profitable. Exhibit 4 reveals what the average shopper desires. One-stop shopping capabilities rates only 26th on the list.

COMPETITION

In recent years, competition in the Southeast has become quite intense. Previously, this area was characterized by predominantly conventional stores. Combination and superstores were scarce. However, many retailers realized that the Southeast was a prime location for the newer formats. In 1984 Cub Foods opened three large, modern stores in the Atlanta area in an attempt to challenge Kroger's dominance in the Southeast. This move marked the beginning of several competitive shakeups in the South.

Kroger

Kroger operates 1,317 supermarkets and 889 convenience stores in the South and Midwest. In 1987 sales were nearly $18 billion. More than 95 percent of the floor space is either new or has been remodeled during the past 10 years.[12] This is a result of the chain's move to larger combination and superstore formats. Kroger has not been as successful as it would like. The company realizes a net profit margin of approximately 1 percent. This is partly due to its new outlets cannibalizing its existing stores and has caused same-store sales comparisons to be relatively flat.[13]

In response to the disappointing profit margins, Kroger is planning to decrease its capital spending plans by about $300 million. It is hoped that this will reduce interest costs as well as keep start-up expenses down. Also, the firm is cutting corporate overhead 20 percent. As for future store designs, Kroger is considering the curtailment of the new super-warehouse stores. These stores combine low grocery prices with high-priced service departments and have not appealed to a large segment of the market. Furthermore, the company is planning to reduce store remodeling in mature market areas.[14]

Winn-Dixie

Winn-Dixie is the fourth largest food retailer in the country with sales of nearly $9 billion. The chain operates 1,271 stores in the Sunbelt area, with the heaviest concentration of stores located

[11] "Retail Operations: The New Basics." p. 62.

[12] *Standard & Poor's Standard Stock Reports*, p. 1318.
[13] *Value Line Investment Survey*, 1987, p. 1511.
[14] Ibid.

in Florida, North Carolina, and Georgia. During the past few years, Winn-Dixie has been hurt by the influx of competition in the Southeast. As a result, profit margins have dipped to just over 1 percent. Net income also declined in 1987. Management points to a lack of investment in new stores and a rather slow response to competitors' underpricing methods as the main reasons for the decline in profits.[15]

Management has adopted several new strategies to combat the competition. Foremost is the move to larger store formats. In the past, the chain operated mostly conventional stores and depended on operating efficiencies to realize sizable profits. However, management believes that it is now necessary to alter the stores in response to changing consumer needs. At the end of 1987, the average supermarket was 27,700 square feet. There are approximately 250 new stores in the 35,000 to 45,000-square-feet range, and they are expected to account for nearly half of all sales in the next five years.[16] The units in the 35,000 square-feet category are combination stores operated under the Winn-Dixie name. The 45,000 square-feet stores employ the superstore format and use the name Marketplace. Emphasis is being placed on service departments as well as price sensitivity.

Other changes involve management. Last year, the company eliminated a layer of management that resulted in 60 layoffs. The firm is also adopting a decentralized strategy which divides the company into 12 operating units. Each division is allowed to develop its own procedures and image. It is hoped that this will help the stores cater to the consumers in each market area more effectively.

Lucky Stores

Lucky operates nearly 500 supermarkets throughout the country. The majority of these are located in California; however, the chain does operate 90 stores in Florida. In 1986 Lucky began a major restructuring. This resulted in the sale of all the nonfood businesses. Also, the company has concentrated on increasing the store size to enable the sale of more service and nonfood items. The average size of the stores at the end of 1986 was 31,000 square feet.[17]

At the end of the year, there was much speculation that American Stores Company would begin to pursue an unsolicited tender offer for all outstanding shares of Lucky common stock. American is a leading retailer in the country and operates mostly combination food and drug stores.

Bruno's

Bruno's operates approximately 100 supermarkets and combination food and drug stores in the Southeast. This chain pursues a strategy of high-volume sales at low prices. Another strategy involves the use of four different formats under various names. Consumer Warehouse Foods stores are relatively small warehouse stores which emphasize lower prices and reduced operating costs. Food World stores are large supermarkets which offer a variety of supermarket items at low prices. Bruno's Food and Pharmacy stores promote the idea of one-stop shopping through the combination store format. Finally, FoodMax stores are superwarehouses which offer generic and bulk foods in addition to the national labels.[18]

The company is also well-known for its innovative forward buying program. Bruno's is able to purchase goods at low prices because of its 900,000-square-feet distribution center which houses excess inventory. This strategy has been very successful as the company boasts high operating and net profit margins.[19] Exhibit 5 presents comparative statistics for Food Lion and its four major competitors.

[15] *Standard & Poor's*, p. 2491.
[16] "Winn-Dixie Strategy," *Supermarket News*, March 3, 1987, p. 12.

[17] *Standard & Poor's*, p. 1387.
[18] Ibid, p. 3358M.
[19] John Liscio, "Beefing Up Profits," *Barron's*, May 25, 1987, p. 18.

EXHIBIT 5 SELECTED STATISTICS FOR MAJOR SOUTHEASTERN SUPERMARKET CHAINS, 1987

	Kroger	Lucky	Winn-Dixie	Bruno's	Food Lion
Stores	2,206	481	1,271	111	475
Employees	170,000	44,000	80,000	10,655	27,033
Sales ($ million)	$17,660	$6,925	$8,804	$1,143	$2,954
Sales/employee	103,881	157,386	110,049	107,265	109,267
Net profit ($ million)	$246.6	$151	$105.4	$31	$85.8
Net profit margin	1.4%	2.2%	1.2%	2.7%	2.9%
Gross margin	22.4	25	22	20.8	19.2
Current ratio	1.1	.83	1.65	1.63	1.41
Return on equity	24.5	46.3	15.2	15.4	25.3
Return on assets	5.5	11.8	7.9	10.3	10.6
Long-term debt/equity	.69	.38	.03	.04	.26
Earnings per share	$3.14	$3.92	$2.72	$.79	$.27
Average price/earnings ratio	15.1	10.2	13.9	23.1	35.3

Source: Standard and Poor's.

EXPANSION AT FOOD LION

Food Lion has continued to grow and expand in the Southeast. During 1987 the chain opened 95 new stores while closing only 8, bringing the total to 475. With the exception of four supermarkets, Food Lion operates its stores under various leasing arrangements. The number of stores has grown at a 10-year compound rate of 24.1 percent.[20] With this expansion has come a 29.7 percent compound growth rate in sales and a 30.9 percent compound growth rate in earnings (see Exhibit 6).[21]

The existence and further development of distribution centers serve as the core for continued expansion. At the end of 1987, four such centers had been completed. These are located in Salisbury and Dunn, North Carolina; Orangeburg County, South Carolina; and Prince George County, Virginia. Two additional centers are planned for Tennessee and Jacksonville, Florida. These distribution centers enable Food Lion to pursue expansion using its "ink blot" formula. Using this strategy, new stores are added

to an existing market area in order to saturate the market. "If anyone wants to go to a competitor, they'll have to drive by one of our stores," explains CFO Brian Woolf.[22] Despite the emergence of new stores, cannibalization has not been a problem. In fact, same-store sales increase

EXHIBIT 6 FOOD LION'S GROWTH AND EXPANSION
(In Thousands)

Year	Stores	Sales	Net income
1987	475	$2,953,807	$85,802
1986	388	2,406,582	61,823
1985	317	1,865,632	47,585
1984	251	1,469,564	37,305
1983	226	1,172,459	27,718
1982	182	947,074	21,855
1981	141	666,848	19,317
1980	106	543,883	15,287
1979	85	415,974	13,171
1978	69	299,267	9,481

Source: Food Lion annual reports.

[20] *1987 Food Lion, Inc. Annual Report*, p. 9.
[21] Ibid.

[22] Liscio, "Beefing Up Profits," p. 19.

approximately 8 percent annually. When Food Lion enters a new area, the strategy of underpricing the competitors is employed. Such a strategy has caused average food prices to decline 10 to 20 percent in some parts of the country.[23] Every new store is constructed no further than 200 miles from a distribution center. With continued expansion, new distribution centers whose radiuses overlap an existing distribution territory are erected to keep warehouse and transportation costs down.

Moreover, Food Lion continues to employ a cookie-cutter approach to its new stores. Rather than purchase existing stores, the firm much prefers to build new ones from scratch. All the stores fall into the conventional store category. The majority are 25,000 square feet and cost only $650,000 to complete. These stores emphasize the fruit and vegetable departments. Approximately 40 percent of the new stores are 29,000 square feet and contain a bakery/delicatessen. These are placed after careful consideration is given to the demographics and psychographics of the area. Normally, new stores turn a profit within the first six months of operation. In comparison, most competitors construct slightly larger stores which cost over $1 million to complete.[24]

The standard size of the stores has allowed the company to keep costs down while sticking to basics. Aside from the bakery departments, Food Lion has stayed away from service departments such as seafood counters and flower shops. Such departments are often costly due to the increase in required labor. Also, Food Lion has remained a retail grocery chain, shunning the idea of moving into the general merchandise area.

With the steady increase in stores over the past 10 years comes an increase in the need for quality employees. In an interview last March, Smith expressed concern over the high dropout rate of high school students.[25] Food Lion relies heavily on recent graduates, and the current trend may signal a decline in the quality of the average worker. Food Lion has responded to the labor problem by setting up an extensive training program for its 27,000 employees. These programs range from in-store training at the operational level to comprehensive training programs for potential managers. In addition, the firm continues to offer programs at headquarters to upgrade the work of the upper staff. Management is also attempting to increase the use of computers within the company. More specifically, Smith is hoping to utilize computer systems to handle much of the financial reporting aspects in the individual stores in an attempt to lessen the need for more employees.

ADVERTISING

Rather than employ costly advertising gimmicks, such as double coupon offers, Food Lion's advertising strategy combines cost-saving techniques with an awareness of consumer sentiment. Smith is the company's main spokesman, appearing in over half of the television commercials. Not only has this method kept advertising expenses down, but it has also made the public aware of both Smith and his discount pricing policy. By producing most of the ads in-house and using only a few paid actors, the cost of an average TV spot is only $6,000. Also, the company policy of keeping newspaper ads relatively small results in annual savings of $8 million. Food Lion's advertising costs are a mere 0.5 percent of sales, one fourth of the industry average.[26]

The content of the ads is another reason for Food Lion's success. Many of the TV spots feature some of the cost-cutting techniques used by the firm. One often-mentioned theme at the end of ads is "When we save, you save." Another commonly used theme states, "Food Lion is coming to town and food prices will be coming down." Before moving into the Jacksonville, Florida, area, Food Lion launched a nine-month

[23]"Food Lion's Roar Changes Marketplace," *Tampa Tribune*, April 5, 1988, p. 1.
[24]Anderson, "That Roar You Hear Is Food Lion," p. 65.
[25]"Food Lion, Inc.," *The Wall Street Transcript*, March 28, 1988, p. 88–90.
[26]Anderson, "That Roar You Hear Is Food Lion." p. 65.

advertising campaign. Many of these ads focused on innovative management methods which permit lower prices to be offered in the stores. For example, one ad demonstrates how a central computer is used to help control freezer temperatures. Other ads attempt to characterize Food Lion as a responsible community member. One such spot describes the importance that management places on preventive maintenance for its forklifts and tractor trailers.

Smith has also used the media to react to potential problems. For instance, Winn-Dixie launched an advertising attack against Food Lion reminding customers how competitors have come and gone. The company countered with an ad featuring Tom Smith in his office reassuring consumers. "Winn-Dixie would have you believe that Food Lion's low prices are going to crumble and blow away. Let me assure you that as long as you keep shopping at Food Lion, our lower prices are going to stay right where they belong—in Jacksonville."[27] Smith also reacted quickly to a possible conflict in eastern Tennessee in 1984. Several rumors circulated which linked the Food Lion logo to Satanic worship. In response, Smith hired Grand Ole Opry star Minnie Pearl to appear in the Tennessee advertisements until the stories disappeared.[28]

INNOVATIONS

The grocery industry is characterized by razor-thin margins. While most retail grocery chains have failed to introduce new innovations in the industry, Food Lion has employed several techniques which enable the firm to offer greater discounts on nearly all its products. These innovations help Food Lion to realize a profit margin of nearly 2.9 percent, twice the industry average. The company's credo is doing "1,000 things 1 percent better."[29] Such a philosophy has re-

sulted in keeping expenses at 14 percent of sales as compared with the industry average of 20 percent.

Examples of the company's cost-cutting ideas are abundant. Rather than purchase expensive plastic bins to store cosmetics, Food Lion recycles old banana crates. These banana boxes are also used for storing groceries in warehouses. These innovations save the company approximately $200,000 a year.[30] Furthermore, the firm utilizes waste heat from the refrigerator units to warm part of the stores. Also, motion sensors automatically turn off lights in unoccupied rooms. Costs are further reduced by Food Lion's practice of repairing old grocery carts rather than purchasing newer, more expensive models. Perhaps the greatest savings can be attributed to the carefully planned distribution system. This system allows management to take advantage of wholesalers' specials. The centralized buyout-and-distribution technique allows products for all stores to be purchased at one volume price.

Moreover, labor costs remain lower than those of many competitors. Smith is vehemently opposed to the use of unionized labor. Despite protests from the United Food and Commercial Workers International Union claiming that Food Lion's wages are well below union standards, management has continued to please its workers and avoid unionization. In fact, Smith believes its employee-benefit package is unequaled in the industry. A profit-sharing plan linking an employee's efforts in making Food Lion profitable with wealth accumulation for the future is already in use. Plans to improve long-term disability insurance benefits are under way.[31] In contrast, several other chains have experienced problems solving labor union problems. For example, a month-long strike by Kroger's Denver-area employees resulted in concessions on wages, ben-

[27] "Food Lion, Winn-Dixie in Animated Squabble," *Supermarket News*, September 14, 1987, p. 9.
[28] Anderson, "That Roar You Hear Is Food Lion," p. 66.
[29] Ibid., p. 65.
[30] "Ad Series Heralds First Florida Food Lion," *Supermarket News*, March 2, 1987. p. 12.
[31] *1986 Food Lion, Inc. Annual Report.*

EXHIBIT 7   SELECTED FINANCIAL RATIOS FOR FOOD LION, 1978–1987

Year	Operating margin	Net profit margin	Return on assets	Return on equity	Long-term debt as a percent of capital
1987	6.8%	2.9%	14.2%	32.4%	26.0%
1986	6.9	2.6	14.1	29.8	24.0
1985	6.3	2.6	14.4	29.1	20.5
1984	6.3	2.5	13.6	30.2	22.8
1983	5.9	2.4	13.0	28.3	25.9
1982	5.6	2.3	15.7	28.1	18.0
1981	6.7	2.9	18.1	32.3	12.4
1980	5.9	2.8	17.7	33.4	15.5
1979	6.7	3.2	20.0	39.0	19.0
1978	6.9	3.2	19.5	38.3	22.8

Source: 1987 Food Lion Inc. Annual Report.

efits, and work rules. Safeway employees were also given quick concessions after threatening to close down several stores.[32]

Other innovations are designed to increase sales. Food Lion often sells popular items such as pet food and cereal at cost in an attempt to draw more customers into the stores. The company makes $1 million a year selling fertilizer made from discarded ground-up bones and fat. Lower prices are also feasible due to the policy of offering fewer brands and sizes than competitors. The company has increased its private label stock, which now includes at least one unit in every category. These two methods allow the company to price its national brand products below many competitors' private brands. As mentioned earlier, the smaller store size and sale of mostly food items have contributed to the high profit margin realized by the company.

FINANCE

Food Lion has been able to expand without becoming overextended or burdened with heavy

[32] Value Line Investment Survey, August 28, 1987, p. 1501.

debt repayments. The firm's capital structure consists of 26 percent long-term debt and 74 percent equity. The majority of growth has been financed through internally generated funds. The company does not want to grow at the expense of profits. Exhibit 7 presents selected financial ratios for the company.

The growth in Food Lion's stock price also reflects the sound financial position of the company. This growth illustrates the continued confidence of investors in the future productivity of the firm. In response to the rapid rise of Food Lion's stock price, management has declared two stock splits since late 1983, when the two separate classes of stock were formed from the previous single class. These splits are designed to keep the price of the stock low enough to be attractive and affordable to all investors. Exhibit 8 shows the adjusted stock prices beginning in 1983, when the two classes were formed.

Furthermore, the per share data reveal the success Food Lion has achieved over the past decade. (See Exhibit 9.) These figures also illustrate investors' desire for Food Lion stock. More specifically, the price/earnings ratio indicates how much investors are willing to pay for

EXHIBIT 8 TRADING RANGE OF FOOD LION'S STOCK PRICES, 1983–1987

	Class A shares		Class B shares	
Quarters	High	Low	High	Low
1983				
4	2⅛	1⅝	2⅛	2
1984				
1	1⅝	1⅜	1¾	1⅜
2	1⅝	1⅜	1⅝	1½
3	1⅞	1⅜	1⅞	1½
4	2¼	1⅞	2⅜	1⅞
1985				
1	2⅝	2⅛	2⅞	2¼
2	3⅛	2¼	3⅛	2¾
3	3	2¾	3	2⅞
4	3¾	2¾	3¾	2⅞
1986				
1	4½	3⅜	4⅞	3⅜
2	6⅛	4⅛	7⅛	4⅝
3	7¼	5½	9	6⅞
4	6⅛	5	7⅜	5⅞
1987				
1	7⅝	6⅛	8½	6⅜
2	8⅛	6⅞	8½	7
3	12¼	7¾	13	8¼
4	13⅜	7¾	14¼	8

Source: Food Lion annual reports.

a dollar of the company's earnings. In 1987 Food Lion's P/E ratio was the 83rd highest of all the companies listed in the Value Line Investment Survey.

FUTURE

Next week, Tom Smith is meeting with the board of directors to discuss and present his ideas for the next few years. Given the recent troublesome trends in the grocery industry as well as the increasing competition in the Southeast, he is reviewing the future strategy of Food Lion. Foremost in his mind is the extent to which Food Lion should continue to expand operations of its conventional stores in this area. He is also pondering movement into other market areas. Smith wants to be sure that the company will be able to finance future growth without greatly changing its current capital structure. Although the current success of Food Lion is quite impressive, Smith realizes that other grocery chains have experienced problems by not responding to the changing environment. He wants to be certain that this does not happen to Food Lion.

EXHIBIT 9 PER SHARE DATA FOR FOOD LION, 1978–1987

Year	Earnings per share	Price/Earnings range	Dividends	Payout ratio
1986	.19	47-17	.01⅞	9
1985	.15	25-15	.01¼	8
1984	.12	20-12	.00¾	6
1983	.09	28-19	.00¾	8
1982	.07	32-12	.00¾	9
1981	.06	17-10	.00⅝	9
1980	.05	13-9	.00½	9
1979	.05	17-8	.00½	9
1978	.03	11-5	.00⅛	4

Source: 1988 Standard & Poor's Corp., p. 3906.

SWATCH

In mid-1986 Chris Keigel returned from military service to become European marketing manager for Swatch, the new watch concept that had revolutionized the watch industry and brought Swiss watchmaking out of a 40-year slump. He knew that Swatch management in Biel, Switzerland, was concerned about maintaining sales growth and agreeing on long-term international strategy. Existing watch brands were renewing their strategies, and new competitors inspired by Swatch were mushrooming worldwide. Chris Keigel had been requested to gather background information for an upcoming top management meeting called to arrive at a consensus on the very concept of Swatch, its international positioning, and viable product line extensions.

COMPANY BACKGROUND

Swatch watches were manufactured by ETA S.A., a century-old Swiss watch movement firm and a subsidiary of SMH (Société Micromécanique et Horlogère), the world's second-largest watch-making concern after the Japanese firm Seiko. SMH was the result of a merger in 1983 between ASUAG (Allgemeine Schweizer Uhrenin-

dustrie) and SSIH (Societe Suisse pour l'Industrie Horlogere), Switzerland's two major watch manufacturers rescued from bankruptcy by the major Swiss banks. In addition to Swatch, the SMH product line included the well-known brands Omega, Longines, Tissot, and Rado. Swatch A.G. was a subsidiary set up in 1984 to handle the international marketing of Swatch watches. Its executive committee was composed of President E. T. Marquardt, Vice President American Operations Max Imgruth, Vice President Continental Operations Felice A. Schillaci, and Vice President Australasian Operations H. N. Tune.

WATCH TECHNOLOGY

Until the late 1950s, all watches were *mechanical*, that is, spring-powered, with movements comprising a hundred or more parts. In 1957, the first electric watch was marketed in the United States. A few years later, the American firm, Bulova, developed a *tuning fork* watch, battery-powered and accurate to within 1 minute per month. The *quartz* watch, that is, electronic watch, was invented in Switzerland in 1968 but first marketed in the United States by Hamilton. It improved accuracy to unheard-of levels. The quartz watch display was either of the traditional "analog" types with hands moving around a face or "digital" with numbers appearing in a frame.

This case was prepared by Helen C. Kimball and Professor Christian Pinson of the European Institute of Business Administration (INSEAD). © 1987 INSEAD-CEDEP. All rights reserved.

EXHIBIT 1   MAJOR COMPONENTS OF FOUR WATCH TYPES

	Mechanical	Tuning fork	Quartz digital	Quartz analog
Energy source	Hair spring	Battery	Battery	Battery
Time base	Balance spring	Tuning fork	Quartz crystal	Quartz crystal
Electronic circuit	—	Simple	Integrated circuit	Integrated circuit
Transmission	Gears	Gears	Gears	Stepping motor/gears
Display	Hands	Hands	Numbers	Hands

Exhibit 1 gives a rough description of the components of four watch types.

The first digital watches used either light-emitting diodes (LEDs) or a liquid crystal display (LCD), which consumed less energy. By 1986 most quartz digital watches had LCDs. The switch to quartz was spectacular: whereas 98 percent of all watches and movements produced in 1974 were mechanical and only 2 percent were quartz, in 1984 the breakdown was 24 percent mechanical and 76 percent quartz.

THE WATCH INDUSTRY

Watchmaking was first developed in Switzerland by Swiss goldsmiths and French Huguenots. Swiss watchmakers were masters of precision workmanship, and "Swiss made" had become synonymous with quality. By 1970, however, the Swiss contribution to world watch production had dropped considerably (Exhibit 2). This trend continued into the 1980s as less expensive and more accurate quartz watches and movements, mainly from Japan and Hong Kong, flooded the market. In 1984, 60 percent of quartz watches and movements produced were from Hong Kong, 30 percent from Japan, and only 7 percent from Switzerland.

Starting in the 1950s, the production of the major American firms (Timex, Bulova, Hamilton) gradually shifted overseas. By 1986, domestic production was considered virtually nil. While Switzerland's contribution to American import volume decreased from 99 percent in 1950 to 4 percent in 1984, the percentage of import volume from Asia increased from 10 percent in 1970, primarily from Japan, to 92 percent in 1984, mostly from Hong Kong.

The Japanese industry was highly concentrated, with the two major firms, Hattori Seiko and Citizen, stressing the development of automated production lines and maximum vertical integration of operations. Compared with the multitude of Swiss watch brands, the combined

EXHIBIT 2   ESTIMATED BREAKDOWN OF WORLD WATCH PRODUCTION, 1948–1985

	World production[a]	Switzerland (%)	Japan (%)	Hong Kong (%)	United States (%)	Rest of world (%)
1948	31	80%	—	—	—	20%
1970	174	43	14%	—	11%	32
1975	218	34	14	2%	12	38
1980	300	29	22	20	4	25
1985	440	13	39	22	0.4	25

[a] Million watches and movements.
Source: Federation of the Swiss Watch Industry.

product lines of these two plus Casio, the third major Japanese watchmaker, did not exceed a dozen brands. In contrast, the industry in Hong Kong was highly fragmented, with several manufacturers producing 10 to 20 million watches per year, and hundreds of small firms producing fewer than 1 million annually. These firms could not afford to invest in quartz analog technology, but with virtually no barriers to entry for watch assembly, they produced complete analog watches from imported movements and modules, often Swiss or Japanese products. The competitive advantages of the Hong Kong firms were low-cost labor, tiny margins, and the flexibility to adapt to changes in the market.

The spectacular rise of Japan and Hong Kong, particularly in the middle- and low-priced categories, was primarily due to their rapid adoption of quartz technology, a drive to achieve a competitive cost position through accumulation of experience, and economies of scale. In 1972 the digital watch module cost around $200, and the same module cost only $0.50 in 1984. The Asian watchmaking industry's expansion had led to a chronic state of world oversupply, mainly in the inexpensive quartz digital range. This had been the cause of a number of bankruptcies and had incited watch manufacturers to turn to the quartz analog market, where added value was higher. In contrast to quartz digital technology, quartz analog technology was available only within the watch industry. Thus, the hundreds of watch assemblers scattered throughout the world were increasingly dependent on the three major movement manufacturers: Seiko, ETA, and Citizen.

THE WATCH MARKET

According to one industry analyst, the European OECD member countries represented around 30 percent of total world watch volume, the United States approximately 20 to 30 percent, and the Japanese market around 10 percent. Estimated annual market growth was approximately 4 percent.

Industry experts estimated 1984 wristwatch purchases in the United States to be 90 to 95

million units, a 400 percent increase over 10 years. By 1985 Americans were buying a new watch once every 2 years compared with once every 6 to 10 years a decade earlier. However, the U.S. market was considered to be near saturation, with an average of 3.5 watches per owner. Buying habits had changed in Europe also, with the 8- to 20-year age group representing nearly half of all watch sales in 1985. When commenting on buying habits, industry experts pointed out that the industry was increasingly committed to the quartz analog, stressing the different meanings the digital and the analog had for the consumer (Exhibit 3). However, some of the more expensive Swiss watch manufacturers seemed to believe in a future trend back to mechanical.

The watch market was generally divided into five retail price segments (Exhibit 4). Swiss watches fell mostly in the mid- to expensive price ranges. To protect its midprice niche, Seiko had adopted a multibrand strategy, offering cheap watches under the Lorus, Pulsar, and Phasar brands, with more expensive watches under the Credor, Seiko, and Lassale brand names.

DEVELOPMENT OF SWATCH

Dr. Ernst Thomke joined ETA S.A. as president in 1978 after proving his success in the marketing department of Beecham Pharmaceuticals. He had been an apprentice in the production division of ETA before taking a Ph.D. in chemistry and a medical degree. In early 1980, after considering the sorry state of the Swiss watch industry, Thomke concluded that the future was in innovative finished products, aggressive marketing, volume sales, and vertical integration of the industry. Quartz analog technology was more complex than digital, but as ETA was known for the technology it possessed for the production of high-priced, ultrathin "Delirium" movements, Thomke decided to develop a "low-price prestige" quartz analog wristwatch that could be mass-produced in Switzerland at greatly reduced cost. Two ETA micromechanical engineers who specialized in plastic injection molding technology, Jacques Muller and Elmar Mock, were given

EXHIBIT 3   A COMPARISON OF DIGITAL AND ANALOG WATCHES

Digital	Analog
1. Time is represented by a sign	1. Time is represented by a symbol
2. The focus is on	2. The focus is on
The instant	Length of time
Numerical code	A pictorial code
Discontinuity	Continuity
Linearity and periodicity	Circularity and cyclical character
3. Signification	3. Signification
The time display is precise	Time display is imprecise
Time is imposed	Time can be negotiated
Monosemy: only one meaning	Polysemy: several meanings

Source: Adapted from Michel-Adrien Viorol "Un Problème d'Evolution du Produit Horloger," in "Les Apports de la Semiotique au Marketing et a la Publicité," IREP Seminar, 1976.

the challenge of designing a product based on Thomke's concept. This required inventing entirely new production technology using robots and computers for manufacture and assembly. By 1981 a semiautomated process had been designed to meet Thomke's goal of a 15 SF factory price, and seven patents were registered. The watch's movement, consisting of only 51 instead of the 90 to 150 parts in other watches, was injected directly into the one-piece plastic case. The casing was sealed by ultrasonic welding instead of screws, precluding servicing. The watch would be simply replaced and not repaired if it stopped. The finished product, guaranteed for one year, was shock resistant, was water resistant to 100 feet (30 meters), and contained a three-year replaceable battery.

In April 1981 Thomke took his idea to Franz Sprecher, a marketing consultant who had worked at Nestlé before setting up his own consulting firm. As background for ETA's project, Sprecher studied prestige products like perfumes, successful mass-market brands like "Bic," and both designer and ready-to-wear fashion. He

EXHIBIT 4   WATCH INDUSTRY PRICE SEGMENTS (SWISS FRANCS), 1984

Segment	Retail price[a]	% units	% value	Examples
A	8–30	60%	10%	Hong Kong LCDs, some cheap mechanicals
B	30–100	15	15	Swatch, Timex, Casio, Guess, Lip, Lorus, Dugena, Junghans, Yema, Jaz, Pulsar, Hamilton
C	80–250	20	45	Tissot, Seiko, Citizen, Casio, Lip, Yema, Jaz, Pulsar, Dugena, Junghans, Bulova, Hamilton, Herbelin
D	120–450	4	15	Omega, Longines, Eterna, Seiko, Citizen, Certina, Rado, Movado, Bulova
E	450+	1	15	Rolex, Piaget, Cartier, Audemars Piguet, Certine, Rado, Lassale, Ebel

[a]$/SF exchange rates: 1983 = 2.10, 1984 = 2.20, 1985 = 2.30, 1986 = 1.84.
Source: Compiled from Federation of the Swiss Watch Industry records.

worked closely with advertising agencies in the United States on product positioning and advertising strategy. In addition to the name "Swatch," a snappy contraction of "Swiss" and "watch," this research generated the idea of downplaying the product's practical benefits and positioning it as a "fashion accessory that happens to tell time." Swatch would be a second or third watch, used to adapt to different situations without replacing the traditional "status symbol" watch.

Launch

Dr. Thomke arranged to have Swatch distributed in the United States by the Swiss Watch Distribution Center (SWDC) in San Antonio, Texas. SWDC was an American firm in which ETA held a minority interest and whose chairman, Ben Hammond, had been instrumental in setting up and building Seiko distribution in the Southwestern states. Swatch was test marketed in December 1982 at 100 Sanger Harris department stores in Dallas, Salt Lake City, and San Diego, without any advertising, public relations, or publicity. The original test product line consisted of 12 rather conventional watches in red, brown, and tan. Opinions on test results were mixed, but the ETA team continued undaunted. Swatch was officially launched in Switzerland in March 1983 and then gradually worldwide. Exhibit 5 shows the fall 1983 collection as pictured in sales brochures.

Max Imgruth took over as president of SWDC in April 1983 and arranged a second test market in December 1983 through both the Zale Jewelry chain in Dallas and the New York department store Macy's, with television support created by Swatch's advertising agency, McCann-Erickson. Test market conclusions were that most of the watches in the 1983 fall/winter collection were not acceptable for the U.S. market. Imgruth recalled:

> Nothing happened. I tried to figure out what was wrong. The product was not very distinctive. It was not just the ad, it was the watches. It was close to the traditional watch. First of all it was its position-

ing, second the product, third pricing, fourth advertising. Basically, I ran down the marketing mix.

Imgruth became increasingly involved in product design and local adaptation of Swatch communication. He was appointed president of the newly created American subsidiary Swatch Watch USA in early 1984. The American pricing strategy was modified and a direct sales force organized to replace SWDC that year. Managers hired to run Swatch Watch USA included Vice President of Operations Don Galliers, formerly in the watch strap business, and Marketing Manager/Creative Director Steve Rechtschaffner, age 27, a former member of the U.S. freestyle skiing team with experience in sales promotion. Exhibit 6 gives the perceived advantages and disadvantages of Swatch, in December 1984, in four countries.

Price

There were initially three prices for the Swiss launch: 39.90 SF for a model with only two hands, 44.90 SF for three hands, and 49.90 SF for three hands and a calendar display. In the United States, however, Swatch was first marketed at seven price points ranging from $19.95 to $37.50. Consumers did not seem to understand why certain watches cost more than others, and so American prices were reduced to three in 1984: $25.00, $30.00, and $35.00. In 1986 one Swatch retail price was set throughout the world, based on the price in the United States of $30.00. Exhibit 7 presents the results of a survey on perceptions of Swatch retail prices in four countries.

From the start Thomke and Sprecher had decided that product contribution would have to be sufficient to finance mass communication. Manufacturing costs had been reduced substantially, and wholesaler and agent margins could be decreased some. Retail margins would have to be kept high enough to motivate retailers. Exhibit 8 gives a comparison of costs and margins for traditional moderate-priced Swiss and Japanese watches, low-priced Hong Kong watches, and Swatch in 1982–1983.

EXHIBIT 5   SWATCH INTERNATIONAL LAUNCH COLLECTION

EXHIBIT 6   PERCEIVED ADVANTAGES AND DISADVANTAGES OF SWATCH

	Total (n = 800)	United States (n = 200)	France (n = 200)	Great Britain (n = 200)	West Germany (n = 200)
Positive features					
Pretty shape	34.5[a]	34.0	33.5	20.0	50.5
Amusing, original	28.6	9.0	31.5	28.0	46.0
Waterproof	28.4	37.5	29.5	29.5	17.0
Fashionable, modern	24.5	7.5	30.5	24.0	36.0
Pretty, varied colors	22.6	31.0	13.5	18.5	27.5
Strong, resistant	22.1	24.5	27.5	24.5	12.0
Can be worn by anyone	16.0	30.5	9.0	12.5	12.0
Quality watches	14.8	28.0	8.0	4.0	19.0
Low price	14.5	3.5	32.0	5.0	17.5
Can be worn anywhere	12.6	13.5	13.5	11.0	12.5
Negative features					
Uncomfortable plastic strap	16.0[b]	13.5	13.0	17.5	20.0
Too fashionable, too modern	10.3	2.0	6.5	9.5	23.0
Looks like a gadget, a toy	9.9	3.5	10.0	8.5	17.5
Does not match all styles of dress	8.4	1.0	4.0	14.0	14.5
Fragile	8.1	0.5	12.0	3.0	17.0
Too sophisticated face	7.4	6.0	3.0	8.5	12.0
Too much plastic	6.6	1.0	7.5	—	18.0
Too noisy	3.6	—	12.5	1.0	1.0

[a] Percentage of respondents indicating this feature in response to the question: "What, in your opinion, are the advantages of Swatch watches in comparison with other watches?"
[b] Percentage of respondents indicating this feature in response to the question: "And what would be their disadvantages?"
Source: Delta International market study, December 1984.

Product Line

Two Swatch collections of 12 different models each were marketed per year, in spring and fall. Styles were based on four major target groups geared to social behavior and trends: "classic," "hi-tech," "sports," and "fashion." Collections were designed by Kathi Durrer and Jean Robert in Zurich, with fashion consultants in New York, Milan, and Paris. At first, there was only one large-size model, enabling mass production. In 1984, a smaller size was added. Limitation of sizes to these two enabled substantial reductions in production costs. Variations in the collections were made possible through face and watchband graphics and style. In the spring of 1984, Max Imgruth decided to name individual watches (e.g., "Pinstripe," "Black Magic," "Mc-Swatch," "Dotted Swiss") and tie each collection in with specific themes starting with the "Skipper" line of sailing-inspired sport watches. Subsequent themes ranged from "Street Smart" paisleys and plaids to "Kiva" American Indian designs. Exhibit 9 illustrates selected watches from the 1984–1986 collections.

By fall 1984, Swatch management realized that a continuous system for pretesting the 80 to 100 models presented by the designers for each collection was essential for constant collection renewal. Franz Sprecher commented:

The strategy should be to create bestsellers. This doesn't mean keeping the same collection for five

EXHIBIT 7   ACTUAL AND PERCEIVED 1986 RETAIL PRICES OF SWATCH

United States (Actual Price = $30)

Perceived price ($)	Total (n = 290)	Buyers (n = 99)	Potential buyers (n = 140)	Non-buyers (n = 51)
Less than 20	8[a]	3	9	16
21–30	57	62	56	49
31–40	26	25	26	25
41–50	6	7	6	2
51–60	2	3	2	2
More than 60	1	—	1	2

United Kingdom (Actual Price = L24)

Perceived price (L)	Total (n = 202)	Buyers (n = 68)	Potential buyers (n = 83)	Non-buyers (n = 51)
Less than 10	4	—	4	12
11–15	10	3	14	14
16–20	39	44	36	35
21–25	22	38	16	12
26–30	8	4	10	12
31–35	1	1	1	2
36–40	2	—	4	2
More than 40	1	1	—	—

France (Actual Price = FF 250)

Perceived price (FF)	Total (n = 200)	Buyers (n = 66)	Potential buyers (n = 99)	Non-buyers (n = 35)
Less than 100	10	2	11	20
100–150	9	2	12	14
151–200	17	8	23	17
201–250	41	74	32	3
251–300	7	9	5	9
301–400	4	3	4	3
More than 400	2	3	1	3

West Germany (Actual Price = 65 DM)

Perceived price (DM)	Total (n = 200)	Buyers (n = 67)	Potential buyers (n = 74)	Non-buyers (n = 59)
Less than 20	3	3	—	7
21–40	11	6	12	14
41–60	38	27	42	44
61–80	39	58	34	22
81–100	7	4	8	8
101–200	3	2	3	3
More than 200	1	—	1	2

[a]Percentage of total responses to the question: "All the [Swatch] watches have the same price—could you estimate the price?"
Source: Qualitest A. G. market study, Zurich, August 1986, and company records.

EXHIBIT 8   BREAKDOWN OF LOW- TO MODERATE-PRICED WATCH COSTS AND MARGINS

	Swiss	Japanese	Hong Kong	Swatch
Retail price = 100%	100%	100%	100%	100%
(Retail margin)	(50%)	(55%)	(50%)	(45%)
Wholesale price	50%	45%	50%	55%
(Wholesale/agent margin)	(25%)	(16%)	(18%)	(11%)
Ex-factory price	25%	29%	33%	44%
(Contribution)	(4%)	(12%)	(3%)	(24%)
Manufacturing cost	21%	18%	29%	20%

Source: Company records.

years but improving the collection by identifying weak models and knowing whether to revamp them or create new models that will be leaders.

A collection of watches, including three scented Granita di Frutta models[1] shown in Exhibit 9, were pretested in December 1984. Test results, presented with the actual ex-factory sales figures for the collection, revealed no significant differences between the four countries involved (Exhibit 10).

Distribution

Until the mid-1970s most medium- and high-priced watches were sold through jewelry and specialty shops. Timex and other low-priced products sold through department and discount stores and some mail-order houses. The Swiss watchmakers, later followed by Seiko, had always placed emphasis on after-sales service and set up dealerships allowing jewelers to take up to 25 percent markups. As prices slipped, however, a gray market[2] developed, fired by a drive for volume and a lack of control over distribution channels.

[1] A line of aromatic Swatches geared to the teenage consumer and consisting of pastel pink, blue, and yellow watches emitting strawberry, mint, and banana fragrances; it represented 80 percent of sales in the United States for the first two months in 1985.

[2] Parallel importing and distribution through unauthorized channels.

In the United States, Swatch watches were sold primarily in "shop-in-shops" at up-market department stores, some specialty watch retailers, sports shops, and boutiques. In Europe, Swatch was sold by the few existing up-market department stores but mostly by traditional jewelers and some specialized sports, gift, and fashion boutiques, mail-order houses, and duty-free shops. In France, as part of his launch strategy, the Swatch distributor Raymond Zeitoun persuaded the prestigious jeweler Jean Dinh Van on the Rue de la Paix in Paris to sell Swatch for a few days. When the jeweler accepted "for the fun of it" and sales boomed, others followed suit. Zeitoun spoke of Swatch in France:

Granted, it's an item without much of a margin, but the profession has to change and widen its horizons. The advantage of Swatch is that it brings a lively atmosphere and a younger clientele to the store.

Discounting by distributors was not allowed, and the trade was warned to keep an eye out for counterfeits. Swatch Watch USA spent close to $1 million in 1984 to buy back Swatches displayed at less than the set price. Don Galliers recalled:

We purchased 85 to 90 percent of gray market watches. Counterfeits appeared in 1985. We set up an international brand protection program with a very sophisticated information network. All new styles were copyrighted, counterfeiters caught at the

CRESTA RUN
Spring-Summer 1985

STREET SMART
(Fall-Winter 1985-86)

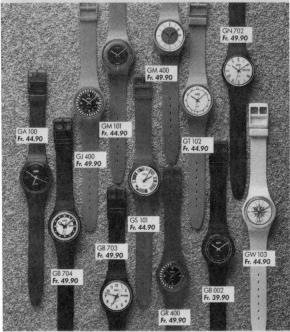

(Spring-Summer 1985-86)

GRANITA DI FRUTTA
Spring-Summer 1985

COLOR TECH
(Fall-Winter 1985-86)

EXHIBIT 9   SELECTED WATCHES FROM THE 1984–1986 COLLECTIONS

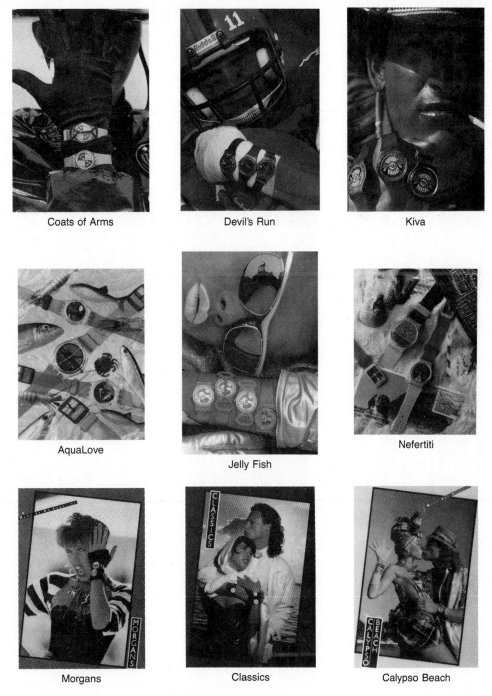

Coats of Arms   Devil's Run   Kiva

AquaLove   Jelly Fish   Nefertiti

Morgans   Classics   Calypso Beach

EXHIBIT 9 (*Continued*)   1986 COLLECTIONS

EXHIBIT 10   PREFERENCES, PURCHASE INTENTIONS, AND SALES DATA FOR 1985 SPRING/SUMMER SWATCH COLLECTION IN FRANCE, WEST GERMANY, GREAT BRITAIN, AND THE UNITED STATES

| Swatch code | Most preferred models[a] | | | Least[b] preferred models Total (n = 800) | Purchase intentions[c] | | | | Ex-factory sales worldwide (000 units) |
| | Total (n = 800) | Men (n = 400) | Women (n = 400) | | For self | | | Gift total (n = 800) | |
					Total (n = 800)	Men (n = 400)	Women (n = 400)		
GB 101	41.1%	63.3%	19.0%	2.0%	33.6%	57.0%	10.3%	27.0%	147
GA 102	36.1	58.8	13.5	3.9	28.4	48.5	8.3	26.0	149
LB 106	20.6	6.5	34.6	1.5	16.6	2.8	30.6	18.3	140
LM 104	20.4	3.3	37.6	2.3	18.1	1.0	35.3	21.0	70
GM 401	19.0	24.8	13.3	3.1	15.9	21.3	10.5	15.0	67
LW 104	18.3	3.8	32.8	3.5	15.1	1.3	29.1	16.6	246
LA 100	17.4	6.5	28.3	1.4	15.1	3.7	27.1	17.3	207
GN 401	17.3	31.8	2.8	4.3	15.1	28.3	2.0	11.8	63
GB 705	13.3	22.8	3.8	8.5	10.5	19.3	1.8	7.8	106
GW 104	12.9	11.8	14.0	7.9	8.0	5.8	10.3	9.9	221
GB 706	10.3	16.3	4.3	10.0	7.5	12.5	2.5	8.0	121
GK 100	9.9	11.5	8.3	48.9	6.3	7.3	5.3	8.0	286
GT 103	9.8	9.3	10.3	5.1	5.6	5.0	6.3	6.8	53
LT 101	9.5	1.8	17.3	3.1	7.1	0.3	14.0	10.3	53
LB 107	6.9	1.8	11.8	6.8	5.5	0.5	10.3	5.6	88
LW 107[d]	6.1	1.0	11.3	27.5	4.5	0.8	8.3	7.1	322
GJ 700	5.8	7.3	4.3	37.4	3.6	4.5	2.8	4.4	104
LN 103	4.1	0.8	7.3	2.6	3.3	—	6.5	5.6	64
LW 105[d]	3.9	0.8	7.0	17.3	3.0	0.3	5.8	4.6	213
GM 701	3.9	5.0	2.8	22.3	2.8	4.0	1.5	2.3	108
GB 403	3.5	4.5	2.5	13.9	2.5	3.5	1.5	2.9	78
LW 106[d]	2.4	0.8	4.0	27.1	1.5	—	3.0	3.1	152
LS 102	1.8	1.0	2.5	28.9	1.1	0.3	2.0	2.1	107
LB 105	1.5	0.8	2.3	5.0	1.3	0.8	1.8	1.6	118
LB 104	1.1	0.5	1.8	3.5	0.6	0.3	1.0	2.3	125

[a] Percentage of total responses to the question: "Here are a number of new Swatch watches. They come in two sizes, standard and small. Which are the three you like best?"

[b] Percentage of total responses to the question: "Which are the three watches you like least?" Responses were virtually the same regardless of sex.

[c] Percentage of total responses to the question: "Would you consider buying such a watch for yourself or as a gift?"

[d] "Granita di Frutta". 69 percent of those interested in these models as gifts claimed the recipient would be a girl under 15 years of age.

Source: Delta International market study, December 1984, and company records.

source, and "confusingly similar" watch marketers taken to court. If we were spending $16–18 million a year on advertising, we could spend a couple of million to protect the brand.

Merchandising was considered fundamental and included sales promotional activities designed to catch the consumer's eye. Backed by 2.5-meter "maxi-Swatches," expensive and carefully designed display racks were "color-blocked," that is, arranged in rows of color. In-store videos played pop or rock music, and sales brochures were available in ample supply. In all countries, parties for the trade were organized for each collection launch to create a feeling of a "Swatch Club," encouraging retailers to give Swatch prime window space and exposure in spite of lower margins. One of Swatch's selling points with distributors was its very low return rate[3] (i.e., 0.3 percent in 1984 compared with the industry average of 5 percent), which virtually eliminated after-sales service problems and customer dissatisfaction.

Exhibit 11 presents consumer preferences with respect to distribution of Swatch and the breakdown of Swatch distribution channels in five countries. A breakdown of sales value and volume by distribution channel was not available.

In general, the attitude of the distributors toward Swatch watches was very positive with the few negative comments limited to low profit margin, production-related delivery problems, skepticism about long-term success, and lack of distributor exclusivity. Don Galliers commented on Swatch's distribution strategy in the United States:

> Swatch's success was built on limited distribution. We should not sell more than 5 million Swatches in the United States in any single year, to keep it rare, in demand. You can't always get what you want so when you see it you'd better buy it. For a trendy article like this, if you accelerate too much into the market, you risk making it become a fad.

[3] Percentage of watches returned on warranty.

Product Line Extensions

While its major competitors — Seiko, Citizen, and others — were diversifying into other applications of electronics and "superwatches" complete with televisions, computers, or health monitoring systems, Swatch, mainly through the initiative of Swatch Watch USA, had moved into a range of accessories and ready-to-wear apparel designed to express a "Swatch" lifestyle (Exhibits 12 and 13).

One of the reasons given for expanding into accessories and apparel was the need to fill out the available space in the shop-in-shops. "Funwear" and "Fungear," manufactured in Hong Kong and the United States, were designed by Renee Rechtschaffner, Steve's wife and the winner of a Swatch-organized contest at the Fashion Institute of Technology. By the last quarter of 1985, nonwatch items accounted for one-third of Swatch sales in the United States. Aided awareness scores for Swatch accessories available only in the United States are presented in Exhibit 14.

Fashion retailing in the United States was stimulated by six "market weeks" per year to launch each new season (i.e., spring, spring-summer, summer, back-to-school, fall-winter, holiday) and introduce products to retailers nationwide. At Swatch Watch USA, preparation of each market week began almost a full year in advance with market and sales analyses, fashion forecasts, and theme development (watches and accessories) covering approximately two months for each season followed by gradual decisions and presentations throughout the rest of the year on design, color, prints, prices, quantities, range, advertising, public relations, and promotion. Coordination of production and delivery with "fickle fashion" was tricky business that relied on very short lead times. Perpetual innovation was also difficult to maintain. Don Galliers commented:

> We don't have the flexibility of the traditional watch industry where if you miss it this year you can launch it next year. We also don't have the normal 18-month development time to field the watch after a one-year design time. Our whole cycle is

EXHIBIT 11   CONSUMER PREFERENCE WITH RESPECT TO DISTRIBUTION
CONSUMER STORE PREFERENCES FOR BUYING SWATCH, 1986

Store	Switzerland (n = 212)	United Kingdom (n = 202)	France (n = 200)	West Germany (n = 200)	United States (n = 290)
"Fine fashion" department stores	68[a]	28	56	57	53
Regular department stores	29	35	16	13	70
Sports shops	14	25	22	22	37
Jewelers	50	73	44	61	35
Boutiques	12	10	28	11	32
Clothing shops	17	12	4	11	31
Discount stores	—	7	—	—	19
Drugstores	—	—	—	—	10
Mail order	5	14	3	2	9
Supermarkets	8	4	6	3	2
Others	6	3	2	2	—

[a] Percentage of total responses to the question: "Listed on this card are different shops where you could buy a Swatch. From which of these shops would you prefer to buy a Swatch?" (Several answers are possible.)
Source: Qualitest A. G. market study, Zurich, August 1986.

SWATCH DISTRIBUTION CHANNELS, 1985–1986

Channel	Switzerland 1985	1986	United Kingdom 1985	1986	France 1985	1986	West Germany 1985	1986	United States 1985	1986
Department stores	10[a]	10	6	9	3	11	19	22	82	71
Jewelers	85	78	87	78	95	79	73	59	3	2
Sports shops	—	—	0.1	0.1	—	—	6	16	1	2
Fashion shops	5	12	6	12	—	—	2	4	6	12
Others[b]	—	0.2	0.4	0.5	2	10	—	—	8	14
Total number of stores (including branches)	590	511	1708	1273	2634	2266	1030	511	6437	4634

[a] Percentage of total number of outlets.
[b] Gift and card shops, drugstores, college bookstores, military exchanges, catalogs, etc.
Source: Company records.

built on the concept that every six weeks there is something new at the Swatch counter.

In the spring of 1986, under license from the Coca-Cola company, the American subsidiary also started marketing a line of Coca-Cola watches. They contained traditional ETA and not Swatch technology quartz movements and did not bear the name Swatch.

Communication

Thomke and Sprecher had adopted a global communication strategy for Swatch to establish a distinctive brand personality. The company issued strict directives on use of the Swatch logo, baselines, layout, and the Swiss cross. The Swatch communication budget was split more or less evenly between advertising/store promotion (50

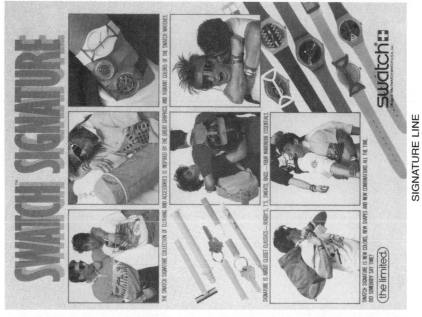

SIGNATURE LINE

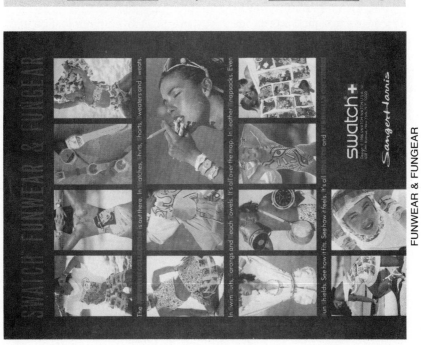

FUNWEAR & FUNGEAR

EXHIBIT 12   SWATCH ACCESSORIES AND APPAREL (USA)

EXHIBIT 13   SWATCH CLOTHING AND ACCESSORIES, 1984–1985

Date	Product	Description	Retail price
Fall 1984	Swatch Guard	Protective, decorative device for watches	$3
Fall 1984	Maxi-Swatch	2.5-meter Swatch wall clock	$150
Spring 1985	Shields	Sunglasses	$35
Spring 1985	Chums	Eyeglass holders	$5
Spring 1985	Signature line	Umbrellas, T-shirts, sweatshirts with watch graphics	$12–$38
Spring 1985	Gift set	Keyholder and Swiss pen-knife	$45
Spring 1985	Paraphernalia	Italian pens, stationery items, key rings, safety razors	$7–$15
Fall 1985	Fungear line	Knapsacks, belts, bags	$10–$65
Fall 1985	Funwear line	Unisex casual wear (pants, tops, sweats, shirts, shorts, skirts) linked to watch themes	$12–$65

percent) and public relations/special events (50 percent). Local agencies were in charge of public relations, promotion, publicity, and special events, including contests, concert tours, and sports events. McCann-Erickson in Zurich was in charge of all advertising and designed ads for local adaptation in different countries through the use of voice-overs for commercials and strips of copy in the respective languages for print ads. Roger Guyard, regional manager for France, explained:

We want to have a global image with the same image in England as in Australia. Where we are different from the others is in our launch events and promotions, adapted to each country and each population.

The Swatch communication target audience was described by McCann-Zurich as "all men and women between 15 and 39 years of age, particularly between 20 and 29, opinion leaders/trend-setters, extroverts who were nonetheless group-dependent, young fashion

EXHIBIT 14   AIDED AWARENESS OF SWATCH ACCESSORIES IN THE UNITED STATES, 1985

	Total sample (n = 895)	Age		
		12–18 (n = 219)	19–24 (n = 234)	25–34 (n = 442)
Shields	17[a]	43	13	8
Bags	16	37	12	8
T-shirts	15	36	13	6
Guards	11	27	10	4
Gift sets	9	20	10	3
Chums	8	20	6	3
Beach boxes	8	18	4	5
Maxi Swatch	8	17	7	3
Pocket knives	6	15	5	2
Pens and pencils	6	13	3	3
Razors	3	5	3	1

[a]Percentage of respondents indicating this accessory in response to the question: "Please tell me which of the following Swatch accessories you are aware of."
Source: "Attitude and Awareness of Swatch in Various Markets" study, McCann-Erickson, July 1985.

wearers and both active and passive sports fans." For Felice Schillaci, vice president of continental operations, Swatch was "a brand for the young at heart, no age group, no 18 to 29, it's a state of mind, an attitude."

Public Relations

Heavy emphasis was placed on testimonials and endorsements by opinion leaders as well as special events including sponsoring of musicians and artists, exhibitions, and competitions at which gadgets, leaflets, and "Swatch magazines" were distributed (Exhibit 15). Swatch promotion was often unsolicited, such as when Lady Diana wore not only her husband Prince Charles's watch at a polo match but also two Swatches, just when Swatch was introducing the ideas of man-sized watches for women and "multiple Swatch accessorizing." Swatch also benefited from massive publicity through the press. According to Elmar Mock,

> Management's stroke of genius was not to hide its engineers. We were on great terms with the newspapers who created an advertising effect, quite naturally, without the slightest solicitation.

Limited edition watches were launched with elaborate parties. The first was designed by Kiki Picasso and distributed to 100 celebrities at a cocktail party in Paris. There was the diamond-studded "Limelight" ($100) available in both Europe and the United States. Then there were the "Breakdance" watch ($30) and four watches designed by New York artist Keith Haring ($50) marketed in the United States only. Swatch's French public relations agency claimed that the strategy behind these serial watches was to manage the production-related scarcity by "creating a frenzy through rarity." Organization of advertising and events revolved around the development of a "Swatch cult" and using connections. In 1984, for instance, Max Imgruth organized a celebrity advertising campaign through a photographer in California who persuaded a number of stars to be in Swatch ads in exchange for a Rolex or Pi-

aget gold watch. These included Lauren Hutton, Donna Mills, Lee Majors, and Ivan Lendl.

Advertising

Swatch advertising and promotion budgets are given in Exhibit 16 with industry media expenditures in the United States. Don Galliers explained that Switzerland had a strict policy whereby roughly 30 percent of the product's retail price would go to advertising. Swatch advertising relied primarily on films for television and cinema. Print ads, accounting for approximately one-third of total advertising expenditure, were used worldwide to reinforce awareness of each collection and current trend themes. They ran from April to June and from September to December every year. Swatch print media plans included sport, fashion, and avant-garde magazines (e.g., *Vogue, Elle, Cosmopolitan, Sports Illustrated, L'Equipe, Rolling Stone, The Face, City*) as well as magazines geared to the young (e.g., *Just 17, Jacinte, Madchen, Seventeen*) and occasionally general news publications (e.g., *Stern, Der Spiegel, Figaro, Tiempo*).

Swatch Watch USA has an in-house department that adapted the McCann ads and created its own ads. Samples of print ads used in the United States are shown in Exhibit 17. Max Imgruth commented on global advertising:

> We adapted the spots in a way that made sense, different wording, cut them a little bit with McCann here, knowing full well that what the Swiss wanted to achieve, a brand created and sent in directly from Switzerland, was impossible. A watch is not consumed like Coca-Cola. It is not a daily need. This is emotional and you have to play local emotions.

Felice Schillaci explained that the loyal Swatch customer in the United States fell in the 10- to 16-year-old age bracket. Reliable data on the Swatch buyer profile in Europe were not available, but buyer age group brackets in the United Kingdom were estimated to be 20 percent under 18, 40 percent between 18 and 24, 30 percent between 25 and 34, and 10 percent over

EXHIBIT 15   MAJOR SPECIAL EVENTS ORGANIZED OR SPONSORED BY SWATCH

Date	Country	Event
March 1984	Germany	13-ton giant Swatch on Commerzbank building, Frankfurt
April 1984	France	Urban Sax saxophonist group at the Eldorado theater in Paris to collaborate launch; first Swatch magazine
August 1984	United States	Ivan Lendl U.S. tennis open
September 1984	United States	World Breakdancing Championship at The Roxy, New York
September 1984	France	First street art painting show with the French artists Les Frères Ripoulin, Espece Cardin theater, Paris
November 1984	United States	The Fat Boys' music sponsorship at Private Eye's, New York, to introduce "Granita di Frutta" to the trade
October '84–January '85	United States	New York City Fresh Festival: breakdancing, rapping, graffiti artists
January 1985	United States	World Freestyle Invitational/Celebrity Classic, Brechenridge, Colorado
March 1985	France	IRCAM "copy art" show, Paris; limited edition (119) Kiki Picasso design watches; second Swatch magazine
Spring 1985	United States	Hi-fly freestyle windsurfing team sponsorship
May 1985	England	Second street art painting show, Covent Garden, London, with Les Frères Ripoulin and English street artists
June 1985	Switzerland	Art fair in Basel; third street art painting show with 50 European artists
Summer 1985	Sweden	Oestersjo Rallyt (Segel-Rallye)
September 1985	France	Cinema festival, Pompidou Center, Paris, with Kuroseauss, *Ran; Mini City* magazine
September 1985	France	"Le Défilé": Jean-Paul Gaultier and Regine Chopinot fashion/dance show, Pavillion Baltard, Paris
September 1985	England	Andrew Logan's Alternative Miss World, London
October 1985	Belgium	"Mode et Anti-Mode" fashion show, Brussels
Fall 1985	United States	Thompson Twins' concert tour sponsorship
November 1985	Spain	Swatch launch party, the Cirque, Barcelona
November 1985	United States	"Limelight" launch party, Los Angeles (for trade)
November 1985	International	Freestyle World Cup sponsorship
November 1985	Japan	Giant Swatch in Tokyo for launch of Swatch
January 1986	United States	Fashion show (for trade) at Private Eye's, New York
January 1986	United States	Pierre Boulez orchestra concert tour
January–November 1986	England	"Time & Motion Competition," Royal College of Art, London
February 1986	England	Feargal Sharkey tour
February–March 1986	Germany	Swatch Freestyle World Cup, Oberjoch
March 1986	Switzerland	"Arosa" freestyle skiing weekend with retailers
March 1986	Austria	"Exposa" jewelry fair with Swatch balloons
March 1986	France	"Waterproof Paris": Daniel Larrieux's subaquatic ballet performance
April–October 1986	Canada	Giant Swatch, Swiss Pavilion, Expo 86, Vancouver
May–September 1986	Sweden	Swatch Funboard Cup sponsorship
June 1986	France	Fourth street art painting show, fourth Swatch magazine
June 1986	Italy	"Sasswatchgala Mailand," launch event
July '86–February '87	Switzerland	First International Swatch Freestyle Youth Camp, Zermatt
July 1986	International	Second Himalaya Super Marathon sponsorship
July 1986	Netherlands	Srachenflug Festival sponsored by Swatch

EXHIBIT 16   SWATCH BUDGETS, 1983–1986   SWATCH ADVERTISING BUDGET[a]
(Thousand Swiss Francs)

Country	Launch	1983	1984	1985	1986
Switzerland	March 1983	459	620	964	1,107
United Kingdom	March 1983	922	2,398	2,398	2,767
West Germany	September 1983	2,275	4,182	2,706	2,706
United States	September 1983		9,480	32,838	33,404
Austria	January 1984		244	429	472
France	April 1984		2,610	2,423	2,583
Belgium	April 1984		199	295	307
Netherlands	May 1984		148	430	369
South Africa	September 1984		301	133	92
Australia	September 1984		562	883	984
Norway	October 1984			243	246
Sweden	October 1984			571	615
Denmark	March 1985			151	184
Finland	May 1985			236	246
Japan	October 1985			NA	NA
Spain	October 1985			1,230	2,460
Italy	June 1986				3,524

NA—not available.
[a] "Advertising" includes production of ads, media spending, in-store programs, etc.

EXHIBIT 16 (*Continued*)   **SWATCH PUBLIC RELATIONS AND SPECIAL EVENTS BUDGET**[a]
(Thousand Swiss Francs)

Country	Launch	1983	1984	1985	1986
Central promotion budget			3,690	4,920	6,150
Switzerland	March 1983			258	184
United Kingdom	March 1983			369	633
West Germany	September 1983			300	209
United States	September 1983			3,978	886
Austria	January 1984		29	29	37
France	April 1984		898	1,204	1,291
Belgium	April 1984		139	253	246
Netherlands	May 1984		118	209	260
South Africa	September 1984		18	31	49
Australia	September 1984			86	123
Norway	October 1984			47	80
Sweden	October 1984			77	209
Denmark	March 1985			[b]	61
Finland	May 1985			[b]	37
Japan	October 1985			NA	NA
Spain	October 1985			492	1,599
Italy	June 1986				1,458

NA—not available.
[a] This budget includes music and sports promotions, special events, etc.
[b] Paid for by distributor.
Source: Company records (disguised data).

EXHIBIT 16 (*Continued*)   1985 WATCH BRAND MEDIA SPENDING IN THE UNITED STATES

Brand	Share of voice[a]	Brand	Share of voice[a]
A-Watch	1.15%	Omega	1.02
Bulova	0.60	Piaget	1.56
Cartier	0.83	Pulsar	9.74
Casio	3.35	Rado	1.87
Certina	0.13	Rolex	5.05
Citizen	10.33	Seiko	11.17
Ebel	0.97	Swatch	7.05
Gucci	2.16	Timex	15.22
Guess	0.03	Tissot	0.32
Hamilton	0.32	Z-Watch	0.01
J. Lassale	7.32	Total	86.32%
Longines	1.77	Others	13.68
Lorus	4.36	Total advertisers	100.00%

NA—not available.
[a]Share of voice = percentage of total industry media spending.
Source: Compiled from 1985 Broadcast Advertisers Reports, Inc., and Publishers Information Bureau, Inc., figures.

34. Management in the United States felt that by catching consumers at an early age they would stick with Swatch as they grew up and the enthusiasm they generated would rub off on those older. By 1986 in New York City and Los Angeles, where Swatch awareness was at a maximum, Swatch Watch USA had limited television commercials to MTV[4] to avoid oversaturation. A firm specializing in TV and radio youth audience surveys conducted an analysis for Swatch of American consumers, based on interviews in 15 cities and including reactions to a random sample of eight Swatch ads (Exhibit 18). Scores for recall of Swatch advertising in five countries are presented in Exhibit 19. Watch brand awareness scores in the same countries are presented in Exhibit 20.

Competition

When asked to define the competition, Swatch management's responses varied. Swatch was generally credited with having opened up a new market niche (Exhibit 21). By 1986, however, the market was flooded with Swatch imita-

[4]A music video cable TV station watched primarily by 12 to 24-year-olds.

tions; some bearing similar brand names are, for example, Watch, Watcha, Swiss Watch, Smash, Swatcher, A-Watch, La-Watch, P-Watch, Q-Watch, Zee-Watch, as well as counterfeits using the brand name Swatch. Many Swatch imitations were produced in Hong Kong or Taiwan for distribution in the United States, Europe, or other major markets. These could look strikingly similar to Swatch, some even similar in quality and very price competitive, and the company was involved in a long series of legal proceedings to fight off the competition.

Timex, one of the companies worst hit by the LCD watch glut, had launched a line of colored fashion watches called "Watercolors," priced slightly below Swatch. Timex was also rumored to be preparing a new advertising campaign for its "Big-Bold-Beautiful" fashion watch line for women, introduced in the summer of 1986 and targeted to an older age group than Swatch. According to one industry expert, the Timex range did not seem to have any "winners," at least not in Europe. Seiko's Lorus line was expanded in 1984 to include "Swatch-like" fashion models, priced lower than Swatch and doing well when they had special design features. The

Spring 1983

Fall 1983

Christmas 1984

Spring 1985

Spring 1985

Summer 1986

Summer 1986

Summer 1986

Summer 1986

EXHIBIT 17 SELECTED SWATCH PRINT ADS IN THE UNITED STATES

EXHIBIT 18   A PSYCHOGRAPHIC SEGMENTATION OF CONSUMERS IN THE UNITED STATES

Age	Children (6–10)	Teeny boppers (11–15)	Young teen rockers (11–15)	Students (11–15)	Rockers (16–22)
Profile/interests	TV: *Jem* rock cartoon, *Nickelodeon*. Males: He-Man, Transformers, G. I. Joe. Females: Care Bears.	Almost 100% female. Middle/middle-upper class suburban, clique oriented, very fashion conscious: trendy, outrageous style, favor Southern California over Europe/NYC look. Like partying, dancing, hanging out at malls. Music: breezy pop love songs, New Wave. Main hero: Madonna.	80% male, 20% female. Middle/upper-middle-class suburban, mall creatures, macho, heavy-metal look. Hard rock concerts, partying (but isolated, not in cliques). Main heroes: Stallone, Schwarzenegger, Iron Maiden ("Madonna is useless").	50% male, 50% female. Middle/lower-middle-class, very conservative, like professional and participation sports. Music: no allegiance to type of music or artist.	60% male, 40% female. Long hair, clique oriented, committed to rock groups, very frequent concertgoers (for music, not as a social event). Like fast cars, comedy and horror movies, 100% American rock 'n roll. Dislike short hair, New Wave, disco. Music: *pure* rock 'n roll (no synthesizers, drum machines). Hero: ZZ Top.
Media	Network TV, MTV.[a]	MTV-crazy, fashion magazines, Top-40 radio.	AOR[b] radio, critical MTV watchers.	Network TV, AM radio.	AOR radio, MTV (77% regular viewers).
Shopping habits	Dependent on parents. Stores: department stores, malls, etc.	Heavy consumers. Stores: department stores, record stores, malls.	*Not* shopping oriented. Stores: record stores, department stores, malls.	Consider shopping not an event. Stores: Sears, Kmart, chain drugstores.	Like all things "American."
Reaction to Swatch	42% awareness (of which 4% ownership, 76% interest in teeny bop models). Consider it "cool," something the big kids wear. Parents' interests: durability, price, large face numbers, traditional styles, models that won't become unfashionable.	*Very positive*—provides a sense of identity—is a lifestyle magnifier but becoming too commonplace, boring. Line extensions: negative. Too expensive, not cool, "Swatch is not a clothing line, but a rock 'n roll time piece."	High awareness due to visibility in schools but strong negative bias: Swatch represents teeny bopper lifestyle. Swatch too wild for their lifestyle yet potential interest to "fit in" (80% unawareness of traditional styles).	Price and function outweigh fashion-ability. Swatch too wild for their lifestyle yet potential interest to "fit in" (80% "price too high for a piece of plastic." Only 16% wear watches, but 72% desire to purchase Swatch if positioned correctly (NB: are currently "undersymboled").	Aware of wild Swatch styles *only*. Like its disposability, price. Dislike what it stands for: glitzy, hi-tech graphics, New Wave, dancing, slick ads, male model geeks. "A girl's/bopper's watch." Consider multiple Swatch ownership too trendy.

	Preppies (16–22)	Trendies (16–22)	Transitionaries (22–32)	Older Casuals (22–43)	Weekend Hippies (33–43)
Age					
Profile/interests	Career-oriented, traditional views, "controlled" wildness in style (designs more than colors), concerts (more as social event than for music), participation sports. Like dating, movies. Music: "Yuppie" rock/folk/pop. Like songs more than artists.	Movement similar to hippies but smaller scale. Exist only in U.S. art and culture capitals. Avant-garde tastes; outspoken on issues they consider important. Left socially and politically. Go to clubs, not concerts. Music: anti rock 'n roll, anti popular groups.	Conservative, social climbers, wildness (as observers, not participants), competitive sports. Music: "intelligent" rock 'n roll.	The hidden mainstream, ultraconservative, very family-oriented, fast-food patrons, socially inactive, disinterested in fashion. Music: traditional.	Mellowed former hippies. Look like but hate being called Yuppies; still subscribe to basic 1960s principles. Music: mood music, "New Age" movement.
Media	Cable TV, some MTV, some fashion magazines, radio (AOR, CHR,[c] light rock mix) but low station loyalty.	Trendy, artsy magazines and newspapers, Anti-MTV, anti-commercial radio.	Females: fashion magazines. Males: Time, Newsweek, Sports Illustrated. Not MTV (only 16% regular viewers).	Network TV. Local newspapers (even National Enquirer–type tabloids).	Cable TV (critical viewers) but not MTV, radio (as background music). Weekend newspaper supplements, traditional magazines (Time, Newsweek, etc.).
Shopping habits	Stores: mainstream department stores.	Consider fashion a vehicle of expression, rejection of anything too popular.	Pro-American but respectful of foreign-made goods; appreciate quality/value; balance between fashion and conservatism. Stores: major mainstream department stores (91% source of potential Swatch purchase for 76% aware).	Traditional brands (e.g., Timex, Bulova, Casio for watches).	Heavy shoppers, appreciate quality products. Stores: upscale department stores (I. Magnin, Saks) for females, mainstream department stores for men.
Reactions to Swatch	92% awareness. Prefer traditional designs, price, fashionability, reliability, practicality. Dislike its young teen image. 73% prefer dressier watches (silver/gold Rolex look) for "special events"; strongly "antidigital." Line extensions: too expensive, unnecessary.	73% wear no watch. Very negative image of Swatch: "a rip-off," "a toy," "the corporate world," "fast-food of time pieces."	Positive: consider it a great leisure tool, like its durability, disposability, price, reliability. Line extensions: high awareness but overpriced for females, not really credible for males.	Watches are functional. Awareness: 12% aided, 4% unaided.	High awareness, but 43% of those have never seen one. Cheap, teen-item image, but like functionality, light weight, durability. Line extensions: overpriced, not functional, too gaudy. High awareness of competing brands.

[a] MTV = a leading national "basic cable" TV music TV station.   [b] AOR = Album-oriented rock.   [c] CHR = Contemporary hits radio.
Source: Compiled from Burkhead, Abrams, Douglas, Eliot Market Study, 1986.

EXHIBIT 19   AIDED RECALL OF WATCH ADVERTISEMENTS

Brand	United States				Switzerland			
	Total (n = 99)	Buyers (n = 99)	Potential buyers (n = 140)	Non-buyers (n = 51)	Total (n = 212)	Buyers (n = 90)	Potential buyers (n = 87)	Non-buyers (n = 35)
Swatch	67[a]	79	66	47	78	88	70	74
Omega	6	9	6	—	19	22	17	14
Rolex	31	32	25	45	20	29	10	23
Seiko	35	35	36	29	16	22	6	23
Cartier	14	7	16	25	16	22	10	11
Timex	41	37	46	35	4	3	2	11
Gucci	16	17	15	16	—	—	—	—
Citizen	18	17	21	12	5	3	3	11
Pulsar	11	12	14	14	—	—	—	—
Bulova	10	6	12	14	—	—	—	—
Casio	10	14	11	—	6	7	5	6
Longines	11	12	11	12	15	18	9	20
Guess	14	18	12	14	—	—	—	—
Tissot	8	12	7	—	50	50	45	60
A-Watch	10	10	13	—	—	—	—	—
K-Watch	—	—	—	—	—	—	—	—
M-Watch	—	—	—	—	13	18	6	20
Club Med	—	—	—	—	—	—	—	—
Dugena	—	—	—	—	—	—	—	—
Kiple	—	—	—	—	—	—	—	—
Lorus	4	—	4	—	—	—	—	—
Yema	—	—	—	—	—	—	—	—

[a] Percentage of total responses to the question: "Which of the watches on this list have you seen or heard advertised recently?" No figure indicates that the brand was not listed on the card.

Source: Compiled from a Qualitest A. G. study, Zurich, August 1986.

EXHIBIT 19 (Continued)

	United Kingdom				France				West Germany			
	Total (n = 202)	Buyers (n = 68)	Potential buyers (n = 83)	Non-buyers (n = 51)	Total (n = 200)	Buyers (n = 66)	Potential buyers (n = 99)	Non-buyers (n = 35)	Total (n = 200)	Buyers (n = 67)	Potential buyers (n = 74)	Non-buyers (n = 59)
	50	56	53	39	50	62	46	34	67	70	69	61
	5	10	—	8	—	—	—	—	19	18	24	14
	17	16	22	12	15	17	12	17	34	31	39	31
	30	35	28	27	30	32	30	26	31	30	36	25
	11	12	13	6	—	—	—	—	—	—	—	—
	23	26	19	24	21	23	23	9	22	24	26	15
	—	—	—	—	—	—	—	49	—	—	—	—
	15	18	18	6	58	64	56	—	6	16	—	—
	—	—	—	—	4	3	5	—	—	—	—	—
	—	—	—	—	—	—	—	14	—	—	—	—
	11	15	11	6	11	11	10	—	13	13	11	14
	3	6	4	—	—	—	—	—	—	—	—	—
	9	13	10	6	—	—	—	—	12	14	11	10
	4	4	6	4	4	6	3	—	—	—	—	—
	—	—	—	—	—	—	—	9	—	—	—	—
	—	—	—	—	5	6	2	—	—	—	—	—
	—	—	—	—	—	—	—	9	15	15	15	15
	—	—	—	—	11	12	10	—	—	—	—	—
	—	—	—	—	14	17	12	14	—	—	—	—

EXHIBIT 20   UNAIDED AWARENESS OF WATCH BRANDS EUROPE AND UNITED STATES

Brand	Switzerland (n = 212)	Great Britain (n = 202)	France (n = 200)	West Germany (n = 200)	United States (n = 290)
Swatch	66ᵃ	49	47	66	62
Timex	—	74	24	17	57
Seiko	15	45	37	26	50
Rolex	26	34	17	58	40
Gucci	—	—	—	—	15
Cartier	8	8	21	20	14
Citizen	—	6	11	19	12
Pulsar	—	2	—	—	11
Bulova	—	—	—	—	11
Casio	—	20	4	3	9
Longines	9	—	—	—	9
Guess	—	—	—	—	6
Tissot	58	—	3	10	6
A-Watch	—	—	—	—	2
M-Watch	5	—	—	—	—
Coca-Cola	—	—	—	—	2
Dugena	—	—	—	26	—
Lorus	—	2	—	—	—
Yema	—	—	8	—	—
Lip	—	—	23	—	—
Kelton	—	—	36	—	—

ᵃ Percentage of respondents mentioning this brand in response to the questions: "What brands of watches can you spontaneously think of?" then "And which else?"
Source: Compiled from a Qualitest A. G. market study, Zurich 1986.

UNITED STATES

Brand	1983 (n = 1641)	1984 (n = 1669)	1986 (n = 1783)
Timex	84ᵃ	84	82
Seiko	36	41	39
Bulova	52	44	38
Elgin	20	21	18
Rolex	8	12	18
Hamilton	14	12	13
Longines	12	10	10
Waltham	12	9	8
Casio	4	4	8
Swatch	NA	NA	7
Pulsar	2	4	7
Omega	7	4	5
Citizen	3	4	5
Caravelle	4	4	2
Piaget	1	1	2
Lorus	—	1	2
Cartier	1	2	1
Tissot	1	1	1
Gucci	NA	NA	1
Guess	NA	NA	1
A-Watch	NA	NA	1

NA—not available.
ᵃ Percent of respondents mentioning this brand in response to the question: "Will you please tell me all the brands of watches you can think of?"
Source: Compiled from The Gallup Organization, Inc., figures.

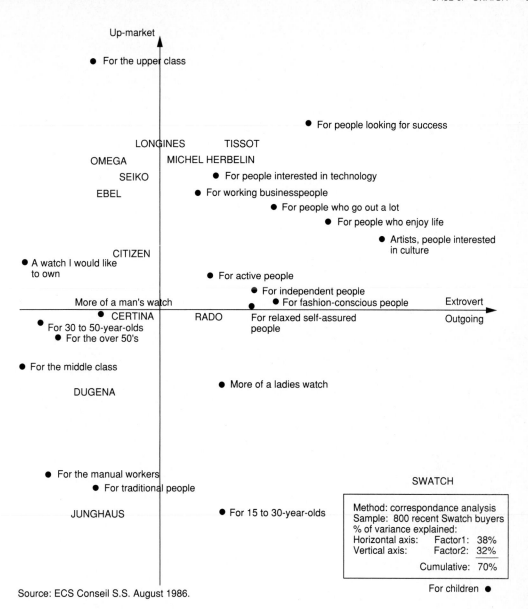

Up-market

● For the upper class

● For people looking for success

LONGINES   TISSOT

OMEGA   MICHEL HERBELIN

SEIKO   ● For people interested in technology

EBEL   ● For working businesspeople

● For people who go out a lot

● For people who enjoy life

● Artists, people interested in culture

CITIZEN

● A watch I would like to own

More of a man's watch   ● For active people

● For independent people

● For fashion-conscious people   Extrovert

● CERTINA   RADO   For relaxed self-assured people   Outgoing

● For 30 to 50-year-olds

● For the over 50's

● For the middle class

DUGENA   ● More of a ladies watch

● For the manual workers

● For traditional people   SWATCH

JUNGHAUS   ● For 15 to 30-year-olds

Method: correspondance analysis
Sample: 800 recent Swatch buyers
% of variance explained:
Horizontal axis: Factor1: 38%
Vertical axis: Factor2: 32%

Cumulative: 70%

For children ●

Source: ECS Conseil S.S. August 1986.

EXHIBIT 21   A PERCEPTUAL MAP OF SWATCH AND OTHER LEADING BRANDS IN WEST GERMANY

first solar-powered wristwatch was also launched under the Lorus brand name in 1986. Competitors wondered, however, if Seiko was really committed to competing with Swatch since non-watch activities—for example, personal computers, printers, and audio and video equipment—were to be increased to 30 percent of worldwide sales by 1989. Don Galliers summarized the challenge in the United States:

> If you want to take significant market share away from the existing well-established brand, you have to spend three times the amount of advertising that brand spends. To kick us where we hurt worse, in delivery and depth, they'll have to build up $75 million worth of initial inventory, in addition to the $100 million investment in production facilities. That's one hell of an investment!

Citizen apparently did not feel it necessary to launch a Swatch-like product, preferring to focus on its specialization, digitals, and technically sophisticated watches. At first Casio, specialized more specifically in calculators and extremely price-competitive multifunction digital watches, did not jump on the Swatch bandwagon either. In 1986, when the shift from digital to analog watches became apparent, however, Casio launched "Color Burst," a line of quartz analog fashion watches, waterproof to 50 meters, retailing at less than the price of Swatch. Sales were reported to be rather disappointing.

Swatch management claimed that only the very large firms could compete with ETA on price and that smaller firms undercutting Swatch on price were left with virtually no margin to compete with Swatch's intensive communication. Swatch refused to enter into a price war with its competitors. According to Jacques Irniger, ETA marketing manager, Swatch spent more than double the watch industry's average ad spending for a *single* brand: "Competitors can copy our watch but not our media spend. They will also have trouble duplicating some of Swatch's promotional stunts." Examples of "Swatch-like" fashion watches with limited market response were the "Twist" by Accurist and the "American Graffiti" watch by Gillex in the United Kingdom. Ac-

cording to Ernst Thomke, "In an era when superbly accurate quartz watches sell for $10, the key is not technology but image." Exhibit 22 presents Swatch's image in five countries.

Brands explicitly positioned as fashion accessories varied from one country to another, and it was difficult to obtain a global view of the situation as well as market share data to determine the relative threat presented by such brands. Designer watches (e.g., Gucci, Dior, Givenchy, Nina Ricci, Yves Saint Laurent, Ralph Lauren, Calvin Klein, Guy Laroche, Lanvin, Hermes, Benetton), although often in a different price range from Swatch, that is, segments C and D (see Exhibit 4), were a growing trend, and the actual concept of "fashion watch" did not appear clear in consumers' minds. Responses to the question "Please tell me all the brands of fashion watches you can think of" included such diverse brands as Timex, Swatch, Bulova, Citizen, and Rolex. Franz Sprecher's definition of a fashion watch was "a watch not only colorful but with accessorizing potential and meaning, a statement of the fashion trends at a specific period of time."

In Europe, moderately priced fashion watches included Kelton, an inexpensive French watch brand launched by Timex in the early 1960s. After initial rejection by the traditional jewelers' network, Kelton had been very successfully distributed through mass distribution channels. The breakdown of Kelton sales in France was estimated to be 45 percent from "tabacs" (registered tobacconists), 30 percent from supermarkets, and 25 percent from department and variety stores. Kelton was also distributed in the United Kingdom, Portugal, and Italy. Prices ranged from 99 to 320 French francs. K'Watch, Kelton's response to Swatch, launched in June 1984, was priced at 249 to 270 FF. Kelton brand awareness was very high in France, and it had a young, inexpensive, active, and fashionable image. Philippe d'Herbomez, Kelton marketing manager, commented:

> When you think about the Swatch strategy, you realize that the product was launched on the Kelton concept: "Vous vous changez, changez, de Kel-

EXHIBIT 22 SWATCH IMAGE IN FIVE COUNTRIES

Swatch	Switzerland				United Kingdom			
	Total (n = 212)	Buyers (n = 90)	Potential buyers (n = 87)	Non-buyers (n = 35)	Total (n = 202)	Buyers (n = 68)	Potential buyers (n = 83)	Non-buyers (n = 51)
is Swiss made	39[a]	43	37	31	15	13	17	14
is reasonably priced	36	44	34	20	32	32	34	27
is a sports watch	33	31	39	23	24	28	23	22
is continuously introducing new models (colors, dials)	32	30	37	26	14	10	23	6
is a watch for all occasions (business, sports)	30	37	32	9	31	35	25	33
is a highly fashionable watch	25	27	31	9	37	25	41	31
is mainly for young people	17	17	18	11	27	25	22	37
is waterproof	15	16	16	9	10	10	8	14
is the ideal present	14	17	16	–	11	15	8	10
has good ads	10	13	7	11	8	6	8	12
is a trendy watch	8	4	8	17	22	16	30	18
is a high-quality watch	7	9	6	3	29	32	23	33
is a quartz watch	6	4	7	9	3	1	6	–
is shockproof	5	4	7	–	10	9	5	20
attracts attention	3	2	3	3	24	25	25	20
I would like to own more than one	1	1	1	–	1	1	–	–

EXHIBIT 22   (Continued)

	France				West Germany				United States			
	Total (n = 200)	Buyers (n = 66)	Potential buyers (n = 99)	Non-buyers (n = 35)	Total (n = 200)	Buyers (n = 67)	Potential buyers (n = 74)	Non-buyers (n = 59)	Total (n = 290)	Buyers (n = 99)	Potential buyers (n = 140)	Non-buyers (n = 51)
	13	12	14	11	21	25	11	29	16	16	16	14
	24	30	19	26	16	15	16	15	26	31	24	18
	43	52	37	43	44	51	47	31	28	30	26	27
	30	29	31	29	50	61	53	32	19	20	20	12
	23	18	25	23	18	21	23	8	14	16	16	8
	18	15	21	14	33	19	39	41	25	27	24	25
	38	23	44	49	40	30	30	63	16	12	13	33
	8	15	5	3	8	9	14	—	17	22	16	10
	23	26	26	9	12	18	14	2	12	12	14	6
	5	8	4	3	16	9	20	19	16	8	21	20
	29	21	28	43	10	3	4	24	25	16	27	35
	6	9	4	6	6	6	4	8	20	28	16	12
	8	5	9	9	8	13	4	7	6	6	7	4
	9	12	5	14	5	6	8	—	8	10	7	6
	14	11	14	17	15	12	12	22	32	35	35	31
	11	15	10	3	1	2	1	—	6	9	5	—

[a]Percentage of total responses to the question: "Which three statements on this card can you think of as the most important ones in describing Swatch?"
Source: Qualitest A. G. study, Zurich, August 1986.

138

ton" (Time to change, change your Kelton!), but the consumer more readily changes his Swatch than his Kelton since with every new Swatch collection the previous ones become virtually obsolete. When Swatch was launched, Kelton was no longer very fashionable and had become expensive in comparison with Asian watches. The 1987 Kelton collection is a series of new lower-priced products. Our distribution is wearing thin also, so we plan to open up new outlets and invest in communication with emphasis on our well-known, successful slogan.

Other fashion watches had mushroomed in the wake of the Swatch success. The M-Watch, an inexpensive (38 SF) traditional quartz watch containing ETA movements, was launched by Mondaine in Zurich at the same time as Swatch and distributed by the Swiss supermarket chain Migros. In May 1984 the French firm Kiple launched "Kip'Marine," priced at 210 to 440 FF and distributed through supermarkets, stationers, "tabacs," and variety stores.

In October 1984, Dr. Konstantin Theile, ETA marketing manager during the development of Swatch, left ETA to launch the new brand TIQ (Time Inter Corporation A.G.). This new nonplastic, leather-strapped, silent, and reparable waterproof quartz watch priced at 70 to 150 SF targeted an "optimistic, individualistic, fashion-conscious consumer" aged 25 to 35 but slightly more conservative than the Swatch consumer. Production costs were three times those of Swatch, and TIQ granted the usual margin to the trade. Distribution was through up-market department stores, established jewelers, and fashion boutiques. To quote Dr. Theile:

> Not everybody wants to wear a noisy irreparable plastic watch. It is frustrating to become attached to your watch only to find out that your model cannot be repaired and is no longer available.

By early 1985 the French firm Beuchat had introduced a series of metal and plastic strap watches with original and fun faces: a sports line illustrating 27 different sports, a "crazy" line including a face with hands turning counterclockwise, and a "corporations" line illustrat-

ing different professions. Distribution was the same as Swatch, and prices were slightly higher. Beuchat's plans were to expand into promotional watches starting with BMW, the German auto company. Under license from Club Méditerranée, the French firm Marckley CDH had launched waterproof metal and plastic quartz watches distributed worldwide through selective channels. Prices were also slightly higher than Swatch. Marckley did not invest in advertising for the "Club Med" watch, but point-of-sales promotion included an aquarium display containing a submerged watch.

The American firm Le Jour started testing a $49 kaleidoscope color fashion watch called "Sixty" in 1986. Sales, mainly through department stores, were reportedly encouraging. In the spring of 1986 a Swiss entrepreneur launched "The Clip," a clip-on waterproof, shock-resistant, silent, and reparable quartz watch designed to be worn "anywhere except on the wrist" and sold through the same distribution channels as Swatch. Launched in Switzerland at 40 SF and 50 SF, The Clip was introduced in France, Spain, West Germany, and England in the summer and would roll out to the United States in the fall. E. A. Day, managing director of Louis Newmark, the Swatch distributor in the United Kingdom, commented:

> It is too early to discuss the future of The Clip. It does appear to sell well when promoted, but once the promotion ends, sales drop back dramatically.

In the summer of 1986, the Swiss firm SAMEL S.A. had introduced "Sweet-zerland," a water-resistant quartz watch with a two-year battery that snapped in and out of interchangeable elastic terrycloth wristbands in different colors, priced at $40. Distribution was through jewelry stores, fashion boutiques, accessory and sports shops, perfumeries, and up-market department stores in France, West Germany, Austria, Benelux, Italy, Spain, and Portugal as well as the United States through a California subsidiary.

Sekonda, an English firm importing watches from the U.S.S.R. and Hong Kong, launched

EXHIBIT 23   SWATCH SALES, 1983–1986
SWATCH WATCHES (Thousand Units or Swiss Francs)

Country	1983		1984		1985		January–August 1986	
	Units	S.F.	Units	S.F.	Units	S.F.	Units	S.F.
World	1319	27,901	4496	114,057	10,168	284,832	8321	209,954
United States	135	NA	1242	42,475	4659	167,562	3817	102,824
Switzerland	NA	NA	1032	23,451	924	21,707	595	14,585
France			399	8,910	756	17,710	667	14,824
England	NA	NA	455	7,140	762	14,288	524	9,694
West Germany	NA	NA	202	4,514	712	17,152	587	16,837
Japan					141	3,374	18	646

EXTENDED PRODUCT LINE
(Thousand Units or U.S. Dollars)

Item	1984		1985		January–August 1986	
	Units	Dollars	Units	Dollars	Units	Dollars
Swatch guards	7	10	3,617	4,280	2,637	3,721
Chums	18	26	104	226	24	6
Bags			224	2,497	134	1,042
Shields			141	2,418	87	1,381
Knives			263	1,236	4	20
Clocks			4	248	1	77
Umbrellas			181	1,606	109	359
Apparel			620	6,279	1,898	18,877
Parafernalia			387	1,175	440	464
Coca-Cola watches					194	3,392

Source: Company records (disguised data).

a new line of fashion watches in 1985, under the brand names "Spangles," "Phantom," and "Nostalgia." Prices ranged from L15 to L20. A mechanical watch named "Hotline," with style variations on the dial and strap, appeared in West Germany and Switzerland in 1986. It was explicitly aimed at preteen age groups and retailed mainly in department stores for 30 DM. Other European fashion watches in roughly the same price category as Swatch included Avia, Alfex, Orion, Zion, Video Clip, and Hip-Hop.

The Meeting

Chris Keigel checked the fashionable collection of Swatches on his wrist. It was time to make major decisions for the future of Swatch, and the meeting with Thomke, Marquardt, Imgruth, and Sprecher was approaching fast. He perused the sales figures in Exhibit 23. Keigel knew that Swatch guards and shields, the Parafernalia line, and the Coca-Cola watches yielded profit margins exceeding that of Swatch watches, whereas those of the other items in the United States extended product line did not. Apparel profit margins had dropped, and sales were lagging behind forecasts. Swatch management knew that the transport and other costs involved in importing this line to Europe might put prices out of line, especially since the clothing was designed specifically for the American market. He also knew that Max Imgruth was pushing for six collection changes per year but remembered hearing Franz Sprecher advocate a more conservative approach:

We can't just announce "Here comes our collection" to the trade. We are an accessory, we are not making fashion. What is most important is what the consumer will think. Are we really enough of a fashion product in the eyes of the consumer to make a planned line extension into fashion wear? If Calvin Klein, Ralph Lauren, or Benetton make a watch, that works because they are established fashion firms, but I have never seen it work the other way around. There is a lot of competition in the department stores, whole floors of T-shirts, so where is our expertise?

THE GOLDEN GATE BREWING COMPANY

At a booth in Harry's, a local bar overlooking the San Francisco Bay, James Cook poured a fresh glass of amber-colored Golden Gate Lager and dropped a bottle cap onto the beer's head. The cap floated like a lily pad on the foam. "That's what you get from using all malt, no rices or corn—a very firm head," he said. "It looks like whipped cream and acts like egg whites, as my father used to say." When Cook's glass was finished, the inside was coated with strips of foam, "Belgian lace" in brewer's jargon, and a sign of a beer's purity. "People usually think of a local beer as crummy, cheap beer. I plan to change the way they think," Cook said.

James Cook, age 36, was president of the fledgling Golden Gate Brewing Company, the brewer of Golden Gate Lager, and sixth consecutive eldest son in the Cook family to become a brewer. Cook was a former high-paid, high-powered management consultant with the Boston Consulting Group. He held a Harvard B.A., M.B.A., and J.D. The Golden Gate Brewing Company was incorporated in 1984, and Golden

Gate Lager was introduced in San Francisco on July 4, an appropriate day, but accidental timing according to Cook. Cook's goal was to establish Golden Gate Lager as a superpremium beer with a distinctive taste:

> I intend to go head-to-head against imported beers. Nowhere in the world but America do they drink so much imported beer. Here, imported beer is popular because our domestic beer is so bad. My work is to give Americans an alternative to drinking foreign beers. I want to start a revolution in the way people think about American beer. There is nothing wrong with standard domestic beers, for what they are. They are clean, consistent, and cheap. But they are also bland and mediocre. They are mass market products. People can recall, off the top of their heads, the advertising, the slogans, and the music for most beers, but they can't remember the taste.

THE SITUATION

For years, small local breweries had either closed down or been acquired by one of the industry leaders. The advent of small boutique breweries—in California, Colorado, and New York— making limited quantities of quality beer, had opposed this trend. Cook acknowledged that

Prepared by Brent Callinicos, research assistant, under the direction of Professor Richard I. Levin, University of North Carolina at Chapel Hill. Copyright ©1988 by the authors.

the odds and history were against small regional breweries. But Cook was betting on a combination of his family's brewing background, management training, and a limited target market to create long-term Golden Gate Lager drinkers.

Golden Gate Lager is currently sold in two locations, San Francisco and Munich. As of November 1985, the current sales volume of 6,000 cases per month represents less than one minute of production for Anheuser-Busch, the long-standing industry leader. Cook reports that he has sold as much beer in the past six months as Anheuser-Busch makes in about six minutes. "They spill more beer every hour than I make in a month." In six months, the Golden Gate Brewing Company has sold 25,000 cases in California. His more than 200 accounts range from liquor stores to exclusive hotels to neighborhood bars, such as Harry's. Exhibits 1 through 3 provide industry background, population demographics of the San Francisco/Oakland area, and general demographics of U.S. beer drinkers.

EXHIBIT 1   BEER INDUSTRY FACTS AND TERMS

Dimensions of the industry

The annual wholesale value of the brewing industry's products in 1985 was $13.7 billion.

Total employment in the industry was close to 40,000 people.

The average hourly earnings of a brewing industry employee was $18.27 in 1985, a 3.2 percent increase over 1984.

In a recent typical year, the industry's gross assets amounted to $6,639,979,000. Its net worth, computed from income tax returns, was $3,377,780,000.

What the industry buys

Agricultural commodities, the output of more than 4 million acres of farm land, worth $700 million plus are used annually by the brewing industry. These include:

- 4.9 billion pounds or 143.8 million bushels of choice malt—worth $380 million
- Other select grains, chiefly corn and rice—worth $221 million
- Hops—value to the grower of $80 million

Some 86.9 percent of all beer sold is packaged in cans or bottles. In one year, the brewing industry uses more than:

- 33.1 billion steel and aluminum cans
- 19.2 billion bottles in returnable and nonreturnable form
- $525 million for interest, rentals, repairs, and maintenance

The industry's annual bill for containers—cans, bottles, kegs, and related packaging materials purchased from other American industries—is close to $4.5 billion. Supplies and services of numerous kinds are also required in brewing and distributing malt beverages. Annual average outlays for these include:

- Fuel, power, and water—$420 million
- Wholesale payroll—$1.8 billion
- Brewery equipment and improvements—$550 million

The industry's products and terminology

Beers fall into two broad categories: those that are top-fermented and those that are bottom-fermented.

Bottom-fermented

Pilsner/Pilsener. The world's most famous beer style, it was named after the excellent beer brewed in Pilsen, Czechoslovakia, for the past 700 years. It is a pale, golden-colored, distinctly hoppy beer.

Lager. All bottom-fermented beers are lagers. This is a generic term, though it is sometimes applied to the most basic bottom-fermented brew produced by a brewery. In Britain and the United States, the majority of lagers are very loose, local interpretations of the Pilsner style.

Top-fermented

Ale. Generic term for English-style top-fermented beers. Usually copper-colored, but sometimes darker. It is usually paler in color and differs in flavor from lager beer.

Stout. Darker in color and sweeter or maltier than ale. The darkest, richest, maltiest of all regularly produced beers.

"Malt Liquor." This is a term conjured up to describe beers that exceed a country's legal alcohol levels—5 percent in the United States. They are most often made as lagers, but the American version can be sweetish or more bitter than the traditional lagers.

Barrel. This refers to a full barrel, which has a volume of 31 gallons.

EXHIBIT 2   POPULATION CHARACTERISTICS OF THE SAN FRANCISCO/OAKLAND AREA, 1980

Year	Population	Percentage change
1960	2,649,000	N/A
1970	3,109,000	17.37%
1980	3,251,000	4.5

Age composition

Age	Population	Percentage of total
Under 18	1,296,000	25.02%
18–24	666,000	12.86
25–34	989,000	19.10
35–44	668,000	12.90
45–54	536,000	10.35
55–64	491,000	9.48
65–Over	533,000	10.29
Under 21	1,571,000	30.33

Ethnic composition

Race	Percentage of total
White	62.37%
Black	10.71
Spanish	9.64
Indian	10.93
Eskimo	0.47
Other*	5.88

Education
(persons 25 years old and over)

Years of education	Percentage of total
Less than five	3%
High school only	71
Four years college or more	26
Median school years completed	13

Occupational profile

Group	Percentage of total
Managerial and professional	28.28%
Technical and sales related	35.43
Service occupations	11.84
Farming/forestry/fishing	1.15
Craft/repair group	11.12
Operators/laborers	12.18

Income breakdown

Income	Households	Percentage of total
Under $5,000	199,763	10.12%
$5,000–$9,999	243,278	12.32
$10,000–$19,999	511,225	25.90
$20,000–$34,999	611,279	30.97
$35,000–$49,999	258,758	13.11
$50,000–Over	149,577	7.58
Total households	1,973,880	
Median income	$20,607	

* Includes Japanese, Chinese, Filipino, Korean, Asian Indian, Vietnamese, Hawaiian, and Samoan.
Source: U.S. Bureau of the Census, *Census of Population,* 1980.

EXHIBIT 3   1983 U.S. BEER DRINKER DEMOGRAPHICS

	Percentage of the population drinking					
	Domestic	Light	Imported	Malt	Ale	Draft
All adults	39.6%	24.4%	15.8%	8.3%	8.6%	26.2%
Males	54.0	28.6	22.0	11.0	12.0	35.6
Females	26.6	20.6	10.3	5.9	5.5	17.7
Age						
18–24	51.2	29.1	26.6	14.8	14.0	36.5
25–34	49.0	30.8	20.8	10.9	10.9	36.1
35–44	39.3	27.8	15.8	7.3	7.8	26.8
45–54	35.5	23.5	13.5	5.6	7.0	22.8
55–64	30.9	16.7	8.5	4.1	5.6	16.9
65 or older	23.4	13.0	4.6	4.3	3.8	9.8
College graduate	47.5	32.2	28.0	6.0	12.4	36.3
Attended college	45.3	30.0	22.0	8.9	11.9	33.5
High school graduate	38.4	23.9	13.6	8.4	7.8	25.8
Not high school graduate	23.6	17.4	8.5	9.2	5.6	16.7
Employed full-time	46.2	30.2	20.4	9.0	10.5	33.2
Part-time	36.7	24.9	17.7	8.0	9.0	26.5
Not employed	32.1	17.3	10.1	7.6	6.2	17.7
Professional	48.2	32.8	27.1	7.4	12.8	37.0
Clerical/sales	38.6	29.8	17.6	7.3	9.2	29.2
Craftsperson/supervisor	52.9	30.7	17.7	9.1	8.4	36.3
Other employed	44.3	25.5	16.2	11.5	9.6	28.9
Single	50.8	28.5	29.0	14.9	14.5	36.5
Married	38.3	24.1	12.9	6.1	7.1	24.6
Divorced	30.7	20.2	11.0	8.7	6.7	19.6
Parents	41.0	26.5	14.5	8.8	7.7	27.9
White	39.8	24.9	15.8	6.1	8.4	27.4
Black	36.8	19.3	14.4	25.4	9.8	16.4
Other	42.0	27.6	25.6	12.7	7.5	27.6
Geographic location						
Northeast	42.9	22.0	22.3	7.2	13.5	27.7
East Central	39.1	24.2	11.6	7.5	9.3	27.2
West Central	42.3	29.0	13.1	7.4	5.6	30.3
South	32.7	22.8	11.1	9.6	6.4	21.0
Pacific	45.1	26.1	22.3	9.5	7.8	28.4
Household income						
$40,000 +	45.6	29.7	24.1	6.0	11.8	32.7
$30,000 +	44.2	28.8	22.5	6.0	10.7	32.0
$25,000 +	44.1	28.4	21.3	6.4	10.3	31.4
$20–24,999	38.1	26.0	14.0	6.8	7.7	27.5
$15–19,999	42.5	26.7	14.5	10.9	8.7	28.8
$10–14,999	36.0	20.9	11.2	9.1	7.1	21.7
Under $10,000	32.3	16.5	9.5	11.3	6.5	16.6

EXHIBIT 4   OPERATING BREWERIES BY CENSUS REGION

Region	1952	1960	1970	1982	Percentage of total	
					1952	1982
Northeast	100	62	45	18	28.0%	22.8%
North Central	164	99	61	25	45.9	31.6
South	42	33	26	20	11.8	25.3
West	51	35	22	16	14.3	20.3
Total United States	357	229	154	79	100.0%	100.0%

"By my standards I have been very successful," said Cook. While demand has been strong, he wondered if it would last. "People who drink imports will try it because it's new, but will Golden Gate Lager be just a flash?" Cook is hoping there are enough beer aficionados in San Francisco, but he is wondering if he should try to expand in Europe, or if he should concentrate on the West Coast, the East Coast, or selected cities throughout the country. How fast should he expand? With several comparable local brews being sold in the area, will his marketing strategy have to change? What are the risks involved? Cook realized he needed to make some strategic decisions.

INDUSTRY OVERVIEW

Historically, the U.S. beer industry had many small local producers, but now it is dominated by the six largest brewers (see Exhibits 5 and 6). In 1876 there were 2,685 breweries; in 1952 there were only 350; and in 1982 there were 79 (Exhibit 4). Major firms were more willing to purchase struggling regional producers or construct new facilities in the South and West so as to establish nationwide distribution of their brands.

Following several years of flat or nearly flat sales, beer consumption declined about 0.7 percent in 1984 (Exhibit 7), the first decline in

EXHIBIT 5   LEADING U.S. BREWERS' DOMESTIC BEER MARKET SHARE

Brewer	1970	1975	1980	1982	1983	1984
Anheuser-Busch	18.2%	23.7%	28.9%	33.5%	34.1%	34.6%
Miller	4.2	8.7	21.5	22.3	21.1	22.1
Stroh	2.7	3.5	3.6	13.0	13.7	13.5
G. Heileman	2.5	3.1	7.7	8.2	9.9	9.3
Adolph Coors	6.0	8.0	8.0	6.8	7.7	7.2
Pabst	8.6	10.5	8.7	6.8	7.2	6.8
Genesee	1.2	1.5	2.1	1.9	1.8	1.9
C. Schmidt	2.5	2.2	2.1	1.8	1.8	1.7
Falstaff	5.4	5.0	2.3	1.8	1.5	1.8
Pittsburgh			0.6	0.6	0.6	0.5
Other	48.7	33.8	14.5	3.3	0.6	0.6
Total	100.0%	100.0%	100.0%	100.0%	100.0%	100.0%

EXHIBIT 6   BARRELAGE OF TOP 10 BREWERS: 1984 COMPARED WITH 1983

| | 1983 | 1984 | Gain/loss | |
			Barrels*	Percent
Anheuser-Busch	60,500,000	64,000,000	3,500,000	5.8%
Miller	37,470,000	37,520,000	50,000	0.1
Stroh	24,300,000	23,900,000	(400,000)	−1.6
G. Heileman	17,549,000	16,760,000	(789,000)	−4.5
Adolph Coors	13,719,000	13,187,000	(532,000)	−3.9
Pabst	12,804,000	11,562,000	(1,242,000)	−9.7
Genesee	3,200,000	3,000,000	(200,000)	−6.3
C. Schmidt	2,800,000	2,500,000	(300,000)	−10.7
Falstaff	2,705,000	2,338,000	(367,000)	−13.6
Pittsburgh	1,000,000	950,000	(50,000)	−5.0
All Others	3,597,000	2,134,000	(1,463,000)	−40.7
Total	179,644,000	177,851,000	(1,793,000)	−1.0%

* In 31-gallon barrels.

27 years; production declined approximately 1.2 percent (Exhibit 8). Per capita consumption of beer also declined (Exhibit 9), and for 1985, per capita consumption is estimated to remain at the 1984 level of 24 gallons. The long-term outlook for the industry is less encouraging. Chris Lole of the Stroh Brewery Company believes that beer sales will remain flat for the next 10, possibly 20, years.

However, there is one segment of growth in this troubled industry—imports. Imported brands have grown from 0.7 percent of total consumption in 1970 to 3.4 percent in 1983 (aided somewhat over the years by a strong U.S. dollar). Imports occupy the high ground in terms of quality in consumers' perception, and trading up continues to benefit imports. As import volume has grown, an increasing number of brands have appeared, and many more are now being advertised. The continued growth in this segment, coupled with the decline in domestic sales, meant an increase in import's share to almost 4 percent in 1984.

For regional and smaller brewers, it is becoming increasingly difficult to move a product which is falling in demand and cannot be backed by the advertising revenues of the large national breweries. Interestingly, the mi-

EXHIBIT 7   U.S. BEER SALES: DOMESTIC BRANDS AND IMPORTED BRANDS, 1983–1984

| | 31-gallon barrels (millions) | | Percent of total | | Percent change |
	1983	1984	1983	1984	
Domestic beer	177.5	175.3	96.6%	96.1%	−1.2%
Imported beer	6.3	7.2	3.4	3.9	14.3
Total sales	183.8	182.5	100.0	100.0	−0.7

EXHIBIT 8   PRODUCTION OF MALT BEVERAGES IN
THE UNITED STATES FOR SELECTED
YEARS
(Thousands)

Year	Barrels	Year	Barrels
1904	48,265	1977	172,229
1914	66,189	1978	171,639
1924	4,891	1979	183,515
1934	37,679	1980	188,374
1944	81,726	1981	194,542
1954	92,561	1982	193,984
1964	103,018	1983	195,664
1974	153,053	1984	193,416

crobrewer/brew pub trend continues. More and more entrepreneurs are allured by the prospects of concocting their own distinctive beer and operating their own business.

EXTERNAL THREATS

Several external threats were affecting the beer industry: First, the U.S. population is more concerned about healthier lifestyles, which potentially reduces beer consumption. Consumption and the purchase-pattern preference of 25- to 40-year-olds have changed dramatically in recent years. This group—because of interests in appearance, exercise, and career advancement—exhibits a preference for drinks with fewer calories and lower alcohol content. Over-40 drinkers are also increasingly health and diet conscious.

EXHIBIT 9   PER CAPITA U.S. CONSUMPTION OF MALT
BEVERAGES, 1974–1984

Year	Gallons	Year	Gallons
1974	20.9	1980	24.3
1975	21.3	1981	24.6
1976	21.5	1982	24.4
1977	22.4	1983	24.2
1978	23.1	1984	24.0
1979	23.8		

An important negative factor for future beer sales is demographics. Growth of the 18-to-34 age group is winding down. Beer sales have closely tracked the baby boom age bulge in the population. The teenage population (the source of most new drinkers) has been decreasing and is forecast to continue its decline. Brewers, therefore, confront a decline in potential new users. In addition, the young adult population (20 to 29 years) is also declining. The beer industry relies on this segment to replace sales lost due to attrition in the drinking population. Finally, people between the ages of 30 and 49 will increase substantially and by 1990 will constitute 30 percent of the population. Historically, this group has been an important beer-drinking group. However, industry analysts say this group is the one most concerned about alcohol abuse and drunk driving.

The beer industry faces another demographic change that will create problems. Blue-collar workers have traditionally been the heaviest consumers of beer. Today, the economy is shifting toward the service sector, and the blue-collar work force is declining.

The emergence of wine coolers is also taking a toll on the beer industry. Wine coolers appeal to beer drinkers and to nonbeer drinkers. Coolers are, to some extent, a beer substitute. Introduced five years ago, there are about 50 cooler brands now available which contain 6 percent alcohol. Retail sales in 1984 were $360 million and in 1985 approached $700 million. However, cooler sales for 1986 are projected at 35 million cases, versus 2.5 billion cases of the beer market. Some analysts believe that wine coolers are firmly established, while others contend that coolers are just a fad.

The market will shrink further due to stiffer penalties for drunk driving and the rise of the national legal drinking age to 21. The growing awareness of the need for responsible drinking habits has been fostered by groups such as Mothers Against Drunk Drivers (MADD). According to MADD, about 55 percent of all highway fatalities in 1983 were alcohol related; 1984 figures indicated a small decline to 54 percent.

In July 1984, President Ronald Reagan signed into law the National Minimum Drinking Age Act, which grants the federal government the authority to withhold federal highway funds from states that fail to raise their legal drinking age to 21 by 1987. When the law was enacted there were 27 states and the District of Columbia with a minimum age below 21, but many have introduced legislation to raise the age, or are expected to. Some 360 new laws regarding drunk driving have been passed nationwide since 1981. Many states and municipalities have banned "happy hours," which encourage increased alcohol consumption through discount prices. Also, there are 37 states with statutes holding the establishments and hosts liable for the subsequent behavior of intoxicated patrons or guests. These could also serve to reduce beer consumption.

INDUSTRY REACTION

Faced with these problems, many other industries would retrench, concentrate on keeping primary profit-making brands afloat, and try to ride out the storm. The brewery industry's response has been almost the opposite. New brands and extensions have appeared on retailers' shelves at a record pace. Beers that had been available only regionally are being moved into broader distribution. New light beers, low-alcohol beers, low-priced beers, superpremium beers, and malt liquors have emerged. Exhibit 10 lists the brands introduced in 1984 by both national and regional brewers.

The major U.S. brewers introduced 26 new products or line extensions in 1984. Two-thirds of these new product introductions were low-alcohol or low-calorie products. Anheuser-Busch (A-B) was the first major brewer to unveil its low-alcohol entry, LA; and regional brewers soon got into the act. To date, however, the low- and no-alcohol products have not worked out well. They are viewed as weak with no zing. They seem to appeal to the drinker who does not drink very much beer to begin with, in contrast to light beers which appeal to the heavy beer drinker.

EXHIBIT 10   DOMESTIC BEER BRANDS INTRODUCED IN 1984

Brand	Brewer
Black Label 11-11 Malt Liquor	Heileman
Black Label LA*	Heileman
Blatz LA*	Heileman
Big Man Malt Liquor	Eastern Brewing
Choice*	F.X. Malt
Golden Hawk	Schmidt
Ice Man Malt Liquor	Pabst
I. C. Golden Lager	Pittsburgh
King Cobra Malt Liquor	Anheuser-Busch
LA†	Anheuser-Busch
Light-N-Lo*	Latrobe
Little Kings Premium	Schoenling
Lone Star LA*	Heileman
Low Alcohol Gold*†	Pabst
Low Alcohol Pabst Extra Light*†	Pabst
Meister Brau Light	Miller
Milwaukee's Best	Miller
Old Style LA*	Heileman
Oscar Wilde's	Pearl
Plank Road Original Draft	Miller
Rainier LA*	Heileman
Schaefer Low Alcohol*	Stroh
Schmidt LA*	Heileman
Select Special 50 Low Alcohol*	Pearl
Sharpe's LA*	Miller
Silver Thunder Malt Liquor	Stroh

* Low in alcohol.
† Repositioned brand.

While new product introductions slowed in 1985, the beer industry is doing everything possible to attact new customers. A shrinking market means that brewers must steal share from competitors. Lower-priced brands have been introduced, and major firms, particularly Anheuser-Busch and Miller, have expanded their advertising budgets.

TAXES

The brewing industry confronts another problem, the ever-present threat of increased taxation. Beer is one of the most highly taxed consumer products. Taxes constitute the largest individual item in the price of beer. The federal excise tax is $9 a barrel, and state taxes average approximately $5.41 a barrel. Combined annual federal, state, and local taxes equal almost $3 billion. While the government earns over $14 for each barrel of beer or ale sold, the brewing industry's average profit rate per barrel after taxes is estimated between $2 and $3. The federal government was debating the merits of increased excise taxes on beer as part of a plan to reduce the federal deficit. It was common for state and local governments to raise taxes on beer periodically. In California, where Golden Gate was headquartered, brewers paid taxes equal to $1.24 per barrel.

INTERNAL/INDUSTRY FACTORS

The major causes of consolidation in the beer industry were economies of scale and product differentiation. Economies of scale, which occur when large plants produce at lower unit costs than smaller ones, existed in both the brewing and bottling processes. The increased capacity attained by many individual breweries over the past 20 years has forced the closing or sale of numerous regional producers. Industry experts contend that the wave of consolidation has not ended. Currently there is excess capacity, and certain plants are inefficient (Exhibit 11). Except for A-B, the industry is operating between 75 percent and 85 percent of capacity.

Even though the U.S. beer industry is suffering from overcapacity, two brewers announced expansion plans during 1985. Adolph Coors Company intends to build a $70 million beer packaging plant in Virginia, and if sales justify it, the facility will be expanded to include full brewing facilities. G. Heileman Brewing Company plans to construct a new brewery in Milwaukee. The facility will specialize in more costly imported-style beers. The industry's overcapacity was accentuated by Miller Brewing's decision to write-down $140 million of its $450 million new plant and Stroh Brewery Company's decision to close its older, underutilized Detroit plant.

EXHIBIT 11   U.S. BREWING INDUSTRY CAPACITY AND USAGE, 1983

Brewer	Plants	Total capacity (million)	Shipments	Percent of capacity
Anheuser-Busch	11	66.5	60.5	91.0%
Miller	7	54.0	37.5	69.4
Stroh	7	32.6	24.3	74.5
G. Heileman	12	25.5	17.5	68.6
Adolph Coors	1	15.5	13.7	88.4
Pabst	4	15.0	12.8	85.3
Genesee	1	4.0	3.2	80.0
C. Schmidt	2	5.0	3.2	64.0
Falstaff	5	5.0	2.7	54.0
Pittsburgh	1	1.2	1.0	83.3
All others	34	7.4	3.7	50.0
Domestic total	85	231.7	180.1	77.7%

Successful product differentiation occurs when a firm convinces customers that real or imagined differences in its beer render it preferable to that of the competitors. Larger brewers, with national sales and multiplant operations, can often more easily attain this high-quality image than local or regional brewers. There also appear to be economies of scale in brand proliferation and product extensions. Large brewers can more easily (and cost-effectively) segment all price and product categories. The high fixed costs associated with advertising new brands can be spread over a large sales volume that smaller brewers do not have. Large firms can realize lower advertising costs on each barrel than small firms.

Advertising has grown considerably in importance and in expense. In 1984 brewers spent an estimated $780 million. Advertising expenditures in 1983 averaged $2.74 per barrel. The evidence that high advertising expenditures and high-profit levels are positively correlated is, however, somewhat mixed. At Schlitz, for example, advertising expenditures on each barrel rose dramatically at a time when sales and operating profit per barrel both fell. Similarly, Coors had higher profit figures when advertising expenditure levels were extremely low and lower profits when advertising outlays accelerated. However, A-B and Miller have increased both profit on each barrel and market share, at a time when advertising expenditures increased.

IMPORTS

Imports are expected to perform well throughout the remainder of the 1980s. Between 1980 and 1984, the quantity of beer imported increased about 12 percent annually. Five countries—the Netherlands, Canada, West Germany, Mexico, and the United Kingdom—account for about 90 percent of all U.S. imports, but over 40 other countries ship beer to the United States. The imports' share of the U.S. beer market has grown from 1.1 percent in 1975 to 3.9 percent in 1984. Many beer wholesalers felt that imports would capture at least 10 percent of the total U.S. beer market by 1990.

Ten years ago, imported beers were esoteric products consumed by a small elite, in a handful of markets. Since then, the industry has exploded with beer drinkers' desire, taste, and imagery fueling this growth. According to industry analyst Emanuel Goldman, "The imports have image. We live in a self-indulgent age that's getting more and more self-indulgent, and people want something different. They can get something different, upscale, and feel good about it with imports. There is a tremendous selection, too. The consumer seems to feel that imports are superior beers."

The top 10 imported brands dominate about 87 percent of the sales (Exhibit 12). Heineken maintains the lead with an estimated 34 percent of the market, while Molson holds second place with 13.4 percent. Fortifying the Canadian segment is Moosehead in the number four spot and Labatt in the fifth place with 6 percent and 4.5 percent of the market, respectively. Beck's is in third place with 8.9 percent of the market, and its closest German competitor, St. Pauli Girl, ranks sixth.

Favorable demographics and an improving economy have aided this segment. The rise of the Hispanic population and the popularity of Mexican cuisine has fared well for Mexican beers, while the growing Oriental population has given rise to a host of Chinese and Japanese brews. Most significant has been the appeal of imported beer to status-conscious consumers. A prime market eager for imported beers has been the young urban professionals, with a desire for unusual and different products, especially those of a foreign bent.

An estimated 10 new imported beers entered the United States every month in 1984. Exhibit 13 provides a partial list of the imported brands introduced in 1984.

There are two major obstacles in trying to capture American market share. The first is

EXHIBIT 12   TOP IMPORTED BEER BRANDS

Top ten	Second ten (alphabetically)
1. Heineken (Netherlands)	11. Carta Blanca (Mexico)
2. Molson (Canada)	12. Dinkelacker (Germany)
3. Beck's (Germany)	13. Dortmunder (Germany)
4. Moosehead (Canada)	14. Grolsch (Netherlands)
5. Labatt (Canada)	15. Guinness (United Kingdom)
6. St. Pauli Girl (Germany)	16. Kirin (Japan)
7. Dos Equis (Mexico)	17. Kronenbourg (France)
8. Foster's Lager (Australia)	18. O'Keefe (Canada)
9. Amstel Light (Netherlands)	19. San Miquel (Philippines)
10. Corona (Mexico)	20. Tecate (Mexico)

EXHIBIT 13 IMPORTED BEER BRANDS INTRODUCED IN 1984

Brand	Country	Brand	Country
ABC Stout	Singapore	Hombre	Mexico
Affligem	Belgium	John Peel Export	Britain
Alfa Beer	Holland	Jever Pilsner	West Germany
Anchor Pilsener	Singapore	Kaiser	Germany
Bamburger Hofbrau	Germany	Koff Stout	Finland
Brador	Canada	Kronenhaler*	Austria
Broken Hill	Australia	Lindener	West Germany
Castillio Beer	Italy	Lorimer	Britain
Castle St.	Britain	Maes Pils	Belgium
China Beer	Taiwan	Oktober Beer	West Germany
China Clipper	China	Oranjeboom	Holland
Danish Light	Denmark	Pacifico	Mexico
De Koninck	Belgium	Rolland Light	Germany
Dempseys	Ireland	Scandia Gold	Denmark
Elan*	Switzerland	Tientan	China
Feingold Pils	Austria	Vaux	Britain
Felinfoel	Britain	Vienna Lager	Austria
Festive Ale	Britain	Warteck*	Switzerland
Glacier*	Sweden	Wolfbrau	Germany
Golden Ox	Germany	Yuchan Beer	China
Grizzly Beer	Canada	Zero*	Germany

* Denotes low or nonalcoholic brand.

Van Munching & Company, which distributes Heineken. Heineken, with its commanding market share, essentially sets the benchmark pricing level for much of the import category. Many feel that you cannot enter the U.S. market if you are above Heineken in price. The second major problem is a paradox created by the very success of the category, namely brand proliferation and the resulting market dilution.

Success hinges on the ability to come up with a unique selling proposition to cut through the multitude of brands competing for available market share. One technique used by imports is a unique packaging profile. The theory behind this is that the consumer knows none of the beers, but will try the one that looks a little different. This is supported by the number of American beer drinkers who first bought Grolsch, if for no other reason than to see what sort of brew was in its distinctive bottle with the old-fashioned wire closure and ceramic stopper. More imports are also moving to green bottles for their products. Consumer research shows that Americans feel green glass is more appealing for a light-colored beer.

Even though beer tasting and tavern promotion nights are the most cost-effective ways to promote public awareness, reliance on heavy advertising is increasing. In 1985 Van Munching spent an estimated $22 million advertising and promoting Heineken. For Molson $15 million was spent. St. Pauli Girl had a $14 million budget, and Mexican Tecate plans regional advertising at $4 million in 1986. Although imports account for less than 4 percent of the beer market, the category held 10 percent of all beer advertising in 1984. About five imported beers represent 78.9 percent of all imported beer advertising. Heineken leads the list of import advertisers with 33.9 percent, Molson has 20.5 percent, Amstel Light follows with 15.8 percent, Moosehead and St. Pauli Girl trail with 4.5 percent and 4.2 percent, respectively. However, some importers are not marketing at all, and some import companies have 10 to 20 restaurants and delicatessens to whom they sell beer.

EXPORTS

Confronted with a static-to-declining domestic market, beer producers are being forced to seek new markets abroad. A-B sees the international market, which is more than twice as large as the U.S. market, as critical to U.S. brewers' long-term success. Miller Vice President Alan Easton echoes this view, "Anybody who is really serious about being in the beer industry is going to have to consider participating in non-U.S. markets." Because substantial foreign opposition exists, brewers are seeking to expand government efforts to negotiate for trade barrier reductions.

Currently, the United States is Canada's major export customer for beer. In contrast, the United States is a residual supplier of beer to Canada. Canadian provinces protect local producers by severely limiting beer imports. But some provinces, particularly in western Canada, are insisting that foreign beers be imported freely. The new Liberal government in Ontario (37 per-

cent of Canada's beer drinkers reside in Ontario) is promising to break up the Ontario brewers' retail monopoly.

Anheuser-Busch is relying on licensees to brew regular Budweiser for its overseas production, marketing, and distribution. To meet A-B standards, the licensees import ingredients from the United States and their production must be approved by Anheuser's four international brewmasters, as well as Chairman August A. Busch III. Licensees are brewing Bud in Britain, Japan, and Israel. Negotiations are being conducted in Australia, Korea, and the Philippines. Anheuser is also considering the purchase of foreign breweries and exports to about 10 other countries. Budweiser has failed, however, to crack the West German market, and Bud sales in France have been a disappointment.

NATIONAL BREWERS

Anheuser-Busch, Inc.

The St. Louis-based "King of Beers" has the most profitable product mix in the industry and is least in need of price increases. The key to its growth has been the world's best-selling beer, Budweiser. Bud has taken a big part of the youth market from Miller High Life and now commands a 24 percent market share (Exhibits 14 and 15). A

EXHIBIT 14　　TOP FIVE NATIONAL BREWERS

1984 rank	Company name	Principal brands
1.	Anheuser-Busch, Inc. St. Louis, Missouri	Budweiser, Bud Light, Michelob, Michelob Light, Busch, Natural Light, LA, King Cobra Malt Liquor
2.	Miller Brewing Co. Milwaukee, Wisconsin	Miller High Life, Miller Lite, Plank Road, Milwaukee's Best, Meister Brau, Sharpe's LA, Lowenbrau, Genuine Draft
3.	The Stroh Brewery Co. Detroit, Michigan	Stroh's, Stroh's Light, Old Milwaukee, Piels, Schlitz, Signature, Schaefer, Goebel, Silver Thunder Malt Liquor
4.	G. Heileman Brewing Co. La Crosse, Wisconsin	Old Style, Old Style LA, Special Export, Blatz, Rainer, Black Label, Lone Star, 11-11 Malt Liquor
5.	Adolph Coors Company Golden, Colorado	Coors, Coors Light, Herman Josephs, George Killian's Irish Red

EXHIBIT 15   TOP 10 BRANDS FOR 1984

Rank	Brand	Market Share	Brand growth
1	Budweiser	24.0%	5.0%
2	Miller Lite	10.0	2.0
3	Miller High Life	7.8	−18.0
4	Coors	5.0	−5.0
5	Old Milwaukee	3.8	1.5
6	Michelob	3.8	−3.5
7	Pabst	3.4	−20.0
8	Stroh	3.2	2.0
9	Old Style	2.9	−5.0
10	Bud Light	2.3	10.5
Top 10		66.2%	−30.5%

good product reputation and a powerful distribution network of virtually exclusive distributors contribute to A-B's success. A-B has marketing muscle; its average wholesaler does a 50 percent greater volume than a Miller counterpart. A-B also has exposure; advertising expenditures in 1985 were $440 million. A-B has created the ability to outspend its competitors, because its gross margin and gross profits are growing while others are not. Moreover, A-B is in the driver's seat as far as pricing goes.

Miller Brewing Company

Acquired in 1970 by Philip Morris, Inc., Miller surged during the 70s and continues to be in the number two position. The premium-priced High Life brand has been losing momentum and its luster as sales erode. However, the Lite brand is doing well, but faces more competition. Miller's strategy of introducing two low-priced, low-profit beers, Meister Brau and Milwaukee's Best, is questioned by analysts. They believe that this maneuver, coupled with a large advertising budget, cannot succeed. Miller is innovating at the higher segment with Plank Road and Miller High Life Genuine Draft. It is trying to reposition Lowenbrau as a brand with worldwide image. Since the Lowenbrau which Miller sells in the

United States is brewed in Milwaukee, not Munich, this campaign has failed in the past. Miller remains hopeful about its future.

The Stroh Brewery Company

Until 1981 this family-owned brewery, founded in 1849, was primarily a regional brewer. Since acquiring F&M Schaefer Brewing Company in 1981 and Jos. Schlitz Brewing Company in 1982, Stroh has carved a comfortable lead over its nearest competitor, G. Heileman. The acquisition of Schlitz gave Stroh a strong national wholesalers' network to distribute the rest of its products. Stroh's national rollout had some bad introductions in the Northeast, but it has a solid product line—Stroh's, Old Milwaukee, Schaefer, and superpremium Signature. A company with good management, Stroh will be a difficult force to contend with since it has minimized unit costs and is operating at full capacity. Moreover, since it is a private company, it does not have to show good quarterly returns; it just has to generate enough cash flow to cover the family's needs.

G. Heileman Brewing Company

The G. Heileman Brewing Company entered 1984 leading the industry in five-year profitability and growth. Its return on equity averaged 31.7 percent. It has 11 breweries—five in the Midwest and two each in the South, Southwest, and Northwest. Heileman's growth is a result of acquisition, and it has expanded its own distribution network by acquiring companies with well-established distribution systems. Despite excellent street-fighting management and good marketing, Heileman lacks a national image for its 50-plus brands. This makes competing with A-B difficult. Heileman is, however, competing with the imports by building a new small plant exclusively for the production of a specialty beer. It does not want to mix the new beer with its domestic brands.

Adolph Coors Company

Famous for using Rocky Mountain spring water in its flagship Coors brands, Coors is expanding its distribution eastward. The rollout has worked very well, especially in New England, where it ran ads at the rate of one TV commercial per second to introduce its brands. Also, Coors seems to have stemmed the market share erosion in its core territories out West and hopes to regain the lost ground. Coors Light is doing very well, and in 1985 accounted for 40 percent of Coors' total barrelage. The success of Coors Light is helping to elevate the confidence that both the consumers and the wholesalers have in the Coors brand name. The imported superpremium George Killian's Irish Red is also making strong headway.

THE REGIONAL/SMALL BREWERS

In an industry increasingly dominated by a few firms, several regional brewers have endured and continue to flourish. Some have 150-year histories, and others have only recently emerged. All stand as evidence that hometown loyalties and the strength of the regional market can be cornerstones of success.

Some of the strategies for survival being used include (1) the specialty brewer serving the moderate beer drinker and catering to the growing market of image-enhanced goods in select markets, (2) the dual-purpose brewer who wants to serve his loyal home market while developing more prestigious and distinctive beers for select markets, and (3) the more traditional regional brewer whose markets are blue-collar and whose customers are more loyal than those in the more transient metropolitan areas.

The Genesee Brewing Company, Rochester, New York

Founded just after Prohibition's demise, Genesee is now the seventh largest brewery in America. Genesee's territory has been expanding and now includes all of the East Coast, Ohio, Indiana, Kentucky, West Virginia, and the province of Ontario. Genesee has implemented major advertising campaigns and has had an impressive growth rate throughout the 1970s, with sales increasing at an average annual rate of 10.3 percent.

The F.X. Matt Brewing Company, Utica, New York

The F.X. Matt Brewing Company reflects the tradition of family involvement that characterizes the industry. Besides a strategy of capital improvements, three other factors have been keys to success: consistent quality, loyal personnel, and a hands-on management philosophy. The extensive product line includes Utica Club; Utica Club Light; Utica Club Cream Ale; Matt's Premium; Matt's Premium Light Choice, a low-alcohol beer; Maximus Super Beer, with a 6.5 percent alcohol content; and Saranac 1888, the newest product. Approximately 125 distributors carry Matt products throughout New York, Pennsylvania, parts of New England, and north-central Colorado. Distributors must have a good game plan, ability to cover the market, competence, and a certain way of doing business.

Anchor Brewing Company, San Francisco, California

In 1965 Fritz Maytag, heir to part of the Maytag appliance fortune, bought this bankrupt brewery. Using his personal finances, he embarked on an extensive capital investment plan to renovate and replace equipment. Anchor, operating at a loss for 10 years, went into the black in 1975. Anchor's initial annual capacity of 600 barrels has been expanded to 50,000 barrels. In 1984 Anchor produced over 37,000 barrels. The brewery's flagship, Anchor Steam Beer, accounts for 80 percent of sales; and Anchor Porter and Anchor Liberty constitute 7 percent of total sales. The remaining sales volume is made up by a barley ale, wheat beer, and its Christmas ale.

While the brewery initially self-distributed its products, it now uses two distributors on the West Coast. With over 100 total distributors, Anchor is available on the West Coast, in parts of Maryland,

Delaware, Virginia, Washington, D.C., New Jersey, Connecticut, and Massachusetts. The company has done almost no advertising, but relies instead on distinctive packaging.

A quasimarket research study provided the following buyer profile: The buyers are young adults, upscale, predominately college-educated, and very knowledgeable about beer. Many drink a variety of beers and consider themselves aficionados. They drink primarily imported brands and enjoy a rich, distinctive taste in the beer they consume.

Maytag explains Anchor's success as follows: "We start with a respect for the brewing tradition and a reputation for integrity. It's a concept that starts with the product. Our brew is low-key, high-quality, and nonestablishment. We actually try to make a beer that most people don't like—heavy, hoppy, and flavorful. It's traditional and distinctive, not designed for high volume but for rapid growth, with relatively high margins on a small scale."

THE MICROBREWERS

The American brewing industry has one small, dedicated group of mavericks. These are the microbrewers, defined as brewers with annual production under 15,000 barrels. Microbreweries are as individual as the personalities of their owners, yet all share an attitude of respect and enthusiasm for the brewer's art.

Jack McAuliffe, an unemployed sailor who started the first microbrewery in 1976 in Sonoma, California, reintroduced top-fermented English-type ale in the United States. His New Albion Brewery survived only a few years, but others have followed. Today there are about 25 micros, and another 30 are set to begin production in 1986. Exhibit 16 provides a comprehensive list of American microbreweries.

Real ale is not the only style produced by microbreweries. A new American-style nouveau lager has emerged on the market. This bottom-fermented beer is decidedly more hoppy and brewed in the German Reinheitsgebot tradition.

Reinheitsgebot dates from 1516, when the Bavarian ruler of that day, Wilhelm IV, limited the ingredients in beer to water, malted barley, hops, and yeast. In West Germany, Norway, and a few other countries, all beer produced for local consumption must be Reinheitsgebot pure, with only those four ingredients, no cereals, no additives, and no enzymes. Nearly all the new wave of micro-beers in the United States are made to these specifications.

The West Coast is a hotbed of microbrewery activity. The area is an ideal geographic market for these niche beers, because of the generally high personal incomes, coupled with a widespread awareness and appreciation of small wineries. The classic flavor and quality these breweries achieve, combined with their anti-establishment stance, has resulted in attractive alternatives for the price-inelastic, high-end beer drinker.

Microbrewing, however, is a risky business, even on the West Coast. In 1982 in the San Francisco Bay area, there were five micros in business. Only two are still brewing. With a failure rate of more than 40 percent, this business is not for amateurs. Micro success is often unattainable, because of competition from imported labels and a high-cost production set-up that requires super-premium pricing to eke out a profit margin. Microbreweries are faced with the dilemma of needing to increase production to build market share and trim unit costs, yet having to contend with a mature and oversaturated market that simply does not justify scaling up.

Because of their low volume sales, it is also difficult to find distributors willing to carry the brands of microbrewers. The few that are receptive are normally attracted by label graphics and by superlative quality. Most distributors cannot, or will not, distribute a label that sells in such small numbers. Therefore, most microbrewers rely on personalized preselling of their brew to retailers, supplemented with point-of-purchase displays to generate buyer interest.

The strategy of the micros involves charging a little more, maintaining a rigorous quality-

EXHIBIT 16   AMERICAN MICROBREWERIES AND BREW PUBS

Name	Location
Riley-Lyon Brewing Company	Little Rock, Arkansas
Palo Alto Brewing Company	Mountain View, California
Sierra Nevada Brewing Company	Chico, California
Stanislaus Brewing Company	Modesto, California
Thousand Oaks Brewing Company	Berkeley, California
Golden Gate Brewing Company	Berkeley, California
Boulder Brewing Company	Boulder, Colorado
Snake River Brewing Company	Caldwell, Idaho
Millstream Brewing Company	Amana, Iowa
Boston Beer Company	Boston, Massachusetts
Montana Beverage Company	Helena, Montana
The Manhattan Brewing Company	New York, New York
Old New York Brewing Company	New York, New York
Wm. S. Newman Brewing Company	Albany, New York
Columbia River Brewing Company	Portland, Oregon
Widmer Brewing Company	Portland, Oregon
Reinheitsgebot Brewing Company	Plano, Texas
Chesapeake Bay Brewing Company	Virginia Beach, Virginia
Hart Brewing Company	Kalama, Washington
Hales Ales Ltd.	Coleville, Washington
Independent Ale Brewing, Inc.	Seattle, Washington
Kemper Brewing Company	Rolling Bay, Washington
Kuefner Brewing Company	Monroe, Washington
Yakima Brewing and Malt Company	Yakima, Washington
Brew Pubs:	
Buffalo Bill's Microbrewery & Pub	Hayward, California
Mendocino Brewing Co.	Hopeland, California
Hopeland Brewery	Hopeland, California

conscious image, and providing more and more beer drinkers with the joys of fresh, wholesome, handmade brews. Their market goal is to make premium an adjective that means something in the beer business.

Sierra Nevada Brewing Company, Chico, California

Located in a farming and college town near Sacramento, this ale brewery has a current sales volume of 3,000 barrels. Started in 1979, the first brew was sold in 1981. Sierra Nevada produces pale ale, porter, and stout, which all retail for about $18 a case. The firm also sells full and half kegs of draft ale and a Christmas ale. Oper-

ating efficiency and a steadily growing reputation among serious beer lovers have proved to be keys for survival. But owner/brewer Camusi predicts a shakeout among microbrewers, a direct result of an overcrowded specialty market.

The critical areas of size and capacity may be the deciding factors in its long-term success. Sierra Nevada has added to its capacity every year and now approaches an annual capacity of 7,500 barrels. Its draft beer, accounting for a large percentage of its volume, enables the brewery to avoid the crowded single bottle market. Camusi believes that growth is essential for survival. According to Camusi, "The really small brewery is just not a viable business anymore."

Mendocino Brewing Company, Hopeland, California

Situated 100 miles north of San Francisco, this brewery was formed from the equipment and staff of the defunct New Albion Brewery. Mendocino has overcome many of the economic viability issues of distribution and scale by operating a "brew pub." Approximately 660 barrels a year of ale, porter, and stout are sold through the pub under the name of the Hopeland Brewery. Mendocino produces a wide variety of products, with Red Tail Ale its mainstay.

This amber, heavy-bodied, English-style brew sells in a one-and-a-half-liter magnum bottle for $6. Its Black Hawk Stout, pale ale, and Christmas, summer, and spring ales sell on draft at the pub. The owners decribe Mendocino as a domestic alternative which provides a small group of beer drinkers with a fresh, premium product. By selling exclusively to a local market, Mendocino has overcome the problem of finding distributors.

Boulder Brewing Company, Boulder, Colorado

Founded in 1979 by a small group of home brewers, this brewery sold its first beer on July 3, 1980. Boulder's products are unpasteurized, English-type brews. The two products, Boulder Extra Pale Ale and Boulder Stout, are sold in 12-ounce nonreturnable bottles. No draft is produced. Accounts are served by wholesale distributors who approached the company. Distribution is confined to the state of Colorado, with a network of 12 outlets currently handling the brewery's products. Although the company enjoys considerable free publicity, word-of-mouth advertising serves as its primary source of demand. Marketing resources are focused on upgrading packaging graphics. A public stock offering in September 1983 financed the company's capitalization and construction of its recently completed $1.1 million brewery. Forty million common shares were issued at 5 cents a share, raising a total of $2 million. The new facility covers about 14,000 square feet, and annual capacity now stands at 15,000 barrels.

The Old New York Beer Company, New York, New York

The first of the nouveau lagers came from New York in 1982, when Matthew Reich introduced New Amsterdam Amber, a rich, hoppy, full-bodied, all-malt lager beer. Reich invested his life's savings, $10,000, and hired Dr. Joseph Owades, an international brewing consultant and director of the Center for Brewing Studies in San Francisco, to design a lager beer similar to Anchor Steam.

Reich had always dreamed of being a brewer. While working as the director of operations at Hearst Magazine, he often wished he was out creating his own beer. He believed that there was room for a connoisseur's beer, the kind poured from kegs, without rice or corn—a pure beer. For two years Reich and Owades slaved over the beer's body, color, and taste, during which time Reich still worked at Hearst.

On the basis of a 15-page business plan, 22 private investors invested $255,000 to form a limited partnership. In the summer of 1982 Reich left Hearst, and that August he began buying brewing time at F. X. Matt Brewing Company in Utica, New York. New Amsterdam Amber ferments for one week and ages for 26 days before being bottled or kegged and shipped to Manhattan.

In 1983, Old New York Beer Company sold 44,000 cases for $600,000. Sales doubled to $1.2 million in 1984, with earnings of $50,000 (after taxes). Reich expects to reach a sales level of $1.8 million in 1985 on 100,000 cases. The average retail price for a six-pack is $6.

Like other micros, Reich personally sold his brew, first approaching trendy restaurants and bars in Manhattan. While he originally intended to target only New York, his beer is now available in 21 states, including the West Coast. Reich's initial success has enabled him to raise an additional $2.2 million from two venture capital firms. He is using the money to construct a new brewery in Manhattan that will also have a restaurant, a tap room, and a visitors' center. Although this action dilutes Reich's holding in the company to 25 percent, it improved Old New York's image and increased its annual production capacity to 30,000 barrels. When the brewery is completed late in 1986, he will be able to triple 1985's expected production.

THE GOLDEN GATE BREWING COMPANY

James Cook, christened Charles James, attended Harvard College, where he majored in government and graduated with honors in 1971. For the next three years, he was a mountaineering instructor with Outward Bound. In 1974 he returned to Harvard to study law and business administration. In 1977 Cook climbed to the snow-covered peak of Alaska's 20,320-foot Mount McKinley. "After traveling for weeks and seeing nothing but white," he recalls, "I wondered what magic sight awaited me at the summit. And when I got to the top, there it was, glowing in the light, an empty beer can, planted like somebody's flag. Ah," he exclaims, "the power of beer is transcendent!"

With a J.D. and M.B.A. degree, Cook joined the Boston Consulting Group (BCG). He spent seven years honing his management skills and advising industrial, primarily international, managers. After six years he got tired of telling other people how to run their companies and decided to start his own. "I wanted to create something; I wanted to make something of my own," said Cook. Cook's choices boiled down to either brewing beer or building a chain of for-profit medical clinics in Seattle. The consultant in Cook voted for the doc-in-the-box setup. But as the eldest son of a fifth generation brewer, he figured he really did not have a choice.

Cook vividly remembers the smell of fermenting beer on days he visited his father at work. "I liked it. I never liked hard liquor and never understood wine. Even now I drink two or three beers a day, rarely less, rarely more. Breweries are neat places, and the brewmaster has the best job. He walks around, tastes beer, and makes changes. It's almost like playing God," notes Cook. Cook believes that he was put on earth for one thing: "to make the greatest beer in the United States." He recalled:

On the surface it was an insane thing to do, but I was convinced there was a small emerging market for what I wanted to do. It was the time for micro-breweries and hand-crafted beers, and it seemed tragic that I was ending a line of five generations of brewers. I realized Americans had begun to appreciate premium beers in recent years, especially on the West Coast, but I felt they relied too heavily on imported beers, which are inherently inferior. I think that the American appreciation of beer is very much in its infancy. We're in the Blue Nun stage of beer drinking. There was a time when people thought that Blue Nun was a great wine, just as now there are people who think Heineken and Beck's are great beers. In fact, they're the Schlitz of Europe. They have a certain mystique, but it's a phony mystique. These beers aren't fresh. Beer has a shelf life that's not a whole lot longer than orange juice. And you'd never think of buying orange juice from Germany.

In Germany, they don't drink Beck's. They drink the local beer. Americans have this notion that the farther away a beer is made, the better it is. But the imports we get in America not only have preservatives, which are illegal in Germany, but by the time they arrive here, they are almost always spoiled, stale and/or skunked. Beer must be fresh. It deteriorates the instant you put it in a bottle. The day it leaves the brewery, it goes downhill. The travel time in importing beer and use of green bottles that expose beer to damaging light can often mean the expensive imported beer is not what it claims to be.

The Start-Up

Although Cook had no formal education in brewing, he studied notes and material his father had saved from the Siebel Institute of Brewing in Chicago, where he learned to be a brewmaster. Although American tastes in mass-marketed beers favor light, paler versions, Cook decided to buck the tide, go with family tradition, and brew a full-bodied lager. He wanted a connoisseur's beer, brewed in an old-world tradition.

His father suggested he revive the old family formula. After searching his father's attic in Cincinnati, Cook found his great-great-grandfather's original recipe, first developed by his ancestor in the 1870s. With his family's formula, Cook hired biochemist and brewery consultant Joseph L. Owades to aid in devising the final formula. In the summer of 1984, Cook traveled to the fermentation lab at the University of California at Davis and worked with Owades on translating Louis Cook's Midwestern American lager into a 1980s West Coast superpremium beer.

The formula is water, malt, hops, and a special yeast strain developed by Owades. The hops is the best in the world, Tettnang and Hallertau Mittlelfreuh hops, imported from Bavaria at a cost of $4.50 a pound. A pound of ordinary hops costs 55 cents. The hops, according to Cook, is key as it gives the beer its flavor. Two-row summer malted barley and some caramel malt are used for color and body. While many people think that water is the most important ingredient that goes into beer, it is, in fact, the least important. The quality of the yeast strain is much more important, but seldom talked about as it lacks advertising appeal. Cook points out, "When you listen to what people advertise about their beers, it's things that have real macho appeal— fire brewing, beechwood aging, mountain spring water. What matters are things like hops, malt, and yeast. Unfortunately, they don't have the advertising appeal of cool mountain streams."

To make this beer formula a reality Cook needed to raise capital. He tossed in all his personal savings, $100,000, and raised an additional $300,000 from friends, business associates, clients, and even his father. "While you can start a small boutique brewery with $400,000, a good lager is difficult to produce in a microbrewery. A lager requires more sophisticated brewing equipment and more careful handling than the ale produced by most micros. I was forced to find an existing brewery, and luckily, I was able to find a brewery in Berkeley that was perfect for my purposes," relates Cook.

The Brewing Process

Golden Gate's hundred-year-old recipe requires a craft brewing process not used by American brewers in this century. The sweetness is drawn from the malt through a process traditional in Germany, but rarely used anymore by American brewers. Fresh hops are added in six stages during the brewing process to give the beer its complex hop character. (The usual process is to add hops only during the cooking stage of production, when boiling extracts the greatest amount of bitterness and, therefore, is more economical.) Cook's beer then goes through a second fermentation that carbonates the beer and also removes some of its impurities for a smoother taste. A final addition of fresh hops is made to the beer as it ages to impart the striking aroma. This is a labor-intensive technique. Golden Gate takes 40 to 45 days to make—one day to cook, seven days to ferment, and about two weeks to ferment the second time. The rest of the time is lagering, or aging. These efforts in the brewing process create the full-bodied flavor, rich with coppery color.

The beer is produced in batches, between 250 and 300 barrels a batch. Cook currently travels to the brewery every one to two weeks to oversee the brewing of a new batch. He follows the process step by step to ensure that his recipe is followed precisely.

Packaging

Golden Gate is currently only bottled; no draft beer is produced. The classic American beer bottle—the 12-ounce longneck, or bar bottle, that requires an opener—is used. This shape and the cap offer the most protection from light and oxidation. The bottle is also a dark brown because a dark bottle protects beer from light, a deadly enemy of beer. Beer left in light for more than ten minutes begins to spoil.

After being bottled in Berkeley, the beer arrives in San Francisco four hours later. Cook has hired two truck drivers and leases trucks. Each trip to San Francisco costs about $800 per truck. Initially, 500 cases per week were delivered, but this has grown to about 1,500 cases per week. (Each truck has a maximum capacity of 2,500 cases.) The beer is delivered to an old San Francisco brewery, where Cook rents office and warehouse space, prior to distribution.

Organization

The employment roster of the Golden Gate Brewing Company numbers five people including James Cook, the brewer and chief salesman. In addition to two truck drivers, there is a part-time bookkeeper and an accounts manager, Rhonda Kallman, who was Cook's secretary at BCG. Her numerous and varied duties include selling and even delivering when necessary. To keep overhead as low as possible, the business has no secretary, no typewriter, and no computer. Cook also took a 75 percent pay cut from his BCG salary.

Financial Information

According to Cook, the Golden Gate Brewing Company "is still in the red, but we're getting back toward recovering our losses. The business after six months is doing remarkably well." Exhibit 17 shows the Golden Gate Brewing Company's income statement for the first six months of operations. Golden Gate sells for about 25 cents more per bottle than Heineken, between $1.75 and $3.50 per bottle retail.

A six-pack retails for about $6.50, and a case varies from $20 to $24. Asked if he thought the high price might limit sales, Cook said, "I don't

EXHIBIT 17　1985 INCOME STATEMENT FOR GOLDEN GATE BREWING CO.

	1985
Sales	$408,000 [1]
Cost of goods sold	273,000 [2]
Gross margin	135,000
Less:	
Shipping	840 [3]
Salaries and wages	101,003 [4]
Office/warehouse rent	4,800 [5]
Truck leasing	20,800 [6]
Marketing and promotion	55,000 [7]
Repairs	1,000 [8]
Depreciation	7,500 [9]
General selling, administrative, and other expenses	9,057 [10]
Net income (loss) before taxes	($65,000)

[1] Includes 25,000 cases sold in California and 500 in Munich.
[2] The first 3,500 cases cost $12/case; the rest cost $10.50/case.
[3] Includes shipping costs of $0.07/bottle for 500 cases shipped. (Larger shipments would decrease the per bottle cost.)
[4] Includes Cook's salary of $25,000 for July–December and average hourly earnings of his four employees of $18.27/hr. (Another 4 percent increase is expected in 1986.)
[5] Office and warehouse rent totals $800 per month.
[6] Twenty-six truck trips were made into San Francisco in the first six months.
[7] Includes $35,000 for booklet and $10,000 for placards used in July and August.
[8] Cost of incidental repairs, including labor and supplies, which do not add materially to the value of the property.
[9] Depreciation is on the straight-line basis, assuming a 20-year useful life, no salvage value, one half year's depreciation taken in the first year, and $300,000 of assets acquired.
[10] Included are salaries and wages not deducted elsewhere, amounts not otherwise reported, such as administrative, general and office expenses, bonuses and commissions, delivery charges, research expenses, sales discount, and travel expenses.

drink wine, but I understand a good bottle of wine costs about $30. Well, for the price of a mediocre bottle of wine, you can go out and buy a six-pack of the best beer in America." Golden Gate wholesales for about $16 a case.

Golden Gate Lager costs two to three times what it costs to brew imported beers. The delivered cost into San Francisco was initially listed at $12 a case, but because of increased volume, it is now down to $10.50 a case. Other expenses include salaries, office/warehouse rent, truck leasing, marketing and promotion, public relations, general administrative expenses, and taxes.

Advertising and Marketing

Golden Gate Lager spends no money advertising its beer. The main marketing element is quality and freshness, and the main marketing tool is personal selling and word-of-mouth. Tabletop display cards are also placed in bars and restaurants in and around San Francisco. In addition, a little blue miniature booklet, each hand-applied, dangles from each long-stem bottle. The booklet is entitled "Why Is This Special Beer Different?" and decribes the beer, brewing process, and flavor. The first order alone cost $35,000.

During the summer of 1985 Cook experimented with advertising. Placards were placed on the sides of San Francisco's tour buses. While it was relatively cheap advertising at $5,000 per month, Cook is not sure it was worth it. "I don't think we generated enough sales to pay for it." This experience confirmed his gut feeling that small specialized companies do better relying on word-of-mouth advertising and publicity. "The first thing you must have in business is a solid, substantial advantage over the alternatives. Somehow you've got to have a reason for people to buy your product, and it's got to be more solid than anything advertising can create. There are very few products that have really lasted long-term on marketing alone," says Cook. "However, nothing is so good that it automatically sells itself. You have to go out and hustle."

While he links the logistics of introducing this beer to those of a fine wine, with the best advertising being word of mouth, Cook was fortunate to gain a credible third-party endorsement. Less than two months after the introduction of Golden Gate Lager, it was crowned the Best Beer in America at the annual Great American Beer Festival in Denver. The 4,000-plus attendees selected one beer as best from over 102 entries. The resulting publicity played a major role in boosting sales. Cook, thrilled by the victory, said, "For a family that has been making beer for 150 years to suddenly get recognized as making the best beer in the country—that is the ultimate accolade."

James Cook also conducts his own market research and studies. Three nights a week he visits local pubs and restaurants. He questions patrons as to why they drink imports when they can have Golden Gate. He asks what they like about imported brands. He asks beer drinkers for their opinion of Golden Gate. If they have not tasted Golden Gate, he describes the flavor and suggests that they try it. After a short conversation, he identifies himself as the brewer. Aside from polling patrons, Cook chats with bartenders and questions waitresses and waiters about sales. According to Cook, "The neatest thing is to come into a bar and see people drinking my beer. The second neatest thing is to take the empty cases out."

Distribution

"Getting the beer on the market boils down to a door-to-door campaign with restaurants, bar managers, and liquor store owners," says Cook. Cook wins new accounts by asking potential carriers to taste the beer. "The response is incredible," boasts Cook. "Bar managers and owners like the personal attention. It shows them how much you believe in your product."

Since Golden Gate requires an amount of personal attention and credibility that the normal beer sales and distribution channels cannot give,

Cook has set up his own distribution company. He even goes as far as making deliveries, pin-striped suit and all, out of his station wagon when regular drivers can't get to a particular account on time. Cook realizes all this costs money, probably twice what traditional distributors pay. Cook is currently negotiating with a major regional beer distributor. Affiliation with a large distributor provides access to numerous established accounts that Cook would otherwise have to pursue one by one. He wonders if this is a sound strategy.

Target Market

The Golden Gate Co.'s target is the beer drinker who knows how to distinguish a well-made beer from an average to below-average one and cares more about quality and taste than advertising appeal. Cook believes that the typical Golden Gate drinker could be anyone, from gourmets to yuppies to construction workers, who likes a good beer. The current diverse cross section of drinkers cuts across traditional demographics.

Export Plunge

In October 1985, Cook shipped 12,000 bottles (500 cases) of Golden Gate Lager to Munich, West Germany, a city with the most finicky beer drinkers in the world, becoming the first U.S. brewed beer to be sold in West Germany outside U.S. military bases. It took four weeks before the Wiehenstathan, or beer institute, gave Cook's beer its seal of approval. Obtaining an import license was the next task.

The 500 cases were sent to George Thaler, a business consultant friend and now part-time beer distributor, who attempts to get Germans to try, and then order, Golden Gate. Thaler explains his sales techniques as follows: "I bring three cold bottles with me; then I tell them what has happened to beer in America and then discuss the brewing process. Then we taste." Thaler says Germans like the beer, which helps both sales of

Golden Gate and the image American products have. "It's a quality image for a U.S. product."

The Munich market is not without problems. In Munich, six breweries own 90 percent of all pubs, and they will serve only their brand of beer. Therefore, Golden Gate is locked out of all but a few of Munich's restaurants, delicatessens, and hotels (the so-called free bars). In addition, while shipping costs add only 7 cents to the price of a bottle of Golden Gate, the beer costs 30 to 50 percent more than German draft beers, or about $5\frac{1}{2}$ marks more per beer. But Thaler explains that this is consistent with the product positioning. "We don't want student beer drinkers to get drunk on Golden Gate. We want the beer connoisseur to drink Golden Gate." Thaler presently has five accounts taking 70 cases per week, which he delivers in the trunk of his Mercedes-Benz. The accounts range from a high-class delicatessen to a New York–style bar.

While Cook's plunge into West Germany is primarily to demonstrate his product's quality, he is now considering expansion. Thaler hopes to expand soon to Düsseldorf and Austria. Cook wonders what other markets he should pursue, how fast he should expand, and how much time he should devote to export possibilities. He is confident that his time-consuming brewing process and choice ingredients make Golden Gate competitive with the best of European brews.

Capital Needs

The Golden Gate Brewing Co. currently rents office and warehouse space at an old San Francisco brewery. This brewery with three-foot-thick walls was abandoned in 1965. It was cheaper to abandon than to tear down. It is now owned by the nonprofit Neighborhood Development Corporation, but Cook has an option on about one-fourth of the building's 170,000 square feet. He hopes to be able to buy the building, renovate it, and brew Golden Gate in 40,000 square feet following funding completion. Cook estimates his needs at $3.75 million, with $1.1 million going for renovations and $2.1 million for new tanks and bottling gear. His goal is an annual capacity of 30,000 barrels. Initially, the project is expected to create 12 to 15 new jobs and potentially 55 to 60. Actual renovation and equipment installation is estimated to take 4 to 10 months.

Cook says it would be cheaper to build a brewery in the suburbs, but "romance" led him to the old San Francisco brewery. "I could save $800,000 if I moved to a suburban industrial park, but I don't want to make California, or West Coast, Lager Beer. I want to make Golden Gate Lager."

Cook has explored several financing possibilities—industrial revenue financing, Urban Development Action Grants, and market rate financing.

Industrial Revenue Financing Industrial Revenue Bonds (IRB) are vehicles that developers and corporations use to raise low-interest financing for construction projects. They are issued by a municipality only to achieve tax-exempt status and are not guaranteed by the full faith and credit of the government. IRB's are backed by the future revenue of the project. IRB's were originally designed to attract industry into communities for employment and economic benefits through the use of tax-exempt financing. IRB loans in San Francisco generally carry interest rates of 70 percent of prime with a 15-year balloon and a 30-year amortization.

The San Francisco Industrial Development Financing Authority (SFIDFA) must give initial approval to an application by Cook's Golden Gate Brewing Company. The revenue bonds must then gain City Council and mayoral approval. Cook is confident that the mayor will bestow enthusiastic support, since he campaigned on revitalizing San Francisco neighborhoods. Once the IRBs are approved, a bank must agree to loan the funds. Most banks require IRB loans to be secured by the personal guarantees of the principals.

Urban Development Action Grants The Urban Development Action Grant (UDAG) is another possibility. The UDAG is a flexible program which offers a source of cheap money. The maturity and interest rate are negotiated between the city and the borrower. The collateral is normally limited to the assets being financed (and personal guarantees). The UDAG can be used for fixed assets whose life expectancy exceeds seven years. The terms and conditions negotiated between the city and the borrower must be approved by the City Council and the U.S. Department of Housing and Urban Development. The UDAG process averages three to four months. Another important advantage of this subsidy is that the UDAG can be mixed with IRBs and other federal programs.

The UDAG subsidy does have one drawback. To raise money for future projects, the local program shares in the profits of the subsidized projects. This can restrict profit potential. Cook was not excited about sharing profits and/or giving up control or ownership.

Market Rate Financing Another option for capital, explored by Cook, is market rate financing from local commercial banks. San Francisco has five major banks, one of which, the Bank of San Francisco, has already solicited the Golden Gate Brewing Co. Cook has yet to supply necessary financial statements or projections, however. The loan would be a mortgage, used to cover all the expenses associated with the completed property. The interest rate would be based on the prime rate. Cook feels that the rate on a commercial mortgage would be prime plus 1 percent for a 15-year balloon with a 30-year amortization.

Expansion/Growth Strategy

Winning the America's Best Beer Award, and the resulting publicity, caused many distributors from other states to solicit the Golden Gate Brewing Company and Golden Gate Lager. Cook has put several possible new accounts temporarily on hold and has turned down requests from distributors in Washington, Colorado, Kentucky, and Alaska. Cook's current agreement with the Berkeley Brewery to brew Golden Gate Lager limits production, and Cook felt that it was important to penetrate and service San Francisco first. Renovating the old San Francisco brewery, however, would provide a much higher production capacity level. Cook also realized that beer is regulated in 50 different ways in the United States. The bureaucratic red tape is complicated and time-consuming. Cook sometimes thinks it is easier to sell Golden Gate in Munich than in the United States. Germany requires only that the beer be pure.

Regardless, Cook wonders if he should expand, how quickly he should expand, and where he should expand. Cook concedes that he will never slay the major domestic giants. "I don't compete with them. I make a different product and sell it for a different price. I compete with foreign beers." But he is uncertain of the strategy he should use.

TEXAS BLUES

"When we left our meeting two weeks ago, Larry, I thought it would be relatively easy to gather information about our growers," Brent was explaining. As President of the Texas Blueberry Growers Association (TBGA), Brent Ramage had volunteered to come up with some facts to describe the operations of blueberry growers in east Texas, where he lived. Two weeks ago he had been in Austin, meeting with Larry Strange, a Texas Department of Agriculture (TDA) official, to review the potential of the Texas blueberry industry. Larry's TDA responsibilities included identifying and analyzing special high-growth potential agricultural projects for the Department, and and Brent was anxious to secure his help. As President of the Association, Brent was interested in good relations with the TDA, and as the owner of a sizable blueberry farm near Hooks, Texas, he was enthusiastic about the rapid increase in blueberry plantings in the state.

"Can we get a handle on the current stage of production in the state, overall?" Larry asked.

"Well, that's harder to estimate than I thought it would be. We know from our TBGA membership lists generally who owns blueberry farms, but estimating acreage is another thing. There's so much variation. On the one hand, you've got a few growers like Don at Fincastle, with a highly developed operation; and on the other hand, some folks have just put plants in the ground. In the middle are quite a few small operators, just trying to do things right.

"I have to agree with you about the information problem. My experience has been similar. I think we've got some pretty good information from the horticultural researchers about growing conditions. And coming up with production and shipment figures wasn't all that difficult. It remains to be seen how much of it will be usable."

As his part of the plan to investigate Texas blueberry potential, Larry had drawn upon his information sources at TDA and his keen investigative skills to ascertain characteristics of blueberry production in east Texas and blueberry production levels in the rest of the nation. The two men intended to pool their information today, April 12, 1985, to determine the current state of blueberry production in Texas, and to define the steps necessary for understanding and planning the future of "Texas Blues."

This case was written by JoAnn K. L. Schwinghammer, Professor of Marketing, Mankato State University; Gopala Krishnan Ganesh, Assistant Professor of Marketing, University of North Texas; and William C. Green, Assistant Professor of Marketing, California State University–Bakersfield.

"Let's start with the growing conditions," Larry went on. "Take a look at what I've found."

HORTICULTURAL FACTORS

By consulting horticultural researchers in the Texas Agricultural Experiment Station system, it had been learned that blueberry production in the United States consists of three varieties that vary by the type of berry and the growing region (hence, length of growing season): highbush, lowbush, and rabbiteye. Each of these three varieties has some distinguishing characteristics.

Highbush berries are predominantly grown in the east coast areas of North Carolina to New Jersey, westward to Michigan, currently the nation's largest producer, and south to northern Arkansas. While these berries are grown in other areas of the country, acreage is limited. Highbush berries are perhaps more susceptible to disease, injury, and frost than other varieties. They are most usually processed or frozen and appear in such products as baked goods, ice cream, and prepared baking mixes. Increasing emphasis has been placed on the fresh market, particularly by Michigan growers.

Lowbush berries are grown only in the very northern regions of Maine and parts of Canada. They are a smaller berry not appropriate for the fresh market, but they grow wild and therefore require little or no care for a prolific crop. The disadvantage of this variety is that the bushes are short-lived, hence to increase production over a period of time, extensive fertilizers are needed. Because this is costly, growers have found that it is cheaper and easier to burn the bushes off every three years. This ensures a fresh crop of productive plants, but requires a time lag while the plants are reaching maturity. Production of these berries is believed to vastly affect the processor market. In fact, it is believed that there is a glut of processed berries currently on the market.

Berries of the rabbiteye variety (so named because in the immature red stage, they resemble rabbit eyes) are those grown predominantly in Georgia, Florida, Mississippi, Louisiana, Alabama, South Carolina, and Texas. Arkansas and Oklahoma have recently experimented with growing rabbiteye berries, as well. These berries are larger and have thicker skins, which means that they are more resistant to damage. They also have a smaller stem scar when picked, which means that they are less susceptible to infection and disease. These berries, because of their size, are most suited for the fresh berry market. They are, however, also well suited for a process called puff drying, in which berries are put under a high-heat, pressurized condition causing a mini-explosion which pinholes the berries (ruptures the skin). They are then tunnel-dried to reduce moisture to 8 to 10 percent of their original content. This process, of course, releases the moisture, allowing for reduced weight and bulk (estimates range from 6–10 to 1), reducing costs of storage and shipment. This process can be done with rabbiteye berries, but it cannot be done with highbush or lowbush varieties. There are, however, only a limited number of puff driers in the country. These driers are reputed to cost as much as three-quarters of a million dollars, which explains partially why there aren't very many of them. The volume of blueberry production necessary to support the operation of a puff drier is believed to be quite large.

Rabbiteye blueberries can be damaged by extensive frost, though they are resistant to damage by only slight frost, which affects the early flowering and reduces slightly the size of the crop. Rabbiteye berries do not require as much chilling to break dormancy as do the other varieties, which, of course, makes them more suitable to growth in the southern regions. Rabbiteye berries, however, must be irrigated. These berries do not suffer greatly from being harvested mechanically. Where mechanical harvesters are used, there are three markets for the produce: (1) the firm berries go to the fresh market, (2) damaged or overripe berries go to the processed and/or frozen market, while (3) green berries may be used for juice stock. Rabbiteye berries may be grown herbicide- and pesticide-free, if other growing conditions are right. In addition, they can be harvested 4 to 6 weeks earlier than the highbush or lowbush varieties.

Rabbiteye berry bushes are relatively long-lived; some are known to have reached 60 years of age. Typically, a new plant must be started in a nursery and will be ready for field planting at about 18 months. During that first year in the field the plant will produce about 1 pound of berries. Its growth and production rates follow, roughly, a pattern of producing 3 pounds in the second year, 5 to 6 pounds in the third year, 6 to 8 pounds in the fourth year, and on to about 30 pounds in the tenth or twelfth year. Where berries are picked with a mechanical harvester, the plants must be kept smaller, and consequently will produce about 20 to 25 pounds per year, maximum. Reasonable production density averages 600 plants per acre, and 12,000 pounds per acre. It is not uncommon that a first commercial harvest occurs in the fifth to seventh year, possibly the third year, if well cared for up to and during this first harvest. Once the plants are mature, there is little maintenance required: some spraying when necessary, fertilization, irrigation, and weeding. While pruning is occasionally necessary for plants that are hand-picked, where mechanical harvesters are used, pruning is an integral part of plant care. The shelf life of these fresh berries is two to three weeks, if they are cooled immediately after picking. If not cooled, shelf life is about one week.

"And blueberries are a healthy fruit: a good source of Vitamins A and C, potassium, phosphorus, and calcium. Most people probably don't know that a half-cup has only 44 calories," Larry explained. "Now, here's what I found out about nationwide production."

NATIONAL PRODUCTION

Blueberries are the third most popular noncitrus fruit in the United States. The largest producer of blueberries in the United States is the state of Michigan, which produces about 12,000 acres of berries. (Exhibit 1 presents national acreage and production figures.) Approximately 90 percent of

Michigan's blueberries go to the processor market. These are sold for about $.40 to $.50 per pound, grower's price. Of the Michigan berries sold to the fresh market (estimates of 12 to 18 percent), growers get about $.90 or a little more per pound. Consumers pay $1.39 to $2.98 per pound at the supermarket. Alliances of Michigan associations with southern growers had been reported in years past, perhaps evidence of Michigan growers recognizing the potential competitive advantage gained by the earlier ripening rabbiteye varieties. Also rumored were feelings among northern producers that there are currently too many frozen blueberries in storage. It is not known what length of time would be necessary for this surplus to be exhausted.

Fresh blueberries grown in New Jersey and North Carolina are shipped nationwide. While these states supply as far west as California with fresh blueberries, in 1984 only 10 truckloads and 1 railcar of blueberries were delivered to Los Angeles grocers. This amounts to about 1,100,000 pounds for the entire Los Angeles market for 1984. California is one western state believed to hold greater potential for blueberry consumption.

Of the southern producers, Georgia is the largest, with Florida in second position. Georgia has the most well-developed fresh and processor market capabilities, producing about 3,000 acres of rabbiteye berries. Among those states with puff driers, Georgia is the only state to use puff drying for processing blueberries. Georgia also has a well-organized grower's association, relying on a centralized structure for cooling, grading, and sorting berries for commercial purposes. Growers in the state are netting approximately $5,000 per acre.

Although Arkansas blueberry production is quite young, it is somewhat more advanced than production in Texas and it has similar growing conditions and problems. Arkansas sold about 850,000 to 1 million pounds of blueberries last year, which didn't meet even the Ozark demand, according to university agricultural researchers. They believe the outlook for sales of their

EXHIBIT 1   NORTH AMERICAN BLUEBERRY

	1983 estimated acreage by John W. Nelson (acres)				Production by J. P. Holbein (000 lbs.)	
	Planted	Harvested	Non-bearing		1983	Projected to 1990
Highbush:						
Northwest						
Oregon	800	700	100		5,250	8,250
Washington	900	800	100		6,512	7,500
British Columbia	2,500	2,000	500		12,000	15,000
Midwest						
Michigan	12,000	10,000	2,000		49,148	60,000
Illinois/Indiana/Ohio	1,000	800	200			
Northeast						
Rhode Island/ Connecticut/New Hampshire/Vermont/ Massachusetts/	1,300	1,000	300			
New York	600	400	200			
Ontario	300	120	180			
Atlantic						
New Jersey	8,000	7,500	500		23,000	28,000
Maryland	500	400	100			
Virginia	100	25	75			
No. Carolina	4,000	3,100	900		5,100	6,900
So. Carolina	200	200	0			
				All others	10,500	15,000

berries to be good where blueberries are not produced: they also sell to California and western parts of the United States, as well as small amounts to Japan. In fact, Arkansas blueberries (as well as some from Georgia and Michigan) had begun appearing in supermarket produce areas in the metropolitan Texas cities in the summer of 1984, selling for as much as $1.89 at the beginning of the season, and closer to $.99 at the end of the season. Arkansas growers are increasingly placing emphasis on the fresh market, although of the fresh blueberries that were sold by Arkansas growers in 1984, only about 15 percent were sold to the fresh market, with 85 percent sold to the frozen market. Of the frozen berries, 70 percent were sold in the United States and 30 percent abroad.

With regard to imports, New Zealand ships blueberries to the United States, although current figures for the amount of these imports are difficult to track. Blueberries are exported to Japan, where there seems to be an appreciation of the berry, not only for its taste and nutrition but also because it is blue.

The North American Blueberry Council, located in New Jersey, represents the interests of those blueberry growers who produce a minimum of 250,000 pounds of berries annually. There are, likewise, state growers' associations, some better organized than others.

TEXAS PRODUCTION

"We may have a long way to go to reach international distribution, but you've got to admit we've

EXHIBIT 1   (continued)

	Planted	Harvested	Non-bearing	1983	Projected to 1990
Central					
Pennsylvania	500	300	200		
Kentucky	100	25	75		
Arkansas/Oklahoma	550	200	350		
Missouri	150	100	50		
Total highbush	33,500	27,670	5,830		
Rabbiteye:					
So. Carolina	500	50	450		
Georgia	3,000	1,500	1,500	1,800	3,800
Florida	1,000	500	500		
Alabama	200	50	150		
Mississippi	400	200	200		
Louisiana	200	50	150		
Texas	250	50	200		
			All others	3,150	9,000
Total rabbiteye	5,550	2,400	3,150		
Total highbush	39,050	30,070	8,980	116,460	153,450
Lowbush:		**New Burn**			
Maine	46,000	23,000	23,000	44,653	55,000
Nova Scotia	20,000	10,000	10,000	19,502	25,000
New Brunswick	12,000	6,000	6,000	8,768	10,000
Quebec	20,000	10,000	10,000	7,300	9,000
Newfoundland	3,500	1,750	1,750	1,440	2,500
Prince Edward Island	2,000	1,000	1,000	800	1,200
Total lowbush	103,500	51,750	51,750	82,463	102,700
			Grand total production	198,923	256,150
			U-Pick and used locally	10,500	21,000
			Total for commercial marketing	188,423	235,150

Note: In the next five years, good yields and increased harvested acreage could produce 235,150,000 lbs. of commercially marketed blueberries, an increase of 25 percent in six years!

come a long way since blueberries were first grown for sale in the state in 1968," Brent laughed. "We didn't get agricultural research on blueberries started until 1971. Here's the rest of the state production information I could come up with."

Blueberry farms are scattered throughout east Texas, from Hooks in the north to Beaumont in the south, encompassing about 250 to 300 sparsely scattered areas. (Exhibit 2 presents Texas blueberry growing areas.) Most of the growers run small operations, many producing berries on under one acre. There are probably under five growers who have up to 35 producing acres. In terms of typical fruit and vegetable retail pallet and shipment sizes, most growers do not produce near pallet size, where one pallet equals 96 flats and a flat equals 12 one-pint containers weighing about 10 pounds. A shipment is equal to about 50,000 to 75,000 pounds volume.

Texas blueberries ripen as early as blueberries anywhere else in the country, with very few exceptions. Texas blueberry bushes often produce blueberries ready for picking in early to mid-June and continue producing through July, a span of six, and sometimes eight, weeks.

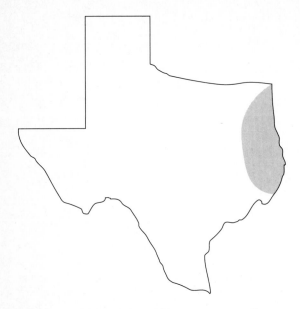

EXHIBIT 2   TEXAS BLUEBERRY GROWING AREAS

Texas berries are of a variety which feasibly could be mechanically harvested (one harvester exists in the state). Mechanical harvesting is ultimately more cost-effective than labor for harvesting where crops equal about 50 acres or more.

No blueberry production in Texas is commercial. A small amount of blueberries are sold at farmers' markets and roadside fruit and vegetable stands. The largest share of production is in pick-your-own (PYO) operations. People seem to be willing to drive from metropolitan and other rural areas to berry farms to pick blueberries for their own use. The PYO farms, however, vary in the services they provide to pickers. Some provide containers or plastic bags, while at other farms pickers must provide their own containers. Some growers grow and sell other kinds of fruit and vegetables, as well as blueberries. Some growers know that they have repeat patrons, but few growers have a very clear understanding of who their customers are, how far they have driven, how long they stay once at the farm, their average size of purchase, why people choose their PYO farm, or even why people choose to pick their own berries. Most PYO operators realize,

however, that once people know that the blueberries are ready to pick, there are almost never any left on the bushes at the end of the season.

Growers were selling blueberries for $.99 to $.69 per pound, the higher prices earned at the beginning of the season. Growers also varied in whether they sold blueberries in pounds or pints, and frequently the two were used interchangeably.

In trying to assess why there seemed to be an increasing demand for blueberries, some growers felt that people who had grown up in the North but had moved to Texas brought with them the taste for blueberries and the habit of berry picking and eating. Not only is the influx of Northerners expected to continue, but these people have "educated" native Texans about picking and eating blueberries.

Competition for blueberries is felt to be from other berries, such as strawberries, cherries, and other fruits that can be put on cereal and in pies and other baked goods. Some growers felt that blueberries might be more like grapes in terms of the costs and risks of production, although the market would be smaller. But no other berry or fruit seemed to offer a model by which to compare growth or consumption patterns.

Nationally, Americans eat an annual average of about 7 ounces of berries of all kinds. With a Texas population of 15 million people, even a conservative estimate points toward a good-sized market for fresh blueberries.

The Texas Blueberry Growers Association is the official organization of the growers, and their membership numbers about 75 to 85 growers. About 90 percent of Texas blueberry growers are members of the Association. It is the intention of the organization to assist growers with whatever problems might arise, to encourage research, and to work toward controlled growth of blueberry acreage.

"That sounds like a fairly thorough summation of where we stand with production, Brent. In your conversations with other growers this week, what appeared to be their concerns about the future?"

"Well, Larry, most feel that this is a good time for blueberries. The Association has picked up a few new growers each year for the past few years, and we're getting more and more people coming out to pick berries. Some Association members are concerned, though, that we ought to have a better handle on how much demand we have—how many pickers we can support. The blueberry industry is relatively new to Texas, and the Association is just beginning to take an active part.

"We don't regularly collect information from the members," Brent continued, "but it would be helpful if we could try to determine how fast we are growing. We don't have a very good idea of how many acres are planted new each year. Of course, the most important thing we want to guard against is reaching a saturation point."

"You're right about that," Larry responded. "It doesn't appear that demand is slacking off. On the other side of the coin, maybe new areas of demand could be tapped. Now might also be a good time to try to assess the commercial market for blueberries, at least on an in-state basis. Let's talk a little more about these two issues—saturation and commercialization. I've got some other figures here we can take a look at."

SATURATION POINT

The two men considered the issue of saturation of prime importance to the Texas blueberry growers. At what level of production, in terms of acres planted or pounds of berries produced, would demand be exhausted? Up to this time, growers agreed that they had more pickers than could be accommodated. But they were certain that with continued rapid growth and assuming present sales methods—PYO operations—would continue as before, there would likely be some point in the future when they would have more berries than could be picked. But how far into the future?

No one, to Larry's knowledge, had studied PYO blueberry farm trade areas, specifically. Researchers at the University of Illinois at Urbana–Champaign's Cooperative Extension Service, in-

vestigating Illinois' PYO strawberry operations in the 1970s and early 1980s, used an adaptation of the Huff retail gravitation model to study trade areas. They defined the retail trade area for PYO strawberry farms to consist of primary (75 percent of all customers living closest to the farm), secondary (the next 15 percent of all customers who lived beyond the primary trade area), and tertiary trade areas (all remaining customers, 10 percent). For the primary trade area, the maximum radii averaged about 20.5 miles, and customers drove an average of about 12.5 miles. More simply, one acre of strawberries would support 2,500 people within a 20-mile radius. Such estimates, of course, depended on the proximity of centers of population and advertising, at the least. Researchers in North Carolina estimated that one acre of PYO blueberries would support 2,000 people within a 25-mile radius. These figures would depend on advertising and the familiarity of the population with blueberry consumption.

The Illinois researchers found that strawberry PYO patrons were more likely to be residents in farm populations, small towns, and small cities surrounding the PYOs. The pickers generally had rural or farm backgrounds, lower incomes, larger families, and relied for PYO information on word of mouth, roadside signs, and local newspapers and radio programs. Residents of larger cities who visited the strawberry PYO farms considered the visits a form of recreation. Though the Illinois researchers collected data from 37 PYO strawberry farms and over 13,300 customer sales, they strongly cautioned against applying their estimates to other crops.

COMMERCIALIZATION POTENTIAL

The saturation issue could be viewed from another standpoint. With an outlook toward expansion of blueberry operations in Texas, commercialization could be viewed as a viable alternative if production exceeded PYO demand.

Commercialization was estimated to take approximately 3 to 10 years and would be feasible for an individual farm of at least 50 acres in size. Initial start-up costs would be high, perhaps up to a half million dollars. Return would be negative for the first three years, if not the first five, with break-even occurring in about the fifth year. A problem for the growers, given the high initial costs, is outside funding. Most bankers are unwilling to lend for unproven operations; there is not a realistically similar model for costing or potential of this market. Other considerations for the growers are the possibilities of sharing facilities for cooling, grading, and sorting, similar to the Georgia example. In Texas, however, growers are more widespread, and distances are much farther. It is estimated that three central locations might be required to perform such a function. In addition, opportunities must be sought for use of the cooling facilities in the off-season, thereby offsetting some of the large initial costs.

Potential markets for fresh blueberries that could be examined include farmers' markets, small and local grocery operations, and large chain grocery operations. A major retail grocery chain has expressed potential need for three truckloads per day, for seven weeks in the summer to the three largest Texas markets (Dallas-Fort Worth, Houston, and San Antonio). This demand alone would require the production of 600 acres of blueberries at current production rates. This is, however, an untested estimate of demand. Rumors hold that retailers would pay $16 per flat FOB for the earliest berries to perhaps a low of $10 to $12 per flat at season's end.

Potential for processing might also be examined. Suggestions include bakeries, ice cream makers, cereal makers, or makers of mass-produced frozen desserts, as well as suppliers for such chains as Wendy's and McDonald's. Processors for frozen or fresh, whole or damaged berries could be sought.

THE RESEARCH TASK

"We have quite a bit of information here, Larry."

"You're right, and most of it is from the production side. We know very little about who picks or eats blueberries, why they pick, or even what they do with blueberries once they get them home. If there's one thing I remember from my marketing classes, it's 'find out who your customers are.' "

"We're really talking about trying to estimate demand, aren't we? To solve the saturation puzzle, we need to know how much demand exists for the PYO farms. And for the commercialization issue, we need to know what overall consumer demand might be."

"Yes, that's all! Now, what we need to do is sit down and develop a research plan. And it would be even better if we could have it ready for this year's blueberry season."

PART THREE

MARKETING STRATEGIES AND PROGRAMS

S trategy determination begins with analyzing the market situation. On the basis of the manager's assessment of the market environment, market opportunity, and competition, target markets are determined. Selecting the target market is the start in marketing strategy development. However, for this to happen, managers will first need to have an understanding of (1) the product objectives to be achieved, (2) the factors that will influence the responsiveness of demand to the marketing offer, (3) the size of the various market opportunities, and (4) the profitability and productivity implications of making changes in prices or in marketing expenditures. The marketing strategy will provide consistency of direction among programs by identifying the kind of total impact on demand that the overall marketing effort is designed to achieve.

One of the unique things about marketing is the great variety of approaches that different companies use. Even firms in the same industries with competing product categories often use different marketing approaches. Marketing programs are the specific marketing decisions and actions that are the responsibility of middle managers.

Included in such programs are product development as well as managing the existing product line, pricing, advertising, sales promotion, and sales distribution. The establishment of specific program objectives can greatly simplify the process of selecting and designing the specific elements of any of these marketing programs.

The variables that managers can control to satisfy the target market and achieve organizational objectives are commonly known as the marketing mix. These variables are usually classified according to four decision areas: product, price, promotion and sales, and distribution. The fourteen cases in Part 3 represent a cross section of those decision areas that are the core of the marketing management process.

METROPOLITAN BANK

"Best ever operating earnings of $207.2 million, up a strong 15 percent, marking our 7th consecutive year of record results." Jack Jones, Chairman and Chief Executive Officer of the Metropolitan Bank in Canada and his top management team were especially pleased not only with 1982 but with the bank's performance over the last decade. In their 1982 annual report they commented that "the past ten years have marked our transformation from a single bank in a single city with only a limited presence abroad into an organization with 428 offices in 10 provinces and 63 facilities in 41 countries. Equally important has been a continuing emphasis on the best traditions of banking by the people who make our organization move. We are committed to even further change—in size and scope, in geographic reach and range of services. But we are also committed to maintaining those values that have always been at the core of our organization: ex-

This case was prepared by Professor Paul Strebel as a basis for class discussion rather than to illustrate either effective or ineffective handling of an administrative situation. Copyright ©1984 by IMEDE, Lausanne, Switzerland. IMD International, resulting from the merger between IMEDE, Lausanne, and IMI, Geneva, acquires and retains all rights. Reproduced by permission.

cellence in delivery of profitable services to our customers."

Metropolitan's earnings were vulnerable, however, to its Latin American exposure, which at approximately 1.9 times equity was the highest of any Canadian Bank. Although Metropolitan had increased its reserves for possible bad loans, the cushion was still small compared to many competitors. As a result, if some of the loans were to go sour, Metropolitan's earnings were likely to suffer more than the earnings of other banks. As an offset, Jones was looking for an expansion of lower-risk activities, especially those with potential for increasing fee-based income.

One area where Jones thought that Metropolitan Bank could improve was the international banking market serving multinational corporations. In the North American market, Metropolitan ranked only fourteenth in terms of the number of "do business with" relationships and tenth in "principal" relationships with multinational companies (see Exhibit 1). He asked Mark Holder, Senior Vice President Corporate Planning, to examine the multinational banking market research report prepared by Bank Marketing Consultants

EXHIBIT 1   NORTH AMERICAN MULTINATIONAL BANKING MARKET PENETRATION

	Do business with %	Principal bank %	Principal as % of do business %
Globalbank	82	66	81
Bank of the U.S.	71	53	75
Big Bank	73	51	70
Topbank	66	48	73
Midwest Bank	62	40	64
British Bank A	55	29	52
Commercial Bank	50	26	52
British Bank B	61	25	41
Canadian Bank	57	25	43
Wall Street Bank	54	24	45
Metropolitan	49	24	50
		Base: Total companies (388)	

Source: 1982 BMC North American Multinational Banking.

Ltd., especially the one on Metropolitan's position in the North American market, and to analyze the economics and potential strategy for more rapid growth in the multinational market worldwide.

Mark Holder had three reports from Bank Marketing Consultants at his disposal: a 1981/1982 report on the North American Multinational Banking market, a 1982 report on the corresponding European market, and a 1982 market research and analysis report prepared for Metropolitan. These reports were based on interviews with senior finance officers (vice presidents, treasurers, controllers, corporate secretaries, directors of international finance) at the participating companies.

The North American report reflected responses from 378 North American multinationals out of a universe of 552 companies with an annual sales size of $250 million or more and with operating subsidiaries or affiliates in two or more national markets in addition to North America. The European report contained responses from 434 companies out of a universe of 726 multinationals in eight European countries, with an annual turnover of $100 million or more and operating subsidiaries or affiliates in at least two countries outside the headquarters country. After reading the reports, Mark Holder decided to summarize the key points as he saw them. His summary follows.

MULTINATIONAL BANKING MARKET

The 1982 banking market for North American Multinational Corporations (AMCs) was dominated by U.S.-based banks. Eight of the top eleven principal international banks used by AMCs were in the U.S., with six based in New York City. The typical AMC had international banking relationships with twenty-two banks. Among these banks, the typical company concentrated its international business with eight principal banks. Over half of the principal international relationships of AMCs were with American banks, one-third of them with foreign banks, and only one-tenth with Canadian banks. (see Exhibit 2)

EXHIBIT 2   EUROPEAN MULTINATIONAL BANKING MAR-
KET PENETRATION

	Do business with %	Principal bank %
Globalbank	65	39
British Bank B	59	28
Bank of the U.S.	50	26
German Bank	58	26
Big Bank	49	25
French Bank A	63	25
French Bank B	62	24
Topbank	44	22
British Bank A	47	21
French Bank C	59	21
Metropolitan	35	8

Source: 1982 BMC European Multinational Banking.

The average European Multinational (EMC) used a comparable total number and distribution of banks for its global international banking needs. The banks most frequently used were American, French, and British. Overall, the use of American banks was common, but not dominant on a country-by-country basis. The large national banks in each of the eight major western European countries were more often lead banks than were American banks. As principal banks, the national banks were used more often than American banks by the multinationals in six of the eight countries surveyed.

In describing why they used particular banks for principal international relationships, AMC financial executives of all reporting company sizes distinguished two sets of closely related reasons: first, the foreign branch network and foreign local currency credit; second, account officer calibre and global account competence. (The industry variation in reasons for principal bank use are shown in Exhibit 3.) EMCs, on the other hand, still cited long-term relationships most frequently as a factor in principal relationships. But because of the increasing volatility in the international fi-

nancial environment, the overall trend was toward principal banks which excelled in delivering unusual value to their clients in credit and services:

The banks that the multinationals concentrate upon are the world-class banks and the best of the national "house banks" that offer these benefits:

• Large international credit capabilities, at favorable prices

• Effective international branch networks providing a wide range of services

• High calibre account managers with authority to deliver global services effectively

This "flight to quality" is strongest among American multinationals. European treasurers are more sensitive to pricing and historical ties than their American counterparts. Fewer European financial executives are yet willing to pay the price that banks providing higher quality service can command.

Nevertheless, a key force for change is the recent climate of unstable interest rates and wide currency fluctuations. A one-half percent difference in interest rate spreads becomes insignificant against the wide swings in interest and currency rates that are now common. It is more important to choose the appropriate financing currency than to find the cheapest deal.

All multinational treasurers need responsiveness, innovation, information, and efficiency from their banks to protect profits from shifting interest rates and exchange rates. There are now clear signs that a growing number of European treasurers are willing to pay for this kind of performance. (Bank Marketing Consultants Ltd., European Multinational Banking Report, 1982.)

In 1982, the international credit facilities used by more than 60% of multinationals on both sides of the Atlantic were overdraft facilities for subsidiaries abroad, foreign local currency credit, export letters of credit, and Eurodollar or Eurocurrency credit facilities. A table of variation in types

EXHIBIT 3   NORTH AMERICAN REASONS FOR PRINCIPAL BANK USE BY INDUSTRY (Cited by at Least 60% of Survey Respondents)

Reasons	Chemicals	Electrical M/C	Food tobacco	Machinery	Paper printing publishing	Petroleum	Primary metals fabrication	Transport equipment
Extent of foreign branch network	*	*	*	*	*	*	*	*
Calibre of account officers	*	*	*	*	*	*		*
Competence in global relations	*	*	*	*	*	*	*	*
Historical relationship		*	*		*	*	*	*
Competence loan price	*	*		*	*			
Foreign local currency credit			*					
International operation capability						*	*	
International financial advice			*		*			
Foreign exchange services			*					

Source: 1981 BMC North American Multinational Banking.

EXHIBIT 4 TYPE OF INTERNATIONAL CREDIT DEMANDED BY MNC HOME COUNTRY (Cited by at Least 60% of Survey Respondents)

Credit service	U.S.	U.K.	Germany	France	Sweden	Neth.	Italy	Switz.	Belgium
Overdraft facilities for sub.	*	*	*	*	*	*	*	*	*
Foreign local currency credit	*	*	*	*	*	*	*	*	*
Export letters of credit		*	*	*	*		*	*	
Eurodollar/currency credit		*	*		*	*			*
Eurodollar/currency S.T. loans		*			*		*		
Performance letters of credit	*				*		*		*
Govt.-supported export credit		*			*				
Eurodollar/currency M.T. loans	*				*		*		
Import letters of credit					*		*		
Credit abroad for parent					*	*			

Source: 1982 BMC European Multinational Banking.

of credit demanded across multinational banking home countries is given in Exhibit 4.

With respect to international services, the most used was international money transfer followed by foreign exchange trading. Exhibit 5 provides a list of the other international services in high demand in different home countries.

Apart from differences between countries on the demand side, a difference existed on the supply side in the perceived distribution of expertise between the top American banks and the leading British and Canadian institutions. The American banks most often had principal relationships based on their overseas branch networks, account officer calibre, and global account competence. The relationships of the Canadian and European institutions rested on foreign-local currency credit, competitive loan pricing, and willingness to lend, as well as long-term historical relationships.

EXHIBIT 5 INTERNATIONAL SERVICES DEMANDED BY MNC HOME COUNTRY (Cited by at Least 60% of Survey Respondents)

Non-credit service	U.S.	U.K.	Germany	France	Sweden	Neth.	Italy	Switz.	Belgium
International money transfer	*	*	*	*	*	*	*	*	*
Foreign exchange trading	*	*	*	*	*	*	*	*	*
Foreign exchange consulting	*		*	*	*	*	*		
Intern. document collection		*	*	*	*	*	*	*	*
Money transfer within foreign country		*	*	*	*	*		*	*
Local currency demand accts. in foreign countries		*			*	*	*	*	
Foreign financial advice			*	*	*		*		
Foreign credit investigation			*	*		*			
S.T. overseas funds investment		*		*	*				

Source: 1982 BMC European Multinational Banking.

METROPOLITAN'S POSITION
IN THE MNC MARKET

In the Canadian financial community, Metropolitan was seen as a bank which "worked hard and substituted quantity for innovation." A competitor suggested that Metropolitan always had a strategy of "following the pack." For example, the bank was slow in building up data processing and automated tellers and also lagged in the development of a sizable bond and foreign exchange trading operation.

Instead of innovating, Metropolitan pushed volume. Standby letters of credit increased five fold between 1979 and 1983 to $6.04 billion, which was much more than at most big banks. Loans rose 4.7 fold to $31.4 billion between 1972 and 1983 compared with 3.3 fold at the ten largest bank holding companies. In the international arena, Metropolitan was the first Canadian bank to establish a merchant bank in London, which led to a doubling of international loan volume after 1976. Metropolitan's desire for loan volume was evident from the way it ran loan syndications: instead of parceling out nearly the whole package as its competitors did, Metropolitan usually held onto at least 10% of these loans.

The bank's main foreign business was correspondent banking. In an approach differing from that of U.S. rivals like Globalbank and Bank of the U.S. which established branches abroad, Metropolitan opened representative offices concentrating on such services as trade financing and dollar settlements for local banks. Metropolitan had a reputation for successfully courting banks overseas. It billed itself as an international bank with excellent correspondent bank relationships, having more than 1600 correspondents. The contribution to Metropolitan's operating earnings grew from $61.9 million or 21% of operating revenue in 1978 to $155 million or 31% of operating revenue in 1980.

In the North American market, Metropolitan Bank was tied for tenth place, and in the European market, it was twenty-fifth in terms of the number of principal relationships among the companies in the Bank Marketing Consultants Ltd. sample (Exhibits 1 and 2). In both markets, Globalbank was the leader, with Bank of the U.S. second in the North American market and third in the European market.

On the other hand, Metropolitan experienced a significant gain in lead bank relationships in the North American market in 1981. During 1982, Metropolitan, two U.K. banks and two U.S. banks all increased their importance sharply in the eyes of their AMC customers, based on the provision of local currency credit, followed much further down the survey list by innovation in tailoring loans to needs, competitive credit pricing, and international account-officer quality (Exhibit 6).

In general, Metropolitan Bank was used mainly because of its willingness to lend, because of long-term relationships, and the competence of its account officers, ranking above the top ten bank average for the first two criteria and average for the third. Very few of Metropolitan's customers used it for its foreign branch network, and there had been no customer-perceived improvement on this aspect since 1980.

With respect to the type of international credit, Metropolitan was employed mostly for its eurocurrency facilities, having the highest percentage usage rate among its customers compared to all the top ten banks. Metropolitan also had above-average usage of its eurocurrency term loans. Since 1981, Metropolitan had strongly increased penetration of the markets for both these services. This occurred despite the fact that, relative to the other banks, Metropolitan had about an average rate of soliciting its customers for new business and an average effectiveness rating for its solicitations among non-customers.

The top international credit type in terms of demand, however, was overdraft facilities for subsidiaries abroad, where two U.K. clearing banks had the highest usage rates. Metropolitan was not rated highly, compared to its major North American competitors, for being consistently willing to lend internationally to meet the needs of multinationals. But when it did lend internationally, Metropolitan was not considered demanding in the pricing of its credit.

EXHIBIT 6   NORTH AMERICAN TRENDS IN PRINCIPAL AND LEAD BANK RELATIONSHIPS

	1980		1981		1982	
	Principal %	Lead %	Principal %	Lead %	Principal %	Lead %
Globalbank	73	35	69	38	66	35
Bank of the U.S.	61	20	54	21	53	17
Big Bank	55	16	48	16	51	15
Topbank	56	21	49	23	48	22
Midwest Bank	41	9	40	13	40	10
British Bank A	22	2	22	1	29	2
Commercial Bank	26	3	22	4	26	5
British Bank B	22	1	21	1	25	1
Canadian Bank	23	2	24	2	25	2
Wall Street Bank	23	3	25	3	24	3
Metropolitan	26	3	22	3	24	6

Source: 1982 BMC North American Multinational Banking.

For non-credit international services, Metropolitan was ranked as one of the most capable banks by only 47% of its principal customers. By contrast, Topbank and Globalbank were ranked as such by over 80% of their principal customers. Exhibit 7 shows the relative ranking of the top banks with respect to the provision of non-credit international services. Topbank rated very highly for international financial advice, and Globalbank rated highest as most capable in foreign exchange trading and international money transfer. Globalbank and Topbank ranked first and second for international cash management. Big Bank and Globalbank were the most used for international trade services, with Bank of the U.S. and Metropolitan forming the second tier well above

EXHIBIT 7   1982 NORTH AMERICAN CUSTOMER EVALUATIONS OF BANKS
MOST CAPABLE IN INTERNATIONAL SERVICES

	Most capable in international services %	International financial advice %	Foreign exchange advice %	International money transfer %
Globalbank	83	57	48	48
Bank of the U.S.	69	36	20	36
Big Bank	58	29	24	25
Topbank	84	71	36	37
Midwest Bank	55	23	17	13
British Bank A	27	7	2	5
Commercial Bank	53	19	33	11
British Bank B	32	11	9	8
Canadian Bank	24	8	10	7
Wall Street Bank	51	22	17	14
Metropolitan	47	10	16	16

Base: each bank's principal customers

Source: 1982 BMC North American Multinational Banking.

the top ten bank average. The top three foreign banks were all used most for foreign local currency demand accounts.

With respect to account officer characteristics, the single most important account officer characteristic looked for by company executives was "following up promptly and effectively." Knowing the companies' international needs and how to use the bank's network ranked next in importance. Metropolitan received its highest evaluations for prompt follow-up and understanding how companies conduct international business, about even with the average top bank scores on these two factors. The top foreign banks received notably low scores on all important account officer criteria.

METROPOLITAN'S OPERATION

Apart from not overlooking potential opportunities in the multinational banking market, Mark

Holder also wanted to make sure that any proposals he might make would fit Metropolitan's portfolio of activities. In Metropolitan's commercial and industrial loan portfolios, which constituted the bulk of its risk asset portfolio in 1982 (see Exhibit 8), domestic borrowers accounted for $7.8 billion out of a total portfolio of $15 billion. The largest portion of commercial loans were to manufacturing firms, many of which were major multinational corporations. This part of the portfolio was well diversified; no single industry group accounted for more than 5% of the total. "Losses relating to foreign lending in this area have grown to approximately $14 million in 1982; however, the majority of the charge-offs in both 1981 and 1982 were domestic in nature. Management believes that 1983 net charge-offs for this category will increase somewhat from the 1982 level."

As a whole, foreign operations accounted for 50% of Metropolitan's net income in 1982, 54%

EXHIBIT 8   1982 PORTFOLIO
(In Millions)

Total loan portfolio	Loans outstanding		Nonperforming loans		Net charge-offs	
	1982 $	1981 $	1982 $	1981 $	1982 $	1981 $
Consumer	2528	2261	—	—	25	25
Real estate	1814	1245	60	66	7	2
Financial institutions	7514	6406	91	85	(1)	(1)
Loans for purchasing or carrying securities	703	1114	—	—	—	—
Loans to foreign governments and official distinctions	2111	1805	95	95	—	—
Commercial and industrial	15023	13490	260	181	45	25
Other	3086	2867	75	16	4	3
	32779	29188	581	443	80	54
Unearned discount	(814)	(725)	—	—	—	—
Total	$ 31965	$ 28463	$ 581	$ 443	$ 80	$ 54
Commercial and industrial portfolio						
Oil and gas	3440	2767	5	4	1	—
Shipping	746	613	1	1	1	—
Metal and mining	1141	1224	46	4	4	—
Other (primarily manufacturing)	9696	8886	207	172	39	25
Total	15023	13290	259	181	45	25

of its total assets, and 56% of total liabilities. The international demand for loans was strong, as shown by the $2.0 billion growth in Metropolitan's foreign loans during 1982. This reflected the bank's expansion of its worldwide network in recent years, coupled with participation in foreign correspondent, corporate, and government markets. A geographic breakdown of Metropolitan's foreign activities is provided in Exhibit 9.

Metropolitan's other operating revenue increased 62% in 1981 to $337 million (including a non-recurring $58 million gain on the sale of the corporation's headquarters) and by 4% to $350 million in 1982. This growth reflected a continuing commitment to increasing fee-based services throughout the corporation

(Exhibit 10). Trading account profits and commissions reflected progress toward the development of capabilities as a securities dealer. The average overseas trading account balance increased 97% from 1981 and was the primary contributor to the overall increase in trading profits. Commissions on letters of credit and acceptance increased as a result of higher letter of credit fees and a greater volume of acceptances. Foreign exchange revenue increased 35% in 1982 following a 148% rise in 1981. Metropolitan increased its participation in the worldwide interbank foreign exchange market, using its global banking system to increase forex service for its multinational customers. Other service revenue grew 42% in 1982 and 58% in 1980. The improvement was based on increased mortgage servicing fees, in-

EXHIBIT 9 1982 FOREIGN LOANS
(In Millions)

December 31, 1982	Due within 1 year	Due from 1–5 years	Due after 5 years	Total foreign loans
Industrialized countries	$2528	$1322	$924	$4774
Centrally planned countries	130	152	11	293
Oil exports	157	17	1	175
Developing countries (per capita income levels)				
High income (over $2500)	979	466	275	1720
Upper-middle income ($1136–$2500)	2106	976	453	3534
Intermediate-middle income ($551–$1135)	1319	914	423	2655
Lower-middle income ($281–$550)	390	204	203	797
Low income ($280 or less)	428	117	52	597
Total	$ 8037	$ 4168	$ 2342	$ 14545

December 31, 1982	Outstandings*	As a percentage of	
		Total outstandings	Total assets
United Kingdom	$1959	5.06%	4.37%
Brazil	1410	3.64	3.14
Mexico	1211	3.13	2.70
Japan	1049	2.71	2.34
Argentina	861	2.23	1.92
West Germany	806	2.08	1.80
France	786	2.08	1.75

* Outstandings (includes loans, interest-bearing deposits with banks, investment securities, lease financing, receivables, and acceptances) represent those of both the public and private sectors and are presented without reductions for guarantees of affiliated parties or world banking institutions.

EXHIBIT 10   FEE-BASED INCOME
              (In Thousands)

December 31, 1982: other operating revenue	1982	1981	1980
Trust fees	$52987	$51334	$44897
Service charges on deposit accounts	21965	16046	14111
Trading accounts profits and commissions	13215	11463	7300
Commissions on letters of credit and acceptances	49948	36644	32764
Foreign exchange	20969	15558	6266
Gain on redemption of sinking fund debentures	—	12849	16969
Gain on sale of corporate headquarters	—	57959	—
Other revenue	191008	134691	85561
Total	$350092	$336544	$207868

EXHIBIT 11   SELECTED FINANCIAL DATA
              (In Millions)

Year ended December 11	1982 $	1981 $	1980 $	1979 $	1978 $
Total interest revenue	4998	4897	3424	2532	1697
Total interest expense	4005	4116	2695	1877	1137
Net interest revenue	993	781	729	655	560
Pension for possible losses	111	95	55	74	55
Net interest revenue after provision	882	686	674	581	505
Other operating revenue	350	337	208	160	140
Other operating expenses	921	750	615	502	434
Income before income taxes and secur.	311	273	267	239	211
Applicable income taxes	104	92	106	92	84
Income before secur. gains (losses)	207	181	161	147	127
Securities gains (losses) net of taxes	(1)	(3)	(1)	—	—
Net income	206	178	160	147	127
Total loans	31965	28463	23131	19097	16552
Total assets	44829	41375	38865	33372	28423
Total deposits	30678	29723	29222	26709	22686
Long-term debt	1182	844	642	594	461
Total shareholders' equity	1732	1330	1196	1089	981
Per common share data	$	$	$	$	$
Income before secur. gains (losses)	5.47	5.33	4.84	4.49	3.91
Net income	5.45	5.24	4.81	4.49	3.91
Cash dividends declared	2.07	1.94	1.80	1.64	1.49

surance income generated by mortgage banking and consumer financing, retail credit card fees, and higher fees on a variety of banking services including securities clearance and the administration of government programs.

As Mark Holder pondered the current distribution of Metropolitan's activities and his assignment from Jones, he wondered whether Metropolitan should try to be all things to as many multinationals around the world as possible, the way some of its U.S., Canadian, and U.K. competitors were doing, or whether a strategy of differentiation would be more appropriate. Should Metropolitan continue to emphasize volume, or should it innovate as well? Given the bank's strengths and weaknesses, was the international multinational market the right place for a new strategic effort?

GERVAIS-DANONE

In December 1982, marketing managers in the German ready-made "pudding-with-topping" market wondered how the industry would evolve in the coming year. The past two years had been characterized by a general decline in prices, accompanied by an increase in advertising spending. As a consequence, industry profitability had declined. Moreover, total industry sales had grown by a mere 2 percent in 1982, after having shown two-digit growth rates for many years. All of this seemed to indicate that the industry was headed for its maturity phase.

Industry participants needed to reassess their market share and profitability objectives in the light of these developments. Of all the firms, the moves of Gervais-Danone and Dr. Oetker would be particularly critical for the industry's future. Gervais-Danone was the industry leader with a market share of about 34 percent. Dr. Oetker, a late entrant, had gained market share rapidly at the expense of Gervais-Danone. The moves and countermoves of these two firms had been a major factor in the industry since 1980.

This case was prepared by Professor Reinhard Angelmar of the European Institute of Business Administration (INSEAD) ©1984 INSEAD, Revised 1988. All rights reserved.

GERMAN PUDDING MARKET

The German pudding market consisted of three major submarkets: pudding powder for preparing homemade pudding, ready-made pudding without a topping, and ready-made pudding with a topping. Pudding powder was the oldest of the three submarkets and was still the largest in terms of volume (about 270,000 tons). Dr. Oetker had a dominant position in this submarket. Sales of pudding powder had been declining regularly since the introduction of the different types of ready-made pudding, which offered the consumer greater convenience. Ready-made pudding without a topping came in water-based and milk-based varieties. Dr. Oetker dominated the former segment, while Elite had a major share of the latter segment. After a promising start, this submarket stagnated and then declined to a level of about 10,000 tons in 1982.

Pudding-with-topping differed from simple ready-made pudding by being creamier and because it had a topping of whipped cream or sauce. Despite being more than twice as expensive as traditional homemade pudding, this submarket had shown double-digit growth rates with the exception of 1982. Sales of ready-made pudding-with-topping amounted to 68,000 tons in 1982. Gervais-Danone was the leader in this market.

COMPETITORS

The pudding-with-topping market was dominated by four national competitors which together accounted for approximately 70 percent of the market: Gervais-Danone, Dr. Oetker, Chambourcy, and Elite. The remainder of the market was shared by approximately 30 local or regional competitors (Exhibit 1).

Gervais-Danone

Gervais-Danone AG, located in Munich, was a wholly owned subsidiary of the French BSN group, Paris. Its 1982 sales of DM 362 million showed an increase of 11 percent relative to 1981, while its profits increased to DM 2 million from 1.1 million. Although the BSN group was active in a number of different product markets (e.g., beer, mineral water, pasta, infant food, and packaging material), Gervais-Danone AG concentrated on dairy products. Its brands in the ready-made pudding, yogurt, and fresh cheese markets gave it the leadership of the German dairy products market with an overall 10 percent share.

All of the Gervais-Danone's pudding-with-topping products were sold under the brand names Dany + Sahne and Dany + Alcohol with the "Danone family" brand umbrella. The products were offered in a variety of flavors such as chocolate, vanilla, coffee, apricot, and strawberry, but only in one-cup size (125 g).

Production took place in Gervais-Danone–owned production units on specialized and highly automatized equipment which could turn out 36,000 cups per hour. The cost per 125 g cup was estimated at DM 0.25 until May 1982. A change in product formulation had subsequently increased the cost to an estimated DM 0.28.

Because pudding-with-topping was produced with fresh milk and cream, cooling trucks were required for transportation to the retailers. Gervais-Danone made direct deliveries to retailers in the areas surrounding the production sites, and to several hundred of its largest customers throughout Germany. It used specialized dairy products wholesalers elsewhere. In the stores, ready-made pudding was displayed in the dairy products section. Gervais-Danone's 150-person sales force was responsible for selling all of the company's products to the retailers. Altogether, the sales force had to carry nine major brands. The average total cost of a salesperson was estimated at DM 85,000. Dany + Sahne was distributed by 89 percent of the German retailers (Exhibit 2).

Although Gervais-Danone had no direct control over the retail price charged for Dany + Sahne, it could influence retail prices by its list price, trade promotions, and other trade condi-

EXHIBIT 1   ANNUAL MARKET SHARES AND INDUSTRY DEMAND, PUDDING-WITH-TOPPING MARKET, 1978–1982

	Annual market share (volume) (%)					
	Gervais-Danone	Dr. Oetker	Elite	Chambourcy	All other	Industry demand (000 tons)
1978	46.8	4.8	9.1	19.0	20.3	42
1979	43.2	6.1	10.1	17.0	23.6	52
1980	35.5	11.3	9.2	14.0	30.0	60
1981	34.0	11.8	9.7	14.4	30.1	67
1982	33.9	11.9	10.4	14.2	29.6	68

EXHIBIT 2   DISTRIBUTION PENETRATION PERCENTAGE, PUDDING-WITH- TOPPING MARKET, 1978–1982

	Gervais-Danone	Dr. Oetker	Elite	Chambourcy	All other
1978	84[a]	49	85	54	70
1979	88	57	86	58	76
1980	89	64	86	63	82
1981	88	65	85	69	84
1982	89	71	86	79	85

[a] The stores that carried Dany + Sahne accounted for 84 percent of the 1978 food sales.

tions. On the average, retail prices were marked up 56 percent above the manufacturer's selling price. The average retail price for Dany + Sahne was 65 pfennigs[1] in 1982 (Exhibit 3).

In the past, Gervais-Danone had attempted to balance expenditures for trade promotions and for consumer advertising. Radio and especially television had been the preferred media. Advertising spending for Dany + Sahne amounted to DM 3.6 million in 1982 (Exhibit 4).

Dr. Oetker

To generations of German housewives, the name Dr. Oetker had been synonymous with packaged dessert products, especially baking and pudding powder products. In fact, the Oetker group was a highly diversified concern with interests in shipping, insurance, banking, and other sectors outside the food industry. But packaged food products still accounted for more than 40 percent of the group's total sales of DM 3.2 billion.

The mother company, Dr. August Oetker in Bielefeld, handled the baking and dessert products which were Oetker's traditional areas of strength. Dairy products were a relatively recent addition to its product line. Industry sources estimated Oetker's total 1982 dairy products sales at DM 30 million. Pudding-with-topping and crème fraîche (a sour cream type of dairy product used for gourmet cooking) were its two major dairy products. Crème fraîche, a traditional French product, had been introduced to the German market in 1977. Although its sales had grown beyond initial expectations and attracted numerous small competitors, distribution remained spotty and usage was restricted to cooking enthusiasts.

Oetker's puddings-with-topping were sold under the Dr. Oetker family brand umbrella, but with different names. The products with chocolate, vanilla, walnut, and coffee flavor were marketed under the Gala brand name. The fruit-based varieties carried the Cremilla brand name, and some other products were marketed under

EXHIBIT 3   ANNUAL AVERAGE RETAIL PRICES (DM) PUDDING-WITH-TOPPING MARKET, 1980–1982

	Gervais-Danone	Dr. Oetker	Elite[a]	Chambourcy	All other	Weighted average price
1980	0.70	0.68	0.78	0.67	0.63	0.68
1981	0.66	0.63	0.74	0.63	0.62	0.65
1982	0.65	0.64	0.72	0.61	0.60	0.64

[a] Weighted average of the prices for the 125-g and 250-g cup size.

[1] One DM (or Deutsche mark) has 100 pfennigs.

EXHIBIT 4   ANNUAL ADVERTISING EXPENDITURES OF NATIONAL BRANDS (DM 000) PUDDING-WITH-TOPPING
            MARKET, 1980–1982

	Gervais-Danone	Dr. Oetker	Elite	Chambourcy	Total
1980	2,700	700	2,400	300	6,100
1981	700	1,000	1,000	1,000	3,700
1982	3,600	1,900	1,200	1,300	8,000

generic names such as Rotwein Creme (red wine cream). All products came in the 125-g size.

Oetker had no production facilities of its own for its dairy products. Instead, it had agreements with three dairy companies which it had equipped with the machinery necessary for the production of 12,000 cups per hour. Oetker's costs per cup of pudding-with-topping were estimated at DM 0.29.

All of Oetker's dairy products were distributed by specialized dairy products wholesalers to the retail stores. Selling these products to the retailers was the responsibility of Oetker's sales force. The sales force carried the entire line of retail-distributed products, or about 200 different products. This made it difficult to obtain sustained support for specific products or product groups. Oetker's pudding-with-topping was distributed by about 71 percent of the German retailers by the end of 1982. On the average, the trade margin for Oetker's pudding-with-topping was similar to that for Dany + Sahne, that is, 56 percent. Slightly more than half of Oetker's consumer advertising effort had gone into television advertising in recent years.

Chambourcy

Chambourcy GmbH of Munich was a wholly owned subsidiary of the Nestlé Erzeugnisse GmbH, which was part of the German Nestlé group. The total 1982 sales of the group in Germany amounted to DM 3.2 billion. Chambourcy concentrated on dairy products, with a line similar to that of Gervais-Danone but lacking fresh cheese. Its 1982 sales were estimated at around DM 100 million.

Chambourcy marketed its pudding-with-topping products under three different brand names. Wiener Becher (Viennese Cup) was Chambourcy's counterpart to Dany + Sahne, and had a similar range of flavors. Mein Lieblingsdessert (My Favorite Dessert) was a three-layer pudding with fruits. Both products were sold under the Chambourcy family umbrella. Milchpudding mit Sahne (milk pudding with cream) was sold as a generic product to the trade. All products came in the 125-g cup size.

Chambourcy had its own production facilities. When necessary, it also used extra capacities from dairy companies. Its twin-cup equipment could turn out 24,000 cups per hour. Production costs per cup were estimated at DM 0.27 per cup.

Chambourcy supplied retailers directly in the areas surrounding its production units and used specialized dairy wholesalers elsewhere. Its sales force carried only dairy products. Chambourcy's puddings-with-topping were present in 70 percent of the German food stores. The total trade margin was similar to that of its competitors. Chambourcy's consumer advertising effort concentrated on radio and television advertising.

Elite

Elite GmbH belonged to the German Unilever concern, which had a total 1982 sales of DM 9.3 billion. Elite concentrated on dairy products. Its sales were estimated at DM 140 million.

Elite's pudding-with-topping products covered a variety of flavors. Although all used the Elite family brand umbrella, they were marketed under different names such as Puddingtraum (Pudding Dream), Schokolust (Chocolate Desire), Schokoliebe (Chocolate Love), and others. In addition to the standard 125-g cup size, the production cost of which was estimated at DM 0.27, Elite also produced some varieties in 250-g cups.

Production and distribution policies were similar to those of Gervais-Danone and Chambourcy. Elite's products were sold to the trade by a sales force which carried the full range of Unilever products. Elite was thought to be highly effective in utilizing Unilever's strengths in other areas, such as margarine, for promoting its pudding products to the trade. Its pudding-with-topping line was carried by 86 percent of all German retailers. Elite's consumer advertising effort concentrated almost exclusively on television.

Other Competitors

The remainder of the market was accounted for by a variety of competitors, including generic and private brands of retailers, and by many small regional dairy companies. The vast majority of the latter were organized as farmers' cooperatives whose main objective was to market their members' milk, either directly or in transformed form. They typically followed new national brands by bringing out me-too products at lower prices and somewhat lower quality. Their main strengths were their production expertise, short distribution channels, and strong local customer base despite a low advertising intensity. The production cost per 125-g cup was estimated at DM 0.24.

A few of the regional companies had been making attempts to broaden their geographic reach. Foremost among them was Ehrmann, a privately managed (i.e., not a farmer's cooperative) dairy products company with a strong base in southern Germany and Nordrhein-Westfalen. Its total 1982 sales were estimated at DM 165 million. Despite a national distribution of only 32 percent at the end of 1982, Ehrmann had managed to reach an 8.5 percent market share in the pudding-with-topping market. Ehrmann produced its own high-quality products and distributed them via specialized dairy wholesalers.

The production cost per cup for its pudding-with-topping products was estimated at DM 0.27. Its 50-person sales force allowed the company to cover only a limited number of specific retail targets chosen for their high sales.

COMPETITIVE DYNAMICS

The first pudding-with-topping was launched on the German market by Gervais-Danone in 1970. Despite its high price compared with traditional pudding powder, the chocolate-flavored Dany + Sahne was very successful and soon accounted for the bulk of Gervais-Danone's sales and profits.

Gervais-Danone faced no competition until 1975 when Chambourcy and Elite entered the market with a similar product. By that time, Gervais-Danone had already added vanilla and coffee flavor to its line. Yet chocolate was, and still is, the dominant flavor, with about 60 percent of sales. Although profit margins were already high, the newcomers attempted to obtain a price premium relative to Gervais-Danone. When this was unsuccessful, they lowered their prices to match the market leader. The newcomers obtained reasonable volumes and expanded the total market. Gervais-Danone responded to the competitive entries by introducing fruit-flavored products under its Dany + Sahne brand.

During 1976, a number of small dairy companies started introducing pudding-with-topping products at prices generally below those of the national brands. All of this competitive activity expanded the total market. It also drove Gervais-Danone's market share down to about 50 percent.

In 1977, Gervais-Danone launched a new variety, three-layer desserts (fruits, pudding, and whipped cream), at a price higher than Dany + Sahne. Although other firms also introduced similar products, this variety never met with consumer success and was eventually abandoned by most competitors including Gervais-Danone. This year also marked the initial entry of Dr. Oetker into the dairy products market with three products: three-layer desserts, crème fraîche, and Cremilla fruit pudding. But these were marginal products. The real entry came during the following year with the launch of Gala, Oetker's chocolate-flavored pudding-with-topping. To gain distribution in a market which already had three national and many regional brands, Oetker offered substantial promotions to the trade. The resulting retail prices positioned Oetker approximately 5 percent below the established national brands. Chambourcy's and Elite's prices started drifting down in order to maintain market share.

Gervais-Danone maintained its prices at previous levels. It responded in two ways to the erosion of its market share that resulted from the stronger price competition. First, it increased its advertising spending. Its television commercial, which simulated a blind taste test by a housewife, argued that it was not worthwhile to save a little money by buying a low-priced yet poor-tasting dessert because that product would be rejected by the family. Second, it launched a consumer promotion program designed to maintain customer loyalty.

In 1979, Gervais-Danone introduced Dany + Alcohol, an alcohol-flavored pudding with a whipped cream topping, at a price slightly above that of a Dany+Sahne. Chambourcy, Oetker, and local competitors soon introduced their versions of the same product. This product variety met with satisfactory consumer response. Despite all of these efforts, Gervais-Danone lost 3.6 points in 1979 and was now down to an average 43.2 percent.

During 1980, Gervais-Danone continued to lose market share to Oetker and to the regional competitors whose products sold at significantly lower retail prices. Its share went as low as 32.4 percent during August and September (Exhibit 5). In the fall of 1980, Gervais-Danone inaugurated

EXHIBIT 5   BIMONTHLY MARKET SHARES (PERCENT) AND INDUSTRY SALES (MILLION 125-G CUPS), PUDDING-WITH-TOPPING MARKET, 1980–1982

Period	Gervais-Danone	Dr. Oetker	Elite	Chambourcy	All other	Industry sales
1980						
December–January	37.97	10.53	10.19	14.73	26.58	77.78
February–March	36.48	11.87	9.93	12.91	28.81	80.03
April–May	34.72	13.05	7.70	14.34	30.19	76.17
June–July	33.37	11.44	9.15	14.27	31.82	80.68
August–September	32.35	12.03	9.77	12.88	32.97	76.39
October–November	38.16	9.48	8.03	14.75	29.58	89.14
1981						
December–January	37.32	10.04	7.66	15.64	29.34	88.94
February–March	35.97	10.76	8.47	14.83	29.97	89.31
April–May	31.69	13.12	10.47	15.10	29.62	89.94
June–July	31.62	12.14	10.64	14.13	31.47	88.96
August–September	33.09	13.06	11.02	12.61	30.22	82.16
October–November	34.33	11.57	10.08	14.09	29.92	93.34
1982						
December–January	34.22	10.98	8.73	16.47	29.60	91.80
February–March	33.48	12.88	9.84	12.76	31.04	92.00
April–May	34.68	12.25	10.43	12.54	30.10	93.39
June–July	31.44	11.87	10.79	15.90	30.00	90.65
August–September	34.07	12.90	11.07	13.17	28.79	84.19
October–November	35.34	10.87	11.60	14.01	28.19	91.90

a new trade promotion program which substantially reduced the trade prices of its products, without actually changing their list prices. As a consequence, their retail prices dropped about 4 percent below those of Oetker (Exhibit 6).

Market share response was immediate: Gervais-Danone's October–November 1980 share increased by almost 6 points to 38 percent, while Oetker's share dropped 2.5 points to below 10 percent. After some hesitation, Oetker responded to the price cut, and by April–May 1981 its retail prices were about 8 percent below those of Gervais-Danone. This drove Gervais-Danone's market share down to 31 percent, while Oetker rebounded to 13 percent.

Gervais-Danone extended its trade promotion program into the summer of 1981. This kept its retail prices at a more or less constant level from October–November 1980 on. Advertising

spending was cut to zero starting in December 1980 (Exhibit 7). But when market share continued to decline, a new advertising campaign was launched in the fall of 1981. Simultaneously, trade promotions were cut while list prices were reduced drastically. The net result of the price moves was a further reduction in the manufacturer's price, and a slight decline in Gervais-Danone's retail prices.

Toward the end of 1981, Oetker's trade promotion activities were becoming less intensive. Its retail prices started moving up and were practically at parity with Gervais-Danone's by April 1982. Oetker's market share was hovering around 12 percent and Gervais-Danone's around 34 percent.

The new advertising campaign launched by Gervais-Danone in the fall of 1981 emphasized the superior "creaminess" of Dany + Sahne. Con-

EXHIBIT 6   BIMONTHLY AVERAGE RETAIL PRICES (DM), PUDDING-WITH- TOPPING MARKET, 1980–1982

Period	Gervais-Danone	Dr. Oetker	Elite[a]	Chambourcy	All other
1980					
December–January	0.70	0.68	0.76	0.67	0.64
February–March	0.70	0.66	0.76	0.67	0.64
April–May	0.70	0.66	0.76	0.67	0.63
June–July	0.72	0.68	0.80	0.66	0.63
August–September	0.69	0.69	0.80	0.67	0.63
October–November	0.66	0.69	0.78	0.65	0.63
1981					
December–January	0.66	0.67	0.78	0.65	0.62
February–March	0.67	0.64	0.75	0.64	0.62
April–May	0.67	0.62	0.71	0.63	0.62
June–July	0.67	0.62	0.74	0.63	0.62
August–September	0.66	0.62	0.74	0.63	0.62
October–November	0.65	0.62	0.72	0.60	0.61
1982					
December–January	0.65	0.65	0.72	0.60	0.60
February–March	0.65	0.62	0.71	0.62	0.59
April–May	0.64	0.64	0.70	0.60	0.59
June–July	0.65	0.65	0.72	0.60	0.59
August–September	0.64	0.64	0.72	0.60	0.60
October–November	0.65	0.65	0.72	0.61	0.61

[a] Weighted average of prices for the 125-g and 250-g cup size.

EXHIBIT 7   BIMONTHLY ADVERTISING EXPENDITURE OF NATIONAL BRANDS (DM 1,000) PUDDING-WITH
TOPPING MARKET, 1980–1982

	Gervais-Danone	Dr. Oetker	Elite	Chambourcy
1980				
December–January	208	35	463	22
February–March	822	130	455	3
April–May	375	190	219	41
June–July	28	98	654	0
August–September	519	245	319	36
October–November	706	10	319	231
1981				
December–January	0	89	3	351
February–March	0	63	28	700
April–May	0	539	531	19
June–July	0	119	430	0
August–September	365	127	6	8
October–November	361	90	19	8
1982				
December–January	518	125	0	3
February–March	790	400	544	601
April–May	532	600	647	237
June–July	856	305	2	0
August–September	2	362	1	34
October–November	862	123	0	415

sumer taste tests carried out during 1982 showed that the chocolate-flavored Dany + Sahne was preferred more often than either Oetker's Gala or the Elite product. However, only the difference between Dany + Sahne and Elite was statistically significant. A blind product test of Cremilla against the equivalent Dany + Sahne products indicated that consumers preferred Oetker's products (Exhibit 8).

In May 1982, Gervais-Danone modified the composition of Dany + Sahne. The resulting products were preferred by a ratio of approximately 80 to 20 to Oetker's products in blind taste tests. During the rest of 1982, retail prices remained more or less at the same levels as in the spring. One could even observe a slight upward tendency during the October–November period. Except for the months of August and September, Gervais-Danone maintained a high advertising pressure throughout the year. Although Oetker al-

most doubled its advertising spending compared with 1981, its absolute level reached only slightly more than half that of the market leader.

By the end of the year, Gervais-Danone's market share reached 35 percent for the first time in almost two years. Oetker's share was slightly below 11 percent, or what it had last been about one year ago.

OUTLOOK FOR THE FUTURE

Growth of the total pudding-with-topping market slowed during 1982. This could indicate that the market was entering its maturity phase and that future volume growth of individual manufacturers could be obtained only at the expense of competitors. Another explanation for the slowdown in industry growth could be the difficult economic situation in Germany during 1982.

EXHIBIT 8   SUMMARY OF CONSUMER PRODUCT TESTS (1981)

A. Chocolate-Flavored Products

Choice	Blind test			As-marketed test		
	Gervais-Danone	Dr. Oetker	Elite	Gervais-Danone	Dr. Oetker	Elite
First	57%	47%	35%	58%	43%	37%
Second	35	46	57	35	50	54
Both equal	7	6	6	6	7	8
No answer	1	1	2	1	–	1

B. Fruit-Flavored Products (Blind Test)

Choice	Dany Erdbeer	Dany Aprikose	Cremilla Erdbeer	Cremilla Pfirsich
First	30%	26%	65%	57%
Second	62	69	28	37
Equal	8	5	7	6

GNP had declined by 1.2 percent relative to 1981, and private consumption declined by 2.2 percent (both in real terms).

Consumer surveys suggested that less than 60 percent of the potential consumers had ever tried pudding-with-topping. The comparable figure for yogurt was about 75 percent. Pudding-with-topping consumption was particularly high among consumers who lived in cities with more than 100,000 inhabitants, had a household income between DM 3000 and DM 4000, were middle- and higher-level civil servants and employees, and were between 14 and 19 years old. Especially low consumption was found among people who were farmers, members of households with four or more children, and those who had a household income below DM 1500. Among the pudding-with-topping consumers, approximately one-third could be considered brand loyal, one-half switched between "good and popular" brands, and the rest systematically bought the least expensive brand.

The competitors in the pudding-with-topping market needed to reconsider their market share and profitability objectives in the light of future growth prospects of this market. Also they had to anticipate competitive behavior and assess their relative strengths and weaknesses. They would also have to decide which prices and advertising levels would best achieve these objectives.

SOFTWARE ARCHITECTS (B): THE MARKETING AUDIT

INTRODUCTION

In early 1982, Harvey Mayerowicz, the President of Software Architects (SA), was reviewing marketing plans and procedures with the other five directors of the firm: Gloria Petersen, Gene Petrie, Edward Wroble, Bruce Parrello, and Fritz Wolf. Harvey had just completed the formulation of the business and marketing strategy for SA, and was eager to ensure that the day-to-day tactical decisions in the marketing area were consistent with the strategic direction that had been adopted.

In the past, there had been no serious problems in marketing for SA. There had always been enough of a backlog of project work to keep all of the SA consultants billable to clients. In fact, the firm had recently had to turn away business because it did not have enough people available to staff the projects. However, in view of the ambitious growth objectives that the directors had set for SA in the next two years, it seemed that additional marketing efforts were going to be necessary.

In order to gain an outsider's perspective on the current state of SA's marketing function, Harvey brought in a consultant who had been recommended to him by Gene Petrie, one of SA's other directors, and the president of another local software services firm. The consultant, affiliated with a well-known western business school, suggested an approach for the project that had been suggested by a prominent marketing professor as the "marketing audit."

Harvey had agreed to the suggestion, and the consultant, Harvey, and Gloria Petersen, an SA

Financial support for this case was provided in part by the Marketing Management Program of the Graduate School of Business, Stanford University.

This case was prepared by Professor Tom Kosnik. Reprinted with permission of Stanford University Graduate School of Business ©1983 by the Board of Trustees of the Leland Stanford Junior University.

director who shared marketing responsibilities with Harvey, explored the major areas of SA's marketing strategy and operations:

1 The marketing environment
2 SA's marketing strategy
3 SA's marketing organization
4 The selling process for SA services
5 Internal marketing information systems
6 Profitability of different SA services
7 SA pricing for various services
8 Advertising/communications to potential clients

THE MARKETING ENVIRONMENT

SA was a software consulting firm. It provided systems and applications programming for a variety of clients whose internal data programming staffs were either too small or lacked specialized expertise to undertake the tasks themselves. SA also developed technical seminars for clients and presented the seminars to the clients' employees.

The software services industry in the Chicago regional area consisted of several hundred consulting companies providing support for a wide variety of private corporations, financial institutions, and public sector organizations. The clients of the software consultants in the Midwest were generally not in the data processing industry themselves. Rather, they used computer systems to process information related to their accounting, production, inventory control, and planning systems.

The Midwest was not a center of high-tech hardware and software manufacturers. The technology that was in place in the potential client organizations was often not the "state of the art." For example, although IBM had introduced the 4300 series of processors several years before, and was not actively pushing the sale of its older 370 series of CPUs, there was still a reasonably large installed base of IBM 370 hardware in the Midwest. In another example, relational database management software, which industry observers on the East and West Coasts were applauding as the new generation in the evolution of database

systems, had not found many early adopters in the Midwest.

Price competition appeared to be fairly keen among the consultants who developed application software for clients in the Chicago area. Many of the firms were "body shops" which used contract programmers to perform the work. The largest proportion of their costs was the salaries of the programmers. Although most firms attempted to charge an hourly billing rate between two-and-a-half and four times the programmer's hourly salary costs, there was ample room for price-cutting to ensure that the firm won the project and kept its people "off the beach." As a result, in a competitive bidding situation, some firms substantially reduced rates below those quoted at the outset of negotiations with a potential client.

There were many types of contracts offered to prospective clients. Whenever possible, the consultants attempted to use a time-and-materials contract. In that situation the total cost of the project was not set in advance. The client agreed to pay a certain rate per hour of the programmers' time for as many hours as it took to get the job done. This put the financial risks of budget overruns on the client's shoulders, and was resisted by most organizations.

At the other end of the spectrum, some contracts were fixed in price. The software firm agreed to deliver software that performed certain functions and met criteria set down in the contract for a flat amount agreed upon in advance. This placed the burden of risk on the consultants, and often had disastrous consequences for them. As a result, most software firms avoided fixed-price contracts except under extreme circumstances, including (1) a large number of their programmers "on the beach" with no other new business in sight, (2) a short project similar to work previously performed by the firm, and (3) high potential for follow-on work in which the consultants hoped to recover the money lost on the first contract.

There was a wide variety of hybrid arrangements in which the consultants and clients sought to share the financial risks of software development. Because the contract was an agreement to deliver a product that did not yet exist and was extremely difficult to specify in advance, both sides had compelling reasons to protect their own interests. However, in most cases both client and consultant appreciated the position of the other party, and saw the need to cooperate in the first phase of what was often a long process of exchanges before the final product was delivered.

SA'S MARKETING STRATEGY

The overall marketing strategy that had been developed for SA is described in Case 2, Software Architects (A). The major components of the strategy were:

1 Maintain high quality of services and charge a premium price.

2 Differentiate SA from its competitors.

3 Focus efforts for client development in companies in the Chicago area with IBM hardware/system software environments.

4 Supplement leads provided by referrals from existing clients with cold calls to organizations which have high potential as prospective clients of SA.

5 Concentrate on obtaining follow-up contracts from clients who have already done business with SA.

SA directors knew that the success of their strategy depended upon external factors as well as their own efforts. They wondered what aspects of the strategy might prove difficult, given the state of affairs in the Midwest, and the deepening recession that was causing many of their potential clients to engage in belt-tightening programs.

THE MARKETING ORGANIZATION

Like most of the management functions at SA, marketing was not the sole province of one individual. Both Harvey and Gloria were actively involved in business development. Often, they made their first visit to new prospective clients together. Once the contact was made, one or the other took responsibility for following up in the hope of closing a contract.

There were several others in the firm who showed promise in the area of client development. Harvey and Gloria planned to groom them to take responsibility for bringing in new business. It was not likely that anyone need become a full-time salesperson in the near future. There were not enough programmers to staff the projects that such a person might generate. Besides, Gloria felt strongly that each member of the firm had to keep his or her technical skills finely honed. It was necessary to work at least 50 percent of the time on projects to prevent the programming skills from becoming atrophied. Harvey was the only member of the team who no longer spent a majority of his time in actual consulting.

THE SELLING PROCESS FOR SA SERVICES

The selling of consulting services in the data processing industry had similarities to the client development activities of law and accounting firms. Typically, senior members of the firm developed a network of relationships with decision makers in the organizations of potential clients. There was a strong "old boy" network, and referrals from one client to another were the most common source of new business. When an organization was considering the proposals of several consulting firms, calls were usually made to references provided by each consultant to verify from other users that the service provided had been satisfactory.

Harvey had a well-established network of contacts at the time he founded SA. These had provided much of the initial business for the firm. Gloria was younger than Harvey and did not have an extensive network at the time she began her marketing efforts. However, her technical competence, empathy with clients, and natural selling ability had helped her to rapidly build a group of loyal clients. The task which confronted both Harvey and Gloria was to expand the network by gaining entry into new organizations and strengthening the bonds with existing or former clients.

Although each prospective client presented a new marketing situation, there was a process which was generally followed in the development of new business for SA. Exhibit 1 provides an illustration of this process. A prospect was first identified, either through a personal referral or a "cold call" via telephone to a target organization. The individual usually contacted was the manager of the systems programming department in the organization's data processing division. How-

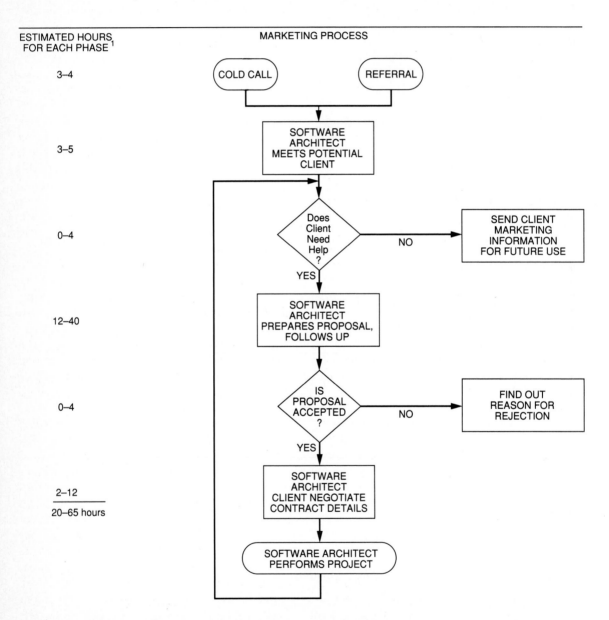

ESTIMATED HOURS
FOR EACH PHASE [1]

MARKETING PROCESS

3–4

3–5

0–4

12–40

0–4

2–12
_____
20–65 hours

[1]Actual hours spent by Software Architect professional. Elapsed time for each phase was considerably longer.

EXHIBIT 1   OVERVIEW OF SOFTWARE CONSULTING MARKETING PROCESS FOR SOFTWARE ARCHITECTS

ever, at times, the person in charge of the application programming department might be the initial contact. In some cases, the senior data processing executive (one or more levels above the two managers mentioned previously) was the point of entry. In many cases that individual had to approve the contract for consulting services before the sale was closed.

In a telephone call to the target individual, Harvey or Gloria arranged a meeting, usually over lunch, to discuss SA. At the one- to four-hour meetings, which both Harvey and Gloria attended, areas of mutual technical interest were discussed, and information about the target organization and SA was exchanged in an informal atmosphere.

At the close of the initial meeting, there was usually one of two outcomes. If the client did not have immediate need for the type of services SA provided, he or she asked for general information on the firm. Gloria subsequently sent a marketing brochure, list of project descriptions, and representative résumés to the prospect. If the client had an immediate need for assistance, a proposal was requested. In SA's experience, approximately 51 percent of the initial meetings resulted in requests for proposals, and 85 percent resulted in requests for general information. The remaining meetings concluded with an explicit statement that the client was not interested in SA's services.

Preparing a proposal was the most time-consuming aspect of the marketing process. The development of a task list, estimation of costs and possible project duration, writing, typing, revisions, and final production took between 12 and 40 hours of Harvey's and/or Gloria's time. The elapsed time to complete a proposal ranged from several days to over a week. Once the proposal was completed, it was delivered to the client. Harvey or Gloria followed up by telephone to ascertain whether the client had questions or whether changes to the proposal were needed.

If the prospect rejected the proposal, SA attempted to find out the reasons for rejection. Exhibit 2 summarizes the reasons that SA did not perform work on 18 proposals that had been written since the company was founded. When Harvey compared the 18 "near misses" with the fact that SA had won 38 contracts from 19 different clients in the same period, he was not sure whether SA was doing well or not. He had no information on the hit rate of other consultants with which to compare SA's results.

On a few occasions, the client appeared ready to accept SA's proposal, but Harvey and Gloria withdrew from the process because they believed that the business was not in the firm's best interest. In one example, a firm wanted SA to commit the majority of Harvey's time for an extended period to give seminars to its employees. It was

EXHIBIT 2 SUMMARY OF REASONS POTENTIAL CLIENTS REJECTED SOFTWARE ARCHITECTS' PROPOSALS FOR CUSTOM PROGRAMMING CONSULTING

Primary reasons Software Architects proposal was not accepted	Number of times cited as primary reason
Software Architects was too expensive relative to competition.	4
Software Architects' competitors had better expertise in a particular area.	3
Software Architects did not follow up after submission of proposal.	5
Software Architects did not want the business.	3
Not sure.	3
	18

Source: Conversations with Software Architects officers.

agreed that SA should turn down the business because he was needed to generate new business for the rest of the firm.

When a proposal was mutually acceptable, additional time was needed to negotiate the details of the contractual arrangement. In some situations the client had a standard contract which was used as the basis for these discussions. If not, SA had a standard contract which it provided the client for review and modification. This process involved the lawyers of both parties, and took from two hours to two days of Harvey's or Gloria's time.

For systems programming and applications programming projects, the process from first contact to signed contract took anywhere from 20 to 65 hours. The elapsed time for the process ranged from three to eight weeks.

Once SA had performed one project for an organization, the time required to negotiate follow-

on work was considerably less than the time taken for the initial selling process. Repeat business was therefore considered more profitable for SA than new client development. Exhibit 3 presents a list of the 19 clients with whom SA had worked since its founding, and the number of contracts performed for each client.

Most of the clients in Exhibit 3 were the result of referrals rather than cold calls. Of the 18 proposals which did not result in new business, 12 had been the result of referrals and 6 had been based on cold calls. Harvey was not sure whether the selling process was likely to change in the future as SA attempted to make increasing numbers of cold calls. He also wondered what he might do to improve SA's ability to successfully use the cold-call approach to generate new business.

Harvey also wondered whether there were ways to improve the overall selling process. SA had maintained a modest marketing budget in the

EXHIBIT 3   SOFTWARE ARCHITECTS' CLIENTS FROM 1979 THROUGH 1981

Client name	Source[1]	Number of contracts	Active project on 12/31/81?	Potential for future work?
AT&T	A	5	Yes	Yes
AT&T Long Lines	R	2	No	?
Bell & Howell	R	1	No	No
Boise Cascade	R	1	No	No
Cambridge Systems	R	1	Yes	?
Chicago Mercantile Exchange	R	1	No	Yes
First National Bank of Chicago	R	1	No	Yes
GATX	C	1	Yes	Yes
GTE Auto Electric Labs	R	1	No	?
Harris Trust	R	1	No	Yes
INC	R	2	Yes	Yes
Illinois Bell	R	2	No	Yes
International Harvester	R	9	No	Yes
Jewell Companies	R	1	No	?
Programmer's Investment Corporation	R	1	No	No
Standard Oil of Indiana	R	5	Yes	Yes
Sunbeam Corporation	R	1	No	No
Tractor Supply	R	1	No	No
White Farms	R	1	No	?

[1] A = Response to article in *Computerworld* written by Harvey Mayerowicz.
R = Referral.
C = Cold call.

past. Was it time to allocate funds for more lavish entertainment of prospective clients? Should SA be doing other things to build their network, such as joining community organizations and social clubs? He knew that such practices were commonplace in other industries and that some of SA's larger competitors also used those techniques.

MARKETING INFORMATION SYSTEMS

Harvey and Gloria each had developed marketing information systems to help them with client development. The systems were manually maintained, and because each was responsible for different clients, the systems were separate.

Harvey maintained a record of all the calls he had made and any future commitments in a day timer. He carried it with him at all times, in order to ensure that he did not set up meetings while on a client call that conflicted with previous arrangements. He also noted important telephone contacts with clients in his day timer for future reference.

In an effort to identify potential customers, Harvey studied the advertisements for data processing personnel in the Sunday edition of the *Chicago Tribune*. If a company repeatedly placed ads for individuals with experience in hardware and software environments that were familiar to SA, he felt that there was a greater chance that the organization might have a need for programming support that SA could satisfy. Although he had collected data from the want ads for over six months, Harvey had not had time to take further action on it. He was planning to hire a new secretary. She would tally the ads each Chicago firm had run in order to identify those which had a continuing need.

The marketing correspondence between Harvey and his prospects was also in need of secretarial support. Although he had saved the letters, proposals, and other documents that had been exchanged over the last several years, they were not organized in a systematic fashion. Setting up a proper file system and a prospect master list

was one of the first projects for the new secretary when she came on board.

Gloria had a system whereby she kept a master sheet on each prospective client for which she was responsible. Exhibit 4 is the form which was used for each prospect. Details on the organization's hardware and software environment, key decision makers' names and phone numbers, and past and future contacts by SA were all included on the form. Gloria used the system as a memory aid during telephone conversations with clients, a "tickler" system to identify prospects which needed to be contacted, and an information source during her meetings with Harvey about marketing.

Gloria also maintained a file of correspondence between her and various prospects and clients for which she was responsible. Included were letters, proposals, contracts, and other information similar to what Harvey maintained for his prospects.

The marketing consultant had taken great interest in skimming through the marketing correspondence files. On the basis of that activity and separate conversations with Harvey and Gloria, he compiled a master list of potential prospects for SA in the Chicago area. Exhibit 5 shows the prospects grouped into three categories: high potential, not sure, and low potential. The consultant asked for reasons that Harvey and Gloria placed organizations in the "low potential" column. The five explanations that were offered were:

1 *Closed shop*: The company had a policy against using consultants in the data processing area.

2 *Hardware*: The organization used non-IBM computer systems.

3 *Budget constraints*: The prospect's data processing budget was too small to afford prices charged by SA.

4 *Out-of-town site*: The firm's data processing facility was not located in the Chicago area, and thus did not satisfy SA's objective of avoiding the personal hardships of extended travel.

COMPANY _____   ORIGINATING DATE _____

ADDRESS _____

_____

_____

PHONE # _____

CONTACT _____   CONTACT _____

TITLE _____   TITLE _____

PHONE # _____   PHONE # _____

ENVIRONMENT

OPERATING SYSTEM _____   DATABASE _____

EQUIPMENT _____   LANGUAGES _____

APPLICATION TYPES _____   TP ENVIRONMENT _____

_____

OTHER _____

_____

CONTACT ROSTER

VISIT/CALL	DATE	RESULTS

EXHIBIT 4   SOFTWARE ARCHITECTS' PROSPECT/CLIENT MASTER SHEET

EXHIBIT 5   CORPORATIONS IN CHICAGO AREA GROUPED BY POTENTIAL AS FUTURE SOFTWARE ARCHITECTS' CLIENTS

High potential	Not sure	Low potential	Reason for low potential
Allstate	Abbott (G)	Ace Hardware	C,B
AT&T	AM International	A.C. Nielsen	H
AT&T Long Lines	American Hospital Supply	Admiral	H
Banker's Life	Amstead	Bliss Laughlin	H
Beatrice Foods	Bally	Bunker Ramo	C
Brunswick	Blue Cross	Clow	C
Baxter Travenol	Borg Warner	DeKalb	O
CBOE	CBI	Ecko	C
Chicago Mercantile Exchange	Combined	F.S. Jones	H
Citibank	Commerce Clearing	Gould	O
CliHouse	Commonwealth Edison	Interstate United	C
CNA	Consol Foods	Kemper	C
CT&T	Continental Illinois	Livingston Communication	H
R.R. Donnelly	R.H. Donnelly	Lowry	B
Federal of Chicago	Control Telephone	MacDonalds	C
First National Bank of Chicago	Esmarck	McGraw Edison	P
FMC	HFC	Midas	B
GATX	Hurtz Schofftner	NAIL	B
GE Credit Corporation	IC Industries	Northern Illinois Gas	H
W. Granger	Illinois Tool Works	Pyle National	B
Harris Bank	Inland	Quaker Oats	H
Homart	Interstate	Santa Fe	H
Illinois Bell Telephone	Kraft	Signal	C,B
INC	Marshall Fields	Sunbeam	P
International Harvester	Master Noswich	Sunstrand	O
International Mining Chemical	Megonite	UARCO	C
Jewel	Metorale	United Airlines	B
Lutheran General Hospital	Murman	Waste Management	H
Mobil Oil	Nalco	W. Heller	H
National Association of Realtors	National Can	Zahn	C
Northern Trust	NW Industries		
NW Hospital	NyCer		
Osco Drugs	OAG		
Ryan Insurance	Old Republic		
Sargent Lundy	People's Energy		
SkilCorp	Pitney		
D. Squave	Scott Foresman		
Standard	Searle		
Symons	Sears		
U.S. Gypsum	SRA		
VISA	Stuart Warner		
Washington National Bank	Trans Union		
WECO	TRW		
White Farms	Walgreen		
	Wilson Sporting Goods		
	Wrigley		
	Zenith		

C = Closed shop.
H = Hardware not IBM.
B = Budget constraints.
O = Out-of-town sites.
P = Previous bad experience.

5 *Previous experience*: In past dealings with the prospects on either proposals or work performed by SA, there had been an unpleasant experience that caused Harvey and Gloria to decide not to do business with the organization in the future.

The companies which fell into the "not sure" categories were those for which neither Harvey nor Gloria had any significant information. Most were taken from a list of the 75 largest companies in the Chicago area which had appeared in the *Chicago Tribune* in April of 1980. The firms in the "high potential" category included many firms with which SA was familiar, which had IBM equipment, and which had shown at least mild interest during initial conversations with SA.

The consultant had launched into an enthusiastic monologue about the merits of an automated marketing information system to keep track of the prospects on the master list in Exhibit 2. Information like that on Gloria's master sheets could be inputted and used subsequently for direct mail marketing with "customized" form letters. Also, the system might automatically report companies for whom a return visit had been promised in a given week, or those which had not been contacted in the previous several months. Moreover, the information for all clients would be centralized for better coordination between Harvey and Gloria. The idea was interesting, but it was not clear that building an automated system was the best use of SA's scarcest resource: the time of its employees.

PROFITABILITY OF DIFFERENT SA SERVICES

The major lines of business in which SA was involved were systems programming, applications programming, and design and implementation of technical education seminars. Systems programming involved the custom development of systems software for use in the client's hardware and operating system. Examples of system software included programs for testing, assessment of system operating efficiency, report writers, and compilers. Application programming was the custom design and implementation of a program to perform specific functions for a non-technical user. Examples of application systems include payroll, accounts receivable, inventory control, and the marketing information system mentioned in the previous section. Details on application and systems software are provided in Case 2, Software Architects (A).

Because of the technical expertise of the SA consultants, they had been asked to develop training programs on several subjects to be presented in a series of seminars to employees in the client organizations. Harvey charged a fee for the development of each seminar and another fee each time the seminar was presented by SA to another group of employees. AT&T had recently agreed to a contract in which a one-week seminar on system network architecture (SNA) was to be given 13 times by SA to different groups around the country in 1982.

SA had also done work with microcomputers for one client, and was considering some additional projects in that area in the next two years.

The target billings for SA in each of the four areas above had been set during the strategy formulation process for 1982 and 1983, and are provided in Case 2, Software Architects (A).

Although they had set target percentages of SA total billings for four types of consulting provided by SA, Harvey and Gloria were not sure whether the mix of business they projected was the most profitable for SA. The percentages were their best estimate of what the market would allow, rather than rigid guidelines which might constrain their marketing efforts.

Because systems programming was more technically complex than application programming, fewer people in the marketplace had the requisite skills, and systems programming commanded a higher hourly billing rate. However, it appeared that the number of clients which required systems programming support in the Midwest was small. Many of the less sophisticated data processing organizations accepted the hardware and systems software provided by the manufacturer and performed application programming within those constraints. In addition, systems programming projects tended to be shorter and less labor-intensive than the implementation of application systems.

Harvey's experience had been that the application programming projects fell into two categories: The first required that the programmer have knowledge of a special operating environment, such as a database management system, in which the application was developed. The second only required that the programmer have a knowledge of a programming language such as COBOL or FORTRAN. Experience in a specialized environment tended to increase the hourly billing rate over that paid for COBOL programming.

In the systems programming area, there was one type of project in which a larger number of clients had needs: database design. This required experience in a particular database management system, such as IBM's IMS or Cullinane's IDMS. However, it did not require other systems programming expertise. As a result, billing rates for database design were higher than application programming rates, but lower than those for other systems programming work.

The consultant felt that the mix of SA's business should be based at least in part on obtaining maximum profits, within the constraints imposed by the market and the hours available to market and perform projects in the various categories. With Harvey's help, he assembled the data in Exhibit 6. The number of consultants assigned to a "typical" project, the elapsed time for the project, and the range of billing rates for each type of service were based on SA's experience of the last two years. Harvey reckoned that it took about the same amount of time (20 to 65 hours) to go from the first visit with a prospect to a signed contract for any of the design and programming services. It was difficult to estimate the time required to market the technical education services. Most of SA's experience in that area had been with AT&T, a large organization which required selling to multiple levels of man-

agement. He felt that it might take anywhere from 40 to 200 hours of his time to close a sale on a technical seminar.

Once the data were assembled, it was unclear to Harvey what the consultant intended to do with them. When he had left Harvey at O'Hare International to fly back to the West Coast, he had babbled excitedly about computer techniques to determine the optimal mix of SA projects. Harvey was curious, although a bit skeptical about such an approach.

In any case, both Harvey and Gloria were interested in gaining a better conceptual understanding of the relative profitability of projects in each area. One particularly thorny issue was how to assess the cost of the people's time spent in programming and in marketing. It was fairly easy to derive an hourly salary cost, by working back from an annual salary using an algorithm whereby salary costs were all loaded into the target hours that an individual was expected to work during the year. SA paid its programmer analysts between $25,000 and $30,000 a year. Determining the cost of Harvey's and Gloria's time was more difficult. Both charged SA $23 an hour to arrive at a "salary," and let the remainder of their compensation come from profit sharing. This figure seemed much too low. Their time was a particularly scarce resource. With the large number of potential clients, every hour spent working on one proposal meant that other potential sources of revenue had to be ignored. Harvey wondered how he might incorporate that aspect into the cost of marketing each of the different types of services.

It was clear that some type of analysis was needed to compare the relative contribution of each type of consulting with SA's overhead and profits.

SOFTWARE ARCHITECTS' PRICING TACTICS

Harvey had attempted to position SA as a high-quality, premium-price source of software consulting. This strategy was not always possible, particularly in a competitive bidding situation for an application programming project. The range of hourly billing rates in Exhibit 6 largely reflected SA's behavior in the face of competition from other firms. When several consultants were bidding on the work and SA sensed that price was a major issue for the client, they lowered their rates to a minimum of $33 an hour. When there did not appear to be price competition, SA charged the highest amount shown in Exhibit 6 for each of its services.

Harvey wondered whether the $33 an hour figure was too low or too high as a floor for SA's rates for application programming. He was also curious about whether he could raise the upper bound of SA hourly rates to reflect higher salary costs as employees received raises and as the starting salary of new graduates increased in the future. He needed a set of guidelines for pricing tactics that were consistent with SA's strategy, and also allowed them to respond quickly if a prospect unexpectedly opened negotiations on billing rates.

In the past, SA had agreed to several fixed-price contracts. In one instance, they had even offered a warranty whereby they worked at no additional cost to repair bugs in software during a certain period after they had completed the project. None of the projects of this type had achieved the target contribution to overhead and profit. In fact, they had barely covered salary costs and direct expenses. As a result, SA had a policy not to accept fixed-price contracts in the future. They had not entirely abandoned the warranty idea, because they felt that it might differentiate them from competitors and enhance the image of quality. Harvey wondered how to assess the conditions and terms under which a warranty agreement might be used successfully.

ADVERTISING AND COMMUNICATIONS TO PROSPECTIVE CLIENTS

In the past, SA had not used any mass media advertising for its services. None of its competitors used radio and television advertising. A few ran print ads in trade journals like *Datamation* and *Computer World*. The marketing consultant indicated that direct mail was also used by firms such as SA, with a relatively small target audience and high need for information before the sale.

Harvey and the consultant had also discussed several less direct forms of creating awareness and interest about SA in the marketplace. The ideas they identified included:

1 Submission of articles about technical issues to industry publications such as *Computer World*, *Datamation*, and *Software News*

EXHIBIT 6   ESTIMATED BILLING RATES, STAFFING LEVELS, AND PROJECT DURATION FOR SOFTWARE ARCHITECTS CONSULTING PROJECTS

Project type	Number of consultants assigned	Elapsed time for a typical project	Range of Software Architects hourly billing rates
System software programming	2	1–3 months	$50
Database design	2	2–6 months	$44–$50
Applications software programming in specialized environment[1]	1–12	1–12 months	$34–$38
Applications programming in standard (COBOL) environment	1–6	1– 6 months	$33–$37
Development of technical education program	2	6–8 months	$50– $65
Execution of technical education program	2	1–2 weeks, 10–15 times a year	$75–$100

[1] Specialized environments included database management systems, such as IMS, and teleprocessing software, such as CICS.

2 Joining Chicago area users groups such as the IMS Users' Group, the Midwest Data Dictionary Group, and the Chicago Database Design Group in order to meet potential clients and demonstrate through discussions and presentations SA's technical expertise

3 Sponsoring a series of free half-day seminars on technical topics of interest to the senior data processing management of SA's target organizations

Gloria had just completed a new marketing brochure for SA which they intended to disseminate to potential clients. The consultant felt that a direct mail campaign might be appropriate with a "personal" letter (using word processing and his proposed marketing information system) and a copy of the new brochure.

Harvey wondered what mix of marketing communication was most effective. How much time and money should be devoted to direct mail, seminars, and user group meetings? How might he encourage SA technical personnel to draft articles aimed for publication in trade journals? There was already time set aside for personal training and development. Did writing an article fall into that category, or should additional time be deducted from the target billable hours for each consultant (currently 1,680 hours a calendar year) and set aside for that purpose? It seemed that the marketing consultant had raised more questions than he had answered.

CONCLUSION

It had been several days since the marketing consultant had left. Although he had promised a written evaluation of SA's marketing function, Harvey and Gloria wanted to make their own assessment of the things that had been discussed. How well did SA's existing marketing tactics fit with their newly formulated strategy for the firm? How well were they doing in the marketing area? What specific improvements were possible?

Harvey also wanted a concrete plan of action for potential changes in SA's marketing organization, selling process, mix of services, advertising and communication program, and pricing tactics. He and Gloria decided to pull together a rough draft of the plan in order to discuss it with their SA colleagues and with the marketing consultant on his return.

TENDERCARE DISPOSABLE DIAPERS

Tom Cagan watched as his secretary poured six ounces of water onto each of two disposable diapers lying on his desk. The diaper on the left was a new, improved Pampers, introduced in the summer of 1985 by Proctor & Gamble. The new, improved design was supposed to be drier than the preceding Pampers. It was the most recent development in a sequence of designs that traced back to the original Pampers, introduced to the market in 1965. The diaper on his right was a TenderCare diaper, manufactured by a potential supplier for testing and approval by Cagan's company, Rocky Mountain Medical Corporation (RMM). The outward appearance of both diapers was identical.

Yet the TenderCare diaper was different. Just under its liner (the surface next to the baby's skin) was a wicking fabric that drew moisture from the surface around a soft waterproof shield to an absorbent reservoir of filler. Pampers and all other disposable diapers on the market kept moisture nearer to the liner and, consequently, the baby's skin. A patent attorney had examined the TenderCare design and concluded that the wicking fabric and shield arrangement should be granted a patent. However, it would be many months before results of the patent application process could be known.

As soon as the empty beakers were placed back on the desk, Cagan and his secretary touched the liners of both diapers. They agreed that there was no noticeable difference, and Cagan noted the time. They repeated their "touch test" after one minute and again noted no difference. However, after two minutes, both thought the TenderCare diaper to be drier. At three minutes, they were certain. By five minutes, the TenderCare diaper surface seemed almost dry to the touch, even when a finger was pressed deep into the diaper. In contrast, the Pampers diaper showed little improvement in dryness from three to five minutes and tended to produce a puddle when pressed.

This case was prepared by Professor James E. Nelson, University of Colorado. Copyright ©1986 by the Business Research Division, College of Business and Administration and the Graduate School of Business Administration, University of Colorado, Boulder, CO. Some data are disguised.

213

These results were not unexpected. Over the past three months, Cagan and other RMM executives had compared TenderCare's performance with ten brands of disposable diapers available in the Denver market. TenderCare diapers had always felt drier within a two- to four-minute interval after wetting. However, these results were considered tentative because all tests had used TenderCare diapers made by RMM personnel by hand. Today's test was the first made with diapers produced by a supplier under mass manufacturing conditions.

ROCKY MOUNTAIN MEDICAL CORPORATION

RMM was incorporated in Denver, Colorado, in late 1982 by Robert Morrison, M.D. Sales had grown from about $400,000 in 1983 to $2.4 million in 1984 and were expected to reach $3.4 million in 1985. The firm would show a small profit for 1985, as it had each previous year.

Management personnel as of September 1985 included six executives. Cagan served as president and director, positions held since joining RMM in April 1984. Prior to that time he had worked for several high-technology companies in the areas of product design and development, production management, sales management, and general management. His undergraduate studies were in engineering and psychology; he took an M.B.A. in 1981. Dr. Morrison currently served as chairman of the board and vice president for research and development. He had completed his M.D. in 1976 and was board certified to practice pediatrics in the state of Colorado since 1978. John Bosch served as vice president of manufacturing, a position held since joining RMM in late 1983. Lawrence Bennett was vice president of marketing, having primary responsibilities for marketing TenderCare and RMM's two lines of phototherapy products since joining the firm in 1984. Bennett's background included an M.B.A. received in 1981 and three years' experience in groceries product management at General Mills. Two other executives, both also joining RMM in 1984, served as vice president of personnel and as controller.

Phototherapy Products

RMM's two lines of phototherapy products were used to treat infant jaundice, a condition experienced by some 5 to 10 percent of all newborn babies. One line was marketed to hospitals under the trademark Alpha-Lite. Bennett felt that the Alpha-Lite phototherapy unit was superior to competing products because it gave the baby 360-degree exposure to the therapeutic light. Competing products gave less complete exposure, with the result that the Alpha-Lite unit treated more severe cases and produced quicker recoveries. Apart from the Alpha-Lite unit itself, the hospital line of phototherapy products included a light meter, a photo-mask that protected the baby's eyes while undergoing treatment, and a "baby bikini" that diapered the baby and yet facilitated exposure to the light.

The home phototherapy line of products was marketed under the trademark Baby-Lite. The phototherapy unit was portable, weighing about 40 pounds, and was foldable for easy transport. The unit when assembled was 33 inches long, 20 inches wide, and 24 inches high. The line also included photo-masks, a thermometer, and a short booklet telling parents about home phototherapy. Parents could rent the unit and purchase related products from a local pharmacy or durable medical equipment dealer for about $75 per day. This was considerably less than the cost of hospital treatment. Another company, Acquitron, Inc., had entered the home phototherapy market in early 1985 and was expected to offer stiff competition. A third competitor was rumored to be entering the market in 1986.

Bennett's responsibilities for all phototherapy products included developing marketing plans and making final decisions about product design, promotion, pricing, and distribution. He directly supervised two product managers, one responsible for Alpha-Lite and the other for Baby-Lite. He occasionally made sales calls with the product managers, visiting hospitals, health maintenance organizations, and insurers.

TenderCare Marketing

Right now most of Bennett's time was spent on TenderCare. Bennett recognized that Tender-Care would be marketed much differently than the phototherapy products. TenderCare would be sold to wholesalers, who in turn would sell to supermarkets, drugstores, and mass merchandisers. TenderCare would compete either directly or indirectly with two giant consumer goods manufacturers, Procter & Gamble and Kimberly-Clark. TenderCare represented considerable risk to RMM.

Because of the uncertainty surrounding the marketing of TenderCare, Bennett and Cagan had recently sought the advice of several marketing consultants. They reached a formal agreement with one, a Los Angeles consultant named Alan Anderson. Anderson had had extensive experience in advertising at J. Walter Thompson. He also had had responsibility for marketing and sales at Mattel and Teledyne, specifically for the marketing of such products as IntelliVision, the Shower Massage, and the Water Pik. Anderson currently worked as an independent marketing consultant to several firms. His contract with RMM specified that he would devote 25 percent of his time to TenderCare the first year and about 12 percent the following two years. During this time, RMM would hire, train, and place their own marketing personnel. One of these people would be a product manager for TenderCare.

Bennett and Cagan could also employ the services of a local marketing consultant who served on RMM's advisory board. The board consisted of twelve business and medical experts who were available to answer questions and provide direction. The consultant had spent over twenty-five years in marketing consumer products at several large corporations. His specialty was developing and launching new products, particularly health

and beauty aids. He had worked closely with RMM in selecting the name TenderCare, and had done a great deal of work summarizing market characteristics and analyzing competitors.

MARKET CHARACTERISTICS

The market for babies' disposable diapers could be identified as children, primarily below age three, who used the diapers, and their mothers, primarily between ages eighteen and forty-nine, who decided on the brand and usually made the purchase. Bennett estimated there were about 11 million such children in 1985, living in about 9 million households. The average number of disposable diapers consumed daily in these households was thought to range from 0 to 15 and to average about 5.

The consumption of disposable diapers was tied closely to birth rates and populations. However, two prominent trends also influenced consumption. One was the disposable diaper's steadily increasing share of total diaper usage by babies. Bennett estimated that disposable diapers would increase their share of total diaper usage from 75 percent currently to 90 percent by 1990. The other trend was toward the purchase of higher-quality disposable diapers. Bennett thought the average retail price of disposable diapers would rise about twice as fast as the price of materials used in their construction. Total dollar sales of disposable diapers at retail in 1985 were expected to be about $3.0 billion, or about 15 billion units. Growth rates were thought to be about 14 percent per year for dollar sales and about 8 percent for units.

Foreign markets for disposable diapers would add to these figures. Canada, for example, currently consumed about $0.25 billion at retail, with an expected growth rate of 20 percent per year until 1990. The U.K. market was about twice this size and growing at the same rate.

The U.S. market for disposable diapers was clearly quite large and growing. However, Bennett felt that domestic growth rates could not be maintained much longer because fewer and fewer consumers were available to switch from cloth to disposable diapers. In fact, by 1995, growth rates for disposable diapers would begin to approach growth rates for births, and unit sales of disposable diapers would become directly proportional to numbers of infants using diapers. A consequence of this pronounced slowing of growth would be increased competition.

COMPETITION

Competition between manufacturers of disposable diapers was already intense. Two well-managed giants—Procter & Gamble and Kimberly-Clark—accounted for about 80 percent of the market in 1984 and 1985. Bennett had estimated market shares at:

	1984	1985
Pampers	32%	28%
Huggies	24	28
Luvs	20	20
Other brands	24	24
	100%	100%

Procter & Gamble was clearly the dominant competitor with its Pampers and Luvs brands. However, Procter & Gamble's market share had been declining, from 70 percent in 1981 to under 50 percent currently. The company had introduced its thicker Blue Ribbon™ Pampers recently in an effort to halt the share decline. It had invested over $500 million in new equipment to produce the product. Procter & Gamble spent approximately $40 million to advertise its two brands in 1984. Kimberly-Clark spent about $19 million to advertise Huggies in 1984.

The 24 percent market share held by other brands was up by some 3 percentage points from 1983. Weyerhaeuser and Johnson & Johnson manufactured most of these diapers, sup-

plying private-label brands for Wards, Penneys, Target, K-Mart, and other retailers. Generic disposable diapers and private brands were also included here, as well as a number of very small, specialized brands that distributed only to local markets. Some of these brands positioned themselves as low-cost alternatives to national brands; others occupied premium ("designer") niches with premium prices. As examples, Universal Converter entered the northern Wisconsin market in 1984 with two brands priced at 78 and 87 percent of Pampers' case price. Riegel Textile Corporation's Cabbage Patch diapers illustrated the premium end, with higher prices and attractive print designs. Riegel spent $1 million to introduce Cabbage Patch diapers to the market in late 1984.

Additional evidence of intense competition in the disposable diaper industry was the major change of strategy by Johnson & Johnson in 1981. The company took its own brand off the U.S. market, opting instead to produce private-label diapers for major retailers. The company had held about 8 percent of the national market at the time and decided that this simply was not enough to compete effectively. Johnson & Johnson's disposable diaper was the first to be positioned in the industry as a premium product. Sales at one point totaled about 12 percent of the market but began to fall when Luvs and Huggies (with similar premium features) were introduced. Johnson & Johnson's advertising expenditures for disposable diapers in 1980 were about $8 million. The company still competed with its own brand in the international market.

MARKETING STRATEGIES FOR TENDERCARE

Over the past month, Bennett and his consultants had spent considerable time formulating potential marketing strategies for TenderCare. One strategy that already had been discarded was simply licensing the design to another firm. Under a license arrangement, RMM would receive a negotiated royalty based on the licensee's sales of RMM's diaper. However, this strategy was unattractive on several grounds. RMM would have no control over resources devoted to the marketing of TenderCare: the licensee would decide on levels of sales and advertising support, prices, and distribution. The licensee would control advertising content, packaging, and even the choice of brand name. Licensing also meant that RMM would develop little marketing expertise, no image or even awareness among consumers, and no experience in dealing with packaged-goods channels of distribution. The net result would be that RMM would be hitching its future with respect to TenderCare (and any related products) to that of the licensee. Three other strategies seemed more appropriate.

The "Diaper Rash" Strategy

The first strategy involved positioning the product as an aid in the treatment of diaper rash. Diaper rash is a common ailment, thought to affect most infants at some point in their diapered lives. The affliction usually lasted two to three weeks before being cured. Some infants are more disposed to diaper rash than others. The ailment is caused by "a reaction to prolonged contact with urine and feces, retained soaps and topical preparations, and friction and maceration" (Nelson's *Text of Pediatrics*, 1979, p. 1884). Recommended treatment includes careful washing of the affected areas with warm water and without irritating soaps. Treatment also includes the application of protective ointments and powders (sold either by prescription or over the counter).

The diaper rash strategy would target physicians and nurses in either family or general practice and physicians and nurses specializing in either pediatrics or dermatology. Bennett's estimates of the number of general or family practitioners in 1985 was approximately 65,000. He thought that about 45,000 pediatricians and dermatologists were practicing in 1985. The numbers of nurses attending all these physicians was estimated at about 290,000. All 400,000 individuals would be the eventual focus of TenderCare marketing efforts. However, the diaper rash strategy would begin (like the other two strategies) where approximately 11 percent of the target market was located—California. Bennett and his consultants agreed that RMM lacked resources sufficient to begin in any larger market. California would provide a good test for TenderCare because the state often set consumption trends for the rest of the U.S. market. California also showed fairly typical levels of competitive activity.

Promotion activities would emphasize either direct mail and free samples or in-office demonstrations to the target market. Mailing lists of most physicians and some nurses in the target market could be purchased at a cost of about $60 per 1,000 names. The cost to print and mail a brochure, cover letter, and return postcard was about $250 per 1,000. To include a single TenderCare disposable diaper would add another $400 per thousand. In-office demonstrations would use registered nurses (employed on a part-time basis) to show TenderCare's superior dryness. The nurses could be quickly trained and compensated on a per-demonstration basis. The typical demonstration would be given to groups of two or three physicians and nurses and would cost RMM about $6. The California market could be used to investigate the relative performance of direct mail versus demonstrations.

RMM would also advertise in trade journals such as the *Journal of Family Practice*, *Journal of Pediatrics*, *Pediatrics*, and *Pediatrics Digest*. However, a problem with such advertisements was waste coverage because none of the trade journals published regional editions. A half-page advertisement (one insertion) would cost about $1,000 for each journal. This cost would be reduced to about $700 if RMM placed several advertisements in the same journal during a one-year period. RMM would also promote TenderCare at local and state medical conventions in California. Costs per convention were thought to be about $3,000. The entire promotion budget as well as amounts allocated to direct mail, free samples, advertisements, and medical conventions had yet to be decided.

Prices were planned to produce a retail price per package of 12 TenderCare diapers at around $3.80. This was some 8 to 10 percent higher than the price for a package of 18 Huggies or Luvs. Bennett thought that consumers would pay the premium price because of TenderCare's position: the pennies-per-day differential simply would not matter if a physician prescribed or recommended TenderCare as part of a treatment for diaper rash. "Besides," he noted, "in-store shelf placement of TenderCare under this strategy would be among diaper rash products, not with standard diapers. This will make price comparisons by consumers even more unlikely." The $3.80 package price for 12 TenderCare diapers would produce a contribution margin for RMM of about 9 cents per diaper. It would give retailers a per-diaper margin some 30 percent higher than that for Huggies or Luvs.

The Special-Occasions Strategy

The second strategy centered around a "special-occasions" position that emphasized Tender-Care's use in situations where changing the baby would be difficult. One such situation was whenever diapered infants traveled for any length of time. Another occurred daily at some ten thousand day-care centers that accepted infants wearing diapers. Yet another came every evening in each of the 9 million market households when babies were diapered at bedtime.

The special-occasions strategy would target mothers in these 9 million households. Initially, of course, the target would be only the estimated one million mothers living in California. Promotion would aim particularly at first-time mothers, using such magazines as *American Baby* and *Baby Talk*. Per-issue insertion costs for one full-color, half-page advertisement in such magazines would average about $20,000. However, most baby magazines published regional editions where single insertion costs averaged about half that amount. Black and white advertisements could also be considered; their costs would be about 75 percent of the full-

color rates. Inserting several ads per year in the same magazine would allow quantity discounts and reduce the average insertion cost by about one-third.

Lately Bennett had begun to wonder if direct mail promotion could instead be used to reach mothers of recently born babies. Mailing lists of some 1 to 3 million names could be obtained at a cost of around $50 per 1,000. Other costs to produce and mail promotional material would be the same as those for physicians and nurses. "I suppose the real issue is, just how much more effective is direct mail over advertising? We'd spend at least $250,000 in baby magazines to cover California while the cost of direct mail would probably be between $300,000 and $700,000, depending on whether or not we gave away a diaper." Regardless of Bennett's decision on consumer promotion, he knew that RMM would also direct some promotion activities toward physicians and nurses as part of the special-occasions strategy. Budget details were yet to be worked out.

Distribution under the special-occasions strategy would have TenderCare stocked on store shelves along with competing diapers. Still at issue was whether the package should contain 12 or 18 diapers (like Huggies and Luvs) and how much of a premium price TenderCare should command. Bennett considered the packaging and pricing decisions interrelated. A package of 12 TenderCare diapers with per-unit retail prices some 40 percent higher than Huggies or Luvs might work just fine. Such a packaging/pricing strategy would produce a contribution margin to RMM of about 6 cents per diaper. However, the same pricing strategy for a package of 18 diapers probably would not work. "Still," he thought, "good things often come in small packages, and most mothers probably associate higher quality with higher price. One thing is for sure—whichever way we go, we'll need a superior package." Physical dimensions for a Tender-Care package of either 12 or 18 diapers could be made similar to the size of the Huggies or Luvs package of 18.

The Head-On Strategy

The third strategy under consideration met major competitors in a direct, frontal attack. The strategy would position TenderCare as a noticeably drier diaper that any mother would prefer to use anytime her baby needed changing. Promotion activities would stress mass advertising to mothers using television and magazines. However, at least two magazines would include a dollar-off coupon to stimulate trial of a package of TenderCare diapers during the product's first three months on the market. Some in-store demonstrations to mothers using "touch tests" might also be employed. Although no budget for California had yet been set, Bennett thought the allocation would be roughly 60:30:10 for television, magazines, and other promotion activities, respectively.

Pricing under this strategy would be competitive with Luvs and Huggies, with the per-diaper price for TenderCare expected to be some 9 percent higher at retail. This differential was needed to cover additional manufacturing costs associated with TenderCare's design. TenderCare's package could contain only 16 diapers and show a lower price than either Huggies or Luvs with their 18-count packages. Alternatively, the package could contain 18 diapers and carry the 9 percent higher price. Bennett wondered if he really wasn't putting too fine a point on the pricing/packaging relationship. "After all," he had said to Anderson, "we've no assurance that retailers or wholesalers would pass along *any* price advantage TenderCare might have due to a smaller package. Either one or both might instead price TenderCare near the package price for our competitors and simply pocket the increased margin!" The only thing that was reasonably certain was TenderCare's package price to the wholesaler. That price was planned to produce about a 3 cent contribution margin to RMM per diaper, regardless of package count.

Summary of the Three Strategies

When viewed together, the three strategies seemed so complex and so diverse as to defy analysis. Partly the problem was one of developing criteria against which the strategies could be compared. Risk was obviously one such criterion; so were company fit and competitive reaction. However, Bennett felt that some additional thought on his part would produce more criteria against which the strategies could be compared. He hoped this effort would produce no more strategies; three were plenty.

The other part of the problem was simply uncertainty. Strengths, weaknesses, and implications of each strategy had yet to be given much thought. Moreover, each strategy seemed likely to have associated with it some surprises. An example illustrating the problem was the recent realization that the Food and Drug Administration (FDA) must approve any direct claims RMM might make about TenderCare's efficacy in treating diaper rash. The chance of receiving this federal agency's approval was thought to be reasonably high; yet it was unclear just what sort of testing and what results were needed. The worst-case scenario could have the FDA requiring lengthy consumer tests that eventually would produce inconclusive results. The best case could have the FDA giving permission based on TenderCare's superior dryness and on results of a small-scale field test recently completed by Dr. Morrison. It would be probably a month before the FDA's position could be known.

"The delay was unfortunate—and unnecessary," Bennett thought, "especially if we eventually settle on either of the other two strategies." In fact, FDA approval was not even needed for the diaper rash strategy if RMM simply claimed (1) that TenderCare diapers were drier than competing diapers and (2) that dryness helps treat diaper rash. Still, a single-statement, direct-claim position was thought to be more effective with mothers and more difficult to copy by any other manufacturer. And yet Bennett did want to move quickly on TenderCare. Every month of delay meant deferred revenue and other postponed benefits that would derive from a successful introduction. Delay also meant the chance that an existing (or other) competitor might develop its own drier diaper and effectively block RMM from reaping the fruits of its development efforts. Speed was of the essence.

FINANCIAL IMPLICATIONS

Bennett recognized that each marketing strategy held immediate as well as long-term financial implications. He was particularly concerned with finance requirements for start-up costs associated with the California entry. Cagan and the other RMM executives had agreed that a stock issue represented the best option to meet these requirements. Accordingly, RMM had begun preparation for a sale of common stock through a brokerage firm that would underwrite and market the issue. Management at the firm felt that RMM could generate between $1 and $3 millon, depending on the offering price per share and the number of shares issued.

Proceeds from the sale of stock had to be sufficient to fund the California entry and leave a comfortable margin remaining for contingencies. Proceeds would be used for marketing and other operating expenses as well as for investments in cash, inventory, and accounts receivable assets. It was hoped that TenderCare would generate a profit by the end of the first year in the California market and show a strong contribution to the bottom line thereafter. California profits would contribute to expenses associated with entering additional markets and to the success of any additional stock offerings.

Operating profits and proceeds from the sale of equity would fund additional research and development activities that would extend RMM's diaper technology to other markets. Dr. Morrison and Bennett saw almost immediate application of the technology to the adult incontinent diaper market, currently estimated at about $300 million per year at retail. Underpads for beds constituted at least another $50 million annual market. However, both of these uses were greatly dwarfed by another application, the sanitary napkin market. Finally, the technology could almost certainly be applied to numerous industrial products and processes, many of which promised great potential. All these opportunities made the TenderCare situation that much more crucial to the firm: making a major mistake here would affect the firm for years.

NABISCO BRANDS, INC.: CIPSTER

In November 1985, Aldo Osti, Area President, Europe—Nabisco Brands, Inc., was reviewing some notes he had made to himself regarding a potential new product launch being planned by one of the company's Italian operations, Saiwa Biscuits. He was trying to reach decisions regarding several strategic concerns with this new product along with some possible organization changes that would affect the product and its management.

Following several successful years as the head of Nabisco's Italian operation, Osti had been appointed President of the European operations in 1976. Presently, he was responsible for the overall operations of Nabisco's companies throughout southern Europe, which included France, Italy, Spain, and Portugal. He reported to the executive vice president of Nabisco Brands International in the U.S. Corporate office.

Headquartered in Paris, Osti had adopted an operating philosophy of decentralization, forcing the decisions for operations, marketing, and planning down to the country and subsidiary managers. He had maintained this organizational arrangement with the belief that those executives closest to the operations were best able to judge individual market trends and to implement strategies appropriate to the specific requirements of local conditions. One result of this was that Osti had a very lean European Headquarters staff, consisting of only one financial executive, one staff executive, two secretaries, and himself.

Over the last several months Osti had conducted informal discussions with the executives of Saiwa regarding a further extension of the company's successful potato formulated snack product, Cipster (pronounced "chipster"). After several years of spectacular growth the brand's sales seemed to be leveling out. Since the product was already dominant in its narrow niche in the Italian snack market, it seemed most reasonable that future growth could be obtained only with new product introductions. Accordingly, he had encouraged his Italian associates either to look for new product ideas for the brand or to plan for brand extensions.

This case was prepared by Professor Robert F. Young as a basis for class discussion rather than to illustrate either effective or ineffective handling of an administrative situation. Copyright ©1986 by IMEDE, Lausanne, Switzerland. IMD International, resulting from the merger between IMEDE, Lausanne, and IMI, Geneva, acquires and retains all rights. Reproduced by permission.

Recently, Luigi Capurro, Saiwa's newly appointed Director of Marketing, had discussed informally with Osti some plans he was formulating to introduce a corn-based extruded snack product under the Cipster label. These plans had not been formalized nor had specific budgetary authorizations been requested. However, Osti thought that some preliminary guidance was appropriate at this time because he did not want the senior management at Saiwa to proceed through the lengthy process of developing written plans and requests if there would be major obstacles to the launch of the new product. Also, if through informal discussions he could raise and perhaps resolve major strategic issues at this preliminary stage, Osti thought he could avoid a lot of rework and delay during the more formal planning and budgeting process.

Nabisco Brands, Inc.

Nabisco Brands was one of the oldest and largest purveyors of packaged food products in the world. Headquartered in New Jersey, Nabisco Brands operated 170 manufacturing plants in 35 countries and had distribution in more than a hundred. In 1985 its worldwide sales were expected to exceed $6 billion, with Europe contributing about 15% of the total. Created in 1981 by the merger of Nabisco, Inc, and Standard Brands, Inc, its product line was diverse and included such well-known brands as Oreo cookies, Planters peanuts and snacks, Ritz crackers, Fleischmann's margarine, Belin biscuits, Baby Ruth candy, and Milk-Bone dog food.

In the second half of 1985, Nabisco Brands was acquired by R. J. Reynolds Corporation, the large U.S.-based tobacco and food processing firm. One result of this merger was that Osti had recently been given the added responsibility for the Del Monte family of canned fruits and vegetables within those countries listed above. Del Monte was an old and well-established brand which had been acquired by R. J. Reynolds in the early 1970s.

Nabisco Brands Operation in Italy

The Saiwa Biscuit Company of Genoa, Italy, had been acquired by Nabisco in 1965. Operated as an autonomous subsidiary, it had grown successfully in recent years and had returned attractive profits to the parent. Among the major products manufactured and sold throughout Italy by Saiwa were crackers, cookies, chocolate-covered biscuits, sugar wafers, and extruded snacks. In 1985 it was expected that Saiwa's sales would be approximately 180 billion Italian lira. (At the time of the case, US$ 1.00 = 1700 Italian lira.)

A second operating arm of the firm in Italy was Nabisco SpA, headquartered in Milan. This firm was run separately from Saiwa with its own chief executive, manufacturing facilities, and sales force. Like other Nabisco subsidiaries the president of Nabisco SpA had total responsibility for the organization's profits and sales growth.

Nabisco SpA processed and marketed an array of brands. Some of these were typical of Nabisco brands found in many other countries such as Ritz crackers and Planters peanuts and snacks. Others were unique to Nabisco SpA in Italy, such as Catari pizza mix and Montania herbal tea. The total sales of this division would be about 60 billion lira in 1985.

Another Nabisco company, Del Monte, Italy, had become Osti's responsibility only within the last few months. This firm concentrated on canned fruits and vegetables and in 1985 was expected to achieve a volume in Italy of 50 billion lira.

CIPSTER

In 1971 Saiwa successfully launched Cipster, an extruded potato-based snack product. The product is made by mixing potato flakes, starch, salt, and coloring. In mix form, the product is extruded in a manner similar to the process used to manufacture spaghetti. The resulting rolls are cut, dried, and then fried briefly in cooking oil. After further drying the product is ready to be packaged.

EXHIBIT 1   CIPSTER'S RECENT SALES HISTORY

	1982	1983	1984	1985 (est.)
Tons	1371	1474	1401	1462
Lira (billion)	9.9	13.2	14.9	17.1

EXHIBIT 2   SALES OF SNACKS IN ITALY, 1981–1985 (In Tons)

1981	1982	1983	1984	1985 (est.)
27,400	28,900	31,130	33,400	36,400

The product was introduced with heavy spending on dramatic television advertising which proclaimed: "It's a potato. No, it's Cipster." The idea was to position Cipster as a "non-potato chip" snack against the category leader, potato chips. Initially, the company spent one lira on television advertising for every lira of sales. Such advertising pressure created almost overnight recognition of the brand and helped the sales force achieve very broad distribution.

In its initial years the product was well received by a broad segment of the population. Cipster was consumed by youngsters as an afternoon snack as well as by adults with a cocktail or aperitif. In 1975 Saiwa began concentrating most of its merchandising for the product on teenagers and young adults. The product was portrayed as "fun" for active, social people. By 1981 this positioning was further enhanced by television commercials using fast rock music. In 1985 this particular "fun" image development was continuing along with a secondary theme of Cipster as the "non-potato chip."

The results of this effort by Saiwa were impressive. By 1985 the sales of Cipster were 17.1

billion lira, and the brand represented about 18% (by tonnage) of the extruded snack market in Italy (see Exhibit 1 for sales history). Also, the brand's contribution to profits was above the corporate average.

The Italian Snack Market

The Italian snack market had experienced substantial growth during the last five years (as shown in Exhibit 2).

While all three major product segments participated in this growth, extruded snacks had clearly grown the fastest (see Exhibits 3 and 4). Within the extruded segment, corn-based products had been the dominant form (see Exhibit 5).

Also, it was apparent that the majority of sales within the extruded segment were in the form of small bags (less than 40 grams) (as shown in Exhibit 6). The distribution of extruded snacks was dominated by the traditional grocery store (as shown in Exhibit 7).

Consumer research indicated that there was a fairly high consumption rate of snacks in the Italian market (as shown in Exhibit 8).

EXHIBIT 3   PRODUCT SEGMENTS IN THE ITALIAN SNACK MARKET, 1981–1985 (Percentage of Tons)

	1981	1982	1983	1984	1985 (est.)
	%	%	%	%	%
Potato chips	65	63	59	58	56
Savory snacks	20	20	21	20	20
Extruded snacks	15	17	20	22	24
	100%	100%	100%	100%	100%

EXHIBIT 4   SALES OF EXTRUDED SNACKS IN ITALY
(In Billion Lira)

1981	1982	1983	1984	1985 (est.)
34.5	46.0	64.9	88.3	114.0

EXHIBIT 5   EXTRUDED SNACKS: PERCENT BY TYPE
(Percentage of Tons)

	1984 %	1985 %
Popcorn	5.4	5.2
Corn-based	67.2	69.1
Potato-based	27.4	25.7
	100%	100%

Cipster's Position

It was Capurro's opinion that Cipster, in its present form, had limited future growth potential. One reason for this was that Cipster had achieved a high share of market within its narrow segment, the extruded potato-based snack market. Currently the brand had about 65% of the volume (in tons) in this particular niche. Although there was no research to support this contention, it was Capurro's opinion that although Cipster competed with the higher-volume corn-based products, consumers did not see the brand as being a direct substitute. Thus, he thought that in its present form, incursion into the more voluminous corn-based segment could not be seen as a significant growth potential.

At the retail level, Cipster was priced significantly higher than the corn-based product (see Exhibit 9). This was due mostly to the more expensive raw material, which had experienced substantial price increases in recent months. It was thought that this price differential was a further inhibitor to the product's growth prospects. Capurro reasoned that this was particularly true in Cipster's case due to the impulse nature of the snack market.

Presently Cipster was bought primarily for consumption in the home. Despite its appeal to young people and teens, the product had achieved only limited success in penetrating the small bag, single-serving, segment. Only 20% of Cipsters' sales were in this package size, although about 70% of the unit volume of the snack category was sold in bags. Sales in this package form were dominated by potato chips. Also, it was believed that within the extruded product area the corn-based product had been more successful in small bags because of its lower price.

As a result of the analysis that led to his conclusion regarding limited growth opportunity, Capurro was informally considering several strategic alternatives. He was suggesting that the Cipster brand strength might be used to launch a new product within the corn-based segment. Such a product would utilize existing equipment and

EXHIBIT 6   SALES OF EXTRUDED SNACKS: PERCENT BY PACKAGE SIZE
(Percentage of Tons)

	1984 %	1985 %
Less than 40 grams (small bags)	57.5	54.5
40–130 grams (large bags and medium-sized cartons)	34.5	36.5
130+ grams (large cartons)	8.0	9.0
	100%	100%

EXHIBIT 7   EXTRUDED SNACKS: SALES BY OUTLET
TYPE
(Percentage of Tons)

	1984 %	1985 %
Supermarkets	13.3	14.0
Superettes	10.9	13.5
Traditional grocery stores	49.3	50.2
Bar/kiosk	26.5	22.3
	100%	100%

EXHIBIT 9   RELATIVE RETAIL PRICES OF EXTRUDED
CORN-BASED AND EXTRUDED POTATO-
BASED SNACK PRODUCTS
(Prices Are Indexed)

	Potato-based	Corn-based
October '84	1.35	1.10
October '85	1.52	1.10

have a texture similar to that of the potato-based product. Its color, taste, and price would be the product's principal distinguishing characteristics.

Although the new product could be produced with minimal new capital investment, the marketing investment for such a brand extension might be substantial. Capurro's tentative plan was to employ the strong Cipster brand recognition and market the product under that consumer franchise. He estimated that by utilizing such a widely recognized brand name, Saiwa would have to spend about 10 billion lira on advertising a corn-based product within the first two years.

The alternative of creating a totally new brand name and identity would probably cost about 20 billion lira. This second alternative also had the drawback that Saiwa would end up with two separate brand names competing for the same consumer usage occasion.

On a per unit basis a corn-based extruded product could be produced for an estimated 60% of the direct manufacturing costs (variable manufacturing plus manufacturing overhead) of the present potato-based product. It would be sold by Saiwa's existing sales force through essentially the same wholesale and retail channels as the potato-based product. There would be, however, additional effort placed on obtaining distribution in kiosks and through various street vendors in order to penetrate more deeply into the impulse-oriented bag snack market.

Along with these tentative ideas for the new product, Capurro was proposing that the 1986 plan for the present Cipster product be a maintenance marketing program. In order to save funds for the eventual launch of the corn-based product he was suggesting an advertising and promotion expenditure of about 1.2 billion lira. This would be used primarily to stimulate trial among teens and young adults. The emphasis would be on a series of sales promotions such as contests, games, premiums, and point-of-purchase price

EXHIBIT 8   SNACK CONSUMPTION
(Percentage of Population over 16 Years Old)

	Potato chips	Savory snacks	Extruded snacks
Consumed within last seven days: winter	18.9%	11.5%	6.9%
Consumed within last seven days: summer	23.5%	11.9%	7.5%
Consume every 2–3 days: winter	5.0%	5.5%	4.0%
Consume every 2–3 days: summer	7.7%	7.2%	4.4%

reductions. There would also be limited television and billboard advertising aimed at the teen market.

Capurro estimated that about 2.5 billion lira was the amount that a brand such as Cipster would normally spend on marketing communications during a year. Thus, there was some risk in reducing the advertising effort, especially in light of the recent increase in the advertising effort of the major competitors.

Osti's View

As Osti was reviewing the proposed Cipster strategy, he had reached several tentative conclusions. It appeared to him that with a reasonable level of advertising support, a new corn-based Cipster had the potential to reach break-even within the second year after its introduction and be profitable in the third. However, the new product's effects on the sales of the current potato-based Cipster were difficult to determine. He thought that the sales and profitability of that product would probably go down. But, it was uncertain how fast that would happen and to what extent the profits would erode.

In addition to the plans for Cipster in Italy, Osti was also considering several broader strategic changes that could potentially affect that product's strategy as well as the way in which the company would be organized to market it. As has been stated, Osti had consistently believed in the many benefits of the highly decentralized marketing decision making that had been practiced by Nabisco in its European operations. Nevertheless, some emerging trends had made him think that perhaps more central coordination would be called for in the future.

Recently there had been substantial publicity given to a concept called "globalization of markets." It was contended by some that throughout the world (and especially in western Europe) there was emerging a common (or "global") consumer culture. Many Europeans were traveling with increasing frequency to countries other than their home. They observed other cultures and local consumer habits. In addition, it was speculated that Pan-European television, with its attendant advertising, would soon be a fact of life. Already homes in border areas and those wired for cable (still a little less than 10%) were receiving broadcasts from other parts of Europe. This Pan-European television would mean that viewers not only would be exposed to alternative lifestyles on a regular basis but would also be watching commercials from several different countries.

It was argued that this cultural binding of both consumer's brand knowledge and lifestyles would justify the development of common brand marketing efforts throughout Europe. It was suggested that marketers approach the entire western European market as a single entity. Pan-European (or global) brand names, package designs, advertising, and promotional programs were being called for.

In addition to these cultural trends, several economic factors were encouraging Osti to consider a Pan-European approach to the firm's marketing programs. In many of the firm's operating divisions there were major brand opportunities which would require substantial investment in marketing tools such as television commercials and innovative packaging. When this investment was weighed against the size of the market opportunity in just one country, such up-front spending could often not be justified. However, if these investments were compared with the revenue opportunity for all of Europe, the marketing plan sometimes became economically attractive.

Along with considering the validity of Pan-European branding programs, Osti was in the process of reviewing with the key operations people in the firm a concept he called "centers of manufacturing excellence." It seemed to some that Nabisco should be consolidating some of its far-flung factory operations. In the current arrangement each country manufactured its own products. Thus, for instance, Saiwa made all of its own products for its home market in its several factories throughout Italy. The same was true of the companies in France, Spain, etc. In each situation there was virtually no exporting to other major markets.

With the advent of more technology in the food processing business (it was still far from a high-tech business, however), it seemed reasonable that the factories should begin to specialize. Thus, perhaps one of Nabisco's French operations, Belin, might make all of the crackers ("biscuits") for the many Nabisco sales organizations throughout Europe, as would perhaps the Italian factory make all of the extruded snack products. This would allow each factory to concentrate on a fewer number of technologies, focus on a limited number of products, and achieve operating efficiencies. While there were not any definite plans for implementing this manufacturing strategy, Osti was confident that this or a similar scheme would be necessary within only a few years.

One of the strategic alternatives that had emerged from these considerations was the idea of establishing Planters as an umbrella snack brand, or "family brand," for all of Nabisco's products in that category throughout Europe. This would mean using the name Planters on all packaging, and with all advertising and promotional effort for snack products. In addition, if this concept were adopted, it seemed reasonable that the familiar deep blue that had come to be identified with the brand would become the dominant color on all packages.

Planters is a "household word" in North America and is synonymous there with peanuts. It is one of the most widely recognized consumer brands in the United States. In addition to peanuts the American operation of Nabisco had recently been successful in expanding the Planters brand to encompass a wide range of snack products. The widely recognized blue package and Mr. Peanut logo were being used to market various snacks including cheese balls, pretzel sticks, and corn chips.

While not as well known in Europe, the Planters brand was gaining momentum. For example, starting from a small base, Nabisco's operations in Germany had doubled the Planters peanut volume over the last several years. Planters peanuts were sold in all the countries under Osti's supervision, but in none of them was the brand franchise what would be considered "well known."

In addition to the arguments presented above, Osti was eager to initiate the concept of Pan-European brands to alter the trend toward brand proliferation. It had been his observation that most of the operating companies tended to develop a new brand for each new product that was introduced. This required that each new brand carry the financial burden of its own unique brand development. If a "family brand," such as Planters for snacks, could be established, there were obvious economic advantages in the areas of advertising and promotion.

The use of a Pan-European family brand for snacks also had the potential benefit of supporting more professional advertising development. Generally, the more financial contribution that is generated by a brand, the more money would be available for this development of advertising materials. Normally, a low-volume brand could not support the best efforts of the leading European advertising agencies. While such agencies might agree to work on a low-volume brand because of their desire to develop relationships with Nabisco, their best creative talent would probably not be assigned. A high-volume umbrella brand such as Osti envisioned for Planters would certainly justify the best of the advertising profession.

Osti saw the launch of a "new" Cipster product as a potential opportunity to begin the broadening of the Planters brand family. It was perhaps possible to widen Nabisco's snack franchise by incorporating successful products under the Planters brand umbrella initially in Italy and then throughout Europe. Cipster could be the first such move in that direction.

At the time of the case there was only one other firm attempting to build a Pan-European snack brand. Bahlsens, a well-established biscuit ("cookies") brand in Germany, was trying to broaden its franchise to encompass a wide range of snack products: peanuts, extruded snacks, and sweet biscuits. In peanuts Bahlsens was well-established only in France, Switzerland, Austria, and Germany. Its biscuit line had long been established in Germany but only recently had the firm attempted to move into other markets with Bahlsens biscuits.

Of course, there were examples of companies that had achieved success with Pan-European or global brands in other categories. The most frequently mentioned were Coca-Cola and Marlboro. However, the extent to which these cases applied to a Pan-European snack brand was uncertain.

At present, the brand name Planters was the responsibility of Nabisco Italy SpA. This company, which reported directly to Osti, was operated independently like all other Nabisco companies. While the firm did sell Planters peanuts throughout Italy, the volume for that product was only about 2.5 billion lira.

Osti's Decisions

Thus far Osti had taken one step in operationalizing his ideas on Pan-European brands. He had been instrumental in establishing a new product coordinating committee with executives from both the southern European operations (his area of responsibility) and Nabisco in northern Europe (which reported to another executive). The purpose of this group was to review the operating companies' new product plans, to encourage the flow of information between the various companies, and to promote Pan-European brand programs where possible. One operating rule that had emerged from this committee was that any totally new brand would be developed in such a way that it could be sold by any of Nabisco's European firms if they so chose. Thus far, the committee had not become involved in the marketing programs of existing brands. (Both Planters and Cipster would be considered existing brands.)

It appeared to Osti that there were several alternatives open to him regarding Cipster. Obviously, he could encourage Capurro and his associates to proceed with their ideas for a corn-based product similar to Cipster under the Saiwa label. Another course of action would be to allow the corn-based product development to continue and transfer its marketing re-

sponsibility to Nabisco SpA in Milan. A further choice was to instruct his operating executives that henceforth the Planters marketing program in Italy would be the responsibility of Saiwa. This alternative would probably also mean moving the operational responsibilities for Planters to the Genoa-headquartered Saiwa from the Milan-based Nabisco SpA.

As he was thinking through these choices, Osti was keenly aware that he had two very fine general managers in place in the two operating companies in Italy. Both had performed well, and Osti was eager to avoid anyone "losing face" with his decision.

The total snack market in western Europe was the equivalent of several hundred million dollars. In organizing a consolidated approach to this market, what type of decisions would have to be made and what form should the organization take? If he were to operationalize his ideas about a Pan-European snack brand called "Planters," Osti wondered if this would call for more centralized marketing planning and control from his Paris office. For instance, would some direction be required when the decision had to be made regarding which names (Nabisco, Saiwa, Planters, Cipster) would be on the package and how much prominence would be given to each? He remembered well how he had fought for three years to obtain complete cooperation from the operating companies regarding the adoption of a common design and typeface for the distinctive Nabisco trademark and colophon on the package of the firm's products.

For many years Osti had encouraged his general managers to be both responsible for their operations and independent in their decision making. Was the implementation of Pan-European branding going to backfire on him and create more interorganizational conflict than it might be worth? Also, he wondered whether introducing the brand Planters on top of a widely recognized name such as Cipster, along with the adoption of blue packaging in place of the present distinctive red package, might serve only to confuse current Cipster customers. There were many consumers in Italy who knew and liked Cipster by Saiwa.

JACOBS SUCHARD: NABOB SUMMIT

"I'm running the most successful new brand that Nabob has introduced in the last twenty-five years, and now you're telling me my sales are too high," Bruce McKay, Summit's product manager, complained. "I feel like the proverbial Canadian grain farmer; the more I sell the less I make."

"That's right. Summit's not making enough money, and you've until year end to solve the problem," John Bell, Nabob's General Manager, told the upset product manager, and as Mr. Bell left the room, he delivered a parting comment, "And don't destroy the brand while you're solving that problem!"

Despondently Mr. McKay looked at the packages and documents that cluttered his office. His eye was caught by the bright blue Summit Decaffeinated package, the line extension that had just been successfully introduced. Beside it was the March/April 1987 A.C. Nielsen report which had arrived that morning. It was open at the section revealing performance in the critical Metro Toronto market. The Summit share had shot upwards and was now close to 8%. The other document that caught his attention was the latest

cost analysis and profitability statement. It confirmed his worst fears. The profitability per case of Nabob Tradition was 30% greater than that of Summit. Every Tradition user who switched to Summit cost the company money.

THE NABOB STORY

Although Nabob had been making food products for 70 years, nothing in its history was as momentous as the purchase of the company in 1976 by Jacobs Suchard of Zurich, Switzerland. Nabob, which made over 150 products, had been owned by Weston, the larger grocery retailer and bread manufacturer. After Jacobs purchased it, Nabob either stopped manufacturing many small brands that had been private labels for Super Valu, a Weston company, or sold those with a solid franchise to other companies. By 1984 the product line had been reduced to only two businesses, ground coffee and tea. Tea was sold only in Alberta and British Columbia. Nabob ground coffee was sold nationally but with very little penetration in Quebec. The size of the Canadian ground coffee market was 78 million pounds, and at an average retail price per pound of $3.50, the dollar value of the market was $275 million.

Jacobs brought to Nabob a singlemindedness of purpose, enthusiasm for the products it sold, and a marketing entrepreneurial zeal with which to take on far larger competitors. This was Jacobs's first entrance into North America, and the company had no intention of remaining content with its dominant position in the Western Canada ground coffee market. Klaus Jacobs, the parent company's chairman, explained one of his management philosophies. "To set high expectations and performance standards for everyone in everything we do," by saying, "We want to be not just as good as our competitors but better. We have to be, in order to equalize their greater size and scale. If they are the Goliaths, we have to be the David." Nabob was Jacobs's window on the North American market.

In 1978 Nabob entered the Ontario market with its Tradition brand of roast coffee. The coffee was packaged in a unique vacuum package, quite different from the soft paper bag packaging that then dominated the Eastern Canadian market.

Nabob test marketed Tradition in Peterborough and Kingston and then rolled out the brand to the rest of Ontario with heavy promotional support and extensive advertising. Memorable advertising copy had the Nabob spokesman compare the difference between Nabob's hard packaging and the competitor's soft paper bags while delivering the message: "Nabob comes in a hard vacuum pack, not in a soft paper bag that lets in stale air. Nabob's fresh flavor and aroma can't get out until you release it. Want a fresher, better-tasting cup of coffee? Start with a fresher, better-tasting coffee. Nabob." The introductory "Microphone" commercial is provided in Exhibit 1.

The major competitor was Maxwell House, from General Foods, with a 15.5% share of the market in 1978 (see Exhibit 2). Ground coffee was considered by many to be a commodity business with pricing as the dominant marketing factor. Maxwell House was also able to rely on the halo effect from heavy advertising behind its instant coffee brand.

By 1982 Nabob had reached an Ontario market share of 22.5%, just below the 24.4% share of Maxwell House, while keeping its 30% market share in Western Canada. During 1982 Nabob introduced a better-tasting Tradition as a result of new high-yield roasting technology, and in 1983 Tradition Decaffeinated was added to the line, giving further impetus to brand growth.

By 1983 Maxwell House had moved to vacuum packaging and was supporting the brand with heavy advertising, featuring the company's long-term spokesman, Ricardo Montalban. In Ontario, Maxwell House remained the best-known brand and had been able to build its market share in the face of Nabob's dramatic growth in this market. Maxwell House Decaffeinated was added in 1982, just months before the Nabob Decaffeinated launch. General Foods also marketed three other ground coffee brands—Sanka, Brim, and Chase and Sanborn.

Nabob, drawing from its European experience, believed that the Canadian roast coffee market, although seemingly a commodity business, could be segmented. "Our objective," said John Bell, "is to segment the roast coffee market as much as we can." Nabob set about testing two premium roast coffees. The first was Signature, a fine blend of arabica coffees featuring high-quality beans from Kenya, test marketed in Alberta. The name, package graphics, and advertising signaled a luxury positioning, reflecting the quality of the coffee. The brand failed to meet its targets. Consumers were accustomed to the taste of their regular brands, often found the premium taste too bitter, and were unwilling to pay the premium price.

The second brand was Select Discoveries, a family of four flavors: Mocha Java, French Bistro, Columbian Classic, and Swiss Chocolate Café. They were sold in 200-gram tins (rather than 369-gram vacuum packaging) and were introduced in Ontario in 1983. A small market developed for this speciality product, but there did not appear to be the same desire for premium quality coffees as in Europe.

NABOB

MAN: Inside these ordinary, old-fashioned, soft paper bags ...

... is ground coffee. You can smell the coffee inside, on the outside.

Stale air keeps getting in, flavour and aroma keep getting out. That's bad. Now for the good news.

Inside this <u>extraordinary</u>...

...hard (knock, knock) foil vacuum pack is a truly superior blend of ground coffee, Nabob. Western Canada's leading fresh ground coffee.

You can't smell a thing. Stale air can't get in, so Nabob's famous flavour and aroma <u>can't</u> get out.

But listen ...

WHOOSH.

Smell that ... <u>that's</u> fresh aroma.

Now I ask you, which one do you think makes a better, fresher cup of coffee?

You're absolutely right.

SCALI, McCABE, SLOVES LTD.

EXHIBIT 1   THE MICROPHONE COMMERCIAL

EXHIBIT 2   ROAST COFFEE SHARES IN EQUIVALENT POUNDS (NATIONAL), %

	1978	1979	1980	1981	1982	1983	1984	1985
Nabob								
Tradition	13.4	17.3	21.8	21.3	22.9	24.9	23.5	21.4
Tradition Decaffeinated						2.0	2.4	2.7
Other Nabob	1.0	0.6	0.2	0.1	0.9	0.4	0.5	0.4
Total Nabob	14.4	17.9	22.0	21.4	23.8	27.3	26.4	24.5
Maxwell House								
Regular	15.5	16.5	16.9	17.2	17.0	18.7	19.0	19.0
Decaffeinated				0.1	0.9	1.3	1.3	1.3
Gold						0.9	1.2	0.9
Total Maxwell House*	15.5	16.5	16.9	17.3	17.9	20.9	21.5	21.2
Sanka*			1.1	1.2	1.7	1.8	1.9	1.6
MJB	3.8	4.4	4.5	5.5	5.2	5.5	5.0	5.2
Chase & Sanborn*	8.3	8.5	8.3	9.6	8.7	5.9	4.6	4.6
Melitta	4.4	4.5	4.4	4.7	4.4	4.4	5.2	4.6
Brooke Bond	5.3	4.5	4.0	3.9	2.6	1.9	2.0	2.4
Hills Bros.			2.0	4.2	3.5	3.1	3.1	2.9
Private Label	39.4	33.9	30.9	26.3	26.6	24.1	26.2	28.5
All other	8.9	9.8	5.9	5.9	5.5	5.2	4.1	4.5
Total	100.0	100.0	100.0	100.0	100.0	100.0	100.0	100.0

*Brands marketed by General Foods.
Note: 1 pound = 453.6 grams.
Source: A.C. Nielsen National Food Index

Maxwell House, in anticipation of an expansion of Nabob Signature from the Alberta test market into Ontario, had launched a premium brand of its own, Maxwell House Gold, sold in a one-pound tin. This brand achieved around a 1% share of the market, making it more difficult for Nabob to introduce another premium brand.

THE DEVELOPMENT OF SUMMIT

It was at this stage that John Bell, then Vice President of Marketing and Sales, Roger Barnes, the Market Research Manager, and Bruce McKay, the Product Manager, met to evaluate new product opportunities. The concept that seemed to offer the greatest promise was coffee that used 100% Colombian beans.

This was not an original idea. General Foods had introduced a premium Colombian coffee, Yuban, in the early seventies that had a lackluster career in the market, peaking at only a 2% share and discontinued in 1978. It still survived as a strong premium brand in parts of the American market. To match the Yuban launch in Canada, Nabob rushed its own premium Colombian brand to market, Boban (Nabob spelt backward). Needless to say, this brand name creativity was not appreciated by consumers, and the brand was quickly withdrawn from the market. Even Safeway entered this market with its own premium Colombian coffee, but it, too, was discontinued in a short time.

Nabob decided to launch a separate brand but one still clearly within its stable of brands. In a study that probed the strength of the Colombian beans proposition, it was found that 65% of a national sample believed that Colombian coffee was the best tasting in the world and that

93% recognized Colombia as a coffee-producing country. This high level of awareness had been developed by the National Federation of Colombian Coffee Growers, which had been spending more that $1.5 million annually on television and print advertising in Canada.

Summit, prepared with 100% Colombian beans, was launched in October 1985. Each aspect of the marketing mix had been carefully developed.

Name and Packaging

Summit, as a name, had many advantages. It was short, not used by other manufacturers, and carried the connotation of high quality. Also, the best beans were grown on the high mountainsides in subtropical countries, and there was an appreciation of this through previous advertising. Consideration was given to calling the brand Nabob Colombian. However, this use of a generic name would have inhibited the development of a distinct brand image and could have been easily matched by the competition. The packaging had to be clearly positioned within the Nabob family. The pack retained the key Nabob logo elements and was red (distinct from the green for Tradition and brown for Tradition Decaffeinated) in order to reinforce Summit's tropical mountain imagery and stand out strongly on the shelf.

Advertising

Creative copy themes were developed to communicate to coffee drinkers that Colombian coffees were known for their rich and distinctive taste and that new Nabob Summit was the best-tasting Colombian coffee. The advertising was to have the same tone consumers had come to associate with Nabob advertising—confident, demanding, and assertive.

Summit's copy strategy was clearly stated on the package: "Like all great-tasting Nabob coffees, Nabob Summit must meet our strict standards for flavour and aroma. That means we don't just pick 100% pure Colombian coffee beans.

We go further by choosing only the few that pass Nabob's test. Only then will you find the rich, distinctive flavour that makes Colombian coffees both legendary and good enough for Nabob."

To provide continuity, Nabob once again turned to Mike Reynolds, spokesman for the Nabob brand since its 1978 introduction in Ontario. The "Sword" commercial (Exhibit 3) was tested, using the day-after-recall technique to measure memorability of the advertising and its ability to communicate the copy strategy. Two hundred women between the ages of 18 and 64 were contacted by telephone the day after the commercial was aired in major centers across Canada. The commercial was remembered as well as the average thirty-second commercial (see following).

	Norm for 30-second commercials
Unprompted recall of ad	20%
Prompted recall	60%

There was concern that the visual device of the sword dominated the commercial and obscured the message that this was a new brand named Summit and that it was made exclusively from Colombian beans. The idea that Nabob used only the best beans in their coffee, a communication objective in all Nabob advertising, was the strongest message recalled in the commercial.

Pricing and Promotion

Summit trade pricing was at parity with Tradition in spite of the fact that Colombian beans were a more expensive blend than regular Tradition. Retail pricing would be slightly above Tradition because retailers would take a higher margin. It was also hoped that Summit could benefit from the leverage of the popular Tradition brand to generate strong retail advertising, merchandising, and price feature support for the new brand.

NABOB

CLIENT :   NABOB
PRODUCT : Summit
TITLE :   "Sword"
LENGTH :   30 sec. T.V.

MIKE: This... is 100%
Colombian coffee, famous
for its legendary flavour.

And this is also 100%
Colombian. New Nabob
Summit.

They're both 100% Colombian,
so they both taste the same,
right?

Wrong.

Some of these Colombian
coffee beans simply don't
measure up...

to Nabob's standards
for flavour and aroma.

Ah, but the ones that
do make all the difference
in Nabob Summit.

A taste we'd call,

a cut above.

EXHIBIT 3   THE SWORD COMMERCIAL

A fifty-five cent direct mail coupon was sent to three million households in Canada in February/March 1986 to initiate trial buying. Total costs including printing, handling, and redemption expenses were expected to amount to $250,000.

Ground coffee was sold extensively on promotion. Summit was to be promoted simultaneously with Tradition so that the new brand could benefit from the merchandising leverage that the larger brand offered. Approximately thirty cents per unit would be offered to the trade, and this was expected to generate trade support and feature pricing at least one week every month.

If, for example, the regular list price to the retailer was $3.19 for a 369-gram package, an off-invoice reduction of 20 cents a unit would be offered on an almost continuous basis to produce a net regular price of $2.99. A fluctuating merchandising allowance would also be offered on a regular basis and could be paid to those retailers who would feature price the brand. The usual merchandising allowance was 10 cents a unit, bringing the cost to the retailer down to $2.89. The feature retail price target would be $2.99. The merchandising allowance might change as the regular list price changed to achieve this feature price. Since ground coffee was often a loss leader for retailers, this slim retail margin was acceptable. In addition other allowance promotions might be run in specific regions and would be used to pay for the retail advertising that supported coffee promotions. Lastly there was a cooperative allowance of 3% off the regular list price. This allowance, based on volume, was accumulated and available to retailers who supported the brand with promotional activity.

Media

The media plan called for 1,800 gross rating points (GRPs) of television advertising in the major television markets in Ontario and Western Canada. The advertising ran in two flights. The introductory flight lasted 12 weeks starting in mid-December. The second, sustaining flight, at a lower weight level of 60 GRPs a week, ran for a further 10 weeks in the fall of 1986.

Nabob, in allocating its media dollars, took into consideration the sales per capita of the regular coffee market by region, its own share of market provincially, and the cost of purchasing air time in each city area (see Exhibit 4). Summit advertising, scheduled to begin in January, was brought forward to December as distribution had grown faster than was anticipated. To maximize Summit awareness, GRP levels were raised to 150 GRPs in mid-January. In March Summit advertising was replaced by Tradition Decaffeinated advertising.

As well, the National Federation of Colombian Coffee Growers was prepared to subsidize Nabob Summit advertising, up to $0.162 per pound. To earn the maximum subsidy, Nabob had to spend $0.23 per pound, and if it did, it would receive a rebate from the National Federation of $0.162 per pound.

SUMMIT MEDIA SCHEDULE (GRPs PER WEEK)

	1985 December		January				1986 February				March
	16	23	30	6	13	20	27	3	10	17	24	3
All markets: numbers of GRPs* per week	←——— 60 ———→				←——— 150 ———→				←—— 100 ——→		

* GRP (gross rating point). A rating point is the percentage of the viewing households tuned in to a television market. If 10% of the potential audience sees the commercial, it has a rating of 10. GRPs are the totals of the ratings for commercials shown during a given period.

EXHIBIT 4   NABOB: 1986 MEDIA PLANNING INDEX

Market	CPM*	MDI†	CPM index‡	MDI/CPM index	1985 weekly GRP levels§
Ottawa E	11.30	100	134	75	50
Barrie	8.50	100	101	99	50
Sudbury	9.60	100	115	87	50
Kingston	11.40	100	136	74	50
Peterborough	9.05	100	107	93	50
Sault Ste. Marie	9.30	100	110	91	50
Kitchener	7.75	100	92	109	60
London	6.50	100	78	128	50
Toronto	7.00	100	84	119	60
Thunder Bay	13.30	180	159	63	50
Winnipeg	6.50	180	78	230	100
Regina	8.00	180	95	189	60
Brandon	12.35	180	147	122	—
Swift Current	18.50	180	221	81	—
Prince Albert	12.50	180	149	121	—
Yorkton	7.60	180	91	198	90
Saskatoon	7.50	180	89	202	70
Lloydminster	6.40	180	76	236	90
Medicine Hat	6.60	179	198	90	—
Red Deer	8.85	179	106	169	80
Edmonton	10.30	179	123	145	70
Calgary	10.50	179	125	143	60
Vancouver	6.45	175	77	227	100
Okanagan	12.50	175	149	117	50
Prince George	17.20	175	205	85	—
Dawson Creek	25.70	175	307	57	—
Weighted average	8.38				

  * CPM is the cost per thousand messages delivered against a target group in a television market over a fifty-two week period. The target group is women 18+.
  †MDI is the market development index for ground coffee, with the Ontario index 100. It reflects the much higher development (sales per capita) of ground coffee in Western Canada. The main reason for this is the lower consumption of instant coffee in the West.
  ‡CPM index is the cost per thousand divided by the weighted average.
  §A rating point is a percent of the viewing households tuned in to a television market. If 10% of the potential audience sees the commercial, it has a rating of 10. GRPs are the totals of the ratings for commercials shown during a given period.

Summit's First Year

The Summit launch must be viewed in the context of worldwide coffee commodity prices. The 1985 Brazilian coffee harvest had been a disaster and had a dramatic effect on coffee futures. Between August 1985 and February 1986, the commodity price of roast coffee rose by 70%. Commodity prices peaked at $3.20 per pound. Consumer prices were to some extent cushioned from this volatile market. The large companies stopped buying at the higher prices. Also, manufacturers squeezed margins as prices rose, hoping to increase them once the prices started to fall. As a result, the retail price of coffee increased from $3 to just over $4 per pound during the first six months of Summit's launch. This spiraling cost of coffee was of grave concern to Nabob, as it could have adversely affected early trial of Summit. Retailers had stocked up with coffee just prior to the Summit launch in anticipation of higher prices. In an escalating price market consumers could

EXHIBIT 5   SUMMIT AVERAGE RETAIL PRICE (369-GRAM UNITS) IN 1986

	Jan.	Feb.	Mar.	Apr.	May	June	July	Aug.	Sept.	Oct.	Nov.	Dec.	Total
Tradition	$3.08	3.37	3.65	3.91	3.86	3.97	3.87	3.64	3.50	3.67	3.75	3.59	3.59
Summit	$3.05	3.52	3.54	4.05	4.12	4.15	4.07	3.74	3.48	3.60	3.89	3.48	3.69
Difference vs. Tradition	−0.03	+0.15	−0.11	+0.14	+0.26	+0.18	+0.20	+0.10	−0.02	−0.07	+0.13	+0.11	+0.10

also be expected to either reduce their purchases or stock up on their regular brand before prices rose. Exhibit 5 provides information for Summit pricing through 1986.

These pricing concerns proved to be illusory. The signals of success were almost immediate. The retail trade was quick to appreciate the value offered by the product and decided to give shelf space to the brand immediately. The trade saw that Nabob was going to market the brand aggressively. As well, ground coffee was a very visible product in that it was heavily promoted, the pricing was extremely competitive, and many retailers used it as a loss leader.

The parity pricing strategy and accompanying trade support plant proved important in determining the product's rapid success and overcoming "price increase" fears. In its first full Nielsen audit, Summit exceeded 50% distribution in all areas where it was marketed, reaching a high of 89% distribution in Alberta. The trade, in turn, supported the product, and a 2% national share was achieved in the first audit. This share was the minimum level at which the trade would begin to give the brand ongoing support. By comparison, the best share ever reached by Signature was 1.9%. In Alberta and British Columbia, market shares of 3.4% and 4%, respectively, were reached. This was achieved before advertising and coupon support had a chance to make an impact. Despite price increases, the trade aggressively priced Summit, averaging only a $0.10/pack premium for the year. In addition, the brand was co-op advertised (featured in weekly supermarket advertisements) and displayed. Summit's share of weighted co-

op averaged 10%, an excellent result of a new product.[1]

By the end of the year, Summit had exceeded all the marketing objectives set out for it, as the following shows (*Exhibits 6 to 8* provide further details of Year 1 performance):

	Objective, %	Actual, %
Year 1 share	2.7	3.3
Distribution where marketed	80	82
Trial of coffee-buying households	12	12
Repeat purchase	35	42

In early May 1986 an awareness, attitude, and usage survey was conducted in Vancouver, Calgary, and Toronto. Nabob contacted by telephone 130 principal grocery shoppers (the individual in the household primarily responsible for grocery shopping), in each of the three cities, who were 18 years and over and who had purchased ground coffee in the last month. At that stage, awareness and trial were still relatively low. Results were more favorable in Calgary than in either Vancouver or Toronto (see pg. 241).

Overall perceptions of Summit were favorable among those who were aware of the brand and prepared to comment. Summit was seen as a "top-of-the-line," "richer," "better" coffee. Summit advertising was reinforcing the consistent

[1] Co-op advertising is retail advertising, in which the cost is shared by the retailer and the national advertiser. Weighted co-op is the percentage of times that a brand, like Summit, was featured in a given time period compared with all coffee brands that were featured.

EXHIBIT 6   GROUND COFFEE SHARES

	1985 total	1986							1987 Dec/Jan
		Dec/Jan	Feb/Mar	Apr/May	June/July	Aug/Sept	Oct/Nov	Total	
Nabob									
Tradition (369 gram)	21.4	19.5	17.0	19.0	18.8	20.7	17.7	18.8	15.9
Tradition (200 gram)	–	–	–	–	0.1	1.4	1.7	0.6	1.7
Tradition Decaffeinated	2.7	2.3	2.5	2.6	2.6	2.6	2.7	2.6	2.6
Summit	–	2.0	3.0	3.7	3.1	4.2	4.0	3.3	3.9
Summit Decaffeinated	–	–	–	–	–	–	–	–	0.2
Other Nabob	0.4	–	–	–	–	–	–	–	–
Total Nabob	24.5	23.8	22.5	25.3	24.6	28.9	26.1	25.3	24.3
Maxwell House									
Regular	19.0	18.3	16.1	17.4	19.3	17.7	17.5	17.7	18.5
Decaffeinated	1.3	1.1	1.4	1.4	1.4	1.3	1.4	1.3	1.3
Gold	0.9	1.0	1.0	1.7	2.0	1.6	1.7	1.5	2.2
Total Maxwell House	21.2	20.4	18.5	20.5	22.7	20.6	20.6	20.5	22.0

Source: A. C. Nielsen Food Index.

EXHIBIT 7   SUMMIT FACT SHEET

	1986						1987	1986
	Dec/Jan	Feb/Mar	Apr/May	June/July	Aug/Sept	Oct/Nov	Dec/Jan	Total
Market shares*								
National	2.0	3.0	3.7	3.1	4.2	4.0	3.9	3.3
Ontario	1.6	3.8	4.7	3.5	5.5	5.3	4.8	4.0
Manitoba/Saskatchewan	1.6	1.8	2.5	3.2	3.1	2.7	3.4	2.4
Alberta	3.4	4.6	5.7	4.7	5.2	6.3	5.3	5.0
B.C.	4.0	4.1	3.7	3.4	4.7	3.9	4.9	4.0
Distribution†								
National	44	51	54	54	55	55	55	
Ontario	54	70	75	77	77	78	78	
Manitoba/Saskatchewan	58	68	77	69	69	74	70	
Alberta	89	91	99	88	89	81	82	
B.C.	78	83	85	82	83	86	89	
Share of weighted co-op‡								
Tradition								
National	24	17	16	21	21	18	16	20
Ontario	31	28	20	22	26	21	15	25
Manitoba/Saskatchewan	47	15	37	33	40	22	34	27
Alberta	38	25	23	31	31	29	22	29
B.C.	18	16	26	23	21	17	19	20
Summit								
National	6	10	11	10	11	9	10	10
Ontario	7	17	14	11	16	18	14	15
Manitoba/Saskatchewan	14	14	13	19	10	5	13	12
Alberta	11	10	18	12	15	12	13	20
B.C.	7	9	13	15	11	6	14	11

* In equivalent pounds.
†In stores accounting for x% of the business.
‡% of stores providing retail advertising support.
Source: A. C. Nielsen National Food Index.

message of Nabob advertising—that Nabob used only the best beans in its coffee.

In the competitive Toronto market where Maxwell House and Nabob Tradition were close rivals, Nabob had after nine years achieved a very strong image. Nabob conducted periodic attitude and image studies which measured consumer perceptions of Nabob and Maxwell House on a number of attributes. In the past, Maxwell House had a strong reputation in the market, based, in part, on the fact that Maxwell House marketed both ground and instant coffee and heavily advertised both product categories. While Maxwell House was still considered the best-selling brand, over the years Nabob had steadily improved its reputation on all taste and quality attributes to the extent that the Maxwell House image advantage had now been eliminated.

Competitor reaction was swift. General Foods reformulated and repackaged its Maxwell House

EXHIBIT 8   SUMMIT COFFEE: CUMULATIVE TRIAL AND REPEAT PURCHASE FREQUENCY, 1986

	Jan.	Feb.	Mar.	Apr.	May	June	July	Aug.	Sept.	Oct.	Nov.	Dec.
Monthly households buying	1.8%	1.8	1.9	1.6	2.1	1.7	1.0	2.1	2.2	1.5	1.7	2.0
New	100.0	85.5	68.4	54.1	55.3	48.4	63.4	44.6	52.6	33.5	32.7	37.3
Repeat	0	14.5	31.6	45.9	44.7	51.6	36.6	55.4	47.4	66.5	67.3	62.7
Cumulative households buying	1.8	3.4	4.7	5.6	6.7	7.6	8.2	9.2	10.3	10.8	11.4	12.1
Households buying once	94.9	83.1	76.4	69.3	67.2	64.9	65.7	60.5	60.6	58.9	58.0	58.1
Repeating once	5.1	14.0	17.2	21.5	18.5	20.4	19.4	22.8	22.1	22.2	22.4	21.0
Repeating twice	—	2.9	4.9	5.4	9.0	7.9	8.2	9.5	8.7	9.4	8.7	7.3
Repeating 3 times	—	—	1.5	2.6	4.3	2.8	2.2	2.8	4.3	4.4	3.2	5.9
Repeating 4 times	—	—	—	1.2	.0	2.2	2.1	.6	.6	1.2	3.9	1.8
More than 4 times	—	—	—	—	1.0	1.8	2.4	3.8	3.7	3.9	3.8	5.9

Source: Consumer Panel of Canada.

	Unaided awareness			
	Total Nabob, %	Summit, %	Summit total unaided and aided awareness, %	Summit purchase, %
Vancouver	65	4	35	9
Calgary	72	13	48	15
Toronto	62	4	25	6

Gold brand. The brand moved from packaging in tins to vacuum packaging and was offered in two varieties, Colombia and Arabica. The pricing strategy was changed from premium to parity with Summit. Maxwell House Gold, share increased from 1% in December/January 1986 to 2.2% in December/January 1987. MJB, an important brand in Western Canada, introduced MJB Colombian, and several generics also introduced Colombian varieties.

THE IMPACT OF THE PRICING DECISION

Success can be your worst enemy. Nabob had planted the seeds for continued growth for 1987. Research conducted on a decaffeinated Colombian product had yielded favorable results. Accordingly Summit Decaffeinated had been introduced in late 1986 to capitalize on the momentum of the brand.

An aggressive marketing plan had been approved to enhance the Summit brand. For example, spending on advertising at $0.17 U.S. per pound on Summit in 1987 would generate advertising support for the brand almost equivalent to that of the main brand, Tradition.

If Nabob continued to fuel the marketing fires behind Summit, the brand would continue to grow. Unfortunately, much of that growth would probably be at the expense of the more profitable Tradition brand. The cost premium for an all-Colombian blend of beans was 10%. However, the cost gap could widen, depending on fluctuating commodity markets, and quite possibly a premium of up to 20% might have to be paid. The Tradition user who switched to Summit might be a satisfied customer but, at the same time, a less profitable one for Nabob. The company, in developing its own projections, had forecasted that a third of Summit volume would be cannibalized from Tradition. The latest figures, particularly from the Toronto market, showed a cannibalization rate in excess of 50%. In 1986 the Summit share was 3.3%, but corporate share had edged ahead only 2%.

Nabob case prices (each case contained twelve 369-gram packages) varied depending on order quantity, as the following shows:

Case order quantity	Price
25–99	$39.81
100–199	39.05
200–399	38.66
400 case plus	38.28

The relative cost and profit ratios on Summit and Tradition were as follows.

	Tradition, %	Summit,%
Gross sales	100	100
Gross profit	50	42
Marketing cost	30	25
Administrative and other	10	10
Profits before tax	10	7

In May 1987 General Foods reintroduced all its decaffeinated ground coffees in smaller 300-gram packages at parity with their regular coffees. Apart from the obvious absolute reduction in price, the big advantage to General Foods was that regular and decaffeinated coffees could now be jointly promoted.

A further complication was the fact that the Federation of Colombian Coffee Growers was starting to put pressure on Nabob to raise the price of Summit. While they found Canadian results satisfactory, they believed that parity pricing was inconsistent with the premium image they were trying to create worldwide. In every previous instance when the Federation had supported and endorsed a Colombian coffee, they had been able to achieve premium pricing.

Mr. McKay felt extremely uncomfortable about the current predicament. He had gained enormous satisfaction from the brand's success and knew it had more potential. Summit Decaffeinated was a superb new coffee. The small retail price differential with Tradition was narrowing as the trade support of the brand was increasing. New copy had been developed that he felt was stronger than the introductory "Sword" commercial. Was it right to put the brakes on the brand before its full potential was realized? Was Nabob over the long haul right to muzzle a brand that was in fact a superior coffee to its leading brand? What would be the repercussions to his own career if he placed the brand's profitability in front of the brand's volume? With these thoughts in mind, he began to decide the future strategy for Summit.

QUAKER OATS COMPANY

The Quaker Oats Company, a large producer and marketer of food products and animal feeds, has long been interested in foods to help solve the serious malnutrition problems that exist in many countries of the world. Such a product is Incaparina, a bland flour that can be used as an ingredient in drinks (similar to low-calorie diet products that are sold in large volume in the United States), soups, sauces, pancakes, muffins, cookies, cake, and bread. Quaker Oats is considering whether or not it should market Incaparina in developing countries. The company is concerned about the impact of such products on long-range growth and profitability.

GENERAL BACKGROUND ON THE QUAKER OATS COMPANY

The Quaker Oats Company was founded in the United States in 1901 to produce oatmeal for human consumption and oat by-products for animal feeds. The company's first plant, and still the largest, was established at Cedar Rapids, Iowa. Today, over 30 manufacturing facilities are located in 16 states; sales offices are located in principal cities throughout the United States and Canada.

The company also operates elevators in Iowa, Kansas, Mississippi, and South Dakota; research laboratories in Barrington, Illinois; and experimental farms in Barrington and Libertyville, Illinois.

Foreign subsidiaries are located in Canada (nine plants), Latin America (plants in Argentina, Brazil, Colombia, Mexico, and Venezuela), Australia, and Europe—plants in Denmark (two), England (three), and Germany, Italy, and The Netherlands (two).

Over the years the company's product line has been broadened to include (1) a variety of food products (for example, Cap'n Crunch and Life cereals, Aunt Jemima mixes, frozen foods, Ken-L-Ration dog food, and Puss-n-Boots cat food); (2) an extensive line of animal feeds (for example, Ful-O-Pep Feeds); and (3) chemicals (for example, QO Furfural, derivatives of furfural, and chemicals for uses in various plastic industries).

In the United States, Quaker Oats products are sold through food retailers and wholesalers. Company representatives handle promotional activities with the trade, especially to obtain adequate shelf space and to assist retailers in promoting and advertising Quaker Oats products. Consumer products are widely advertised, especially on network television.

The chief executive officer of Quaker Oats is the chairman of the board. The vice chairman, president, and two executive vice presidents report directly to the chairman. Top management responsibility and authority is divided among these four.

The vice chairman has general responsibility for the Chemicals Division and several corporate staff functions—legal, purchasing, planning, and finance.

The president has general responsibility for the marketing activities of the Burry Biscuit Division, the Grocery Products Division, and the corporate staff functions of sales, advertising, and research and development.

The executive vice president of operations has general responsibility for the Feed Division and the remaining corporate staff functions, including production, traffic, personnel, and public relations.

The executive vice president of the International Division has basic responsibility for exporting and for manufacturing and marketing outside the United States. The world is divided into areas, headed by a general manager (Australia), a president (Canada), or a corporate vice president (Europe and Latin America).

Although the vice chairman, president, and executive vice president of operations have primarily domestic authority and responsibilities, they are gradually working toward "internationalizing" by fostering the idea among domestic officers and operating personnel that they should "think international" and be concerned about the types of problems and activities that are being handled in the International Division. Close cooperation with international operations is encouraged.

LATIN AMERICAN AND PACIFIC ORGANIZATION AND OPERATIONS

Both the vice president and the general manager for Latin American and Pacific Operations are located in New York City. These two officers have the general responsibility for exports, including sales, advertising, and physical distribution; also, line authority extends through them to the general managers of subsidiaries located in Argentina, Brazil, Colombia, Mexico, and Venezuela.

The export sales manager and the Far East sales director are concerned primarily with exports. Foreign subsidiaries each have their own sales manager and sales force. The production manager, the advertising and new products manager, and the manager of administrative services have responsibilities for coordinating and guiding subsidiaries.

The production manager has responsibility for directing the production and engineering activities of subsidiaries. He maintains continued liaison with domestic production, engineering, and research and development activities; makes or disseminates policies to guide subsidiary manufacturing; and provides assistance and direction in solving subsidiary manufacturing and engineering problems.

The office manager and manager of administrative services for subsidiaries has responsibilities similar to those of a financial officer, working to implement the policies of the domestic controller with regard to accounting and credit policies. He serves as the link between the domestic controller and subsidiary controllers. He also supervises those who are responsible for the preparation of documents for exports.

The advertising and new product manager (A&NP manager) has dual responsibilities, as his title suggests. With regard to advertising, he has responsibility of two kinds: export and subsidiary advertising.

Export Advertising

The A&NP manager works with an export advertising agency in much the same way that domestic advertising managers work with domestic agencies. After products are selected to be advertised, after countries are chosen in which the selected products are to be advertised, and after budget limitations are determined, the advertising agency prepares advertisements and makes media recommendations for review and approval by the A&NP manager. The recommendations of the advertising agency often include (1) selection of foreign media (that is, local media such as foreign newspapers, radio, cinema, and outdoor) and (2) selection of international media (that is, media that circulate in a number of countries, for example, *Selecciones, Hablemos, Life en Español*).

Subsidiary Advertising

Subsidiaries have basic responsibility for planning and preparing their own advertising budgets and campaigns, but they are submitted to the A&NP manager in the New York office for final approval. A substantial degree of local independence is felt to be necessary because market and competitive conditions differ from country to country and people on the scene have the needed detailed knowledge to handle advertising properly. Likewise, subsidiaries usually have the freedom to employ whichever local advertising agency they feel is the best available to meet their needs. They are under no pressure to choose any one agency over another.

Subsidiaries prepare their proposed advertising budgets and programs and submit them to New York for approval, comments, and advice. Budgets that are out of line with established percentage of sales guidelines or are based on unrealistic estimates could be rejected or revised. The New York advertising manager also reviews materials (for example, television storyboards) sent in by the subsidiary's advertising agency and can exercise some influence if he feels that his advice is warranted.

The A&NP manager is also responsible for the exchange of advertising information and ideas between domestic and subsidiary operations and among subsidiaries. He handles requests for assistance from subsidiaries and forwards successful materials and ideas to any location where he thinks they might be useful.

With regard to new products, the A&NP manager performs a coordinating function. Although subsidiaries have their own product planning personnel and laboratory facilities, many new ideas come from the corporate research facility in Barrington, Illinois. The A&NP manager attends a meeting every two months with research personnel in Barrington to learn about their new product projects. He sends ideas or samples of new products to any subsidiaries that could have an interest.

Every month subsidiaries prepare a new product progress report in which they report on the status of new products that are being developed by subsidiaries. Other divisions in the company also prepare such a report. These reports are then circulated to all general managers and research personnel, domestically and in Europe, Canada, and Australia. By this method Quaker Oats personnel throughout the company are kept informed of activities elsewhere in the company. The report sometimes leads to direct exchange of detailed information and to cooperation among interested parties from several countries in the development of new products.

The A&NP manager, working with the general manager of Latin American and Pacific Operations, also influences priorities that subsidiaries give to the development of products. Occasionally, the priority accorded to a new product by a subsidiary (based on local considerations) is different from the priority that corporate considerations require.

The corporate staff uses all available sources of information on competitors' new products, both within the company (for example, subsidiaries) and outside the company (for example, newspapers, trade publications). Any division or subsidiary, domestic or foreign, can query Chicago for information and samples of competitors' products.

Since the company has unparalleled experience in oat products, Quaker Oats capitalizes on this strength to sell oat products wherever they can be sold. Thus, in all South American subsidiaries, the basic product is rolled oats.

In addition, subsidiaries examine local foods that are widely used and seek to "instantize" them. The policy is to take a well-established food and to add "convenience."

Thus, in Mexico, in addition to rolled oats, the company produces and sells such products as Aunt Jemima Pancake Mix, Chocavena (an oat-based powder used to prepare a chocolate-flavored drink), and Atolvena (a powdered drink preparation that is stirred into milk or water). Atolvena is an instant *atole* (the Spanish word for "thin gruel").

In Colombia a major product is Frescavena (a powdered formula of oat flour, sugar, and various ingredients). Frescavena is a quick version of a popular drink that consumers formerly made by grinding oats into oat flour and adding sugar. The drink is popular in restaurants, as well as in the home, and is considered to be a refreshing, cooling beverage.

Another major product in Colombia is Areparina, a precooked corn flour. Arepas are a staple in the Colombian diet, much as bread is a staple in the United States and Europe. Arepas are long and tedious to prepare, and Areparina, an "instant version" of Arepa, has met with considerable success. Other major products sold in Colombia include animal feeds and oat flour in tins (Chocavena).

The major products in other South American countries are:

1 Argentina: Magica, a precooked corn meal
2 Venezuela: rolled oats, oat flour, and Frescavena
3 Brazil: Vitavena (a version of Frescavena), a line of soups, Polentina (similar to Magica), and Milharina (similar to Polentina but prepared somewhat differently to meet the preferences of a substantial segment of the Brazilian market which desires this variation)

MALNUTRITION IN THE WORLD

It has been estimated that between one-half and two-thirds of the world's population suffers from malnutrition or undernutrition. In many Latin American countries the net food supply per person in terms of calories per day is less than two-thirds of the food supply available to U.S. residents. Even more important, high-nutrition foods are in short supply. One of the most serious nutritional problems is lack of protein. The supply of meat and milk in many Latin American countries is about one-third of the supply in the United States. Moreover, the traditional sources of protein—meat, eggs, fish, milk, and dairy products—are too expensive for impoverished consumers in low-income nations; per capita income in most Latin American countries ranges between one-fifth and one-third of the U.S. level.

Due mainly to the synergism of malnutrition and infection, mortality rates are 20 to 40 times higher for preschool children in less-developed areas compared with those of more favored countries.[1] Since preschool malnutrition may retard irreversibly the mental and physical development of the survivors, the adult population of some areas probably has less vigor and enterprise and therefore is unable to contribute as fully as they might to economic, industrial, and social development. Some countries are finding it difficult to break out of the vicious circle of population explosion–malnutrition–slow economic development.

However, essential proteins are contained not only in expensive foods; they are readily available in legumes, fish, and oilseed residues such as soy, cottonseed, or peanut meal. Since the technology exists to prepare foods from such sources at a cost that can be afforded by low-income consumers, one solution to the malnutrition problem may be to interest public or private organizations, with the manufacturing know-how and marketing capabilities, in producing and marketing such products.

INCAP

In 1949 the Institute of Nutrition of Central America and Panama (INCAP) was established in Guatemala City by the governments of

---

[1]G. E. Belden et al., *The Protein Paradox* (Boston: M. R. Management Reports): v.

Costa Rica, El Salvador, Guatemala, Honduras, Nicaragua, and Panama. The purpose of INCAP was to forge a cooperative effort to study nutritional problems and to find ways of solving them.

After determining that protein malnutrition was a critical problem, INCAP set about developing vegetable protein mixtures that could be made from local resources at low cost. After a few years the results of INCAP's work began appearing in the nutrition literature. Through papers presented at nutrition and food technology conferences and through continual publication in the literature, INCAP efforts received considerable attention. After more than a decade of research, INCAP, with a substantial reputation in the international medical and scientific community, took steps to arrange for commercialization of the products that had been developed.

INCAP had developed a number of vegetable mixture formulas based on raw materials that were available locally in Central and South American countries. The formulas contained corn flour or sorghum flour as a base; sesame, cottonseed, or soy meal as a source of concentrated protein; calcium carbonate; yeast; and several vitamins, especially vitamin A.

INCAP had tested its formulas with normal children, comparing them with milk, and found no significant difference in nutritional value. Tests were also made with children suffering from protein malnutrition to compare recovery by the use of the formula and by the use of milk. In all tests the INCAP product resulted in satisfactory progress toward recovery. When tested as a cure for kwashiorkor, the malnutrition disease that is a major child killer in tropical and subtropical areas of the world, the formula again was judged as satisfactory. Babies in advanced stages of kwashiorkor recover rapidly when they receive an adequate quantity of the formula. They often show signs of recovery within three or four weeks and substantial improvement in six to eight weeks.

But since INCAP intended its formula for foods rather than medicines, additional testing was necessary to establish its acceptability. In Guatemala acceptability trials were conducted in four villages. Mothers who regularly attended the health centers in these villages were given a mixture to feed to their children as an *atole*. *Atole* (gruel) made with this mixture is prepared by adding water and boiling for 15 minutes. It is consumed hot. Over the 16-week test period, 75 percent of the children drank two or three glasses of the new *atole* every day, and parents showed great interest in the product.[2]

At this point INCAP selected a trade name for the product. The combination of INCAP and *harina,* the Spanish word for "flour," led to Incaparina, the registered trademark for INCAP-developed mixtures containing 25 percent or more of proteins comparable in quality to those of animal origin and that have proved suitable for feeding young children.

Before making arrangements for commercialization, INCAP undertook a pilot test to see how the product was accepted when offered for sale. With the assistance and cooperation of the Ministry of Health and some interested commercial firms, a three-month sales test was carried out in a town of 3,600 near Guatemala City. The product was sold in 75-gram polyethylene bags, enough to prepare three glasses of *atole,* or one day's supply for a child. The retail price was set at $0.03 (U.S.) per bag. About 750 pounds of Incaparina were sold during the first four weeks. INCAP considered the test a success and made arrangements for a larger test to be conducted over a seven-month period in Guatemala City and other urban areas. Sales during this test amounted to 120,000 pounds, convincing INCAP that commercial introduction was feasible.

INCAP felt that the most effective way to make the fruits of its research available to the greatest number of people would be through commercial production and distribution, rather than relying on public organizations.

Since INCAP wished to protect its reputation as a scientific research institute, it felt that only responsible firms should be permitted to manu-

[2]Ibid., p. 32.

facture and market the product. In addition, INCAP wished to maintain some degree of control over product quality, advertising, promotion, and price.

Therefore, INCAP prepared a resolution which set forth the basic policies for licensing Incaparina. Commercial firms are required to:

(1) get the approval of the local government; (2) meet the general requirements of INCAP (see next paragraph); (3) submit samples to INCAP for analysis and approval prior to distribution; (4) maintain the specified quality and submit production samples required on a regular basis; (5) get INCAP approval of all packaging and descriptive matter relating to the product; and (6) pay the cost of analyses and other services in accordance with a schedule of fees.[3]

In explanation of the second requirement, that is, the "general requirements of INCAP," it was decided that a commercial firm must:

(1) present proof of financial capacity; (2) describe the facilities to be used including laboratory equipment and machinery; (3) report the background of the technical and laboratory personnel involved; (4) describe the methods of distribution, storage, and transportation; (5) describe the arrangements for promotion, publicity, and advertising; (6) report on the sources of raw material supply to insure uninterrupted production throughout the year; and (7) present production estimates and request specific authorization for retail prices and special reduced prices to public and private charitable institutions.[4]

INCAP's policies with regard to consumer advertising are worth special mention. Some of the highlights of the policies are:

1 All advertising claims and other promotion should be based on well-established facts that have been substantiated by the scientific method.

2 The product should be advertised as a balanced vegetable mixture of high nutritive value. The protein content of 27 percent, while very important, should not be overstressed to the extent that the other valuable dietary elements are overlooked.

3 The product should be promoted as a suitable supplement to the daily diet. Advertising based solely on the approach that Incaparina is a substitute for other recognized protein-containing foods should be avoided.

4 Incaparina is a food that has been found to be beneficial to all age groups. Nevertheless, because of high nutritive value, its use by pregnant and lactating mothers and growing children is recommended.

5 Any claims implying properties to the product that it does not contain must be avoided in the interest of ethical advertising and the protection of the consumer.

6 The following are a few of the descriptive phrases that must not be used in connection with the product: "Miracle Food," "High-Energy Food," "Complete Diet," etc.[5]

In essence INCAP's restrictions on advertising prohibit a firm from advertising Incaparina as "better than milk." The restrictions also prohibit the licensee from engaging in "unethical" practices or from using exaggerated or unfounded claims. In some areas where Incaparina might be sold, standards or government controls on labels, advertising, and claims are nonexistent, and INCAP felt that the product, consumer, and producer need protection.

LICENSING OF INCAPARINA TO PRODUCTOS QUAKER, S.A.

INCAP decided to license the production and sale of Incaparina in countries where suitable licensees could be found. When Quaker Oats learned that INCAP was ready to license Incaparina, inquiries were made to determine if such a venture would be desirable for the company.

The Quaker Oats Company has long been interested in the development of foods to solve

---

[3] Ibid., p. 35.
[4] Ibid.

[5] Ibid., p. 36.

nutritional deficiencies of large numbers of low-income people in underdeveloped areas of the world. The company has been interested not only in selling such products profitably but also in helping low-income undernourished people to obtain an adequate diet at a cost that they can afford. Moreover, Quaker Oats realized that to market a product such as Incaparina involves considerable risk and very likely a relatively long payout period. Since margins must be low, profits must depend on high sales volume, and this takes time to develop.

Quaker Oats had devoted laboratory efforts to developing a low-cost, high-protein food since World War II. In fact, Quaker Oats had developed products that were as good as or better than Incaparina, but it had not marketed them. The company had planned to enter the market with its own brand, but INCAP had gained such a tremendous amount of favorable publicity that consideration was given to exploiting it by licensing Incaparina. It would have been costly and time-consuming for Quaker to put its own product through extensive clinical testing and to achieve acceptance from health, hospital, and medical authorities, such as that enjoyed by Incaparina. It was felt that a basic advantage of affiliating with INCAP was that it would facilitate obtaining the support of the medical profession and public health authorities quickly. Such support was considered essential.

The INCAP license was considered desirable for additional reasons. INCAP licenses were granted on an exclusive basis in each country. Thus, Quaker Oats need not fear that INCAP would license a competitor in the same market. Moreover, if Quaker Oats found this arrangement satisfactory in Colombia, there was a good possibility that Quaker Oats would be able to obtain an exclusive license from INCAP in other countries in which Quaker Oats had subsidiaries.

The Quaker Oats Company received from INCAP the exclusive right to produce and market Incaparina through its subsidiary, Productos Quaker, S.A., in Colombia. Terms of the licensing agreement were in accordance with the established policies of INCAP. Although INCAP agreed to provide technical assistance in accordance with a schedule of modest fees, Quaker Oats paid no royalties.

Prior to making a final determination of whether or not to go ahead with the commercial introduction of Incaparina in Colombia, and prior to making final decisions on such matters as the precise nature of the product, package, marketing channels, promotional program, and the price, Productos Quaker executives studied the experience with Incaparina in Guatemala, El Salvador, Nicaragua, and Mexico.

Guatemala

Three months before signing the licensing agreement with Quaker, INCAP had negotiated a licensing agreement with Cerveceria Centro Americana, S.A., a locally owned company with 75 years of experience in the production and marketing of soft drinks, beer, and other food products. It took the firm six months after the date of the licensing agreement to take over the pilot facilities previously used by INCAP for testing Incaparina and to begin its commercial sales efforts.

The retail price of the product was $0.04 (U.S.) for a 75-gram package, with the wholesaler and retailer getting approximately 14 percent and 13 percent margins, respectively.

Since Incaparina was already well known in Guatemala because of testing done by INCAP, the initial response of the trade strained production capacity. Sales within two months peaked at 23,000 pounds per month. Thereafter, sales declined somewhat to an average between 15,000 and 20,000 pounds per month for the next five months, which concluded the calendar year with an eight-month total of 153,000 pounds.

Sales in the first months of the next calendar year averaged about 17,000 pounds per month and peaked in October when sales hit 30,000 pounds. However, sales in the last part of the year dropped off sharply as the supplier of cottonseed flour ran out of stock. Total sales for the year were about 238,000 pounds, a monthly average of nearly 20,000 pounds.

In cooperation with INCAP, the Guatemalan company developed during the first year a promotional campaign centered on public hospitals and health centers operated by the Guatemalan Ministry of Health to serve large urban and rural low-income populations.

Before the campaign, a sales supervisor and demonstrator had been trained in INCAP. During the campaign they were employed to promote Incaparina in rural areas. They used a panel truck especially equipped with a generating unit, a motion picture projector, and a tape recorder and loudspeakers to demonstrate the preparation and use of the product. Efforts were made to inform church officials, physicians, charitable organizations, schoolteachers, and other influential people about Incaparina and to request that they advise people to purchase it.

Typically, the sales supervisor called first on the doctor in charge of the local medical center to inform him or her about Incaparina and to distribute technical information and samples. Then, a series of demonstrations was arranged for the medical center staff, teachers, mothers' clubs, church groups, and so on at which an *atole* or some other application was prepared and samples given to the audience. Several movies dealing with nutrition were shown in public squares or in auditoriums. The movies presented information on malnutrition and the development and use of Incaparina. Since movies are a rare and special event for rural areas, they tended to be well attended.

Following the film, some of the product was sold from the mobile van. The sales supervisor then contacted as many local retailers as possible to gain distribution or to obtain reorders if Incaparina had been stocked previously. The mobile van campaign made it easy to get rural merchants to carry Incaparina.

The sales supervisor was also charged with the task of assisting and promoting local "Healthy Baby Contests." These contests are part of the regular efforts of most of the governmental medical centers to encourage better child care. The sales supervisor helped to organize and publicize the contests, to solicit prizes from local business managers, and to demonstrate Incaparina in connection with the award ceremony.

During the third year of sales in Guatemala, a researcher from Productos Quaker, S.A., in Colombia interviewed 86 retailers and 139 consumers in Guatemala City. He found that 56 percent of the retailers carried Incaparina and that the product had a good reputation among consumers. Sales appeared to be better in small stores in poor neighborhoods than in other types of stores. Retailers, however, complained that they were not visited often enough by the distributor, a wholly owned subsidiary of the producer, and that more and better consumer advertising was required. Subsequently, at the suggestion of INCAP, the producer opened up the sales of Incaparina to regular food wholesalers. This greatly improved retail distribution, and sales increased to a monthly rate of 80,000 pounds; the trend continued, and not long thereafter the increased volume and concomitant economies of scale permitted a reduction of over 20 percent in the retail price.

About 43 percent of consumers interviewed had purchased Incaparina. Usage was split about evenly between adults and children. The main application was in the form of the *atole,* although frequently consumers mentioned that they used Incaparina in soups. Consumers had a generally favorable attitude toward the product, price, and package. They reported that they had learned of the product primarily through demonstrations at medical centers and to a lesser degree from friends, stores, doctors, and the mobile unit. Average consumption appeared to be about 2.5 packages per family per week, a rather small amount.

El Salvador

INCAP authorized the firm of Productos Alimenticios, S.A., to produce and sell Incaparina in El Salvador. This company was a major processor of food products in El Salvador and had some experience with packaged foods.

Governmental health officials and the local medical profession were strong supporters of Incaparina and offered to help in any way they could. For example, the Nutrition Section of the Ministry of Health provided training in nutrition to persons who were to be used as field demonstrators.

A formula for the product was selected (from among those that had been developed by INCAP) that utilized locally available grains. Productos Alimenticios, confident of success, purchased and installed the best production equipment it could find. Several hundred thousand packages were ordered in advance as well as several thousand pamphlets and descriptive materials.

Introduction of the product was delayed a few months until a supply of cottonseed meal could be obtained from the only Central American producer of this material (another firm in El Salvador).

Once production began, Productos Alimenticios put the full weight of its sales organization behind the product. Heavy advertising was initiated, using local health centers as much as possible. No consumer acceptability or market tests were done by the producer prior to launching the product nationally.

Almost immediately it was clear that the program was not successful. The taste of the product was not palatable to the El Salvador consumer; apparently the product needed to be sweetened and flavored. Also the El Salvadorian preferred to let the boiled mixture cool before drinking; unfortunately when it cooled the mixture became too thick to drink. Moreover, the package was not considered attractive. Finally, it seemed that promotion had been directed too strongly to the "pharmaceutical characteristics" of the product and that an approach was needed that concentrated on telling the consumer, in understandable terms, what Incaparina could do.

To correct the situation, Productos Alimenticios added sugar and cinnamon to the product to improve the taste and an enzyme suggested by INCAP to help keep the product liquid after it cooled. A new package was designed, slightly larger to accommodate the sugar, with a price per package increase of 50 percent. All the previous promotion materials were scrapped, and new materials were prepared.

However, rather than launch another national campaign, Productos Alimenticios decided to test market the product in Zacatecoula, a small agricultural town that was considered by the producer to be representative of the population of El Salvador.

The new product, named "Campeon," was introduced, and for two months the company made an intensive selling effort in the test market. Leaflets and samples were distributed, and up to 100 announcements per day were made on the local radio station. A truck equipped with a loudspeaker and movie projection equipment was utilized also.

In spite of this effort, no "real demand" for the product developed. Thus, after two years, the license agreement was terminated.

INCAP, after reviewing the situation, felt that some preliminary consumer research and better use of carefully controlled market tests might have led to more effective packaging and promotion. Productos Alimenticios felt, however, that the *atole* concept was not suited at all to El Salvador. In Guatemala consumers were familiar with the use of an *atole;* but El Salvadorians were not. Also, the company felt that the Guatemalan effort might have been helped by the publicity surrounding INCAP's research and development work.

Nicaragua

INCAP licensed the newly established firm of Alimen-Infantiles in Nicaragua to manufacture and distribute Incaparina. The firm was founded by a group of physicians who were interested in having a local supply of an inexpensive, nutritious food. Their primary motive was humanitarian rather than commercial.

Since the Nicaraguan government was interested in the project, the laboratory of the Ministry of Health was made available for product testing and development of facilities to meet INCAP requirements for product quality.

Production was started eight months after licensing. Since the Guatemalan tests had indicated that the product was acceptable (to Guatemalans), they used basically the same product formula as had been used in Guatemala. Also, since the product was acceptable, they anticipated that sales would develop with relatively little promotional effort. Therefore, no consumer or market testing was done in Nicaragua.

However, sales did not go well; at the end of the first seven months of production, only 4,000 pounds had been sold. At this point the company decided to dispose of its equipment and dissolve the enterprise.

Mexico

In contrast with the foregoing ventures, INCAP licensed, at the request of the Mexican government, the production and sale of Incaparina in Mexico to a nonprofit government-owned corporation, Compania Distribuidora de Subsistencias Populares, S.A. (CONASUPO).

CONASUPO is a part of the Mexican government's social welfare program and, among other things, distributes food, clothing, and other basic necessities to low-income Mexican families at low cost. The company operates retail stores throughout Mexico in which are sold a complete line of basic consumer products such as clothing, food, and household utensils. Prices are below prevailing retail prices.

Since corn is more abundant locally than is sorghum, CONASUPO selected an INCAP formula based on corn. Efforts were initiated to develop a local source of cottonseed flour, but until a local source was available, it had to be imported from El Salvador.

For some time CONASUPO had marketed successfully to low-income families an *atole* that is packaged in attractive, multicolored, heavy-gauge, polyethylene bags. Atole Popular CONASUPO, regular variety, sold for 35 centavos ($0.028 U.S.) for a 100-gram bag; and Atole con chocolate CONASUPO, the flavored variety, sold at 70 centavos ($0.056 U.S.) for a 140-gram bag.

The experience of CONASUPO indicated that a flavored product might be best for Mexico; therefore, a formula containing Incaparina, natural chocolate, a sweetener, and an enzyme was developed that had the consistency and taste of the chocolate drink that CONASUPO had previously marketed successfully to low-income families. Tentatively, it was planned to package and price the Incaparina chocolate drink similar to the *atole* already on the market.

Within 16 months after the licensing agreement with the INCAP, CONASUPO had developed several flavors of Incaparina *atoles*—cinnamon, rum and coconut, vanilla, rice, and chocolate.

For testing the consumer acceptance of the product, CONASUPO incorporated the product into a mass feeding program to provide food for people living in an area ravaged by drought. The program utilized a field headquarters, a grain and basic food packaging plant, 33 retail stores, and pilot centers in five towns. Each center consisted of one retail store, a tortilla factory, a sewing center, and a public kitchen and restaurant.

In the public restaurant in each of the five towns, the daily menu consisted of a rice dish with fish, a bean dish, and an Incaparina *atole*. The flavors of the *atole* were varied from day to day. Two serving lines were used, one inside and one facing outside for those who wanted to take the food home. The price of the meal was 50 centavos (about $0.04 U.S.).

Between 2,000 and 3,000 persons visited each of the five restaurants each day. The Incaparina *atole* apparently was well accepted, and it was noted that considerable numbers of preschool children and lactating mothers consumed Incaparina in the dining hall or took it home.

In addition, CONASUPO decided to test Incaparina in five field kitchens that it operated for 10,000 workers on an irrigation project. At each of the five field kitchens, as many as 2,000 workers were fed each day. The Incaparina *atole* was well received, and there were frequent requests for second helpings. Many workers who were not familiar with *atoles* prior to the program liked them as part of their meals.

It has been estimated that about 12,000 people out of the 500,000 in the drought area used Incaparina regularly. At this rate, extending usage to the entire Mexican population would result in a total market potential of about 25 tons per day. CONASUPO felt that these tests indicated that the product had been well accepted and that, with proper promotion and advertising, the potential for the product would be even higher.

PLANNING AND DEVELOPMENT OF INCAPARINA FOR SALE IN COLOMBIA

Productos Quaker, recognizing the many possible pitfalls in entering into the production and marketing of Incaparina, concerned itself first with the development of an adequate and reliable supply of cottonseed flour suitable for human consumption. Negotiations with Grasas, S.A., a principal oilseed processor in the area, led to a modification of the production process that provided cottonseed flour meeting specifications. Modification of the production process was necessary to eliminate a toxic ingredient that was present. A year after the licensing agreement, the first satisfactory batch of cottonseed flour finally was produced successfully.

Although Productos Quaker had done considerable laboratory and survey work during the first 12 months, the assurance of an adequate supply of cottonseed flour permitted the company to begin broader field testing.

During the next year, Productos Quaker conducted product acceptability tests at four hospitals and medical centers to demonstrate the nutritive value of the product. Although INCAP had already done such tests in Guatemala, it was felt that local work would provide greater impact with the Colombian medical profession as well as give an indication of the acceptance and toler-

ance of Incaparina by children under Colombian conditions. The tests were completely successful.

Before making a decision on the product formula. Productos Quaker conducted a consumer survey among 150 low-income families in Cali and the surrounding area. Since the interviews showed a preference for corn, it was decided to develop a product with a corn base.

In May, two years after the licensing agreement was signed, Productos Quaker held a series of conferences with public officials to acquaint them with the product and the work that had been done to date. Leading public officials of the national and local government—including the National Institute of Nutrition, the medical and public health professions, and others—participated in the conferences. They reacted favorably to the proposed plans for production, quality control, promotion and advertising, and distribution of Incaparina, and they indicated their support.

In July, two years and four months after licensing, a comparison test was run to see if the consumer preferred a formula with cottonseed as the prime protein source or a formula that substituted toasted soy flour for half of the cottonseed flour. The sample included 400 housewives, children, and other persons. No significant preference was found.

A few months later Productos Quaker, convinced that it had an acceptable product, began a large-scale, 12-month test-marketing program in Cali, a city with a population of about 700,000, representing about 5 percent of the population of Colombia. The objective of the test was to determine how well the product would move through regular retail and wholesale channels.

After placement of Incaparina in retail outlets was obtained, a promotional program was begun. The basic promotional approach was to use a "shock theme." A poster was prepared that compared sickly, emaciated-looking children suffering from malnutrition with healthy, smiling pictures of the same child a few months later after having been fed on an Incaparina-based diet. The "before and after" approach was used as the basis for the message that Incaparina was a matter of life and death. Additionally a 5-minute movie was prepared, dramatizing the devastating effects of kwashiorkor in an infant. This promotional approach was not inconsistent with INCAP advertising guidelines.

The reason for this severe, dramatic theme was that there was already a large number of other products being advertised as "good foods." It was felt that Incaparina's special characteristics must be stated in a way to clearly separate the product from others.

For a slogan, Productos Quaker coined *Es Mucho Alimento Y Cuesta Menos,* which means "a great deal of nourishment at a low price." The slogan has more "punch" in Spanish than when it is translated into English.

In the development of the promotional campaign, full advantage was taken of the fact that the product had the active support of public health officials, social welfare groups, the medical professions, and others interested in supporting the basic social welfare objectives of the product. Much free publicity and advertising time and space were donated by advertising media.

In addition, the following media were utilized in the test campaign:

1 *Radio.* Four major radio stations each carried 360 commercial spots per month. The content of these spots was developed from information obtained during the Cali consumer survey. The messages dealt with concepts regarding nutrition as well as presenting facts about Incaparina, especially its nutritive value.

2 *Newspapers.* Because of the widespread community interest in the product, newspapers carried a number of news releases and feature stories on Incaparina, reporting on the reaction of various public officials and physicians. Newspapers were used only for publicity; it was felt that no paid advertising was required.

3 *Point-of-purchase and sales aids.* Posters for use in stores, institutions, and other public places were distributed widely. A special folder containing the basic facts about Incaparina in graphic form was utilized by sales representatives in presenting the product to retailers.

4 *Television and cinema.* The 5-minute film was shown in movie theaters and on television.

5 *Demonstrations before groups.* One of the key aspects of the promotional program was the practical demonstration before a wide variety of groups of how Incaparina is prepared in the home. These demonstrations were given at schools, mothers' clubs, parochial centers, and other organizations. The same movie that was prepared for television and cinema was used in these presentations. Additional visual aids were also used.

6 *Seminars and conferences.* Meetings with physicians, nurses, teachers, and social workers were conducted on a regular basis to inform them of the views of prominent Colombian and foreign doctors and scientists. Special tape recordings of their views were presented.

In view of the need to make Incaparina available to low-income families, the basic pricing policy was to set the price as low as possible, based on estimated potential sales volume that could be obtained in the national market and consistent with raw material, manufacturing, and marketing costs plus a reasonable return on investment.

Since the price had to bear a reasonable relationship to basic food staples if Incaparina were to be used as a staple food, and since the prime market was the 80 percent of the Colombian market that was not in the habit of purchasing any packaged foods in significant quantity, Productos Quaker felt that at a maximum the price could be set at only a very small premium over staples.

No studies were made to determine price elasticity. The company relied on the price of other food products and the judgment of executives in estimating demand at the planned price. After all factors were taken into consideration, the retail price was set at 1.3 Colombian pesos for a 500-gram package ($0.13 U.S. on the basis of a 10-to-1 exchange rate).

Wholesalers and retailers were allowed 5 percent and 10 percent margins, respectively, which were normal margins for such products in Colombia. Institutions were quoted the wholesale price ($0.105 per 500 grams) when they bought in 35-kilogram quantities.

At that price, a consumer could prepare a glass of Incaparina *colada* (a popular drink in Colombia similar to the Guatemalan *atole*) containing protein and other nutritive elements found in a glass of milk at less than one-fifth the price of a glass of milk. In terms of protein per peso, Incaparina compared favorably with other products, as shown in Exhibit 1.

In view of the need to keep the price low, inexpensive packages were required. Producers of Incaparina in other countries had used relatively expensive 75-gram bags. But in Colombia it was noted that grocery retailers often bought products like Areparina in bulk and then repackaged them into small brown bags. Therefore, it was decided to sell Incaparina in 12- and 35-kilogram bags and include, separately from the product, sufficient empty 500-gram paper bags for repackaging at the sales point. The small bags were printed in attractive red and black. On the back of each package were four suggested recipes for home preparation. The recipes were for colada, soups, baby foods, and meals.

Although the repackaging method was not normal trade practice for Quaker products, retailers were approached with the observation that to sell at prices their customers could pay, many retailers were buying other products (for example, Areparina) in large quantities and repackaging them in small bags. Since retailers had to buy the bags themselves and Productos Quaker provided the bags free, they took the approach: "This is what we are going to do for you." Retailers were quite pleased and did not resist doing the packaging job.

RESULTS OF THE FIRST THREE MONTHS OF THE TEST IN CALI

In the initial placement (the first month of the test), 40,000 pounds of Incaparina were distributed to 984 stores and 16 health centers. Of the stores contacted, about 70 percent accepted the product on the first offering.

All subsequent orders from retail outlets were turned over to four wholesalers. In the second month of the test, wholesalers moved 32,000 pounds to retailers and institutions. An additional 23,600 pounds were ordered for delivery in the third month.

In addition to factory sales figures, Productos Quaker made a weekly audit of sales of Incaparina and similar products in a sample of 25 retail stores. The audit revealed, tentatively, that Incaparina sales appeared to be cutting into the sales of other flour products and tinned powdered milk.

Contacts with wholesalers and retailers indicated also that purchases being made in the third month were largely repurchases, indicating a favorable level of acceptance beyond the "curiosity sales volume" that might be expected for this kind of new product.

ESTIMATED INVESTMENT AND PRODUCTION COSTS

During the first two and one-half years of development work leading up to the test market, total costs were between $30,000 and $40,000 (U.S. dollars). This included staff time, materials, laboratory work on ingredient improvement, produc-

EXHIBIT 1   AMOUNT OF PROTEIN THAT CAN BE PURCHASED PER PESO

Product	Protein per peso (grams)
Incaparina	114.5
Eggs	14.0
Powdered milk	10.7
Corn flour	7.0
Plantain flour	6.8

EXHIBIT 2   PRODUCTION COSTS

Nature of the cost	Cost (pesos)
Package material	5.95 per 35-kilo sack
	2.57 per 12-kilo sack
Grain and other ingredients	40.00 per 35-kilo sack
	13.75 per 12-kilo sack
Direct manufacturing, packaging, and other variable costs	30.00[a] per 35-kilo sack

[a] This figure is fictitious. Since the actual costs are confidential and cannot be released, this figure is included for purposes of case analysis.

tion facilities needed to produce pilot quantities of Incaparina, and the services rendered by the company's U.S. research facilities.

The installed production equipment needed to produce Incaparina in adequate volume to reach and exceed the point where it will become profitable is estimated to cost about $60,000. In addition, since the break-even volume of about 2,000 tons per year is about two years away, the operation will operate at a loss of about $20,000 (including the net loss on the test mar-

ket project). Thus, if the forecasted volume is achieved four and one-half years after the licensing agreement was signed, Productos Quaker will have an investment in Incaparina of approximately $120,000. But if volume does not increase as rapidly as planned, the loss could be as high as $30,000 or $40,000 per year; these additional "sunk costs" that would have to be amortized could increase the break-even volume to as high as 3,000 tons per year. Variable production costs are shown in Exhibit 2.

BIG SKY OF MONTANA, INC.

Karen Tracy could feel the pressure on her as she sat at her desk late that April afternoon. Two weeks from today she would be called on to present her recommendations concerning next year's winter-season pricing policies for Big Sky of Montana, Inc.—room rates for the resort's accommodation facilities as well as decisions in the skiing and food service areas. The presentation would be made to a top management team from the parent company, Boyne USA, which operated out of Michigan.

"As sales and public relations manager, Karen, your accuracy in decision making is extremely important," her boss had said in his usual tone. "Because we spend most of our time in Michigan, we'll need a well-based and involved opinion."

"It'll be the shortest two weeks of my life," she thought.

BACKGROUND: BIG SKY AND BOYNE USA

Big Sky of Montana, Inc., was a medium-sized destination resort located in southwestern Montana, 45 miles south of Bozeman and 43 miles north of the west entrance to Yellowstone National Park.[1] Big Sky was conceived in the early 1970s and had begun operation in November 1974.

The 11,000-acre, 2,000-bed resort was separated into two main areas: Meadow Village and Mountain Village. Meadow Village (elevation 6,300 feet) was located two miles east of the resort's main entrance on U.S. 191 and seven miles from the ski area. Meadow Village had an 800-bed capacity in the form of four condominium complexes (ranging from studios to three-bedroom units) and a 40-room hostel for economy lodging. Additional facilities included an 18-hole golf course, six tennis courts, a restaurant, a post office, a convention center with meeting space for up to 200 people, and a small lodge serving as a pro shop for the golf course in the summer and for cross-country skiing in the winter.

Mountain Village (elevation 7,500 feet), located at the base of the ski area, was the center of winter activity. In this complex was the 204-

---

This case was written by Anne Senausky and Professor James E. Nelson, University of Colorado at Denver. Copyright © 1978 by the Endowment and Research Foundation at Montana State University.

[1] Destination resorts are characterized by on-the-hill lodging and eating facilities, a national market, and national advertising.

room Huntley Lodge offering hotel accommodations, three condominium complexes (unit size ranged from studio to three-bedroom), and an 88-room hostel, for a total of 1,200 beds. The Mountain Mall was also located here, next to Huntley Lodge and within a five-minute walk of two of the three condominium complexes in Mountain Village. It housed ticket sales, an equipment rental shop, a skiers' cafeteria, two large meeting rooms for a maximum of 700 persons (regularly used as sack lunch areas for skiers), two offices, a ski school desk, and a ski patrol room—all of which were operated by Boyne. Also in this building were a delicatessen, drugstore/gift shop, sporting goods store/rental shop, restaurant, outdoor-clothing store, jewelry shop, T-shirt shop, two bars, and a child day-care center. Each of these independent operations held leases, due to expire in one to three years.

The closest airport to Big Sky was located just outside Bozeman. It was served by Northwest Orient and Frontier Airlines, with connections to other major airlines out of Denver and Salt Lake City. Greyhound and Amtrak also operated bus and train service into Bozeman. Yellowstone Park Lines provided Big Sky with three buses daily to and from the airport and Bozeman bus station (cost was $4.40 one way, $8.40 round trip), as well as an hourly shuttle around the two Big Sky villages. Avis, Hertz, National, and Budget offered car-rental service in Bozeman, with a drop-off service available at Big Sky.

In July 1976 Boyne USA—a privately owned, Michigan-based operation—purchased Huntley Lodge, Mountain Mall, the ski lifts and terrain, the golf course, and the tennis courts for approximately $8 million. The company subsequently invested an additional $3 million in Big Sky. Boyne also owned and operated four Michigan ski resorts.

Big Sky's top management consisted of a lodge manager (in charge of operations within Huntley Lodge), a sales and public relations manager (Karen), a food and beverage manager, and an area manager (overseeing operations external to the lodge, including the mall and all recreational facilities). These four positions were occupied by persons trained with the parent company; a fifth manager, the comptroller, had worked for pre-Boyne ownership.

Business figures were reported to the company's home office on a daily basis, and major decisions concerning Big Sky operations were discussed and approved by "Michigan." Boyne's top management visited Big Sky an average of five times annually, and all major decisions, such as pricing and advertising, were approved by the parent company for all operations.

THE SKIING

Big Sky's winter season usually began in late November and continued until the middle of April, with a yearly snowfall of approximately 450 inches. The area had 18 slopes between elevations of 7,500 and 9,900 feet. Terrain breakdown was as follows: 25 percent novice, 55 percent intermediate, and 20 percent advanced. (Although opinions varied, industry guidelines recommended a terrain breakdown of 20 percent, 60 percent, and 20 percent for novice, intermediate, and advanced skiers, respectively.) The longest run was approximately three miles in length; temperatures (highs) ranged from 15 to 30 degrees Fahrenheit throughout the season.

Lift facilities at Big Sky included two double chairlifts, a triple chair, and a four-passenger gondola. Lift capacity was estimated at 4,000 skiers per day. This figure was considered adequate by the area manager, at least until the 1980–1981 season.

Karen felt that the facilities, snow conditions, and grooming compared favorably with those of other destination resorts of the Rockies. "In fact, our only real drawback right now," she thought, "is our position in the national market. We need more skiers who are sold on Big Sky. And that is in the making."

THE CONSUMERS

Karen knew from previous dealings that Big Sky, like most destination areas, attracted three distinct skier segments: local day skiers (living within driving distance and not utilizing lodging in the area); individual destination skiers (living out of state and using accommodations in the Big Sky area); and groups of destination skiers (clubs, professional organizations, and so on).

The first category was typically composed of Montana residents, with a relatively small number from Wyoming and Idaho. (Distances from selected population centers to Big Sky appear in Exhibit 1.) A 1973 study of four Montana ski areas, performed by the advertising unit of the Montana Department of Highways, characterized Montana skiers as:

1 In their early twenties and male (60 percent)
2 Living within 75 miles of a ski area
3 From a household with two skiers in it
4 Averaging $13,000 in household income
5 Intermediate- to advanced-ability skiers
6 Skiing five hours per ski day, 20 days per season locally
7 Skiing four days away from local areas
8 Having taken no lessons in the past five years

EXHIBIT 1   DISTANCES FROM SELECTED CITIES TO BIG SKY

Population Centers in Proximity to Big Sky (distance and population)

City	Distance from Big Sky (Miles)	Population (U.S. 1970 Census)
Bozeman, Montana	45	18,670
Butte, Montana	126	23,368
Helena, Montana	144	22,730
Billings, Montana	174	61,581
Great Falls, Montana	225	60,091
Missoula, Montana	243	29,497
Pocatello, Idaho	186	40,036
Idaho Falls, Idaho	148	35,776

Approximate Distances from Selected Major U.S. Population Centers to Big Sky (in air miles)

City	Distance to Big Sky[a]
Chicago	1275
Minneapolis	975
Fargo	750
Salt Lake City	375
Dallas	1500
Houston	1725
Los Angeles	975
San Francisco	925
New York	2025
Atlanta	1950
New Orleans	1750
Denver	750

[a] Per-passenger air fare can be approximated at 20 cents per mile (round trip, coach rates).

Karen was also aware that a significant number of day skiers, particularly on the weekends, were college students.

Destination, or nonresident, skiers were labeled in the same study as typically:

1 At least in their mid-twenties and male (55 percent)
2 Living in a household of three or more skiers
3 Averaging near $19,000 in household income
4 More likely to be intermediate skiers
5 Spending about six hours per day skiing
6 Skiing 11 to 14 days per season, with three to eight days away from home
7 Taking ski school lessons

Through data taken from reservation records, Karen learned that individual destination skiers accounted for half of last year's usage, based on skier days.[2] Geographic segments were represented approximately as follows:

Upper Midwest (Minnesota, Michigan, North Dakota)	30%
Florida	20%
California	17%
Washington, Oregon, Montana	15%
Texas, Oklahoma	8%
Other	10%

Reservation records indicated that the average length of stay for individual destination skiers was six to seven days.

The individual destination skier was most likely to buy a lodging/lift package; 30 percent made commitments for these advertised packages when making reservations for 1977–1978. Even though there was no discount involved in this manner of buying lift tickets, Karen knew that it was fairly popular because it saved the purchaser a trip to the ticket window every morning. Approximately half of the individual business came through travel agents, who received a 10-percent commission.

[2] A skier day is defined as one skier's using the facility for any part of one day of operation.

The third skier segment, the destination group, accounted for a substantial 20 percent of Big Sky's skier-day usage. The larger portion of the group business came through medical and other professional organizations that held meetings at the resort, as this was a way to combine business with pleasure. These groups were typically composed of couples and individuals between the ages of 30 and 50. Ski clubs made up the remainder, with a number coming from Florida, Texas, and Georgia. During the 1977–1978 season, Big Sky drew 30 ski clubs, with membership averaging 55 skiers. The average length of stay for all group destination skiers was about four to five days.

Some of these group bookings were made through travel agents, but the majority were made directly with Karen. The coordinator of the professional meetings or the president of the ski club typically contacted the Big Sky sales office to make initial reservation dates, negotiate prices, and work out the details of the stay.

THE COMPETITION

In Karen's mind, Big Sky faced two types of competition, that for local day skiers and that for out-of-state (i.e., destination) skiers.

Bridger Bowl was virtually the only area competing for local day skiers. Bridger was a "no-frills," nonprofit, smaller ski area located some 16 miles northeast of Bozeman. It received the majority of local skiers, including students at Montana State University, which is located in Bozeman. The area was labeled as having terrain more difficult than that of Big Sky and thus was more appealing to the local expert skiers. However, it also had much longer lift lines and had recently lost some of its weekend business to Big Sky.

Karen had found through experience that most Bridger skiers usually "tried" Big Sky once or twice a season. Season passes for the two areas were mutually honored (by charging the half-day rate for an all-day ticket), and Big Sky occasionally ran newspaper ads offering discounts on lifts to obtain more Bozeman business.

Big Sky considered its competition for out-of-state skiers to be mainly the destination resorts of Colorado, Utah, and Wyoming. (Selected data on competing resorts appear in Exhibit 2.) Because Big Sky was smaller and newer than the majority of these areas, Karen reasoned, it was necessary to follow an aggressive strategy aimed at increasing its national market share.

PRESENT POLICIES

Lift Rates

It was common knowledge that there existed some local resentment concerning Big Sky's lift-rate policy. Although comparable to rates at Vail or Aspen, the price of an all-day lift ticket was $4 higher than that of the ticket offered at Bridger Bowl. In an attempt to alleviate this situation, management at Big Sky instituted a $9 "chair pass" for the 1977–1978 season, entitling the holder to unlimited use of the three chairs, plus two rides per day on the gondola, to be taken between specified times. Because the gondola served primarily intermediate terrain, it was reasoned that the chair pass would appeal to the local, more expert skier. A triple chair serving the bowl area was located at the top of the gondola; two rides on the gondola would allow those skiers to take ample advantage of the advanced terrain up there. Otherwise, all advanced terrain was served by another chair.

However, Karen believed that if Big Sky was to establish itself as a successful, nationally prominent destination area, the attitudes and opinions of all skiers must be carefully weighed. Throughout the season she had made a special effort to grasp the general feeling toward rates. A $12 ticket, she discovered, was thought to be very reasonable by destination skiers, primarily because Big Sky was predominantly an intermediate area and the average destination skier was of intermediate ability, and also because Big Sky was noted for its relative lack of lift lines, giving the skier more actual skiing time for the money. "Perhaps we should keep the price the same," she thought. "We do need more business. Other destination areas are likely to raise their prices, and we should look good in comparison."

Also discussed was the possible abolition of the $9 chair pass. The question in Karen's mind was whether its elimination would severely hurt local business or would instead sell an all-lift $12 ticket to the skier who had previously bought only a chair pass. The issue was compounded by the unknown number of destination skiers who also opted for the cheaper chair pass.

Season pass pricing was also an issue. Prices for the 1977–1978 all-lift season pass had remained the same as last year's, but a season chair pass had been introduced that was the counterpart of the daily chairlift pass. Karen did not

EXHIBIT 2   COMPETITORS' 1977–1978 PACKAGE PLAN RATES,[a] NUMBER OF LIFTS, AND LIFT RATES

	Lodge double (2)[b]	Two-bedroom condo (4)	Three-bedroom condo (6)	Number of lifts	Daily lift rates
Aspen, CO	$242	$242	$220	19	$13
Steamboat, CO	230	230	198	15	12
Jackson, WY	230	242	210	5	14
Vail, CO	230	242	220	15	14
Snowbird, UT	208	none	none	6	11
Bridger Bowl, MT	(No lodging available at Bridger Bowl)				

[a] Package plan rates are per person and include seven nights' lodging and six lift tickets (high-season rates).
[b] Number in parentheses denotes occupancy of unit on which price is based.

like the relationship between the number of season chair passes purchased and the number of all-lift passes purchased and was considering recommending the abolition of the season chair pass as well as an increase in the price of the all-lift pass. "I'm going to have to think this one out carefully," she thought, "because skiing accounted for about 40 percent of our total revenue this past season. I'll have to be able to justify my decision not only to Michigan but also to the Forest Service."

Price changes were not solely at the discretion of Big Sky management. As was the case with most larger Western ski areas, the U.S. government owned part of the land on which Big Sky operated. Control of this land was the responsibility of the U.S. Forest Service, which annually approved all lift pricing policies. For the 1976–1977 ski season, Forest Service action had kept most lift-rate increases to the national inflation rate. For the 1977–1978 season, larger price increases were allowed for ski areas that had competing areas nearby; Big Sky was considered to be such an area. No one knew what the Forest Service position would be for the upcoming 1978–1979 season.

To help Karen in her decision, an assistant had prepared a summary of lift rates and usage for the past two seasons (Exhibit 3).

EXHIBIT 3   SUMMARY OF LIFT RATES AND USAGE

Ticket	Consumer cost	Skier days[a]	Number of season passes sold
1977–1978 lift rates and usage summary		*(136 days of operation)*	
Adult all-day, all-lift	$12	53,400	
Adult all-day chair	9	20,200	
Adult half-day	8	9,400	
Child all-day, all-lift	8	8,500	
Child all-day chair	5	3,700	
Child half-day	6	1,200	
Hotel passes[b]	12/day	23,400	
Complimentary	0	1,100	
Adult all-lift season pass	220	4,300	140
Adult chair season pass	135	4,200	165
Child all-lift season pass	130	590	30
Child chair season pass	75	340	15
Employee all-lift season pass	100	3,000	91
Employee chair season pass	35	1,100	37
1976–1977 lift rates and usage summary		*(122 days of operation)*	
Adult all-day	10	52,500	
Adult half-day	6.50	9,000	
Child all-day	6	10,400	
Child half-day	4	1,400	
Hotel passes[b]	10/day	30,500	
Complimentary	0	480	
Adult season pass	220	4,200	84
Child season pass	130	300	15
Employee season pass	100	2,300	70

[a] A skier day is defined as one skier's using the facility for any part of one day of operation.
[b] Hotel passes refer to those included in the lodging/lift packages.

Room Rates

Room-rate pricing was particularly important because lodging accounted for about one-third of the past season's total revenue. It was also difficult because of the variety of accommodations (Exhibit 4) and the difficulty in accurately forecasting next season's demand. For example, the season of 1976–1977 had been unique in that a good portion of the Rockies was without snow for the initial months of the winter, including

Christmas. Big Sky was fortunate in receiving as much snow as it had, and consequently many groups and individuals who were originally headed for Vail or Aspen booked in with Big Sky.

Pricing for the 1977–1978 season had been determined on the premise that there would be a good amount of repeat business. This came true in part, but not as much as had been hoped. Occupancy experience had also been summarized

EXHIBIT 4   ROOM RATES FOR VARIOUS ACCOMMODATIONS

Accommodation	Low-season range	High-season range	Maximum occupancy
		Nightly room rates[a] 1977–1978	
Huntley Lodge			
Standard	$42–62	$50–70	4
Loft	52–92	60–100	6
Stillwater Condo			
Studio	40–60	45–65	4
One-bedroom	55–75	60–80	4
Bedroom w/loft	80–100	90–110	6
Deer Lodge Condo			
One-bedroom	74–84	80–90	4
Two-bedroom	93–103	100–110	6
Three-bedroom	112–122	120–130	8
Hill Condo			
Studio	30–40	35–45	4
Studio w/loft	50–70	55–75	6
		Nightly room rates, 1976–1977	
Huntley Lodge			
Standard	32–47	35–50	4
Loft	47–67	50–70	6
Stillwater Condo			
Studio	39–54	37–52	4
One-bedroom	52–62	50–60	4
Bedroom w/loft	60–80	65–85	6
Deer Lodge Condo			
One-bedroom	51–66	55–70	4
Two-bedroom	74–94	80–100	6
Three-bedroom	93–123	100–130	8
Hill Condo			
Studio	28–43	30–45	4
Studio w/loft	42–62	45–65	6

[a]Rates are determined by the number of persons in the room or condominium unit and do not include lift tickets. Maximums for each rate range apply at maximum occupancy.

for the past two seasons to help Karen make her final decision (Exhibit 5).

As was customary in the hospitality industry, January was a slow period, and it was necessary to price accordingly. Low-season pricing was extremely important because many groups took advantage of the lower rates. In addition, groups were often offered discounts in the neighborhood of 10 percent. Considering this, Karen could not price too high, with the risk of losing individual destination skiers, nor too low, such that an unacceptably low profit would be made from group business in this period.

Food Service

Under some discussion was the feasibility of converting all destination skiers to the American plan; each guest in Huntley Lodge would be placed on a package that included three meals daily in a Big Sky–controlled facility. There was a feeling both for and against this idea. The parent company had been successfully utilizing this plan for years at its destination areas in northern Michigan. Extending the policy to Big Sky should find similar success.

Karen was not so sure. For one thing, the Michigan resorts were primarily self-contained and alternative eateries were few. For another, the whole idea of extending standardized policies from Michigan to Montana was suspect. As an example, Karen painfully recalled a day in January when Big Sky "tried on" another successful Michigan policy of accepting only cash or check payments for lift tickets. Reactions of credit-card–carrying skiers could be described as ranging from annoyed to irate.

EXHIBIT 5   SUMMARY OF OCCUPANCY RATES

	1977–1978 lodge-condominium occupancy (in room-nights[a])				
	December (26 days of operation)	January	February	March	April (8 days of operation)
Huntley Lodge	1,830	2,250	3,650	4,650	438
Condominiums[b]	775	930	1,350	100	90

	1976–1977 lodge-condominium occupancy (in room-nights)				
	December (16 days of operation)	January	February	March	April (16 days of operation)
Huntley Lodge	1,700	3,080	4,525	4,300	1,525
Condominiums[c]	600	1,000	1,600	1,650	480

Lodge-condominium occupancy (in person-nights[d])				
December 1977 (1976)	January 1978 (1977)	February 1978 (1977)	March 1978 (1977)	April 1978 (1977)
7,850 (6,775)	9,200 (13,000)	13,150 (17,225)	17,900 (17,500)	1,450 (4,725)

[a] A room-night is defined as one room (or condominium) rented for one night. Lodging experience is based on 124 days of operation for 1977–1978, whereas Exhibit 3 shows the skiing facilities operating 136 days. Both numbers are correct.
[b] Big Sky had 92 condominiums available during the 1977–1978 season.
[c] Big Sky had 85 condominiums available during the 1976–1977 season.
[d] A person-night refers to one person's using the facility for one night.

If an American plan were proposed for next year, it would likely include both the Huntley Lodge dining room and Lookout Cafeteria. Less clear, however, were prices to be charged. There certainly would have to be consideration for both adults and children and for the two independently operated eating places in Mountain Mall (see Exhibit 6 for an identification of eating places in the Big Sky area). Beyond these considerations, there was little other than an expectation of a profit to guide Karen in her analysis.

THE TELEPHONE CALL

"Profits in the food area might be hard to come by," Karen thought. "Last year it appears we lost money on everything we sold" (see Exhibit 7). Just then the telephone rang. It was Rick Thompson, her counterpart at Boyne Mountain Lodge in Michigan. "How are your pricing recommendations coming?" he asked. "I'm about done with mine and thought we should compare notes."

"Good idea, Rick—only I'm just getting started out here. Do you have any hot ideas?"

"Only one," he responded. "I just got off the phone with a guy in Denver. He told me all of the major Colorado areas are upping their lift prices one or two dollars next year."

"Is that right, Rick? Are you sure?"

"Well, you know nobody knows for sure what's going to happen, but I think it's pretty good information. He heard it from his sister-in-

EXHIBIT 6   EATING PLACES IN THE BIG SKY AREA

Establishment	Type of service	Meals served	Current prices	Seating	Location
Lodge dining room[a]	A la carte	Breakfast Lunch Dinner	$2–5 2–5 7–15	250	Huntley Lodge
Steak House[a]	Steak/lobster	Dinner only	6–12	150	Huntley Lodge
Fondue Stube[a]	Fondue	Dinner only	6–10	25	Huntley Lodge
Ore House[b]	A la carte	Lunch Dinner	0.80–4 5–12	150	Mountain Mall
Ernie's Deli[b]	Deli/restaurant	Breakfast Lunch	1–3 2–5	25	Mountain Mall
Lookout Cafeteria[a]	Cafeteria	Breakfast Lunch Dinner	1.50–3 2–4 3–6	175	Mountain Mall
Yellow Mule[b]	A la carte	Breakfast Lunch Dinner	2–4 2–5 4–8	75	Meadow Village
Buck's T-4[b]	Road house restaurant/bar	Dinner only	2–9	60	Gallatin Canyon (2 miles south of Big Sky entrance)
Karst Ranch[b]	Road house restaurant/bar	Breakfast Lunch Dinner	2–4 2–5 3–8	50	Gallatin Canyon (7 miles north of Big Sky entrance)
Corral[b]	Road house restaurant/bar	Breakfast Lunch Dinner	2–4 2–4 3–5	30	Gallatin Canyon (5 miles south of Big Sky entrance)

[a]Owned and operated by Big Sky of Montana, Inc.
[b]Independently operated.

EXHIBIT 7   SKI SEASON INCOME DATA (PERCENTAGE)

	Skiing	Lodging	Food and beverage
Revenue	100.0%	100.0%	100.0%
Cost of sales			
Merchandise	0.0	0.0	30.0
Labor	15.0	15.9	19.7
Maintenance	3.1	5.2	2.4
Supplies	1.5	4.8	5.9
Miscellaneous	2.3	0.6	0.6
Operating expenses	66.2	66.4	66.7
Net profit (loss) before taxes	11.9	7.1	(25.2)

law who works in Vail. I think he said she read it in the local paper or something."

"That doesn't seem like very solid information," said Karen. "Let me know if you hear anything more, will you?"

"Certainly. You know, we really should compare our recommendations before we stick our necks out too far on this pricing thing.

Can you call me later in the week?" he asked.

"Sure, I'll talk to you the day after tomorrow; I should be about done by then. Anything else?"

"Nope—gotta run. Talk to you then. Bye," and he was gone.

"At least I've got some information," Karen thought, "and a new deadline!"

ISLAND SHORES

In February 1982, Tom Smith, vice president and project manager of Enterprise Developers, Inc., was contemplating marketing alternatives available to the firm and the associated risks inherent in real estate development during such turbulent economic times. As Mr. Smith sat in his St. Petersburg, Florida, office trying to organize his thoughts and the market information at his disposal in some meaningful fashion, he was well aware that should the firm act on his recommendation, tens of millions of dollars would be at stake. Within the firm Smith was known for his good insights and solid judgment. While his previous decisions had successful outcomes, there was no guarantee that he was immune from mistakes, and in this business mistakes were costly. Corporate expectations to meet a target return on investment of 18 percent added to the pressure that the selected project be more than marginally successful. The final plan to be submitted to the board of directors would have to include consideration of the designated target market, site selection, and architectural design requirements as well as price and promotional strategy.

This case was written by Cynthia J. Frey, Assistant Professor of Marketing, Boston College, and Maria Sannella as a basis for class discussion rather than to illustrate either effective or ineffective handling of an administrative situation.

COMPANY BACKGROUND

The history of Enterprise Developers was characterized by risk taking and an unusually high rate of success. The firm was founded by three businessmen from New York who had grown up in one of the worst boroughs in the city. They had banded together in the late 1950s to renovate and refurbish a neighborhood tenement building. After buying the burned-out shell from the city for $1,000 they rebuilt it themselves with sweat equity into a model example of low-income housing worth several hundred thousand dollars. The group invested the profits from the sale of this building into other pieces of real estate. Middle-income housing, apartment buildings, and townhouses followed. With each renovation success the profits were reinvested in more property. The group was always alert to a new opportunity.

Encouraged by a friend and the possibility of more lucrative ventures, the trio moved to Miami in 1969. The next five years were spent developing rental units in the central city area. Close to the major business district, these mid-rise-style buildings provided convenient access to the city for office workers. The skills that Enterprise acquired in New York City developing high-density urban living units were equally successful in Miami.

During this time period extensive condominium development was occurring along Florida's east coast, particularly in the Fort Lauderdale area. Two of the primary groups of buyers were retirees desiring low-maintenance home ownership in a warm climate, and investment buyers who might spend three or four weeks a year in their unit and rent the remaining weeks to Florida vacationers looking for an alternative to high-priced, crowded hotel accommodations. While this was a time of extraordinary growth for east coast condominium building, with units being sold before construction was even started, little of this development was occurring on the west side of the state.

In an attempt to take advantage of the condominium boom in the early 1970s, Enterprise investigated possible sites throughout the Florida peninsula but found most of the areas best suited to resort or retirement communities vastly overpriced or unavailable. One alternative which caught the trio's interest was a so-called spoil spot in Boca Ciega Bay, 350 miles from Miami between St. Petersburg and Clearwater. From dredging operations by the Army Corps of Engineers, a 320-acre island had been formed. Two bridges connected the island with the northernmost portions of the city of St. Petersburg 25 minutes away by car. The island was comprised of coarse bottom sand from the Bay. Vegetation was sparse and uncultivated giving the area a decidedly remote and desolate atmosphere.

The 320-acre island was offered for sale by a prominent insurance company. Although friends and business associates advised against the acquisition of the parcel for the planned high amenity community, Enterprise purchased the site for $18 million. While clarification of zoning ordinances was the first concern for the developers, taming the wilderness to support human creature comforts would be a time-consuming task.

ST. PETERSBURG AREA

St. Petersburg is known for its mild temperatures and beautiful year-round weather. According to the local paper, the *St. Petersburg Independent*, 361 days of sunshine per year are guaranteed. On days when the sun does not appear by 3 P.M., the newspaper distributes the afternoon edition free of charge. Since 1910, only 30 editions have been given away. The record for consecutive days with sunshine is 546.

St. Petersburg, the fourth largest city in Florida, is located on the southern tip of the Pinellas Peninsula. This point of land takes its name from the Spanish Punta Pinales, or Point of the Pine Trees. Tampa Bay is on the east and to the south; the Gulf of Mexico on the west. St. Petersburg Beach, on Long Key, is one of the Holiday Isles, a ribbon of keys separated from the mainland and St. Petersburg by Boca Ciega Bay. (See Exhibit 1.)

Although the Spanish explorer Narvaez landed on the peninsula in 1528 and marched to Tampa Bay, John C. Williams of Detroit is credited as the city's founder. Williams acquired 1,700 acres of wilderness land in 1876, which later became the nucleus of downtown St. Petersburg. Williams's intention was to establish a resort community to take advantage of the fine weather. However, his remote location had no transportation connection with other Florida population centers. As a result, he agreed to a partnership with Russian exile Piotr Alexeitch Dementieff (a.k.a. Peter Demens) contingent on Demens's completion of a railroad trunk line into the area.

The Orange Belt Line from Lake Monroe near Sanford, Florida, was completed in 1888 when Williams's little community had a population of 30. As the story goes, Williams and Demens flipped a coin to decide who would name the new town. Demens won and elected to name the town St. Petersburg after his birthplace. Williams's resort hotel, completed around 1890, was fittingly named The Detroit.

As early as 1885 the American Medical Association praised the climate and healthful surroundings as ideal. With its accessibility improved by the Orange Belt Line, the population had climbed to 300 by 1892 when the town was incorporated. Many of the early settlers were British who had emigrated to the Bahamas and Key West. In an effort to expand the resort reputa-

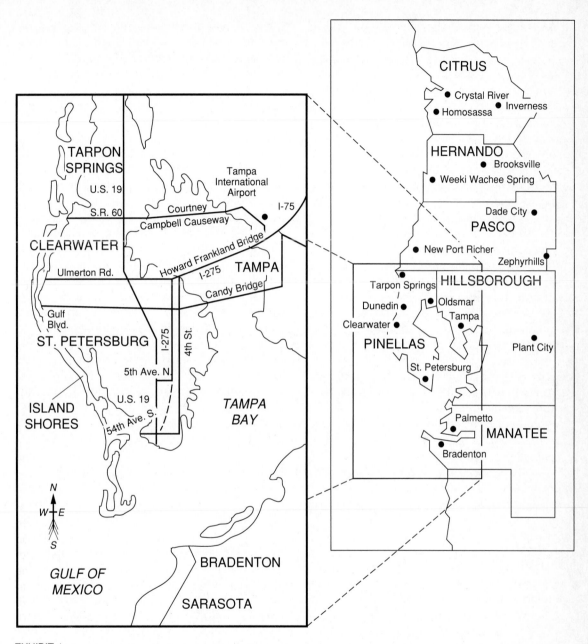

EXHIBIT 1

tion of St. Petersburg, the Chamber of Commerce established its first promotional budget of $150 in 1902. In 1907 a special tax was levied on year-round residents to support tourist promotion.

Today, thousands of people arrive daily at the Tampa International Airport, which also serves St. Petersburg and Clearwater. Considered one of the most modern and efficient airports in the world, Tampa International has shuttle trains from the main terminal to the gates, an assortment of restaurants and boutiques, and a hotel with a revolving penthouse. Fifteen major air carriers fly into the airport, many with international routes to Central and South America and Europe.

St. Petersburg is also known as the Boating Capital of the United States. With boating activity supported by the Municipal Marina downtown and the St. Petersburg Yacht Club, St. Petersburg is home base to some of the most important sailboat and power boat races in the Gulf. The Swift Hurricane Classic, Isla de Mujeres Race, and the Southern Ocean Racing Conference championships represent the highlights of the season.

Fishing is also a favorite pastime in St. Petersburg, where people can be seen lining the bridges fishing late into the night. Golf courses are widely available as are tennis courts.

While St. Petersburg has become a preferred retirement community for many, the city has tried to promote business development in the area to balance the population demographics. Since 1970, construction of new plants and plant expansions have totaled 1,196, and 19,005 new jobs have been created. Changes in population demographics in St. Petersburg and the surrounding counties between 1970 and 1979 are presented in Exhibit 2.

A survey of newcomers to the St. Petersburg area conducted by Suncoast Opinion Surveys in 1980 reveals some further information. This group of newcomers is considered to represent approximately 19 percent of the adult population in Pinellas County. Survey results are presented in Exhibit 3.

BACKGROUND ON ISLAND SHORES

Management at Enterprise was convinced that careful planning and gradual development would be critical to the success of the Island Shores project given their previous experience. In order to appeal to both retiree and second-home vacationers, Island Shores had to represent a distinct combination of benefits. While many of the Florida condominium complexes were just places to hang one's hat and residents were dependent on the Ft. Lauderdale or Miami communities for things to do and places to go, the loca-

tion of Island Shores required that many of these entertainment and recreation options be available on the island. Enterprise's plan called for development of the following amenities: angling, beaches, golf, jogging and bicycle paths, open areas, clubhouse and restaurant, sailing, shopping, sunbathing, swimming pools, tennis and racquetball courts, and water skiing. In order to attract buyers in the early stages of development, at least some of these planned benefits had to be apparent; and so the golf course and clubhouse went into construction immediately.

The plan for the island called for high density residential units to be built on the water's edge and a golf course in the center. Since the golf course was considered a major drawing feature, the problems associated with growing grass where none had grown before had to be faced immediately. In 1974 work on the golf course began at the same time as condominium construction. After several false starts and experimentation with many varieties of grass, ground covers, and shrubs, reasonably well-manicured greens appeared three years later. It became painfully clear that landscaping a "spoil spot" would take perseverance, patience, and a great deal of money. Costs associated with construction of the golf course alone totaled a million dollars.

Michele Perez, an award-winning architect from California, was responsible for designing the residential structures in harmony with the island environment. Because of the priority given the 18-hole golf course in the 320-acre parcel and the desire to maximize picturesque views from each condo unit, the residential development plan called for high-density construction along the water's edge. The land utilization goal of 14 condominiums per acre was met by Perez's plan for positioning units diagonally to the water rather than lining them up parallel to the beach frontage in traditional fashion. These clusters form miniature neighborhoods while maximizing ocean views. For each cluster a swimming pool and sunbathing deck was constructed, which acts as a social gathering spot and pro-

EXHIBIT 2   POPULATION AND POPULATION CHARACTERISTICS CHANGE, 1970 TO 1979

	Metro area			Pinellas			Pasco			Hillsborough		
	April 1, 1979 population	Percent of total	Percent change since 1970	April 1, 1979 population	Percent of total	Percent change since 1970	April 1, 1979 population	Percent of total	Percent change since 1970	April 1, 1979 population	Percent of total	Percent change since 1970
Total population	1,521,799	100.0%	+39.8%	725,457	100.0%	+38.9%	161,873	100.0%	+113.1%	634,469	100.0%	+29.4%
0–14 years	285,296	18.8	+14.7	112,546	15.5	+14.8	25,662	15.9	+93.7	147,088	23.2	+7.0
15–24 years	217,866	14.3	+43.3	82,771	11.4	+40.1	17,515	10.8	+111.6	117,580	18.5	+38.8
25–44 years	323,700	21.3	+51.2	129,227	17.8	+49.0	23,962	14.8	+122.1	170,511	26.9	+46.3
45–64 years	338,423	22.2	+38.4	171,011	23.6	+37.3	39,528	24.4	+101.5	127,884	20.2	+27.4
65 and over	356,514	23.4	+55.6	229,902	31.7	+49.4	55,206	34.1	+129.8	71,406	11.2	+39.5
18 and over	1,165,496	76.6	+47.9	584,955	80.6	+45.5	130,413	80.6	+117.6	450,128	70.9	+38.1
Median age	40.9 years	—	+2.5 years	49.5 years	—	+1.4 years	52.0 years	—	−1.4 years	31.2 years	—	+2.7 years
White	1,385,288	91.0%	+42.5%	671,331	92.5	+40.4	157,783	97.5	+119.4	556,174	87.7	+31.8
Nonwhite	136,511	9.0	+17.2	54,126	7.5	+22.2	4,090	2.5	+1.5	78,295	12.3	+14.9
Male	716,075	47.1%	+39.1%	334,017	46.0	+38.9	77,599	47.9	+110.7	304,459	48.0	+28.1
Female	805,724	52.9	+40.4	391,440	54.0	+38.8	84,274	52.1	+115.4	330,010	52.0	+30.6

271

EXHIBIT 2 *(Continued)*

	Manatee			Citrus			Hernando		
	April 1, 1979 population	Percent of total	Percent change since 1970	April 1, 1979 population	Percent of total	Percent change since 1970	April 1, 1979 population	Percent of total	Percent change since 1970
Total population	141,188	100.0%	+45.4%	42,397	100.0%	+120.9%	38,182	100.0%	+124.5%
0–14 years	23,837	16.9	+27.2	7,155	16.9	+ 85.1	7,399	19.4	+ 73.8
15–24 years	15,049	10.6	+37.1	3,717	8.8	+ 81.7	4,166	10.9	+ 93.8
25–44 years	24,504	17.4	+58.1	6,215	14.6	+113.4	7,104	18.6	+120.7
45–64 years	33,874	24.0	+50.1	11,909	28.1	+121.4	10,268	26.9	+161.9
65 and over	43,924	31.1	+49.8	13,401	31.6	+168.4	9,245	24.2	+167.4
18 and over	112,346	80.0	+51.3	33,869	79.9	+134.5	29,253	76.6	+144.9
Median age	49.2 years	—	+.5 years	51.9 years	—	+2.8 years	45.8 years	—	+7.6 years
White	128,068	90.7	+50.1	40,622	95.8	+134.3	35,833	93.8	+146.1
Nonwhite	13,120	9.3	+11.5	1,775	4.2	− 4.4	2,349	6.2	− 3.9
Male	66,700	47.2	+46.7	20,397	48.1	+119.9	18,833	49.3	+125.7
Female	74,488	52.8	+44.2	22,000	51.9	+121.8	19,349	50.7	+123.5

Source: University of Florida, Bureau of Economic and Business Research, "Age, Race, and Sex Components of Florida Population—1979," and 1970 Census. Prepared by Research Department, *St. Petersburg Times* and *Evening Independent,* May 1980.

272

EXHIBIT 3   DEMOGRAPHIC PROFILE OF PINELLAS RESIDENTS

	Total Pinellas adults	By length of residency		
		Newcomers (2 years or less)	Midterm residents (3–10 years)	Long-term residents (over 10 years)
Total population	100%	19%	35%	46%
Sex				
Male	45%	46%	51%	40%
Female	55	54	49	60
Age				
18–24 years	10%	25%	7%	6%
25–34 years	17	20	22	13
35–49 years	21	24	18	22
50–64 years	22	19	23	22
65–74 years	18	10	22	18
75 years and over	12	2	8	19
Median adult age (years)	51.4	38.1	52.0	56.1
Where born:*				
Pinellas County	8%	1%	1%	16%
Other Florida	5	7	4	5
Northeast	32	31	37	29
Midwest	31	35	31	29
South	15	17	14	14
West	3	3	4	2
Outside United States	6	6	9	5
Education				
Grammar school	4%	1%	4%	6%
Some high school	11	6	12	12
High school graduate	34	28	32	37
Technical, business school graduate	7	8	8	7
Some college	21	24	21	20
College graduate	23	33	23	18
Employment status				
Employed full-time	43%	56%	46%	35%
Employed part-time	7	5	7	7
Temporarily out of work	3	6	1	3
Retired	32	19	35	34
Housewife	11	11	7	15
Disabled	2	1	3	3
Other	2	2	1	3

* *Northeast* includes Connecticut, Maine, Massachusetts, New Hampshire, New Jersey, New York, Pennsylvania, Rhode Island, and Vermont.

   Midwest includes Illinois, Indiana, Iowa, Kansas, Michigan, Minnesota, Missouri, Nebraska, North Dakota, Ohio, South Dakota, and Wisconsin.

   South includes Alabama, Arkansas, Delaware, Washington, D.C., Georgia, Kentucky, Louisiana, Maryland, Mississippi, North Carolina, Oklahoma, South Carolina, Tennessee, Texas, Virginia, and West Virginia.

   West includes Alaska, Arizona, California, Colorado, Hawaii, Idaho, Montana, Nevada, New Mexico, Oregon, Utah, Washington, and Wyoming.

EXHIBIT 3   *(Continued)*

	Total Pinellas adults	By length of residency		
		Newcomers (2 years or less)	Midterm residents (3–10 years)	Long-term residents (over 10 years)
Women				
Employed outside home	40%	49%	41%	36%
Not employed outside home	60	51	59	64
Household income				
Under $10,000	23%	21%	18%	28%
$10,000–$15,000	18	24	16	17
$15,000–$20,000	19	12	23	19
Over $20,000	40	43	43	36
Median	$17,400	$17,100	$18,500	$16,300
Own/rent residence				
Own, with mortgage	47%	37%	52%	47%
Own, no mortgage	33	19	32	40
Rent	19	42	15	13
Other	1	2	1	†
Type of residence				
Single family	69%	53%	68%	77%
Apartment	11	19	10	7
Condominium	9	11	10	7
Mobile home	9	11	10	7
Other	2	6	2	2
Household size				
1 person	21%	14%	16%	26%
2 persons	41	45	48	35
3 persons	13	15	9	14
4 persons	15	15	15	16
5 or more persons	10	11	12	9
Average	2.5	2.6	2.6	2.5
Children present in houshold				
No children present	69%	68%	69%	69%
Child(ren) present	31	32	31	31
Race				
White	96%	97%	98%	94%
Nonwhite	4	3	2	6
Household income sources				
Wages/salaries only	40%	53%	39%	36%
Wage/salary and other regular sources‡	25	21	26	26
Other regular sources only	34	26	34	37
No income sources	1	—	1	1

† Less than one half of 1 percent.

‡ Other regular sources = Other than wages and salaries; includes social security, dividends, interest, alimony, child support, disability, pension, welfare, or other benefits.

EXHIBIT 3 *(Continued)*

	Total Pinellas adults	By length of residency		
		Newcomers (2 years or less)	Midterm residents (3–10 years)	Long-term residents (over 10 years)
Number of wage earners in household				
None	35%	26%	35%	39%
One wage earner	31	30	33	30
Two wage earners	26	36	19	27
Three wage earners	6	6	11	2
Four or more	2	2	2	2
Average	1.1	1.3	1.1	1.0
Residence				
North of Ulmerton Road	43%	55%	44%	37%
South of Ulmerton Road	57	45	56	63
Daily newspapers read regularly				
St. Petersburg Times	83%	83%	82%	84%
Evening Independent	22	15	18	27
Clearwater Sun	23	23	28	20
Tampa Tribune	3	6	4	2
Other	3	4	2	3
None	4	3	3	5
Daily newspapers read yesterday				
St. Petersburg Times	67%	59%	68%	69%
Evening Independent	16	11	8	23
Clearwater Sun	18	18	21	15
Tampa Tribune	2	3	2	2
Other	1	1	—	2
None	15	21	13	14
Sunday newspaper read last Sunday				
St. Petersburg Times	74%	72%	70%	78%
Clearwater Sun	17	16	19	15
Tampa Tribune	1	2	2	—
Broadcast media				
Watched television yesterday:				
6:00–8:59 A.M.	8%	7%	6%	8%
9:00–10:59 A.M.	10	7	10	11
Noon–5:59 P.M.	34	37	27	35
6:00–8:59 P.M.	67	66	70	65
9:00–10:59 P.M.	61	63	63	59
11:00 P.M. or later	30	26	30	31
Don't know when watched	1	—	2	1
Did not watch TV yesterday	11%	13%	8%	13%
Subscriber to cable TV	11	11	14	9
Not cable TV subscriber	89	89	86	91

EXHIBIT 3   *(Continued)*

	Total Pinellas adults	By length of residency		
		Newcomers (2 years or less)	Midterm residents (3–10 years)	Long-term residents (over 10 years)
Listened to radio yesterday:				
6:00–8:59 A.M.	34%	39%	38%	30%
9:00–11:59 A.M.	28	28	29	26
Noon–5:59 P.M.	32	27	37	31
6:00–8:59 P.M.	15	13	14	16
9:00–10:59 P.M.	9	2	11	10
11:00 P.M. or later	7	2	10	8
Don't know when listened	2	2	1	3
Did not listen to radio yesterday	37	38	34	40
Checking account	90%	92%	91%	88%
Savings account	89%	82%	92%	90%
At bank	74	76	77	71
At savings and loan	43	34	38	51
At credit union	26	21	30	24
MasterCard or Visa	55%	56%	59%	52%
MasterCard	36	39	41	31
Visa	46	48	46	45
Other credit cards:				
American Express	10%	18%	13%	6%
Diners Club	3	4	4	2
Carte Blanche	2	2	3	2
Passport	18	11	22	18
Base	(501)	(93)	(175)	(233)

vides a recreational area with a relatively large amount of privacy. The large "community pool" concept was considered by Enterprise to be unappealing to many potential residents who were expected to value easy access to the pool's ambience more than its Olympic proportions. Resident parking was designed underneath the buildings to minimize the asphalt perspective so typical of high-density living environments.

Four-story and 12-story high-rise units, 2-story townhouses, and free-standing condominium villas were constructed. The units in greatest demand between 1975 and 1980 were villas. Many of them sold before construction was even begun. Two-bedroom units in the mid- and high-rise buildings were also very popular. One-bedroom high-rise units and townhouses were still avail-

able, although on a limited basis. The primary construction materials were stucco and wood, which blended with the Spanish architectural influence throughout the St. Petersburg area. As each building was completed, landscaping was carefully undertaken. The landscape architects working for Enterprise were sent to Disney World in Orlando to study plantings. Using similar shrubs which could adapt to conditions at Island Shores, sculptured shrubs and ever-blooming varieties of plants created a garden atmosphere. In 1981 alone, the cost of landscaping approached $1.5 million not counting individual building phases.

In 1975 the condominiums on Island Shores ranged in price from $42,000 to $50,000. The average market value of these units for resale in

1982 was $108,034. Smith's records showed that in December 1981, 70 units had been sold for a total of $7,562,389. Overall, new sales in 1980 were $32 million and sales in 1981 were $34 million. Prices for units still under construction in the Colony Beach portion of the project as of 1982 are shown in Exhibit 4.

Prices vary for the models depending on what floor they are on in the building and their relative exposure. Each unit has its own balcony, carpeting, a full set of appliances, and assigned parking. Two-bedroom–two-bath models had been the most in demand with different square footage and floor plans distinguishing Sevilla, Villa, and Barcelona models. Recent prices at Island Shores for villas had been in the range of $79,000 to $112,000, mid-rise units from $70,000 to $150,000, and high-rise units $95,000 to $166,000. Smith was concerned that as costs escalated the project was being priced out of the reach of most people in the market for vacation homes. While the number of one-bedroom units could be increased, in the future they did not appear to be the most desirable. He wondered if square footage in the two-bedroom–two-bath models could be reduced further or if the target market should be narrowed to primary home buyers rather than including vacation home buyers. This would have implications

EXHIBIT 4

Colony Beach (6-story)		
Model	Size	Price
Madrid	1 bedroom–1½ bath	$70,000–$ 92,900
Sevilla	2 bedroom–2 bath	$90,900–$125,000
Villa	2 bedroom–2 bath	$86,900–$107,000

Colony Beach (12-story)		
Model	Size	Price
Barcelona	2 bedroom–2 bath	$133,000–$162,000
Sevilla	2 bedroom–2 bath	$135,000–$166,000
Villa	2 bedroom–2 bath	$110,000–$117,000

for the physical design of the units and the required storage space. The Colony Beach area with a planned 1,200 units was not scheduled for completion until 1988. Based on previous experience, it was currently estimated that the 340 units, as yet unsold, would be fully occupied by the end of 1984.

COMPETITION

Smith knew from friends in the business and his own observations that competitors' sales had declined in recent months. While he felt that Island Shores was more desirable than similar high-rise condominium units located on the Intracoastal Waterway or the Mandalay Channel, he had collected pricing information hoping it would help him develop his marketing plan. In general, unit square footage ranges from 950 to 1,450 and the selling price from $77 to $115 per square foot. Exhibit 5 presents data for projects comparable to the units in Colony Beach.

It was clear that the development firms behind the competition were aggressive and unlikely to give market share to Island Shores without a battle. Smith didn't know for sure how they would respond to the recent market downturn, but he suspected it would be through strengthened promotional efforts. It was likely that the promotion budget for the Colony Beach community would have to be increased just to keep pace with the competition and maintain the build-out schedule for 1984–1985.

BUYER PROFILES

In 1975 the average age of Island Shores condominium buyers was 58. More recently, the average age had decreased to approximately 52 with many buyers in their late 40s. Smith was unsure how to interpret this trend. During the early stages of development, many retirees and investment buyers came from Illinois, Ohio, and Michigan. As economic conditions in these areas worsened, fewer and fewer newcomers seemed to come from the Midwest. To Smith's surprise,

EXHIBIT 5   COMPETITIVE PRICES

Marina Walk			
Model	Description	Price range	Units/building
J	2 bedroom–2 bath	$125,000–$150,000	20
K	2 bedroom–den–2 bath	$140,000–$165,000	20
L	2 bedroom–2 bath	$112,500–$142,000	20
M	1 bedroom–1 ½ bath	$ 90,000–$110,000	20
NE	2 bedroom–2 bath	$155,000–$185,000	20
NW	2 bedroom–2 bath	$167,500–$202,500	20

Sailfish Key			
Model	Description	Price range	Units/building
Sunfish	1 bedroom–1 bath	$ 97,900–$ 99,900	6
Yacht	1 bedroom–1 ½ bath	$110,000–$126,400	10
Corsair	2 bedroom–2 bath	$136,500–$149,500	12
Brigantine	2 bedroom–2 bath	$167,000–$175,000	6
Galleon	2 bedroom–2 bath*	$171,000–$179,500	10
Frigate	2 bedroom–2 bath–den	$215,000	2
Clipper	3 bedroom–2 ½ bath	$270,000	2

* Corner.

an increasing number of Europeans and South Americans were coming to Island Shores over any number of other condominium areas. It seemed that there were growing numbers of buyers from West Germany, France, Venezuela, Argentina, and Mexico. Each nationality tended to cluster together at Island Shores and to maintain close social ties. Whether this pattern would present problems in the long run for the total community was unclear.

A growing concern voiced by condominium residents was the issue of security. The small groupings of units actually facilitated security since neighbors knew each other's comings and goings and watched out for one another. The problem seemed to be caused by transients. When investment buyers rented their condominiums long distance, they could exercise very little control over their tenants. Similarly, management at Island Shores had scant information about

renters and no power to intervene unless explicit rules and regulations were being violated. Compared with other condominium developments in the St. Petersburg area the relative crime rate at Island Shores was very low. St. Petersburg itself had little crime compared with other major cities like Miami. Smith began to wonder whether the residents' perceptions of security were more at issue than the occasional burglary. Since one of the objectives of the management was to create an atmosphere of stability in a relaxing environment, any tensions caused by real or imagined security problems would have to be resolved.

Smith wondered if there was some way to encourage more permanent residents and fewer speculative investors to minimize the transient issue. If security personnel were increased, it was not clear whether the result would be to alarm or calm the residents and potential buyers. As it had turned out so far, some of the individuals sampling life at Island Shores by renting from absentee owners eventually purchased units on the island, although the number of such individuals was small.

MARKETING DECISIONS

Before Smith could recommend a marketing program, he needed to establish the basic target market and whether or not to continue building at Island Shores. Secondary data showed that more people leave New York for the South every year than from any other state. If this market was to be reached, however, there would be a lengthy process of registering Enterprise with New York state authorities in order to promote land sales to New York residents. Smith estimated that this process would take about a year. Enterprise was already registered in Michigan, Illinois, Indiana, Ohio, and Pennsylvania.

Another possible market consisted of people already in the St. Petersburg area. Considering the escalation of land values in recent years, many individuals could sell their existing property for twice its purchase price. In this event, the extensive amenity package at Island Shores, offering both quality golf and boating, might prove very attractive. Promotional efforts would certainly be reduced in reaching this market segment, Smith thought.

The international market seemed to be one of growing importance. If this market was actively pursued, the cost and methods of reaching buyers were difficult to determine. The long-run potential of this market was unclear. Smith became even more unsure as he thought about international currency fluctuations and the recent devaluation of the peso.

Expanding on the plan for development at Island Shores was by far the easiest plan of action to adopt in the short run, but Smith wondered if perhaps a lower amenity package with a golf course but no ocean access might not recapture the Midwest market. He knew of projects such as The Westside near Tampa Airport which con-

centrated on patio homes, both attached and detached, with prices from $45,000 to $70,000. The patio home concept was relatively new. There was no yard to speak of with the house, just the fenced patio. In some parts of the country they were known as zero-lot homes. They offered single-family housing with very low maintenance, which might prove appealing to retirees and young families. Patio homes had gained acceptance as starter homes for young couples, and there seemed to be encouragement to expand the target market.

A parcel of 200 acres just east of Bradenton in Manatee County was available for purchase which might prove suitable. With the lower yield per acres of about 6 units compared to 14 units per acre at Island Shores, Smith felt that there would be a potential 350 to 380 units, with the remaining land used for a golf course. While the price of the parcel was open to negotiation, the asking figure was $6 million. Smith had 10 days to pick up a 90-day option on this property. This would mean a commitment of $5,000.

If building was continued immediately at Island Shores, the mix of high-rise, mid-rise, and villas needed to be considered as did the two-bedroom and one-bedroom proportion. If prices were to be reduced, something would have to change. Existing plans called for development of the Ocean Watch portion of the project, which was a mid-rise building series with 50 two- and three-bedroom condominium units from $175,000 to $260,000. This was a 1982 estimate, but completion was not scheduled until 1985, when prices would certainly be higher. The current plan called for surface preparation of the area beginning in 1983. If the market became highly price sensitive, a potential option was to sell the units under a time-sharing arrangement. Smith knew that existing owners in Colony Beach had voiced objection to such a proposal earlier, but then again, Ocean Watch was a different situation. The target market for this type of vacation home would be a totally new one for Enterprise.

Smith realized that forecasting the demand for seasonal vacation homes versus year-round retirement homes was a critical issue that would strongly influence project location and physical design decisions. Until the best target market was identified, little in the way of price or promotional decisions could be resolved. The person interested in a $200,000 condominium would not likely be the same individual considering a $60,000 patio home.

Since the attributes and amenities of the projects would be very different, the promotional messages would also be very different. Smith was responsible for developing the overall marketing strategy for his projects and would make deci-sions on promotional strategy as well. A local advertising agency would handle the details of implementation, such as art, collateral materials, production, and media buying.

Smith felt strongly that when the real estate market picked up, the Tampa–St. Petersburg area would be among the first to lead the upturn. It was difficult to determine, however, which segments of the market represented the best opportunities for Enterprise. As Smith tried to evaluate the different opportunities facing him, he knew that it was going to be a long weekend. Next Wednesday's board meeting would come all too soon.

CASE 20

S.C. JOHNSON AND SON, LIMITED (R)

Four months ago, in November, George Styan had been appointed division manager of Innochem, at S.C. Johnson and Son, Limited[1] (SCJ), a Canadian subsidiary of S.C. Johnson & Son, Inc. Innochem's sole product line consisted of industrial cleaning chemicals for use by business, institutions, and government. George was concerned by the division's poor market share, particularly in Montreal and Toronto. Together, these two cities represented approximately 35 percent of Canadian demand for industrial cleaning chemicals, but less than 10 percent of Innochem sales. It appeared that SCJ distributors could not match the aggressive discounting practiced by direct-selling manufacturers in metropolitan markets.

Recently, George had received a rebate proposal from his staff designed to increase the distributor's ability to cut end-user prices by "sharing" part of the total margin with SCJ when competitive conditions demanded discounts of 30 percent or more off the list price to end users. George had to decide if the rebate plan was the best way to penetrate price-sensitive markets. Moreover, he wondered about the plan's ultimate impact on divisional profit performance. George had to either develop an implementation plan for the rebate plan or draft an alternative proposal to unveil at the Distributors' Annual Spring Convention, three weeks away.

THE CANADIAN MARKET FOR INDUSTRIAL CLEANING CHEMICALS

Last year, the Canadian market for industrial cleaning chemicals was approximately $100 million at end-user prices. Growth was stable at an overall rate of approximately 3 percent per year.

"Industrial cleaning chemicals" included all chemical products designed to clean, disinfect, sanitize, or protect industrial, commercial, and institutional buildings and equipment. The label

[1] Popularly known as Canadian Johnson Wax.

was broadly applied to general-purpose cleaners, floor maintenance products (strippers, sealers, finishes, and detergents), carpet cleaners and deodorizers, disinfectants, air fresheners, and a host of specialty chemicals such as insecticides, pesticides, drain cleaners, oven cleansers, and sweeping compounds.

Industrial cleaning chemicals were distinct from equivalent consumer products typically sold through grocery stores. Heavy-duty industrial products were packaged in larger containers and bulk and marketed directly by the cleaning chemical manufacturers or sold through distributors to a variety of end users. Exhibit 1 includes market segmentation by primary end user categories, including janitorial service contractors and the in-

EXHIBIT 1   SEGMENTATION OF THE CANADIAN
             MARKET FOR INDUSTRIAL CLEANING
             CHEMICALS

By end-user category	
End user	Percent total
Retail outlets	25%
Contractors	17
Hospitals	15
Industrial and office	13
Schools, colleges	8
Hotels, motels	6
Nursing homes	5
Recreation	3
Government	3
Fast food	2
Full-service restaurants	2
All others	1
Total	100% = $95 million

By product category	
Product	Percent total
Floor care products	40%
General-purpose cleaners	16
Disinfectants	12
Carpet care products	8
Odor control products	5
Glass cleaners	4
All others	15
Total	100% = $95 million

house maintenance departments of government, institutions, and companies.

BUILDING MAINTENANCE CONTRACTORS

In Canada, maintenance contractors purchased 17 percent of the industrial cleaning chemicals sold during 1980 (end-user price). The segment was growing at approximately 10 to 15 percent a year, chiefly at the expense of other end-user categories. *Canadian Business* reported, "Contract cleaners have made sweeping inroads into the traditional preserve of in-house janitorial staffs, selling themselves on the strength of cost efficiency."[2] Maintenance contract billings reached an estimated $1 billion last year.

Frequently, demand for building maintenance services was highly price-sensitive, and since barriers to entry were low (small capitalization, simple technology), competition squeezed contractor gross margins below 6 percent (before tax). Variable cost control was a matter of survival, and only products bringing compensatory labor savings could command a premium price in this segment of the cleaning chemical market.

A handful of contract cleaners did specialize in higher margin services to prestige office complexes, luxury apartments, art museums, and other "quality-conscious" customers. However, even contractors serving this select clientele did not necessarily buy premium cleaning supplies.

MAINTENANCE DEPARTMENTS

Last year, cleaning chemical sales to various government offices (federal, provincial, and local) approached $2 million. Typically, a government body solicited bids from appropriate sources by formally advertising for quotations for given quantities of particular cleaning chemicals. Although bid requests often name specific brands, suppliers were permitted to offer "equivalent substitutes." Separate competitions were held for each item and normally covered 12 months' supply with provision for delivery "as required."

[2] "Contract Cleaners Want to Whisk Away Ring-around-the-Office," *Canadian Business*, 1981, p. 22.

Contracts were frequently awarded solely on the basis of price.

Institutions

Like government bodies, most institutions were price-sensitive owing to restrictive budgets and limited ability to "pass on" expenses to users. Educational institutions and hospitals were the largest consumers of cleaning chemicals in this segment. School boards used an open-bid system patterned on the government model. Heavy sales time requirements and demands for frequent delivery of small shipments to as many as 100 locations were characteristic.

Colleges and universities tended to be operated somewhat differently. Dan Stalport, one of the purchasing agents responsible for maintenance supplies at the University of Western Ontario, offered the following comments:

> Sales reps come to UWO year 'round. If one of us (in the buying group) talks to a salesman who seems to have something—say, a labour-saving feature— we get a sample and test it. Testing can take up to a year. Floor covering, for example, has to be exposed to seasonal changes in weather and traffic.
>
> If we're having problems with a particular item, we'll compare the performance and price of three or four competitors. There are usually plenty of products that do the job. Basically, we want value— acceptable performance at the lowest available price.

Hospitals accounted for 15 percent of cleaning chemical sales. Procurement policies at University Hospital (UH), a medium-sized (450-bed) facility in London, Ontario, were typical. UH distinguished between "critical" and "noncritical" products. Critical cleaning chemicals (i.e., those significantly affecting patient health, such as phenolic germicide) could be bought only on approval of the staff microbiologist, who tested the "kill factor." This measure of effectiveness was regularly retested, and any downgrading of product performance could void a supplier's contract. In contrast, noncritical supplies—such as general-purpose cleaners, floor finishes, and the

like—were the exclusive province of Bob Chandler, purchasing agent attached to the Housekeeping Department. Bob explained that performance of noncritical cleaning chemicals was informally judged and monitored by the housekeeping staff:

> Just last year, for example, the cleaners found the floor polish was streaking badly. We (the Housekeeping Department) tested and compared five or six brands—all in the ballpark price-wise—and chose the best.

Business

The corporate segment was highly diverse, embracing both service and manufacturing industries. Large-volume users tended to be price-sensitive—particularly when profits were low. Often, however, cleaning products represented such a small percentage of the total operating budget that the cost of searching for the lowest cost supplier would be expected to exceed any realizable saving. Under such conditions, the typical industrial customer sought efficiencies in the purchasing process itself, for example, by dealing with the supplier offering the broadest mix of janitorial products (chemicals, paper supplies, equipment, etc.). Guy Breton, purchasing agent for Securitech, a Montreal-based security systems manufacturer, commented on the time economies of "one-stop shopping":

> With cleaning chemicals, it simply isn't worth the trouble to shop around and stage elaborate product performance tests. I buy all our chemicals, brushes, dusters, toweling—the works—from one or two suppliers...buying reputable brands from familiar suppliers saves hassles—back orders are rare, and Maintenance seldom complains.

DISTRIBUTION CHANNELS FOR INDUSTRIAL CLEANING CHEMICALS

The Canadian market for industrial cleaning chemicals was supplied through three main channels, each characterized by a distinctive set of strengths and weaknesses:

EXHIBIT 2   EFFECT OF GEOGRAPHY ON MARKET SHARE OF DIFFERENT DISTRIBUTION CHANNELS

Supplier type	Share nationwide	Share in Montreal and Toronto
Direct marketers	61%*	70%
Private label distributors	14	18
National brands distributors	25†	12

* Dustbane	17%	† SCJ	8%
G. H. Wood	31	N/L	4
All others	13	Airkem	3
		All others	10
Total	61%	Total	25%

a Distributor sales of national brands
b Distributor sales of private label products
c Direct sale by manufacturers

Direct sellers held a 61 percent share of the Canadian market for industrial cleaning chemicals, while the distributors of national brands and private label products held shares of 25 percent and 14 percent, respectively. Relative market shares varied geographically, however. In Montreal and Toronto, for example, the direct marketers' share rose to 70 percent and private labelers' to 18 percent, reducing the national brand share to 12 percent. The pattern, shown in Exhibit 2, reflected an interplay of two areas of channel differentiation, namely, discount capability at the end-user level and the cost of serving distant, geographically dispersed customers.

Distributor Sales of National Brand Cleaning Chemicals

National brand manufacturers—such as S.C. Johnson and Son, Airkem, and National Labs—produce a relatively limited range of "high-quality" janitorial products, including many special-purpose formulations of narrow market interest. Incomplete product range, combined with shortage of manpower and limited warehousing, made direct distribution unfeasible in most cases. Normally, a national brand company would negotiate with middlemen who handled a broad array of complementary products (equipment, tools, and supplies) by different manufacturers. "Bundling" of goods brought the distributors cost efficiencies in selling, warehousing, and delivery by spreading fixed costs over a large sales volume. Distributors were, therefore, better able to absorb the costs of after-hour emergency service, frequent routine sales and service calls to many potential buyers, and shipments of small quantities of cleaning chemicals to multiple destinations. As a rule, the greater the geographic dispersion of customers, and the smaller the average order, the greater the relative economies of distributor marketing.

Comparatively high gross margins (approximately 50 percent of wholesale price) enabled national brand manufacturers to offer distributors strong marketing support and sales training along with liberal terms of payment and freight plus low minimum order requirements. Distributors readily agreed to handle national brand chemicals, and in metropolitan markets, each brand was sold through several distributors. By the same token, most distributors carried several directly competitive product lines. George suspected that some distributor salesmen used national brands only to "lead" with and tended to offer private label whenever a customer proved price-sensitive, or a competitor handled the same national brand(s). Using an industry rule of thumb, George estimated that most distributors needed at least 20 percent gross margin on retail sales to cover sales commission of 10 percent, plus delivery and inventory expenses.

Distributor Sales of Private Label Cleaning Chemicals

Direct-selling manufacturers were dominating urban markets by aggressively discounting end-user prices—sometimes below the wholesale price national brand manufacturers charged their distributors. To compete against the direct seller, increasing numbers of distributors were adding low-cost private label cleaning chemicals to their product lines. Private labeling also helped differentiate a particular distributor from others carrying the same national brand(s).

Sizable minimum order requirements restricted the private label strategy to only the largest distributors. Private label manufacturers produced to order, formulating to meet low prices specified by distributors. The relatively narrow margins (30 to 35 percent wholesale price) associated with private label manufacturers were characteristically provided to distributors. Private label producers pared their expenses further still by requiring distributors to bear the cost of inventory and accept rigid terms of payment as well as delivery (net 30 days, FOB plant).

In addition to absorbing these selling expenses normally assumed by the manufacturer, distributors paid salesmen higher commission on private label sales (15 percent of resale) than on national brands (10 percent of resale). However, the incremental administration and selling expenses associated with private label business were more than offset by the differential savings on private label wholesale goods. By pricing private label chemicals at competitive parity with national brands, the distributor could enjoy approximately a 50 percent gross margin at resale list, while preserving considerable resale discount capability.

Private label products were seldom sold outside the metropolitan areas, where most were manufactured. First, the high costs of moving bulky, low-value freight diminished the relative cost advantage of private label chemicals. Second, generally speaking, it was only in metro areas where distributors dealt in volumes great enough to satisfy the private labeler's minimum order requirement. Finally, outside the city, distributors were less likely to be in direct local competition with others handling the same national brand, reducing value of the private label as a source of supplier differentiation.

For some very large distributors, backward integration into chemical production was a logical extension of the private labeling strategy. Recently, several distributors had become direct marketers through acquisition of captive manufacturers.

Direct Sale by Manufacturers of Industrial Cleaning Chemicals

Manufacturers dealing directly with the end user increased their gross margins to 60 to 70 percent of retail list price. Greater margins increased their ability to discount end-user price—a distinct advantage in the price-competitive urban marketplace. Overall, direct marketers averaged a gross margin of 50 percent.

Many manufacturers of industrial cleaning chemicals attempted some direct selling, but relatively few relied on this channel exclusively. Satisfactory adoption of a full-time direct-selling strategy required the manufacturer to match distributor's sales and delivery capabilities without sacrificing overall profitability. These conflicting demands had been resolved successfully by two types of companies: large-scale powder chemical manufacturers and full-line janitorial products manufacturers.

Large-Scale Powder Chemical Manufacturers Economies of large-scale production plus experience in the capital-intensive manufacture of powder chemicals enabled a few established firms, such as Diversey-Wyandotte, to dominate the market for powder warewash and vehicle cleansers. Selling through distributors offered these producers few advantages. Direct-selling expense was almost entirely commission (i.e., variable). Moreover, powder concentrates were characterized by comparatively high value-to-bulk ratios, and so could absorb delivery costs even where demand was geographically dispersed. Thus, any marginal benefits from using middlemen were more than offset by the higher margins (and associated discount capability) possible through direct distribution. Among these chemical firms, competition was not limited to price. The provision of dispensing and metering equipment was important, as was 24-hour servicing.

Full-Line Janitorial Products Manufacturers   These manufacturers offered a complete range of maintenance products, including paper supplies, janitorial chemicals, tools, and mechanical equipment. Although high margins greatly enhanced retail price flexibility, overall profitability depended on securing a balance of high- and low-margin business, as well as controlling selling and distribution expenses. This was accomplished in several ways, including:

Centering on market areas of concentrated demand to minimize costs of warehousing, sales travel, and the like
Increasing average order size, either by adding product lines which could be sold to existing customers, or by seeking new large-volume customers
Tying sales commission to profitability to motivate sales personnel to sell volume, without unnecessary discounting of end user price

Direct marketers of maintenance products varied in scale from established nationwide companies to hundreds of regional operators. The two largest direct marketers, G. H. Wood and Dustbane, together supplied almost a third of Canadian demand for industrial cleaning chemicals.

S.C. JOHNSON AND SON, LIMITED

S.C. Johnson and Son, Limited (SCJ), was one of 42 foreign subsidiaries owned by the U.S.-based multinational, S.C. Johnson & Son, Inc. It was ranked globally as one of the largest privately held companies. SCJ contributed substantially to worldwide sales and profits and was based in Brantford, Ontario, close to the Canadian urban markets of Hamilton, Kitchener, Toronto, London, and Niagara Falls. About 300 people worked at the head office and plant, while another 100 were employed in field sales.

Innochem Division

Innochem (Innovative Chemicals for Professional Use) was a special division established to serve corporate, institutional, and government customers of SCJ. The division manufactured an extensive line of industrial cleaning chemicals, including general-purpose cleansers, waxes, polishes, and disinfectants, plus a number of specialty products of limited application, as shown in Exhibit 3. Last year, Innochem sold $4.5 million of industrial cleaning chemicals through distributors and $0.2 million direct to end users. Financial statements for Innochem are shown in Exhibit 4.

INNOCHEM MARKETING STRATEGY

Divisional strategy hinged on reliable product performance, product innovation, active promotion, and mixed channel distribution. Steve Remen, market development manager, maintained that "customers know our products are of excellent quality. They know that the products will always perform as expected."

At SCJ, performance requirements were detailed and tolerances precisely defined. The Department of Quality Control routinely inspected and tested raw materials, work in process, packaging, and finished goods. At any phase during the manufacturing cycle, Quality Control was empowered to halt the process and quarantine suspect product or materials. SCJ maintained that nothing left the plant "without approval from Quality Control."

EXHIBIT 3   INNOCHEM PRODUCT LINE

Johnson Wax is a systems innovator. Frequently, a new product leads to a whole new system of doing things—a Johnson system of "matched" products formulated to work together. This makes the most of your time, your effort, and your expense. Call today and see how these Johnson systems can give you maximum results at a minimum cost.

For all floors except unsealed wood and unsealed cork

Stripper:	**Step-Off**—powerful, fast action
Finish:	**Pronto**—fast-drying, good gloss, minimum maintenance
Spray-buff solution:	**The Shiner Liquid Spray Cleaner or The Shiner Aerosol Spray Finish**
Maintainer:	**Forward**—cleans, disinfects, deodorizes, sanitizes

For all floors except unsealed wood and unsealed cork

Stripper:	**Step-Off**—powerful, fast stripper
Finish:	**Carefree**—tough, beauty, durable, minimum maintenance
Maintainer:	**Forward**—cleans, disinfects, deodorizes, sanitizes

For all floors except unsealed wood and unsealed cork

Stripper:	**Step-Off**—for selective stripping
Sealer:	**Over & Under-Plus**—undercoater-sealer
Finish:	**Scrubbable Step-Ahead**—brilliant, scrubbable
Maintainer:	**Forward**—cleans, disinfects, sanitizes, deodorizes

For all floors except unsealed wood and unsealed cork

Stripper:	**Step-Off**—powerful, fast stripper
Finish:	**Easy Street**—high solids, high gloss, spray buffs to a "wet look" appearance
Maintainer:	**Forward**—cleans, disinfects, deodorizes
	Expose—phenolic cleaner disinfectant

For all floors except unsealed wood and unsealed cork

Stripper:	**Step-Off**—for selective stripping
Sealer:	**Over & Under-Plus**—undercoater-sealer
Finishes:	**Traffic Grade**—heavy-duty floor wax
	Waxtral—extra tough, high solids
Maintainer:	**Forward**—cleans, disinfects, sanitizes, deodorizes

For all floors except asphalt, mastic and rubber tile
Use sealer and wax finishes on wood, cork, and cured concrete; sealer-finish on terrazzo, marble, clay, and ceramic tile; wax finish only on vinyl, linoleum, and magnesite.

Sealer:	**Johnson Gym Finish**—sealer and top-coater, cleans as it waxes
Wax finishes:	**Traffic Wax Paste**—heavy-duty buffing wax
	Beautiflor Traffic Wax—liquid buffing wax
Maintainers:	**Forward**—cleans, disinfects, sanitizes, deodorizes
	Conq-r-Dust-mop treatment
Stripper:	**Step-Off**—stripper for sealer and finish
Sealer:	**Secure**—fast-bonding, smooth, long-lasting
Finish:	**Traffic Grade**—heavy-duty floor wax
Maintainer:	**Forward or Big Bare**
Sealer-finish:	**Johnson Gym Finish**—seal and top-coater
Maintainer:	**Conq-r-Dust**—mop treatment

EXHIBIT 3   *(Continued)*

General cleaning:
   Break-Up—cleans soap and body scum fast
   Forward—cleans, disinfects, sanitizes, deodorizes
   Bon Ami—instant cleaner, pressurized or pump, disinfects
Toilet-urinals:
   Go-Getter—"Working Foam" cleaner
Glass:
   Bon Ami—spray-on foam or liquid cleaner
Disinfectant spray:
   End-Bac II—controls bacteria, odors
Air freshener:
   Glade—dewy-fresh fragrances
Spot cleaning:
   Johnson's Pledge—cleans, waxes, polishes
   Johnson's Lemon Pledge—refreshing scent
   Bon Ami Stainless Steel Cleaner—cleans, polishes, protects
All-purpose cleaners:
   Forward—cleans, disinfects, sanitizes, deodorizes
   Break-Up—degreaser for animal and vegetable fats
   Big Bare—heavy-duty industrial cleaner
Carpets:
   Rugbee Powder & Liquid Extraction Cleaner
   Rugbee Soil Release Concentrate—for prespraying and bonnet buffing
   Rugbee Shampoo—for power shampoo machines
   Rugbee Spotter—spot remover
Furniture:
   Johnson's Pledge—cleans, waxes, polishes
   Johnson's Lemon Pledge—refreshing scent
   Shine-Up Liquid—general purpose cleaning
Disinfectant spray air freshener:
   End-Bac II—controls bacteria, odors
   Glade—dewy-fresh fragrances
Glass:
   Bon Ami—spray-on foam or liquid cleaner
Cleaning:
   Break-Up—special degreaser designed to remove animal and vegetable fats
Equipment:
   Break-Up Foamer—special generator designed to dispense Break-Up cleaner
General cleaning:
   Forward—fast-working germicidal cleaner for floors, walls, all washable surfaces
   Expose—phenolic disinfectant cleaner
Sanitizing:
   J80 Sanitizer—liquid for total environmental control of bacteria; no rinse necessary if used as directed
Disinfectant spray:
   End-Brac II Spray—controls bacteria, odors
Flying insects:
   Bolt Liquid Airborne or **Pressurized Airborne**, P3610 through E10 dispenser
Crawling insects:
   Bolt Liquid Residual or **Pressurized Residual**, P3610 through E10 dispenser
   Bolt Roach Bait
Rodents:
   Bolt Rodenticide—for effective control of rats and mice, use with Bolt Bait Box

EXHIBIT 4   S. C. JOHNSON AND SON, LIMITED
Profit Statement of the Division
(In $ Thousands)

Gross sales:	$4,683
Returns	46
Allowances	1
Cash discounts	18
Net sales	4,617
Cost of sales	2,314
Gross profit:	2,303
Advertising	75
Promotions	144
Deals	—
External marketing services	2
Sales freight	292
Other distribution expenses	176
Service fees	184
Total direct expenses	873
Sales force	592
Marketing administration	147
Provision for bad debts	—
Research and development	30
Financial	68
Information resource management	47
Administration management	56
Total functional expenses	940
Total operating expenses	1,813
Operating profit	490

"Keeping the new product shelf well stocked" was central to divisional strategy, as the name Innochem implies. Products launched over the past three years represented 33 percent of divisional gross sales, 40 percent of gross profits, and 100 percent of growth.

Mixed Distribution Strategy

Innochem used a mixed distribution system in an attempt to broaden market coverage. Eighty-seven percent of divisional sales were handled by a force of 200 distributor salesmen and were serviced from 50 distributor warehouses representing 35 distributors. The indirect channel was particularly effective outside Ontario and Quebec. In part, the tendency for SCJ market penetration to increase with distances from Mon-treal and Toronto reflected Canadian demographics and the general economics of distribution. Outside the two production centers, demand was dispersed and delivery distances long.

Distributor salesmen were virtually all paid a straight commission on sales, and were responsible for selling a wide variety of products in addition to S.C. Johnson's. Several of the distributors had sales levels much higher than Innochem.

For Innochem, the impact of geography was compounded by a significant freight cost advantage: piggybacking industrial cleaning chemicals with SCJ consumer goods. In Ontario, for example, the cost of SCJ to a distributor was 30 percent above private label, while the differential in British Columbia was only 8 percent. On lower value products, the "freight effect" was even more pronounced.

SCJ had neither the salesmen nor the delivery capabilities to reach large-volume end users who demanded heavy selling effort or frequent shipments of small quantities. Furthermore, it was unlikely that SCJ could develop the necessary selling and distribution strength economically, given the narrowness of the division's range of janitorial products (i.e., industrial cleaning chemicals only).

THE REBATE PLAN

The key strategic problem facing Innochem was how best to challenge the direct marketer (and private label distributor) for large-volume, price-sensitive customers with heavy service requirements, particularly in markets where SCJ had no freight advantage. In this connection George had observed:

> Our gravest weakness is our inability to manage the total margin between the manufactured cost and consumer price in a way that is equitable and sufficiently profitable to support the investment and expenses of both the distributors and ourselves.

> Our prime competition across Canada is from direct-selling national and regional manufacturers.

EXHIBIT 5   DISTRIBUTORS' REBATE PRICING SCHEDULE: AN EXAMPLE USING PRONTO FLOOR WAX

Code: 04055
Product description: Pronto Fast-Dry Finish
Size: 209-Litre
Pack: 1

EFF DATE: 03-31-81
Resale Price List 71 613.750
Distributor Price List 74 349.837
Percent Markup on Cost with Carload and Rebate

Discount percent[1]	Quote (federal sales tax included)[2]	Rebate		2%		3%		4%		5%	
		Percent[3]	Dealers[4]	Net[5]	Markup percent[6]	Net	Markup percent	Net	Markup percent	Net	Markup percent
30.0	429.63	8.0	27.99	314.85	36	311.35	38	307.86	40	304.36	41
35.0	398.94	12.0	41.98	300.86	33	297.36	34	293.86	36	290.36	37
40.0	368.25	17.0	59.47	283.37	30	279.87	32	276.37	33	272.87	35
41.0	362.11	17.5	61.22	281.62	29	278.12	30	274.62	32	271.12	34
42.0	355.98	18.0	62.97	279.87	27	276.37	29	272.87	30	269.37	32
43.0	349.84	18.5	64.72	278.12	26	274.62	27	271.12	29	267.63	31
44.0	343.70	19.0	66.47	276.37	24	272.87	26	269.37	28	265.88	29
45.0	337.56	20.0	69.97	272.87	24	269.37	25	265.88	27	262.38	29
46.0	331.43	20.5	71.72	271.12	22	267.63	24	264.13	25	260.63	27
47.0	325.29	21.0	73.47	269.37	21	265.88	22	262.38	24	258.88	26
48.0	319.15	21.5	75.21	267.63	19	264.13	21	260.63	22	257.13	24
49.0	313.01	22.0	76.96	265.88	18	262.38	19	258.88	21	255.38	23
50.0	306.88	23.0	80.46	262.38	17	258.88	19	255.38	20	251.88	22
51.0	300.74	24.0	83.96	258.88	16	255.38	18	251.88	19	248.38	21
52.0	294.60	25.0	87.46	255.38	15	251.88	17	248.38	19	244.89	20
53.0	288.46	26.0	90.96	251.88	15	248.38	16	244.89	18	241.39	19
54.0	282.33	28.0	97.95	244.89	15	241.39	17	237.89	19	234.39	20
55.0	276.19	30.0	104.95	237.89	16	234.39	18	230.89	20	227.39	21

[1] Discount extended to end user on resale list price.
[2] Resale price at given discount level (includes federal sales tax).
[3] Percentage of distributor's price ($613.75) rebated by SCJ.
[4] Actual dollar amount of rebate by SCJ.
[5] Actual net cost to distributor after deduction of rebate and "carload" (quantity) discount.
[6] Effective rate of distributor markup.

EXHIBIT 6 EFFECT OF REBATE PLAN ON MANUFACTURER AND DISTRIBUTOR MARGINS: THE EXAMPLE OF ONE 209-LITRE PACK OF PRONTO FLOOR FINISH RETAILED AT 40 PERCENT BELOW RESALE LIST PRICE

I. Under present arrangements	
Base price to distributor	$349.84
Price to distributor, assuming 2 percent carload discount*	342.84
SCJ cost	174.92
∴SCJ margin	$167.92
Resale list price	613.75
Resale list price minus 40 percent discount	368.25
Distributor price, assuming 2 percent carload discount	342.84
∴Distributor's margin	$ 25.41
II. Under rebate plan	
Rebate to distributor giving 40 percent discount off resale price amounted to 17 percent distributor's base price	$ 59.47
SCJ margin (minus rebate)	108.45
Distributor margin (plus rebate)	84.88
III. Competitive prices	
For this example, George estimated that a distributor could buy a private brand "comparable" product for approximately $244.	

* A form of quantity discount, which, in this case, drops the price the distributor pays to SCJ from $349.84 to $342.84.

These companies control both the manufacturing and distribution gross margins. Under our pricing system, the distributor's margin at end user list on sales is 43 percent. Our margin (the manufacturing margin) is 50 percent on sales. When these margins are combined, as in the case of direct-selling manufacturers, the margin becomes 70 percent at list. This long margin provides significant price flexibility in a price-competitive marketplace. We must find a way to profitably attack the direct marketer's 61 percent market share.

The rebate plan George was now evaluating had been devised to meet the competition head-on. "Profitable partnership" between Innochem and the distributors was the underlying philosophy of the plan. Rebates offered a means to "share fairly the margins available between factory cost and consumer price." Whenever competitive conditions required a distributor to discount the resale list price by 30 percent or more, SCJ would give a certain percentage of the wholesale price back to the distributor. In other words, SCJ would sacrifice part of its margin to help offset a heavy end-user discount. Rebate percentages would vary with the rate of discount, following a set schedule. Different schedules were to be established for each product type and size. Exhibits 5, 6, and 7 outline the effect of rebates on both the unit gross margins of SCJ and individual distributors for a specific product example.

The rebate plan was designed to be applicable to new, "incremental" business only, not to existing accounts of the distributor. Distributors would be required to seek SCJ approval for end-user discounts of over 30 percent or more of resale list. The maximum allowable end-user discount would rarely exceed 50 percent. To request rebate payments, distributors would send SCJ a copy of the resale invoice along with a written claim. The rebate would then be paid within 60 days. Currently, Innochem sales were sold by distributors at an average discount of 10 percent off list.

Proponents of the plan maintained that the resulting resale price flexibility would not only enhance Innochem competitiveness among end

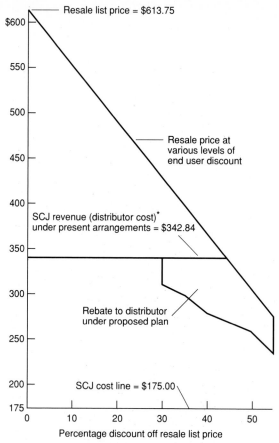

*Assuming 2 percent quantity ("Carload") discount off price to distributor.

EXHIBIT 7   EFFECT OF REBATE PLAN ON MANUFAC-
TURER AND DISTRIBUTOR MARGINS UNDER
PROPOSED REBATE PLAN: THE EXAMPLE OF
ONE 209-LITRE PACK OF PRONTO FAST-DRY
FINISH RETAILED AT 40 PERCENT BELOW RE-
SALE LIST PRICE*

users but also diminish distributor attraction to private label.

As he studied the plan, George questioned whether all the implications were fully understood and wondered what other strategies, if any, might increase urban market penetration. Any plan he devised would have to be sold to distributors as well as to corporate management. George had only three weeks to develop an appropriate action plan.

*Assuming 2 percent quantity ("carload") discount off price to distributor.

CSX SYSTEM

Edwin E. Edel, vice president for corporate communications of CSX Corporation, was experienced in "start-ups." He was the first public affairs director for railroads for the Department of Transportation and was involved in the early phases of AMTRAK. He was vice president for corporate communications at Seaboard Coast Line Industries, Inc., before accepting his present position on November 1, 1980. Two months later, Edel reflected upon this experience, as well as the issues and actions of the past few hectic months, and reviewed his newly completed corporate communications strategy for 1981. Was it an appropriate strategy for the complicated entity that was CSX?

BACKGROUND

CSX Corporation was created on November 1, 1980, through the merger of Chessie Systems, Inc., and Seaboard Coast Line Industries, Inc. Its major units were two rail systems—Chessie System Railroads and the Family Lines Rail System. These rails formed a north-south transportation system that covered 27,000 miles and 22 states

This case was prepared by Margo W. Hoopes under the direction of Professor Paul W. Farris, Colgate Darden Graduate School of Business Administration, University of Virginia. Copyright ©1982 by the Darden Graduate Business School Foundation, Charlottesville, Virginia.

(see Exhibit 1). The two rail systems accounted for approximately 95 percent of revenues and 85 percent of net income for CSX (Exhibit 2).

CSX also had holdings in natural resources, communications, aviation, and hotel services. CSX Minerals, Inc., held the mineral rights to over 677,000 acres of land in West Virginia, Kentucky, and Maryland, containing an estimated 1.3 billion tons of recoverable coal reserves. CSX Resources managed and developed extensive real estate holdings, directed corporate participation in oil and gas exploration, and managed 350,000 acres of forestry lands. The New River Company operated coal mines in West Virginia, while CSX Mineral Development Company assisted coal companies in acquiring coal reserves and in opening coal mines throughout the territory served by CSX's rail units. Florida Publishing Company, another CSX holding, published daily and weekly newspapers in Jacksonville and northern Florida, and the Greenbrier Resort Hotel was a wholly owned subsidiary of CSX. Beckett Aviation managed a fleet of executive aircraft and offered related services in nine major airports.

THE RAILROAD INDUSTRY AND CSX

The railroad industry was considered mature at best, characterized by low profit margins, a

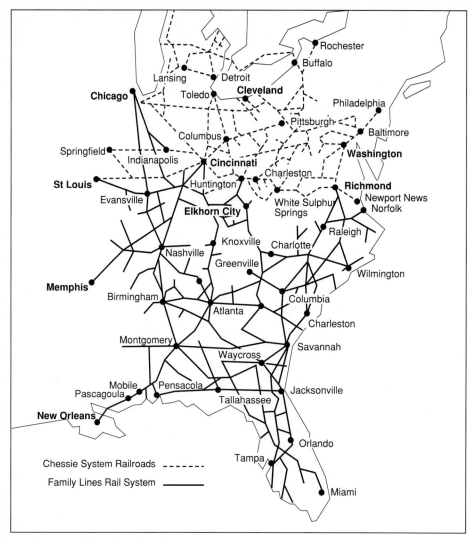

EXHIBIT 1   CSX CORPORATION

declining share of transportation services, and labor strife, all of which were brought to public attention with the well-publicized bankruptcy of Penn Central. Ironically, railroading was also perceived as a static, unexciting industry. Industry and management had recently been buoyed by a feeling of optimism, however, due to three factors: deregulation, mergers, and coal. The Harvey O. Staggers Rail Act of 1980 gave railroads the right to change rates within prescribed zones without seeking ICC permission. This right, for which the industry gave up its right to collective rate-making, allowed more aggressive competition in the marketplace.

CSX sold its rail services through a direct sales force that maintained close contact with customers. This sales force was organized into "commodity modules." There was a group of direct

EXHIBIT 2   CONSOLIDATED STATEMENT OF EARNINGS
Year Ended December 31
($ Millions)

	1980	1979
Operating revenue:		
Merchandise	$2,948.4	$2,792.4
Coal	1,357.3	1,039.3
Other	191.3	195.3
Transportation	4,497.0	4,027.0
Nontransportation	344.4	326.9
Total operating revenue	4,841.4	4,353.9
Operating expenses:		
Labor and fringe benefits	2,063.1	1,974.7
Materials, supplies, and other	1,395.2	1,202.9
Locomotive fuel	462.2	334.0
Depreciation	158.0	160.7
Transportation	4,078.5	3,672.3
Nontransportation	255.0	253.5
Total operating expenses	4,333.5	3,925.8
Income from operations	507.9	428.1
Other income—net	37.9	46.9
Interest expense	180.7	185.8
Earnings before income taxes	365.1	289.2
Income taxes	83.5	52.1
Earnings for the year	$ 281.6	$ 237.1
Earnings per share*	$7.13	$6.12

*Primary earnings per share are based on 41,204,845 shares for the year, 1981; 39,498,853 shares for the year, 1980; and 38,742,897 for the year, 1979.

salespeople devoted to the paper and lumber industry, another dedicated to "piggyback" services, and still another for the coal industry.

When standard services were required by the customer, the prices were determined by merely referring to the published tariff rates. Other arrangements were quite common, however. For example, contract rates were negotiated for a fixed time and predetermined amount to be shipped, either in trainload or less-than-trainload quantities.

The newly favorable atmosphere for mergers created opportunities for such systems as CSX. The merger made possible more efficient routing of traffic by eliminating high-cost short hauls and frequent switching. Equally important was the creation of a more competitive service and what this meant to marketing and sales.

As a result of energy conservation, greater use of gas by utilities, and environmental regulations, there had been little or no growth in coal traffic in recent years. But industry sources predicted that export coal would be a vital source of new business, and European markets promised continuing strong demand for coal. For a major coal hauler, such as CSX, this prediction was particularly significant. Export coal yielded a higher revenue per ton at less expense since it was moved in trainload lots from the mines to port.

The major constraint on greater export coal

volume was inadequate port facilities. These delay-causing inadequacies, which might lead European users to look elsewhere for coal, inspired efforts by railroads, mining companies, and the government to increase port facilities. Chessie reopened Pier 15 at Newport News in August 1980, and construction was begun on three new facilities in Baltimore and Newport News. Additionally, four coal companies agreed to build a $60 to $100 million coal export facility in Portsmouth, Virginia.

THE MERGER

The merger that created CSX placed it in a favorable position in several respects. The 27,000 miles of rail, which connected Michigan with the southern tip of Florida, allowed CSX to offer the better and cheaper service of a single system while enjoying the savings and efficiency obtained from the merger. Management believed that this efficiency would lead to improved operating revenues and corporate earnings. CSX was dominant in key natural resources, most significantly as a major carrier and holder of reserves of coal, which promised to become more and more important. In addition to its coal development activities and mineral rights, CSX was the leading carrier of coal in the United States.

The real test of the merger's success would be whether CSX could compete successfully for new traffic. With its 27,000 miles of rail, CSX had the potential to originate and terminate a lot of traffic formerly shared with other lines. A single system reduced or eliminated paperwork, crew changes, locomotive changes, sorting of cars, delays, expense, and sharing of revenue. As a major Seaboard customer said, "The fewer problems that railroads have with the division of revenue and the more shipments they can haul on a single-line basis, the better opportunity I have to get improved service and more competitive rates."

CSX expected $70 million in annual operating savings by the third year. Efficient utilization of assets was expected to produce rapid benefits.

For example, Louisville & Nashville, a subsidiary line of Seaboard, was frequently short of locomotives and hopper cars. Chessie had a predicted surplus of 30 diesels, which were put at L&N's disposal along with the Chessie-operated hopper car plant in Kentucky.

Southern Railway estimated that it would lose $50 million a year in freight business to CSX because of the merger.[1] In addition, CSX expected the efficiency and resulting lower rates not only to convince shippers to switch business from competitive rail lines but also to capture freight business from truck lines. Growth was anticipated in refrigerated shipments, steel shipments, and grain shipments. Both railroads, however, saw the greatest growth possibility in an operation known as *piggybacking*—hauling of truck trailers and containers on flatcars in high-speed trains over long distances, such as from Jacksonville, Florida, to Philadelphia. As the cost of diesel fuel increased, piggybacking became ever more attractive to trucker lines.

The rest of the railroad industry was well aware of the benefits of merger and single-system service. A merger of the Norfolk and Western Railway and the Southern Railway was on the horizon. The merger would probably be approved within the next two years, and CSX would face a direct and possibly stronger competitor in its own regions.

Certain aspects of the merger and the resulting corporation complicated this positive situation, however. Early in the merger discussions it was agreed by Chessie and Seaboard to preserve the identities and general operating independence of each company. The merger was viewed and accepted as a 50/50 partnership. CSX was created by Hays T. Watkins and Prime F. Osborn III, chief executive officers of the two companies, without incurring conversion costs, without affecting the current identities in the marketplace, and with little disruption in day-to-day operations. Even the new name, CSX Corporation, began as a deliber-

---

[1] "CSX: A Gradual Consolidation," *Railway Age*, October 13, 1980.

ately nondescript, temporary designation. It was adopted because it had been well received prior to and during the ICC merger hearings and because, according to President Hays T. Watkins, "Prime [Prime F. Osborn, chairman of CSX] and I thought it up and like it because it's so anonymous and nondistinctive—the way we want the parent to be in relation to its operating railroads."

The economy and logic of this sort of transition were apparent. There were attendant disadvantages, however, such as the inconsistency of a two-part identity with the image and benefits of the corporate entity; the complications of a multifaceted identity for marketing and communications; the confusion of a two-part identity for customer perceptions; and the added costs of advertising, promotion, printing, etc.

The seriousness of the identity issue became more obvious when the systems were examined in detail. Both Seaboard and Chessie had evolved over several decades and possessed complex identities composed of their many different elements (see Exhibit 3). For example, the line in Nashville was the L&N Railroad, not CSX or even Family Lines. The Baltimore Railroad was the B&O, not Chessie. The creation of CSX added another layer of complexity to this multifaceted entity. Yet the strength of CSX, its short- and long-term potential for increased growth and profitability, was created by the very fact of its new corporate identity.

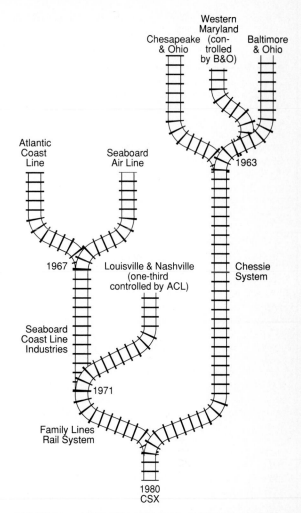

EXHIBIT 3   HOW THE CSX RAIL SYSTEM CAME TO-GETHER

THE ROLE OF COMMUNICATIONS

Edwin Edel outlined his philosophy of how his function would relate to the communications officers on the company level in an early memo. An initial interim plan covering the period from November 1, 1980, to the end of the fiscal year on December 31, 1980, dealt, of necessity, with start-up issues of a new name, merger details, new headquarters, etc. (see Exhibit 4).

The overall objective of the start-up corporate communications effort was to begin to achieve the recognition, understanding, and support that

CSX needed from all of its publics in order to operate successfully as a new business entity. Edel identified several key goals in reaching this objective. They included developing an accurate picture of CSX as the parent company of Chessie and SCL; conveying a reputation for success, good management, even better service, and responsible civic behavior; fostering broad understanding of the benefits of the new corporation and its subsidiaries; and building confidence in both its operations and its people.

EXHIBIT 4   L&N MERGER INTO CSX TO IMPROVE FREIGHT SERVICE
By Ben Eubanks

Louisville and Nashville Railroad's new ability to speed freight to large Northern cities could attract more new industry to Tennessee, L&N officials say.

On Nov. 1, L&N became part of one of the world's largest privately-owned railroads, when its parent corporation, Seaboard Coast Line Industries, Inc., and the Chessie System, Inc., merged to form CSX Corp.

CSX will be the nation's No. 1 railroad with assets of more than $7.4 billion and 75,000 employees. It will be No. 2 in track length with 27,000 miles of rail in 22 states stretching between Miami, Fla., and Ontario, Canada.

Direct service will also be available between cities such as Detroit, Chicago, Pittsburgh, St. Louis, Birmingham, and New Orleans. Before the merger, freight traveling from these cities often had to be handled by several different rail services.

Seaboard, concentrated in the Southeast, was comprised of railways such as L&N, Clinchfield and Georgia Railroad called the Family Lines. Chessie's concentration is in the Northeast and has railroads such as the Baltimore and Ohio, Chesapeake and Ohio, and Western Maryland.

Hooper said L&N customers will now get quicker delivery of freight going north since the Cincinnati gateway will be avoided. Before the merger, Seaboard's track ended at Cincinnati and the cars were turned over to other railways.

Hooper said switching through the Cincinnati yard, operated by Con Rail, usually takes two or three days now because of the vast number of railcars passing through the city.

"If we can get through Cincinnati without wasting two days in the gateway, we are improving everybody's service," Hooper said.

CSX will be using C&O's (Chessie) Stephens Yard in Cincinnati for its Piggyback Service which will be expanded with three of the six new routes CSX is planning coming through Nashville. L&N already operates two lines: St. Louis to Atlanta and Chicago to Birmingham.

Hooper said the economics of the CSX line will make it more competitive with trucking lines and may return some business lost several years ago.

"One thing trucks always got us on was quicker delivery and better scheduling," Hooper said. "But these customers will find that with the increasing gasoline and fuel costs and with quicker service time the costs of railroads will have become more attractive."

Source: The Tennessean, November 16, 1980.

RAIL MERGER CREATES NO. 2 TRANSPORTATION COMPANY IN U.S.
By Carole Shifrin
Washington Post Staff Writer

Take the 50 largest transportation companies in the 1980 Fortune Double 500 Directory. Cross off number 11—Seaboard Coast Line Industries—and number 13—Chessie System. Make a new entry: number 2—CSX Corp.—just between Trans World Corp., number 1, and UAL, Inc., old number 2.

The merger of Chessie and Seaboard into CSX was formally consummated this month, less than two years after their joint application to the Interstate Commerce Commission.

Along with the increased competition that is expected to come from rail deregulation legislation, the merger is just one of many developments that is expected to make the rail industry more dynamic than it has been in decades.

Source: Washington Post.

RAILROAD MERGER BECOMES FINAL

The merger of Chessie System, Inc., and Seaboard Coast Line Industries, Inc., into CSX Corporation was formally consummated Nov. 1 as members of the new CSX board of directors met for the first time in Richmond, Va.

Prime F. Osborn III, chairman, and Hays T. Watkins, president, termed the meeting "a significant milestone" in the history of the railroad industry. "Our forefathers long dreamed of a strong north-south railroad system that would link the industrial Northeast with the Southeast, tying together these two vital areas of the country. Today that dream is a reality," they said.

Source: Wilmington Morning Star, November 9, 1980.

Edel's start-up program contained three major elements. First, the new corporate identity required a logo that was a strong and positive symbol communicating the essence of a well-managed company that united two strong and complementary railroads and included a group of diverse nonrail companies. The logo was to reflect unity, strength, innovation, and diversity, and be adaptable to a wide range of uses. It must fit when used in conjunction with subsidiary materials, such as Chessie Railroad advertising.

Second, the advertising of the new corporation was to define and explain the corporation to important audiences. The message was to be geared to the business and financial communities, and to emphasize innovation, efficiency, improved operating ratios, and profitability. The advertising was to use both reach and frequency and maintain a continuity in its "look." There was to be an introductory and a sustaining phase.

The third element of Edel's initial plan was a public relations program to disseminate basic information on the new corporation to interested publics. While all required much of the same information, each needed a different treatment as to emphasis and means of presentation. These publics included the following:

1 Financial and business press
2 Shareholders
3 Analysts
4 Investors
5 Employees
6 Trade press
7 General print media
8 Electronic media
9 Legislative and executive branches of federal government
10 State and local governments in states served

Next in determining his strategy for 1981, Edel attempted to balance the complicated issues created by the merger with the goals of the new corporation. The role of corporate communications was to create a recognition of CSX as a purposeful, future-directed, and profit-oriented corporation in the business and financial community. The external analyses of CSX available to the financial community predicted growth and increased profitability,[2] and the corporate

advertising program was designed to develop a high and positive awareness of CSX. Edel's objective was to enhance CSX's image with both current and potential shippers and the financial community. He had researched the effects of corporate advertising on stock prices, and he believed that the research results supported the idea that an advertising campaign could have a measurable impact (see Exhibit 5).

Edwin Edel formulated some specific objectives for corporate advertising in 1981. Taking advantage of the interest inherent in being "new" and the opportunity to take the initiative rather than the defensive, he intended to focus on the following:

Informing individual investors about CSX and its increased importance in the economy

Establishing increased awareness to facilitate future acquisitions

Supporting the rail and other units of CSX through positive association with the CSX name

Creating awareness and understanding among the "influentials"—that small and exclusive group of security analysts, brokers, investment bankers, and financial writers and editors

The results of achieving these objectives would be:

To establish CSX as a dominant U.S. corporation, competing successfully with consumer-oriented "nifty-fifty" corporations for investment dollars and management talents.

To inform analysts who do not specialize in rails, assist those with less research time and those who do not favor conglomerates while expanding beyond the "railroad holding company" image.

---

[2] Examples of such analyses:
"Superior market performance is expected from CSX Corporation as the economy strengthens and the newly formed system attracts greater volume."

"From a valuation standpoint, CSX's P/E ratio of 6.3 for 1980 represents a 36 percent discount to the Standard & Poor's 500. With a favorable outlook for 1981, the stock would appear undervalued at current levels."
"Railroad deregulation, allowing for upward revision of rates and a higher level of coal export loadings, leads to projected increases in 1981 earnings."
"The major port expansions under way both at Chessie and Seaboard indicate that CSX should garner more than its share in the increased coal shipments in future years."

EXHIBIT 5   EFFECTS OF CORPORATE ADVERTISING

Is Financial/Corporate Advertising Effective?

A survey among professional money managers who are readers of *Barron's* indicated the following:*

1.   81 percent said they take financial/corporate advertising seriously and, as a result, look into a company's investment qualifications.
2.   78 percent said their investigations led them to purchase securities.

Does Corporate Advertising Affect Stock Prices?

A three-year study by E. P. Schonfeld and J. H. Boyd, Jr., professors of advertising and finance, Northwestern University, led to the following conclusions:

1.   Corporate advertising has a statistically significant positive effect on stock prices.
2.   Based on three years' data, the impact of corporate advertising seems greatest in an up market.
3.   Firms that could report *stable* earnings growth had more favorable results from their corporate advertising than those that could not.

   A study among some 600 upper-echelon executives across the country revealed the following:†

1.   *47 percent* of those who had *not* been exposed to a financial corporate campaign had a favorable general impression of the average company.
2.   *63 percent*, on the other hand, who had been exposed had a favorable opinion, showing a "lift" factor of 33 percent.

   A three-year study, analyzing 460 major U.S. corporations, revealed the following:‡

1.   Corporate advertising adds about 4 percent per share to the price of a corporation's stock.
2.   About 55 percent of a corporation's stock price is determined by economic performance, such as revenue and earnings growth, dividends, net sales, debt/equity ratio, etc.
3.   About 40 percent is due to market influences or company disasters.
4.   There is approximately a 30-to-1 return on corporate advertising expenditures.

---

*Source: Erodos & Morgan, Inc.   †Source: Time, Inc., study.   ‡Source: Dr. Jaye S. Niefield, executive vice president, Independent Research.

To support the selling efforts by creating a recognizable name for prospective rail service customers.

   To anticipate and preempt the competition. Norfolk/Western and Southern would be a reality in eighteen months at the most, and the lead time would be used to establish CSX's single-system service.

   Edwin Edel carefully reviewed the results of an awareness study (Exhibit 6) and telephone interviews (Exhibit 7). He glanced once more through his plan for 1981–82 (see Addendum). Now, as before, the fundamental communications problem centered on the following question: If we must preserve the two railroad identities, how do we "sell" a completely new, complicated corporate identity with clarity and bring simplicity to this maze?

EXHIBIT 6   STUDY OF *THE WALL STREET JOURNAL* **SUBSCRIBERS**

Method and Sample

One thousand (1,000) survey forms were sent to *W.S.J.* subscribers randomly selected from the newspaper's files. These names were provided on self-adhesive labels and selected by zip code from the top ten (10) major markets. The questionnaire addressed the following areas:

1. Name recognition
2. Areas of business activity

Summary of Findings

Table 1   Corporate Awareness

		Position		
	Total	CEO	Other top management	All other
Base: Total respondents	(269)	(62)	(85)	(104)
	%	%	%	%
CSX	18	15	22	19
Esmark	64	58	72	69
TRW	86	92	95	88
PepsiCo	84	79	95	89

Table 2   Corporate Image

	Percentage who rate company as excellent or good			
	CSX	Esmark	TRW	PepsiCo
Base: Aware of company	(48)	(171)	(231)	(225)
	%	%	%	%
Progressiveness	35	47	68	63
Earnings record	25	23	38	37
Potential investment	29	26	44	40

Table 3   Lack of Familiarity Among Respondents
Who Claim Awareness of Company

	Base: aware of company	Unable to rate company
		%
CSX	(48)	(46)
Esmark	(171)	40
TRW	(231)	26

Table 4   Advertising Awareness Among Those Aware of Company

	Base: Aware of company	Position			
		Total	CEO	Other top management	All other
		%	%	%	%
CSX	(48)	31	44	26	30
Esmark	(171)	73	68	75	77
TRW	(231)	84	81	86	85
PepsiCo	(225)	79	74	86	74

Table 5   Familiarity with CSX's Business

Base: Aware of CSX	Total (48)
	%
Railroads	63
Natural resources	35
Coal mining	25
Resorts	23
Publishing	15
Aviation	13
None of the above	15
Don't know	17

EXHIBIT 7   STUDY OF REGISTERED REPRESENTATIVES

The objectives of this study were:

To establish benchmark data on awareness of CSX Corporation among a limited number of registered representatives.

To provide guidelines for developing the design and specifications of further research.

Method/Sample

Data were collected via telephone interviews with 100 registered representatives from East and Midwest United States.

Awareness of CSX

Q# 1: "I'm going to read down a list of companies. As I read each name, please tell me whether or not you are familiar with the company."

Base total	Familiar with company percentage 100
Esmark, Inc.	93
CSX Corporation	44
IC Industries, Inc.	68
NWS Corporation	11
Beckett	24
TRW, Inc.	91
PepsiCo, Inc.	98
Burlington Northern, Inc.	98
None	1

Companies' Progressiveness

Q# 2: "I'm going to read down the same list of companies. This time, as I read each name, please tell me how you would rate the company in terms of its progressiveness. Please rate each company either excellent, good, only fair, or poor on progressiveness."

	Base total	Excellent	Good	Only fair	Poor	Don't know/ no opinion
Esmark, Inc.	(100)	21	44	14	3	18
CSX Corporation	(100)	4	25	10	—	61
IC Industries, Inc.	(100)	13	28	17	1	41
NWS Corporation	(100)	1	6	6	—	87
Beckett	(100)	3	8	7	—	82
TRW, Inc.	(100)	32	40	10	—	18
PepsiCo, Inc.	(100)	31	35	20	2	12
Burlington Northern, Inc.	(100)	32	41	15	—	12

EXHIBIT 7 *(Continued)* STUDY OF REGISTERED REPRESENTATIVES

Earnings Records of Companies

Q# 3: "Next, I'd like to ask your opinion of the earnings record of each of these companies. As I read each name, please tell me whether you consider the company's earnings record to be excellent, good, only fair, or poor."

	Base total	Excellent	Good	Only fair	Poor	Don't know/ no opinion
Esmark, Inc.	(100)	12	36	17	3	32
CSX Corporation	(100)	4	18	7	1	70
IC Industries, Inc.	(100)	7	31	11	—	51
NWS Corporation	(100)	2	3	4	—	91
Beckett	(100)	1	8	2	2	87
TRW, Inc.	(100)	27	37	5	—	31
PepsiCo, Inc.	(100)	28	28	18	2	24
Burlington Northern, Inc.	(100)	25	34	15	—	26

Companies' Qualities as an Investment

Q# 4: "Now, I'd like to ask you to classify the common stock of each company in terms of its quality as an investment. As I read each name, please tell me whether you consider the company's stock suitable for growth-oriented portfolios, suitable for income-oriented portfolios, suitable for speculative portfolios, or not suitable for any portfolio at this time."

	Base total	Growth oriented	Income oriented	Speculative	Not suitable	Don't know/ no opinion
Esmark, Inc.	(100)	58	7	8	5	22
CSX Corporation	(100)	27	9	2	1	61
IC Industries, Inc.	(100)	39	11	8	1	41
NWS Corporation	(100)	5	3	4	1	87
Beckett	(100)	10	2	8	—	80
TRW, Inc.	(100)	70	5	1	1	23
PepsiCo, Inc.	(100)	67	16	5	2	10
Burlington Northern, Inc.	(100)	56	21	5	3	15

Number of Years as a Registered Representative

Q# 7: "How long have you been a registered representative?"

Base total	Percent 100
Less than one year	13
1–5 years	35
6–10 years	16
11–15 years	17
16–20 years	8
21–25 years	6
26+ years	5

Number of Industries Followed

Q# 8: "How many industries do you follow regularly as part of your job?"

Base total	Percent 100
1–5	36
6–10	26
11–15	7
16–20	2
21–25	—
26+	6
No answer	18
None	3
Don't know	2

Number of Companies Followed

Q# 9: "In all, about how many companies do you regularly follow as part of your job?"

Base total	Percent 100
Less than 10	19
11–20	25
21–30	13
31–40	7
41–50	11
51–100	8
101+	7
No answer	7
Don't know	3

ADDENDUM

CSX CORPORATION: 1981–1982

Media Objectives

1 Direct advertising to a target audience consisting of (1) the financial community and (2) the broad business community.

2 Provide for both a high-impact introductory campaign designed to build awareness quickly and a strong base-level continuity campaign designed to sustain awareness levels throughout 1982.

Media Strategy

1 During the Introductory Campaign utilize a combination of financial magazines, business publications, newsweeklies, and selected network television news programs to effectively and efficiently reach large numbers of the target audience.

2 After the introductory awareness effort, utilize a shorter list of publications selected to sustain advertising exposure primarily among the financial community and owners of corporate stock.

CSX Print Media

The following publications are recommended to effectively and efficiently reach CSX target audiences:

Professional investors	Individual investors
Barron's	*The Wall Street Journal* (E&MW)
Financial World	*New York Times*
Institutional Investors	*Dun's Review*
Financial Analysts' Journal	*Forbes*
	Fortune
	Business Week
	Money
	Time
	Newsweek
	U.S. News & World Report

These publications will provide a monthly reach of 80 percent of all people who own securities. Frequency of exposure will be 2 to 3 times per month. Total reach 85 percent: frequency 6 to 7 times.

Media Budget Summary

	4th quarter 1981	1981/2 (12 months)
CSX Corporation:		
Magazines	$1,164,000	$2,868,200
Television	307,000	307,500
	1,471,000	3,175,700
Freight:		
Magazines	118,300	631,200
Industrial:		
Magazines	13,700	195,000
	1,603,000	4,001,900
Production	200,000	300,000
	1,803,000	4,301,900

1981–1982 Corporate Media Plan

I. *Magazines*

A. *Financial Publications*—These magazines are recommended during both the introductory and the sustaining campaigns. Each emphasizes the professional investor.

	Circulation	Approximate unit cost	1981 schedule	
			Number of ads	Total cost
Barron's (weekly)	262,000	$ 6,061*	3	$18,182
Financial Analysts' Journal (bimonthly)	19,000	11,236	1	11,236
Financial World (semimonthly)	100,000	11,385	2	22,770
Institutional Investor (monthly)	32,000	15,985	2	31,970
Registered Rep (monthly)	37,000	9,120	1	9,120
				$93,278

* Full-page black and white; all others 4-color spreads.

The above publications, plus three additional magazines, are recommended during 1982 to sustain strong exposure among this primary target.

	Circulation	Approximate unit cost	1982 schedule	
			Number of ads	Total cost
Barron's (weekly)	262,000	$ 6,061	12*	$ 72,732
Financial Analysts' Journal (bimonthly)	19,000	11,236	6	67,416
Financial World (semimonthly)	100,000	11,385	12	136,620
Institutional Investor (monthly)	32,000	19,125	6	114,750
Registered Rep (monthly)	37,000	9,120	6	54,720
Fortune (financial) (bimonthly)	160,000	23,012	12	276,144
Pensions & Investments (26/year)	32,000	6,411†	6	38,490
Survey of Wall Street Research (bimonthly)	20,500	1,485*	6	8,190
				$769,782

* Full-page black and white.
† Half-page 4-color spread; all others 4-color full-page spreads.

B. *Business Publications*—These magazines are also recommended during both the introductory and sustaining campaigns. Each is a major business publication long established and read by the broad business community.

	Circulation	Approximate unit cost	1981 schedule	
			Number of ads	Total cost
The Wall Street Journal	1,325,000	$20,500* 30,625†	2	$163,550
Dun's Business (monthly)	285,000	15,230	2	30,460
Forbes (biweekly)	690,000	43,677	2	87,354
Fortune (26/year)	670,000	52,382	1	52,382
Business Week (weekly)	770,000	53,866	3	161,598
				$495,344

* 888-line OpEd.
† Full-page black and white; all others 4-color spreads.

With one exception (*Fortune*, financial, rather than full-run), each of these publications is recommended during 1982 to continue advertising emphasis directed to the corporate business executive and stockholder. In addition, *Harvard Business Review* is recommended as an efficient means of supplementing the 1982 effort.

	Circulation	Approximate unit cost	1982 schedule	
			Number of ads	Total cost
The Wall Street Journal	1,325,000	$34,625*	24	$ 834,000
Dun's Business (monthly)	285,000	15,230	6	91,380
Forbes (biweekly)	690,000	46,715	6	280,290
Business Week (weekly)	770,000	57,500	9	517,500
Harvard Business Review (6/year)	225,000	12,190	3	36,570
				$1,759,740

* Full-page black and white; all others 4-color spreads.

C. *Introductory Emphasis Publications*—To build awareness quickly, additional publications are recommended to be discontinued after the first few months of the advertising effort. These publications broaden the campaign's exposure considerably to reach not only the professional investor and the corporate business community but the individual investor as well. These "emphasis" vehicles are judged important to enhance the campaign's overall visibility.

	Circulation	Approximate unit cost	1981 schedule	
			Number of ads	Total cost
New York Times (daily)	930,000	$ 18,432*	3	$ 55,296
Money (monthly)	875,000	42,389	1	42,389
Time (top management)	590,000	49,784	1	49,784
Newsweek (weekly)	2,950,000	127,116	2	254,232
U.S. News & World Report (weekly)	2,000,000	86,705	2	173,410
				$575,111

* Full-page black and white; all others 4-color spreads.

During the first quarter of 1982, the upper-management demographic editions of the three newsweeklies are recommended to efficiently extend the high visibility introductory print effort.

	Circulation	Approximate unit cost	1982 schedule	
			Number of ads	Total cost
Time (top management)	590,000	$49,784	2	$ 99,568
Newsweek (executive)	575,000	49,467	2	98,934
U.S. News (blue chip)	450,000	37,471	2	74,942
Washington Post (daily)	618,100	9,980**	4	39,920
				$313,364

**Half-page black and white; all others 4-color spreads.

II. *Television*

Like the introductory emphasis publications, television is recommended as a supplementary medium to help build awareness quickly and en-hance the visibility of the CSX corporate aware-ness advertising campaign. The following sched-ule was placed during 1981:

Network/program:	Estimated 25–54 rating	Day	Time	Number of announce-ments	1981 total cost
ABC/Issues & Answers	2.0	Sun	12 N–12:30 P.M.	2	$20,470
ABC/This Wk w/Brinkley	2.0	Sun	11:30 A.M.–12:30 P.M.	3	30,705
ABC/World News Tonight	7.3	M–F	6:30–7 P.M.	1	40,235
CBS/AM News	1.0	M–F	7:30–9 A.M.	8	46,776
CBS/Dan Rather News	8.1	M–F	6:30–7 P.M.	1	50,406
	Estimated 25–54 rating	Day	Time	Number of announce-ments	1981 total cost
NBC/Today Show	1.5	M–F	7:30–9 A.M.	6	57,500
NBC/Nightly News	7.3	M–F	6:30–7 P.M.	1	45,400
CNN/Financial News	0.6	T–Th	7–7:30 P.M.	7	10,815
CNN/Inside Business	0.6	Sun	6:30–7 P.M.	7	4,690
				36	$306,997

A similar schedule is recommended in 1982, beginning in mid-January as follows:

Preliminary schedule					
Network/program:	25–54 rating	Day	Time	Number of announce-ments	1982 estimated total cost
ABC/This Wk w/Brinkley	2.8	Sun	11:30 A.M.–12:30 P.M.	6	$ 61,410
ABC/World News Tonight	8.4	M–F	6:30–7 P.M.	1	35,235
ABC/Good AM America	1.8	M–F	7:30–9 A.M.	7	62,662
CBS/Sun Eve. News	6.2	Sun	6:30–7 P.M.	2	44,812
NBC/Today Show	1.5	M–F	7:30–9 A.M.	7	54,180
NBC/Nightly News	7.0	M–F	6:30–7 P.M.	1	31,500
CNN/Financial News	0.6	T–Th	7–7:30 P.M.	8	12,360
CNN/Inside Business	0.6	Sun	6:30–7 P.M.	8	5,360
				40	$307,519

III.   *Reach & Frequency Estimates*

	1981 (3 months)		1982 (3 months)		Total	
	Reach	Frequency	Reach	Frequency	Reach	Frequency
Introductory period						
Financial & business publications	50%	1–2×	50%	1–2×	60%	2–3×
Introductory emphasis publications	60%	1–2×	55%	1–2×	65%	2–3×
Total print	70%	2–3×	70%	2–3×	85%	4–5×
Television news	40%	1–2×	50%	1–2×	60%	2–3×
Sustaining period			(average monthly)			
Financial & business publications	—		30%	1–2×	85%	9–10×

Source: Media Mark Research (MRI) Manager and Administrator; Readership by publication, 25–54; Nielsen Television Ratings, TW & Co. estimates.

CHESSIE/FAMILY LINES (FREIGHT): 1981–1982

Media Objectives

1 Direct advertising to the shipping public and industrial business community (i.e., traffic managers or individuals who make decisions on the shipping of goods in large manufacturing companies).

2 Schedule advertising support on a sustaining basis beginning in the fourth quarter 1981 and throughout 1982.

Media Strategy

Selected business trade publications.

1981–1982 Freight Media Plan:

I.   *1981*—The following magazines are recommended:

	Circulation	Approximate unit cost	Number of ads	1981 schedule total cost
Chemical Week	53,000	$10,340	1	$ 10,340
Coal Industry News	10,400	1,245	1*	1,245
Commerce Magazine	N.A.	1,048	1†	1,048
Container News	30,000	4,870	2	9,740
Distribution	61,000	6,480	2	12,960
Handling & Shipping	75,000	6,850	2	13,700
Industry Week	280,000	17,712	2	35,424
Purchasing Magazine	95,200	8,125	1	8,125
Railway Age	122,800	4,745	1	4,745
Traffic Management	70,000	6,250	2	12,500
Traffic World	13,500	4,250	2	8,500
				$118,327

N.A. means not available.
* Jr. Page.
† Full-page black and white; all others 4-color spreads.

II. *1982*—The use of most of the above publications is recommended to continue in 1982. Two publications, *Business Week* (industrial edition) and *Chemical Business*, are also recommended.

	Circulation	Approximate unit cost	Number of ads	1982 schedule total cost
Business Week (industrial)	315,000	$37,200	3	$111,600
Chemical Week	53,000	12,200	3	36,600
Chemical Business	17,350	4,300	3	12,900
Container News	30,000	4,900	6	29,400
Distribution	61,000	6,500	6	39,000
Handling & Shipping	75,000	6,850	6	41,000
Industry Week	280,000	19,900	8	159,200
Purchasing	95,200	8,125	6	48,750
Traffic Management	70,000	6,250	6	37,500
Traffic World	13,500	4,250	12	51,000
Savannah Port Handbook	N.A.	1,140	1	1,140
Modern Railroad	18,125	5,920	3	17,760
Railway Age	22,800	4,745	3	14,235
				$600,185

III. *Media Cost Summary*

Freight	$118,330	$600,185
Industrial development	13,670*	—
	$132,000	$600,185
Ports campaign reserve		25,000
Rate increase reserve	—	6,000
	$132,000	$631,185

* *Jacksonville Magazine* 11/12 issue @ $989.
Nation's Business Nov. I.D. issue @ $12,673.

FAMILY LINES (INDUSTRIAL DEVELOPMENT)—1982

Media Objectives

1 Direct advertising to a broad number of manufacturing companies that may be interested in establishing a manufacturing and/or distributing operation in the 13-state area served by the Family Lines.

2 Utilize vehicles that are likely to generate inquiries regarding Family Lines Industrial Development Services.

Media Strategy

Selected business trade publications.

I. *1982 Industrial Development Media Plan:*
The following publications are recommended: (see table on p. 312)

	Circulation	Unit cost	Total number of ads	1982 Schedule total cost
Area Development	32,000	$1,610 (5)	12	$ 20,335
		1,755 (7)		
A.I.P.R.	30,600	1,700	10	17,000
Chemical Week	53,000	4,025 (2) pg.	8	18,790
		1,790 (6) $\frac{1}{3}$		
Dun's Business Month	285,000	6,525 (2) pg.	8	27,240
		2,365 (5) $\frac{1}{3}$		
Industry Week	280,000	6,961 (2) pg.	8	30,632
		2,785 (6) $\frac{1}{3}$		
Plant Location Annual	42,000	2,650	1	2,650
Site Selection Handbook	28,000	1,865	4	7,460
Plants Sites & Parks	30,900	1,955	6	11,730
The Wall Street Journal				
(East)	780,000	4,679	3	28,077
		(420 li)		
		1,560	9	
		(140 li)		
				$163,914
			Reserve	31,086
				$195,000

OTHER CORPORATE COMMUNICATIONS PROGRAMS

Corporate communications programs will be implemented to maintain an easily understood and consistent flow of information on those corporate activities that impact on each public and, thus, move the company toward the aforementioned overall goals. The CSX activities will center on the following:

1. *A broad Financial Relations Program* will improve communications with our stockholders, increase demand for CSX shares, and educate the investment community about our business, our growth opportunities, and the strengths of our management team.
   a. Multicity briefings will be held in January and February with security analysts.
   b. Early-on meetings will be initiated with institutional investors in major on-line and off-line cities.
   c. A corporate profile will be produced for broad distribution.
   d. A new quarterly publication will be ini-

tiated and called the *CSX Investor Update*. The publication will be designed to supplement the usual interim reports and to give shareholders, present and future, more timely "product" information in greater depth that can be included in the present interim and annual reports.
   e. A center of information will be installed for analysts and brokers. (An 800 line is recommended in the Finance Department as it opens up communications to brokers, most of whom have to pay for their own phone calls!)
   f. Quarterly and annual results will be disseminated to employees, the trades, and financial and general media.
2. *A Corporate Information Program* will disseminate the news from the top to the various nonfinancial publics.
   a. A new publication, tentatively called *CSX Dialogue*, will be developed to give us a controlled forum on national and other issues that affect the business environ-

ment in which we operate. This publication will be directed at not only the investment community but also the political community, transportation professionals, national opinion leaders, and potential shareholders, and can accomplish three things:

    (1) It will provide the opportunity to speak out on any pertinent issue (e.g., energy, worldwide or coal development).

    (2) It will help build long-term credibility.

    (3) It will provide the opportunity for commissioned articles by national authorities to be an important force.

  b. A strong program of public appearances and speeches by top executives will be supported.

  c. A planned flow of information to top-level business writers of all major publications will be initiated and maintained.

3. *A steady flow of news from the two railroad systems* to both external and internal publics will be planned and managed.

  a. Each railroad system now generates news almost every week that is of interest to one or more publics regarding new capital projects, a new traffic record, or a new service, etc. Each railroad group, therefore, will be expected to maintain a steady flow of such stories to be coordinated to obtain the maximum reach without flooding the market.

  b. Each railroad system will maintain its specialized information programs now in place for employees and shippers, for Operation Lifesaver, and regarding safety activities. Again, coordination will be required to obtain the most mileage in reach and budget.

  c. At the same time, a new *CSX Management Digest* will be proposed that will sharpen communications from top management to supervisors and above. As its name implies, this publication will consist of pertinent excerpts and reprints of a whole range of self-help and generally informative items on how to better manage affairs.

HENKELL SEKT

Dr. Franzjosef Hoefler, CEO of Henkell and Company, had just boarded a plane on his way back home to Weisbaden, West Germany, and was trying to sort out his options for pursuing the U.S. market for champagne and sparkling wines. He had had the opportunity to review several recent market research reports and had spent the last week in January 1983 in New York with Henkell's importers and U.S. ad agency. Volume in the United States had increased steadily over the past eight years, with sales reaching 480,000 bottles in 1982. Although Hoefler did not feel this came close to realizing the potential of Germany's premier brand of sparkling wine, he was uncertain about what constituted reasonable sales volume and market share goals. Questions of product positioning, distribution, advertising, and promotion policies would also require resolution if the Henkell brand was to rise from its 0.3 percent U.S. market share.

Dr. Hoefler had just been CEO of Henkell for a year. He had been persuaded by the family owners to join in January 1982, following a period characterized by large losses and declining market share. His academic training included

a doctorate in economics, and his business experience included 26 years with Gervais-Danone, A.G., serving as president of the company during his last several years. Gervais-Danone, A.G., a subsidiary of the French corporation with the same name, produced and sold cheeses, yogurts, and dessert products. Under Hoefler's leadership, sales had grown significantly, primarily from the introduction of a wide range of new products. Hoefler's management responsibilities included coordination of other subsidiaries in Europe and the Near East.

EARLY COMPANY HISTORY

Henkell was founded in 1832 by Adam Henkell (1801–1866) as a wine brokerage and export business. In 1856, he produced the first bottles of sekt (sekt is the name given to German sparkling wines). Soon the company exported to England, and, from 1885 to 1890, Henkell was the leading wine exporter to the United States. The production of sekt remained a very small part of the business, however, until Otto Henkell joined the company in 1891. He spent three years in New York and London, during which time he developed some of the ideas that contributed to the company's expansion:

In any case I learned how much easier and more lucrative it is to sell a brand name. Once it has been

This case was prepared by Barbara M. Bruner and Professor Paul W. Farris. Copyright ©1983 by the Darden Graduate Business School Foundation, Charlottesville, Virginia.

Note: DM 1 equals $0.42. A bottle is 750 ml. unless otherwise specified. One case is 12 bottles, or 2.4 gallons.

introduced, millions of consumers will demand it again instead of always having to offer them a new and unknown wine with the label of an American wine importer on it. I also believe that we should concentrate on the sekt market, but to this purpose we first need to make the name of Henkell known. (Translated from the German, *150 Jahre Henkell & Co.*)

In 1894 the brand Henkell Trocken (*trocken* is German for "dry") was registered, and the first advertising was undertaken: "Connoisseurs prefer a sekt that accents the taste of the wines used to make it." Famous artists were employed to design advertising for Henkell Trocken. By 1906, the firm sold 3 million bottles, five times the volume sold at the turn of the century.

In celebration of the company's recent success, Otto Henkell sponsored a competition in 1906 among a group of Germany's leading architects for the design of a new headquarters building. The result was a complete "sekt kellerei" made to look like an old chateau converted for business use. The reception area was adorned with an ornate chandelier in the center of a 60-foot ceiling. The colonnades on either side were of almost cathedral proportions, and every wall and ceiling was covered with decorative relief. Priceless works of art and numerous family portraits were prominently displayed among elegant antique furniture. The ornate staircase leading from the center of the grand reception hall led to five stories of cellars, which stored enormous quantities of wine. A train terminal and truck docks were concealed on the back side of the building.

Both World War I and II brought trouble to the company because of shortages of grapes and packing materials. Soon after recovering from the first war, the headquarters building suffered bomb damage while serving as temporary headquarters for a U.S. army unit in the second war.

POST WW II EXPANSION

Otto Henkell II, who was thrust into the presidency in 1945 at age 23, proved to be an able manager. A combination of investment in new production technology and the introduction of new labels enabled him to reestablish Henkell and Company as a leading domestic producer.

Production

Otto Henkell was one of the first European producers to adopt modern production methods developed in California after WW II. In Europe, the word *champagne* can appear only on those bottles produced from white (chardonnay) and/or purple (pinot noir) grapes grown in the Champagne region of France and processed according to the *methode champenoise*. This traditional production method begins with a first fermentation in an oak cask or stainless steel vat. The resulting wines are usually blended (the *cuvee*) before the second fermentation takes place. The *cuvee* is bottled with sugar and yeast (the *liqueur de tirage*) and laid to rest for a year for nonvintage blends, or three years for vintage bottles. During this time the bubbles form. After resting, the bottles are placed in a riddling rack, where they are turned daily and gradually tipped almost upright to induce the sediments to the neck of the bottle. The end is quickly frozen, the cap and frozen sediment removed, the volume replenished with the *dosage* (a blend of sugar to control the sweetness, brandy to stop the fermentation, and champagne from the first bottle to make up the volume), and the final cork inserted.

The newer method adopted by Otto Henkell was known as the *Charmat* or *bulk process*. In this case, the second fermentation takes place in large pressured tanks, instead of individual bottles, and the sediment is filtered out before final bottling.

The quality of the sparkling wines produced in this way were subject to intense debate around the world. Some argued that the precise temperature and pressure control possible with the Charmat method allowed the production of a superior product. Others argued that there was no substitute for the original *methode champenoise*. The Charmat process cost approximately 25 cents less per bottle. The second major factor affecting production costs was the quality of grapes being used. In 1982, the costs ranged from as little as 25 cents per bottle for some sparkling wines to $7 for some from the Champagne region.

New Labels

The use of the Charmat method allowed Henkell to introduce several new labels in its domestic market, mostly at lower prices. In 1981, the firm sold over 31 million bottles (12 bottles equal 1 case) of sekt in the home market. They were marketed under five labels. *Henkell Trocken*, the original company label and the only one to carry the family name, carried a fairly high price in the German market. *Adam* was a low-volume premium sekt, comparable in quality to the French champagnes. *Kardinal* was known as a high-quality sparkling burgundy. *Carstens, A.G.*, had been acquired by Henkell and has been a very successful product at three quarters of the retail price of Henkell Trocken. Finally, the largest-volume and fastest-growing label was *Ruttgers Club*, which retailed at only half the price of Henkell Trocken and among the lowest prices available for a dry sekt.

These five labels, introduced separately to avoid confusing the customer, gave Henkell a position in several segments of the domestic market. Segmentation in the sparkling wine business was usually examined along two dimensions: price and dryness. The matrix shown in Exhibit 1 shows the positioning of the five Henkell labels, their 1981 volume, and the relative strengths of their numerous competitors. All of the French labels, including Vin Mousseaux, shared less than 7 percent of the market. The spumantes represented a number of labels from Italy and were the only other significant imports, with a 15 percent market share.

Performance

Henkell's performance was aided by the size and growth of its home market. Exhibit 2 shows that the market for champagne and sparkling wine in

Germany was more than twice the size of the U.S. market in 1981. Although per capita consumption was already high, growth in consumption had increased from 1977 to 1980 at the same rates as in the United States.

During the last few years of Otto Henkell's presidency, however, the firm's performance started to decline. Health and other concerns had caused frequent turnover among managers during the period. The financial statements shown in Exhibit 3 show the declining contribution from domestic sekt sales and the flat performance in the importing and distribution business. The one brighter spot had been exports. Most of the 6 million export bottles (versus 31 million domestic shipments) carried the Henkell Trocken label and above-average profits.

NEW MANAGEMENT

The declining performance convinced the owners of Henkell (two other families had been brought in to provide cash immediately following WW II) to look for a new president. When Franzjosef Hoefler was approached, he made some independent inquiries before agreeing to join.

Henkell had become an important agent for a number of wines and spirits immediately after WW II to help build cash flow for the ailing company. One of the principal brands it handled was Hennessey, which had 15 percent of the German brandy and cognac market. Others had been concerned about the deteriorating relationship with Hennessey, but Hoefler saw it as an opportunity when he learned that Remy Martin, with 30 percent market share, was unhappy with its distributor in Germany. He proposed an exclusive arrangement with Remy; then, in his first week on the job, he offered Hennessey the opportunity to buy its contract for DM 4 million, compensating Henkell for goodwill built up over the years.

Henkell then founded a joint venture with Remy Martin, the market leader in the cognac category in Germany. Henkell owned 51 percent

EXHIBIT 1   1981 GERMAN MARKET AND LEADING BRANDS
(Millions of 750 ml. Bottles)

Price (DM)	Brut	Blend Trocken (extra dry)	Lieblich (dry)	Süss (sweet)	Total Market
High 10	French labels 4.5 von Metternich 5.3 Adam* 0.2	Deinhard Lila 1.9	Kardinal* 0.2	Krim 3.0	16
Mid 6–10		Henkell Trocken* 10.8 Kupfersberg 10.6 Matheus Miller 7.6 Deinhard Cabinet 7.3		M & R Asti 20.0 Cinzano Asti 10.1	75
Low 6		Carstens* 8.0 Ruttgers* 12.0 Sohnlein 16.0 Vin Mousseaux 20.4	Faber Kronung 52.6 König 12.0 Römer 10.3 Private labels 75.0	Other Spumante 20.7	272
Total market†	11.0	110.0	182.0	60.0	363

* Henkell & Company labels.
†Figures do not sum because of omitted brands.
Note: DM 1 equals $0.42.

EXHIBIT 2 WORLD CHAMPAGNE MARKETS AND HENKELL'S SHARE BY COUNTRY, 1981

Country	Market size (millions bottles)	Per capita consumption	Henkell volume	Henkell market share
W. Germany	363	5.9	31.20	8.6%
Austria	10	1.4	1.89	18.9
Canada	36	1.5	1.16	3.2
U.S.A.	151	0.6	0.46	0.3
Switzerland	4	0.6	0.39	9.8
Sweden	2	0.2	0.33	16.5
Great Britain	23	0.4	0.24	1.0
Italy	95	1.6	0.21	0.2
Denmark	1	0.2	0.13	13.0
Belgium/Lux'g	12	1.2	0.13	1.1
France	210	3.9	N.M.	0.0
Other			0.72	
			36.86	

EXHIBIT 3 CONTRIBUTION
(DM Millions: DM 1 = $0.42)

	1978	1979	1980	1981
Henkell Trocken	29.0	28.5	26.9	26.9
Kardinal	1.0	0.1	(4.3)	(0.3)
Adam	0.8	0.3	(0.1)	0.2
Carstens	7.9	9.2	9.8	10.3
Ruttgers	25.9	20.4	20.0	9.3
Other	0.4	0.4	0.4	0.4
Domestic sekt	65.2	58.8	55.6	46.9
Export sekt	5.6	5.5	6.1	8.2
Total sekt	70.8	64.3	61.7	55.1
Larent Perrier (wine & champagne)	0.6	0.9	1.1	1.3
Mateus	1.8	1.9	1.8	2.7
Hennessey	2.9	2.5	3.0	2.9
Black & White	2.0	1.3	1.4	1.3
Grand Marnier	2.4	2.4	2.4	2.3
Other	1.9	0.8	1.0	0.9
Total imports	11.6	9.8	10.7	11.4
Total contribution	82.4	74.1	72.4	66.5

and Remy Martin 49 percent. Henkell brought 35 men from its sales force, as well as all of the brands carried for other manufacturers (e.g., Grand Marnier, Mateus Rosé), to the new organization. The salespeople staying with Henkell (65) were thus able to devote their time completely to Henkell's own brands.

The next area to which Hoefler turned his attention was the U.S. champagne market. Henkell had had a presence since the late 19th century. Although the firm's volume had grown by a factor of seven within the most recent 10 years and it was a larger bottler of sparkling wine than all but one of the U.S. producers, its 0.3 percent market share placed Henkell about 50th in share of the U.S. market.

Stories about the explosion of wine sales in the States abounded in the popular press. The market was large already, and per capita consumption was far below the levels seen in most of Europe. The opportunity for growth seemed almost without limit. Hoefler had heard that a couple of Spanish companies had introduced sparkling wines in the United States recently and built volume of three to five times Henkell's in a very short time. He decided to make a determined effort to find out why Henkell couldn't do the same thing. As a starting point, he contracted with a couple of research firms in New York and California to obtain a more precise picture of the market. The next section of the case is abstracted from these reports.

THE U.S. CHAMPAGNE AND SPARKLING WINE MARKET

For over 20 years, the consumption of wines had been increasing in the United States, reflecting a consumer shift away from spirits and beer. In 1981, 2.525 billion bottles of wine entered the distribution channels, compared with only 1.335 billion a decade earlier. California produced 71 percent of the total volume, and other states only 8 percent. Imports had increased their share from 11 percent to 21 percent of the market during the same period. The U.S. wine producers exported less than 2 percent of their volume, and most of that went to Canada.

The champagne or sparkling wine segment had shown particular strength in 1980 and 1981, increasing at almost twice the rate of the total market. The imports had been the chief beneficiaries (Exhibit 4).[1] The strong dollar during the

[1] Estimates of market size vary from source to source. Some of the differences are due to efforts to capture consumption (lower estimates) versus volume entering distribution.

EXHIBIT 4   U.S. SPARKLING WINE MARKET
(Millions of 750 ml. Bottles)

Source	1970	1975	1980	1981	1981 average retail price
California	72.0	75.0	106.0	116.0	
Other states	28.0	15.0	20.5	18.5	
Total U.S.	100.00	90.0	126.5	134.5	$4.26
Italy			13.6	19.4	
France			7.2	9.7	
Spain	(not available)		2.0	4.7	
Germany			1.0	1.1	
Other countries			0.3	0.5	
Total imports	9.0	9.5	24.1	35.4	$12.05
Total market	109.0	99.5	150.6	169.9	$6.07

period aided all imports, but the largest gains fell to Spanish and Italian producers who had also undertaken aggressive expansion programs.

Although Germany was the fourth largest source of imported sparkling wines, it represented only 3 percent of imports and less than 1 percent of total consumption.

CONSUMER AND DEMOGRAPHIC PROFILES

Champagne consumption in the United States was concentrated both geographically and seasonally. For most consumers, champagne was identified with "occasions." This was reinforced by the fact that a bottle did not keep after opening. Each consumer was found to have his own definition of what constituted enough of an "event" to open a bottle. The market was heavily skewed toward the end of the year, with the Thanksgiving–Christmas–New Year's celebrations running back to back. Over 40 percent of sales took place during the fourth quarter. A second but far smaller peak showed up in May, June, and July (25 percent of annual volume) boosted by weddings, graduations, and Mother's and Father's Days.

Only 30 percent of champagne was consumed in bars, clubs, or restaurants. The majority was consumed at home (32 percent), at the home of a friend (22 percent), or at a party (9 percent). This was significantly different than other forms of wine and spirits, for which closer to 50 percent was consumed on premise. Research had indicated that as much as two-thirds of the champagne was consumed by 7 percent of the population. Psychographic studies indicated that the champagne drinker had a higher than average income, was college educated, and "inner-directed."

These findings were consistent with other data that showed consumption to be geographically concentrated. Three states accounted for almost 50 percent of sales, and the top seven states accounted for 70 percent. Exhibit 5 shows total and per capita consumption by state. Even within these states, consumption was concentrated in the major metropolitan areas. Only 12 metropolitan areas accounted for over 50 percent of the total market.

PRICING AND THE PURCHASE DECISION

The market research reports received by Mr. Hoefler also contained information on retail pricing patterns. Prices in 1981 broke down as follows:

Price range	Percent of units
$2.76–4.25	53%
$4.25–5.75	28
Over $5.75	19

While names like Dom Perignon and Moët & Chandon were widely recognized, their $15 to $35 or higher price tags meant that they were not widely consumed.

Market surveys had shown that the consumer's decision to purchase a champagne or sparkling wine could be divided into three steps: (1) the decision that an occasion was sufficiently "special," (2) how much money he or she wanted to spend for the occasion, and (3) familiarity (name and package) with a product in that price range. One survey indicated that brands were chosen on the basis of the following:

25%	Brand
21%	Friend's recommendation
13%	Flavor
12%	Price
8%	Geographic source of the wine

As with the still wine market, many perceptions of quality existed which were not based on fact. The debate over which production method produced the superior beverage was mentioned earlier in the case. A similar issue was that of the preferred bottle closure. Cork was associated with quality in the minds of consumers, although plastic was believed by many producers to be far superior. Because of the occasional nature of the beverage, few consumers ever made the side-by-

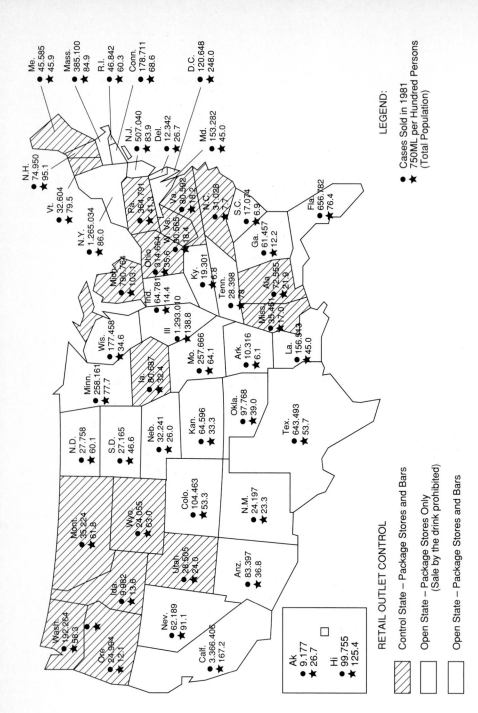

TOTAL U.S. CONSUMPTION ● 12.521.782 Cases
NATIONAL AVERAGE ★ 66.9 750ML per Hundred Persons

EXHIBIT 5   CHAMPAGNE AND SPARKLING WINES: MARKETING MAP

Source: Decus Reports and Liqour Handbook Estimates

side comparisons that might diminish the pervasiveness of these myths.

The range of choices often seemed overwhelming to the consumer. For instance, a spot check of one Kroger's grocery store in Virginia revealed 65 different labels on the shelf (Exhibit 6). In this environment, the endorsements of the wine critics in local newspapers and the gourmet magazines could be quite influential.

COMPETITION

The growth of the U.S. wine market had attracted many new entrants and caused several large beverage and consumer goods companies to enter the market through acquisitions. Coke had purchased Taylor, Sterling, and the Monterey vineyards, forming a group it called the Wine Spectrum. Prior to its being acquired by R.J. Reynolds, Heublein had assembled a portfolio with Beaulieu at the high end, Inglenook in the middle, and Italian Swiss Colony at the bottom. Seagram's had acquired Paul Masson, and National Distillers & Chemical Corporation had acquired Almaden. Gallo was alone among the major domestic producers in remaining privately owned.

The heavy advertising and promotion budgets brought to bear by these companies (e.g., Heublein and Coke each spent $14 million on advertising in 1980, mostly on television) were believed by many to have pulled the market growth at least as fast as consumer demand pushed it. An industry consultant was quoted in *Fortune* (4-18-83) as saying, "Coke has had more impact on the industry than anything since Prohibition."

Despite the presence of large companies, new wineries were still opening. An unusually well-financed venture was that of Frank S. Berger, the former president of the House of Seagram who started a champagne import venture in 1982, saying, "My own people get annoyed when I say this, but it's all the same junk. Wine and spirits, soda, and cosmetics are all parity products that sell on image—the sizzle, not the steak" (5-28-

82, *Marketing News*). He planned to spend $5.5 million on TV advertising to introduce a $5.99 French sparkling wine in the New York, New Jersey, Connecticut, Florida, Illinois, and Texas markets for the next holiday season.

The tables in Exhibits 7 and 8 show the 10 leading domestic and imported champagnes, respectively. Data are given on volume, retail price positions, and advertising expenditures. Exhibits 9 through 11 offer additional perspectives on the positions of the leading brands.

Two labels that were cited frequently in the market research reports and which caught Mr. Hoefler's eye were Freixenet and Cordoniu, both from Spain, where the government provided a 12 percent to 17 percent subsidy for champagne exports. They had both made rapid inroads in the U.S. market and were expected to end up in first and fourth positions, respectively, among imports when the 1982 final count came in. Both had been introduced at about $4 per bottle retail. After gaining recognition, they had managed to raise prices to $7 or more in some markets. A controversial issue was whether the new brands would be able to maintain the higher price and still retain volume and distribution. Neither of them had spent heavily on advertising and consumer level promotion. Much to the surprise of industry watchers, Freixenet had established its own importing firm, rather than using an established importer. More recently, it had purchased land in California.

THE DISTRIBUTION SYSTEM

The 21st Amendment, which marked the end of the Prohibition era, allowed each state to regulate the sale of alcoholic beverages. Fifty years later, the distribution systems were still highly regulated and extremely fragmented. The three-tier system was strictly adhered to: producers, importers, wholesalers, and retailers/on-premise licensees. Wholesalers were allowed to operate only within one state. All retail and on-premise licensed vendors (bars, restaurants, and clubs)

EXHIBIT 6   MAY 1983 CHAMPAGNE SELECTION: KROGER'S, CHARLOTTESVILE, VIRGINA

Origin	Label	Price	Production method
France	Veuve Amoit—brut	$ 5.99	MC
	Piper-Heidsieck—extra dry	23.19	MC
	Charles-Heidsieck—extra dry	19.99	MC
	Bouvet—brut	10.33	MC
	Mumm's—Cordon Rouge	21.99	MC
	—extra dry	20.09	MC
	Moët & Chandon—extra dry	17.99	MC
	Veuve Clicquot Ponsardin—brut	23.19	MC
	Taittinger—brut	24.19	MC
	Pol Roger & Co.—reserve—brut	23.55	MC
	Club Montmarte—brut	5.99	Vin Mousseaux
Italy	Pinot Noir—brut	7.73	—
	Castello di Bossi—brut	7.49	MC
	Asti Spumante (Villa Banfi)	8.63	—
	Asti Cinzano	9.17	—
	M & R Asti	10.69	—
	Cella Asti—750 ml.	9.99	—
	Cella Asti—375 ml.	5.49	—
	Grand Cavit—brut	7.29	—
	Ballabio Brut	18.99	MC
Spain	Nadal—brut	6.99	MC
	Grand Nador—extra dry	4.99	CH
	Delapierre—brut	6.87	MC
Germany	Adolph Rheinart—Trocken	7.99	MC
	Blue Nun	7.29	CH
California	Le Domaine—brut (750 ml.)	5.15	MC
	Le Domaine—extra dry (375 ml.)	2.95	MC
	Le Domaine—extra dry (750 ml.)	3.99	MC
	Le Domaine—extra dry (1.5 l.)	9.99	MC
	André—extra dry	2.99	CH
	André—pink	2.99	CH
	André—sparkling burgundy	3.19	CH
	André—cold duck	2.99	CH
	Franzia—light champagne	3.43	CH
	Franzia—pink	2.99	CH
	Franzia—extra dry	2.99	CH
	Jacques Bonet—extra dry	2.99	CH
	Jacques Bonet—pink	2.99	CH
	Jacques Bonet—cold duck	2.99	CH
	Paul Masson—brut	7.03	MC
	Paul Masson—extra dry	7.03	MC
	Paul Masson—pink	7.03	MC
	Paul Masson—Cracklin' Chablis	4.73	MC

EXHIBIT 6 *(Continued)*

Origin	Label	Price	Production method
	Korbel—brut	9.64	MC
	Korbel—extra dry	9.64	MC
	Korbel—blanc de noirs	12.95	MC
	Korbel—rose	7.39	MC
	Korbel—rouge	7.89	MC
	Korbel—natural	11.03	MC
	Almaden—chardonnay nature	8.93	MC
	Almaden—Eye of the Partridge	9.23	MC
	Almaden—Blanc de Blanc	9.23	MC
	Almaden—extra dry	6.29	MC
	Almaden—vintage brut	6.39	MC
New York	J. Roget—cold duck	3.09	MC
	J. Roget—American spumante	3.09	MC
	J. Roget—pink	3.09	MC
	J. Roget—extra dry	3.09	MC
	Chateau Laurent	4.33	MC
	Taylor—brut	6.19	MC
	Taylor—pink	6.19	MC
	Taylor—extra dry	6.19	MC
	Great Western—natural	8.79	MC
	Great Western—extra dry	7.63	MC
	Great Western—pink	7.63	MC

EXHIBIT 7 1981 TOP 10 DOMESTIC WINERY SALES: ESTIMATED

Winery	Major brands	Production method	1981 sales (million bottles)	Volume trend	Retail Price	Advertising expend ($000)
E & J Gallo	André, Gallo	Charmat	56.4	Up	$2.99	$3,539
United Vintners (Heublein)	Leju		15.0	Declining	N.A.	N.A.
	Jacques Bonet				2.99	N.A.
The Wine Spectrum (Coca-Cola)	Taylor	M. Ch.	7.2	Up	6.19	3,305*
	Great Western	M. Ch.	5.4		7.63	283
Almaden (National Distillers)	Almaden	M. Ch.	7.8	Up	7.99	290
Franzia	Franzia	Charmat	6.0	Flat	2.99	N.A.
Paul Masson (Seagram)	Paul Masson	M. Ch.	5.1	Flat	7.03	N.A.
Korbel (Brown-Foreman)	Korbel	M. Ch.	5.9	Up	10.99	52
Weibel (Nabisco)	Weibel		5.1	Up	N.A.	178
Guild	N.A.		3.6	Flat	N.A.	N.A.
Christian Brothers	Christian Bros.		1.7	Flat	N.A.	N.A.
Total			119.2			

* Includes all Taylor wines.
N.A. means not available.

EXHIBIT 8   1981 TOP 10 IMPORT BRAND SALES: ESTIMATED

Brand	Origin	Production method	Importer	1981 sales (million bottles)	Volume trend	Retail price	Advertising expend. ($000)
M & R Asti Spumante	Italy		Renfield	3.9	Up	$10.69	$1,165
Moët & Chandon	France	M Ch.	Schieffelin	2.8	Up	17.99	432
Freixenet	Spain		Freixenet	2.5	Strong	6.74	130
Gancia Asti Spumante	Italy		Paterno	1.9	Up	N.A.	153
Mumm's	France		Brown Vintners	1.8	Up	20.09	352
Zonin Asti Spumante	Italy		F. Bonanno	1.7	Strong	N.A.	N.A.
Cinzano Asti Spumante	Italy		Wine Spectrum	1.3	Up	9.17	84
Piper-Heidsieck	France	M. Ch.	Renfield	1.2	Flat	23.19	228
Cordoniu	Spain	M. Ch.	Jos. Victori	1.2	Strong	N.A.	N.A.
Cella Asti Spumante	Italy		Jos. Garneau	1.2		9.99	N.A.

N.A. means not available.

were required to buy from wholesalers within their own state. Major supermarket chains, like Safeway, had to deal with separate sources of supply in each of the states that allowed wine to be sold in grocery stores. Eighteen states were "control" states, meaning the state owned and operated the majority of retail outlets. In these states, bar and restaurant owners received a discount but had to make all of their purchases through the state store as well. "Noncontrol" states required licensing but allowed competitive pricing. The 35 states which allowed sale of wine through grocery outlets averaged almost 25 percent higher per capita consumption than those that did not.

For most brands of sparkling wine and champagne, taxes and distribution costs exceeded production costs by a substantial margin. Federal taxes alone amounted to $3.40 per gallon (10 times the level imposed on still wine). State taxes ranged from $0.25 to $1.50 per gallon in noncontrol states (one gallon = 5 bottles). Control states used a markup, instead, which ran as high as 50 percent. Transportation to the East Coast might easily be $17 per case from Europe versus $3 to $4 from California. Wholesalers typically marked up their goods 30 percent, and retailers 40 to 50 percent. The following price comparison was presented in one of the reports:

	Henkell			Taylor	
Case	Bottle			Case	Bottle
$ 40.54	$3.38	FOB taxes paid*		$42.90	$3.58
57.62	4.80	Delivered to Boston		46.40	3.87
74.75	6.23	After distributor markup		59.99	5.00
107.88	8.99	Suggested retail price		83.88	6.99

* Includes importer's margin, advertising, and promotional expense.

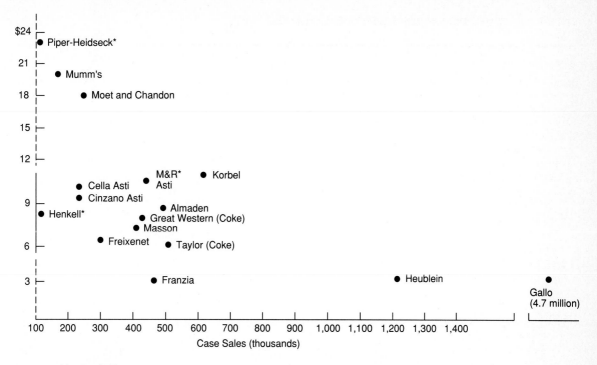

* Imported by Renfield.

EXHIBIT 9   PRICE-VOLUME RELATIONSHIP OF LEADING DOMESTIC AND IMPORTED CHAMPAGNES (FROM EXHIBITS 7 AND 8)

Despite the legal constraints, changes had been taking place in the distribution system. Consolidation was taking place at the producer/importer level. In 1981, the top 10 domestic wineries producing champagne accounted for 88 percent of domestic champagne shipments. The same year, the top 10 import labels accounted for 55 percent of imported champagne volume. The large domestic producers, like Coca-Cola's Wine Spectrum, were complementing their own lines with imported products, providing major competition for the independent importers, of whom few remained.

The role of the importer was to work with the producer as his marketing and sales arm in the United States. The importer worked out media programs and budgets, point-of-sale displays, wholesaler promotions, incentives for both wholesalers and on-premise licensees (e.g., mirror, table-top tents), coupon refund offers, and pricing to the wholesaler. Most champagne was shipped directly from the winery to the wholesaler, enabling the importer to avoid inventory costs.

Wholesalers obtained the brand from numerous producers/importers. Normally there was heavy competition among them.

An industry observer commented:

Traditionally the wholesalers have regarded themselves as pure distributors, that is, as performing a service. They do not see themselves as sellers with marketing activities, nor do they see themselves as supporters of the marketing measures employed by producers/importers.

This meant that direct actions from the producers/importers to the retail trade were necessary to

EXHIBIT 10   20 LEADING BRANDS: SALES, SHARE, PRODUCT TYPES

Brand	Sales 1981 (in 000 cases)	Market share	Extra dry	Brut	Natural	Other
			Product type			
U.S.-produced	10.221	81.6%				
Charmat	7,868	62.8				
André, Gallo	5,175	41.3	X	X		
Leju, J. Bonet	1,237	9.9	X			
Franzia	525	4.2	X			
Weibel	419	3.3	X	X		
Guild	392	3.1		N.A.		
Chris. Brothers	120	1.0	X	X		
Transfer	1,887	15.0				
Taylor, Gr. Western	875	7.0	X	X		
Almaden	666	5.3	X	X	X	
Paul Masson	336	2.7	X	X		
Champenoise						
Korbel	476	3.8	X	X	X	B/B
Imported	1,635	13.1				
Asti Spumante	840	6.7				
M & R	320	2.5				
Gancia	160	1.3				
Zonin	145	1.2				
Cinzano	110	0.9				
Cella	100	0.8				
Champagne	485	3.9				
Moët & Chandon	235	1.9	X	X		
Mumm's	150	1.2	X	X		
Piper-Heidsieck	100	0.8	X	X		
Other						
(Champenoise)	310	2.5				
Freixenet	210	1.7	X	X	X	Sweet
Cordoniu	100	0.8		X	X	

N.A. means not available.

influence the activities of the retailers. For example:

- Letters to the retailer
- Advertising in trade journals/magazines
- Employing one's own merchandiser without a selling or distribution function
  - Renting a display company
  - Telephone campaigns

The wholesaler covered a specific geographic region, always within the confines of one state. In 1982, there were approximately 500 wholesalers in the United States, down significantly from 1970. In NYC, for instance, the number of wholesalers had fallen from 21 to 5 over a 15-year period. They typically carried 4,000 to 4,500 items and frequently serviced overlapping territories. A few industry observers expected to see the resurrection of specialty wholesalers in the 1980s, and in fact, some of the large whole-

EXHIBIT 11   MARKET RESEARCH SUMMARIES OF COMPETING BRAND STRATEGIES

Martini & Rossi

Product:	1
Assortment:	3 sizes
Design:	light color "typical" Asti from Italy
Advertising:	simple, "manufacturer advertising"
Familiarity:	aided + unaided = 74%
Positioning:	high-priced, imported

Freixenet

Products:	Rosé, Extra Dry, Brut, Nevada, Negro Brut Natural
Assortment:	only 1 size
Design:	not typical for this product
Price:	medium price
Advertising:	superficial, aimed at shelf recognition
Familiarity:	aided + unaided = 7%
Positioning:	reasonably priced, ur.~omplicated "imported" champagne

Cordoniu

Products:	Blanc de Balncs, Brut, Dry Brut de Noirs, Rosé, Brut Natural
Assortment:	only 1 size
Design:	heavy dark, no high-value image
Price:	medium price
Advertising:	. . .
Familiarity:	aided + unaided = 22%
Positioning:	reasonably priced, uncomplicated "imported" champagne

Bouvet

Products:	Brut
Assortment:	3 sizes
Design:	look of champagne
Price:	relatively high
Advertising:	"champagne advertising" Loire wines and champenoise method.
Familiarity:	. . . ?
Positioning:	me-too champagne at reasonable price

André

Products:	Cold Duck, Pink, Burgundy, White
Assortment:	1 size
Design:	look of champagne
Price:	low
Advertising:	. . .
Familiarity:	aided + unaided = 75%
Positioning:	simple, all-around American product but having high claim to value

Piper Sonoma

Product:	Brut
Assortment:	1 size
Design:	100% champagne
Price:	high
Advertising:	. . .
Familiarity:	. . . ?
Positioning:	a valuable champagne from California at a relatively favorable price

Korbel

Products:	Blanc de Blancs, Natural, Extra Dry, Blanc de Noirs, Rosé, Rouge, Sec
Assortment:	3 sizes
Design:	look of champagne
Price:	medium to high price
Advertising:	special occasions and romantic occasions for two
Familiarity:	aided + unaided = 22%
Positioning:	Champagne with atmosphere, the more valuable reasonable alternative to champagne, "uncork the magic"

Chandon

Products:	Blanc de Pinot Noirs Brut, Special Reserve Brut
Assortment:	1 size
Design:	look of champagne, but relatively cheap; appearance of value
Price:	high
Advertising:	. . .
Familiarity:	aided + unaided = 18%
Positioning:	reasonably priced champagne from California

Taylor

Products:	Dry, Pink, Brut, Burgundy, Cold Duck
Assortment:	4 sizes
Design:	limited look of champagne
Price:	medium
Advertising:	. . .
Familiarity:	no data
Positioning:	an alternative to champagne from New York, partially with pretensions of appealing to connoisseurs, partially "American"

Great Western

Products:	Brut, Pink, Cold Duck, Pink Sparkling Burgundy, Extra Dry, Natural
Assortment:	2 sizes
Design:	unusual, not typical for this product
Price:	upper end of medium-priced products
Advertising:	. . .
Familiarity:	aided + unaided = 25%
Positioning:	the "American," independent version, good price/value relationship

salers had already divided their own sale forces to provide more focus. The wholesaler had full liberty to set prices at his level in the distribution system as long as he did not sell below cost (except during a closeout). The wholesalers competed with one another primarily on the basis of price and service (which usually meant the ability to deliver in small quantities on an almost daily basis). There was little loyalty in the field.

The retail tier in the distribution system was highly fragmented. Nationwide there were 428,964 licenses to sell wine by retail. Of these, 195,725 were on-premise licenses; 137,079 were for off-premise sales; and 96,160 were combined licenses. The mix and type of off-premise outlets varied considerably by state. New York State prohibited chains from selling alcoholic beverages; licenses were granted for single locations. This restriction had led to the formation of buying cooperatives to deal with the increasing strength of the wholesalers. In California, by contrast, over 60 percent of the volume was handled by large grocery chains. In the total U.S. market, less than 25 percent of sparkling wines were sold through co-ops and grocery chains.

FORECAST TRENDS

Several of the reports obtained by Mr. Hoefler forecasted continued growth in the U.S. champagne market. In one from Find/SVP, Daniel Mirassou of Mirassou Valley Vineyards was quoted as saying that he expected consumption to triple by 1990 and was planning to triple his own production to meet the demand. Another cited figures from the Wine Marketing Handbook (figures are millions of 750 ml. bottles):

	1981	1986	Percent of growth
United States	115	157	37%
Imports	35	91	159
Total	150	248	65

Impact Data Bank's forecast indicated compound growth rates of about 5 percent. Even if the more optimistic forecast was realized, sufficient acreage had been planted that, despite the long lead times required to produce champagne, no shortages were expected.

In terms of consumer preferences, some people felt that tastes would mature in favor of drier champagnes; but a favorite line in the industry remained: "Label it dry and blend it sweet for the American market." The other trend, being supported by the producers, was to encourage the use of champagne consumption as a cocktail or with a meal, rather than always waiting for a special occasion.

Further concentration was expected at virtually every level in the production and distribution chain but within the constraints imposed by the existing legal environment.

HENKELL'S U.S. SALES

Sales of Henkell Sekt had doubled from 240,000 bottles in 1977 to 480,000 in 1982. But Dr. Hoefler did not feel satisfied when he examined those results compared with the total market. Although the Henkell growth had kept up with that of total imports, other German champagnes had outpaced it.

The market research reports had also noted that Henkell's brand recognition was still very low, although those who had tried it seemed to like the taste. The distribution of Henkell Sekt was characterized as "spotty," although 7 of Henkell's top 10 markets were also top 10 category markets. But the kind of volatility exhibited in Exhibit 12 worried Dr. Hoefler. Year-to-year volume changes were all over the map: California was up 50 percent, but Illinois and Massachusetts were each down 36 percent from 1980.

RENFIELD IMPORTERS, LTD.

Since 1974, Henkell had been represented in the United States by Renfield Importers, Ltd. The relationship had started quite by chance when the

EXHIBIT 12   APRIL–DECEMBER NATIONAL DEPLE-
TIONS (BOTTLES)

Top 10 markets	1980	1981	Percent change
Illinois:			
Metro Chicago	50,232	32,328	−36
Downstate	9,264	10,824	+17
New York:			
Metro New York	59,628	74,700	+25
Upstate	5,076	5,520	+ 9
Florida	34,176	39,552	+16
Washington, D.C.	21,924	18,756	−14
Texas	14,928	16,560	+11
New Jersey	26,880	29,916	+11
California	9,684	14,520	+50
Massachusetts	11,448	7,272	−36
Pennsylvania	6,936	8,124	+17
Virginia	7,344	8,784	+20
Total top 10 markets	257,520	266,856	+ 4
Total other	65,256	64,932	− 1
Total	322,776	331,788	+ 3

individual who had been handling Henkell for years sold his small import business to Renfield. At the time, the Henkell product was distributed only in New York and New Jersey. Volume was 60,000 to 70,000 bottles and was mostly in seven-ounce bottles, called *pikkolos*, which were packaged in threes in fancy wooden gift boxes. Herman Merinoff, chairman and CEO of Renfield, had decided to keep Henkell Sekt in his portfolio "because I liked the taste and I liked Otto Henkell."

Renfield claimed to be the largest independent importer in the United States. The firm's offices in midtown Manhattan were adorned with a fine collection of old posters advertising wines and spirits. Among the successes the firm claimed was its role in pushing Martini and Rossi Asti Spumante into the number 1 imported sparkling wine position. Renfield also represented Gordon's gin and vodka; Pinch, Haig & Haig, and King William IV Scotch; Martini & Rossi Vermouth; Giacobatsi pop wine; Coin-

treau; Piper-Heidsieck champagnes and several smaller-volume liqueurs and cordials. Renfield also owned 53 percent of Sonoma Vineyards in California and distributed its fall line of wines. In July 1980, Renfield announced a joint venture with Piper-Heidsieck to build a $4.5 million facility on the grounds of the Sonoma winery to produce premium California sparkling wines; the announced goal was to produce 1.2 million bottles a year by 1985. Measured in volume, Renfield sales were split almost equally between wine and spirits.

The Renfield sales organization had grown from 59 people to 146 in five years. Most of them were salaried salesmen, although a few states required them to use independent brokers. They dealt with approximately 230 of the 500 wholesalers in the country, attempting to give exclusive access to their products in most markets.

POSITIONING HENKELL SEKT FROM 1974–1982

With a taste similar to premium champagnes, both domestic and imported, Henkell had been priced at about $9 per bottle retail, above most domestics and most of the faster growing imports. Twenty-five percent of its volume was in gift packs, and sales were even more skewed to the holiday season than average. The pikkolo had been reduced to only a small portion of sales, as emphasis had shifted to the more profitable 750 ml. bottles.

Mr. Merinoff described most of the marketing effort during the period as based on a push, rather than a pull, strategy, emphasizing such programs as contests for the salesmen. But a variety of complementary strategies had been attempted. The firm had tested television advertising one holiday season but with no obvious success. A limited radio series based on the light theme of "Have you had your Henkell today?" had also been disappointing.

After trying spring advertising in 1980, Henkell went back to holiday only in 1981. In 1981, it focused on NYC, rather than the three investment markets it had identified the year before. After the brief trials with consumer advertising, it shifted emphasis in 1981–1982 back to increased distribution efforts and promotional activities.

One experiment along the way had met with immediate success. The firm had so reduced the price in the Chicago market that it was available at $3.99 retail. Volume soared. But Otto Henkell "got off the plane and told them to put the price back up because they were bastardizing the family name!"

JANUARY 1983 STRATEGY MEETING

Armed with this data, Dr. Hoefler flew to New York in January 1983 for a strategy development meeting with Mr. Merinoff and his managers.

The Renfield team outlined a strategy calling for rapid growth over the following three years:

In bottles			
1982	1983	1984	1985
516,000	600,000	750,000	960,000

Mr. Merinoff proposed to do this with the Henkell Sekt label only, emphasizing the 750 ml. bottles. Merinoff said all of the success stories he knew of had concentrated on building one brand. Merinoff felt that you confuse the customer by offering different prices, images, and labels before cementing one of them. He pointed out that the volume to date had been built on a push strategy; but that, in his opinion, obtaining the million-bottle level would require more pull. He, therefore, recommended increasing the spending levels for a number of marketing programs and maintaining them at a fairly high per case level for at least the three-year planning horizon.

Mr. Casciari, Renfield's champagne product manager, followed up with the detailed spending proposal shown in Exhibit 13. He recommended that $300,000 of the 1983–84 investment be made by Renfield and $450,000 by Henkell.

In terms of geographic coverage, the proposal was to concentrate in a few markets to ensure adequate levels of support and to maximize efficiency. Starting with the New York market, in which Renfield had already invested advertising and sales promotion dollars, it planned to add one market each year. The firm would probably choose from Florida, Illinois, New Jersey, Texas, and Washington, D.C., which, with New York, already represented 67 percent of sales. The advertising and sales promotion dollars would be spent in the key markets, with marketing allowances in other areas.

The definition of sales promotion had been broadened to include not only point-of-sale material but refund offers, direct mail, sales promotion, and tastings. Particular emphasis was to be placed on refund offers for retailers and coupons for consumers (either media-delivered or as case cards).

Advertising would continue to be focused in support of promotional activities. Radio would be used to build brand awareness and to announce special offers. Newspapers would be used to deliver coupons or refund offers in new markets. Two flights of advertising were suggested for each of New York and one other market—three weeks in June and three weeks in December.

Public relations efforts would be primarily trade oriented (retailers and wine press). The goal would be to inform the trade of the positive product attributes and price/value relationship of Henkell. Means of accomplishing this would include a press kit, tastings, and a quarterly mailing in key markets.

Sales incentives had been successful in pushing the brand previously. A Henkell trip had stimulated brand interest before. The firm planned to involve the Renfield sales personnel in similar contests in 1983 and 1984.

One of the challenges presented was that of coordinating/integrating the merchandising effort. Mr. Merinoff emphasized repeatedly that

EXHIBIT 13   RENFIELD BUSINESS PLAN ($000)

	1982/83	1983/84	1984/85	1985/86
Budget Allocation				
Advertising	$125	$215	$250	$350
Sales promotion	230	200	270	300
Gift cartons	30	40	70	85
Sales incentive	20	50	50	50
Wine list	25	50	50	50
Public relations	—	10	10	30
Other	50	35	50	71
Total	$480	$600	$750	$936
Incremental Spending Plan				
Marketing allowances	$ 50	$ 75	$ 95	$125
Sales incentives	50	—	—	—
Advertising/sales promotion	—	75	105	125
Total	$100	$150	$200	$250
Dollars per bottle (includes incremental spending)	$1.12	$1.25	$1.27	$1.24

Henkell was competing in a very crowded and varied category, in which there appeared to be a very low level of brand awareness and much confusion on the part of the consumers. While French champagnes and Italian spumantes were usually regarded as distinct segments, he was not sure it made sense to view German sparkling wines as a separate segment in the U.S. champagne market. Brand awareness and brand positioning had to be reinforced in both the retailer's and consumer's mind.

Finally, with regard to pricing, Renfield recom-mended that Henkell maintain its FOB price from 1982 into 1983, allowing it to achieve "competitive pricing" in the U.S. market.

DR. HOEFLER'S RESPONSE

Dr. Hoefler was disappointed when he returned to his hotel room that night. He wanted to see faster results. After some consideration, he decided to offer a challenge to Renfield the next day. He pulled out a set of slide pens and drafted the presentation which follows:

Henkell Objective: 3% of U.S. sparkling wine market by 1986			
Year	U.S. mkt. (bottles)	SOM	Henkell volume (bottles)
1981	171MM	0.3%	0.51MM
1982	180MM		
1983	189MM	0.5%	1.0MM
1984	198MM		
1985	208MM		
1986	219MM	3.0%	6.57MM

QUESTIONS TO BE RESOLVED

1 Can we achieve our objective with one brand? Existing or new ones? German or international-sounding brands with a French touch?

2 Do we need a range of tastes to cover the market segmentation?

3 Is Renfield prepared to invest?

4 Is Renfield in a position to achieve objectives if desired?

5 What kind of advertising is required: PR, advertising, sales promotion, consumer promotion, media, which?

6 What's the required advertising impact (spending and what is the ROI? Who pays for what? Who's responsible for our operations?)?

Dr. Hoefler presented his thoughts the following morning, but absolutely no closure had been achieved when he had to run to the airport for his return flight to Weisbaden. He was reluctant to relinquish his goal of the tenfold increase in volume over the following four years in favor of Renfield's goal of doubling volume.

ROLM CORPORATION (A)

In October 1973, Kenneth Oshman, President of the ROLM Corporation, and other members of ROLM's top management team were finalizing a business plan to market a private branch exchange system (PBX), thereby entering the telecommunications industry. The plan was to be presented to ROLM's Board of Directors at their November meeting in order to obtain approval for market entry. The initial product was to be a computer-controlled electronic PBX with capacity to handle from 100 to 800 telephone extensions.

The Company

ROLM Corporation had been founded in 1969 by four electrical engineers: Mr. Richeson, Mr. Oshman, Mr. Loewenstern and Mr. Maxfield. In fact, the name of the corporation was an acronym based on the first letters of their names. All were in their late twenties to early thirties at the time of the founding, and all were, or had been, em-

ployed by electronic or computer firms in the San Francisco Bay Area.

In the fall of 1968, Bob Maxfield and Gene Richeson attended the Fall Joint Computer Conference. Data General, subsequently to become a major factor in the minicomputer industry, and a dozen other new manufacturers announced their first products at this show. A few months later, while the four of them were sitting around "blue skying" about potential businesses, Gene Richeson suggested that what the world really needed was a low-cost off-the-shelf military minicomputer. The major manufacturers of militarized computers ("mil-spec") were IBM and Sperry Univac, who manufactured the computers on a custom basis resulting in long lead times and high cost—often $150,000 for a system. The Data General commercial NOVA minicomputer, on the other hand, cost about $10,000, and Gene Richeson, on the basis of his knowledge of the requirements of the various military applications, felt that such a computer would have sufficient power for most of these applications. Bob Maxfield, who had the most experience with computers, felt that a militarized version of the Data General computer could be manufactured to sell

This case was prepared by Professor Adrian Ryans. Reprinted with permission of Stanford University Graduate School of Business ©1979 by the Board of Trustees of the Leland Stanford Junior University.

for less than $30,000. They phoned Edson de Castro, President of Data General, and told him they were thinking of starting up a company to manufacture mil-spec computers and asked him if he would be interested in licensing hardware and software designs to them. Mr. de Castro was interested, and so they flew to Data General's home office in Boston and negotiated an agreement with him.

On the basis of their idea, they developed a business plan and were successful in getting sufficient money to start the business. ROLM began operation on June 1, 1969. In the first quarter of fiscal year 1971, which began in July 1970, ROLM showed a profit and remained profitable thereafter.

The ROLM mil-spec computers were typically purchased by contractors of the U.S. Department of Defense, the Defense Department itself and certain industrial customers who required computers that could operate in severe environments. The company employed a direct sales organization which totaled about eight people in 1973.

The Decision to Diversify

By fiscal 1973, sales had reached $3.6 million. An income statement and balance sheet for ROLM are included in Exhibit 1. Early in 1973, top management of ROLM became concerned about the potential size of the segment of the military computer market in which ROLM competed. There was a strong feeling among ROLM's top management that their market segment would be saturated by the time their annual sales reached $10 to $20 million. Given that they had an objective to build a major company, they began to look for areas of diversification that would allow ROLM to continue its growth. They felt that any diversification should build on their main technological expertise in computers, and so they investigated other computer-related businesses that they might enter. The PBX market was an obvious candidate. As Oshman pointed out, "The computer-based PBX is very much a computer system, and we already had 80% of the technology; we figured we could get the other

20% easier than the telephone companies could get the computer technology." The idea was initially abandoned when they realized that the cost of setting up a national sales and service organization would be beyond ROLM's resources.

EXHIBIT 1   ROLM CORPORATION FINANCIAL DATA

Income Statement for Fiscal Year Ending June 29, 1973	
Net sales	$3,637,000
Costs and expenses	
Cost of goods sold	1,572,000
Product development	455,000
Marketing, administrative, and general	964,000
Interest	14,000
Total costs and expenses	3,005,000
Income before taxes	632,000
Provision for income taxes	311,000
Net income	$321,000

Balance Sheet for Quarter Ending September 28, 1973	
Current assets	
Cash	$202,000
Receivables	442,000
Inventories	994,600
Other current assets	43,100
Total current assets	$1,681,700
Other assets	
Capital equipment	$440,700
Accumulated depreciation	228,300
Net capital equipment	$212,400
Other assets	24,100
Total other assets	$236,500
Total assets	$1,918,200
Current liabilities	
Accounts payable and accrued payroll	$306,700
Income tax payable	139,400
Other current liabilities	31,900
Notes payable	24,400
Total current liabilities	$502,400
Lease contracts payable: long-term	$97,500
Stockholders' equity	
Capital stock	$170,800
Paid in surplus, net	610,800
Retained earnings	536,700
Total equity	$1,318,300
Total liabilities and equity	$1,918,200

Source: Company records.

Nevertheless the proposal kept resurfacing during the following months. As Bob Maxfield recalled: "We all felt it would be fun to develop a computer-controlled telephone system, so we decided to look at it more carefully in March 1973."

To head the product development side of the project, Maxfield was successful in recruiting Jim Kasson from Hewlett-Packard. Kasson had a background in data acquisition and control systems and was very knowledgeable about computers. He also brought with him from Hewlett-Packard another very good engineer. Together with ROLM's top computer software specialist they became, in June 1973, the three-person ROLM PBX technical feasibility team. In August 1973, Dick Moley, a marketing manager in Hewlett-Packard's computer division, joined ROLM to do the market analysis for the PBX.

TELECOMMUNICATIONS INDUSTRY IN THE UNITED STATES

The telecommunications system in the United States was operated by American Telephone and Telegraph (AT&T) and some 1760 independent telephone companies.

AT&T consisted of several major operations. Bell Telephone Laboratories conducted basic research and designed equipment for use by AT&T.

Western Electric was the manufacturing arm of AT&T and as the result of a consent decree with the Justice Department sold its products exclusively to the Bell System operating companies and to the U.S. government. The Long Lines Department installed and operated the interstate long distance telephone network and international calls. The twenty-four Bell System operating companies provided telephone service at the local level. They covered about 85% of the telephones in the United States. In 1972, AT&T had telephone revenues of $21.4 billion and had 109 million phones in service. Fourteen million of these phones were business phones connected to PBXs.

The 1760 independent telephone companies provided local telephone service in areas not served by AT&T. They varied greatly in size from very small rural telephone companies to major corporations such as General Telephone, which had operating revenues in the United States of almost $2 billion. The ten largest independent telephone companies are shown in Exhibit 2.

The Emergence of the Telephone Interconnect Industry

Prior to 1968, all telephone company tariffs in the United States had contained a prohibition against the attachment of customer-provided ter-

EXHIBIT 2   TEN LARGEST INDEPENDENT TELEPHONE COMPANIES

Name and addresses	Telephones	% of total independent telephone industry	Total operating revenues
1. General Telephone & Electrical Corp. (U.S. only), New York, N.Y.	10,622,000	45.81	$1,881,000,000
2. United Telecommunications, Inc., Kansas City, Missouri	2,642,300	11.40	448,684,000
3. Continental Telephone Corporation (U.S. Only), Chantilly, Virginia	1,774,200	7.65	299,536,000
4. Central Telephone & Utilities Corporation, Lincoln, Nebraska	1,059,600	4.57	194,055,000
5. Mid-Continent Telephone Corporation, Hudson, Ohio	593,500	2.56	82,842,000
6. Rochester Telephone Corporation, Rochester, New York	535,100	2.31	89,502,000
7. Puerto Rico Telephone Company, San Juan, Puerto Rico	357,400	1.54	64,277,000
8. Lincoln Telephone & Telegraph Company, Lincoln, Nebraska	239,800	1.03	37,176,000
9. Commonwealth Telephone Company, Dallas, Pennsylvania	154,900	.67	18,857,000
10. Florida Telephone Corporation, Ocala, Florida	143,600	.62	29,068,000

minal equipment (such as telephones, answering machines and PBXs) to the telecommunications network. The 1968 Carterfone decision of the Federal Communications Commission (FCC) held that these blanket prohibitions were unreasonable, discriminatory and unlawful, and the FCC required that the telephone companies file new tariffs that did not contain such blanket prohibitions. This decision opened up the vast market for terminal equipment to a variety of new competitors.

PBXs and Key Systems

Interconnect equipment was any equipment attached to where incoming telephone company lines terminated on a customer's premises. In the business market most of the sales volume was in two product classes; private branch exchanges (PBX) and key telephone systems.

A PBX was a local telephone switching system within a company which handled incoming, outgoing and intraoffice calls. As shown schematically in Exhibit 3, a PBX consisted of four major parts:

1 Switching equipment and control system. The switching system was the electromechanical or electronic equipment that connected the various internal (telephone extensions) and external lines in the system and provided ringing, busy signals, dial tone and intercom services.

2 Trunk circuits. These were lines connecting the PBX to the public switched network.

3 Attendant console.

4 Telephone station equipment. These were the individual telephones and key systems (a telephone that allows a person access to several lines with a single push-button set).

While key systems were commonly part of the PBX telephone system in large companies, stand-alone key systems were commonly used in smaller organizations (typically those with forty or fewer telephones) as the sole system.

The technology involved in automatic PBXs had evolved in recent years—from electrome-

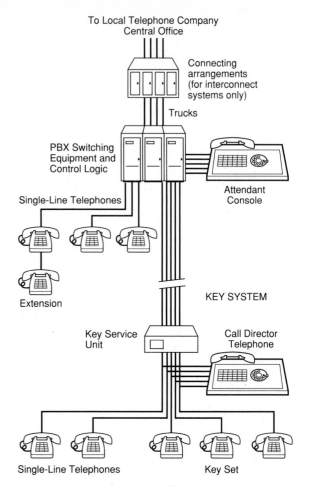

EXHIBIT 3   PBX SYSTEM INCLUDING KEY SYSTEM

chanical step-by-step systems, to electromechanical crossbar systems, to electronic systems.[1]

Step-by-step systems were first offered at the beginning of the century and were the primary PBX product of the telephone companies for many years. These electromechanical systems were very bulky and had only limited features, but provided economical and reliable service.

Crossbar systems were the next step in PBX evolution. These were again electromechanical switches that were more compact than the step-by-step systems, and had lower labor and mainte-

---

[1] A brief description of the switching and control systems technology can be found in Appendix A.

nance costs. They provided very reliable service, but were costly to expand beyond the capacity of the original installation.

Electronic telephone switching systems were the most recent technological development. The original work on electronic switching systems had been done at Bell Laboratories in the mid-1950s, and the first commercial electronic central office (i.e., a switching system within the Bell System) was opened in 1965. Electronic switching technology began to be used in the PBX market only in the early 1970s, and by 1974 there were about 20 electronic PBX models on the market. Most of these electronic systems used space division multiplexing (SDM). Electronic systems with time division multiplexing (TDM), which allowed several signals and calls to go over one pair of wires, promised to significantly simplify and reduce the costs of cabling a building for the PBX system. Electronic systems contained both memory and logic capabilities. PBXs with stored program logic allowed the user to make changes in the system by entering the changes at a terminal. Besides providing the normal control (connection) functions and a range of features to aid the telephone user, a computer-controlled electronic PBX could be used to record details of all toll calls (call detail recording), could monitor usage of the system, and could even perform self-diagnostic functions if there were problems with the equipment. In addition, if a company placed Tie Lines and WATS (Wide Area Telephone Service) lines on direct access (i.e., no operator was needed), the electronic switch could be programmed to seek the least-cost route for a long distance call. With additional memory an electronic PBX could be programmed to provide a wide range of features beyond those available on crossbar systems, including automatic dialing and speed calling, call forwarding, automatic distribution of calls to free telephones in a department, and multiple classes of service (i.e., some telephones could be given access to a limited range of the services available on the system, such as long distance).

Electronic systems could therefore provide a range of useful features to the user. They promised to be more reliable than electromechanical systems, although experience with electronic systems was not yet large enough to provide a convincing maintenance and reliability record. Electronic systems, particularly those based on the TDM technology, were also more suitable for tying into data communication terminals. This was expected to become an increasingly important consideration by the late 1970s.

COMPETITION IN THE PBX AND KEY SYSTEMS MARKET

After 1968 a customer could purchase a PBX or key system from one of two basic types of suppliers: (1) the telephone company providing service in his area or (2) an interconnect company. As Exhibit 4 suggests, the structure of the interconnect market was quite complex.

Manufacturers of PBX and Key Systems

The manufacturers of PBX equipment were a pretty diverse group. Western Electric, the supplier of the Bell System, Northern Telecom, the U.S. subsidiary of Northern Electric (the Bell Canada manufacturing arm), and the major suppliers to the independent telephone companies (such as GTE-Automatic Electric, North Electric and Stromberg Carlson) were all well established in the North American market—having supplied equipment to the various telephone companies since prior to the 1968 Carterfone decision. The PBX equipment manufactured by these suppliers for the independent telephone companies was, in 1968, generally similar to Western Electric's and offered only traditional features. The Carterfone decision provided an opportunity for another group of manufacturers to enter the U.S. market. These were largely European and Japanese manufacturers who had extensive experience with PBXs and key systems in other markets. With the encouragement of the interconnect suppliers (i.e., the companies selling to the end users), they modified their equipment and were able to offer end users features previously unavailable in the United States. By the early 1970s the Japanese and European companies had captured about 75% of the U.S. PBX and key system interconnect market.[2] The major companies in this group were Oki, Nippon Electric, Hitachi and Nitsuko (all Japanese) and L.M. Ericsson (Swedish). International Telephone and Telegraph (ITT) also entered the U.S. market after the Carterfone decision, and some industry observers

[2]That is, 75% of PBX and key system market which was not serviced by the AT&T operating companies or the independent telephone companies.

felt that in 1973 it had the best line of PBX equipment available in the United States. A list of the major manufacturers ranked in terms of their estimated 1973 sales to U.S. interconnect suppliers is shown in Exhibit 5. Some of these companies had also been quite successful in selling their products to some of the telephone operating companies. This resulted, in some cases, in end users being able to obtain identical equipment from either the telephone operating company or an interconnect supplier. The opening of

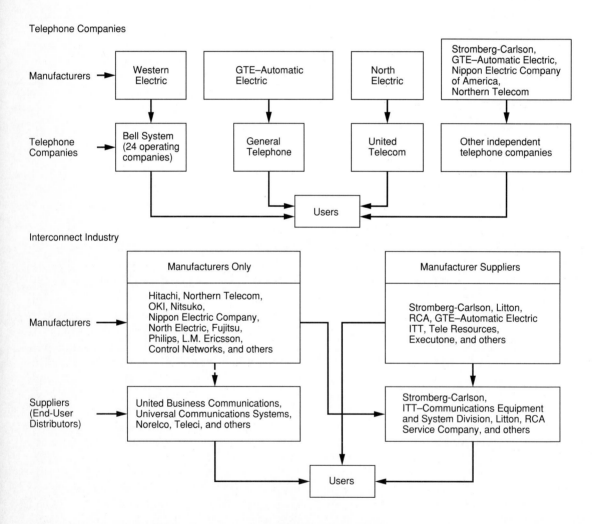

EXHIBIT 4   STRUCTURE OF THE MARKET FOR PBXs AND KEY SYSTEMS

Source: SRI Long Range Planning Service

EXHIBIT 5 MAJOR MANUFACTURERS OF INTERCONNECT EQUIPMENT RANKED IN ORDER OF ESTIMATED 1973 SALES TO U.S. INTERCONNECT COMPANIES

Company	Manufacturing locations
OKI Electronics of America/OKI Electric of Japan	Japan and U.S.
Nippon Electric Company	Japan and U.S.
Hitachi	Japan and U.S.
Nitsuko*	Japan
International Telephone and Telegraph (ITT)	U.S. and Spain
L. M. Ericsson	Sweden
Northern Telecom (subsidiary of Northern Electric of Canada)	Canada and U.S.
Stromberg Carlson	U.S.
North Electric (subsidiary of United Telecommunications)	U.S.
Fujitsu	Japan
General Telephone and Electronics (GTE)-Automatic Electric	U.S.
North American Phillips-Norelco	Netherlands and U.S.
CIT/TELIC	France and U.S.
Iwatsu*	Japan
Meisei	Japan
Siemens	Germany
Lynch	U.S.
Toshiba*	Japan

* Key systems only.
Source: SRI long range planning service.

the interconnect market had also brought a number of new U.S. manufacturers into the market. Wescom, Tele/Resources and Philco Ford had all developed electronic PBXs and were supplying them to the independent telephone companies or to interconnect suppliers. Litton and RCA, which had entered the market as national interconnect companies, were buying PBXs from others and were both rumored to be developing electronic PBXs. Other large manufacturers, active in foreign markets, were also believed to be ready to enter the market. IBM was viewed as a possible entrant, since it had developed a very strong position in the European PBX market with two expensive electronic PBXs. The major manufacturers of electronic PBXs and a brief description of their equipment and market position is contained in Exhibit 6.

Notable in their absence from the list of manufacturers in Exhibit 6 were the Japanese and European manufacturers. The major Japanese manufacturers (Nippon, Hitachi, Fujitsu and Oki) and the leading European manufacturer, L.M. Ericsson, produced high-quality electromechanical PBX equipment. Until the devaluation of the dollar in 1973, the Japanese PBX equipment had been very competitively priced. Ericsson had always sold its equipment at premium prices in the United States. The major Japanese manufacturers and Ericsson were all rumored to be developing electronic PBXs.

Interconnect Companies

The number of interconnect companies had grown rapidly since 1968, and by 1973, there were thought to be about 300 of them in the United States. These interconnect companies analyzed customer needs for PBXs and key systems, designed and recommended a system, installed it and serviced it. Interconnect companies could be subdivided into two basic groups: national

EXHIBIT 6   ELECTRONIC PBX MANUFACTURERS AND THEIR PRODUCT OFFERINGS IN 1973

Manufacturer	Model	Technologies used[a]		Number of lines PBX can handle	Comments
		Control	Switching		
Western Electric	801A	Electronic-wired logic	Space division (SDM)-reed relay[b]	46–270	Western Electric produced a very broad line of PBXs, most of which were still electromechanical. The 801A and 812A were both semielectronic. In the 101 systems, all switching was actually done in a Bell System central office, not on the customer's premises. An electronic central office was needed for the ESS. Only a small proportion of Bell central offices were electronic.
	812A	Electronic-wired logic	SDM-crossbar	400–2000	
	101 ESS (3A)	Electronic-computer	Time division (TDM)-electronic (PCM)[c]	400–800	
	101 ESS (4A)	Electronic-computer	TDM-electronic (PCM)	2000–4000	
ITT	TD-100	Electronic-wired logic	TDM-electronic (PAM)[d]	40–100	ITT's fully electronic PBXs covered all line sizes. Many observers felt it had the best line of PBXs on the market in 1973. Shipment of the TD-100 PBX was expected to begin in early 1974.
	TE-400A	Electronic-wired logic	SDM-electronic	100–400	
	TE-400G	Electronic-wired logic	SDM-electronic	400–800	
	TCS-2	Electronic-computer	SDM-electronic	600–6000	
Stromberg-Carlson	400A	Electronic-wired logic	SMD-reed relay	100–400	Both were semielectronic PBXs.
	800A	Electronic-wired logic	SDM-reed relay	400–800	
Wescom	501	Electronic-wired logic	SDM-electronic	40–120	This PBX was being sold to independent telephone companies. Shipments were expected to begin in early 1974.

| Manufacturer | Model | Technologies used[a] | | Number of lines PBX can handle | Comments |
		Control	Switching		
Tele/Resources	TR-32	Electronic-wired logic	TDM-electronic (PAM)	40–164	This PBX required unique and expensive phones and was sold only to interconnect suppliers. There were large order backlogs in late 1973.
Philco Ford	PC-192	Electronic-computer	SDM-electronic	64–192	The PC-512 was introduced in 1972 and was marketed to independent telephone companies. It was very expensive in relation to competitive offerings and was not believed to be selling well.
	PC-512	Electronic-computer	SDM-electronic	128–512	
IBM	2750	Electronic-computer	SDM-electronic	256–756	IBM had been successfully selling these very expensive PBX's in Europe. They were really feasible only for installations requiring more than 500 telephones.
	3750	Electronic-computer	SDM-electronic	256–2264	
Northern Telecom	SG-1	Electronic-wired logic	TDM-electronic (PAM)	40–80	The SG-1 was introduced in 1972 and had been selling very well in the U.S. and Canada. The SG-2 was not yet in production.
	SG-2	Electronic-wired logic	TDM-electronic (PAM)	80–120	
ROLM	Proposed	Electronic-computer	TDM-electronic (PCM)	100–800	

[a] See Appendix A for a brief discussion of the technological issues.
[b] Reed relay was an evolutionary switching approach that bridged the gap between electromechanical crossbar and fully electronic switching.
[c] PCM—pulse code modulation. Here all signals that are transmitted are digital signals.
[d] PAM—pulse amplitude modulation. Here all signals that are transmitted are analog signals.

EXHIBIT 7   ESTIMATED SALES BY INTERCONNECT COMPANIES IN 1973

Company	Sales (millions of dollars)
Litton Business Telephone Systems	25
Stromberg-Carlson Communications (subsidiary of General Dynamics)	25
ITT-Communications Equipment and Systems Division	18
United Business Communications (subsidiary of United Telecommunications)	14
Universal Communications Systems (subsidiary of American Motor Inns)	9
RCA Service Company (subsidiary of North American Philips)	8
GTE-Automatic Electric*	7
Teleci (subsidiary of Holiday Inns)	3
Tele/Resources	4
ITT-Terryphone**	4
Others (about 300, mostly local)	60
Total	182

* Excluding sales to local suppliers, figures for which are included under "Others."
** Key system sales only.
Source: SRI long range planning service.

suppliers and regional suppliers. Estimated sales for the major interconnect suppliers in 1973 are shown in Exhibit 7.

The four largest national companies—Litton, Stromberg-Carlson, ITT and United Business Communications—had offices throughout the United States and were divisions of much larger corporations. In 1973, ITT was the only one of the four that had a wholly owned manufacturing subsidiary. Stromberg-Carlson Communications was the result of the acquisition by General Dynamics, in June 1973, of Arcata Communications, Inc., and Arcata Leasing from Arcata National. The two Arcata National units had offices in twenty major metropolitan areas across the United States, and had generated losses of close to $4 million after taxes on sales of $25 million in the final year before General Dynamics acquired them. Eventually, as the acquired interconnect supplier was integrated with the Stromberg-Carlson manufacturing unit, Stromberg-Carlson would have, like ITT, an integrated manufacturing and distribution organization. There were also three other companies that were national in scope. Universal Communications Systems, a subsidiary of American Mo-

tor Inns, and Teleci, a subsidiary of Holiday Inn, both specialized in the hotel/motel segment of the market, and RCA Service Company specialized in hospitals and universities. Industry observers believed that these three companies were profitable. The hotel/motel segment of the market had some fairly unique characteristics that made it a good candidate for specialization. It required only a voice communications system, phones were not moved, key sets were rarely used, most calls were ingoing or outgoing, and a record of all outgoing calls had to be made for billing purposes. Universal Communications Systems and Teleci chose to meet the needs of this segment by importing Japanese electromechanical PBXs that could meet these requirements at low costs.

The regional interconnect suppliers were generally small companies which typically served a geographical area within a 50- or 100-mile radius of their home office. Among the major regional interconnect suppliers were Tele/Resources (New York), the Other Telephone Company (Minnesota), Fisk Electric (Texas) and Scott-Buttner Communications (California). Most of the interconnect companies were small with telecommunications sales generally being less than $2 million; Tele/Resources, believed to be the largest of these companies, had sales of about $4 million. Industry observers believed that these companies, unlike many of the national suppliers, were profitable. This was probably the result of lower overheads, knowledge of local requirements, and the flexibility of small companies. Many of these companies were seriously undercapitalized.

Some industry observers felt that the interconnect suppliers had been unable to fully exploit what they believed to be the major weaknesses of the telephone companies, namely, their fairly obsolete product line and their inability to respond quickly to the changing market and technology. Much of the Japanese and other PBX equipment the interconnect suppliers were handling was only marginally superior in terms of features to the equipment manufactured by Western Electric. Thus, they were forced to compete largely on the basis of lower price, more flexible pricing arrangements and greater installation flexibility. Even the Tele/Resources PBX, while fully electronic and easy to install, was not a great deal more flexible than conventional PBX equipment and, in addition, required expensive special phones. Also, it was said to be difficult to maintain. Nevertheless the first two years of production of this PBX were sold out within a few months of it being introduced.

Interconnect companies, both regional and national, stocked spare parts for their customers' PBXs so that they could rapidly get a customer's malfunctioning telephone system operating again. The faulty parts were then returned to the manufacturer for repair. Since this could take weeks or months, the interconnect companies generally carried substantial inventories of spare parts.

The Response of the Telephone Companies

The AT&T operating companies and the independent telephone companies were vigorously resisting the encroachment of the interconnect suppliers into the PBX and key systems market by actions on the regulatory front and by improving their PBXs. In 1970 AT&T had established a huge task force with people from Bell Labs, Western Electric and AT&T marketing and engineering at a new facility in Denver, Colorado, to develop a new, more competitive PBX product line. This resulted in four new competitively priced electronic or semielectronic PBXs (shown in Exhibit 6) being introduced between 1971 and 1973. ROLM management felt that AT&T's intensive product development efforts were likely to result in further products that were technically much more competitive with the proposed ROLM offering, although ROLM would probably have a year or so lead time.

Current Status of the Interconnect Market and Future Prospects

In a proprietary report published by the Long Range Planning Service (now the Business Intelligence Program) of SRI International, it was estimated that sales by interconnect suppliers had grown from virtually zero in 1968 to $182 million (at end-user prices) in 1973. Manufacturers' selling prices were approximately 50% of end-user prices, and given that there was a substantial amount of inventory at the supplier level, manufacturers' shipments were expected to total $120 million in 1973.

The $182 million sales estimate was broken down into three categories:

1 $130 million in PBX sales. This included 3300 PBXs with 248,000 telephones. This was estimated to be 12.4% of the dollar value of all new and replacement PBX installations in 1973.

2 $47 million in key systems sales. This included 6000 key systems with 72,000 telephones. This was estimated to be 6.7% of the dollar value of all new and replacement key system installations in 1973.

3 $5 million in service and maintenance revenues which included charges for telephones added to the original system, moving telephones within an office, etc.

SRI also attempted to project the market growth through 1985. Given the uncertainties surrounding the interconnect market, both conservative and optimistic projections were made. These projections took into account probable shakeouts in the industry, stronger competition from the telephone companies, regulatory factors and a shortening life cycle (hence more frequent replacement) for this type of equipment. On the basis of SRI's assumptions, total interconnect supplier sales were expected to be in the range of $1.1 to $1.7 billion by 1985; this was expected to give interconnect suppliers an installed base penetration of 21% to 30% for PBXs and 15% to 21% for key systems. During this period SRI expected rapid technological development to continue with computer-controlled or stored-logic electronic switching systems being standard in PBX and key systems by 1980.

PBX AND KEY SYSTEMS CUSTOMERS

One of the first things Dick Moley had done after joining ROLM in August 1973 was to talk to several large companies about their communication problems. Commenting on these interviews Moley said: "What they came up with was very interesting—because what they said their problems were, were problems that were not being addressed by the interconnect equipment or the Bell System equipment at the time, and that is where we saw our opportunity. What they said was that the largest portion of their bill, frequently 70% to 80%, is toll expenses. If you are a large electronics company, for example, you have foreign Exchange lines, Tie lines and WATS lines. Trying to get people to use these—to get them to go to the proper tables and look up how to call a number in a particular city, say Los Angeles (to dial 76 for Los Angeles, then dial 9 for an outside line, and then dial the telephone number)— is very difficult. Even if a person does all this, the line frequently will be busy. Similarly, to gain access to a WATS line the caller may have to call a special operator and wait for a line to become available. So what happens in many companies, of course, is that many people make many long distance calls without bothering to use these expensive facilities. Furthermore, many companies wish to keep track of who was calling which numbers, both to control abuse and to bill departments for their real use of facilities, rather than simply making an arbitrary allocation. Many people also felt that restrictions on toll calling on a telephone-by-telephone basis and automated queuing for WATS lines seemed to be needed features. The equipment available in 1973 simply did not address these needs and the Bell System obviously didn't have a great incentive to optimize the use of toll calling facilities, since it would negatively impact its revenues."

A second major area of concern that surfaced in these interviews was the cost of making, and the time required to make, changes in the telephone system when people were relocated. This was particularly true in firms that used a project type of organization or in organizations that were experiencing rapid growth, where the average times between moves of a phone could be as short as six months. Every time personnel changes were made and people were relocated, the telephone company had to be called in to change wires and relocate the phones, and sometimes the companies had to wait quite a long time for these changes to be made. One very large firm of consultants in San Francisco was already spending over $400,000 per year on moves and changes.

"Another area that was an absolute nightmare was key phone systems," commented Dick Moley. "We saw that in our office last year when Ken Oshman's office had to be relocated. Two men spent a whole day recabling 125-pair cables to the new location for the key phone system. We then asked ourselves, Why are key systems so difficult to move? The reason is that each light on the call director's push-button set takes six wires to activate, and so you may need a very thick (1 inch in diameter) 125-pair cable from the switching equipment to the call director telephone with 20 or so lines, and you clearly can't afford to run such a cable all over the building. That seemed to us to be totally insane with the available electronics. So we said we can do it differently. What we can do is use a key phone with a three-pair cable—one pair for voice, one pair to power the electronics and the third pair to digitally signal which button is depressed and to indicate which button to light. Thus, if we standardize the building wiring completely on three-pair cables, which connect to wall sockets much like electrical wiring, the user will not have to rewire the building if some phone is moved."

Large customers would be critical to ROLM's success in the marketplace, since the computer-controlled PBX system that they were developing was designed to handle 100 to 800 lines. This line range had been chosen because cost-effective computer-controlled models that would provide the kind of benefits customers desired could not yet be cost competitive for installations of less than 100-line capacity. In 1973 only a very small number of Fortune 500 companies were buying from interconnect suppliers. Most of the sales by the interconnect companies had been made to smaller organizations. In fact about 75% of the interconnect equipment was sold to hotels and motels, wholesalers and retailers, stockbrokers, insurance agencies, hospitals and clinics, attorneys, banks, stockbrokers, manufacturers and service industries. Few of the installations made by the interconnect companies had more than 100 lines. For these reasons a final issue Dick Moley raised in his interviews with the large companies was why they had not bought equipment from interconnect suppliers. A major reason the companies cited was that they saw few economic benefits from buying from interconnect suppliers. The main benefit was that they could purchase the equipment and hence freeze their equipment cost (since they would be unaffected by telephone company rental rate increases). But since equipment was usually only 20% to 30% of their costs, and when a discounted cash flow analysis of the purchase versus rental choice was made, the savings often turned out to be minor. Meanwhile if the equipment was purchased, the company was locked into equipment that might soon become obsolete. It seemed that smaller companies were much less likely to do a discounted cash flow analysis and seemed to be largely attracted to the interconnect PBXs by their marginally better features and the belief that they would get better service from these companies than they would from the telephone operating companies. An additional factor that might help explain the failure of the interconnect companies to penetrate larger companies was that few of the interconnect suppliers appeared to have sales organizations that were capable of conducting a sales campaign at several levels of decision making in prospective large companies.

From his discussions with the large companies Mr. Moley also gained a better appreciation of the decision-making process for PBXs and key systems. Voice communication decision makers were generally low-level office managers or communication managers. The office or communications manager often relied greatly on the recommendations of the telephone company salesperson, and in fact, frequently the manager was a former Bell System employee. The main responsibilities of the manager were largely those of placing orders with the telephone company and coordinating installation and service activities. When alternative suppliers to the telephone companies became available, they were very cautious about recommending them, since the risks of poor service and the possibility of the interconnect supplier going out of business were not inconsequential. Furthermore since switching to an interconnect supplier typically required that the equipment be purchased rather than leased, they usually lacked the authority to make the decision themselves, and the capital expenditure had often to be approved at very high levels in the organization—sometimes even at the board level. The communication manager was not usually accustomed to preparing these types of proposals and doing the necessary internal selling to get the proposals approved.

The results of the customer interviews made ROLM management very enthusiastic about their potential entry into the telecommunications market. As Mr. Moley remarked, "Out of our discussions I and the others in ROLM management became really enthusiastic, because clearly here is a vast market where we potentially have the capability to solve meaningful customer problems and save companies large amounts of money. Computer technology was the key to solving these problems: we could optimize call routings, handle toll restrictions, etc. If there are telephones in place, handling moves and changes becomes simply a matter of remotely reprogramming the switching equipment: nobody needs to visit physically the customer's office or plant."

THE ROLM PBX

By October 1973, Jim Kasson and his two associates had made considerable progress on the technical aspects of the ROLM product. The conventional wisdom in the telephone industry trade magazines at the time was that time division multiplexing (TDM) with pulse code modulation (PCM) switching technology and stored logic (computer control) control technology would not be viable and cost-effective until the late 1970s or early 1980s. Jim Kasson was now convinced that it was a viable technology in 1973. As a result of some clever circuit work and ROLM's knowledge of minicomputers, software and PCM technology, they were convinced that their approach would work and would be cost-effective. They had already "breadboarded" (i.e., laid out the electronic circuitry in a crude way) key technology elements that were new to ROLM, and they even had a couple of telephones in the laboratory working with their switching circuitry. In effect, the technological advances they were taking advantage of promised to change the nature of PBX manufacture from a labor- and capital-intensive operation to a technology-intensive electronic assembly operation which would require the manufacturer to have minicomputer, software and solid-state switching expertise. These were all technologies in which ROLM management felt that their company had significant strengths.

The management of ROLM was convinced that the flexibility of a computer-controlled PBX built on a TDM technology would change the economics of a business communication system's installation, maintenance and operation, besides providing excellent user convenience. For example, with their PBX it would be possible to prewire a building with standard three-pair cable connected to wall outlets. Then all that was necessary to install a complete system was to connect the cables to the PBX, plug the standard telephone sets into the sockets, and enter into the computer the locations and extension numbers of the telephones. In the case of a multiline key set, the information entered into the PBX would include information on all the extensions which are to be routed to the set. Moves and changes of extensions would be a straightforward matter of entering the new configuration information into the computer. No longer would it be necessary to have the wiring tailored to the specific configuration and have ancillary key-set switching equipment located remote from the PBX. Furthermore, the ROLM PBX was expected to be price-competitive in the range of 100 to 500 extensions, a range which, they estimated, accounted for 60% of the dollar value of all PBX systems.

DECISIONS FACING ROLM IN OCTOBER 1973

ROLM's Board of Directors, in preliminary discussions of the proposed entry, were not totally convinced of the wisdom of ROLM, a $4 million company, moving against such formidable competitors, and some directors openly questioned whether this was the best area in which to invest the company's limited resources. Investment bankers also raised similar concerns. Even within the top ranks of ROLM management there were executives who were quite unsure about whether a move into the telecommunications market was in ROLM's best interest.

From a manufacturing cost viewpoint, ROLM management was not concerned about the disparity in size between ROLM and its competitors, whose manufacturing experience base for the most part was built on electromechanical equipment (which was labor- and capital-intensive) whereas ROLM's equipment was largely electronic. In their view, this made it feasible for ROLM to compete with the likes of Western Electric. Kasson and his team had concluded that with a further investment of $500,000 in engineering and manufacturing they could get the product into production. If given the go-ahead, they expected to have a prototype working in the laboratory by mid-1974 and to begin shipping systems in early 1975.

Detailed estimates of manufacturing costs had been developed by Kasson and others on the PBX team. With a sales price based on two and one-half times manufacturing cost (direct materials, direct labor and overhead based on direct labor cost) the ROLM PBX promised to be cost-competitive with the most closely competitive models available in the United States. They anticipated that volume discounts would be given to customers ordering multiple PBXs, if they decided to market the product through telephone companies or interconnect companies. Since the ROLM PBX made heavy use of electronic components (e.g., the minicomputer, the computer memory and integrated circuits), the cost of the PBX was expected to decline over time as the cost of electronic components continued their decline. Electromechanical PBXs, and even electronic PBXs based on analog technologies, were expected to experience a much more static cost future.

Channels of Distribution for the PBX

In many respects ROLM's management felt that the most crucial decision facing them in 1973 was the choice of channels of distribution for their PBX system. Dick Moley felt they had several alternatives open to them:

1 Sell to the Bell System. The operating companies of the Bell System had traditionally relied exclusively on Western Electric for all their equipment. However, the competitive pressures from the interconnect companies had resulted in several of the operating companies— including the largest one, Pacific Telephone— buying equipment from other suppliers. Pacific Telephone had bought electromechanical PBX systems from Japanese suppliers, and more recently it had bought Northern Telecom's fully electronic PBX which handled up to 120 lines. The former move was not a very radical one since the Japanese designs were similar to Western Electric designs and could be installed and maintained by their field service force without any extensive retraining. The Northern Telecom purchase was more significant since this did require retraining the field service force. Since the Bell operating companies were still believed to control some 80% of the installed PBX base, even a small share of this market would represent a huge sales volume to ROLM.

2 Sell to the independent telephone companies, such as General Telephone. While the independent telephone companies covered about 15% of the phones in the United States and were more concentrated in rural areas, they were growing about 50% more rapidly than AT&T. This reflected the movement of industry and population away from major metropolitan areas. Since larger companies still tended to concentrate in major metropolitan areas, the independent telephone companies' share of the large PBX (greater than 100 lines) market was much less than 15%. Their captive manufacturing subsidiaries were not as strong as Western Electric, and the independent telephone companies had never relied on them as much.

3 Sell to the interconnect companies. These were concentrated in the larger metropolitan areas. Here ROLM had two alternatives: (a) the national companies such as Litton Business Systems, ITT, RCA Service Company, United Business Communications and Stromberg-Carlson Communications; or (b) the regional companies such as Tele/Resources,

Fisk Telephone Systems and Scott-Buttner Communications. Many of the national suppliers were in trouble due to the lack of experienced managers, higher than anticipated investments, heavier than anticipated installation and maintenance expenses, too-rapid geographic expansion resulting in loss of control, and the difficulty of providing quick and adequate service capability on a nationwide basis. These problems were exacerbated by the fiercely competitive nature of the markets, the heavy legal expenses, and the drain on management time necessary to challenge some of the telephone companies' new pricing schemes before the regulatory commissions. These chaotic market conditions had resulted in some companies getting into difficulties and being forced to merge with others. Some of the regional interconnect companies were doing quite well in their local markets. They bought their equipment from a variety of manufacturers including Nippon, Stromberg-Carlson and Tele/Resources. Generally the manufacturers required them to handle the equipment on a nonexclusive basis so that two or more interconnect companies in the same market area might carry the same PBX line. The regional companies typically were undercapitalized and sold small systems. It was very seldom that one handled a PBX with a capacity larger than 100 lines. Most of the equipment they were handling was still electromechanical. While marketing through regional interconnect companies had some advantages, particularly from a servicing perspective, there was a real question of whether large companies with multiple locations would want to deal with multiple interconnect companies. Some of the other manufacturers using regional interconnect companies, including Northern Telecom, handled large sales directly, and simply subcontracted with the regional interconnect companies for installation and maintenance service.

4 Sell direct. ROLM had given little thought to this alternative, since they felt that they were simply too small. But from a sales viewpoint it had some obvious advantages, especially when it came to dealing with large accounts with multiple locations around the country.

Dick Moley's Task

Dick Moley had to make decisions with respect to channels of distribution and pricing and also with respect to such closely related issues as the amount and nature of advertising and sales promotion to be directed at end users. By the November 1973 board meeting he hoped to have selected and laid out in some detail the marketing plan for the ROLM PBX. He hoped he would be able to present a convincing case for ROLM's entry into the PBX market.

APPENDIX A

PBX AND KEY SYSTEMS TECHNOLOGY

Much of the technological change in PBX systems was occurring in the switching and control systems. The technological alternatives in both the switching and control systems are shown in Exhibit A1. With respect to the switching system, two major alternatives were possible: space division multiplexing (SDM) and time division multiplexing (TDM). An SDM system was one in which separate individual transmission paths were set up for the duration of the call. A TDM system was one in which the speech on each active line was sampled at a very high rate so that no information was lost, and the samples were assigned to unique time slots on a common transmission line. The original signal could be reconstructed from these samples when needed. The ability to handle many calls on one line promised to lower costs. In a TDM system the samples could be transmitted as either an analog (pulse amplitude modulation, or PAM) signal or a digital (pulse code modulation, or PCM) signal. If pulse code modulation was used, then all signals were digital—making such a system ideal for transmitting data as well as voice. This was expected to be an increasingly valuable feature by the late 1970s, as more and more companies wished to transmit both data and voice over the same telecommunications system. Furthermore, if a digital signal was sent over a reliable trans-

mission line, there was no cross-talk or distortion, which one could get if an analog system were used. ROLM engineers believed that a PBX with a TDM analog system could not (with the technology then available) be designed to handle more than 120 lines without excessive cross-talk. Partly for this reason, TDM with pulse code modulation was carrying an increasing share of the Bell System's long distance traffic. Nevertheless many observers in the early 1970s did not expect that the pulse code modulation technology would be cost-effective in PBXs until the late 1970s.

The control system could be either distributed control or common control. A distributed-control system was one in which the control logic was distributed throughout the PBX system (e.g., if key phones were used, some of the control logic was in the key phone unit), whereas a common-control system was one in which all the control functions were centralized in one set of logic. With a common-control system the control equipment was tied up only during the time the connection was made and not during the conversation. A wired logic common-control system basically did with electronic components what was otherwise done by electromechanical relays. On the other hand, a computer-controlled common-control system added a new dimension to the PBX. New circuits had to be added to a wired logic system in order to alter its properties and capabilities, but a computer-controlled system's functions could be altered by changing its pro-gram. This gave a computer-controlled system great flexibility and the potential to meet future demands that wired logic systems could not match.

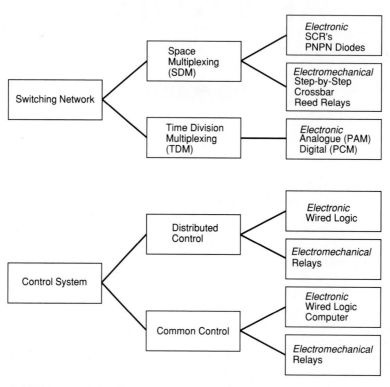

EXHIBIT A1   PBX TECHNOLOGICAL ALTERNATIVES

COLGATE-PALMOLIVE FRANCE (A)

In late 1982, Paul Jarrot,[1] National Account Manager at Colgate-Palmolive France, was drawing up a proposal for the 1983 sales conditions he would be presenting at a December 23rd meeting with "Intermarché," a large national supermarket chain. During a recent meeting the representatives from Intermarché's central purchasing office had demanded a substantial improvement in the sales and promotional terms for Colgate's hygiene-toiletry products. Paul Jarrot now wondered how he could best answer their request.

COLGATE-PALMOLIVE

Colgate-Palmolive was an American firm that manufactured and sold branded consumer goods, mainly for household cleaning and personal care. It was one of the world leaders in this category consisting of soaps, toothpastes, shampoos, shaving products, and other toiletries. The Colgate-Palmolive France group was the corporation's largest subsidiary with 1982 sales of 3 billion French francs,[2] 8.5% of Colgate's sales worldwide.

Marketing and sales

Two groups handled all consumer good marketing activities at Colgate-Palmolive France (Exhibit 1). Marketing was mainly responsible for designing, developing, and managing products, with particular emphasis on pricing and advertising. Sales (household goods) was broken down into two parallel divisions: "Household Cleaning" and "Hygiene-Toiletries," which represented 60% and 40% of sales, respectively (Exhibit 2). Each division had regional sales forces reporting to regional managers and sales supervisors (Exhibit 3). The two sales forces operated independently when calling on individual stores.

In addition, each sales division had national account managers, each responsible for a portfolio of national accounts. Although the sales forces did not report to them, the national ac-

---

This case was prepared by François Canivet, INSEAD M.B.A. participant, under the supervision of Reinhard Angelmar, Associate Professor at INSEAD. It is intended to be used as a basis for class discussion rather than to illustrate either effective or ineffective handling of an administrative situation.

[1] All names have been changed.

[2] 10 F ≈ 1 US$.

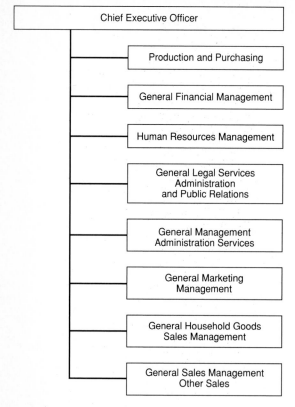

EXHIBIT 1   PARTIAL ORGANIZATION CHART

count managers set and monitored objectives, product line strategy, and promotional plans for their clients, thus influencing sales force work. Within the constraints of Colgate's general sales policy, they were granted considerable autonomy in decision making, especially during the annual negotiation of sales and promotional terms.

HYGIENE-TOILETRY PRODUCTS IN FRANCE

These included soaps, toothpastes, shampoos, shaving products, bubble baths, shower products, hair sprays, and powders.

Consumption of these products showed a slight annual growth of 2%. The world leaders— Colgate, Procter & Gamble, Lever/Gibbs, L'Oréal —represented a substantial portion of the market (Exhibit 4), and competed vigorously using all elements of the marketing mix: consistent improvement of formulae and products, intense advertising (Exhibit 5) and heavy presence with distributors through large sales forces and sophisticated promotional plans.

Consumer research indicated strong brand loyalty, from around 30% for soaps and shampoos to nearly 50% for some toothpastes.

DISTRIBUTION IN FRANCE

Retail sales of hygiene-toiletry products through medium- and large-sized outlets accounted for 60% to 70% of sales depending on the product (Exhibit 6). In recent years, retailers had been joining forces to form central purchasing offices ("Centrales d'Achat"). Their main functions were to negotiate with the manufacturers the amounts of year-end discounts and the conditions for accepting new products. Agreement between a manufacturer and a purchasing office was often the first phase in a lengthy negotiation process. In the case of accepting a new product, for example, a framework agreement was signed with the purchasing office, authorizing the supplier to propose his product to its members, who might then revise the conditions if deemed necessary and allow the manufacturer to conduct final negotiation with their individual retail outlets. Procedures could be simpler in other purchasing offices (Exhibit 7). In all cases, the product reached the shelves of the retail stores only through heavy involvement of the manufacturer's entire sales organization, from top to bottom.

The emergence of central purchasing offices had created considerable concentration at the retail level. For example, the largest purchasing office represented 13% and the ten largest accounted for 80% of Colgate's sales (Exhibit 8). Each manufacturer carried far less weight with each of the retailers since the top hundred manufacturers represented approximately 50% of the retailer's grocery sales. Colgate usually ranked fifth among suppliers.

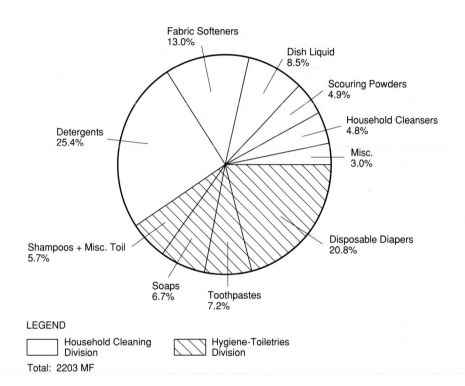

LEGEND

☐ Household Cleaning Division   ▨ Hygiene-Toiletries Division

Total: 2203 MF

EXHIBIT 2   COLGATE-PALMOLIVE: HOUSEHOLD GOODS SALES—FRANCE
STRUCTURE OF 1982 SALES BY PRODUCT GROUP

EXHIBIT 3   COLGATE-PALMOLIVE: 1982 HOUSEHOLD GOODS SALES ORGANIZATION

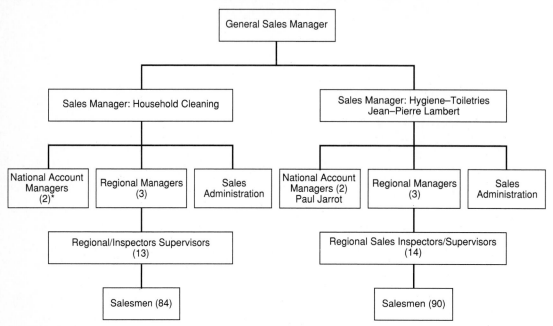

* The numbers in brackets refer to the number of persons in each position.

Source: Colgate-Palmolive.

EXHIBIT 4   HYGIENE-TOILETRY PRODUCTS

Development of Sales (81/80) and 1981 Market Shares (in Volume) of the Major Brands and Companies on the French Market

Soaps	81/80	MS 81(%)	Toothpastes	81/80	MS 81(%)	Shampoos	81/80	MS 81(%)
Palmolive	−8	12.9	Tonigencyl	−2	9	Palmolive	+3	10.3
Cadum	+7	9.4	Colgate Fluor	+4	7.5	**Total Colgate**	−5	**12.1**
Donge	+8	9.3	**Total Colgate**	−4	**26.5**	Dop	−2	12.8
Total Colgate	0	**33.4**				**Total SCAD**	−7	**20.6**
Monsavon	+2	11.1	Signal	−3	20.9	Moëlle Garnier	−5	7.6
Camay	+4	13.0	**Total Gibbs**	−5	**32.8**	Mixa Bébé	+13	7.0
Total P&G	+3	**29.3**	Fluocaril	−9	10.1	**Total Roja Garnier**	−1	**16.3**
			Teraxyl[1]	−	4			
Lux	+1	9.1				**Total L'Oréal**	−5	**40.7**
Total Lever	−5	**14.5**				L'Empereur	+23	6.4
						Corinne de Farme	+24	5.4

[1] New 1981 Henkel product.
Source: Colgate-Palmolive.

EXHIBIT 5   HYGIENE-TOILETRY PRODUCTS: 1981 ADVERTISING EXPENDITURE
(in Million French Francs)

Soaps	MF	% of sales	Toothpastes	MF	% of sales	Shampoos	MF	% of sales
Palmolive	2.2	4.5	Tonigencyl	19.8	37	Total Colgate	4.4	5.4
Cadum	3.3	10	Colgate Fluor	10.5	31	Total L'Oréal	23.8	N.A.
Total Colgate	5.5	4.2	Total Colgate	27.3	19			
Monsavon	3.5	N.A.						
Camay	4.7	N.A.	Signal	10.5	N.A.			
Total P&G	8.2	N.A.	Total Gibbs	25.0	N.A.			
Lux	2.8	N.A.						
Total market	33.5	N.A.	Total market	79.0	N.A.	Total market	34.8	N.A.
81/80	+14%		81/80	+31.0%		81/80	+10.0%	N.A.

Source: Colgate-Palmolive.

In the battle for the consumer, competition among retailers was fierce, even between members of the same central purchasing office. Competition focused primarily on prices as reflected in retailer advertising.[3] In accordance with this policy, national brands, like those of Colgate-Palmolive, were used as "loss leaders," sold at minimum margin to attract the clientele. Average retail prices supplied by retailer panels revealed prices that were at most 10% above Colgate list prices and as much as 18% below for some products.

Another facet of retailer strategy was to develop "private label" (store brand) and especially "no-brand" (generic) products. The market shares controlled by such products were greater for commodity-type categories (e.g. sugar, jam) than for "image" categories like hygiene-toiletry, where they never exceeded 3%.

COLGATE'S SALES POLICY

Manufacturers were required by French law to comply with non-discriminatory sales practices. This meant that they had to offer identical sales conditions for "identical" products and services. This applied to both general sales terms (price lists, functional discounts, terms of payment, year-end discounts) and promotional conditions (promotional discounts and cooperative promotion).

[3] In France, retailers were the heaviest users of advertising, with copy often limited to "reduced prices," "unheard-of prices," "prices shattered," "lowest prices," etc.

EXHIBIT 6   HYGIENE-TOILETRY: SALES BY RETAIL OUTLET 1981/82
(All Brands Together, in % of Tonnage)

	Hypermarkets	Supermarkets	Mini-markets	Department stores	Others[1]	Comments
Soaps	34	37	6	8	15	
Toothpastes	26	31	6	7	30*	* Including 25 pharmacies
Shampoos	32	33	6	7	22	

[1] For example, pharmacies, perfume and beauty shops, hairdressers, mail-order houses.
Source: Colgate-Palmolive.

EXHIBIT 7   NEW PRODUCTS ACCEPTANCE: EXAMPLES OF PRODUCT SELECTION PROCEDURES

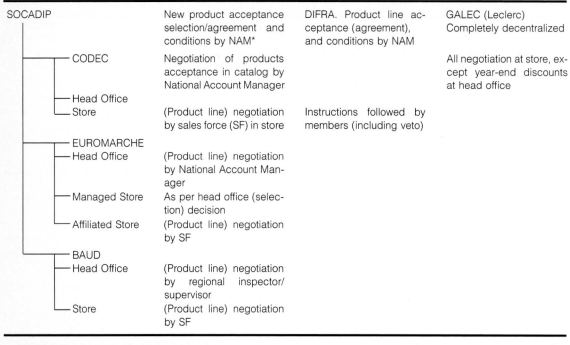

SOCADIP		New product acceptance selection/agreement and conditions by NAM*	DIFRA. Product line acceptance (agreement), and conditions by NAM	GALEC (Leclerc) Completely decentralized
	CODEC	Negotiation of products acceptance in catalog by National Account Manager		All negotiation at store, except year-end discounts at head office
	Head Office			
	Store	(Product line) negotiation by sales force (SF) in store	Instructions followed by members (including veto)	
	EUROMARCHE			
	Head Office	(Product line) negotiation by National Account Manager		
	Managed Store	As per head office (selection) decision		
	Affiliated Store	(Product line) negotiation by SF		
	BAUD			
	Head Office	(Product line) negotiation by regional inspector/supervisor		
	Store	(Product line) negotiation by SF		

* NAM: National Account Manager.
Source: Colgate Palmolive.

Price List

Colgate's price list was identical for all clients, private and public. Volume discounts were given. The price list was not negotiable. This had now been totally accepted by retailers.

Functional Discounts

A functional discount might be granted to compensate distributors for storage and redistribution services. Only distributors with warehouses benefited from this discount, which was independent of quantities ordered. It amounted to 2% off invoice and was not negotiable.

Terms of Payment

Since Colgate's parent company was extremely sensitive to funds tied up in accounts receivable, terms of payment were watched very carefully by sales management. Terms of payment could be discussed with the retailers[4] but had to remain non-discriminatory. Colgate-Palmolive made an effort to maintain a relationship between its terms and the inventories financed by the client (Exhibit 9).

Exceptions to the rules shown in Exhibit 9 existed, mainly for historical reasons, but they were gradually disappearing. Financial factors could also be involved, leading to shorter payment periods if a client's creditworthiness was doubtful.

Year-End Discounts (YED)

Discounts could be tied to sales level, sales growth, the acceptance of new products, etc.

[4] Terms of payment were rarely discussed at the purchasing office level because of the widely varying nature and creditworthiness of members.

EXHIBIT 8   COLGATE SALES BY ACCOUNT, 1982

	Total (MF)	Sales (%)	Colgate hygiene toiletry (MF)	Colgate hygiene toiletry (%)	Channel	Main member companies
Socadip	294	13.3	57	13	Chain + wholesale stores	Viniprix-Baud Euromarché, Codec Primistères
Galec	230	10.4	35	8	Group of independents	Leclerc
Metca/Vita C/M	224	10.2	46	10.6	Indep, HM + direct	Carrefour Comptoirs Modernes
Interdis	217	9.9	37	8.5	Wholesalers	Promodès
Difra	211	9.6	38	8.8	Chain + wholesale stores	Camas, Francap Genty Cathiard
Paridoc	192	8.7	37	8.5	Chain stores	Stam, Cedis, Cofradel
SGCC	113	5.1	22	5.1	Coop.	Coop (regional)
Auchan	111	5.0	21	4.8	Independent HM + direct	Auchan
ITM	93	4.2	20	4.6	Group independents	ITM
Guichard-Perrachon	87	4.0	16	3.7	Chain of stores	Casino-Epargne
Total	1772	80.4	329	76.0		
Total France	2204	100.0	433	100.0		

	Main store names	Assortment decision	Number of stores HM	Number of stores SM	Number of stores Mini
Socadip	Idem + Rallye La Parisienne	Local after agreement from Central Purchasing Office (CPO)	70	655	1100
Galec	Leclerc	Warehouse	49	266	
Metca/Vita C/M	Carrefour, Comod	Store	52	147	194
Interdis	Continent, Champion	idem SOCADIP	23	176	440
Difra	Radar, Sodim, Record	Members after agreement CPO	36	582	568
Paridoc	Mammouth, Suma	Members-minimum common assortment	75	382	163
SGCC	Rond-Point, Coop	National catalog recommended by type of store	40	346	1084
Auchan	Auchan	Catalog negotiation at head office and store	32	1	-
ITM	Intermarché	National local promo.	2	366	-
Guichard-Perrachon	Casino-Epargne	National, by type of store	18	76	2022
Total			397	2997	5571
Total France			443	3968	6746

Source: Colgate-Palmolive.

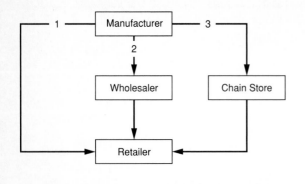

Channel	Account	Inventory to finance	Colgate Conditions[1]
1	Retailer	Retailer	30 days
2	Wholesaler	Warehouse	45 days
3	Chain store	Warehouse + retailer	60 days

[1] Conditions are typically from "end of month" of the invoice. The "end of month" clause means an additional 15 days, on the average. That is, "30 days end of month" correspond to a payment 45 days after the invoice date, "45 days end of month" to 60 days, and so forth. Sometimes, conditions are quoted "net." On the average, "net" conditions are 15 days shorter than "end of month" conditions.

EXHIBIT 9   HYGIENE-TOILETRY PRODUCTS TERMS OF PAYMENT

They were negotiated annually with the purchasing offices as a function of detailed objectives and represented the most controversial element of sales terms, varying widely across product categories and competitors. Manufacturers were under constant pressure from the retailers to increase discounts, make them unconditional, and reduce their payment periods, since the retailers often deducted their anticipated discounts during the year to establish low prices. In spite of resistance from the manufacturers, quarterly advance payments on year-end discounts were becoming increasingly common.

Promotional Discounts

Colgate proposed promotional actions to its clients, which ordinarily resulted in reduced consumer prices. Typically, the client was granted a promotional discount on one order during the promotion period, usually two months. Promotional actions were discussed locally by the sales force, which later checked to see that the reduction had actually been passed on to the consumer. The sales force had a six-month promotion schedule specifying the promotions planned for each product. In principle, promotional discounts also had to comply with the rule of non-discrimination.

Promotional discounts granted by Colgate varied from 5% to 15% depending on product category. At any point in time, around one-third of its products were on promotion.

Cooperative Promotion

Cooperative promotion meant that a retailer agreed to sell certain services to the manufacturer. Such services included shelf space for new products, rental of end-of-aisle displays, special in-store displays, etc. Agreement on cooperative promotion would involve subsequent signature of a contract and invoicing of services by the retailer. Since the retailer was selling the service, it was he who had to comply with the principle of non-discrimination. There were two main forms of cooperative promotion: long- and short-term.

Long-term cooperative promotion usually involved an annual contract, stipulating the supply of a number of services throughout the year. For example, a chain of stores might agree to place 12 end-of-aisle display racks in each store at the manufacturer's disposal for the year. Such contracts were negotiated by the national account manager at the head office, and payment was made at the end of the year. The sales force supervised implementation of the contract at retail outlets.

Short-term cooperative promotion involved the supply of services (shelf space, end-of-aisle displays, special displays, etc.) at the specific time of the promotion, in a specific store, and was negotiated and controlled locally. Even if a contract were signed nationally, payments would have to be made to each store. The cost of renting an end-of-aisle display rack could be as much as 3,000FF per week per store.

Whenever a new product was launched, special conditions would be negotiated, sometimes starting at the central purchasing office level. Certain offices demanded compensation that could reach as much as 20% of the new product's sales.

Colgate-Palmolive intended to offer sales terms comparable to those of its major competitors. However, comparison of sales terms was often complicated by the diversity of lines. The detergent manufacturers (Procter & Gamble, Lever) usually offered less advantageous conditions than the toiletry producers (Gibbs, L'Oréal). These differences were mostly due to differences in inventory turnover rates, volume-surface occupied-price ratios, and logistical considerations. Colgate's hygiene-toiletry product range included both detergent (soap) products, and toiletries, and so its sales terms were somewhere between the two extremes. This meant that its soaps had a stronger position, toothpastes parity, and shampoos, shaving products and other toiletries a slight disadvantage relative to competitors.

The competitive environment for disposable diapers, which were also the responsibility of the hygiene sales division, was very different from that of the other products in the line. The sales terms on this market, therefore, were very different.

In all its contacts with the distributors, Colgate stressed the logic of its marketing policy and the consistency and non-discriminatory character of its sales terms.

INTERMARCHÉ

The Intermarché (ITM) group of independent supermarkets was founded in 1969. Its 1982 domestic sales were estimated at 14 billion French francs, 4.5% of grocery retailing in France. As of late 1982, the group numbered 470 supermarkets throughout France, 90 of which had opened that year.

The typical Intermarché outlet was a supermarket covering approximately 1000 sq. m. (3048 sq. ft.), offering merchandise consisting mainly of food products (i.e. very little clothing,

furniture, etc.), and located near the center of a medium-sized city. Intermarché pursued a pure discounter strategy. The product line was limited and concentrated on a small number of suppliers in each category of products, to obtain their best conditions. Advertising stressed low prices and store gross margins could not exceed 12% (after all discounts).

Each Intermarché store was bound by a membership and franchise contract to the group and was managed by a member who had to be the majority stockholder of his company. No member could run more than two stores. With an average of 1.2 stores per member, ITM had grown mainly by recruiting new members.

Each member agreed to volunteer around one-third of his time to group management. Most members changed volunteer position approximately every 18 months to encourage a flow of new ideas and experiences. The few non-members, or so-called "permanents," involved in group management were generally considered potential members. After a period of approximately 18 months, ITM judged whether they had the necessary qualities to become members. If they qualified, ITM helped them find the funds they would need to open a store. If not, they were encouraged to leave.

ITM France was in charge of group coordination and operational management and had, in turn, founded nine regional companies, called "bases," in which it had a 65% interest; the rest was owned by the members running Intermarché stores in the particular region.

Intermarché's Purchasing Policy

Purchasing policy was set nationally (ITM France) for important products. National Purchasing Management consisted of two managers, one a member and the other a permanent. They were assisted by five departments, specialized by group of products: packaged goods, hygiene-household cleaning, perishables, drinks, others. Each department had two national buyers, one a member and the other a permanent, who negotiated sales conditions with the suppliers.

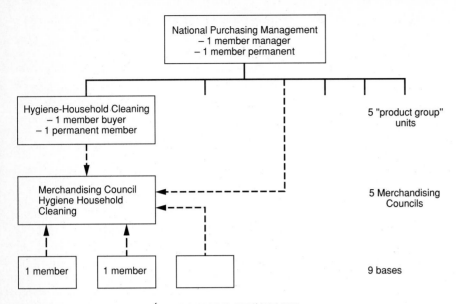

EXHIBIT 10   INTERMARCHÉ: PURCHASING STRUCTURE

The purchasing policy for each group of products as well as all final agreements with the suppliers were decided by the "Merchandising Council," which met twice a month. It consisted of the two buyers, the two managers, and nine member-representatives from the bases (Exhibit 10).

When a product was accepted by the council, it became a "national" item, meaning that it would be carried by all Intermarché stores. The bases could add "complementary items" to their range that were therefore negotiated locally. The bases were also responsible for negotiating promotion for all products with the suppliers.

ITM placed its suppliers in four categories depending on types of item: privileged, monopolistic, "local," and "other" (Exhibit 11). A supplier could change categories as, for example, when ITM discontinued a supplier's products because of disagreement on sales terms.

Type of Supplier / Type of products	Privileged	Monopolistic	Local	Excluded (Other)
National (mandatory stocking at all stores	yes	yes	no	no
Complementary (negotiated by bases)	yes	no	yes	no

EXHIBIT 11   INTERMARCHÉ SUPPLIER CLASSIFICATION (1982)

In the past, ITM had not hesitated to discontinue items produced even by national leaders in markets like beer, coffee, detergents, and disposable diapers for periods ranging from three months up to even three years. Dropping a leader was nonetheless a rare event, and was most likely intended to intimidate suppliers as a whole.

In 1982, Intermarché generated 4.63% of Colgate's hygiene-toiletry product sales with account sales growth exceeding that of Intermarché itself (Exhibit 12). Colgate-Palmolive was a "monopolistic" supplier in ITM classification.

COLGATE-PALMOLIVE/INTERMARCHÉ NEGOTIATIONS

1982 Sales Terms

In 1982, ITM benefited from the following conditions:

- Functional discounts for delivery to the warehouses: 2% off invoice
- Payment in 30 days from end of month or 1.5% off for payment in cash
- Year-end discounts of 7.2% maximum (including a 4% unconditional base), payable at the end of the year

These conditions were comparable to those Colgate granted other retailers (Exhibit 13). No cooperative promotion agreements had been concluded with the central purchasing office in 1982. Except for the price list, sales terms were not made public, and so only Colgate was aware of the information in Exhibit 13. However, the retailers often managed to obtain information on the conditions granted to their competitors, particularly since there was considerable mobility of personnel. On the other hand, such information was not always reliable, complete, and recent.

The Negotiators

Paul Jarrot, age 35 and with Colgate for 12 years, dealt with the ITM central purchasing office for all hygiene division products, including disposable diapers. After gaining experience in different departments (Transport, Administration), Paul Jar-

rot had joined Sales where he had successively held the positions of Head of Sales Administration, Sales-Trainee, and Regional Sales Supervisor before becoming National Account Manager 18 months earlier. In his discussion with ITM, as with other clients, Paul Jarrot always tried to stick to the actual facts and stay calm while remaining very firm on conditions.

In the event of serious disagreement, Jarrot called on Jean-Pierre Lambert, his Sales Manager. Lambert, age 42, had a doctorate in Economics and had been with Colgate for 18 years, the last 12 as Sales Manager. His responsibilities included developing and implementing sales policy for the hygiene division. Since he was most often summoned when the situation became dramatic, Lambert first tried to ease the tension in the air. Then he studied the possibilities for agreement without compromising the consistency of Colgate's sales policy.

André Roland (member) and Jacques Marcadet (permanent) were the ITM hygiene–household cleaning buyers. André Roland, age 40, had worked his way up from the bottom, and had previously been National Buyer for a large hypermarket chain. He had been an ITM member for only six months. Jarrot had had very little contact with him until now. On the other hand, he was very familiar with Jacques Marcadet, who had been with ITM for 20 months. Marcadet, age 35, previously with a cash-and-carry company, was known to be in search of "sponsors" at ITM who would support his candidacy for membership and provide the necessary funds. During prior meetings with Colgate representatives, Marcadet had appeared highly emotional, seldom analytical in his reasoning, and susceptible to dramatization.

First Discussion

On November 30, 1982, Paul Jarrot met with André Roland and Jacques Marcadet at ITM to examine the results of 1982 and discuss the sales terms for 1983.

To the satisfaction of both companies, examination of the preliminary results for 1982 in-

EXHIBIT 12   GROWTH OF ITM AND OF COLGATE-PALMOLIVE SALES AT ITM

Sales in 000F*	1980	80/79 % growth	1981	81/80 % growth	1982	82/81 % growth
Total ITM sales	6,900,000	27.2	9,600,000	39.1	14,000,000	45.8
Number of stores	310	12	380	22.5	470	23.6
Colgate sales at ITM	38,072	29	55,336	45	92,611	68
Total Colgate sales-household	1,578,140	18	1,859,816	18	2,203,858	18
ITM weight in Colgate total	2.41	—	2.81	—	4.20	—
Colgate hygiene-toiletry sales at ITM	9,584	27	12,926	35	20,062	55
Total Colgate hygiene-toiletry sales	348,209	18	402,897	16	433,231	8
ITM weight in Colgate hygiene-toiletry sales	2.75	—	3.21	—	4.63	—

* Unless specified otherwise.
Source: Colgate-Palmolive.

BREAKDOWN OF COLGATE SALES BY TYPE OF PRODUCT IN 1982

	At Intermarché[1]			Total sales-household goods: France			
	1982 sales	%	81/82% growth	1982 sales	%	82/81 % growth	%
Soaps	5,683	28.3	51	145,702	33.6	10	3.90
Toothpastes	7,352	36.6	52	161,791	37.3	13	4.54
Hair care products	4,272	21.3	63	73,891	17.1	-8	5.78
Shaving products	1,507	7.5	36	28,726	6.6	11	5.25
Others	1,248	6.2	108	23,121	5.3	15	5.40
Total hygiene-toiletry	20,062	100	55	433,231	100	8	4.63
Disposable diapers	11,700	—	317	465,367	—	40	2.51
Household cleaning products	60,848	—	54	1,305,261	—	16	4.66
Total	92,610	—	68	2,203,858	—	18	4.20

Source: Colgate-Palmolive.

EXHIBIT 13   EXAMPLES OF SALES CONDITIONS GRANTED BY COLGATE-PALMOLIVE IN 1982

Accounts (type)	Hygiene-toiletry sales (MF)	Functional discount (% off invoice)	Terms of payment	Y.E.D. (% of sales)	Annual cooper-rative promotion (% of sales)	Point of delivery
ITM	20	2	30 d.e.m.[1]	7.20	0	Warehouses
Hypermarket	21	0	30 d.e.m.	7.25	0.75	Direct Stores
Chain store	22	2	60 d.e.m.	6.00	1.00	Wholesaler
Associated retailers chain	12	2	60 d. net	8.46[2]	0	Wholesaler
Hypermarket chain	46	0	60 d. net	8.00	1.00	Store

[1] d.e.m. = days "end-of-month."
[2] Benefits from the conditions of its central purchasing office that generates 57 MF in sales for Colgate.
Source: Colgate-Palmolive.

dicated that all newly accepted items had performed well, especially disposable diapers, and there was a significant increase in Colgate hygiene product sales at ITM. This qualified ITM for the maximum year-end discount rate allowed. When it came time for comments, Roland criticized Colgate on two points:

1 A lack of promotional activity
2 A failure to adapt packaging to ITM's logistical requirements

Jarrot's response to the first comment stressed the strong points of Colgate's promotional policy, and the second criticism proved to apply to only a portion of the product range. Roland claimed that this was not the first time Colgate had reneged on logistical requirements but was unable to cite specific cases.

Jarrot then presented Colgate's plans for 1983. He announced product improvements, relaunches, one launch, and increased advertising spending. On the other side, Roland pointed out that ITM was forecasting 35% to 40% growth resulting from the expected opening of 80 new stores. This would generate an estimated 28 million FF for Colgate in sales of hygiene-toiletry products at ITM in 1983. At the same time, he informed Jarrot of a plan to give the bases greater autonomy in determining product lines. The central purchasing office would nonetheless continue to specify a certain number of mandatory national items.

Finally, it came time to discuss the 1983 sales terms for hygiene-toiletry products. Roland compared the conditions offered by Colgate with those offered by toiletry manufacturers (shampoos, shaving products, etc.) and claimed that Colgate's conditions were far less advantageous. Jarrot insisted on the necessity to include soap and toothpaste competitors in the comparison. After a fair amount of discussion, Roland conceded. When Colgate conditions were compared with those of the major competitor, in each class of products, differences that were sometimes substantial appeared between the information provided by Roland and Jarrot's own estimates (Exhibit 14). At the end of the analysis Roland requested an improvement in year-end discounts for 1983. Jarrot then suggested different rates for different types of products. Roland accepted the idea but specified that the increase in year-end discounts had to be 1 point for soaps and toothpastes, and from 2 to 3 points for toiletry articles (Exhibit 15). He suggested that another meeting be scheduled for December 23 when Colgate could present a proposal along such lines.

At the end of his meeting report, Paul Jarrot noted that "discussion was relaxed on the whole." Now, however, he had to prepare a proposal for the upcoming meeting.

EXHIBIT 14   ITM SALES CONDITIONS: COMPARISON WITH COLGATE COMPETITORS

	Functional discount	Terms of payment	Year-end discount (YED)
Colgate-Palmolive	2	30 d.e.m.	7.2
Major competitor			
Soaps			
According to ITM	1	60 d.e.m.	8.2
Colgate estimate	0.5	30 d.e.m.	6.2
Toothpastes			
According to ITM	2.4	60 d.e.m.	7.2
Colgate estimate	2	30 d.e.m.	7.2
Toiletries			
According to ITM	4/5	60 d.e.m.	10
Colgate estimate	2/3	60 d.e.m.	8.5/9

Source: Colgate/Palmolive.

EXHIBIT 15   INTERMARCHÉ SALES CONDITIONS

	1981	1982	ITM request 30 November 1982	Comments
Functional discount (% of invoice)	2	2	2	
Terms of payment	30 d.e.m.	30 d.e.m.	30 d.e.m.	
YED (in % of sales)				
Base	4.00	4.00		Unconditional
Growth	0.50 or 1.00	0.50 or 1.00		If sales equal to previous year. If growth exceeds Colgate average
Sales lever brackets		1.5>15 MF 1.75>17 MF 2.00>19 MF		
New products acceptance	0.20	0.20		% of total sales if products added
Additional YED, toiletries	-	-	1.00/2.00	On sales other than soaps/toothpastes
Maximum total YED (in % of sales)				
Soaps and toothpastes	5.20	7.20	8.20[1]	
Toiletries	5.20	7.20	9.20/10.20	
Overall	5.20	7.20	8.70[2]	Annual payment
Cooperative promotion	1.50	-	Not discussed	

[1] Breakdown not discussed.
[2] $(8.20 \times 0.65 + 1/2(9.20 + 10.20) \times 0.35) = 8.70$
Source: Colgate-Palmolive.

PART FOUR

COORDINATION AND CONTROL

G ood marketing strategies and programs are essential for the survival and long-term success of nearly all organizations. However, these programs must be well-conceived or else substantial resources can be wasted and the firm's revenue-generating capability and link to the consumer can be seriously endangered. Integrating all the organization's marketing activities is a major undertaking. Because a variety of programs may be employed to carry out a marketing strategy and because more than one individual may be involved in managing these programs for a product or product line, some method of coordinating the programs is necessary. One of the key means to integrate marketing activities is through the marketing planning process. Furthermore, how well marketing strategies and programs are executed will determine their effectiveness. Even then, a well-designed, closely coordinated, and properly executed plan may fail to achieve the product objectives because of uncontrollable factors such as economic forces or competitors' actions.

In spite of all the attention and carefully planned activity that goes into the development and implementation of a marketing program, it is necessary to establish controls and monitor the program.

Conditions may change rapidly, and adjustments to the program are essential if goals are to be achieved. A number of alternative approaches for structuring the organization and for managing those human resources necessary to achieve effective coordination and execution of marketing strategies and programs exist. The cases in this section illustrate some of the problems and decisions managers must face when controlling, evaluating, and revising marketing strategies and programs.

K MART STORES: WHERE AMERICA SHOPS AND SAVES

The S. S. Kresge Company opened hundreds of K mart stores throughout the United States after its first store opened for business in the early 1960s. The company maintained a practice of keeping the stores very uniform in layout and appearances throughout most of this period. Each store was a simple box-like building usually located as freestanding away from shopping malls. K mart stores sold low- to medium-quality merchandise that was priced lower than its competitors. This approach proved to be very successful, especially among price-conscious shoppers who left full-service department stores to shop at K mart and other discounters. The K mart logo itself became a symbol of low prices in the minds of many shoppers.

In the dynamic 1980s, important changes were taking place in the retail industry. Younger shoppers had become more discriminating than their parents, and many had a greater amount of disposable income to spend. These younger shoppers wanted higher-quality merchandise, and they were willing to pay for it. While K mart stuck with its traditional approach, other retailers had moved in to satisfy this new consumer group. In the process, these competitors created a retail environment that had never been more competitive. Furthermore, the successful market penetration of warehouse clubs and specialty stores into the retailing industry meant even more intense competition for discount stores such as K mart.

How K mart should respond to these and other issues remained unclear. One thing did seem certain. Unless K mart made changes to remain aligned with a changing retail environment, its future financial performance would probably decline.

This case was written by John L. Little, Assistant Professor of Strategic Management at the University of North Carolina at Greensboro, and Larry D. Alexander, Associate Professor of Strategic Management at Virginia Polytechnic Institute and State University © 1988 by John L. Little and Larry D. Alexander.

HISTORY

The S. S. Kresge Company was founded in 1899 with the opening of a single store in downtown

Detroit, Michigan. Its founder, Sebastian Kresge, who followed a slogan of "Nothing over ten cents," rapidly opened more stores in new locations. He standardized the mix of merchandise, continued to emphasize low prices, and centralized the purchasing function. This latter move greatly increased the bargaining power that Kresge had over suppliers while at the same time reducing administrative overhead. This made the opening of new stores easier by spreading startup costs over a wider base. Kresge soon developed operating procedures that permitted centralized control over a growing number of uniform stores. The lower prices charged by Kresge caused individual store volume to increase and profits to rise, which provided the necessary funds to open still more stores. When the company was incorporated in 1912, Kresge's "five and ten" style stores numbered 85 and had a combined annual sales of more than $10 million.

Variety stores—which carried a variety of inexpensive kitchen, stationery, toy, soft good items, and hard goods—grew in popularity throughout the 1920s and 1930s as a more convenient means of shopping than the earlier established specialty stores. A number of variety store chains had been established by 1940, with their limited selection of a wider array of product lines. The greater buying power available to these chain stores allowed them to underprice the specialty stores that concentrated in just one product line. The combination of lower prices and a wider selection of different product categories was a powerful attraction to customers. Furthermore, since more and more shoppers had their own cars, they were willing to travel farther from home to save money.

During the 1950s, the introduction of shopping centers and supermarkets began to draw customers away from variety stores. To counter this, some variety retailers began looking for new ways to attract customers. In 1954, for example, Marty Chase converted an old mill in Cumberland, Rhode Island, into a discount store named Ann and Hope. The store sold ribbon, greeting cards, and women's clothing. As other discount stores opened throughout the 1950s, then Kresge President Harry Cunningham began to consider a similar approach. Finally, in 1962, Kresge responded by opening its first K mart discount store in Garden City, Michigan.

K mart discount stores were nothing more than a large-scale version of the earlier Kresge retail stores. They still emphasized low prices, a wide selection, and low overhead costs, which combined to create profits. The first K mart stores were stocked primarily with Kresge merchandise. A number of licensees, who operated departments within the store, added their merchandise to the selection. Later, licensee merchandise was replaced entirely with K mart's own merchandise. The initial stores were a great success, and by 1966, they numbered 162 with a combined sales of over $1 billion.

The K mart success formula remained relatively unchanged for many years. Many new stores were added each year, sometimes by the hundreds. Almost all of them were uniform, freestanding stores located away from large shopping centers. By erecting simple, freestanding buildings in suburban areas, K mart opened its stores more quickly than competitors, who had to wait for shopping centers to be completed. This also helped to keep overhead costs down since its freestanding stores were not located in expensive shopping malls, where rent was high. Over time, K mart stores became located in almost all major U.S. metropolitan areas. During the 1960s and 1970s, annual sales grew by an average of 20 percent per year, primarily due to the fact that consumers found K mart's blend of low price and wide selection very attractive. The company's smaller Kresge stores, unlike its K mart stores, were not as profitable, and many were closed during this period.

By 1976, the Kresge Company had become the second largest general merchandise retailer in the United States, behind only Sears. During the next year, the corporate name was changed from the Kresge Company to the K mart Corporation because K mart stores accounted for 94.5 percent of all corporate sales.

By the late 70s, several problems were impacting on K mart. Good locations for new K mart stores were becoming more difficult to find. Other discount chains were drawing some K mart shoppers away. Industry surveys indicated that the needs of the customers were changing. While other discounters started upgrading their stores and started emphasizing brand name merchandise, K mart continued to sell primarily low-priced K mart private label and generic goods in their same austere-looking stores. Furthermore, during these same years, K mart sales growth started to flatten.

In 1980, Bernard Fauber was named K mart's new chief executive officer. He replaced an unusual arrangement in which three men shared the office of the president. Fauber quickly moved to refurbish its dated K mart stores, and to upgrade the quality of goods which it carried. New display racks, better point-of-purchase displays, and improved traffic flow through the stores helped to make K mart stores more attractive to customers.

FUNCTIONAL AREA STRATEGIES WITHIN THE K MART STORES

Marketing

Early on, K mart stores emphasized low prices as an important marketing weapon. Its low prices often meant that the product being offered was of a lower quality. For hard goods such as kitchen appliances, this usually meant that just the basic product was carried, without the extra features that competing retailers' higher-priced models offered.

K mart focused on satisfying the needs of low- and middle-income families with limited budgets. Customers in this market segment were unwilling to pay higher prices for similar products with extra features. Still, it was estimated in the 1980s that 80 percent of all Americans shopped at K mart at least once during a calendar year.

The sales promotion of K mart's products was accomplished in several ways. First, sales promotion was emphasized by more attractive in-store point-of-purchase displays. Second,

K mart's well-known "blue light specials" were used to promote specific products for short periods of time during the day. Third, its products were promoted in numerous newspaper ads.

K mart relied heavily on newspaper advertising to promote its goods. Newspaper inserts were designed at corporate headquarters and sent to newspapers throughout the country for publication. Advertising copy was sent to store managers in advance so they could prepare for the sales. The company placed approximately 120 million inserts in 1,700 different newspapers each week throughout the United States by the mid-1980s. While the company continued to emphasize newspapers, increased attention was being given to television advertising. This advertising only became relatively economical once K mart had opened thousands of stores across the nation.

With its high level of market penetration, K mart initiated a new effort to get customers to buy more goods per trip. Management felt that this would be possible because disposable family income of many K mart customers was rising. This rise in family income was partially the result of a significant increase in the number of two-income families. K mart estimated that 19 percent of its customers were from households with annual incomes of at least $40,000; however, this customer group typically bought only low-priced items such as tennis balls, batteries, and shampoo at K mart.

K mart added more national brand merchandise and higher-quality private labels, and then displayed them in a more attractive manner. Brand name products such as Casio, Minolta, Nike, MacGregor, Wilson, and General Electric were increasingly found throughout the stores. K mart hoped that this action would help attract higher-income customers to other product areas and increase their per sale purchases. At the same time, the company hoped to retain its less affluent customers by continuing to offer an assortment of lower-priced, lower-quality merchandise.

K mart did extremely well in certain departments, but performed weakly in others. It was the leader in housewares and the second largest appliance retailer behind only Sears. Many customers were attracted to its brand name appliances and housewares by K mart's low prices. These same customers, however, were turned off by K mart's cheap clothing, which had a low image among many consumers. Its apparel departments, in fact, had been a major shortcoming for K mart throughout the years. K mart tried to address this problem by upgrading many lines of clothing. Furthermore, the responsibility for ordering apparel was taken away from store managers and given to professional staff buyers at corporate headquarters, who were more knowledgeable about fashion.

K mart had also moved into specialty discount stores through several acquisitions. The first Designer Depot, which was a discount-price specialty apparel store, was started in Detroit during 1982. These stores sold quality brand-name merchandise at discounts of 20 percent to 70 percent. Some stores also sold shoes, while others sold bedroom and bathroom soft goods.

The company also acquired several other impressive specialty chains. Waldenbook Company, Inc., another K mart acquisition in 1985, operated 943 stores in all 50 states. Builders Square, Inc., a warehouse-type home improvement center chain, was acquired in 1984. By 1985, the company had 25 stores located in eight states. Frederick Stevens, executive vice president of specialty retailing operations, argued that 400 locations across the country could support the volume requirements of these huge discount builders' supply warehouses. Builders Square was hoping to capture a 25 percent share of that market.[1]

Pay Less Drug Stores Northwest, another K mart acquisition in 1985, was the 10th largest drug chain in the nation. Pay Less was a discount chain, supported by a very cost efficient operation and strong management. With sales approaching $1 billion and 176 stores, the chain

hoped to penetrate rapidly in its present markets in California, Oregon, Washington, Idaho, and Nevada.

Two final K mart acquisitions were in the restaurant industry. Furr's Cafeterias, acquired earlier in 1980, and Bishop Buffets, acquired in 1983, had a total of 162 units by 1985. Because of slow growth in the cafeteria industry, however, future growth for new cafeterias in this acquisition was expected to be limited to 10 percent per year.

K mart Corporation had limited involvement in overseas markets. It did have, however, a 20 percent interest in G. L. Coles and Coy Limited, a food and general merchandise retailer in Australia. It also had a 44 percent interest in Astra, S.A., which operated a food and general merchandise chain in Mexico.

Store Operations

During the 1980s, K mart was approaching market saturation, with its stores located almost everywhere throughout 48 states. By the end of 1985 its 2,332 stores were located in 250 of this country's 255 Standard Metropolitan Statistical Areas (SMSA). From a record 271 new stores opening in 1976, only 18 new K mart stores were opened in 1985.

Because of market saturation, K mart switched its emphasis from opening new stores to renovating existing ones. This effort, which started in the early 1980s, was intended to increase productivity as well as to upgrade the store image. Wider and taller display cases carried more merchandise and made better use of cubic space. This allowed for a wider assortment of merchandise to be displayed within the same square footage. It also reduced the need for additional backroom storage. A new store layout was developed around a wide center aisle which let consumers walk through every department without leaving the aisle. As one K mart store manager put it, "We want to encourage people to go into areas where they would not normally go . . . to pass by merchandise they were not planning to buy!"[2]

---

[1] "K mart: A Look inside the Nation's Largest Discounter," *Mass Market Retailers*, December 16, 1985, p. 42.

[2] Ibid., p. 20

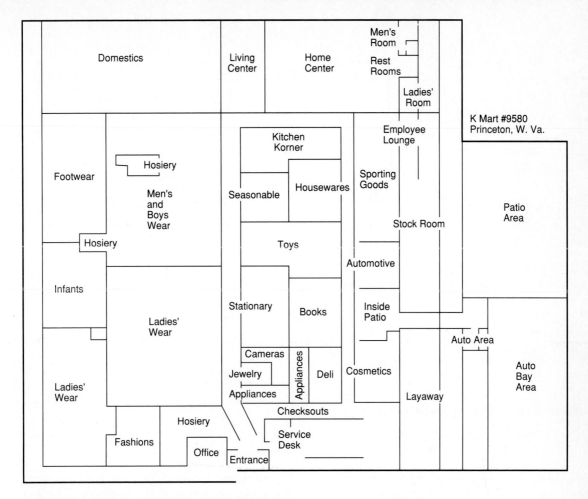

EXHIBIT 1   TYPICAL K MART STORE FLOOR LAYOUT

Source: K Mart Pamphlet, 1985.

All K mart stores were designed around the same basic floor plan, as shown in Exhibit 1. As shoppers entered the store, they were no longer confronted with the smell of popcorn and the sight of gumball machines. Instead, they might be greeted by the jewelry department with a wide selection of watches and jewelry of various price ranges. The main aisle down the center of the store separated soft goods from hard goods. Located on the soft goods side of the store were women's apparel, then men's apparel, with infants' wear, and children's clothes nearby. Popular crafts and yarn were also located on this side,

where homemakers were most likely to look for them. In the hard goods half of the store, housewares, sporting goods, automotive supplies, and hardware were located at the rear of the store, drawing men and women past the high-impulse, high-margin merchandise in the greeting cards, jewelry, and toy departments. The health and beauty items and the pharmacies, for the minority of stores that had them, were typically located in the right front section of the store.

Electronic communications systems connected all stores to 10 enormous regional distribution centers. These centers were located in Califor-

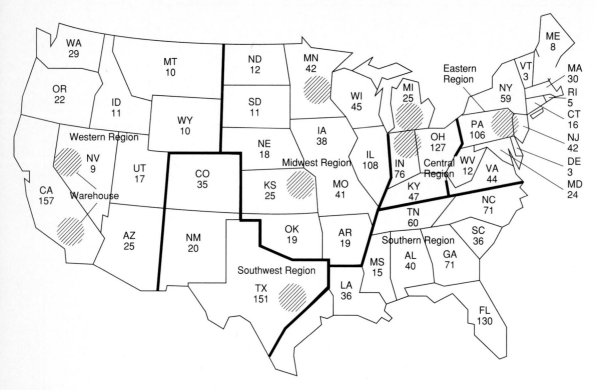

EXHIBIT 2   STORE DISTRIBUTION NETWORK

Source: Mass Market Retailers, Dec. 16, 1985, p. 42.

nia, Nevada, Texas, Kansas, Minnesota, Michigan, Indiana, Ohio, Pennsylvania, and Georgia, as shown in Exhibit 2. These highly automated distribution centers contained a combined 15 million square feet of warehouse space. Together, they operated a fleet of 250 tractors and 1,000 trailers, which provided weekly delivery to every K mart store requesting it.

Approximately 25 percent of K mart's merchandise was handled by these distribution centers. In contrast, 75 percent of all store purchases were shipped directly from suppliers to the stores in order to minimize shipping cost. The delivery of products from suppliers was usually fast in order to keep such a large account as K mart satisfied. This reduced inventory level requirements at stores to minimum levels. A significant reduction in reorder time had been achieved by installing optical scanners on cash registers at

K mart stores. Scanning, coupled with a companywide computer network, permitted automated replenishment of merchandise, and made it possible to differentiate the seasonal needs of each region.

As part of its efforts to upgrade its image, K mart was completing a major remodeling program of store interiors to present a more modern store appearance to shoppers. This new effort, called "The K mart of the Eighties," incorporated a new color scheme on interior walls and floors, broader aisles, and more attractive displays. Low-volume lines were dropped or consolidated to achieve a store within a store format. The Kitchen Corner, Home Care Center, and Domestic Center were arranged along the back wall and emphasized fashion and style at discount prices. The early success of the plan was encouraging. Sales per square foot had risen from $139 in 1980 to

$168 four years later. While this was superior to the $128 per square foot typical among discounter department stores, it was far behind such discounters as Target and Wal-Mart.

Product categories no longer in demand were eliminated. For example, K mart's 360 automotive service departments in rural stores were closed in 1982. Unprofitable stores were closed altogether, freeing up more than $1 million each in capital for use elsewhere in the corporation.

The more than 2,000 K mart stores were organized into six regions, each of which had from 266 to 422 stores. Each region consisted of about 20 districts, while each district had from 10 to 20 stores.

K mart stores came in five basic sizes. The smallest was the 40,000-square-foot-size store, which was placed in smaller markets. At the other end, the jumbo 120,000-square-foot store was placed in large metropolitan markets. These freestanding stores were located in suburban areas with large parking lots, and were usually leased rather than owned. Buildings were usually erected by local contractors, but a K mart subsidiary built several stores each year to allow the company to remain knowledgeable about building costs and procedures.

K mart's decision to avoid shopping center locations was part of its low overhead philosophy. Leasing costs at shopping centers were very high compared to K mart locations. Shopping centers generally did not want discounters as tenants anyway, because of the negative image associated with them. Also, specialty stores did not want to locate next to a discount store because of the significant price difference between their products and a discounter's. Sometimes, K mart would buy existing buildings in shopping centers or develop properties in good locations and sublease retail space to specialty stores.

FINANCE

Total sales for the K mart Corporation, as shown in its consolidated statement of income in Exhibit 3, were $22.4 billion for fiscal year 1985, which ended on January 29, 1986. This represented a 6.3 percent increase over the sales for the previous year. Net income after taxes for that same year was $221.0 million. The consolidated balance sheet for fiscal 1985 and 1984 is shown in Exhibit 4. Finally, a comparison of sales and various financial data for K mart over a 10-year period is presented in Exhibit 5.

Retail sales at K mart were extremely seasonal with a high proportion of sales and profits coming during the Christmas shopping season. For example, some 33 percent of K mart's 1984 sales and 41 percent of its profits came during the fourth quarter alone.

K mart did not offer a charge card and did not encourage credit sales. By comparison, approximately 58 percent of arch rival Sears' sales were on credit. MasterCard and VISA credit cards were accepted at K mart, and limited in-house credit was provided on appliance sales. Many K mart stores required customers to follow a rigid two-step procedure for writing checks. The customer first had to get approval from the service desk, and then wait at a checkout line to pay for the purchased items.

K mart's policy for granting exchanges or refunds, on merchandise which did not satisfy the customer, was quite liberal. Most items could be returned for cash by customers without a hassle. This policy was inherited from the old Kresge variety stores. Similarly, K mart customers could get a rain check on any advertised item not found in stock at the time of the sale.

INNOVATION

The K mart approach to innovation was to adopt new ideas only after they had been developed and proved successful by someone else. This approach avoided risk and had served K mart well throughout the years. Once a good idea was identified, however, K mart showed its genius on applying and perfecting it. For example, when the discount store idea emerged, Kresge was the first to refine the concept with its K mart stores. K mart pursued rapid expansion while other retailers looked on with amazement. The idea of standardizing the store floor plan and layout was

EXHIBIT 3   K MART CORPORATION CONSOLIDATED STATEMENTS OF INCOME
(Millions, except Per-Share data)

	Fiscal year ended		
	January 29, 1986	January 30, 1985	January 25, 1984
Sales	$22,420	$21,096	$18,598
Licensee fees and rental income	225	207	191
Equity in income of affiliated retail companies	76	65	57
Interest income	24	40	38
	22,745	21,408	18,884
Cost of merchandise sold (including buying and occupancy costs)	16,181	15,260	13,447
Selling, general and administrative expenses	4,845	4,428	3,880
Advertising	567	554	425
Interest expense:			
Debt	205	147	84
Capital lease obligations	191	193	189
	21,989	20,582	18,025
Income from continuing retail operations before income taxes	756	826	859
Income taxes	285	327	366
Income from continuing retail operations	471	499	493
Discontinued operations	(250)	—	(1)
Net income for the year	$ 221	$ 499	$ 492
Earnings per common and common equivalent share:			
Continuing retail operations	$3.63	$3.84	$3.81
Discontinued operations	(1.90)	—	(.01)
Net income	$1.73	$3.84	$3.80

Source: K mart Corporation, 1985 Annual Report, p. 30.

another example of how K mart borrowed a good idea from elsewhere and perfected it.

HUMAN RESOURCES/PERSONNEL

K mart Corporation employed more than 290,000 people in 1985, but tried to encourage a small business feeling within its individual stores. Loyalty among store managers was unusually high; consequently, their turnover rate was low. Many K mart managers had never worked for any other employer, and 25-year-service pins were common. Furthermore, promotion to managerial positions was almost entirely done from within. For those selected, management training consisted of a 16-week program on all phases of a K mart store's operation. After the program, the trainees became assistant managers with responsibility for several departments. Typically, trainees were rotated through various departments and stores for 6 to 10 years before they were ready to manage their own stores.

The opportunity for promotion was strong in the 1970s when new stores were being opened at the rate of several per week. That changed in the 1980s when K mart greatly curtailed its new store openings. This threatened to increase employee turnover as assistant managers became impatient

EXHIBIT 4   K MART CORPORATION CONSOLIDATED BALANCE SHEETS
(Millions)

	January 29, 1986	January 30, 1985
Assets		
Current assets:		
Cash (includes temporary investments of $352 and $294, respectively)	$ 627	$ 492
Merchandise inventories	4,537	4,588
Accounts receivable and other current assets	363	231
Total current assets	5,527	5,311
Investments in affiliated retail companies	293	188
Property and equipment—net	3,644	3,339
Other assets and deferred charges	527	220
Investments in discontinued operations	—	204
Total assets	$9,991	$9,262
Liabilities and shareholders' equity		
Current liabilities:		
Long-term debt due within one year	$ 15	$ 2
Capital lease obligations due within one year	76	74
Notes payable	127	235
Accounts payable—trade	1,908	1,917
Accrued payrolls and other liabilities	548	362
Taxes other than income taxes	218	200
Income taxes	198	99
Total current liabilities	3,090	2,889
Capital lease obligations	1,713	1,780
Long-term debt	1,456	1,107
Other long-term liabilities	345	163
Deferred income taxes	114	89
Shareholders' equity	3,273	3,234
Total liabilities and shareholders equity	$9,991	$9,262

Source: K mart Corporation, 1985 Annual Report, p. 31.

to move up. At the same time, K mart was reducing the number of assistant managers from three to two per store in order to cut administrative costs.

K mart relied heavily on part-time employees to operate its stores. The company goal was to have 60 percent part-time and 40 percent full-time employees within each store. This gave the store manager greater flexibility in matching the work force with the amount of traffic during different periods of the day. Also, the labor costs for part-time employees were considerably lower because they started at minimum wage and were not paid benefits. The great majority of these employees were women who preferred to work part-time because of their family obligations. The company, however, did have an employee savings plan, even for part-timers, in which K mart contributed 50 cents in K mart stock for every one dollar that the employee contributed.

EXHIBIT 5   K MART CORPORATION: 10-YEAR FINANCIAL SUMMARY

	1984	1983	1982	1981	1980	1979	1978	1977	1976	1975
Summary of operations (*millions*)										
Sales	$21,096	$18,598	$16,772	$16,527	$14,204	$12,731	$11,696	$9,941	$8,382	$6,798
Cost of merchandise sold	$15,260	$13,447	$12,299	$12,360	$10,417	$9,283	$8,566	$7,299	$6,147	$4,991
Selling, general and administrative expenses	$4,982	$4,305	$4,049	$3,810	$3,326	$2,839	$2,503	$2,085	$1,750	$1,409
Interest expense—net	$300	$235	$219	$230	$200	$149	$132	$116	$103	$89
Income before income taxes	$820	$854	$419	$323	$436	$625	$634	$564	$484	$395
Net income	$499	$492	$262	$220	$261	$358	$344	$298	$262	$196
Per-share data (*dollars*)										
Earnings per common and common equivalent share	$3.84	$3.80	$2.06	$1.75	$2.07	$2.84	$2.74	$2.39	$2.11	$1.61
Cash dividends declared	$1.24	$1.08	$1.00	$.96	$.92	$.84	$.72	$.56	$.32	$.24
Book value	$25.87	$23.35	$20.89	$19.81	$18.99	$17.79	$15.68	$13.56	$11.62	$9.69
Financial data (*millions*)										
Working capital	$2,422	$2,268	$1,827	$1,473	$1,552	$1,403	$1,308	$1,231	$1,074	$904
Total assets	$9,262	$8,183	$7,344	$6,657	$6,089	$5,635	$4,836	$4,489	$3,983	$3,336
Long-term obligations—Debt	$1,107	$711	$596	$415	$419	$209	$209	$211	$211	$210
—Capital leases	$1,780	$1,822	$1,824	$1,752	$1,618	$1,422	$1,294	$1,266	$1,155	$989
Shareholders' equity	$3,234	$2,940	$2,601	$2,456	$2,343	$2,185	$1,916	$1,649	$1,409	$1,169
Capital expenditures—owned property	$622	$368	$306	$361	$302	$292	$217	$162	$123	$112
Depreciation and amortization—owned property	$203	$168	$157	$141	$119	$93	$77	$65	$56	$52
Average shares outstanding	126	125	124	124	123	123	122	122	121	121

Source: K mart Corporation, *1984 Annual Report*, pp. 16, 17.

MANAGEMENT

Harry Cunningham developed the basic K mart strategy and led the company during its rapid growth from 1962 to 1972. When he stepped down in 1972, he appointed K mart's Robert Dewar, Ervin Wardlow, and Walter Tennga to collectively run the company. Dewar, with 32 years of legal and financial background but no store experience, was named chairman. Wardlow, with strong merchandising experience, was named president. Finally, Tennga, a real estate and financial executive, was named vice chairman. These three executives ran the company for eight years. Although sales tripled during this period, the three could not agree on which direction K mart should take.

In 1980, Bernard Fauber was named the new chief executive officer at the suggestion of Dewar, who felt that K mart needed a store man at the top, rather than a staff man. Since then, K mart has made dramatic changes in its approach to business. As Fauber conceded:

> For 20 years we had been just about the most successful retailer in America, so it was not easy getting our people to admit that some changes were advisable and others were necessary.[3]

In explaining the reasons behind K mart's decision to diversify into other areas, Fauber added:

> We realized that we must do something else for growth since it was no longer possible to open 100 to 120 K mart stores each year.[4]

Fauber, like all but one previous CEO, was not a college graduate. He first came to work for the company in 1941 as an 18-year-old stockroom boy in a Kresge store. Nine years later, he joined the management training program. Later he gained experience as a store manager and district manager and, in 1968, became vice president of the Western Region. Like nearly all K mart executives, Fauber had never worked for any other company.

[3] Ibid., p. 54.
[4] Ibid.

K mart's philosophy was to train their store managers as generalists, and then allow them wide discretion in running their stores. They had an incentive plan based on store profits to avoid the mistakes Sears made in the 1970s when it tied its department managers' incentive plan to sales volume. The Sears incentive system, which has since been changed, caused its managers to focus on low-margin merchandise which boosted sales and their bonuses, but which hurt profits.

Store managers at K mart were encouraged to involve themselves and the store in community activities, such as the United Way. One socially responsible effort K mart undertook was its "Lost Child Program" in 1985. The prime exposure available nationwide at its stores made K mart a good vehicle for the program and enhanced the corporate image.

THE RETAIL INDUSTRY

Market Segments

The retail industry was divided into several general segments which somewhat overlapped one another. There were full-line department stores, discount department stores, discount drugstores, specialty stores, supermarkets, and convenience shops. Exhibit 6 shows the top 15 general merchandise chains for 1985, and includes many of these store types. The trend toward one-stop shopping had blurred the distinctions among these various kinds of stores in recent years. For example, shoppers could find food items in drugstores and discount stores, and clothing and hardware in supermarkets. Within the discount department store category, the emerging warehouse stores were the fastest growing segment along with discount specialty stores.

External Threats

By the mid-1980s, the retail environment was extremely competitive. Retailers were also being squeezed by two powerful factors. One factor was slower growth in customer demand for

EXHIBIT 6   TOP 15 GENERAL MERCHANDISE CHAINS FOR 1985

Rank and company	Net sales ($000)	Net income ($000)	Earnings per share	Location of headquarters
1. Sears Roebuck	$40,715,300	$1,303,300	$3.53	Chicago
2. K mart	22,420,002	221,242	1.73	Troy, Mich.
3. J. C. Penney	13,747,000	397,000	5.31	New York
4. Federated Department Stores	9,978,027	286,626	5.88	Cincinnati
5. Dayton Hudson	8,793,372	283,620	2.92	Minneapolis
6. Wal-Mart Stores	8,580,910	327,473	1.16	Bentonville, Ark.
7. F. W. Woolworth	5,958,000	177,000	5.50	New York
8. BATUS	5,881,408	163,532	—	Louisville
9. Montgomery Ward	5,388,000	(298,000)	—	Chicago
10. May Department Stores	5,079,900	235,400	5.38	St. Louis
11. Melville	4,805,380	210,812	3.90	Harrison, N.Y.
12. Associated Dry Goods	4,385,019	119,696	3.00	New York City
13. R. H. Macy	4,368,386	189,315	3.69	New York City
14. Wickes Companies	4,362,454	76,130	0.47	Santa Monica, Calif.
15. Allied Stores	4,135,027	159,275	3.70	New York City

Source: "The 50 Largest Retailing Companies," Fortune, June 9, 1986, pp. 136–137.

general merchandise in recent years. Industry forecasts suggested a continuing trend in this direction with a declining proportion of disposable income being spent on general merchandise in coming years. The other factor was the excess number of stores that existed in the industry. These two realities along with several others were making retail merchants somewhat worried about the future.

The decline in the teenage population had decreased per capita spending on apparel. Apparel chains, which had expanded so rapidly in the 1960s and 1970s to capitalize on the lucrative teenage market, were now facing an older customer base with less interest in fashion. As Americans grew older, their spending patterns were shifting toward health and leisure services and away from general merchandise.

Another source of trouble for retailers was the extremely high level of consumer credit in the mid-1980s. Some industry observers feared that this would lead to a decline in consumer spending and increased woes for retailers. Part of this was due to the catch-up spending that people

did for consumer durables after the 1981–1983 recession.

Competition

A recent challenge within the retail industry was wholesale clubs and specialty stores. They were at opposite ends of the retailing spectrum. Still, both of these store types were very profitable, and they were making it harder for stores in the middle.

The wholesale club concept was first introduced in 1976 by Sal and Robert E. Price with their first Price Club in San Diego. For a $25 membership fee, small businessmen could buy such diverse goods as food, office supplies, and appliances at wholesale prices. This membership approach meant that the Price Club got an interest-free loan in advance and locked in the customer with switching costs if they decided to move to another such club. By stocking 4,000 high-moving items, as compared to 60,000 items found in typical discount stores, Price Club stores turned over their inventory 15 times a year, compared to just 5 times for a full-line discount store. The Price Club had grown to 25 stores, and the concept was being copied by other retailers.

Specialty stores enjoyed strong growth in the early 1980s. A number of large retailers had established chains of small stores specializing in single product lines like shoes, women's apparel, and books. Woolworth had found success in stationery supplies with Harold's Square, Lucky Stores with its Minnesota Fabrics, and Allied Stores with its Catherine's Stout Shoppes. The attraction of such stores was the greater depth of choice in a specific line for which many consumers were willing to pay extra.

Between the wholesale clubs and the specialty stores were full-line department stores. This was where the primary battle within the retailing industry was taking place. The saturation of the market with these one-stop shopping stores had caused many changes. For example, both Sears and J. C. Penney had curtailed most new store openings. Instead, they both were moving to upgrade their existing stores with higher-quality, higher-priced merchandise. Both sought to establish a fashion image to differentiate themselves with the discount chains.

Sears

K mart's greatest competition came from Sears Roebuck & Co., the world's largest retailer with its 435 full-line department stores, 397 medium-sized department stores, and 1,971 catalog sales offices. Sears stores generated sales of $21.5 billion in 1985, which rose to a staggering $40.7 billion when all other Sears strategic business units were included. For its full-line department stores, Sears' breadth in departments was unsurpassed by any competitor.

During the 1970s, Sears first moved to higher-priced, more stylish merchandise. This confused many customers who preferred to go to discounters for lower prices and specialty shops for greater product line depth. Under CEO Edward Telling, who took office in 1978, the company made drastic changes. Twenty percent of its work force was cut, 200 stores were closed, and the remaining stores renovated. Many Sears clothing labels were replaced by fashion labels associated with such names as Arnold Palmer, Joe Namath, and Cheryl Tiegs.

With its move into financial services, Sears envisioned the day when a customer could walk into a Sears store and buy a house through its Coldwell Banker realty division, insure it through its Allstate Insurance division, and furnish it before he or she left. Sears' charge card was already held by 58 percent of Americans. Visa cards, on the other hand, were held by only 53 percent of all households. The opportunity existed for Sears to convert its ordinary credit accounts into savings and checking accounts. Furthermore, the deregulated banking environment of the 1980s made it possible to offer multiple financial services in retail stores, an option Sears seemed to be pursuing.

J. C. Penney

While Sears had its strength in hard goods, J. C. Penney Company, Inc., had a well-established reputation for quality in soft goods. The company got its initials J. and C. from G. Johnson and T. Callahan, who founded the firm back in 1902. During the 1960s and 1970s, Penney's tried to move into hard goods to counter Sears' well-established strength there. Penney's did this in several key instances by teaming up with well-known suppliers. For example, it formed an alliance with General Electric to sell its washers, dryers, refrigerators, stoves, etc., in its retail stores.

During 1985, when Penney's had total sales of approximately $13.7 billion, it made a retrenchment of sorts. It discontinued its auto accessories department, eliminated children's toys, and even discontinued selling many hard goods such as G.E. appliances. Instead, it renewed its commitment to emphasize soft goods in its 574 metropolitan market stores, 133 metropolitan market soft-line stores, and 696 geographic market stores in nonmetropolitan markets. With

EXHIBIT 7   GENERAL MERCHANDISE RETAILERS, 1985: YARDSTICKS OF MANAGEMENT PERFORMANCE

Company	% in segment— sales/profits	Profitability: return on equity					Growth: sales			Earnings per share		
		Rank	5-Year average	Latest 12 months	Debt as % of equity	Net profit margin	Rank	5-year average	Latest 12 months	Rank	5-year average	Latest 12 months
Department stores:												
R. H. Macy	●●	1	21.4%	16.3%	14.0%	4.3%	4	14.2%	7.5%	2	21.1%	−15.6%
Lucky Stores	25/13	2	19.2	17.5	61.3	1.1	12	9.5	6.5	12	−0.3	12.8
Dillard Dept. Stores	●●	3	18.6	19.8	70.4	3.9	1	25.2	49.3	1	40.5	32.0
Mercantile Stores	●●	4	16.3	15.0	28.0	5.0	7	10.9	6.8	4	17.5	4.2
May Dept. Stores	68/72	5	16.0	17.3	41.2	4.4	10	9.8	10.2	5	14.6	9.3
Federated Dept. Strs	67/89	6	14.6	13.1	27.9	3.3	8	10.8	8.0	10	8.5	11.0
Allied Stores	●●	7	12.8	15.3	70.9	3.9	5	13.8	5.7	9	9.9	25.5
J. C. Penney	79/NA	8	12.7	10.1	54.7	2.9	13	3.0	2.3	8	13.3	−18.6
Strawbridge	●●	9	12.5	16.0	125.8	3.7	6	11.5	12.5	3	20.1	16.6
Associated Dry Goods	61/73	10	11.8	12.2	33.8	2.8	2	19.6	9.5	6	13.6	−0.7
Carson Pirie Scott	50/45	11	10.8	13.4	104.2	2.0	3	19.6	23.2	11	4.2	132.5
Sears Roebuck	67/57	12	10.6	10.7	87.4	2.9	9	10.4	4.6	7	13.5	−19.9
Carter Hawley Hale	73/52	13	9.4	7.3	84.6	1.6	11	9.6	−2.0	13	−0.3	−50.0
Equitable of Iowa	41/2	14	7.0	4.3	9.2	2.6	14	2.7	4.9	14	−15.0	−10.2
Alexander's	●●	15	1.4	7.4	87.0	1.0	15	1.9	0.5		NM	24.7
Medians			12.7	13.4	61.3	2.9		10.8	6.8		13.3	9.3
Discount and variety:												
Wal-Mart Stores	●●	1	34.9	30.7	49.6	3.9	1	39.9	32.2	1	43.0	24.1
SCOA Industries	84/●	2	24.8	22.6	88.5	2.9	8	10.4	5.1	8	9.3	9.8
Ames Dept. Stores	●●	3	23.1	19.7	60.6	3.1	2	20.1	30.8	5	23.5	19.4
Stop & Shop Cos	48/73	4	19.2	12.8	52.8	1.3	7	11.2	12.8	2	33.6	−26.9
Dayton-Hudson	71/73	5	16.8	16.1	43.2	3.3	4	19.0	12.2	9	9.1	10.3
Zayre	70/65	6	15.7	19.0	46.5	2.6	5	16.0	19.9	3	28.7	22.1
Rose's Stores	●●	7	15.6	14.2	16.6	2.1	6	14.0	9.2	4	28.1	−13.9
K mart	●●	8	13.2	12.4	89.3	1.8	9	10.0	13.4	7	10.5	−23.2
Household Intl.	26/8	9	12.0	13.6	236.0	2.6	10	9.1	5.3	10	4.7	−4.6
Associated Dry Goods	38/26	10	11.8	12.2	33.8	2.8	3	19.6	9.5	6	13.6	−0.7
Heck's	86/DD	11	9.3	def	89.3	def	11	2.0	6.5		NM	P-D
F. W. Woolworth	68/39	12	3.5	14.5	35.4	2.6	13	−5.6	3.2		NM	20.6
Cook United	●/DD	13	def	def	NE	def	12	−2.8	−47.7		NM	D-D
Medians			15.6	14.2	49.6	2.6		11.2	9.5		10.5	−0.7

Source: Industry Survey-Retailing, Forbes, January 13, 1986, p. 202.

this move, the firm refocused its efforts on selling quality clothing to men, women, boys, girls, and infants. In addition to clothing, Penney's continued to emphasize its towels, sheets, etc., for which it was noted.

Discount Chains

In 1985, there were more than 8,700 general merchandise discount stores in the United States. Exhibit 7 gives a comparison of profitability and growth performance of the top discount, variety, and department store chains. The average discount store had 55,792 square feet of selling space, which had been rising in recent years. The average customer transaction was $12.35. The annual sales per square foot, as shown in Exhibit 8, varied from the $603 in the photography department to $132 in men's and boys' wear.

There were a number of regional chains within the discount segment of the retail industry. They included Mervyn's in the West, Target in the Midwest, Caldor in New England, and Richway in the Southeast. For the most part, they had done very well by differentiating themselves from K mart. Some firms had accomplished this by appealing to the high end of the discount market. Other discounters sold department store quality merchandise at discount prices in attractive stores. As a result, they succeeded in attracting many affluent shoppers who would not normally shop at K mart.

One of the most successful retailers in recent years was Wal-Mart, a discount chain headquartered in Bentonville, Arkansas. Much of its success was due to the location of its stores. Its 834 discount stores and 19 Sam's Warehouse Clubs were concentrated in small towns in the South and Midwest. By clustering up to 150 stores within several hours drive of a central warehouse and stocking only name brand merchandise, Wal-Mart consistently led the industry in return on investment.

EXHIBIT 8   DISCOUNT STORE SALES BY CATEGORY

Category	Volume ($ billions)	Sales per store ($ millions)	Annual sales per sq. ft.	Annual turns	Initial markup (%)	Gross margin (%)
Women's apparel	$14.3	$1,763	$176	4.6	48.0%	37.2%
Men's and boys' wear	8.2	1,011	132	3.4	44.6	36.0
Housewares	6.3	777	135	3.2	41.1	30.2
Consumer electronics	5.9	728	316	3.2	31.4	19.4
Health and beauty aids	5.6	691	219	4.5	26.9	20.5
Automobile	5.2	641	279	2.8	34.9	28.7
Hardware	4.8	592	184	2.4	41.9	32.1
Toys	4.1	506	202	3.1	36.5	28.4
Sporting goods	3.8	469	187	2.0	36.9	26.9
Photo/camera	3.3	407	603	3.2	24.5	16.6
Domestics	3.2	395	126	2.5	43.4	35.3
Personal care	2.9	358	421	3.3	30.4	20.0
Stationery	2.1	259	140	3.5	46.7	40.1
Paint	1.8	222	175	2.4	43.9	35.2
Electric housewares	1.7	210	238	3.4	33.2	21.4
Jewelry	1.4	166	290	1.8	49.9	37.7
Glassware	0.7	80	129	4.0	40.7	34.9

Source: *Standard & Poor's Industrial Survey*, July 4, 1985, p. 120.

SUPPLIERS

Retailers dealt with thousands of suppliers to stock the wide range of merchandise they carried. This was due in part to the fact that most retailers did not manufacture the merchandise they carried. The bargaining power of large retail chains in relation to their suppliers was great. Sears, J. C. Penney, K mart, and others were such large and welcome customers that suppliers often became overly dependent on them.

Each year, many new products were introduced by the major chains, replacing old products which were discontinued. Each supplier knew that their products were expected to generate targeted levels of sales. Those that didn't achieve these goals were dropped with little regard for the supplier. On occasion, suppliers were encouraged to increase production capacity only to find their product dropped a short time later on. Often, orders were cancelled at the last minute, leaving suppliers in a difficult position. At times, chain retailers would take merchandise on a consignment basis, paying for it only if sold, thus shifting the risk to the supplier. Payment to the suppliers was, at times, delayed by retailers in order to enhance cash flow and obtain free short-term financing.

Sears and K mart were good examples of firms making sizable use of private label merchandise. Often their private label products were made by a brand name manufacturer to similar or the exact same specifications as the brand label. The manufacture of private label products could then be contracted out to other manufacturers, giving a great deal of leverage to the retailer and reducing the bargaining power of suppliers.

In spite of such treatment by chain retailers, many suppliers were willing to take the risk and abuse. In return, they hoped to get enormous volume and nationwide distribution which high-volume retailers could provide. In response to this one-sided relationship, a number of general merchandise manufacturers had broadened their product lines. By producing a wide variety of items, a supplier could reduce dependence on a single product and increase its bargaining power with the retailer.

BUYERS: THE NEW CONSUMERS

Several important demographic shifts were affecting retailers during the mid-1980s. Population shifts from the cities to the suburbs were reducing the sales volume of urban stores while helping suburban stores. Population shifts from older industrialized areas of the Northeast to the Sun Belt states had similar effects. The baby-boom teenagers of the 1960s were approaching middle age. Better educated than their parents, their perception of value, attitude toward quality merchandise, and response to promotional techniques were changing the way retailers did business.

Price still remained a key consideration, but quality and brand image had increased in importance. Many consumers were willing to trade dollars for time, as was proved by the demand for fast food, microwave ovens, and other time-saving products and services.

While the number of households was growing rapidly, the population growth was slowing. This caused changes in the type of merchandise demanded, the way to market it effectively, and the price/quality trade-off. Health-related products, prescriptions, and leisure products were in greater demand reflecting the needs of older customers. At the same time, the market for baby food, toys, and children's clothing had declined.

Women were working in greater numbers than ever before. This contributed to the rise in discretionary income and increased the demand for products needed by working women, such as clothes and cosmetics. A K mart survey showed that the percentage of K mart customers with household incomes from $25,000 to $40,000 had increased from 23.3 percent in 1980 to 28.1 percent in 1984.[5] Some 18.9

[5] K mart Corporation, *1984 Annual Report*, p. 3.

percent of K mart's customers in 1984 came from households with incomes greater than $40,000 as compared with 8.3 percent in 1980. A profile of who shops at a K mart, broken by income, occupation, education, sex, and age is shown in Exhibit 9.

With more women working, men were doing retail shopping more than ever before. Men tended to be less value conscious and more likely to trust the advertising of national brands. The trend was clearly toward a more mature, affluent customer with a preference for value, quality, and fashion in merchandise.

K MART AND THE FUTURE

Sales at the average K mart store were good, but there was tremendous room for improvement. Overall, K mart's per store sales were about one-third that of Sears stores. K mart's appliances and housewares departments were strong areas; however, its clothing and other soft goods, which took up almost half of the typical K mart store, had low appeal to many customers. Clearly, K mart needed to address its clothing dilemma, perhaps by reducing store space allocated for it or by improving the clothing being offered. Overall, K mart needed to decide which product lines and departments should be emphasized. Exhibit 10 provides a breakdown of total retail trade by major product areas.

Since the appointment of Bernard M. Fauber as chief executive officer in 1980, K mart had made a number of substantial changes. By the end of 1985, the store renovation program had been going for some time, and the move toward higher-quality national brand merchandise was well under way. Still, as 1986 began, there were a number of important issues still facing K mart. Would the repositioning program succeed in attracting more affluent customers to buy its higher-priced name-brand merchandise? What additional steps could be taken to upgrade K mart's stores? Would the new image result in a substantial loss of lower-income customers, which had historically been the backbone of its business? Might K mart customers be confused by the move as happened to Sears in the 1970s? How could K mart improve the performance of its clothing and soft goods? If it did, could fashion-seeking customers really be convinced that K mart was a trendy place to shop? These and other questions came to mind as CEO Fauber looked ahead to the remainder of the 1980s and into the 1990s.

EXHIBIT 9   DEMOGRAPHICS OF K MART SHOPPERS

	% of K mart shoppers
Occupation:	
Professional	12.5%
Technical	5.5
Manager	13.4
Clerical	4.5
Salesworker	6.4
Craftsman	11.7
Operative/kindred worker	9.8
Service worker	4.7
Laborer	3.1
Retired	20.7
Income:	
Over $20,000	38.7
Under $20,000	60.6
Education:	
High school or less	52.2
Some college or more	46.5
Sex:	
Male	46.6
Female	53.4
Age:	
Under 25	12.8
25–34	24.1
35–44	19.6
45–54	12.7
55–64	14.5
65+	15.3

Source: Chain Store Age, December 1984, p. 54.

EXHIBIT 10   TOTAL RETAIL TRADE
(In Millions of Dollars)

	1984	change 1983–84	10-year growth rate
Retail trade total	$1,297,015	+10.5%	+ 9.0%
Durable goods stores total	464,287	+17.1	+ 9.6
Nondurable goods stores total	832,728	+ 7.1	+ 8.8
General merchandise group	153,642	+10.2	+ 7.9
General merchandise stores	144,575	+10.6	+ 8.4
Department stores	129,284	+10.9	+ 8.6
Variety stores	9,067	+ 5.1	+ 1.8
Apparel group	66,891	+10.8	+ 8.8
Men's and boys' wear stores	8,432	+ 5.9	+ 3.1
Women's apparel accessory stores	27,899	+13.9	+ 9.3
Family & other apparel stores	17,567	+13.8	+11.1
Shoe stores	10,339	+ 5.6	+ 9.9
Furniture & appliance group	63,581	+16.3	+ 8.9
GAF total	325,938	+11.7	—
Automotive group	277,008	+19.0	+ 9.5
Gasoline service stations	100,997	+ 2.2	+10.2
Lumber, building material hardware	59,304	+15.2	+ 9.7
Eating and drinking places	124,109	+ 8.2	+10.8
Food group	269,959	+ 5.9	+ 8.3
Drug and proprietary stores	44,165	+10.3	+ 9.2
Liquor stores	19,494	+ 2.5	+ 6.3

Source: Standard & Poor's Industrial Survey, July 4, 1985, p. 111.

HANOVER-BATES CHEMICAL CORPORATION

James Sprague, newly appointed northeast district sales manager for the Hanover-Bates Chemical Corporation, leaned back in his chair as the door to his office slammed shut. "Great beginning," he thought. "Three days in my new job and the district's most experienced sales representative is threatening to quit."

On the previous night, James Sprague, Hank Carver (the district's most experienced sales representative), and John Follett, another senior member of the district sales staff, had met for dinner at Jim's suggestion. During dinner Jim had mentioned that one of his top priorities would be to conduct a sales and profit analysis of the district's business in order to identify opportunities to improve the district's profit performance. Jim had stated that he was confident that the analysis would indicate opportunities to reallocate district sales efforts in a manner that would increase profits. As Jim had indicated during the conversation, "My experience in analyzing district sales performance data for the national sales manager has convinced me that any district's allocation of sales effort to products and customer categories can be improved." Both Carver and Follet had nodded as Jim discussed his plans.

Hank Carver was waiting when Jim arrived at the district sales office the next morning. It soon became apparent that Carver was very upset by what he perceived as Jim's criticism of how he and the other district sales representatives were doing their jobs—and, more particularly, how they were allocating their time in terms of customers and products. As he concluded his heated comments, Carver said:

This company has made it darned clear that 34 years of experience don't count for anything... and now someone with not much more than two years of selling experience and two years of pushing paper for the national sales manager at corporate headquarters tells me I'm not doing my job.... Maybe it's time for me to look for a new job...and

This case was prepared by Professor Robert E. Witt, the University of Texas, Austin.

EXHIBIT 1   HANOVER-BATES CHEMICAL CORPORATION: SUMMARY INCOME STATEMENTS, 1984–1988

	1984	1985	1986	1987	1988
Sales	$19,890,000	$21,710,000	$19,060,000	$21,980,000	$23,890,000
Production expenses	11,934,000	13,497,000	12,198,000	13,612,000	14,563,000
Gross profit	7,956,000	8,213,000	6,862,000	8,368,000	9,327,000
Administrative expenses	2,606,000	2,887,000	2,792,000	2,925,000	3,106,000
Selling expenses	2,024,000	2,241,000	2,134,000	2,274,000	2,399,000
Pretax profit	3,326,000	3,085,000	1,936,000	3,169,000	3,822,000
Taxes	1,512,000	1,388,000	790,000	1,426,000	1,718,000
Net profit	$1,814,000	$1,697,000	$1,146,000	$1,743,000	$2,104,000

since Trumbull Chemical [Hanover-Bates's major competitor] is hiring, maybe that's where I should start looking . . . and I'm not the only one who feels this way.

As Jim reflected on the scene that had just occurred, he wondered what he should do. It had been made clear to him when he had been promoted to manager of the northeast sales district that one of his top priorities should be improvement of the district's profit performance. As the national sales manager had said, "The northeast sales district may rank third in dollar sales, but it's our worst district in terms of profit performance."

Prior to assuming his new position, Jim had assembled the data presented in Exhibits 1 through 6 to assist him in analyzing district sales and prof-

its. The data had been compiled from records maintained in the national sales manager's office. Although he believed that the data would provide a sound basis for a preliminary analysis of district sales and profit performance, Jim had recognized that additional data would probably have to be collected when he arrived in the northeast district (District 3).

In response to the national sales manager's comment about the northeast district's poor profit performance, Jim had been particularly interested in how the district had performed on its gross profit quota. He knew that district gross profit quotas were assigned in a manner that took into account variation in price competition. Thus he felt that poor performance in the gross profit quota area reflected misallocated sales efforts ei-

EXHIBIT 2   DISTRICT SALES QUOTA AND GROSS PROFIT QUOTA PERFORMANCE, 1988

District	Number of sales reps	Sales quota	Sales: actual	Gross profit quota[a]	Gross profit: actual
1	7	$3,880,000	$3,906,000	$1,552,000	$1,589,000
2	6	3,750,000	3,740,000	1,500,000	1,529,000
3	6	3,650,000	3,406,000	1,460,000	1,239,000
4	6	3,370,000	3,318,000	1,348,000	1,295,000
5	5	3,300,000	3,210,000	1,320,000	1,186,000
6	5	3,130,000	3,205,000	1,252,000	1,179,000
7	5	2,720,000	3,105,000	1,088,000	1,310,000
		$23,800,000	$23,890,000	$9,520,000	$9,327,000

[a] District gross profit quotas were developed by the national sales manager in consultation with the district managers and took into account price competition in the respective districts.

EXHIBIT 3   DISTRICT SELLING EXPENSES, 1988

District	Sales rep salaries[a]	Sales commission	Sales rep expenses	District office	District manager salary	District manager expenses	Sales support	Total selling expenses
1	$177,100	$19,426	$56,280	$21,150	$33,500	$11,460	$69,500	$388,416
2	143,220	18,700	50,760	21,312	34,000	12,034	71,320	351,346
3	157,380	17,030	54,436	22,123	35,000[b]	12,382	70,010	368,529
4	150,480	16,590	49,104	22,004	32,500	11,005	66,470	348,153
5	125,950	16,050	42,720	21,115	33,000	11,123	76,600	326,558
6	124,850	16,265	41,520	20,992	33,500	11,428	67,100	315,655
7	114,850	17,530	44,700	22,485	31,500	11,643	58,750	300,258
								$2,398,915

[a] Includes cost of fringe benefit program, which was 10 percent of base salary.
[b] Salary of Jim Sprague's predecessor.

ther in terms of customers or in terms of the mix of product line items sold. To provide himself with a frame of reference, Jim had also requested data on the north-central sales district (District 7). This district was generally considered to be one of the best, if not the best, in the company. Furthermore, the north-central district sales manager, who was only three years older than Jim, was highly regarded by the national sales manager.

THE COMPANY AND THE INDUSTRY

The Hanover-Bates Chemical Corporation was a leading producer of processing chemicals for the chemical plating industry. The company's products were produced in four plants, located in Los Angeles, Houston, Chicago, and Newark, New Jersey. The company's production process was, in essence, a mixing operation. Chemicals purchased from a broad range of suppliers were mixed according to a variety of user-based formulas. Company sales in 1988 had reached a new high of $23.89 million, up from $21.98 million in 1987. Net pretax profit in 1988 had been $3.822 million, up from $3.169 million in 1987. Hanover-Bates had a strong balance sheet, and the company enjoyed a favorable price-earnings ratio on its stock, which traded on the OTC market.

EXHIBIT 4   DISTRICT CONTRIBUTION TO CORPORATE ADMINISTRATIVE EXPENSE AND PROFIT, 1988

District	Sales	Gross profit	Selling expenses	Contribution to administrative expense and profit
1	$3,906,000	$1,589,000	$388,416	$1,200,544
2	3,740,000	1,529,000	351,346	1,177,654
3	3,406,000	1,239,000	368,529	870,471
4	3,318,000	1,295,000	348,153	946,847
5	3,210,000	1,186,000	326,558	859,442
6	3,205,000	1,179,000	315,376	863,624
7	3,105,000	1,310,000	300,258	1,009,742
	$23,890,000	$9,327,000	$2,398,636	$6,928,324

EXHIBIT 5   NORTHEAST (#3) AND NORTH-CENTRAL (#7) DISTRICT SALES AND GROSS PROFIT PERFORMANCE BY ACCOUNT CATEGORY, 1988

District	(A)	(B)	(C)	Total
Sales by account category				
Northeast	$915,000	$1,681,000	$810,000	$3,406,000
North-central	751,000	1,702,000	652,000	3,105,000
Gross profit by account category				
Northeast	$356,000	$623,000	$260,000	$1,239,000
North-central	330,000	725,000	255,000	1,310,000

Although Hanover-Bates did not produce commodity-type chemicals (e.g., sulfuric acid), industry customers tended to perceive minimal quality differences among the products produced by Hanover-Bates and its competitors. Given the customers' perception of a lack of variation in product quality and the industrywide practice of limiting advertising expenditures, field sales efforts were of major importance in the marketing programs of all firms in the industry.

Hanover-Bates's market consisted of several thousand job-shop and captive (in-house) plating operations. Chemical platers process a wide variety of materials including industrial fasteners (e.g., screws, rivets, bolts, and washers), industrial components (e.g., clamps, casings, and couplings), and miscellaneous items (e.g., umbrella frames, eyelets, and decorative items). The chemical plating process involves the electrolytic application of metallic coatings such as zinc, cadmium, nickel, and brass. The degree of plating precision required varies substantially, with some work being primarily decorative, some involving relatively loose standards (e.g., 0.0002 zinc, which means that anything over two ten-thousandths of an inch of plate is acceptable), and some involving relatively precise standards (e.g., 0.0003–0.0004 zinc).

Regardless of the degree of plating precision involved, quality control is of critical concern to all chemical platers. Extensive variation in the condition of materials received for plating requires a high level of service from the firms supplying chemicals to platers. This service is normally provided by the sales representatives of the firm(s) supplying the plater with processing chemicals.

Hanover-Bates and the majority of the firms in its industry produced the same line of basic processing chemicals for the chemical plating industry. The line consisted of a trisodium phosphate cleaner (SPX); anesic aldahyde brightening agents for zinc plating (ZBX), cadmium plating (CBX), and nickel plating (NBX); a protec-

EXHIBIT 6   POTENTIAL ACCOUNTS, ACTIVE ACCOUNTS, AND ACCOUNT CALL COVERAGE: NORTHEAST AND NORTH-CENTRAL DISTRICTS, 1988

District	Potential accounts			Active accounts			Account coverage (total calls)		
	(A)	(B)	(C)	(A)	(B)	(C)	(A)	(B)	(C)
Northeast	90	381	635	53	210	313	1,297	3,051	2,118
North-central	60	286	499	42	182	218	1,030	2,618	1,299

tive post-plating chromate dip (CHX); and a protective burnishing compound (BUX). The company's product line is detailed as follows:

Product	Container size	List price	Gross margin
SPX	400-lb. drum	$80	$28
ZBX	50-lb. drum	76	34
CBX	50-lb. drum	76	34
NBX	50-lb. drum	80	35
CHX	100-lb. drum	220	90
BUX	400-lb. drum	120	44

COMPANY SALES ORGANIZATION

Hanover-Bates's sales organization consisted of 40 sales representatives operating in seven sales districts. Sales representatives' salaries ranged from $22,000 to $30,000, with fringe-benefit costs amounting to an additional 10 percent of salary. In addition to their salaries, Hanover-Bates's sales representatives received commissions of 0.5 percent of their dollar sales volume on all sales up to their sales quotas. The commission on sales in excess of quota was 1 percent.

In 1986 the national sales manager of Hanover-Bates had developed a sales program based on selling the full line of Hanover-Bates products. He believed that if the sales representatives could successfully carry out his program, the following benefits would accrue to both Hanover-Bates and its customers:

1 Sales volume per account would be greater, and selling costs as a percentage of sales would decrease.

2 A Hanover-Bates sales representative could justify spending more time with such an account, thus becoming more knowledgeable about the account's business and becoming better able to provide technical assistance and identify selling opportunities.

3 Full-line sales would strengthen Hanover-Bates's competitive position by reducing the likelihood of account loss to other plating-chemical suppliers (a problem that existed in multiple-supplier situations).

The national sales manager's 1986 sales program had also included the following account call-frequency guidelines:

A accounts (major accounts generating $12,000 or more in yearly sales)—two calls per month

B accounts (medium-sized accounts generating $6,000–$11,999 in yearly sales)—one call per month

C accounts (small accounts generating less than $6,000 yearly in sales)—one call every two months

The account call-frequency guidelines were developed by the national sales manager after discussions with the district managers. The national sales manager had been concerned about the optimum allocation of sales effort to accounts and felt that the guidelines would increase the efficiency of the company's sales force, although not all of the district sales managers agreed with this conclusion.

It was common knowledge in Hanover-Bates's corporate sales office that Jim Sprague's predecessor as northeast district sales manager had not been one of the company's better district sales managers. His attitude toward the sales plans and programs of the national sales manager had been one of reluctant compliance rather than acceptance and support. When the national sales manager succeeded in persuading Jim Sprague's predecessor to take early retirement, he had been faced with the lack of an available qualified replacement.

Hank Carver, who most of the sales representatives had assumed would get the district manager job, had been passed over in part because he would be 65 in three years. The national sales manager had not wanted to face the same replacement problem again in three years and also had wanted someone in the position who would be more likely to be responsive to the company's sales plans and policies. The appointment of Jim

Sprague as district manager had caused considerable talk, not only in the district but also at corporate headquarters. In fact, the national sales manager had warned Jim that "a lot of people are expecting you to fall on your face...they don't think you have the experience to handle the job, in particular, and to manage and motivate a group of sales representatives, most of whom are considerably older and more experienced than you." The national sales manager had concluded by saying, "I think you can handle the job, Jim....I think you can manage those sales reps and improve the district's profit performance ...and I'm depending on you to do both."

APPLE COMPUTER

In 1983, Dataquest, a San Jose, California, market research firm, estimated computer sales to the education market at $492 million. Of these, 35 percent were made for use by elementary students, 24 percent for secondary school students, 5 percent for trade and technical school students, and 32 percent for college and university students.

In the college and university market, Apple Computer, Inc., was clearly the leader with a 19 percent market share, while Zenith Electronics captured 14 percent. Other major competitors were Commodore Business Machines with 13 percent and International Business Machines with 6 percent market share. Apple had achieved its strong market share with its Apple II line of computers, which had been marketed through programs that involved student discounts, "giveaways" in areas where the company could get a tax break, and computer clubs designed to interest students in computers even before entering college. Apple executives believed the growth of the educational market to be 50 percent per year and were committed to growing Apple's market

share along with it. To attain this goal Apple began a new strategy in early 1984.

APPLE'S CONSORTIUM STRATEGY

In 1984, Apple Computer introduced a revolutionary computer called the Macintosh. It was the first computer that a novice could learn to use in a matter of hours; it allowed cut-and-paste integration of text and graphics between applications. The Macintosh was the first computer that used software applications so consistent that once users had learned one application, they then understood the basics of all applications. It was a computer ideally suited to the higher education market. To reach this market, Apple placed free computers in member schools that signed a consortium agreement prior to public release of the Mac. This agreement specified that members, called the Apple University Consortium (AUC), had to order a minimum quantity of equipment per year, usually $100,000, and establish at least one student laboratory outfitted with Apple Macintoshes on campus. These labs acted as experimental networking projects paralleling what industry was attempting to do in factories and offices. Participating schools were also expected to design and develop software for university and student use that would be run

Reprinted with permission of Prof. Charles Schewe, University of Massachusetts, Amherst. This case was prepared as the basis for class discussion rather than to illustrate either effective or ineffective handling of an administrative situation.

on the Macintosh. To create their own software and networking, universities were given the tool kits, program debuggers, and technical support needed. In return, consortium members dealt directly with Apple and, through its University Purchasing Program (UPP), received the lowest pricing available.

Schools chosen for membership were top leading-edge universities that would provide, in accordance with the "trickle down" strategy, a mentor model for other universities among the 3,100 colleges and universities in the United States. Apple ensured that at least one university in each of its sales territories was included. (See Table 1.)

The plans at these institutions ranged from ambitious (Drexel had each of its 1,800 freshmen buy a Macintosh) to conservative (several schools planned to offer only discounts on machines).

Underlying this approach was the strategy to firmly entrench Macintosh as the key higher education computing tool. When students left campus to pursue their careers, they would take with them knowledge of and preference for Apple products, especially the Macintosh. It was anticipated that targeting leading-edge schools that others looked up to would foster a penetration down through the college and university ranks. Apple held annual educational college computing forums where these prestigious consortium schools would give addresses about what they were doing so that other schools could follow. Furthermore, Apple hoped to generate a flurry of educational software development for the Macintosh machine and make it the standard for academic applications. Finally, this strategy gave Apple high visibility in the education market. This consortium strategy remained Apple's mainstay approach to marketing to higher education until 1987.

The Competition

Zenith Data Systems' marketing strategy had been based on offering a quality but low-priced IBM compatible computer. The firm believed that IBM's PC with its DOS operating system was the "business standard" and that many universities believed that to prepare students for the real world meant using compatibles. Being a major supplier of component parts for IBM, Zenith was well-suited to offer a competitive product.

In 1983, Zenith negotiated a contract with Clarkson University in Potsdam, New York, which was one of the first colleges to require that each freshman have a computer. Zenith was chosen to provide computers for each of its incoming freshmen. Students were charged $200 per semester to lease the machines and were given the right to buy them when they graduated. This rental cost was built into the school's tuition. By the end of 1984, more than 50 colleges and universities had become Zenith customers.

The cornerstone of Zenith's strategy was price. Rock-bottom prices, the company believed, were necessary to compete with bargain-priced PC clones. To provide this low price, little technical support was offered to buyers. Zenith's approach was to send out its sales force to sell on price and to avoid the use of resellers by

TABLE 1   APPLE CONSORTIUM MEMBERS

Boston College	Columbia	Northwestern	Rochester
Brigham Young	Cornell	Notre Dame	Stanford
Brown	Dartmouth	Pennsylvania	Texas
Carnegie-Mellon	Drexel	Princeton	Utah
Chicago	Harvard	Reed	Washington
City University of New York	Michigan	Rice	Yale

selling directly through the school. While this lack of support was not very reassuring, of the 900 computers sold to Clarkson in 1984, only eight malfunctioned, and the shaving of support service was one way Zenith managed to hold its low price. The company firmly believed that the right price for attracting students was $999, while other companies pointed to $1200 as the winning price point. Zenith negotiated with a school directly, signed a contractual agreement, and became vendor through the university. Any problem with machines meant that the student had to seek repair from a local Zenith dealer.

To boost sales, Zenith often provided free software. On occasion, the company also sent a computer-filled truck to college campuses, where students bought the machines right off the tailgate. At the first "truckload sale" at Northwestern University, the company sold 130 computers in one day. The Zenith truck also appeared during spring break in Fort Lauderdale, Florida.

Throughout the period 1983–1987, Zenith's goal appeared to be to remain a market nicher and not aggressively pursue the higher education market. Having moved into this market earlier than even Apple and IBM, the company's strategy appeared to be to hold market share or capture only a modest amount.

Commodore Business Machines had been a low-price marketer as well, but the scaled-down power of its machines did not approximate the value, as Commodore sold the disk drive and computer for about $700, several hundred dollars below the price of other competitors. Hence, Commodore shunned the practice of discount marketing. The company also refused to give away equipment to schools or clubs to generate interest in its computer products. By 1987, Commodore was no longer a viable competitor in the college market but remained strong in the pre-college market. However, at this time, Commodore began an attempt to gain a foothold within the college market with its Amiga 2000. Playing up its graphics capabilities, the company

started targeting specific areas in universities. Its plan appeared to be to take a slow approach to building a presence in the higher education marketplace.

Throughout this period, IBM did not appear to aggressively pursue the higher education student market. Because of their business applications, IBM PCs were the computer of choice of college and university administrators. But in the student market, IBM steered a course of confusion. Its PC product was viewed as much more complicated to learn than Apple's Macintosh, and its software was much less conducive to students' needs than Apple's. Its price list was unwieldy and difficult to read, while the ordering procedure to purchase directly from IBM was cumbersome. Universities and bookstore managers found IBM salespeople more interested in making a sale than in helping them carry out their mission of supplying educational tools to the academic community. Too often legal and policy restrictions at IBM headquarters reduced sales force flexibility. IBM's promotions and advertising often seemed to miss the mark with the student market. Despite these shortcomings, IBM remained a viable competitor. Its strength came from its name and compatibility with its own and other machines used in the after-college marketplace.

In August 1987, IBM introduced the PS/2 Model 25 at a price of $1350 for the monochrome version and $1695 for the color version. Designed to conserve space on the desktop, the Model 25 covered an area of just 13 inches by 15 inches. The bottom of the chassis was hinged for easy maintenance and featured a security bar that allowed the chassis to be bolted to the desk. This safeguard made the unit ideally suited for the college environment. Discounts for the Model 25 were offered at up to 40%. IBM began marketing it through virtually all of its reseller channels, including IBM Personal Computer Dealers, Advanced Products Dealers, Value Added Dealers, and Advanced Products Value Added Dealers.

THE SITUATION IN 1987

In 1987, Apple Computer began a strategic push to gain market share in the business market, a market that had long been dominated by IBM. At the same time, the education market remained a continuing focus at Apple. "Apple's roots are in education," said Katie Povejsil, Apple's Higher Education Market software solutions manager. Added Lloyd Mahaffey, newly appointed director of educational marketing, "We're definitely focused on education. [The educational marketing group] is very much a key business sector within the company." Both felt that over the long run, higher education was a better market than almost any other because it is "refreshable," both with its need to have the latest equipment and with the millions of new students coming into the system every year. The two executives, along with John C. "Burt" Cummings, Higher Education Sales Manager, were reviewing the current market situation as well as the newly refined marketing strategy and tactics employed at Apple to move the higher education sales program ahead. The group was wondering how their strategy and programs might be improved and what they might anticipate in the way of competitive reaction in the future.

The Market's Buying Behavior

In 1986, higher education's computer purchases totaled $3 billion by most estimates. Data were difficult to come by in this market, but industry research sources estimated that one-third of this figure represented sales to students while the other $2 billion was the estimated amount of purchases by institutions. About 40 percent of those institutional sales were for desktop computers, 40 percent for mid-sized computers, and 20 percent for mainframe and supercomputers. More important was the potential size of the educational market. Industry sources believed that sales of microcomputers to students could bring the higher education market to more than $4 billion by 1990.

Reaching the higher education market requires special approaches, special skills, and a lot of time. Colleges' and universities' needs are very different from those of business and of consumers seeking computers for their homes. Furthermore, the market is made up of many diverse types of schools: leading-edge universities, four-year public colleges, technical and professional schools, national liberal arts colleges, regional liberal arts colleges, and two-year colleges. Each has its own unique buying characteristics.

The Decision-Making Unit   Smaller schools, especially two-year colleges, have few computers and little discretionary funds, and their decisions are often made by large committees. However, at top-ranked institutions where there are many computers already, decisions are often made by departmental committees or even by individuals. Because so many decisions in higher education are made by committees and at many levels, more people have to be "sold" than is the case for businesses.

No pattern seems to exist for who (the computer vendor or the university personnel) contacts whom first. When university administrators decide to pursue the possibility of a vendor contract, they may call the vendor's company headquarters, regional sales office, or salesperson directly if that person is known. In most cases, the Apple salesperson would contact the central administration (Provost's office, President's office, or some variant) first. Other alternatives might be the computing center, purchasing (especially at smaller schools), or the university store. Yet still other people may be the key persons. At San Diego State, for instance, interesting the faculty themselves seemed to result in the determination of which computer students would use. There the faculty was the key market, and the Macintosh was the preferred computer in departments such as journalism and mathematics.

University Motivation   Institutions of higher education are totally committed to computers as a tool, just like professors and textbooks, necessary to carry out their educational mission. More than other markets, colleges and universities set a high priority on having and utilizing the latest in hardware and software. Such associations with cutting-edge technology bring peer school recognition and educational prestige to their institutions. Universities and other higher education schools see facilitating student purchase of computers to be consistent with their academic mission but strongly feel that they cannot actively "push" computer sales on their student bodies. Offering unbiased advice about buying low-priced hardware and software is generally perceived as the maximum extent of the school's domain of activity. Schools also use their commitment to microcomputers as a mechanism for attracting students. Many display their coursework and classroom computer integration in their brochures and other school marketing literature.

University Retailer Motivation When a school enters into a contract with a vendor to sell its computers, it has a number of options for outlets: university stores, university-sponsored computer stores, retail outlets set up in the computer center or other places on campus, as well as simply taking orders, placing them directly with the vendor, and having the product shipped to a local dealer for installation. In all these alternatives, the school's main goal is to provide an educational tool to its students at the lowest possible price. In these circumstances, the school views itself as providing a service leading to enhanced learning opportunities. In addition, the institution wants to be sure that students buy machines and software that meet their educational needs, are properly installed, and are repaired when needed. Getting the machines back in service when broken is a very important facet of university service, especially at larger institutions.

Student Motivation The biggest use of computers by students is for word processing. Productivity is a key decision criterion. At Apple, many advertisements to students emphasized the MicroSoft software to illustrate that feature. Students are also interested in ease of use, which is the Macintosh's strongest feature. The use of the Macintosh can be learned in one day, whereas IBM and compatible products might often take several days to learn. Peer pressure is also a prime factor in motivating students to purchase. Seeing friends' personal or laboratory usage, reinforced with academic programs, can provide a momentum to propel a major vendor into the forefront on a given campus.

Another student buying feature is compatibility with other machines. Apple's technology has consciously been kept proprietary, while IBM has strategically opened its hardware architecture to generate increased software opportunities. One result of this is that IBM has created a clone environment while Apple has established a monopoly position. Apple's strategy has been to maintain its proprietary orientation and ignore the compatibility feature. Apple's promotion decidedly does not counter IBM's "take it to the business world" promotional argument.

Students, realizing that they are receiving the lowest price available when buying through the school, appear to be less concerned with delivery time; they are willing to wait to get that low price. While price is certainly a major criterion, some of the larger, more prestigious schools find students opting for the more expensive models. At an October 1987 Apple promotional sale on the University of Michigan campus, for instance, 70 percent of the sales were at a price of $2200 or more.

Dealer Motivation Throughout the consortium strategy years, Apple emphasized building dealer loyalty by having its computer sales filter through its dealer channel. Dealers appear to have a short-term ("How can I make the most money right now?") outlook. Hence, large margins, high volumes, and exclusive relationships become key motivators. With the long-standing "stand by the dealer" strategy, Apple found that it needed to shift focus away from providing high margins to offering low prices as it moved more directly into the higher education institutions.

THE NEW "EXPAND AND FOCUS" STRATEGY

The consortium strategy was intended as a two-tier strategy. Top schools by Apple territory (AUC) were used as opinion leaders who seeded the value and use of Apple computers to other colleges and universities. Simultaneously, dealer loyalty was stressed as the backbone of marketing. In 1987, Apple entered a new strategic phase that emphasized a long-term perspective. The goal turned explicitly toward building higher education institutional commitment rather than simply "selling boxes." All the programs at Apple began being directed toward actively integrating the college or university with the computer. It was felt that this institutional relationship would be gained by offering full support to the institution—student financing plan; training, promotion, and merchandising assistance for campus bookstores; academic software guides and a quarterly publication; and seminars for educators.

Apple also came to realize that computer dealers were trying to be all things to all customers, selling to businesses and home users, as well as students and institutional buyers. It also believed that dealers could not satisfactorily cover the university/college market and that it must get universities involved as participative channel members. Additionally, Apple began to broaden its base of universities by targeting an additional 250 large schools over and above the then 32 AUC member schools (8 additional schools had been gradually added to the original 24). These 250 had been dealer-serviced, but under a newly formed Higher Education Purchase Program (HEPP II), they gained the right to resell products to students, faculty, and administrators. These schools would buy directly from Apple and had to offer a resale program. In return, Apple would offer substantial discount programs based in steps upon volume. These discounts would approximate those offered to consortium members. This new approach was known as the expand and focus strategy.

Market Segmentation

The 3,100 colleges and universities were viewed in separate groups by Apple. At the top were the leading-edge schools—those that enjoyed the prestige that accrues with being one of the nation's top institutions. These schools formed the basis for the Apple University Consortium. The next tier consisted of large advanced public institutions that began getting involved in the computerization of campus and student body. It was these two segments that formed the target for the "expand and focus" strategy. Apple also viewed a third group, small liberal arts schools, which the firm believed were not yet ready for computers. By the end of 1987, only about 100 of the 250 large schools targeted had actually been contacted by Apple representatives. Additionally, within targeted schools, strategic areas were designed for further targeting. English and computer science were among those key departments. For instance, at one large Texas school, Apple targeted English, geography, electrical engineering, chemistry, physics, and teacher education as the important departments.

Apple Products

Computers The focal product offered to the higher education student market was the Macintosh Plus and its technologically advanced newer models. The Mac Plus, the Macintosh SE (an expandable Macintosh Plus), and the Macintosh II (a high-performance personal computer and advanced function workstation) were available to students but only under very strict restrictions. Under terms of the Apple University Consortium or University Purchase Program (UPP), the precursor to HEPP II, a qualified full-time student could purchase only one Macintosh computer. All buyers had to have their full-time status verified prior to purchase. The monitoring of all restrictions was the responsibility of the university. Purchased computers were not to be resold, as reselling would have created a gray market by bypassing the dealer, causing dissatisfaction among these intermediaries. To allow an upgrade to a Mac SE or Macintosh II, a set of restrictions was mandated. (See Exhibit 1.)

In some instances, the Mac Plus was bundled with other peripherals and software to reduce the decision-making confusion on the part of the student. In 1987, the Mac Plus was offered with an ImageWriter printer and MicroWord word processing software. Three such product bundlings were offered during 1986. Various university outlets could also and did bundle Apple products on their own.

School Developed Software As part of the consortium arrangement and strategy, members' schools agreed to write software for the Macintosh product line. By 1987, this part of the consortium agreement was not widely adhered to or enforced; however, the spirit of software development still existed. Strategically, creating an abundance of software for the Macintosh increased the value and usage of the machine and indirectly stimulated hardware sales. Such software was shared with Apple and with other universities and colleges. One mechanism for this was the Kinko's Academic Courseware Ex-

EXHIBIT 1 POLICY FOR PURCHASE OF A MACINTOSH SE OR MACINTOSH II

Under the terms of the Apple University Consortium or University Purchase Program (UPP) purchase agreement with Apple, a qualified full-time student, faculty member, or member of the professional and research staff may purchase only one Macintosh™ computer. It is Apple's desire, however, to give the higher education community access to the increased benefits provided by evolving technologies. Technological advances make upgrades of previous Macintosh systems to the Macintosh SE and II unfeasible. Because of this, our policy is being modified as follows:

A qualified full-time student, faculty member, or member of the professional and research staff defined as eligible for purchase of product under the terms of the purchase agreement with Apple may purchase a Macintosh SE or Macintosh II personal computer under the following conditions:

   1 Such individual has not previously purchased a Macintosh under the terms of the agreement; or
   2 Such individual had purchased a Macintosh prior to March 2, 1985, under the terms of the agreement, two years prior to the introduction of the Macintosh SE and Macintosh II products; or
   3 An institution may resell or allow purchase of a Macintosh SE or II even if such individual had purchased a Macintosh between March 2, 1985, and March 2, 1987, under the terms of the agreement, provided the institution repurchases the equipment (which could then be resold to another eligible individual) and/or agrees to comply with the following:

   • institution executes an addendum to its agreement allowing for such resale; and
   • institution obtains a letter or form provided by the institution stating that the Macintosh previously purchased by the individual has been sold to another eligible individual at the same institution;
   • institution verifies that the individual purchasing this used equipment is eligible for purchase under the terms of the agreement; institution will register the purchase and have the individual purchasing this used equipment sign an Individual Purchase Agreement, which states that the purchase of the used equipment represents the individual's one-time purchase of a microcomputer under the terms of the agreement, (that is, they will not be able to buy another Macintosh at a later date).

As with all sales of Apple products under these agreements, it is the responsibility of the institution to monitor this policy and keep adequate records on file. Institutions are urged to examine their procedures to ensure maximum compliance with the terms of individual purchases under the program.

February 26, 1987

---

change (ACE) program. Kinko's, a copy center chain headquartered in Santa Barbara, California, published the *Academic Courseware Exchange Catalog* three times a year. Catalogs were distributed through Kinko's network of 300 stores nationwide, and by mail to those calling a toll-free number.

Courseware in the catalog was priced between $8 and $40. To minimize production costs, software distributed through ACE was not copy-protected, and prices were kept low to discourage unauthorized copying. The library of courseware included templates, applications, and tools. Authors contracted directly with Kinko's and had a number of options for services rendered by Kinko's, payment for those services, and royalty arrangements.

To enhance greater software development, in June 1987, Apple initiated a graduate fellowship program for one student at each of 26 institutions belonging to the InterUniversity Consortium for Educational Computing, a group of colleges and universities interested in the next generation of desktop computers for education. Each of the fellows would work on software development and receive a $2,500 stipend, a Macintosh II, and training from Apple.

Wheels for the Mind   *Wheels for the Mind* was developed as a quarterly publication of Apple University Consortium and Apple Computer, Inc. Each quarter, 30,000 copies were published and distributed to Apple higher education representatives worldwide and to Apple education dealers. *Wheels* was also distributed at Apple events and education meetings, and could be purchased by subscription.

The publication contained a wealth of information about the Apple Macintosh computer and how it was being used at institutions of higher education around the world. A typical issue included a theme with articles addressing that theme: descriptions of applications, projects, or programs going on at colleges and universities that support that theme; technical items of interest to hardware and software developers; Mac-

intosh product information; listings of books and articles in other publications about Macintosh; and a cumulative collection of projects involving Macintosh in academic computing around the world.

AppleWorld   AppleWorld was an annual event held by Apple to inform its various constituencies about Apple's direction and intent. The higher education focus of this event was designed to enhance the partnership Apple has with its higher education customers and to continue to explain and demonstrate Apple's Academic Program, the umbrella term used at Apple for all non-price programs. The emphasis of AppleWorld was on new products and positioning. AppleWorld afforded customers the opportunity to see the "big picture," that is, what Apple is doing in all of its market channels: business, education, consumer, government, international, and so on.

MacAdemia   The MacAdemia conference was an event that was implemented by field sales offices and co-sponsored by a local Apple University Consortium school. The primary focus was to provide faculty members with a chance to learn more about computer resources and to network with their peers and also with Apple personnel. It also provided faculty members an opportunity to demonstrate their software development work and to gain recognition for their accomplishments. MacAdemia conferences often included special sessions that brought together participants and attendees with specific interests in particular disciplines such as "Computing for Liberal Arts" and "Medical Applications."

MacWorld Conference   Other than AppleWorld, MacWorld was the only event that involved participation by all the market segments, allowing Apple customers to see what was happening in the other markets. In addition to this, there were many third-party developers demonstrating their products. MacWorld attendees had the opportunity to experience the breadth of what was happening in the world of Macintosh.

Macintosh Programming Seminars These programs were intended for people who plan to develop Macintosh applications. The seminars served as the first step in the development process. In 1987, four seminars were available: Introduction to Macintosh Programming (one day, $325); Developing a Macintosh Program (three days, $770); Using MPW—Macintosh Programmer's Workshop (one day, $325); and MacApp and Object-Oriented Programming (four days, $1095). Additionally, Apple offered a two-day course that trained university personnel to act as network administrators. It cost $300 and provided the necessary knowledge to set up, maintain, and control a network system. Participants also received the tools to provide on-site desktop communications user support.

AppleLink AppleLink, Apple's information and communications network, is a fast, interactive support system that runs on the Macintosh personal computer. With AppleLink, one can easily obtain information about Apple and Apple products. It also provided an electronic-mail network for communication with Apple sales personnel.

AppleLink offered a direct link to Apple—almost 24 hours a day, seven days a week. By possessing AppleLink software, a Macintosh, and a modem, and by dialing a local telephone number, university personnel could obtain information vital to doing business with Apple: press releases, product announcements, and program descriptions and procedures. It also allowed communication with third parties who might be working on a particular problem of interest.

Technical Support: Apple Support Coordinator Self-supporting customers contracted directly with Apple for support and assigned an individual at the school to become the Apple Support Coordinator (ASC) for the account. The ASC handled the support and training needs of the users at his or her university. Apple provided ASCs with support tools, reference materials, and ongoing backup support. At an orientation program, ASCs learned what they were expected to do, what tools were available to assist them, and how they would be supported by Apple. To keep them informed of new developments at Apple, ASCs received the *Apple-Gram* newsletter with a special insert that included such items as product reviews, hints, and tips; a special ASC newsletter; and reference materials. They also received a support programs binder that contains *Apple Support and Resource Guide*, "how to" guides such as *How to Sponsor a User's Group*, and additional reference materials. This binder also held the materials received in the monthly mailings. The AppleLink information and communications network provided ASCs with Apple and third-party technical support, Apple and third-party product descriptions, and communication with Apple and other universities and ASCs. Additionally, Apple offered a 24-hour, seven-days-a-week hotline, a toll-free number, to obtain technical assistance directly from Apple. The Self-Supporting Customer Program was available to approved Apple higher education customers who met the following conditions:

• Agreed to the Training and Support Guidelines for Self-Supporting customers
• Completed the Self-Supporting Customer Information Checklist, available from the Apple higher education representative
• Designated a key support person (or persons) as the Apple Support Coordinator(s)

AppleGram *AppleGram for Higher Education* was a monthly publication sent to Apple's University Consortium and University Purchase Program accounts, as well as certain Apple internal people and Apple field personnel associated with the higher education channel. *AppleGram* contained the following: new product information, promotional information, success stories (ideas and solutions that may be applicable to many campuses), technical information, AppleLink user updates, information on Apple conferences and events, information on third-party solutions, and miscellaneous information pertaining to computing in higher education.

AppleCare   *AppleCare* was an extended carry-in service agreement that covered customers' Apple systems and peripheral products after the initial 90-day limited warranty expired. Products were covered against all unexpected repair costs. Only self-servicing and reselling UPPs can sell *AppleCare*. This service agreement was usually sold as a package with the Apple system and peripheral products—as an integral part of selling the "Apple Solution." Resellers received a 50% margin on each *AppleCare* sale. The program provided 25% parts margin and a labor reimbursement for repairs. It was designed to enhance the reseller's service department. Additional revenue was derived when Apple sent customers a renewal letter encouraging them to return to the reseller to renew their contract. The program featured an annual price less than that of a single typical repair and was transferable to a new owner. It covered an unlimited number of repairs.

Pricing at Apple

Apple's pricing strategy rested on a four-tier approach based on volume and commitment to Apple. At the same time, the level of pricing offered to a school was negotiable. Apple continued to maintain strong ties to consortium schools, and they were assured of the best pricing available. However, even within consortia members, variability existed in the contracts offered. The University of Michigan, for instance, had its own very favorable contract. While many consortia agreements mandated a minimum total annual purchase quantity of $100,000 (which most consortia meet easily anyway), Boston College in 1987 entered into a contract committing it to $2 million in hardware purchases over three years. A sample contract appears in Exhibit 2. Orders had to be placed to Apple for minimum shipment quantities of $10,000 per order. Larger schools normally made much larger orders and gained even deeper discounts, whereas smaller schools took orders from students and accumulated them until they reached a $10,000 order quantity. This, of course, would cause delays in deliveries to students.

In 1987, Apple introduced its HEPP II purchase program, which was targeted at larger universities and focused on the university becoming the reseller. The university would take on the function of the installing dealer and fulfill the technical aspects of receiving, checking, and installing the machines as well as training the customer. Alternatively, the school might use a local dealer for these activities, wherein the dealer received some amount (which varies by agreement but is usually about $75 per order). The university would add a markup to its cost (usually 10 percent of invoice price or 6 percent of list price—although some university outlets went as low as 5 percent). While college/university resellers were far more interested in accomplishing their educational mission than making money, they were concerned that they covered their operating costs. In fact, some university outlets were explicitly mandated to cover their costs. With some expectation, university dealers did not hold any inventory and placed all orders directly with Apple. When the university did keep some stock, it was generally for only 10 to 20 machines. All repair parts were purchased through the local dealers. When the university chose to utilize an outside dealer to be the installing dealer, it would choose only from a set of dealers that Apple specified. Sometimes only one dealer in the area could be chosen. In other situations, schools had an "open market" policy and could specify more than one dealer. This policy ensured that the dealer selected was in tune with the university system.

At smaller schools, sales were made through dealers on a non-exclusive basis. No sharp discounts were offered, no commitment was exacted from the school or dealer, and no method of doing business was specified. Apple was not committed to this lower end of the market. Because of its diverse needs and methods of procurement and student resale, Apple consciously decided not to specify a pricing approach for this segment of the market.

Apple Credit Card   The Apple Credit Plan was run in cooperation with General Electric Credit Corporation (GECC), one of the largest and most

EXHIBIT 2   HIGHER EDUCATION PURCHASE PROGRAM II AGREEMENT

THIS AGREEMENT is entered into between Apple Computer, Inc. ("APPLE") and _____ ("INSTITUTION") as of this _____day of_____ , 198____.

The parties do hereby agree as follows:

1. PURCHASES.

A.   During the term of this Agreement, INSTITUTION, its colleges, laboratories, libraries, and departments may order from Apple those products as set forth on the Higher Education Purchase Program ("HEPP II") Product List as generally in effect from time to time ("Apple Products") for its own use in its facilities in the United States.

B.   In addition, INSTITUTION may resell such products designated on the HEPP II Product Lists as available for resale to its full-time students, faculty, professional and research staff, provided that INSTITUTION shall not resell more than one personal computer to any given student, faculty member, or staff member without Apple's prior consent, nor shall INSTITUTION resell or otherwise transfer such products or service stock as defined below to third parties (including, without limitation, independent contractors and maintenance organizations) except as provided above or in the course of actually rendering repair services contemplated hereunder.

INSTITUTION's right to resell may be terminated as per Paragraph 2 below.

INSTITUTION agrees that products purchased hereunder are intended for academic use and that INSTITUTION shall not resell products to students, faculty members, and staff members for the purpose of further resale, and INSTITUTION agrees that any resale of products purchased hereunder shall be in accordance with Apple's then current sales guidelines for institutional resale. In the event products are purchased from INSTITUTION for the purpose of further resale Apple shall have the right to immediately terminate this Agreement upon written notice to INSTITUTION.

INSTITUTION shall provide space on campus to display and demonstrate Apple Products. INSTI-TUTION shall also provide its faculty, staff and students with product literature, prices and other information necessary to purchase Apple Products.

C.   Each order shall be binding upon the parties only after acceptance in writing by an authorized representative of Apple. No term or condition set forth on any order or other document submitted by INSTITUTION shall be of any force or effect whatsoever.

2. TERM; PURCHASE REQUIREMENT.

The term of this Agreement shall commence on the date it is signed by Apple and shall continue for a period of one year. INSTITUTION shall purchase $100,000.00 (ONE HUNDRED THOUSAND DOLLARS) worth of Apple Products under this Agreement in accordance with the following milestones: INSTITUTION shall purchase no less than ten percent (10%) of the Products within the first three (3) months of the term, thirty percent (30%) within the first six (6) months of the term, sixty percent (60%) within the first nine (9) months of the term and the balance of the Products prior to the expiration of the term. In the event INSTITUTION shall fail to meet any of these purchase milestones, then the prices for Apple Products shall be those prices set forth on Apple's then current Education Purchase Price List and INSTITUTION's right to resell under 1.B. shall be terminated.

Further, within sixty (60) days from the date of this Agreement, INSTITUTION shall install a minimum of one (1) public access lab. Each lab shall have a minimum of seven (7) systems, with a system consisting of a Macintosh, printer and disk drive. During the term of this Agreement, INSTITUTION shall install on campus a minimum of one (1) system for every one thousand (1,000) students, up to a maximum of twenty (20) systems.

3. PRICE.

Prices shall be as set forth on the HEPP II Product List in effect upon receipt by Apple of INSTITUTION's order. Prices may vary on certain Apple Products depending upon whether the Products are purchased for internal use by Institution or for resale by Institution, as per paragraph 1.B. of the Agreement. It shall be the responsibility of Institution to purchase the Products at the appropriate price, depending upon the use of the Products. Institution shall maintain such records as may be necessary to ensure to Apple that it is in compliance with the terms of this Agreement and Apple shall have the right at reasonable times to inspect such records. INSTITUTION shall submit purchase orders for products having total purchase price, net of discount, of no less than One Thousand Dollars ($1,000.00). Apple shall give INSTITUTION no less than 30 days prior written notice of any price increase. All applicable local sales and use taxes, duties and other imposts due on account of purchases hereunder (other than those based upon Apple's net income) shall be paid by INSTITUTION. INSTITUTION shall be invoiced upon shipment of product and shall pay each invoice at the designated Apple Support Center within THIRTY (30) DAYS of date of invoice.

4. DELIVERY.

Delivery shall be F.O.B. Apple's shipping location best way by common carrier, minimum insurance, unless otherwise directed by INSTITUTION in writing. INSTITUTION shall pay all transportation and insurance. Apple will endeavor to ship according to INSTITUTION's scheduling, but cannot be liable for failure to do so or for delay caused by forces beyond Apple's control. INSTITUTION shall designate one location as a receiving site, and Apple shall ship all products to that site.

5. LIMITED WARRANTY AND LIMITATION OF LIABILITY.

A.   All products, including service stock, sold or licensed by Apple to INSTITUTION hereunder shall be free from manufacturing and material defects for NINETY (90) DAYS from the date of delivery. Provided INSTITUTION notifies Apple of any such defect in writing received by Apple within NINETY (90) DAYS of delivery, Apple shall, at its option and expense, either (a) repair the defective product, (b) replace the defective product, or (c) accept prompt return of the defective product and, upon its return, refund to INSTITUTION any sums paid to Apple for such product.

   This limited warranty is non-transferable and is contingent upon proper use of the products and does not cover products which have been modified or which have been subject to unusual physical or electrical stress. APPLE MAKES NO OTHER EXPRESS OR IMPLIED WARRANTY WITH RESPECT TO PRODUCTS SOLD OR LICENSED TO INSTITUTION OTHER THAN THE LIMITED WARRANTY SET FORTH HEREIN. No Apple dealer, agent or employee is authorized to make any modification, extension or addition to this warranty.

   Unless unenforceable or unlawful, ALL IMPLIED WARRANTIES, INCLUDING, WITHOUT LIMI-TATION, THE IMPLIED WARRANTIES OF MERCHANTABILITY AND FITNESS FOR A PARTICULAR PURPOSE ARE HEREBY LIMITED IN DURATION TO NINETY (90) DAYS FROM THE DATE OF DELIV-ERY. THE LIABILITY OF APPLE, IF ANY, FOR DAMAGES RELATING TO ANY ALLEGEDLY DEFECTIVE PRODUCT SHALL UNDER ANY LEGAL THEORY BE LIMITED TO THE ACTUAL PRICE PAID FOR

SUCH PRODUCT AND SHALL IN NO EVENT INCLUDE INCIDENTAL, CONSEQUENTIAL, SPECIAL OR INDIRECT DAMAGES OF ANY KIND, EVEN IF APPLE IS AWARE OF THE POSSIBILITY OF SUCH DAMAGES.

Some states do not allow the limitation of implied warranties or liability for incidental, consequential, special or indirect damages, so the above limitation may not always apply. This warranty gives INSTITUTION specific legal rights, and INSTITUTION may also have other rights which vary from state to state.

B.   IN NO EVENT SHALL APPLE BE LIABLE FOR INCIDENTAL, CONSEQUENTIAL, INDIRECT OR SPECIAL DAMAGES, INCLUDING WITHOUT LIMITATION, LOST REVENUES.

C.   Notwithstanding the foregoing, with respect to product purchased for resale by INSTITUTION hereunder, the warranty shall be as set forth on the standard written limited warranty statement which accompanies the product. (The individual purchaser shall receive a limited warranty from Apple which shall commence upon date of his purchase from INSTITUTION and extend for a period of 90 days, however the period shall in no event exceed 180 days from date of shipment to INSTITUTION.)

6.   ORIENTATION, SUPPORT AND TRAINING.

Apple shall provide orientation, support and training, as set forth below, for all Apple Products purchased under this Agreement. Apple shall have an authorized Apple Education dealer, selected by INSTITUTION, perform such services on its behalf.

A.   Apple shall provide basic user orientation to all users of Apple Products purchased under this Agreement. INSTITUTION shall implement such procedures as necessary to ensure that the eligible faculty, staff and students purchasing Apple Products from INSTITUTION receive such orientation.

B.   Apple shall provide INSTITUTION with a minimum of 8 hours per month of training and seminars for Apple Products. INSTITUTION and the authorized Apple Education Dealer shall work together to determine the type of training and seminars which shall be provided.

C.   Apple shall provide INSTITUTION with a telephone hot-line number for 40 hours per week which Institutional users may call with technical questions. Institution and the authorized Apple Education Dealer will work together to provide problem resolution within 2 working days.

D.   Apple shall provide INSTITUTION on-site pick-up and return warranty services. Institution and the authorized Apple Education Dealer shall determine a reasonable time within which Dealer shall accomplish such pick-up and return.

7.   PATENT INDEMNITY.

Apple agrees to defend, indemnify and hold INSTITUTION harmless from any and all losses, damages, liabilities, costs and expenses (including but not limited to attorney's fees) incurred by INSTITUTION as a result of any judgment or proceeding against INSTITUTION in which it is determined or alleged that the use of any Apple Product sold by Apple infringes any patent, copyright, trademark, trade secret or other proprietary or contractual right of any third party, provided that the INSTITUTION promptly notifies Apple of any such claim or proceeding in writing, tenders to Apple the right to defend or settle such claim or proceeding at its expense, and cooperates with Apple in defending or settling any such claim or proceeding.

Apple shall have no liability for claims based on the use of Apple Products that have been modified or used in combination with other products.

8. TRADEMARKS.

Neither party shall use the other's name, logo, or trademarks or trade names in any of its advertising, communications, or publications without the prior written permission of the other, nor shall either party disclose this Agreement or any portion thereof to any third party without prior written permission of the other.

9. NOTICES.

All notices, requests, demands and other communications given or to be given under this Agreement shall be in writing and shall be deemed to have been duly given when served if served personally, or on the second day after mailing if mailed by first class, registered, or certified mail, postage prepaid, and properly addressed to the party to whom notice is to be given as set forth below.

If to Apple:

Apple Computer, Inc.
20525 Mariani Ave.
Cupertino, CA 95014
ATTN: Counsel

with a copy to:

_____
_____
_____
ATTN:_____

If to the INSTITUTION:

_____
_____
_____
ATTN:_____

10. TERMINATION.

Either party may terminate this Agreement upon thirty (30) days prior written notice.

11. CHOICE OF LAW.

This Agreement shall be construed in accordance with and governed by the laws of the state in which INSTITUTION is located.

12. ENTIRE AGREEMENT.

This Agreement constitutes the entire agreement between the parties pertaining to the subject matter hereof and the purchases and sales contemplated hereunder, and any written or oral agreements heretofore existing between the parties or modifications to this Agreement (including any of the terms of any purchase order documentation of INSTITUTION) shall be of no force or effect as regards the subject matter hereof unless incorporated herein by a writing signed by both parties specifically referencing this paragraph. In the event any portion of this Agreement should be determined to be void or invalid for any reason, its remaining terms shall be interpreted so as to reflect the basic intentions and objectives of the parties.

IN WITNESS WHEREOF, the parties to this Agreement execute it through their representatives duly authorized.

INSTITUTION

By:_____

Title:_____

Date:_____

APPLE COMPUTER, INC.

By:_____

Title:_____

Date:_____

---

successful consumer financing organizations in the world. Apple offered an "instant credit" option that allowed customers to open an Apple Credit Plan account of up to $2,500 if they met certain qualifications that ensured their ability to pay. If the qualifications could not be met, a cosigner was needed.

Apple's Distribution Approach

The distribution strategy was at the heart of Apple's 1987 strategic thrust. Apple management realized that the higher education market was not being sufficiently served by the existing dealer network. Dealers were marketing to many diverse markets—home, business, retail, and schools—and were spreading themselves too thin. Since the higher education market was central to Apple's corporate mission, the company decided to move toward bypassing the traditional computer store and gaining commitment from the college or university to be the self-supporting outlet for student sales.

Under the new approach, the school became an order taker and had the option to handle the computer merchandise or pass that activity along to an existing dealer. Whoever took on the tasks of accepting delivery, inspecting the machine, installing it, and instructing the buyer was called the "installing dealer." When the school chose not to be the "installing dealer," Apple examined the territory surrounding the school and chose one or several of the retail dealers, who could

then be designated as the school's "installing dealer." Such a choice rested upon Apple's assurance that the dealer could and would be able to render the needed services to the school's customers. When only one dealer was deemed so qualified, the school was limited to funneling all purchased products through that dealer. When a set of dealers was indicated, the school could choose one of the set or take an "open market" approach and let all designated dealers participate and compete for the student/buyer's installation business.

The Details of Being a University Dealer As order taker, the university was responsible for advising buyers about product, verifying their student status, collecting their money, and (in purchase lots of at least $10,000 per order) conveying orders directly to Apple. The university was also responsible for keeping records on purchases to disallow multiple purchases by individual students and to monitor hardware upgrade behavior. The policing of meeting purchase restrictions was the responsibility of the university dealer.

Apple recognized that selling computers was new to many universities. To make the transition easy, Apple offered merchandising assistance and repair training to all "self-supporting" schools. With merchandising aids, Apple offered but did not demand that the school take its advice and marketing tools. Apple offered resellers a copy of *Delivering the Campus Microcomputer*, a guide providing detailed information on effective marketing and advertising on campus. If the school outlet wished to have fliers or advertising help, Apple responded quickly to tailor a program to the desires of the dealer. While promotional programs came from a set developed at corporate headquarters, the particular needs of the dealer were responded to rather than forcing the dealer to bend to a structured promotional program. Apple welcomed participation in school-sponsored computer fairs and demonstrations and was generally receptive to all requests for help from school dealers.

Repair training was conducted for university personnel at Apple distribution centers, with training resulting in levels of certification for school repair persons. Such training was offered only to "self-supporting" institutions.

Repair of Apple products was handled in a wide range of different ways. Some schools handled only university computer repairs themselves, while others did both student product repairs and their own. For instance, at San Diego State, five full-time technicians operated a factory repair station on campus for all Apple products. Each machine purchased by the university or by students was given a San Diego State sticker and qualified to be serviced at this repair station. The school even committed itself to inventorying its own parts at a large carrying cost to the school. Its service goal was to put machines back in use in two hours. Schools did not generally carry their own parts but purchased them through the local dealer. In contrast, at Rutgers the repair function was given in a five-year contract to Xerox, which in turn maintained all personal computers through its maintenance center. Apple's policy was not to provide parts or training to third-party organizations since they were not technically "self-supporting" schools. At Rutgers, for instance, all parts and training were funneled through the university.

The type of outlet used by a college or university varied. Many used their bookstores as the retailer while others spun off a separate store to sell computers only. Still others used informal outlets often adjacent to the computer center or com-

puter service area. All worked with a "lowest cost to the student" mission; hence, amenities such as atmosphere and expensive technical and marketing services were rarely found.

Apple executives made delivery time a high priority for university dealers and students. Apple's delivery schedule was 7 to 10 days after the placement of the order. Machines were shipped from the closest regional distribution center, called an Area Support Center. These were located in Charlotte, North Carolina; Rolling Meadows, Illinois; and Sunnyvale, California. Orders could also be placed over AppleLink. Schools using AppleLink needed to complete a Higher Education Purchase Program AppleLink Ordering Agreement prior to placing the orders. Hard copies were not accepted once the agreement was approved.

Apple's return policy for finished-goods products stated that returns would be accepted only under the following situations:

A shipping error had been made by Apple. (or)
The product was "dead on arrival" (DOA).

In both cases, prior approval from Apple was required before goods could be returned. Unauthorized returns were refused by Apple and were sent back to the university at the university's expense. Apple warranted that Apple products were free from manufacturing and material defects at the time they were shipped to the university. If products were found not working (DOA), a return request was required within 20 days of their receipt. Freight expense for products shipped by Apple to replace defective products was borne by Apple.

Reseller Conferences   Annual conferences were held in different regions for university and reseller personnel to provide information about the direction Apple was taking as well as assistance in retailing Apple products. These conferences also provided a feedback mechanism to Apple so that reseller problems could be aired and solved. At the two-day conference, the agenda included both business and relaxation. The vacation feature was there to make the event consistent with Apple's image. The agenda for the 1987 Eastern Region reseller's conference is shown in Exhibit 3. The reseller's program also included small workshops where four to five schools were joined by two Apple representatives for a pointed discussion of positive and negative aspects of doing business with Apple. Issues surrounding Apple policies, product direction, and restrictions were discussed openly, and main points were put on paperboard that hung on the walls. Top officials attended, and all non-Apple attendees signed nondisclosure agreements ensuring confidentiality of session content.

Resolving Dealer Conflict   To better understand expected reactions from existing dealers to its channel change, Apple established a Dealer Advisory Council for advice. Council members helped design the new higher education distribution system to minimize negative feelings on the part of the dealers who had been the backbone of Apple's prior distribution system. The strategy of using the school as "self-supporting" dealer was met with varied response by retailers who were being bypassed. In larger locations, dealers were generally complacent. They realized that students were buying at a much lower price than they could afford to offer and that this "price" segment would not buy at a higher price from them anyway. And if they were designated as "installing dealer," they would receive a dollar amount on each machine for undertaking that activity—and without bearing the cost of carrying inventory. Furthermore, the dealer would also make money on all parts used in repair. And the "installing dealer" would also have access to the student buyer (with name and address), who would likely buy other equipment and software. Many dealers were very content with this new arrangement.

Others, especially those in smaller locations, relied more heavily on students for sales and were less than pleased. Complaints, rumor spreading, and other uncooperative tactics emerged. Such problems were met in many ways.

Some universities cut dealers back in by shifting all merchandise sold (where the university was the "installing dealer") back through the dealer. Here the dealer would receive a higher margin and the university a much lower margin. In some cases merchandise delivered to the university was actually moved from the university to the local dealer. At the University of Wisconsin at Madison, the university held inventory. Students paid Wisconsin with a check, and the merchandise was sent to the local "installing dealer" for delivery to the students. The dealer remitted vouchers to the university and was paid in installments. Dealers were satisfied because they had no inventory to carry. In other cases, local chambers of commerce interceded for local retailers and initiated compromise agreements between the university and the local dealers. At Western Washington at Bellingham, for instance, countering what dealers and the chamber of commerce thought unfair competition resulted in marketing all Macintosh machines through downtown dealers. There, merchant dealers received a 10% discount and the university 3%, thereby diluting the 35% discount offered the university by Apple to less than 25%. Still other schools used subtle mechanisms to reduce conflict. At the University of Michigan, a fall 1987 "kickoff" weekend sale involved both many computer manufacturers and local retailers, who worked side by side to sell computers. The university held a party after the sale. The camaraderie of the entire event resulted in a continuing dialogue between the school and dealers and dispelled much conflict. Dealers even sent flowers to university officials.

Apple's Promotional Activities

Apple's promotional strategy was to be responsive to the university's or college's wants for promotional and merchandising assistance. In its personal selling component, a young, relaxed, and flexible sales force of sales representatives *pushed* the product through the new university dealer channel. Advertising, but more importantly sales promotion with highly coordi-

EXHIBIT 3   AGENDA
1987 Higher Education Reseller's Conference

August 4

6:00–8:00 PM   Pre-registration and cocktail party at the Sheraton for participants arriving the night before the conference

August 5

8:00–9:00 AM   Continental breakfast and registration
9:00–9:30 AM   Welcome
9:30–10:15 AM   Trends in Campus Reselling: A Recent Survey by Apple
10:15–10:30 AM   Break
10:30–11:45 AM   Critical Success Factors for a Campus Resale Operation
11:45–12:30 PM   Impact of Resale on Campus—The Importance of a Student/Faculty Support Structure
12:30–1:45 PM   Lunch
1:45–3:15 PM   Promotion and Advertising to Generate Awareness on Campus
3:15–3:30 PM   Break
3:30–4:45 PM   Merchandising to Make the Most of Your Resale Space
4:45–5:00 PM   Walk to Penn's Computer Connection
5:00–5:30 PM   Tour of the Computer Connection
5:30–6:15 PM   Return to the Sheraton and relax before dinner
6:15 PM   Buses depart for the Moshulu for the evening activity. The Moshulu is an old masted shipping vessel built at the turn of the century permanently docked at Penn's Landing on the Delaware River. We will have cocktails and dinner there.
6:30–8:00 PM   Cocktails topside
8:00–10:00 PM   Dinner inside the ship

August 6

8:00–9:00 AM   Continental Breakfast
9:00–10:15 AM   Financing Programs
10:15–10:30 AM   Break
10:30–11:30 AM   Service Programs and Apple Care
11:30–1:00 PM   Lunch
1:00–1:15 PM   Return to main conference room
1:15–2:00 PM   Apple Open Forum—Apple people to field questions and comments from attendees.
2:00–2:30 PM   Wrap-up

nated programs to students, *pulled* the product through the channel. Appeals to the image of a young, fun-loving company mirrored the lifestyle values of the college student.

Personal Selling   Within Apple there were five separate sales forces: K-12, dealer, value-added reseller, national accounts, and the university sales forces. The university sales force consisted of more than 50 reps who called on the targeted schools. This sales rep/school ratio was about 1:6. Some schools, though very few, had their own full-time representative. Those reps not only directly solicited orders but also participated in demonstrations, Apple- and university-sponsored computer fairs, and met with various directly and indirectly responsible parties on and off campus.

The sales representatives were assisted by more than 50 marketing support representatives. These individuals provided backup activities that coordinated with the selling efforts of the sales reps. Such activities included sending out letters to targeted individuals and coordinating sales promotional campaigns. They taught classes on Apple products. Much of the marketing support representative's emphasis was on post-sales to ensure that installation went smoothly.

Apple also employed student sales representatives on many campuses. Those individuals possessed both technical and promotional skills, and their assignments varied depending on the desires of the university. Generally, those students distributed fliers around the campus; helped set up demonstrations on campus; met with department faculty, chairpersons, and deans; and set up meetings for sales representatives. Some worked (often one to two hours per day) in the college's computer store, if so desired by university resellers. All activities that they undertook were approved first by the university. Student representatives were remunerated in money and/or computer equipment.

Advertising Apple controlled all advertising on campus. While the company offered cooperative advertising to its regular dealers, this program was not used with higher education resellers. Its media program consisted almost entirely of print advertising. The vast majority of it was placed in college newspapers. All advertising was prepared by its advertising agency, BBDO Worldwide, located in New York and Los Angeles. The agency's media department, when the local newspaper was not known, would call the central administration of the school to get the name and telephone number of the paper and would place the advertising directly. The program stressed the fun, ease of use, and productivity of a Macintosh. Apple also placed advertising in *Newsweek*

on Campus and *Business Week Careers* issues distributed to campuses and offered free to students. Apple was not sure how effective these two publications actually were. The only other vehicle used to reach college students was a limited amount of television advertising on MTV, the music/video cable channel.

Sales Promotion The *pull* emphasis of the promotional program clearly rested on sales promotion activities. Apple sponsored its own computer fairs, called MacFests. These events focused on the image of fun and student involvement with Apple products. Demonstrations and product counseling were the main thrusts. Similarly, Apple sales and student reps participated in any university-sponsored computer fairs open to them. In addition, Apple would donate Macintoshes to schools and other worthy causes to gain school commitment.

A number of sales promotion vehicles were available. Banners and computer stands were employed by resellers or student reps to create awareness. Note boards with pads for writing notes were left on dorm doors, offering still another unusual vehicle for keeping the Apple "fun" theme visible. Numerous fliers were also used as sales tools. Some were as follows:

- *Student Flier.* "I wish I'd had a Macintosh when I was in college" was directed to students as well as parents. It discussed how using the Macintosh would help students become more productive and successful. The flier could be used as an in-store point-of-sale piece, a registration stuffer, or a direct mail piece to students and parents.
- *Apple Credit Card Flier.* This flier invited students to purchase the Apple system they needed and establish credit at the same time.
- *Higher Education Product Family Flier.* This flier showed how each Macintosh—the Plus, the SE, and the II—fit into the campus community.
- *Higher Education Product Family Brochure.* This introduced and described the Macintosh family of products. It outlined the features of the Macintosh Plus, the SE, and the II, and helped

potential customers select which model best met their needs.

- *Faculty Brochure.* This was a compilation of interviews with nine prominent university faculty members and administrators, discussing why they selected the Macintosh and the sometimes unusual ways they used it.
- *Higher Education Desktop Publishing Brochure.* The theme of the higher education desktop publishing brochure was "For Every Voice, a Means to Be Heard." The brochure illustrated this theme through interviews with college and university faculty, researchers, and staff. Their examples demonstrated how desktop publishing made a significant and beneficial impact on their day-to-day work.

In addition, Apple provided a variety of special promotions to stimulate interest and sampling. A number of contests were run that featured as prizes a bicycle, a compact disk system, or a Honda motor scooter. Apple usually featured a Christmas promotion. In 1987, the company offered $100 off if the student purchased a printer with a Macintosh computer.

REVIEW OF THE EXPAND AND FOCUS STRATEGY

After closely reviewing the Apple strategy and programs planned for 1988, the group was still uncertain as to two things. Although they felt that the extensive programs planned for the higher education market would provide them with a competitive edge, they were still concerned that IBM might shift its strategy to place more emphasis on supplying educational tools to the academic community. The higher Apple gross margins (25% greater than those of other PC makers) were felt necessary to fund the research needed to keep Mac ahead of the IBM-PC and its clones. However, the educational market was beginning to find it more difficult to afford new Macs, and there was a concern that fewer new customers would be willing to pay the premium to buy their first Macintosh. In addition, at the same time, the whole proprietary approach, which allowed Apple to follow a high-priced strategy, might be called into question by the so-called open systems. Those computers, based on standardized software, were able to promise not only low hardware costs but easy inter-connections as well. In addition, MicroSoft Corp. was rumored to be ready to release Windows 3, the IBM-PC program that would finally match the Mac's big advantages.

In discussing the expand and focus strategy, the Apple Marketing group began to wonder what IBM's strategy might be if they decided to concentrate on the educational market. In addition, although they felt that they had developed an extensive program for this market, they began to discuss how they would measure or ascertain whether it had succeeded or not. In an effort to focus on these areas, they decided to try and identify any possible gaps or weaknesses in the existing program as well as anticipate what a competitor's strategy and subsequent programs would be if they were to compete for the educational segment. At that point, the group decided to meet again in one week and focus on those areas.

ERICSSON DO BRASIL: ERICALL SYSTEM

After several months of careful investigation, Mr. José Castanheira, Director of Ericsson do Brasil's General Sales Division, was approaching a point where he had to make a decision on how to relaunch ERICALL in the Brazilian market. ERICALL was an electronic paging system that had been on the Brazilian market for several years. The last two years had shown the first significant sales growth, and Mr. Castanheira was considering a major effort in this area. The General Sales Division (GSD) was to lead Ericsson do Brasil away from its traditional overdependence on the government sector. Both the Brazilian company and its Swedish parent, L. M. Ericsson, believed strongly that ERICALL could make a major contribution for a company reorientation toward the private sector. With the product launch date of August 1982 only three months away, it was now up to Mr. Castanheira to approve the marketing plan for ERICALL's introduction.

This case was prepared by Professor Jean-Pierre Jeannet as a basis for class discussion rather than to illustrate either effective or ineffective handling of an administrative situation. Copyright ©1984 by IMEDE, Lausanne, Switzerland. IMD International, resulting from the merger between IMEDE, Lausanne, and IMI, Geneva, acquires and retains all rights. Reproduced by permission.

THE ERICALL SYSTEM

The ERICALL contactor was a personal paging system. A person, if equipped with a pocket receiver, could receive various types of signals via a radio transmitter operated from a central system. Depending on the configuration of central, transmitter, and receivers, the system could simultaneously handle several thousand different receivers (see Exhibit 1).

Four types of battery-powered receivers were available. The basic model, EC 401, was able to emit a sound signal, or "beep," plus a light-coded signal. The EC 401 was equipped with two small lights and could receive up to four flashes on any one of them. Consequently, a maximum of eight types of combinations could be received. The model EC 400V was also equipped with the double-light feature. It differed from the more basic version because of its vibration mechanism. When activated, the person carrying the EC 400V would feel a single vibration once, twice, three, or four times. The combination of light color and pulsations indicated the type of message. As a result, eight different signals could be transmitted, but the signals were only noticeable to the intended receiver because of the absence of sound.

415

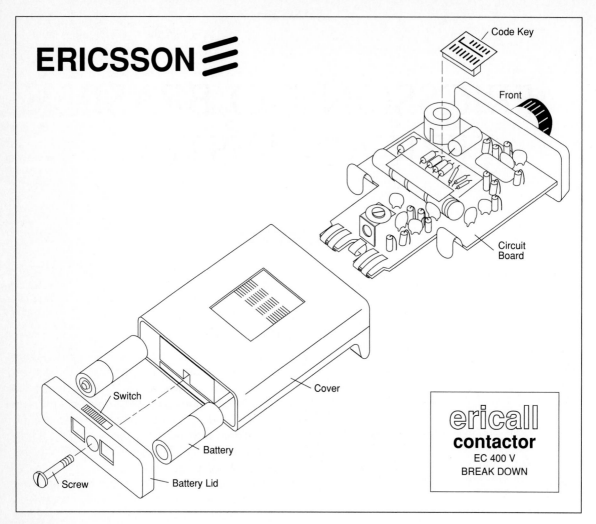

ERICSSON

Code Key

Front

Circuit
Board

Cover

Switch

Battery

Screw

Battery Lid

ericall
contactor
EC 400 V
BREAK DOWN

EXHIBIT 1

Receivers EC 400 and EC 401

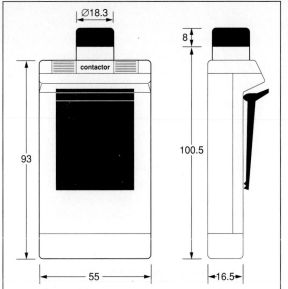

Cylindric piece on top of receiver: lower section applies to high audio level model, both sections to vibrating receiver. Available in yellow and brown (all models), Beige and green (EC 400, EC 401).

Receiver EC 405

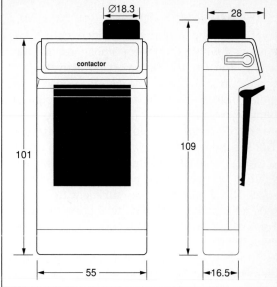

Black top applies to vibrating receiver. Available in yellow and brown.

Technical Data

Order No.	EC 400
	EC 400 vibrator
	EC 401 high audio level
	EC 405 display
	EC 405 display and vibrator
Order key	SRA 1316-R3-167080
Radio frequency	25-42 MHz
Frequency stability	±0.2%
Selectivity	
at > 6 dB	±120 kHz
at > 40 dB	±300 kHz
at > 60 dB	±400 kHz
Sensitivity	
Code	< 30µ V/m
Speech	< 100µ V/m at 12 dB S/N
Alerting signal frequency	3.2 kHz
Sound level at 30 cm distance (not applicable on vibrating receiver)	EC 400 68 dB(A)
	EC 401 87 dB(A)
	EC 405 87dB(A)
Dimensions	
standard receiver	93 × 55 × 16.5 (28) mm
display receiver	101× 55 × 16.5 (28) mm
Weight excluding batteries	93-105 g
Weight of 1 battery set	20-27 g

Power supply	2 Alkaline cells 1.5 V/700 mAh* e.g. Mallory MN9100 or 2 Mercury cells, 1.4 V/800 mAh* e.g. Mallory RM 401 or 2 NiCd cells 1.25 V/150 mAh* e.g. DEAC 151 D Reservation for variations in battery quality.	
Approx. operating time	330 h/100 mAh with 5 calls per day incl. lamp indication, display or vibrator.	
Current consumption	Stand-by	<270µ A
	Tone signal	< 30 m A
	Tone and lamp signal	< 90 m A
	Tone and LED signal	< 50 m A
	Speech	< 15 m A
	Vibration	<100 m A
	Vibration and LED signal	<130 m A
	Tone and display	< 90 m A
	Vibration and display	<160 m A
Battery test	Press reception button (sound or vibration).	
Ambient temperature (max 6 dB sensitivity decrease)	-10 C° to +55° C	
Options	Light indication using lamps, (EC 400/401) Light indication using LEDs (EC 400/401) Vibrator. Display.	

We reserve the right to change technical data or modify the equipment without previous notice.

EXHIBIT 2

The Model EC 405V receivers were substantially more sophisticated since both came equipped with a display for alphanumeric characters. The EC 405 had a sound activator and could transmit voice. The EC 405V had a vibrator instead of sound/voice. The four-digit alphanumeric display unit could be used to transmit codes of up to 8 alphanumeric characters. The second set of four was activated by simply pressing a button. The message remained activated, or available, until erased by the next message. The display unit was sufficient to accommodate Brazil's seven-digit telephone numbers. For a sketch of the four types of receivers see Exhibit 3.

The central switching unit was an important element in the ERICALL system. Two types existed: a compact version and a modular system. The simpler compact version required that the operator activate manually any type of receiver. The receiver capacity in the simpler compact version was 3,375, independent of the mix of receivers. The EC 405 or 405V types permitted the user to send more than 30 million different alphanumerically coded messages to each receiver in any combination of one to eight characters consisting of digits between 0 and 9 and letters from A to E. The compact system alowed for the direct connection of up to three alarm points without operator interference. See Exhibit 4 for additional details.

The modular system was a more powerful paging system. It could be connected into a PABX system which allowed calls to be routed directly to the intended person without operator interference. Furthermore, up to 256 different alarm points could be connected automatically. The modular system could be expanded by the possible simultaneous use of more than one transmitter or codifier. Its key advantage, however, was automatic operation compared with the manual compact system. For more details see Exhibit 5.

For both systems, the keyboard allowed the selection of three-digit receiver codes, i.e., 000 through 999, or letters A, B, C, D, and E, or an alphanumeric combination such as AA3, C23,

D14, etc. This allowed for a combination of up to 4,096 different codes, or the maximum number of receivers which could be handled on one system. The ERICALL system also included a transmitter with an output in watts that depended on the particular application and on distances to receivers.

Ericsson do Brasil manufactured the smaller transmitters in its own factory. The company helped customers in the purchase of the required transmitter from a supplier in Brazil if a stronger signal was needed. If necessary, several transmitters could be combined into a single system to ensure that all intended receivers could be contacted.

POTENTIAL APPLICATIONS FOR ERICALL

The ERICALL system was adaptable to a very wide range of applications. Its principal advantage was automatic activation without operator interference. Consequently, through Ericsson's advanced centrals any receiver could be activated individually through its internal code. The system was adaptable to interface with any alarm system. For example, a company could connect smoke detectors through the central system. If one of the detectors was activated, the alarm would be transmitted automatically to the intended receivers. The respective codes indicated the location of the activated smoke detector, allowing for immediate action. Similar alarm systems could be coupled with burglar alarms.

Receivers with alphanumeric displays provided transmission of various messages. When the receiver was activated through either sound or vibration, the person carrying it could check for the coded message on the display unit. It might contain a telephone number to call, or any prearranged coded message. For units with voice, a verbal message could be transmitted from the central unit. The range of possible applications appeared limitless.

In terms of pager systems technology, the ERICALL was considered advanced, although pager systems technology in general was fairly stable. ERICALL was the only pager system in Brazil to offer a choice of contact by either sound,

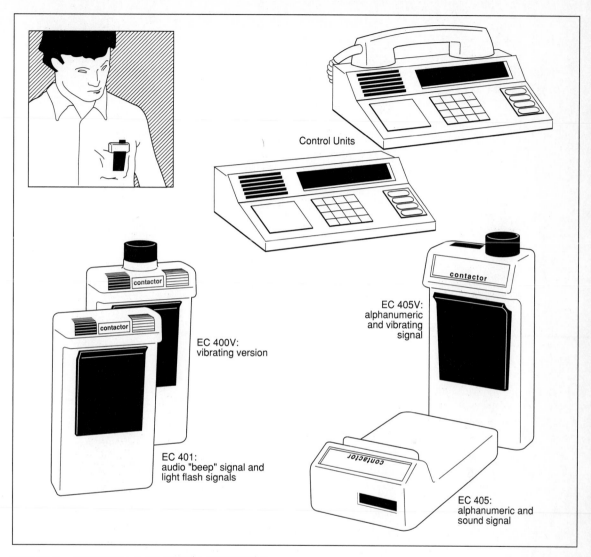

Control Units

EC 400V:
vibrating version

EC 401:
audio "beep" signal and
light flash signals

EC 405V:
alphanumeric
and vibrating
signal

EC 405:
alphanumeric and
sound signal

EXHIBIT 3   TECHNICAL DATA RECALL RECEIVERS

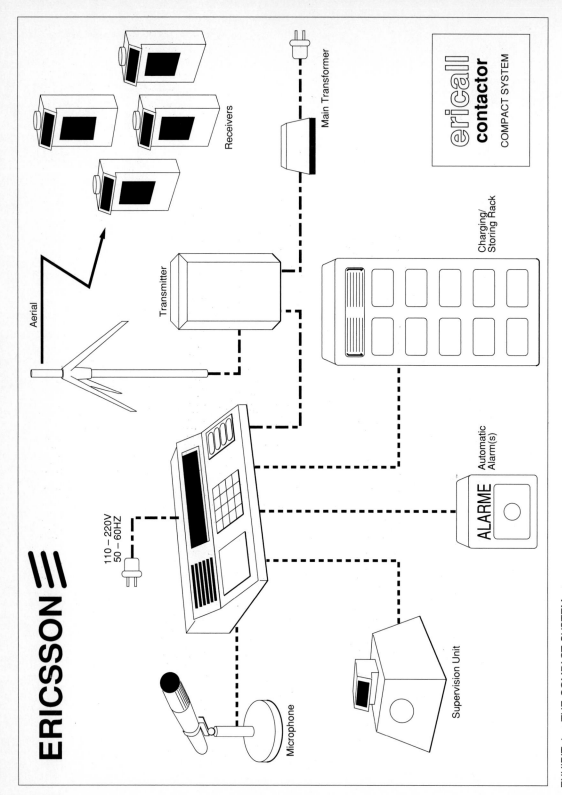

EXHIBIT 4   THE COMPACT SYSTEM

420

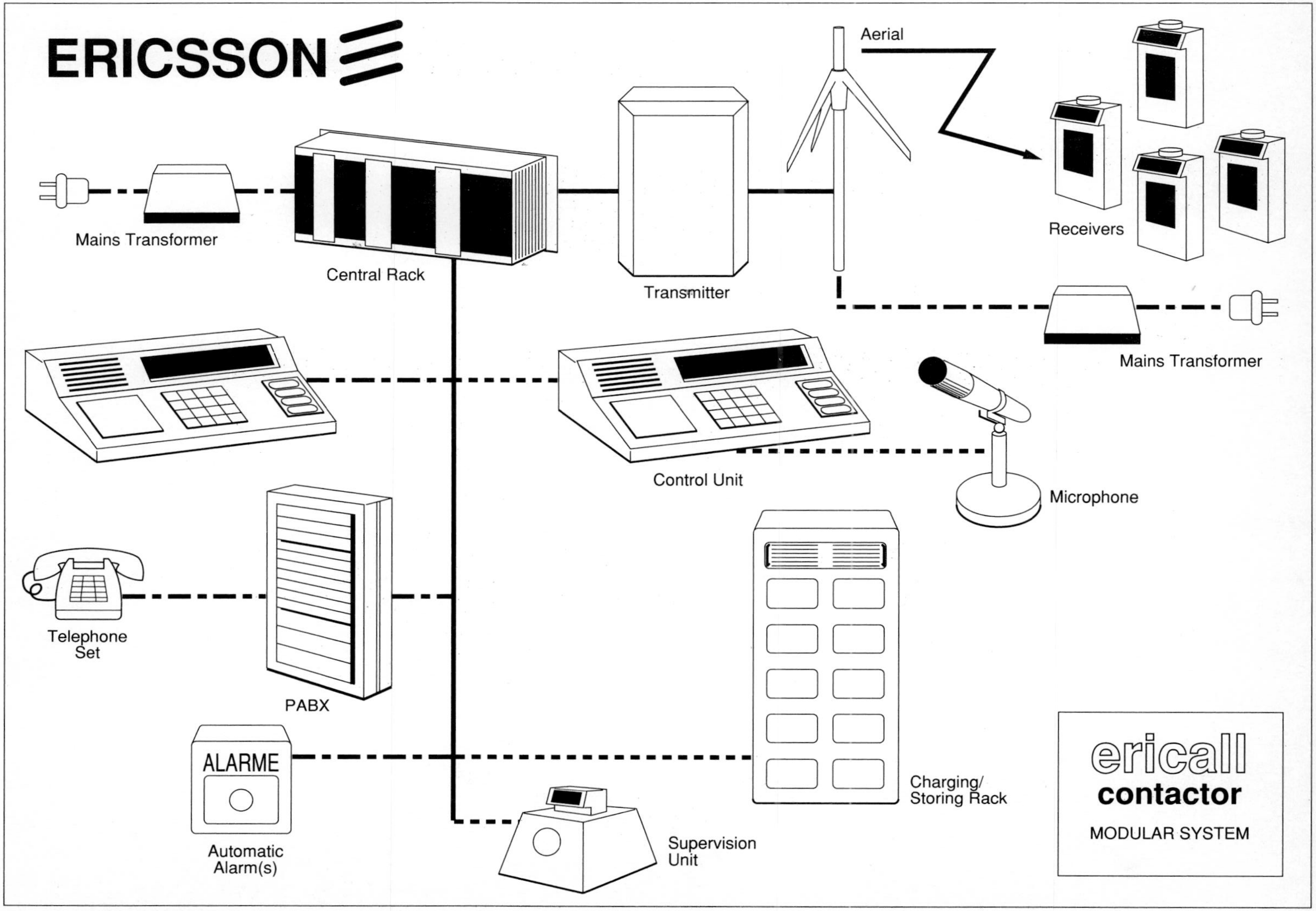

ERICSSON

ericall
contactor
MODULAR SYSTEM

Aerial

Receivers

Mains Transformer

Microphone

Transmitter

Control Unit

Charging/
Storing Rack

Central Rack

Mains Transformer

PABX

Supervision
Unit

Telephone
Set

ALARME

Automatic
Alarm(s)

EXHIBIT 5   THE MODULAR SYSTEM

421

vibration, voice, or alphanumeric code. Competitors in the Brazilian market offered systems with sound contact only. The feature of either voice and/or alphanumeric code eliminated the need of finding a telephone and calling a central switching office to receive the message. Voice data or code data could instantly convey the action required by the recipient provided the action was based on pre-arranged signals as in the case of alphanumeric codes. Mr. Castanheira and his colleagues at Ericsson do Brasil believed that this direct contact capability would create an entirely new range of applications for this pager system. They were particularly excited about its use in the medical and security fields.

COMPANY BACKGROUND

Ericsson do Brasil Comercio e Indústria S/A. (EDB) was an associated company of L. M. Ericsson (LME). LME, a Swedish-based multinational company, had annual sales of about $2.5 billion in 1981. With its more than 160 subsidiaries, associated companies, or technical offices, LME had installed some of the world's most advanced telephone switching equipment. More recently, LME had started a major effort to enter the high-

technology market for office systems and radio communication devices.

LME owned 64 percent of EDB's outstanding capital but controlled only 26 percent of its voting shares. The remainder of the voting shares were in the hands of Brazilian investors. Despite the de jure independence of EDB, the operation relationship between LME in Sweden and EDB was similar to that of any other parent-subsidiary relationship. LME tended to appoint the chief operating executive, who at that time happened to be from Sweden, and the Brazilian partner appointed the majority of the directors.

EDB was organized along functional lines. Reporting to top management were six directors, one each for administration, commercial, finance, production, public relations, and research and development. The commercial director, Mr. Falcao, had responsibility for both the General Sales Division, headed by Mr. Castenheira, and the telephone exchange division. Mr. Castanheira's GSD employed about 900 people. For an organization chart see Exhibit 6.

Marketing at GSD was divided into two regions: south and north. The Southern Department included the two large branches in Rio de Janeiro and São Paulo. "There is a basic differ-

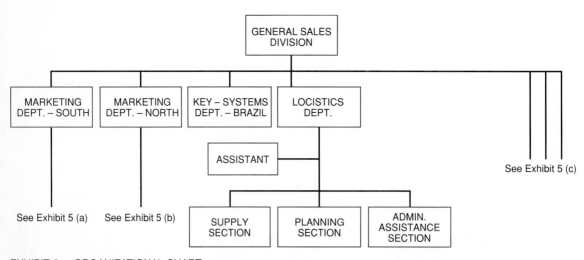

EXHIBIT 6   ORGANIZATIONAL CHART

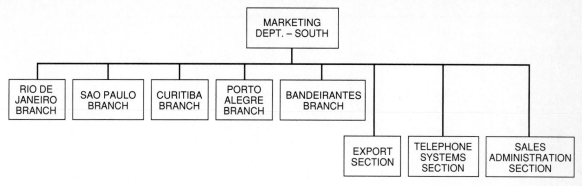

EXHIBIT 6a   ORGANIZATIONAL CHART

ence in business between the more industrialized south and the more rural north," said Mr. Castanheira. In the south of Brazil where about 70 percent of the population was concentrated, economic activity was dominated by large manufacturing companies. In the north, small companies engaged in trade and commerce were relatively important.

This difference between north and south was also reflected in GSD's sales mix. In the south, sales of larger PABX systems dominated and the average system had about 200 lines. In the north, systems had up to 50 lines with an average of about 30. Furthermore, the sales approach was reflective of the cultural differences. Business in the north was more informal. Ericsson salesmen frequently had direct access to the company's top

person. Many businessmen did not wear ties to work. In the south, business was more formal and sales contacts at larger firms were usually at a lower level than in the north.

Each of the 10 branches had a sales group and service and administrative personnel. In the larger branches of the south, sales were specialized according to PABX or key systems.[1] In the north, where sales of smaller key systems were

[1] PABX was a commonly used abbreviation for "private access business exchange" with a capacity of up to several hundred lines. Installed by businesses and government agencies, they required skilled manpower to operate. Key system was a PABX with a small capacity for internal and external communications. For this system, companies did not use specialized operators, and the user received and started his own telephone calls. In the United States, the abbreviation PBX is preferred.

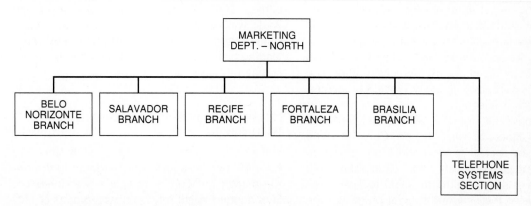

EXHIBIT 6b   ORGANIZATIONAL CHART

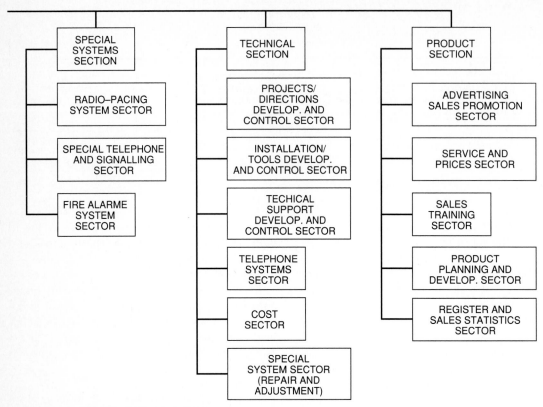

EXHIBIT 6c   ORGANIZATIONAL CHART

common, the same sales force tended to sell both systems.

In the market for PABX systems, EDB had a dominant market share of about 45 percent. The company sold about 1,000 systems annually and had a separate maintenance and service organization for its approximately 10,000 clients in Brazil. It competed against Siemens, Philips, ITT, NEC, and GTE, as well as two local companies, Daruma and Telequipo.

Responsibility for the ERICALL system had been assigned to Mr. Arnaldo Curvello, who headed the special systems section. This section was created shortly after Mr. Castanheira had taken over responsibility for GSD to give more emphasis to the new and special products. The signal systems and fire alarm systems were under Mr. Curvello as well.

With a total employment of more than 7,000 persons, EDB was LME's largest unit in its worldwide network of subsidiaries, affiliates and companies. EDB's factory on the outskirts of São Paulo was, with its 4,000 employees, the largest single LME factory in the world. EDB enjoyed a leading position in its markets and had been operating profitably for several years.

ERICSSON DO BRASIL'S PAST EXPERIENCE WITH ERICALL

ERICALL had been imported by EDB since the early 1970s. Sales had been sporadic to the onsite market for which the system was intended. EDB depended entirely on direct imports of ERICALL elements from Sweden. Though it was marketed successfully, SRA, an Ericsson subsidiary

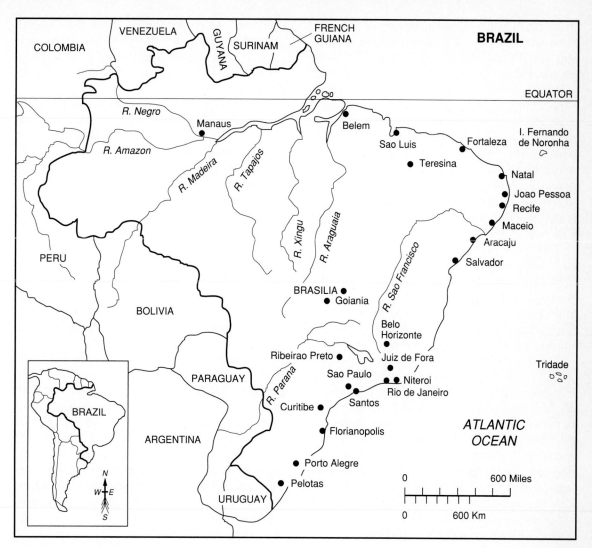

EXHIBIT 7   MAP OF BRAZIL

that manufactured the ERICALL system in Sweden, tried in vain to get EDB to push for more volume. An older executive was responsible for the system at EDB, and he told SRA executives on several occasions that he "just couldn't get the support he needed to push up the volume."

Following Mr. Castanheira's appointment as director of the General Sales Division in 1979, GSD was entirely reorganized. "I wanted everybody to be responsible for their own budget and

to concentrate on a particular product," recalled Mr. Castanheira. It was at that time that he appointed Mr. Arnaldo Curvello as Chief of Special Systems, a department consisting of all specialized products sold through GSD. Mr. Curvello at first found considerable resistance to ERICALL, as the sales force was accustomed to selling PABX systems only. The salesmen viewed ERICALL as a system that could not be sold and that had an image of lesser importance.

To change the negative attitude of the sales force, Mr. Curvello convinced the sales supervisors that if presented properly, the ERICALL system could be sold to the same client who bought Ericsson's PABX system. His insistence paid off, and suddenly, EDB's volume in ERICALL systems took off. "Two years later, in 1981, the SRA people came back, but this time they wanted to know what we did to suddenly increase the volume," remembered Mr. Castanheira. With volume up, it was becoming increasingly difficult for EDB to rely on imports alone. At this point EDB suggested that SRA arrange for a license to produce ERICALL locally.

Though sales had barely totaled 50 systems, each averaged about 20 receivers. Most of these sales had come during the last two years. SRA would have preferred to export finished products to Brazil but realized that the strict import licensing practices of the Brazilian government did not support a continuation of the export business.

A major breakthrough came in the second half of 1981. The Ericsson salesman who visited the IBM head office, a part of his territory, picked up a hint that IBM was in need of a paging system to manage its service representatives in the major Brazilian cities. However, the need was for a company-owned citywide system and not the on-site system for which ERICALL had been designed. IBM, which liked the various features of ERICALL, subjected the system to intensive testing. After several months of negotiations, IBM ordered ERICALL for several of its branch offices. The total contract amounted to about US$ 1 million. "We suddenly felt ourselves reconsidering the 4 percent salesman's commission we allowed on our equipment. We just hadn't thought that such large-scale applications would be in the cards," said Mr. Castanheira.

The IBM contract, signed in early 1982, had a substantial effect on the GSD sales force. Suddenly, ERICALL looked like a winner. On the other hand, it also was an eye opener for Mr. Castanheira. "Here we were pursuing an on-site system for the citywide applications. In fact, we had to convince our people in Sweden that we could sell the system to IBM. They had ERICALL pegged as strictly an on-site system. They only gave in once we showed them the IBM test results. But they continue to prefer that we sell for on-site use only."

The IBM contract, having come through at the time when EDB was ready to gear up for a larger effort for ERICALL, made everybody at EDB question the more traditional on-site strategy. With a successful application for citywide use, Mr. Castanheira found himself in a situation where two alternatives became available where before there was only one: on-site usage. "The IBM contract changed our view of things."

Mr. Castanheira knew, however, that there were two basic reasons why LME and SRA would have preferred a concentration on the on-site market. In Sweden, for some time a competitive company had made available a citywide paging system based upon FM-band radio. That system had functioned well and allowed for a direct call via radio to a specific telephone set. With this market in Sweden firmly in the hands of the competition, a broadcasting company, there had been little interest at LME to enter the public paging market with ERICALL. Secondly, Mr. Castanheira believed that SRA and LME wanted to go into the public or citywide market with a new and more sophisticated system, currently in the developing stage. However, Mr. Castanheira was of the opinion that Brazil did not need a system more sophisticated than ERICALL.

EDB'S PRODUCTION LICENSE

The resurgence of ERICALL sales brought about some inquiries by SRA in Sweden, the L. M. Ericsson unit which was responsible for the ERICALL system. SRA suggested a willingness to extend a production license to EDB as it became increasingly difficult to obtain import licenses for the growing volume. Mr. Arnaldo Curvello, as Section Chief of Special Systems, made several trips to Sweden to negotiate an agreement with SRA. The major difficulty was not in coming to terms with SRA but striking a deal that was also acceptable to the various Brazilian authorities: the Carteira de Comércio Exterior (CACEX), or Brazilian Foreign Trade Authority; the Conselho de Desenvolvimento Industrial (CDI), or Industrial Development Council; and the Instituto Nacional de Propriedade Industrial (INPI), the National Institute of Industrial Property.

To arrange for the introduction of ERICALL, all three of these Brazilian authorities had to be consulted, each playing a special role. Mr. Curvello started with CDI, where he first gave a general presentation of the ERICALL project. CDI was responsible for deciding on the important index of nationalization. The index represented the percentage of local content required for the production of a product. For its decision, CDI looked at each component of ERICALL. Whatever could be sourced in Brazil had to be part of the local content. Furthermore, CDI would check if a local producer already manufactured such a product. If that were so, CDI might not grant permission for local production at all. CDI certification was needed to compete for official tenders. Since both government and semi-government agencies accounted for a substantial part of the Brazilian economy, the nationalization indexes certified by CDI were important to many companies. In the case of ERICALL, Mr. Curvello negotiated for 64 percent nationalization in year one, rising to 68 percent in year two, and to 70 percent in year three. "At that point we will have to negotiate with CDI for another three years", explained Mr. Curvello.

In the next step, Mr. Curvello took his plan to INPI. "The Brazilian government does not allow for the royalty payment from affiliated and associated companies," said Mr. Curvello. Since the licensing agreement with SRA had to be negotiated through LME, ERICALL did not qualify for royalty payments. INPI's role was to look at all contracts that entailed payments for technology to assure a fair deal and to prevent excessive payments. INPI allowed a lump sum payment of $ 700,000.[2] This amount was made up of pay-

ments for documentation (40 percent), training and technical visits (40 percent), and for technical assistance (20 percent).

With both CDI and INPI approval, Mr. Curvello could now approach CACEX. This agency controlled both the nature and volume of imports into Brazil through a system of import licenses. CACEX followed its own rules, and, occasionally, earlier agreements with CDI and INPI had to be renegotiated because CACEX might not approve a certain component for importing. For the approved components, EDB would have to pay import duties averaging 118 percent of c.i.f. value. CACEX could be a strong ally for companies producing locally as it had the power, and often used it, to outlaw the import of finished products once a production existed.

The negotiations with CACEX could not be successfully completed without submitting a production schedule on ERICALL. "Each year", Mr. Curvello went on, "we negotiate our production levels for the coming year with CACEX. As a net importer of components, Ericsson do Brasil has to get CACEX approval for import levels which are tied to our production or sales forecasts. If we are over our goals, it might be difficult to get additional foreign exchange. If we are consistently under our own estimates, we might not get as much as we want the next year. Therefore, we have to be quite accurate in our forecasts."

The production level was finally set at 100 ERICALL systems for 1982, increasing by 10 percent each of the following years. It was estimated that 26 receivers would be sold with each system. Sufficient capacity existed to produce the necessary components. EDB's flexibility was such that a volume of 20 percent in excess of target could still be handled. Anything above would have to be accommodated only after a renegotiation with CACEX.

Production Planning

ERICALL systems and receivers were to be manufactured at EDB's factory near Sao Paulo where about 4,000 people were employed. For the ERICALL systems, about 50 new semiskilled

[2] US$ 1.00 = Cruzeiros Cr$ 93.125

assembly jobs were to be created. The only skilled labor needed were four testers for the equipment after final assembly. Production was planned in batch form with assembly concentrating on one individual product at a time. Focus would thus shift from centrals to receivers on to other components, etc. The additional investment needed for production equipment was minimal since most of the components could be produced by EDB's existing machinery or sourced from local suppliers.

Total investment for the ERICALL system was estimated at 12.5 million cruzeiros. This cost was relatively low since the plastic case for the keyboards and receivers could be imported. EDB thus saved the investment into plastic molding equipment.

Unit production costs for the modular system consisting of centrals connected to PABX and transmitters amounted to Cr$ 1.1 million. The compact system including transmitter had a unit cost of Cr$ 1 million. The receivers' unit costs amounted to Cr$ 25,000 for the simple 401 model and Cr$ 35,000 for the 405. Total unit costs were further subdivided into variable costs of 85 percent and a fixed cost contribution of 15 percent. The variable costs consisted to 80 percent of material and to 20 percent of direct labor. Imported components made up almost two thirds of direct material costs.

The Market for Pager Systems in Brazil

Two major market segments existed in the Brazilian pager market. The industry differentiated between city-wide and on-site systems. City-wide systems were equipped with stronger radio transmitters and thus had a wider reach. They were operated by independent companies who sold or rented their services to a wide range of companies and individuals. On-site systems were installed for a company's or institution's use and were typically restricted to the client's premises. Although technically the systems only differed in the power of their radio transmitters, substantial differences existed between the two segments in terms of applications, buyer behavior,

competition, volume, and future growth possibilities. One of Mr. Castanheira's principal strategic decisions with respect to the relaunch of ERICALL was in connection with the appropriate weighing the importance of each of these two segments. Any decision had to be founded on a complete understanding of the dynamics involved with each segment.

The Market for City-Wide Paging Systems

City-wide paging systems had existed in Brazil for about 15 years. According to information collected by EDB, about 130 systems had been licensed throughout the country. Licenses were granted by Dentel, an agency at the Brazilian Ministry of Communications, who controlled radio communications. Since paging systems required the use of radio transmitters, it was Dentel who opened areas for bidding. The company receiving the award for a license in a given city would install a central system; a radio transmitter equipped with the stipulated power, or watts, and the licensed frequency; and make its services available to private subscribers. EDB executives estimated that by 1981 a total of 45,000 individual receivers were in operation throughout Brazil. In Sao Paulo alone, some 25,000 receivers were estimated to be in use. Presently, EDB research had estimated the annual volume of new receivers in this segment to be 4,000 to 4,800 receivers for 1982. Annual growth for the next four years was estimated at anywhere from 10 to 20 percent.

The currently operating citywide paging systems were limited, however, by their existing technology. All systems used sound activated receivers only, signaling via a high-pitched sound, or "beep." The person receiving the signal was then obliged to go to a telephone and call a central operator, who would transmit the message. Furthermore, the receiver had to be manually activated by a central operator for the system.

The paging service companies promoted their services through a variety of channels to the general public. EDB executives believed that professionals—such as lawyers, doctors, and architects—accounted for about 80 percent of the subscribers. Other users were people employed as service technicians, in transport, in construction, and in the news media.

Two companies dominated the market of supplying equipment for citywide paging systems. The largest one, Intelco Radio Comunicacão S/A., was located in Sao Paulo and accounted for about 80 percent of the market. Established in 1968, Intelco had used a double strategy. In the largest cities of Brazil, Intelco was the licensee for the operation of its own paging systems. For smaller cities, Intelco made the entire package available to independent companies, who then bid for the license. Typically, Intelco sold the equipment outright to the independent paging service operators. Service subscribers, however, rented receivers for the duration of their subscription period.

Intelco's receivers were equipped for sound only. Their design was based on an early model of Motorola, a U.S. company. Motorola was the original supplier of components, which were then assembled in Brazil by Intelco. This agreement was discontinued when import restrictions made it impossible for Intelco to continue importing components. Intelco then began manufacturing receivers similar to Motorola's using Brazilian components only. All official licensing or royalty relationships between Intelco and Motorola have been severed.

Intelco employed about 270 persons and depended entirely on paging systems for its revenues. The company was believed to be quite profitable and had an estimated annual output of about 2,000 receivers. Throughout Brazil, Intelco employed 28 salesmen. Of these, eight were concentrated in Sao Paulo and six in Rio de Janeiro. Intelco was actively advertising its service in high-volume newspapers and magazines. Mr. Castanheira personally estimated Intelco's advertising expenditures at about Cr$ 50 million. Some full-page ads in the popular *Veja* magazine were priced at about Cr$ 500,000 alone. Intelco was known to have had service and maintenance problems with their receivers.

Earlier this year, the company had started to replace older receivers with a smaller but still only sound-activated model.

Telefones em Automóveis Sitam S/A. was the second competitor in the market for citywide paging systems. Believed to produce about 600 receivers annually, Sitam also operated its own service "Ondafone" in larger cities and supplied entire packages to operators elsewhere. The company employed about 85 people and maintained a relatively large sales force. Ten of its seventeen salesmen were concentrated in the Sao Paulo area. Its advertising budget was estimated by Mr. Castanheira at about Cr$ 5 to 10 million. Sitam was known to be price-competitive, offering lower rental fees than Intelco. Mr. Castanheira, however, suspected that a pricing agreement existed between the two companies because Intelco could easily lower prices to drive Sitam out of the market. Sitam operated in fewer cities than Intelco. Actually, Mr. Castanheira believed that Sitam's large sales force stimulated business for Intelco as well. Typically, potential customers contacted by Sitam would check with Intelco before signing up. This allowed Intelco to strike back and try to sign the customer up before Sitam finalized the sale.

Sitam's receivers employed a technology similar to Intelco's. Its receivers' designs were based upon a mix of Motorola-like components and elements from other U.S. firms. No official licensing agreement had ever existed between Sitam and the foreign firms. Sitam produced its receivers from Brazilian-sourced components only. Sitam receivers were sound-activated only.

Brazil's local telephone companies offered a message system that could be considered an alternative to the paging systems. Incoming telephone calls could be routed to a central message office where all messages were recorded. At any time during the day, the subscriber could call the center and ask for messages, usually telephone numbers, which had been left. The service's major disadvantage was the delay as the message recipient could not be contacted immediately. However, the local telephone companies offered this service because it generated additional traffic. In Brazil, all calls, even local, were metered. With switching equipment underutilized during the off-peak hours of 11 to 12 a.m. and 4 to 5 p.m., the telephone companies looked for any opportunity to get additional usage and increase "traffic."

In the opinion of Mr. Castanheira, EDB's ERICALL system offered major advantages to present operators and users of existing paging systems. First of all, the modular system allowed direct connection into a PABX system. Incoming calls could be routed directly to the intended receiver via radio communications without the manual operation of an operator. Secondly, the ERICALL receivers, even the most basic ones, allowed for the transmission of signals, and the more sophisticated models for the direct transmission of a telephone number. Thus the time-consuming first call to the central switchboard was avoided, and the message recipient could get in touch with the person looking for him or her without delay. Consequently, the ERICALL system promised substantial improvements in both service and efficiency.

But Mr. Castanheira was looking even further ahead. He became intrigued by the possibility of connecting ERICALL receivers directly to the telephone companies' central switching equipment. If such a connection were feasible, then the market for receivers would literally explode. When he inquired about the technical feasibility of such an installation, Mr. Castanheira found out that LME technical staff in Sweden had no test results available as yet. Instead, LME engineers had been involved heavily with the development of a mobile telephone for Sweden. "That's O.K. for Sweden," Mr. Castanheira replied, "but such an installation would cost about US$ 35,000 in Brazil. And then it still works only as long as you are in the car. What about when you are away from the car?"

Despite the attractiveness of the citywide paging systems market, Mr. Castanheira felt that there were several unresolved questions. First of all, he was not at all sure how Intelco and Sitam might react to Ericsson's entry into that market. He was concerned that they might be able to secure new technology to compete with receivers that could also display alphanumeric characters. He was certain, however, that they would not get any import licenses easily. Somehow, they would have to source their components in Brazil.

Still unresolved was how Ericsson could compete in the citywide market. Mr. Castanheira had little interest in getting involved with the operations of the competing paging services. Licenses for top markets had already been granted. There existed, however, a possibility of acquiring either Intelco or Sitam. He had no idea if either of the companies would be for sale or even what the acquisition price might be. At the present time, both companies were profitable. An acquisition would certainly accomplish the elimination of competitive suppliers of paging equipment. Since EDB was primarily concerned with the sale of paging equipment, Mr. Castanheira was wondering how an acquisition might fit in with his long- to medium-term strategy. And yet there was no doubt that the citywide segment offered the largest potential growth opportunities.

THE MARKET FOR ON-SITE PAGING SYSTEMS

The market for on-site paging systems appeared to be much less developed than the citywide market. Typically, on-site installations were limited to the use of a single company or organization. The radio transmitters were less powerful and usually did not exceed a range of more than three miles. Technically, the equipment for on-site paging systems was identical to those used for citywide systems with the exception of the transmitter. A major difference was the preponderance of outright sales to users instead of rentals. The company also obtained a license for their radio transmitter from Dentel, which determined the allowable signal strength and frequency.

Only one company was active in the on-site field. Embracom Eletrónica S/A., located in Sao Paulo, was a company formed in 1972 and active in a range of electronic applications. The company employed about 350 persons and was active in the manufacture of transmission equipment. Embracom, a Brazilian-owned company, actively cooperated with the government in the development of various electronic products. The company distributed its on-site systems through independent distributors located in major Brazilian cities. Embracom was believed to install about 50 systems annually and to produce about 1,000 receivers in an average year. Last year, however, they were believed to have built 2,800 receivers.

On the basis of market research data, EDB executives believed that about 15,700 companies existed in Brazil for whom it was worthwhile to own a system. They estimated that annual receiver sales would grow from about 2,500 annually in 1981 to 3,800, by 1985. Primary users today were hospitals, with 23 percent of the market; industrial companies, with 30 percent; banks, with 7 percent; hotels, with 10 percent; and the rest scattered over a wide range of applications. EDB research identified top executives as the primary decision makers in about 80 percent of all cases. Purchasing departments were influencing the decisions in about 12 percent of the situations, and the actual user played a role in only about 8 percent of all situations.

"We know that Embracom has a poor reputation for quality of equipment and service," explained Mr. Castanheira. They were believed to be slow in responding to service calls. Its systems were based on outdated Motorola technology and allowed for sound signaling only. The equipment, though closely resembling Motorola designs, was not based upon any formal licensing agreement. Embracom paging systems required manual operation on the part of a company's central switchboard operator. Its equipment was not compatible with central telephone equipment, and only one transmitter could be handled by the same system. A maximum of 100 receivers could be accommodated by the Embracom system.

"You have to know the special government regulations concerning telephone operators to understand our situation in Brazil," explained Mr. Castanheira. The regulations stipulated that central switchboard operators could work no longer than six hours. To cover a full working day at its corporate offices, EDB employed two shifts of two operators each. But smaller companies could not afford this. "In our Rio de Janeiro branch office, we just have the operator arrive two hours later in the day," said Mr. Castanheira. "During the first two hours, our phone traffic is traditionally light, and we equipped executive phones with direct lines." In general, companies were concerned with overloading operators. In the opinion of Mr. Castanheira, the Embracom system required an unnecessary additional call for the company operator and was thus likely to create a bottleneck if too many receivers were part of the system.

THE MARKETING PLAN FOR ERICALL

Mr. Castanheira had been assigned the responsibility of proposing a marketing plan to Mr. Curvello, who, as Section Chief, had been in charge of the product's sales for almost three years. His preliminary proposal—which was based upon his successful negotiations with SRA, LME, and the Brazilian government—addressed the major decisions Mr. Castanheira would face. Basically, ERICALL could be targeted to both city-wide and on-site use. The sales responsibility was to be delegated to a specialized sales force of about a dozen people divided into two groups, one for each segment. Both groups would be based on Sao Paulo, the head office of EDB. In terms of pricing, the proposal suggested setting prices for the basic sound-only systems, equal to those of EDB's competitors, and asking for a 15 to 20 percent premium for the systems with alphanumeric receivers. This proposal, combined with a detailed budget, was now in Mr. Castanheira's hand. The preliminary budget was based on sales of 100 systems in year one, 120 systems in year two, and increasing to 160 systems by year five. Likewise, receivers were to increase from 2,100 to 3,360 in five years. The total market in receivers was forecast to grow from 7,100 units to 11,000 units over the same time period, giving EDB a market share of about 30 percent.

As Mr. Castanheira looked at the proposal, three key areas stuck out in his mind. First of all, the target group selection was likely to cause considerable discussion with LME in Sweden. Secondly, the sales force decision had to be reviewed in light of past experiences he had in GSD. And finally, the pricing strategy would have to be carefully looked at in view of the various competitors' responses. If he could come to a conclusion in these areas, the final budget could be drawn up, he thought.

TARGET MARKET SELECTION

As the proposal stood, LME and SRA executives, who would eventually review the plan, preferred a concentration on the on-site segment. Mr. Castanheira remembered the discussions when IBM wanted to acquire ERICALL for what amounted to be a citywide system operated by IBM in key Brazilian cities.

Though designed as an on-site system with a maximum reach of about three miles, EDB executives and its technical staff were convinced that ERICALL could function well in citywide systems. The only difference was the need for a stronger transmitter depending on the reach required. IBM had subjected ERICALL to intensive testing before it accepted the system. "Somehow, back at LME they find it difficult to believe that it really works."

ERICALL's successful performance in several European markets in the on-site segment had obviously had its impact at LME head office and at SRA as well. Even Mr. Castanheira had to admit that the system was extremely well-suited for on-site use. On the other hand, the citywide segment, or public use of paging systems, was a larger market than on-site uses only. He did not want to miss out in what he believed to be the much larger market. Mr. Castanheira did not believe that LME would actually stop him from entering the citywide market. He also wanted to take such a step only after careful consideration.

After all, targeting both segments meant competing with different companies. It might also influence his sales force decision.

THE SALES FORCE DECISION

Mr. Castanheira was well aware of the reasons why Mr. Curvello had asked for a small but specialized sales force. When he had assumed his present position as director of GSD, he had moved toward a strategy concentrating on one product that eventually led to a reorganization of the entire division. "To fully understand the difficulties with our sales organization you have to understand the situation I found when I took over the division," said Mr. Castanheira. The division's principal products were telephone equipment sold to the private market, as opposed to the switching division which sold primarily to telephone companies. The product line consisted of PABX systems, or inhouse telephone central switching equipment for companies. Ericsson's PABX could accommodate up to 200 external trunk lines and up to 10,000 internal lines. In this market, Ericsson was the leader in Brazil.

Also marketed by GSD were key systems, or telephone central systems with a small capacity of up to 25 incoming lines and a maximum of 50 internal lines or connections. Of much smaller importance, but also within the responsibility of GSD, were ERICALL, railroad signaling equipment and signaling systems for traffic lights. The major challenge for Mr. Castanheira, however, was to redress the balance between PABX and key systems sales. PABX, key systems, and Ericall had been sold through the same geographically organized sales force. Originally, each salesman was responsible for selling all three product lines. In reality, however, all the attention went into PABXs. As Mr. Castanheira remembered: "I found our sales force made offers for a PABX system to a client who did not really need one. Then our competitors moved in with an offer for a key system. By the time our salesman realized what was going on, it was too late. Our sales force would rather sell a PABX than a key system. However, I would rather sell a key system than no system at all."

The market for key systems was much larger than the market for PABXs. Most firms in Brazil were too small to warrant a PABX. While Ericsson enjoyed a market share of almost 40 percent in PABXs, it trailed in key systems with a market share of only 10 to 15 percent. The leaders in the key systems segment were GTE, a U.S. firm, and NEC of Japan. To obtain a better coverage for the key systems market, Mr. Castanheira decided to split his sales force with each regional office assigning salesmen to only one of the two markets. Later on, the specialization for the smaller branch offices in the north was discontinued.

The EDB sales force of about 100 was paid a fixed salary of Cr$ 37,250 per month and a commission of about 4 percent of sales. A good salesman could thus earn about Cr $ 185,000 per month. Special government regulations required that each salesman be assigned an exclusive selling territory. If a salesman was reassigned, the company was liable to maintain his income for another twelve months. Consequently, a change in sales territories was something that had to be thought through carefully.

Mr. Castanheira remembered the long discussions they had after one of their salesmen brought in the IBM contract. The 4 percent commission amounted to almost two years of income for the salesman. There were many executives who believed that the commission in such a case need not be paid. In the end, the salesman was granted his commission, and the rate remained unchanged at 4 percent.

Past experience indicated strongly that an organization that focused responsibility more directly did show positive results. This was also born out with ERICALL under Mr. Curvello. However, a new sales force would represent additional fixed costs that would not arise if ERICALL was sold through the existing organization. If the existing organization was given ERICALL, then sales territories would have to be assigned carefully. At this point, Mr. Castanheira had little indication as to which salesmen were the best for ERICALL. Secondly, if a salesman's territory in-

cluded a very large company, he wanted to make sure that the potential was actually realized. Later reassignment might turn out to be a problem.

THE PRICING DECISION

EDB research had attempted to determine the possible price premium for ERICALL. Since none of EDB's potential competitors offered systems with comparable sophistication and capabilities, the research department had asked potential users how much more they would be willing to pay for the ERICALL system. The consensus was that users would be willing to pay a 25 to 40 percent premium for ERICALL's most advanced systems equipped with modular central and the alphanumeric display receivers. Currently, Embracom offered its system for about Cr $ 1,115,000. If the user wanted to have the Embracom paging system connected to the PABX, an additional connection charge would arise. "Marketers of PABX systems had little interest in such modifications," explained Mr. Castanheira. "If we were approached by one of our PABX clients to connect an Embracom paging system, we would probably try to convince them to buy our system. And other PABX suppliers would most likely price the same way."

Currently, receivers were priced at Cr$ 31,500 by all competitors. This price applied to the basic sound-activated receivers only, since no others were on the market. For citywide subscribers, a one-time fee of Cr$ 1,500 was charged, and the receiver rental was currently about Cr$ 2,600 per month. Mr. Castanheira was concerned how the local competitors might react to any kind of pricing decision he might take. If possible, he wanted to come close to the gross margin EDB earned in its PABX business of about 40 percent. His general administrative overhead for launching the ERICALL system would amount to about Cr$ 30 million annually.

BRAZIL'S ECONOMIC OUTLOOK

José Castanheira was very concerned about one aspect of the ERICALL introduction that he could do very little to change: the ERICALL was to be introduced at a time when Brazil's economy was entering a recession. Would his demand forecasts hold up if the economy continued with its decline, or was further decline inevitable?

Economic growth in Brazil had been strong, but erratic, since 1972. The oil price increases of 1974 and 1976 had a strong negative impact on the economy and led to sharp increases in Brazil's external debt and a deteriorating trade balance as Brazil struggled to pay its increased oil bill. In order to reduce its dependence on imported oil and to increase export earnings, the Brazilian government had launched a range of investment projects during the mid 1970s that had been financed with foreign debt. By 1979 debt service requirements were absorbing most of Brazil's export earnings, and inflation was soaring. Under these circumstances the government decided to cool down economic activity. Interest rates were allowed to increase dramatically in order to restrict the money supply. Consequently, industrial output increased slightly in 1980 before it nose-dived in 1981. Similarly, exports, which had grown an average of 17 percent every year between 1974 and 1981, were actually decreasing by 9 percent in the first months of 1982.

Inflation had peaked at 120 percent annualized in April 1981 and declined to 91 percent per year in early 1982, only to show signs of increasing again in May 1982. Inflation was not an insurmountable problem to wage-index-linked Brazilian wage earners, but the number of unemployed who received no form of government assistance was increasing at an alarming rate. In 1981, Brazil's GNP declined by 3.5 percent. It was Brazil's worst recession in many years. High debt charges and worldwide recession were compounded by falling prices for Brazil's most important commodity exports. Sugar prices were less than 40 percent of their 1975 level. Soy bean prices were below 1979 and 1980 levels, and coffee prices had plunged from an index-linked 410.6 in 1977 to 168.2 in 1981 (1975 = 100).

These economic difficulties were aggravating problems that had already begun to plague the government's efforts to reduce the considerable disparities between Brazil's industrialized south and rural north. In São Paulo, for example, the per capita GNP in 1980 was US$ 3,300, while for the rest of the country it was US$ 1,432, which was barely higher than that of other Latin American countries. The government's projects in the country's northwest region had been expected to greatly increase employment opportunities in that area. An oil substitution project involving substantial sugar cane production for an alcohol-based fuel had run into problems. It was discovered that the ethanol engine fuel created ecological problems if expensive automobile engine alterations were not made. This led to a slowdown of sales volume for alcohol-powered cars. The second project, named Carajas, was aimed at increasing Brazil's mineral exports. The project was being implemented, but world demand and prices for iron ore, copper, bauxite, nickel, and manganese were falling as a result of the persistent worldwide recession.

EXPORT POSSIBILITIES FOR ERICALL

José Castanheira had also discussed with LME the possibility of producing and exporting ERICALL systems to other Latin American countries. As Brazil was strategically placed on the Latin American continent, it would be easy for EDB to give the necessary support to other LME subsidiaries and to sell and offer technical assistance on ERICALL. LME currently sold very few ERICALL systems in other Latin American countries.

The Brazilian market combined with export sales would permit EDB to reach a volume of production which would result in economies of scale. Labor costs in Brazil would be another contributing factor that would lead to a lower-cost product. Possible opportunities for LME included selecting EDB to produce and sell ERICALL to the world market, providing the same level of quality at a lower price.

Export volume would substantially strengthen Mr. Castanheira's hand in negotiations with

Brazilian authorities to obtain the necessary import license for key components. Also, exporting would be profitable since the Brazilian government granted considerable subsidies on export sales amounting to about 20 percent of sales and access to subsidized low interest loans. On the other hand, Mr. Castanheira believed that his division's performance in marketing ERICALL in Brazil might have considerable bearing on whether he might be granted export rights by LME.

CONCLUSION

Reviewing all the data his staff had collected over the past few months, José Castanheira felt that he had about as much information as he could hope to get on the relaunch of ERICALL. It was not up to him to make the required decisions on the target market, as well as the related decisions on sales force organization and pricing. The final budget could be completed once these key decisions had been made.